LEONARD COVELLO AND
THE MAKING OF BENJAMIN FRANKLIN
HIGH SCHOOL

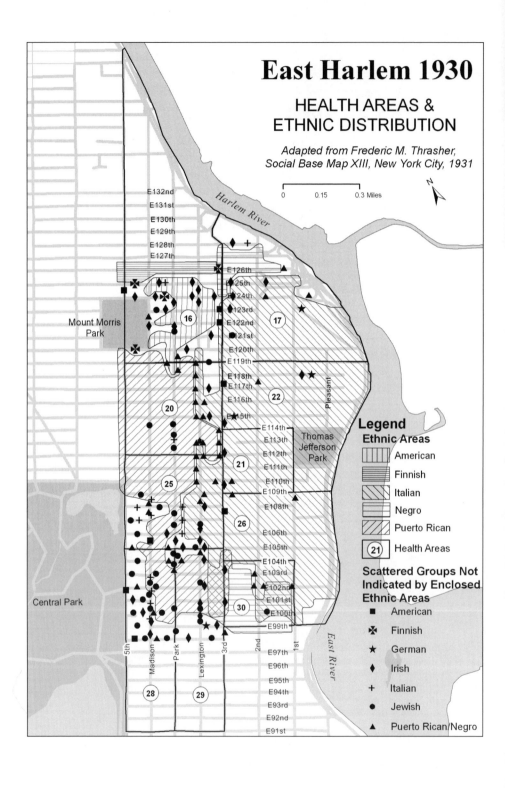

Leonard Covello *and* *the* Making *of* Benjamin Franklin High School

Education as if Citizenship Mattered

MICHAEL C. JOHANEK

JOHN L. PUCKETT

TEMPLE UNIVERSITY PRESS
Philadelphia

For Rosario and Karin

TEMPLE UNIVERSITY PRESS
1601 North Broad Street
Philadelphia PA 19122
www.temple.edu/tempress

Copyright © 2007 by Temple University
All rights reserved
Published 2007
Printed in the United States of America

The paper used in this publication meets the requirements
of the AmericanNational Standard for Information Sciences—
Permanence of Paper for Printed Library
Materials, ANSI Z39.48-1992

Library of Congress Cataloging-in-Publication Data
Johanek, Michael C.
Leonard Covello and the making of Benjamin Franklin High School :
education as if citizenship mattered / Michael C. Johanek, John L. Puckett.
p. cm.
Includes bibliographical references and index.
ISBN 1-59213-521-8 (hardcover : alk. paper)
1. Community schools--New York (State)--New York. 2. Community and
school--New York (State)--New York. 3. Benjamin Franklin High School (New
York, N.Y.) 4. Covello, Leonard, 1887-1982. I. Puckett, John L., 1947- II.
Title.
LC221.3.N38J64 2007
371.0309747'1--dc22
2006015211

2   4   6   8   9   7   5   3   1

Frontispiece: Frederic M. Thrasher, *Final Report on the Jefferson Park Branch of the Boys' Club of New York*, "Social Base Map (No. II), Local Neighborhoods, New York City, 1931," map XIII, 84, Rockefeller Archive Center, Bureau of Social Hygiene collection, series 3, box 12.

CONTENTS

Photographs follow page 181

ABOUT THE AUTHORS

Michael C. Johanek is a Vice President at Teachscape, a professional development services company.

John L. Puckett is Associate Professor in the Policy, Management, and Evaluation Division of the University of Pennsylvania Graduate School of Education.

ACKNOWLEDGMENTS

D URING THE EIGHT YEARS of research and writing needed to bring this book to fruition, scores of people provided invaluable assistance. We take great pleasure in acknowledging our considerable debt to them.

At Teachers College, Columbia University, Mike Johanek studied with the late Lawrence Cremin, whose broad and humane vision of educational history inspired him profoundly. He was fortunate to continue his studies under the wise guidance of his doctoral advisor, Ellen Condliffe Lagemann, Professor Cremin's colleague and former student, who continues a proud legacy of formidable historical scholarship that extends the boundaries of our civic commitments and intellectual imaginations. Under Ellen, Mike's dissertation explored the origins and evolution of community-centered schooling at Benjamin Franklin High, distilling from its rich historical context the fundamental tensions involved in the public purposes of education.

John Puckett's work on this book originated in his close association with Lee Benson and Ira Harkavy, historians at the University of Pennsylvania who invited him to undertake a study of community school history in the early 1990s. This unpublished study provided historical materials for the community schools project of the West Philadelphia Improvement Corps, which Lee, Ira, and their undergraduate students had founded in the mid-1980s. Lee has been an unstinting and indispensable source of bibliographical suggestions and insights, in particular for our narrative of community school history and our analysis of John Dewey's involvement in this history. Ira collaborated with John Puckett on several publications that identify the Progressive Era roots of the community school idea.

We could not have completed this book without the benefit of release time for research and an ample pool of travel funds. For these necessities, we gratefully acknowledge the generous financial support of the Spencer Foundation, which awarded a postdoctoral fellowship to John and a grant for our joint endeavor to develop the book. We are also grateful for a grant from the University of Pennsylvania Research Foundation.

Libraries and archives are the keystones of this book. Skilled and energetic staff at Penn's Van Pelt Library provided indispensable services, especially Lee Pugh, Lauris Olson, Patty Lynn, and Hilda Pring. We are deeply indebted to several fine archivists—Joseph Anderson of the Balch Institute for Ethnic Studies; David Ment and Betty Wenick of Milbank Special Collections, Teachers College, Columbia University; and Thomas Rosenbaum of the Rockefeller Archive Center. We also thank the archivists at the Historical Society of Pennsylvania; New York City Public Library, Archives and Manuscript Division; Museum of the City of New York; City Hall Library, New York City; Morris Library Research Collection, Southern Illinois University; New York University Archives; Robert F. Wagner Labor Archives, New York University; West Virginia and Regional History Collection, University of West Virginia; Arthurdale Heritage Inc.; Immigration History Research Center, University of Minnesota; Center for Southwest Research, University of New Mexico; Regenstein Library, University of Chicago; and Seeley G. Mudd Manuscript Library, Princeton University. We owe special thanks to Barbara Levine of the Center for Dewey Studies at Southern Illinois University, a superb bibliographer who helped us navigate Dewey's extensive correspondence and answered John's many questions during a weeklong sojourn in Carbondale. For their assistance with photographic reproductions and copyrights, we thank R. A. Friedman of the Historical Society of Pennsylvania, Faye Haun of the City Museum of New York, Danny Stockdale of Morris Library Special Collections, and Leonora Gidlund of the New York City Municipal Archives. Thanks also to staff members of the National Center for Community Education, who allowed John to rummage freely in their library and donated back issues of community education journals to our project. And thanks to Carol Ricciardelli of the Manhattan School of Science and Mathematics (formerly Benjamin Franklin High School) for her assistance with BFHS yearbooks.

We owe an immeasurable debt to David Tyack, Jonathan Zimmerman, Jeffrey Mirel, Marvin Lazerson, and Eric Schneider, who generously and rigorously critiqued a presentable draft of the book. Their carefully weighed comments and criticisms inspired a more precise elaboration of several key arguments in the manuscript and a restructuring of some of the chapters. We wish, however, to make abundantly clear that these scholars bear no responsibility for any errors or weaknesses in the final version.

In 2002 Susan Fuhrman and Marvin Lazerson invited us to write a chapter on the state of civic education for the Annenberg Foundation's Institutions of American Democracy series. Our research for the Annenberg project led us fortuitously to political theory and some of the theoretical perspectives that inform our book. We are grateful to Susan, Marvin, and the foundation for having encouraged our participation in their work. Portions of our Annenberg essay, "The State of Civic Education: Preparing Citizens in an Era of Accountability," published in *Institutions of American Democracy: The Public Schools*, ed. Susan Fuhrman and Marvin Lazerson (New York: Oxford University Press, 2005), appear in our book with the permission of Oxford University Press.

We were fortunate to have four talented research assistants at various stages of our research and writing on community schools. Christina Collins collected materials from multiple archives and helped us think about the broader meanings of Leonard Covello's work; Jamie Clark compiled New York City census and health district data; Ingrid Boucher tracked down numerous sources on civic education and rendered a valued second opinion on our interpretations of that material; Leah Gordon helped us situate and often restate particular arguments in the manuscript—her occasional, always emphatically asserted question "Where's the argument?" still rings in John's ears.

Our work also benefited from superb technical assistance. Donald Kaufmann, Steven Nachsin, and Zachary Nachsin provided invaluable computer support; Daniel Raduta Krista and Heinka Vicky Tam constructed our GIS map of East Harlem; and Daniel McGrath provided statistical consultation. We are also indebted to Andrea DeAngelis, Ruth Ebert, Maureen Cotterill, Elizabeth Deane, Joyce Cook, Teresa Singleton, and Patricia Friess for their capable and always cheerful administrative support.

Friends and colleagues lent valuable assistance and encouragement to the project. David Brownlee advised us on the architectural details of Benjamin Franklin High School. Jonathan Sher suggested our subtitle, an adaptation from a famous book by E. F. Schumacher. The late Professor George Abernethy shared with us his memoir of DeWitt Clinton High School in the 1920s. For their interest and support, we also thank Cory Bowman, Joann Weeks, Cynthia Lurio, Rebecca Maynard, Tom Kecskemethy, Catherine Lacy, Kathleen Hall, Michael Morris, William Denton, and Francis Johnston.

We are particularly indebted to Micah Kleit, senior editor at Temple University Press, who shared our great enthusiasm for Leonard Covello's project and shepherded this book to publication. We also wish to thank Bobbe Needham, our copy editor, for her careful scrutiny and adroit handling of the manuscript.

Lastly our loved ones sustained us through all of the vicissitudes of completing this work. Mike thanks his wife, Rosario Conde, whose graceful inspiration and patient support makes all possible, and their two daughters, Francisca and Camila, early authors themselves, who tolerated all the times Dad escaped to a coffee shop to write. John thanks his wife, Karin Schaller, whose devotion and unstinted support are the mainstays of his life and work.

INTRODUCTION

T HE SPEAKERS and other dignitaries gathered on a landing above the crowd that warm, sunlit day in East Harlem in May 1941. The early afternoon celebration featured the cornerstone laying for the school district's long-awaited new high school building. Draped across the building's west portico some fifteen feet above the podium, a U.S. flag at least thirty feet wide and fifteen feet high brushed against a row of scaffolding attached to the as yet unfinished colonnaded façade. Below the speakers, halfway down the wide staircase, an honor guard stood at attention, flags held aloft. Assembled on the sidewalk in front of the staircase, a marching band struck up the national anthem. Facing the oversize flag, their hands raised in salute, stood the students of Benjamin Franklin High School, all boys, in rows fifteen to twenty deep along Pleasant Avenue.

Thousands of spectators crowded the main entrance to the splendid cupola-crowned late-Georgian building of red brick and limestone on a campus bounded by Pleasant Avenue and East River Drive between 114th and 116th streets. Years of unremitting hard work and political struggle had culminated in the board of education's authorization of this capacious, well-appointed building, designed to function as a "community-centered" high school for boys in East Harlem.

The new building finally opened in the winter of 1942. In mid-April Vito Marcantonio, the district's radical third-term congressman, and Leonard Covello, Marcantonio's mentor and Franklin's founding principal, spoke at the dedication ceremony, having spearheaded the multiyear campaign to obtain this "new, completely equipped high school" for East Harlem. They envisioned the new Franklin as an institution that would function as a center for educational and democratic development in this densely populated, chronically poor, and ethnically divided area of the city. The school would serve as a catalytic hub for creating and strengthening social networks and fostering community norms of civility, trust, and reciprocity.[1] It was explicitly designed to play a central role in the social reconstruction of East Harlem.

Since the mid-1930s the idea of community-centered schooling had achieved partial realization in the programs and activities of the original Benjamin Franklin High School. Located on East 108th Street between First and Second Avenues, the original building stood in the tenement heart of East Harlem about seven blocks southeast of the new Franklin building. The new high school on Pleasant Avenue was expected to continue and expand the work started at the first site into a fully realized community school. By special decree of the board of education, the new Franklin would be open "every hour of every day of the year" to provide an array of educational, cultural, recreational, social, and health services to the residents of the 271 square blocks that constituted this highly stressed district. Projecting an image of democratic openness and liberality of spirit, the new building and its park-like venue contrasted sharply with the crowded tenement houses that defined most of East Harlem and characterized the neighborhood where the community school idea had first been planted. This dignified Georgian structure was literally and symbolically a beacon on a hill. On the east side of the new building a spacious terrace offered an unobstructed view of the East River, Randall's Island, and the Triborough Bridge; a manicured lawn and sidewalk provided direct access to 114th Street and the green spaces and playgrounds of neighboring Jefferson Park; and on the west side the main entrance and staircase fronted the intersection of Pleasant Avenue and 115th Street, with a view to the nearby Church of Our Lady of Mount Carmel, Italian Harlem's spiritual center.

Marcantonio hailed "this great building" as "indeed a monument to democracy in education, . . . truly a people's school." Covello, the educator most responsible for Franklin's creation, solemnly pledged the new high school "to exercise *an influence outside the school* which will help to produce a community worthy of the greatest democracy on earth" (original emphasis).[2] Yet for all the pride, sense of accomplishment, and hopeful anticipation felt at this long-awaited moment, the nation's entry into World War II cast a long shadow over the ceremony. Covello, Marcantonio, and their silent partner in city government, New York's flamboyant mayor Fiorello La Guardia, feared the worst for their social experiment in the face of the global conflagration.

JOHN DEWEY NOTED FAMOUSLY that "the true starting point of history is always some present situation with its problems."[3] Recalling Dewey's maxim, our true starting point in this book is the contemporary crisis of America's underserved schools and neighborhoods, whose dire conditions are symptomatic of a broader crisis of U.S. democracy. Our present civic dilemma involves the corrosive cynicism, alienation, and political disengagement of the American people; the pervasive distrust of our major institutions; and the accelerating movement away from the ties that bind Americans as neighbors and citizens. Emblematic of and integral to the crisis of diminishing citizenship is the widespread civic and political disaffiliation of the present generation of U.S. youth and young adults, the subject of a legion of fire-bell surveys and research reports. Most evidence suggests that young Americans have a limited understanding and appreciation of citizenship consistent with "thin" democracy. They view citizenship in terms of individual responsibilities and helping behaviors, and they do not consider civic participation or political engagement to be a citizen's responsibility. Though they are volunteering in unprecedented numbers, their volunteerism is largely individualistic, emphasizing altruism and charity, lacking civic or political content.

Writing at the turn of the last century, at a time of great societal disruption and dizzying technological change, Dewey argued that young people's direct participation in solving the problems of their local community, a "first-hand contact with actualities," should be made the foundation of the school curriculum; thus reconstructed, public education would become the "deepest and best guaranty" of a democratic society.[4] More than a century later, the priorities of public education stand at a very far distance from Dewey's deepest and best guaranty. At a critical juncture when the U.S. schooling system and the larger society cry out for a renewal of imagination and a reinvented sense of public possibility, the role of schooling in the democratic development of the nation and the enhancement of the public sphere is not a central concern expressed in our educational reform era of test scores and standards. Unfortunately, even as we hold schools increasingly accountable for student achievement, we rarely seem to hold them accountable for their performance in citizenship preparation, an inauspicious "accountability gap" for a democracy.

Consistent with this observation, sociologist David Labaree writes compellingly that contemporary public education and school reform are dominated by the goal of individual social mobility and status attainment, which justifies public schooling as a private good; the school's mission is increasingly weighted toward the promotion of private advantage through the competitive allocation of educational credentials.[5] While equity, the raison d'être of accountability, is often stated as an explicit concern in policy agendas and proposals, it is all too often implicitly, and narrowly, defined as equal preparation for individual competition in a market economy. The emphasis on students' market viability contributes to reducing democracy to an economic concept—one that too often breeds selfishness, promotes a narrow conceptualization of the social responsibilities of citizenship, and undermines a vision of community.[6] Inadequate attention is given to the public purposes that are necessary for schooling to be genuinely a public good—one that has far-ranging benefits that are more than simply an aggregation of private ends.

By no means do we disagree with the argument that public schools should be held accountable for the academic achievement of their students. The inequities in academic opportunities mock any basic sense of fairness and certainly impair societal development. It is clear, however, that schools are not being held accountable for how well they prepare young people as citizens. The omission of citizenship in educational reform debates is a deafening silence, implying that citizenship is a marginal concern, noble-toned rhetoric for commencements. This is ironic, since the primary justification for the school's existence as a publicly funded entity is citizenship training, unequivocally a public purpose.[7] More recent turns in foreign policy foregrounding a renewed proselytizing posture on behalf of democracy and the urgent need for civic reconstruction in foreign lands only highlight and complicate our challenge in preparing future citizens of this republic. Perhaps the greatest obstacle to solving the crisis of diminishing citizenship and the threat to democracy it entails is the paucity of imagination and vision reflected in the nation's understanding of the role of public schooling. Shortcomings in ideas produce real shortfalls in institutions and wasted resources in the education of children and youth. The failure of remedies in the present situation compels us to look backward critically to educational history for promising ideas and strategies. The past must be mined for other visions and models, not to transplant panaceas wholesale across time and space, but rather to nourish rigorous thinking about the broader purposes of public schooling and the lessons of past efforts to attain those purposes, even if incompletely realized. Educators, policy makers, and school reform advocates alike need to recapture past conversations such as those around community-centered schooling and civic development in East Harlem in the 1930s and 1940s, in which the role of public schooling was deemed to be the very foundation of a democratic republic. That civic role implied concrete actions and strategies in which school leaders saw social context as both educational constraint and opportunity.

HOW WE ENVISION the civic role of schools depends on how we understand citizenship. Western democracies are legatees of two traditions that stand in uneasy tension with one another. On the one hand, a tradition of republicanism (a legacy of the ancient Greeks and Jacobin France) envisions citizenship as "an office, a responsibility, a burden proudly assumed"; on the other hand, liberalism (a legacy of imperial Rome and the Enlightenment) regards citizenship as "a status, an entitlement, a right or set of rights passively enjoyed." In theory, writes political theorist Michael Walzer, "the passive enjoyment of citizenship requires, at least intermittently, the activist politics of citizens"; in practice, however, "democratic citizenship in its contemporary form does not seem to encourage high levels of involvement or devotion."[8]

Liberalism is the dominant public philosophy of our era. Liberal political theory envisions a nation of individual citizens freely choosing their own ends and values within a framework of basic rights and liberties that are provided and protected by government. We are, in philosopher Michael Sandel's apt phrase, a "procedural republic." This theory appeals alike to egalitarian liberals and libertarian liberals (conservatives, in contemporary political parlance), the former arguing that freedom to pursue one's own ends is contingent on the state's guarantee of "minimal prerequisites of a dignified life," the latter defending the market economy and "a scheme of civil liberties combined with a strict regime of private property rights." On both views, liberal political theory has no vision of citizens deliberating about the common good or sharing in collective efforts to shape their political community. "The procedural republic cannot secure the liberty it promises," Sandel concludes, "because it cannot sustain the kind of political community and civic engagement that liberty requires."[9]

This critique is supported in Benjamin Barber's 1983 book *Strong Democracy*. Barber makes an impassioned yet carefully reasoned plea for activist politics, taking direct aim at the passivity of contemporary democratic citizenship and sharply criticizing liberal democracy, which he derides as "thin," a "minimalist" conception that "is concerned more to promote individual liberty than to secure public justice, to advance interests rather than to discover goods, and to keep men safely apart rather than to bring them fruitfully together."[10] Barber champions "strong" democracy, which he associates with communitarian politics. "In strong democracy," he writes, "politics is something done by, not to citizens. Activity is its chief virtue, and involvement, commitment, obligation, and service—common deliberation, common decision, and common work—are its hallmarks."[11]

A coterie of U.S. scholars has suggested ways of thinking about democratic citizenship and provided, usually implicitly, guidance on how expectations for citizenship might be translated into civic education in the schools. Others have been more explicit in extending their understanding of citizenship into the educational arena. A typology presented by social studies educators Joel Westheimer and Joseph Kahne provides one such example, through their notion of the "personally responsible citizen" and the "participatory citizen." The personally responsible citizen, an individualistic conception, is described as the helping neighbor who picks up litter, donates blood, recycles, stays out of debt, obeys laws, and volunteers on an individual basis, perhaps at a soup kitchen or a senior center—salutary behaviors, yet insufficient to sustain an effective democratic society. By contrast, the participatory citizen has a collective orientation. According to Westheimer and Kahne, the participatory citizen is actively involved in community organizations and civic affairs, and he or she helps

TABLE I.1   WHAT DO WE MEAN BY "CITIZEN"? A CONTINUUM

PERSONALLY RESPONSIBLE CITIZEN	PARTICIPATORY CITIZEN	PUBLIC WORK CITIZEN
Helping citizen who obeys laws and performs individual acts that demonstrate social responsibility, kindness, and compassion.	*Corporate citizen* who participates in collective action to address a need or alleviate a crisis—action that typically involves a self-selected "little public," i.e., one that is collectively not equivalent to the larger public in its range of interests and perspectives.	*Public-building citizen who* engages with members of diverse groups constituting a non-self-selected "larger public" to address and resolve a problem by dealing with underlying causes—a resolution that requires the cooperation and resources of all groups with a vested interest in the problem.
Volunteers in a homeless shelter.	Helps organize a clothing drive on behalf of the shelter.	Engages with members of diverse groups to address and resolve the problem of access to quality housing in a community.

organize such efforts as community economic development initiatives and environmental cleanups.[12]

The most advanced conception in this literature is the "public work citizen." According to activist scholars Harry Boyte and Nancy Kari, public work harnesses the cooperative efforts of diverse categories and groupings of people, even ones in conflict, to accomplish shared civic and political goals. Examples include, among others, the Civilian Conservation Corps forestry management and Appalachian Trail programs, the Citizenship Schools associated with the civil rights movement, and, more recently, the development of Seattle's Union Lake as a multiple-use (recreational, commercial, residential) environmental resource.[13] In its strongest form, public work engages citizens in problem-solving efforts that can succeed only through the collaborative efforts of all the groups that have a vested interest in the problem—and their joint initiative is directed toward the underlying causes of the problem.[14]

Table I.1, an adaptation of Westheimer and Kahne's schematic, shows the continuum of citizenship models on which the status and progress of citizenship preparation may be charted.[15]

Given this continuum of citizenship constructs, the need to address the civic ends of schooling will depend in part on how we see that function fulfilled today. What do we know about citizen development outcomes for youth in terms of their knowledge, behaviors, and dispositions? Acknowledging that there are many factors that prepare citizens—home, community, media, peers, schools, and so on—within this mix, how well do schools contribute to citizenship preparation? To answer the questions about the present and thereby preface our study of the past, we briefly sketch the state of civic education in the United States.[16]

In the lower grades, children are taught, both formally and informally, that good citizenship means being patriotic, voting, helping others, obeying laws, and respecting individual liberties. At the high school level, the point of heaviest concentration, this version of citizenship is taught through a combination of a textbook-based civics or government curriculum, with a content emphasis on the structure and functions of U.S. government (for example, the Constitution and Bill of Rights, the three branches, "how a bill becomes law"), perhaps supplemented by a We the People program and/or some form of individualized community service. Yet, as noted in *The Civic Mission of Schools*, an authoritative 2003 report authored by leading scholars and foundation officers, "most formal civic education today comprises only a single course on government—compared to as many as three courses in civics, democracy, and government that were common until the 1960s," in sum, a civic education decline.

In most cases where civics is taught, informed participation in conjoint civic or political activities is not emphasized as a hallmark of responsible citizenship. Service-learning, an increasingly popular approach, usually takes the form of one-to-one volunteerism—it is less frequently participatory and rarely involves public work. Widely distributed cocurricular programs, such as We the People, focus on political knowledge, a necessary but insufficient condition for the more advanced forms of citizenship.[17] Innovative approaches that support participatory or public work citizenship operate in only a fraction of schools, and even here an ambitious program such as Public Achievement is on the margins of the civics curriculum.[18] In sum, civic education seems to be progressing out of its traditional textbook-based, didactically taught *spectator* mode largely by dint of service learning and opportunities for volunteerism, but it is still a far cry from what might be called "change-agent" civics. And as Westheimer and Kahne suggest, it is largely about cultivating personally responsible citizenship.

Viewed holistically and taken at face value, the weight of civic education research supports mapping young people's citizenship performance to that conception, and that worries knowledgeable observers. While being personally responsible is unquestionably a necessary disposition for a strong democracy, it is a very far cry from a sufficient condition. Survey after survey and a raft of research studies reveal worrisome gaps in young Americans' civic/political knowledge, behaviors, and dispositions, to the extent that their civic deficits have become a fire bell in the night, and a veritable cottage industry, for social scientists, think-tank researchers, and foundation officers gravely concerned that U.S. democracy has reached a critical juncture.

Readers who are comfortable with personally responsible citizenship are probably content with the current direction of civic education in the schools. Yet if citizenship means something that lies between participatory and public work, the evidence suggests the need for a significantly different approach than current activities. Certainly schools could do a great deal to promote movement along the citizenship continuum by adopting participatory and social problem–focused service-learning programs. Some observers call for a comprehensive, or hybridized, model that combines some of the best examples of existing efforts. Given the incremental impact individual components appear to have, this would be a good start. Real movement toward public work citizenship, however, requires far more; namely, an *institutional* commitment and *institutional modeling of citizenship* are necessary. Schools would need to move from course and cocurricular components to the *institutional performance* of public work citizenship. The history of community-centered schooling that follows can powerfully inform that institutional transformation.

ONE MORNING IN JUNE 1999 we met at the College Board in New York City to discuss writing a book about Leonard Covello and Benjamin Franklin High School. Earlier in the 1990s each of us, working on separate projects, had reviewed the Covello Papers, an extensive collection at the Balch Institute for Ethnic Studies in Philadelphia. We were drawn to Covello's vision of urban community revitalization, his profound understanding of school-community relations, his brilliance as a community organizer and a practical theorist, and his conceptualization of the role of public schooling in a democratic society. We agreed that Covello and Franklin High School would make a good story, but we wanted the book to be more than an engaging read. Later that day, as we walked along the bustling avenues and streets of East Harlem below 116th Street, Covello's old haunts, and visited the Manhattan Center for Science and Mathematics, the former Benjamin Franklin High School, we decided that our book would focus conceptually on the major themes of Covello's theory and practice.

At the outset we also recognized that a thorough understanding and appraisal of Covello's work would require an analysis of the origins and early development of the community school idea in the United States and the various strands of that idea which coalesced in the creation of Benjamin Franklin High School. We also wanted to know what became of the idea after World War II and what explained its growing popularity at the fringes of public school reform in the 1990s and into the new century. And, most importantly, we were interested in the lessons of this history for public school reform and democratic renewal.

With an eye to the present situation, our historical inquiry led us to confront two unavoidable questions: What is the appropriate role for the school as a publicly funded institution in terms of preparing citizens? What is the school's appropriate role vis-à-vis the underlying social and economic forces that affect its capacity to educate? Our book lays out a history of how these issues have been addressed over the last century or so through the tradition of community schools. A part of this tradition, highlighted in BFHS, posits a particularly ambitious, public work–oriented vision of citizenship and a correspondingly distinctive approach to the role of the school as an educational institution. This "outlier" historical case provides an unusual foil to how the country now envisions citizenship and the role it assigns to schools in preparing citizens.

U.S. public schools educate young people for a "thin" version of citizenship, hoping to produce law-abiding, helpful, neighborly citizens who may volunteer from time to time, are basically informed of government structures, and vote. As a nation we seem to have little expectation of a more active participation or any effort to work across the community to solve underlying issues. There is no such required senior project, no such exit assessment tied to community problem–solving competency.

Leonard Covello expected much more of citizenship. At Benjamin Franklin he promoted and, to a certain extent, enacted his ideal of an informed, active citizenry equipped with knowledge, skills, and dispositions to participate in cooperative activity that would involve the contributions of diverse cultural groups, even groups in conflict, to solve trenchant community problems. Put another way, public work would be the means to mobilize the "little publics" of fragmented communities such as East Harlem around a common democratic vision, creating a larger public of shared interests. Public schools would be the primary agency and training ground for public work citizenship.

Our argument to support this position in the present situation is based on the following premises. First, democratic society should aspire to this kind of "active" citizenship, and more adults should be prepared to engage publicly in this way. U.S. democracy has not achieved its full development, and it must do so in order to claim leadership in a world of emerging democracies. Major social problems such as health and environmental issues resist solutions that are not collective by design; individuals acting freely in a market will not suffice. Further, diversity, to be a fully realized resource, requires citizens who can work effectively across social boundaries, being more than just "sensitive" to other cultures and social perspectives; the ability to forge deliberative, principled compromise becomes a strategic asset for achieving a more just and humane society. In sum, to maintain international leadership as a democracy, to resolve critical social issues, to make diversity work toward these ends, and to reconcile divergent interests, democracy requires individuals who are skilled in public work citizenship. If we recognize that public work citizens are fundamental to our national wellbeing, and unless we think this happens by accident or osmosis, we need some mechanism to prepare people for this role.

Is preparing this kind of citizen an appropriate role for the school or does it overburden the institution and jeopardize the school's educational mission? With Covello we argue that the school, *in order to carry out its educational mission*, has a clear interest and a role to play in resolving issues that affect the education of its students. If, for example, community health or housing issues impinge on classroom learning, the school has a clear interest in these issues; it also *may*, as in Covello's conception, play a central role in educating young people to resolve them. This training role enhances the school's effectiveness in two key ways. First, by institutionally modeling public work citizenship, the school strengthens its capacity to engage and prepare young people to be active citizens. Students see the adults "walking the walk" of active citizenship, a critical counter to dangerous cynicism and real food for youth's appetite for inspiration. Second, by helping to resolve community issues that affect students' learning, the training can help lower barriers to their educational success overall. If the school, a centrally placed community institution, were not to assume this training role, then some other institution or configuration of institutions would have to undertake it.

Our argument does not preclude other institutional solutions, such as school-community partnership arrangements that provide health and social services (a direction that is currently in vogue). But integrating health, social, and educational services, while a clear step forward, is at best palliative and may even foster dependency unless it also trains youth to do the work of identifying and resolving underlying social issues across the community and its diverse groups. By no means does this role minimize the school's obligation to prepare students in academic subject matter or in the other skills deemed necessary by a community—but the need to prepare young people for citizenship duties must still be addressed. This need, we argue with Covello, can be met through a community-centered approach in ways that benefit students morally, intellectually, and motivationally.

WHAT DO WE MEAN BY A COMMUNITY SCHOOL? The definition provided by Paul Hanna and Robert Naslund in *The Community School*, a landmark book on the subject published in 1953, informs our research and analysis. Hanna and Naslund emphasize the role of community schools as agents of social and democratic revitalization. Beyond its purpose of educating young people to become productive workers, the community school, they write forcefully, is "*directly concerned with improving all aspects of living in the community* in all the broad meaning of that concept in the local, state, regional, national, or international community. To attain that end, the community school is *consciously used* by the people of the community." Through the school's curriculum and community program, youth and adults work together to analyze the problems of the community, research and formulate solutions to those problems, and mobilize resources and support for putting solutions into operation. The community school is cosmopolitan in the sense that community problems are always treated as local manifestations of broader societal or global problems.[19] Hanna and Naslund describe an ideal-type community school—a standard against which social reality can be compared.[20] Benjamin Franklin High School was the most extensive and longest-standing effort in the twentieth century to build the kind of community school envisioned by Hanna and Naslund—through its community program and occasionally the regular school curriculum, the East Harlem high school functioned as a community problem–solving institution. Progressing beyond Hanna and Naslund's conceptualization, Covello recognized that a community-based problem-solving approach could spur democratically motivated community development in a complex multicultural setting—Franklin's East Harlem initiatives, which started in the mid-1930s and resumed after World War II, were attempts to achieve that goal.

The "ecology" of urban neighborhoods and their problems figured prominently in Covello's formulation. A trained sociologist and committed activist, Covello recognized that myriad educational influences, positive and negative, were in play in East Harlem shaping the lives of his students, for better or worse. Accordingly, a vigorous agenda of social research was undertaken under Benjamin Franklin's aegis to specify precisely those local factors. Building on this local research base, Covello and his allies organized a community advisory council (CAC) and a set of affiliated programs as coordinating mechanisms to align the district's constructive forces with the work of the high school.

Every facet of Franklin's community program was education centered, designed to reinforce the high school's instructional program. CAC committees and social clubs, for instance, educated East Harlem parents about interethnic tolerance and cooperation at the same time their sons were learning these lessons in the high school's intercultural education program. Community-centered schooling was at heart an enterprise for the education of East Harlem youth and the cultivation of a leadership class that would continue the project of democratic development and social revitalization after Covello, Marcantonio, and their cohort of community organizers had moved on.

The approach pursued in East Harlem, including its origins and its evolving conceptualization, speaks directly to enduring questions of the relationship of public schooling to its community, and thus the role of public education in a democracy. The evolution of community-centered schooling at Benjamin Franklin High School also reveals the complexity of defining and implementing public purposes in the U.S. schooling system. Leonard Covello and his East Harlem allies defined Benjamin Franklin's primary goal as the democratic development of its local geographic community and constituent ethnic groups. Their goal presupposed that public schools have public purposes independent of, yet interwoven with, the education of individuals; that the school's educational mission includes building and strengthening social networks, developing local democratic processes, and advancing social welfare; and that achieving and sustaining these locally defined ends is an essential precondition for educating the community's youth, as well as for reconciling the claims of individual social mobility and the need for knowledgeable, publicly engaged citizens.[21] Implementing these purposes required agreement among Franklin's various and shifting constituencies that these were indeed legitimate aims for a comprehensive high school. In practice, Franklin was buffeted by claims that often supported the high school's credentialing (social mobility) role as its primary purpose. At its best, however, community-centered schooling in East Harlem was able to reconcile these claims with Covello's democratic vision, drawing from both academic and civic goals, often for the same set of activities.

Aptly named, Benjamin Franklin High School stood squarely in the tradition of public service represented by its namesake American founder. In his 1749 *Proposals Relating to the Education of Youth in Pensilvania,* Benjamin Franklin, a natural philosopher and public servant par excellence, advocated a decidedly public purpose for American schooling: to cultivate in youth "an *Inclination* join'd with an *Ability* to serve mankind, one's Country, Friends and Family" (original emphasis). The civic themes that permeated Franklin High School's classrooms, corridors, and community programs were markedly Franklinean, notably the emphasis on the institutional modeling of citizenship and the attention paid to collective community problem solving as a civic responsibility.[22]

EMERGENT WITHIN AND COMPLICATING our case study of Franklin High School and our broader narrative of community school history are four recurring critical tensions. The first is the tension within the history of U.S. progressivism between a reform tradition that Arthur Link and Richard McCormick identify as "social progressive" and another they call "reforming professional."[23] These two traditions are reflected in different conceptions of the community school idea, which we label "citizen-centered" and "client-centered," respectively. The former conception envisions community schools as agencies for social change and democratic development. The latter sees them as centers for the delivery of a variety of community services. The client-centered approach, which was infused by an ideology of science, efficiency, and expertise, became the dominant version of the community school idea after World War I and for the remainder of the twentieth century. At present the client-centered approach is evident in the trend toward school-based health and social services, or what one of our colleagues calls the "service-center model" of community schools.[24] In some instances in this history, these different conceptions of community schools were combined, the service-delivery role complementing and supporting the democratic development role, as was conspicuously the case at the service-rich, citizen-centered Benjamin Franklin High School. Accordingly, how Covello and his allies were able to achieve such an integration and what its trade-offs and limitations were—viewed in the context of urban social forces and the constraints of the world's largest school bureaucracy—are issues of vital concern to this study.

The second tension involves the claims of academic, or disciplinary, studies and community studies, or community problem–solving efforts, on the U.S. curriculum. This tension arises largely from a market concern that community studies will dilute the school's academic program and its value for individual social mobility. It was manifested in the Depression era when a minor community school movement was underway and social issues were made the emphasis of curriculum development in the most publicized projects. Recognizing this tension within his own high school, Covello argued that Benjamin Franklin's community focus was an enhancement of the academic curriculum and an attraction for youth who were otherwise alienated from schooling. Here we explore the extent to which Covello was able to balance the demands of disciplinary studies and the New York State Regents' examinations with his commitment to civic education and democratic community development through a community-studies approach.

The third tension relates to the heavy demands community-centered schooling puts on schoolteachers. Our study highlights and specifies the play of this tension at Franklin and other community school sites, providing a cautionary tale about the complexities of community school teaching and the professional commitments needed to sustain a fully realized community school. Franklin's accomplishments as a community school were attributable in no small way to a group of stalwart teachers who identified themselves professionally as scholars and social activists, *and* who responded with alacrity to Covello's galvanic energy.

The fourth tension arises in the interaction of local and nonlocal influences in a community school. A school eager to serve its local community, though subject to forces beyond the community, Benjamin Franklin was often caught between purposes determined at local and nonlocal levels. Moreover, the nature of those purposes often varied according to who was understood to constitute the local community or the nonlocal authority. The shifting ethnic composition of East Harlem, the variety of distinct groups within it, and their varying roles in community affairs presented an uncertain and changing picture of who "the local community" was. Identifying the nonlocal authority offered similar ambiguity—was it the board of education, the state government, university professors, Italian associations, political parties, educational organizations, or some combination of these entities? Or was it East Harlem's professional class, which represented cosmopolitan values and a vision of cultural democracy that challenged the ethnic parochialism, cultural prejudice, and anti-intellectualism of the district's many de facto communities. Embedded in this particular tension is the problem of how to define the meaning of "community."

TWO PERIODS OF INSTITUTIONAL development mark Benjamin Franklin High School's history as a community school, which was coterminous with Covello's tenure as principal. The first period, 1934–41, witnessed the rise of community-centered schooling in East Harlem. These were Franklin's halcyon years, when the center of operations was a terribly cramped, sparingly appointed brownstone edifice on East 108th Street. At this location the structures and programs of community-centered schooling East Harlem–style were developed and linked in dramatic fashion to districtwide housing, health, and citizenship campaigns. Before World War II, Franklin's main constituency was East

Harlem's Italian population, and the problems of poor Italian immigrant families and their adolescent male children played a defining role in the high school's early phase. Any account of this period in Franklin's history must reckon with the salient contributions of the federally sponsored Works Progress Administration (WPA), which provided, at virtually no cost to the high school, indispensable human capital for Franklin's community programs.

The second period, 1942–56, saw the gradual decline of community-centered schooling in East Harlem. After the move to Pleasant Avenue, Franklin was increasingly buffeted by social forces that were beyond the control of Covello and his staff. After losing hundreds of students to the war effort and suffering a debilitating loss of resources to support community-centered schooling, Covello attempted to adapt the high school to the postwar Puerto Rican migration and other seismic changes engulfing East Harlem, unhappily with more losses than gains. By the time he retired in 1956, community-centered schooling was virtually a dead letter in East Harlem.

Threading this history is Covello's formidable presence. Benjamin Franklin High School was virtually inseparable from Covello, indelibly stamped by his charismatic leadership and unstinted devotion to the high school and its community. Covello's boyhood experience as an Italian immigrant in East Harlem, his prominent career as a teacher of second-generation Italian Americans at DeWitt Clinton High School in central Manhattan, his extensive involvement in East Harlem community organizations, and his apprenticeship with educational sociologists at New York University were fertile seedbeds that nourished Covello's social acuity and political savvy, and pushed him inexorably to the decision to undertake the revitalization of East Harlem through the agency of a community high school. While Covello had powerful friends and allies like Vito Marcantonio and Fiorello La Guardia who supported his project, "the zeal, the energy, and the intelligence with which he pursued the ideal" brought it to fruition in 1934 and sustained it for twenty-two years.[25] Covello's biography, therefore, constitutes an indispensable component of the historical background of Benjamin Franklin High School.

Social historians and scholars of Italian American culture have long acknowledged Covello's pioneering contributions to the field of ethnic studies, in particular his dissertation study, *The Social Background of the Italo-American School Child*, completed at New York University in 1944 and published in 1967; and his research at the Casa Italiana, Columbia University, in the 1930s.[26] Other scholars have written glowing encomiums on Covello's contributions as a teacher and school leader qua activist and urban sociologist. In *Beyond the Melting* Pot, a landmark study of five major ethnic groups in New York City, Nathan Glazer and Daniel Moynihan (one of Covello's former students) hail Covello as "the most subtle and perceptive writer on the Italo-Americans" and "one of New York City's great educators."[27] In *Managers of Virtue*, an important historical study of public school leadership in the United States, David Tyack and Elisabeth

Hansot call Covello "a pioneer in creating bilingual, bicultural education; store-front schools; community advisory committees for schools; multicultural education; programs to prevent school dropouts; school-based community service and political action programs; methods of troubleshooting in race riots; and much else."[28] Paula Fass, in *Outside In*, an oft-cited study of the role of minorities in shaping the U.S. schooling system, notes of Covello: "His efforts were praised by contemporaries and have remained a model of cultural contact aimed at the alleviation of the conflicts between the school and the local community within which it was often an alien presence."[29] In *Teacher with a Heart*, "an extended reflection" on Covello's autobiography, The *Heart is the Teacher*, teacher educator Vito Perrone salutes Covello's "vision of what a school at the center of a community, being integral to a community's well-being, an important resource, a place where children and young people are understood to be genuine citizens, prepared to make ongoing contributions, can be like."[30]

The most important previous treatment of Covello and Benjamin Franklin High School is Robert Peebles's *Leonard Covello: An Immigrant's Contribution to New York City*, which the author completed as a Ph.D. dissertation at New York University in 1967 and published in 1978. In addition to researching the Covello Papers, which were then in Covello's possession in East Harlem, Peebles conducted multiple interviews with Covello and gathered material from sixty-five other informants, many of whom were former pupils of "Pop" Covello. Peebles's study is a thorough and reliable source for Covello's career to 1934 and the founding of the community high school. As a descriptive analysis of Benjamin Franklin, however, the study must be viewed with caution. Peebles did not raise difficult questions or render a critical appraisal; for example, he failed to note that the community high school was in decline after World War II.[31]

No account of Covello and Benjamin Franklin High School is yet available that situates the East Harlem project in relevant historical contexts, attends to the social forces that gave impetus to and shaped the community high school, or highlights the tensions within Covello's project and his legacy of community-centered schooling. To fill these lacunae, we have organized what is properly viewed as both a case study of Benjamin Franklin High School and a history of community schools in the United States. Here we address the following questions:

1. What were the origins and development of the community school idea in the United States before and during the 1930s and the making of Benjamin Franklin High School?
2. What were the local contexts and social forces that shaped community-centered schooling in East Harlem? How did these factors influence Covello's career path?
3. How was Benjamin Franklin organized to accomplish its goals and public purposes? What was Covello's philosophy and how did it shape

and reflect the community high school in action? How was Covello able to advance his civic and political agendas given the constraints of New York City's public school bureaucracy?

4. What explains Benjamin Franklin's decline as a community school? More broadly, what happened to the community school idea after World War II? What explains the resurgence of this idea at the opening of the twenty-first century?

5. What do we learn from the East Harlem community school about how to advance U.S. democracy and citizenship development through public education in the twenty-first century?

We are mindful of Franklin High School's exceptionality. The combination of Covello's visionary, indefatigable leadership, powerful political allies such as Marcantonio and La Guardia, and a New Deal funding agency make Franklin a problematic "model" of community-centered schooling. Yet here we make no claim for replicability. We are interested primarily in Covello's community-centered approach as an alternative vision to the current conception of the role of schools. We take readers to a place where the public purposes of schooling were taken seriously, where a very different set of decisions than the ones governing our era of accountability were involved.

Our study locates BFHS within a chronological progression of ideas and developments in the history of the "wider use" of schools as social centers, community centers, and community schools, applications of what is variously called the "community school idea," "community schooling," and "community-centered schooling" (Covello's preferred term). This historical framework spans a period of some 120 years from the early Progressive era to the present day. We also examine Covello's project within East Harlem, using the lenses of ethnic history, Depression-era sociological studies, and contemporaneous accounts of East Harlem life, work, and welfare. We analyze key developments and trends in community school history, holding the Franklin High School case study continuously in view for purposes of comparison and critique. Finally, we sift our findings through a hopper of relevant social and political theory to specify the bearings of this history upon public school reform and civic education in particular.

This book is divided into three parts. Part One, "Contexts and Social Forces," looks at historical and sociological/demographic factors that illuminate Leonard Covello's life and career, his educational philosophy, and the structure of community-centered schooling in East Harlem. Chapter 1 specifies, through a narrative historical framework, the different institutional forms and ideologies associated with the community school idea in the Progressive era and between the world wars, and it locates Covello's project within this national context of ideas and developments. Chapter 2 shifts our focus to East Harlem and the local contexts of Covello's project, highlighting the growth and expansion of Italian Harlem, the emergence of East Harlem's Puerto Rican colony, and the immediate social contingencies of community-centered schooling. Chapter 3 presents Covello's biography from 1887 to 1934, with particular attention to the varied influences that shaped his conception of Franklin High School.

Part Two, "The Making of Benjamin Franklin High School," looks at the structure, programs, and evolving philosophy of the East Harlem community high school. Chapter 4 describes Franklin's organization at the East 108th Street location from 1934 to 1941, with particular attention to the school's innovative community program and the committee work of the Community Advisory Council. Chapters 5 and 6 include Benjamin Franklin's efforts to overcome ethnic and racial divisiveness in East Harlem and to organize the district's disparate groups around critical quality-of-life issues; these two chapters illustrate the linkages that were made between the high school curriculum and East Harlem's social problems. Chapter 7 looks at the community high school from 1942 to 1956, focusing on Franklin's wartime programs, the effects of the postwar Puerto Rican migration to East Harlem, and the social forces and internal tensions that combined to undermine the community high school.

Part Three, "The Community School Idea since World War II," traces the community school idea from the 1930s to the present. In Chapter 8 we take up the downgrading of the community school idea in the years following the Depression. Here we sketch the history of the community education movement, which built a national organizational apparatus under the aegis of the Charles Stewart Mott Foundation from the 1940s to the 1990s and conveyed a somewhat more limited version of community-centered schooling. We also describe variants of the community school idea that at this writing appear to be coalescing into a minor social movement. Chapter 9 concludes the book with discussion of the implications of the Benjamin Franklin case study and our broader historical analysis for a renewal of public purposes and reinvigoration of citizenship preparation in the U.S. schooling system.

We list our names alphabetically on the cover of this book. This arrangement denotes that our work has been truly a collaborative endeavor, a coequal partnership of intellectual inquiry, lively conversation and debate, and shared decision making about every aspect of the study.

PART ONE

Contexts and Social Forces

CHAPTER ONE

The Community School Idea:
Social Centers, Community Centers,
Community Schools

FROM THE EARLY PROGRESSIVE ERA to World War II, proponents of community schooling embraced the "wider use" of schools as "social centers," "community centers," and "community schools." The community school idea was contested, in that progressive reformers of different ideological suasions often used the same language and institutional forms to further their social agendas. Social progressives advanced a citizen-centered conception of community schooling, which they associated with the political goal of local democratic development. By contrast, reforming professionals—social workers and professional community organizers, health-care experts, recreation specialists, and university professors, among others—supported a client-centered conception that limited community schooling to service delivery, a goal that had nothing to do with politics.

In the citizen-centered approach, which was evident to some extent in pre–World War I school social centers, and more strikingly in Benjamin Franklin High School during the interwar years, community services functioned side by side with democratic development activities, the services complementing and building support for the agenda for participatory citizen action. Highlighting tensions within U.S. progressivism, our narrative of the community school idea illustrates the rarity and fragility of the citizen-centered approach.

In this chapter we look at the progress of the community school idea from its origins in the American settlement movement to the rise of "community schools" in the Depression era, highlighting turning points and main decisions, actions, and processes and influential actors.[1] This analysis allows us to locate and interpret Benjamin Franklin High School and other Depression-era community schools in a national context of ideas, trends, and developments. It shows that Covello and his cohort of community school pioneers did not create a sui generis social innovation, but rather that they improved on a preexisting idea of schools as centers and catalysts for building a democratic communal life. Here we give particular attention to the rise of community schools, profiling two other notable community schools of the 1930s, Nambé and Arthurdale, which serve as points of comparison with Benjamin Franklin High School.

The American Settlement Movement, 1886–1902

Identifying the various intellectual and ideological threads that wove the complex tapestry of the American settlement movement poses the problem of "infinite regress to the Garden of Eden."[2] To avoid this problem, we begin our analysis in England in the 1880s, a decade of buoyant optimism and faith in the moral character of the working poor. Numerous philosophical and experimental influences coalesced in the English settlement movement, of which Toynbee Hall, a secular settlement house founded in 1884 in London's East End by Samuel Barnett, an Anglican vicar, was the first and quintessential example. Barnett established Toynbee Hall as a residence for recent graduates of Oxford and Cambridge, who used the Hall's facilities and resources in the evenings and on weekends to educate and edify the working poor of St. Jude's Parish through classes, lectures, and discussion groups in humanistic, elementary, and utilitarian subjects.[3]

Transfer of the British model to America began in 1886, when Stanton Coit visited Toynbee Hall and then returned to New York City to establish the Neighborhood Guild, a settlement house on the Lower East Side. The American settlement movement grew apace in the 1890s, with six settlement houses by 1891, seventy-four by 1897, and more than one hundred by 1900.[4] On a much larger scale than did their British counterparts, the American settlement pioneers confronted the problem of teeming immigration from eastern and southern Europe. They subsequently adapted the English settlement model by giving it a uniquely pragmatist twist. For example, the early settlements experimented with, and in some cases pioneered, social, health, vocational, and recreational services that were widely adopted by urban public schools.[5]

The most famous settlement was Hull House, founded by Jane Addams and Ellen Starr on Chicago's West Side in 1889, its philosophy and programs adapted from Toynbee Hall with a significant modification: The residents of Hull House were both community service providers *and* social activists. Organized along four lines that Addams designated the social, educational, humanitarian, and civic, the settlement's programs included college extension classes, clubs and literary offerings, ethnic festivals, art exhibits, recreational activities and neighborhood shower-baths, a summer-camp program, a cooperative boardinghouse for working women, and kindergarten, visiting-nurse, and legal services. The civic category included the settlement's role as a center for labor union activities, public forums, social science research, and advocacy for progressive social change.[6] More specifically, Hull House residents—among their number, famously, Florence Kelley, Julia Lathrop, and later, Edith Abbott and Sophonisba Breckinridge—developed a hard-nosed political agenda and an applied research process that included observing social conditions, compiling statistics, writing reports (memorably *Hull-House Maps and Papers*, published in 1895), and lobbying for such reforms as sweatshop legislation, child labor laws, compulsory schooling, and juvenile courts.[7] That the residents acted too frequently for rather than with their neighbors (treating them as clients) must be weighed against their dedication to an ideal of universal democratic participation.[8]

In sum, Addams and her colleagues provided a holistic institutional approach to the social problems of the U.S. city, a strategy that combined amelioration and reformist social science.[9] John Dewey, a frequent visitor to Hull House in the 1890s and a close friend of Addams, understood that the settlement was "primarily and in the broadest sense, an educational institution."[10] Rethinking his own theory of "school and society" under Addams's influence, Dewey would propose the settlement idea as a strategy for advancing democracy through the public schools.

The Social Center Movement and the
Social Reform Ideal, 1902–1917

From the turn of the century to World War I school social centers played the role of settlement houses in the public schools. Spearheaded by social progressives like Dewey, Edward J. Ward, and Mary Parker Follett and publicized by the Russell Sage Foundation, social centers were sites for community education and recreation, as well as democratic public forums for social and political reform. The most fully developed social centers were those in midsize and large cities, notably Rochester, Boston, and New York City—although social centers in one form or another also appeared in rural towns and hamlets across the country. The spirit of Jane Addams and the women of Hull House infused this social movement, which was ameliorative, reformist, and participatory in its general approach. In the Depression era, Covello would appropriate and recast the social progressives' school as social center in the form of a citizen-centered community school. The social progressives' influence, however, was short-lived in the 1910s—professional expertise and a client-centered approach increasingly dominated the social center movement in the years before World War I.

Dewey's Seminal Essay

As Dewey astutely recognized, the settlement house provided a new way to conceptualize the role and organization of public schools in an advanced industrial society. Hull House directly inspired his idea of the school as "a center of life for all ages and classes, . . . a thoroughly socialized affair in contact at all points with the flow of community life."[11] In "The School as Social Centre," his 1902 address to the National Council of Education, Dewey emphasized the centrality of the neighborhood school in modern community life and its potential as a center and catalyst for stabilizing and strengthening the local community. The school social center would provide an easily accessible neighborhood site for continuous lifelong learning, which Dewey recognized as a sine qua non of modern industrial life. It would also be a "social clearing house" where face-to-face communication would be the stock-in-trade, "where ideas and beliefs may be exchanged, not merely in the arena of formal discussion—for argument alone breeds misunderstanding and fixes prejudice—but in ways where ideas are incarnated in human form and clothed with the winning grace of personal life. Classes for study may be numerous, but all are regarded as *modes of bringing people together, of doing away with barriers of caste, or class, or race, or type of experience that keep people from real communion with each other*" (emphasis added). Lastly, the school social center would provide constructive amusement and recreation for adults: "The social club, the gymnasium, the amateur theatrical representation, the concert, the stereopticon lecture, these are agencies the force of which social settlements have long known; and which are coming into use wherever anything is doing in the way of making schools social centers."[12]

Properly organized, school social centers would be alive with the spirit and activities of "social intercourse," a term by which Dewey seems to mean the collaborative production of goods. Yet he only posited "certain general lines" as to how all this might actually work—the details of implementation were of marginal interest to him. Moreover, Dewey failed to consider the role that social centers might play as community problem–solving institutions, in particular how local social problems might become grist for children's active learning.[13]

That stated, it is important to note that "The School as Social Centre" marked a radical shift in Dewey's writing during the Dewey School era at the University of Chicago (1896–1904). As political philosopher Alan Ryan observes, Dewey's Chicago writings, in particular the essays in *The School and Society* (1900) and his famous monograph on *The Child and Curriculum* (1902), were largely concerned with deriving a set of principles and abstractions from what was unambiguously a *laboratory school* experiment.[14] Dewey and his staff cleverly used the theme of "occupations"—their term for generic cultural developments like weaving, sewing, cooking, and metalworking—as the organizing framework for the curriculum. Children worked experimentally and "conjointly" on problems like building a miniature smelting furnace, "discovering" why wool predated cotton in the evolution of cloth manufacture, and testing the effects of scalding, simmering, and boiling water on egg whites; the children, in effect, were guided to recapitulate, in a laboratory setting, the evolution of human culture writ large.[15] For all the intellectual excitement and learning these activities elicited, there was very little if anything about the Dewey School that engaged fin de siècle Chicago and little that might have been replicated by ordinary teachers in nonlaboratory settings. That is to say, the school was neither the "miniature community" nor the "embryonic society" that Dewey claimed it to be. In fact, the Dewey School contradicted a basic proposition in Dewey's theory: that urban/industrial-age schooling must somehow retain the advantages of the intellectual, social, and moral education embedded in the "apprentice-like, household-and-community problem solving, informal natural learning system of preindustrial society."[16]

Strongly influenced by the women of Hull House, Dewey turned, in "The School as Social Centre," toward grounding his theory in real-world contingencies. That he failed to follow up on that promising start, and the implications of that failure, are complex issues that we take up in Chapter 8. "The School as Social Centre" signals a turning point in community school history: Capturing an idea that was "in the air" at the turn of the last century, Dewey gave it his prestigious imprimatur. A social movement was starting to coalesce.[17]

Edward J. Ward and the Rochester Social Centers

A bellwether of the social movement toward school social centers was the New York City public school system, where the board of education sponsored thriving "wider use" programs. Vacation schools, evening elementary schools, public lecture centers, and evening recreation centers attracted what Clarence Perry of the Russell Sage Foundation described as a "cosmopolitan multitude" of New York's immigrant working class.[18] The settlement-style public school envisioned by Dewey, however, did not originate on a citywide basis in New York, but rather in Rochester in 1907. Edward J. Ward, a grassroots progressive, Social Gospeler, and communitarian who "wanted to connect the primary bonds of familial association to the entire neighborhood through the local schools," directed the Rochester social centers. Ward encouraged the development of self-governing adult centers and civic clubs, with a premium on free speech and the give-and-take of the open forum. Notable for their heated debates on politically charged topics freely chosen by the participants, the

Rochester social centers were organized to cultivate deliberative skills and "to educate citizens for the responsibilities of self-government."[19]

By the end of 1907–8, three social centers were operating in Rochester as evening recreation centers and neighborhood clubhouses for "the discussion and understanding of civic questions and the development of a good community spirit." In 1908–9, sixteen social centers involved 1,500 active members organized under the umbrella of the Citywide Federation of Civic Clubs. In 1909–10, with eighteen social centers in operation, Rochester witnessed the first opening of a dental office inside a public school, the use of schoolhouses as art galleries and local health offices, the introduction of motion pictures in schools, and the establishment of employment bureaus in the neighborhood libraries of the social centers.[20]

The Rochester social centers received support from an annual school board appropriation that amounted to $20,000 by 1909–10, and the endorsement of the city's labor and trade council and women's associations. Governor Charles Evans Hughes told the Federation of Civic Clubs: "You are buttressing the foundations of democracy." Yet the participatory democratic features of the social centers raised the hackles of Rochester's business community, five local newspapers, and "Boss" George Aldridge and his loyal Catholic constituents, who anathematized Ward's uncensored public forums and attacked the centers as hotbeds of socialism and atheism.[21]

By 1909–10, the social center movement in Rochester was, in Ward's words, "continually under the fire of misrepresentation from the press and of hostility from the city hall."[22] Entrenched opposition by business leaders and elite conservative groups to the open examination of social injustice forced curtailment of the civic clubs and led to the dismissal of Ward and his associates. Consequently, "Rochester's centers after 1910 were almost indistinguishable from those in many parts of the nation, as they increasingly emphasized recreational programs to the virtual exclusion of adult civic participation."[23]

In hindsight it is important to note the genuine strengths of Rochester's brief experiment with democratic social centers. The social centers garnered support from diverse civic groups along the political spectrum, including women's clubs, settlement workers, trade unionists, socialists, and even the Daughters of the American Revolution. The civic clubs were racially integrated and inclusive of people from all walks of life—for example, one debate paired a Polish washwoman and the president of the Women's Christian Temperance Union against a day cleaner and a college professor. Significantly, the clubs' political agendas were planned and organized by participants themselves.[24] In an era when administrative progressives were imposing their templates of centralized school governance and expert management on urban schools, Rochester's social centers provided an alternative model of bottom-up civic participation and grassroots social action that challenged the growing hegemony of social efficiency schooling.

After Rochester, Ward carried the banner of the social center movement to Wisconsin, where he worked out of the extension division of the University of Wisconsin, serving for several years as an advisor for social center development and helping organize hundreds of social centers in the state's hinterlands.[25] As historian William Reese concludes: "After 1910, Ward continued to publicize the value of neighborhood civic clubs, the wider use of the schools, and general educational extension. He never let his failures in Rochester dim his optimism."[26]

Building a Social Movement: From City to Hinterland

Giving impetus to a national social center movement was the First National Conference on Social Center Development, conducted in the fall of 1911 under the auspices of the University of Wisconsin's extension division, described ebulliently by one observer as follows: "It was a conference to be remembered from New York to California, from Texas to North Dakota. Delegates came representing city clubs, boards of education, welfare committees, churches, universities, and various associations for civic and social betterment. A new spirit of enthusiasm, a new hope for the future, a fresh and eager interest in the interchange of ideas and experiences seemed to fill the air." The conference, whose participants included New Jersey governor Woodrow Wilson, created the Social Center Association of America, avowedly "to promote the development of intelligent public spirit through community use of the common schoolhouse—for *free discussion of public questions* and all wholesome, civic, education and recreational activities" (original emphasis).[27]

In 1911 Mary Parker Follett, a Boston social worker and chairperson of the Women's Municipal League's Committee on Extended Use of School Buildings in that city, helped establish the East Boston High School Social Center, which included a dramatic club, a recreation club, an orchestra—and most important in Follett's view, a "city council," which met weekly to debate, as Follett put it, "practical municipal questions." City councils, identical to Ward's civic clubs, were a major component of the other Boston school social centers that Follett helped organize between 1911 and 1913. Follett was both a theorist and proponent of democratic deliberation; she regarded local neighborhood social centers as wellsprings of democratic living and behavior.[28]

L. J. Hanifan, West Virginia state superintendent of rural schools, shared Follett's perspective on the democratizing potential of social centers. Describing the situation of a rural West Virginia school district in 1913, Hanifan apparently coined the term "social capital," which he defined as "good will, fellowship, sympathy, and social intercourse among the individuals and families who make up a social unit." Social centers in the town of Hundred created social capital through school-based community forums, fairs and exhibits, adult education and public lecture programs, student presentations on community

history, and a district school baseball league. Hanifan noted that Hundred's
social capital became civically oriented; weekly community meetings pro-
gressed in stages from recreation to a successful campaign to secure better
roads in the district.[29]

By 1913, seventy-one cities in twenty-one states reported having social
centers; by 1914, seventeen states had enacted wider-use legislation. "The
social center movement had captured the imaginations of educational decision-
makers and legislators alike," writes Edward Stevens. "It administered to both
urban and rural constituencies."[30] At its annual meeting in San Francisco in
1912, the National Education Association endorsed social centers, declaring
that "the school buildings of our land . . . should become the radiating centers
of cultural and social activity in the neighborhood in a spirit of civic unity and
cooperation."[31] Clarence Perry, who joined the Russell Sage Foundation's
Recreation Department in May 1909, helped popularize social centers through
his widely read book, *Wider Use of the School Plant* (1913), two monographs,
and some twenty pamphlets.[32] Indeed, the foundation, through its publication
of Perry's tracts, played a pioneering, catalytic role in creating a national social
center movement.[33]

Social centers exerted enormous appeal for efficiency-minded administrators and policy makers. Extended use of the school building ensured that valuable public property would not sit idle after the regular school day or school
week had ended. In Perry's view, the social centers promoted not only a more
stable social order, but also a more humane, healthier, happier one. Perry
claimed that social centers prevented "considerable loss of life" by keeping children off the streets and out of their mothers' kitchens, and by providing young
men with wholesome diversions to compete with the local saloon.[34]

The social center movement preached participatory democracy, but the
reality of social center operations often belied the rhetoric of citizen participation. As Robert Fisher writes, social center development in the cities relied
heavily on outside organizers. While volunteers secured funds from local officials, they often hired trained organizers to develop support for a "neighborhood group" that would represent the social center's clubs; often the same hired
organizer would serve as a "community secretary," planning and administering the center's activities with varying levels of support from community members.[35] In practice the professional organizer's role was increasingly dominant.
Although the aim may have been to transfer governance and administrative
roles to the local citizenry, "the lack of any concrete evidence of citizen participation in the neighborhood groups, and the comments of more detached
observers, suggest strongly that organizing from the bottom up remained, at
best, an unfulfilled ideal."[36]

Rhetoric began to match reality as the zeitgeist of scientific management and
reforming professionalism took hold in the social center movement. After 1915,
newly established social centers, now using the label "community centers," more

and more reflected an ideological shift that subordinated process goals of participatory democracy, self-reliance, and community building to a technical emphasis on increasing the efficiency of social programs and services in the neighborhoods through centralized planning. The new task goals enunciated the role of professional community organizers and social workers, with particular attention to scientific management of the centers. John Collier, of the People's Institute of New York City, declared: "Democracy needs science, and the community movement aims to put science—which means experts—into the people's hands." Increasingly, on the eve of World War I, centralized planning units were administering the local community centers.[37]

The People's Institute of New York City epitomized these changes in the theory and practice of social centers. Founded in 1897 by Charles Sprague Smith, a former professor at Columbia University, the People's Institute rented quarters in Cooper Union, where, among other events, it used the Great Hall for the People's Forum, a Friday-evening venue for lectures and discussions of social problems and a program of grassroots political reform. Straw votes were taken on pending legislation and the results published, often with potent effect, for example, helping to secure public ownership of New York's rapid transit system in 1913.[38]

After 1910, the People's Institute pioneered the development of social centers in New York, replicating Ward's Rochester model.[39] In 1912, the board of education authorized the institute to organize "an experimental self-supporting, self-governing social center" at P.S. 63 at East Fourth Street and First Avenue. With elected representatives and a professional organizer as its chairperson, P.S. 63 Social Center generated operating funds from membership fees and various entertainments. The social center sponsored a weekly People's Forum, neighborhood civic clubs, more than forty social and literary clubs, and such activities as drama, music, debating, athletics, and social dancing. In 1914, the People's Institute opened a second school social center at P.S. 17 in Hell's Kitchen. The success of the two programs convinced the board of education to take over the institute's work of organizing the city's social centers. In 1915 the board created a standing committee on community centers and appointed a citywide director of community centers; by 1918, New York was sponsoring eighty community centers.[40]

In October 1915, the People's Institute opened the New York Training School for Community Workers in Gramercy Park. Its purpose was "to discover men and women possessed of social insight and of the capacity for leadership, and to equip them to carry forward the new community movement." The training school sponsored the 1916 National Conference on Community Centers and Related Problems, which organized the National Community Center Association; the training school also provided staff and resources for the new association's monthly magazine, the *Community Center.* Although the training school continued to provide administrative and financial support, the National

Community Center Association, with permanent headquarters in Chicago, operated independently of the People's Institute. Social workers, not community center members, attended the annual meetings of the National Community Center Association. Increasingly, local neighborhood efforts were being coordinated and unified at the national level.[41]

By World War I, the social/community centers were distancing themselves from the civic purposes that had animated the institutions founded by social progressives such as Ward, Follett, and Smith.[42] The home-front mobilization during the war would accelerate that trend and set the stage for a postwar decade of growth in the community center movement. Developments in the 1920s would be marked by the professional control of community centers and a predominant emphasis on community recreation.

World War I and the
Withering of Reform, 1917–29

As relations with Germany deteriorated, on 29 August 1916 Congress established the Council of National Defense. The purpose of this new agency was to create "relations which render possible in time of need, the immediate concentration and the utilization of the resources of the nation." When the United States entered the war in 1917, the council "concentrated its efforts on the mobilization of industries, resources and people of the United States for the effective conduct of the war."[43] The nation's community centers, supported in thirteen states with public funds and responsible to state and local subsidiaries of the Council of National Defense, shifted their primary focus from neighborhood issues to war mobilization. The community centers sponsored Americanization programs, Red Cross relief, Liberty Loan drives, soldiers' aid work, and community thrift, food austerity, and nutrition programs. Consonant with the repressive political climate of 1917–18, they restricted free speech in their forums and propagandized the war effort through motion pictures, civic activities, and social clubs. The trend toward professional control continued unabated. At the P.S. 40 community center in Gramercy Park, the community governing board included twenty-eight professional representatives of public and private war-related agencies.[44]

In 1919–20, Clarence Perry reported that 667 school centers operated in 107 cities.[45] Community center development accelerated in the 1920s. Citing data from a 1924 national study, Eleanor Glueck wrote in 1927 that "school houses are being very generally utilized throughout the United States for community purposes," with the greatest use reported by states where laws provided for extended use of schools and public financing for such activity. As for regular community participation: "Only 5 percent of the school houses in the United States are being regularly used . . . as often as once a week for two types of activities or twice a week for one, not including night schools." Seven hundred and twenty-two cities, townships, and villages met this criterion for regular use. Glueck observed that "the regular use of schoolhouses is growing, as there has been an increase of 128 per cent since 1919 in the number of cities over five thousand population which have school centers (according to the definition used), and of 55 per cent in the total number of school centers in cities over five thousand population. There has also been some increase in the length of season of school centers and the number of evenings weekly that such centers are open. There is every certainty, then, that the use of schoolhouses for community purposes is growing rapidly throughout the country."[46]

Those community purposes were increasingly recreational in the 1920s—to the chagrin of social progressives who had imagined that the wartime community center movement would usher in an era of social reconstruction.[47] Glueck noted dourly: "The recreational phase of the school center movement has been the first to develop and the civic feature which Ward and others emphasized is having a very slow growth." An ardent communitarian, Glueck envisaged the primary role of the school community center as "that of acting as a medium for the integration of the life of the *individual* neighborhood" (original emphasis).[48]

The distancing of school community centers from social reform in the 1920s resonated with the ethic of normalcy that pervaded virtually every institution in that conservative decade.[49] Mass consumerism and social mobility fueled a national climate of narcissism that obtained quasi-scientific legitimacy from Freudian psychology. In New York, the People's Institute abandoned its community centers to concentrate on developing a liberal education program for adults—a conservative emphasis the institute maintained until its merger with Cooper Union in 1934.[50]

The point of view that schools can serve larger community purposes than recreation had few adherents outside a small circle of social visionaries that included Clarence Perry.[51] After 1924 Perry advocated the "neighborhood unit" as the primary locus of city and regional development.[52] Carefully planned to promote family life, the neighborhood unit, "with its physical demarcation, its planned recreational facilities, its accessible shopping centers, and its convenient circulatory system—all integrated and harmonized by artistic designing—would furnish the kind of environment where vigorous health, a rich social life, civic efficiency, and a progressive community consciousness would spontaneously develop and permanently flourish."[53] Perry based his visionary idea on an analysis of Forest Hills Gardens, a successful residential development in the Borough of Queens, New York City. Modeled after developments in England's City Garden movement, Forest Hills Gardens was financed by the Russell Sage Foundation, landscaped by Frederick Law Olmsted, Jr. and constructed by architect Grosvenor Atterbury. Perry claimed that the general principles embodied in the development of Forest Hills Gardens, "a highly satisfactory neighborhood" where he and his family had lived since 1912, could be effectively applied in any city or suburb. Perry pitched his argument especially to city planners intent on replacing metropolitan slums with apartment house developments.[54]

At the center of Perry's neighborhood unit stood the neighborhood elementary school. In the 1929 *Regional Plan of New York and Its Environs,* sponsored by the Russell Sage Foundation, Perry wrote that a neighborhood unit's "desirable area" was 160 acres, with the school site centrally located to serve families living within one-quarter to one-third of a mile from the school.[55] He described the neighborhood-unit community school as the "focussing point, both physically and psychically, for the life of the neighborhood, . . . the core of a live community." (Perry encouraged what he saw as a trend toward building "commodious auditoriums" to be used for public events, even partisan political rallies; he also advocated extension libraries, open to the public in the evenings, which he claimed to find in many new city schools.)[56]

Although Perry's plan had the endorsement of Lewis Mumford and the Regional Planning Association of America, the neighborhood unit made little headway within the city planning profession in the 1930s.[57] By the mid-1940s the central orientation of city planning was to redevelop blighted areas to attract white middle-income residents to the city; perhaps the quintessential statement of that orientation was Stuyvesant Town, built on Manhattan's Lower East Side as "a self-contained new community, a virtual suburb within the city." Financed by a private redeveloper, the Metropolitan Life Insurance Company, Stuyvesant Town had no public school, a nondecision ensuring that children on the periphery would not sully the racial and class homogeneity of the white middle-class housing project.[58] Enthralled city planners hailed Stuyvesant Town as the wave of the future[59]—so far had the planners distanced themselves from Perry's neighborhood unit and the school reform tradition of the school as social center.

Set adrift from its Progressive era moorings, the community center movement merged with the mainstream of the U.S. playground and recreation movement in the 1930s.[60] In New York City, community centers qua recreation centers thrived up to and well beyond World War II, as evidenced by board of education reports from the thirties, forties, and fifties.[61] While the community centers turned away from the civic and social meliorist agendas of the social center movement, a small group of determined social progressives in the 1930s struggled to maintain the reform tradition of community-centered schooling. By middecade a community school movement was aborning. Disparate community-centered educational projects, in some cases fully functioning community schools, sprang up in response to the Depression, more often than not in unrelated ways. In a sense this was a social movement in search of itself—that is, it required the efforts of progressive educators to find a common ground and to coalesce projects that already existed in far-flung and often isolated areas into a national movement.

The Rise of Community Schools, 1929–1942

Mounted by leading progressive intellectuals, a trenchant social critique of capitalism and the U.S. schooling system fortified activist educators who wanted to achieve social justice and a reasonable quality of life for all Americans, albeit without social upheaval. Leonard Covello belonged to this demimonde group of educators, who may be said to have reinvented and updated Dewey's idea of "the school as social centre." Working far out of the mainstream, community school organizers found a favorable venue for disseminating their ideas in professional journals such as *Progressive Education, Clearing House,* and the *Journal of Educational Sociology,* which occasionally featured articles on the "community-centered school," a term that had currency by the mid-1930s. Two books in particular signified attempts to unify and extend the various projects, and to engender a social movement toward community schools: Paul Hanna's *Youth Serves the Community* (1936) and Samuel Everett's edited volume *The Community School* (1938).

Working under Works Progress Administration (WPA) auspices, Hanna and his research associates collected descriptive information from hundreds of youth-service projects in the United States and abroad. The youth-service projects, most of which were school based, fell into six broad categories: public safety; civic beautification; community health; agricultural and industrial improvement; civic arts; and local history, surveys, and inventories and protection of resources. Teachers College professor William Heard Kilpatrick, who wrote the book's introduction, hailed the projects as exemplars of "cooperative activities for community improvement."[62] The book also had a critical edge. In the concluding chapter, Hanna reported his impression that "rural youth has more leadership and more opportunity for socially useful work than has urban youth." This disparity was "chiefly due to the fact that the rural environment is more often owned or controlled by the adults who are directly concerned with its improvement. The urban environment is usually controlled by impersonal corporations, set in a complex economic and political milieu which is so impregnable that youth cannot really have access to it."[63]

Hanna believed that the obstacles to youth service in the nation's cities could be overcome through a radically reconstructed schooling system. "The school is the universal, continuing, well-equipped and locally-controlled, institution in every community," he wrote. Having stated that, he articulated a unifying civic purpose for schooling. "But if the American school should desire to provide the leadership for socially-useful work of children and youth," he concluded, "school people must vastly *increase* their vision and their techniques.

The school program must shift its emphasis from the classical and academic approach to an emphasis on the solution of problems facing children and youth here and now, and it must foresee the problems of the future" (original emphasis).[64] It would be a short analytic leap from Hanna's call for "a coordinated movement on a national scale" to Samuel Everett's effort two years later to launch a national community school movement.

In *The Community School* Everett, a Northwestern University education professor, showcased a handful of community school projects in diverse settings. The venerable Kilpatrick introduced the book with a laudatory piece similar to the introduction he had written for Paul Hanna's book. Leonard Covello contributed one of his most cogent essays, "The School as a Center of Community Life in an Immigrant Area," highlighting Benjamin Franklin's role as a public space for intercultural and intergenerational education.[65] Two of the community schools described in this volume operated in the multiethnic agricultural district of Waialua, on the island of Oahu, Hawaii. Their school-community programs were jointly governed by a community coordinating council whose standing committees played an analogous role to Franklin's community advisory council.[66]

Everett's book also included a description of the Highlander Folk School near Monteagle, in mountainous Grundy County, Tennessee—a project that in the 1930s and 1940s helped educate and unionize southern textile workers, coal miners, and other industrial groups. Highlander was founded in 1932 by Myles Horton, a theology-trained labor organizer who was influenced by Reinhold Niebuhr, Robert Park, John Dewey, Jane Addams, and Bishop Grundtvig, founder of the nineteenth-century Danish folk school movement.[67] Horton envisioned the folk school functioning as a community center, with an adjoining nursery school, elementary school, "neighborhood school" (the latter replacing the conventional junior and senior high school), and adult program. Starting in the elementary school "the struggle for democracy" would permeate every aspect of the child's education. This was a radical and certainly dangerous position, considering the repressive racial and labor climate of the South in the 1930s; for example, in the neighborhood school "a study would be made of the extra-legal functions of vigilante organizations which openly and secretly commit acts of violence against union organizers and radical political leaders. The segregation, inequality of opportunity, and lynching of negroes would be analyzed. Other infringements considered might be the herding of unorganized industrial workers, farm laborers, and the share-croppers to the polls by their employers. Such studies should lead to a critical attitude towards political democracy and the knowledge of its limitations without a basis in economic democracy."[68]

Significantly absent in *The Community School* are two important rural community schools of the Depression era—the Nambé School (Santa Fe County, New Mexico, 1937–42) and the Arthurdale School (Preston County,

West Virginia, 1934–36). Although they were short-lived, Nambé and Arthurdale were fully functioning community schools that mediated health, social, and recreational services, and systematically integrated community themes and issues into the day-school curriculum.[69] Recent scholarship offers a critical reappraisal of these projects—a much needed corrective to the accounts published by the projects' founders, Lloyd S. Tireman at Nambé and Elsie Ripley Clapp at Arthurdale.

Nambé

The school at Nambé, New Mexico, which operated from 1937 to 1942, was a noteworthy yet relatively obscure community school experiment. Populated mainly by the descendants of Spanish American settlers who arrived from Mexico as early as 1711 and built their adobe houses on the red-clay banks of the shallow Nambé River, a tributary of the Rio Grande, the village of Nambé was a drought-stricken, erosion-blighted village located eighteen miles north of Santa Fe at the foot of the heavily forested Sangre de Cristo mountains. The villagers, some six hundred people and 152 families, etched out a hardscrabble subsistence from their farm fields, which were dependent on three long irrigation ditches running out of the Pojoaque River to the north. Water and grazing rights were a persistent source of conflict with the native peoples of the adjacent Pueblo lands.[70]

Santa Fe resident Cyrus McCormick, the founder and publisher of the *New Mexico Sentinel,* a Republican weekly, and his wife, Florence, provided the original impetus for the Nambé community school. (The grandson and namesake of the founder of International Harvester, McCormick had a strong civic conscience.) Convinced that the local school, a preschool through eighth-grade facility, could better serve the economically distressed area in a radically altered form, the McCormicks arranged with Joseph Granito, the Santa Fe County superintendent of schools, and Professor Lloyd S. Tireman of the University of New Mexico, a reforming professional, to help create a community-centered school. The McCormicks agreed to underwrite the school for five years—in the end the couple would donate a total of $19,000 and contribute to a new school building. Tireman, who agreed to direct the venture, persuaded the General Education Board to approve a transfer of $8,000 from his previously funded project, the San José Demonstration and Experimental School in Bernalillo County, to Nambé. In addition to these funds, Santa Fe County continued to provide Nambé's usual county school allotment. It was the McCormicks' philanthropy, however, that was indispensable to the operation of the community school.[71]

Following a town meeting at which a majority of the villagers approved the project, Granito and Tireman began to organize the school and hired teachers who were deemed to be "open-minded, familiar, and sympathetic with the problems of Spanish-speaking children; who were familiar with rural areas and endowed with the vision and experience which would be necessary for the realization of the aims of the project." The pedagogical aim was unambiguously community centered: "The starting point in every part of the curriculum will be Nambé. The pupil may go to the farthest point of the earth but must follow the plan of going from something that is familiar and well known to something that is over the horizon. Unless that connection can be established by the pupils, we will relentlessly omit that part of the curriculum no matter how sanctified it may be by tradition and academic respectability." There is more than an inkling here of hostility to subject matter: "If one honestly and consistently follows it, the formal and familiar course of study is subjected to rough treatment. Whole sections of organized knowledge rendered sacred by long use are omitted! This method places a premium on social utility and removes 'knowledge for its own sake' to a secondary place." (The planners stipulated that reading lists would be available to the children to ensure a broader coverage of subject matter.)[72]

By 1939 the school plant included three buildings, two preexisting and one donated by the McCormicks, housing a nursery school, lower school (prefirst to third grade), and upper school (fourth to eighth grade). Consistent with the results of a community survey, Nambé curricula focused on the natural sciences, with a particular emphasis on health education and land management. Second- and third-grade work, for example, included studies of indigenous flora and fauna (in connection with the school garden), nutrition, and sanitation. Fourth and fifth graders focused on the physical properties and public health/social dimensions of water use and conservation. Students in the upper grades investigated problems of land use.[73]

Literacy was taught in the context of Nambé community studies. The teachers grouped students in their classes according to achievement levels for instruction in reading and arithmetic; appropriate activities based on the community theme were worked out for each level. The arrangement was flexible, and a student could advance to a higher level. English was the only language of instruction. Whereas Tireman apparently wanted a bilingual program in the higher grades, one that emphasized both English and Spanish in written and oral form, the teachers and parents insisted on, and got, an English-only program. Any use of Spanish, including singing Spanish folk songs, was openly discouraged, even on the playground. Principal Mary Watson relented to the extent of sending notes home in Spanish after instructions in English to bring in products made in Nambé resulted in a student's presenting a Navajo rug.[74]

Beyond its educational role, the Nambé School was a center for community health and social services. As Nambé lacked any accessible medical services (the nearest hospital was in Santa Fe, the nearest doctor in Española), the McCormicks paid the salary of a Spanish-speaking public health nurse, who organized a school-community health education program and community clinic that provided prenatal and infant-welfare services, venereal-disease treatment, and immunization services. Promoting land-use management skills, the school helped link the community's farmers to county and state extension, forest, and conservation services. It also connected unemployed youths and adults to federal National Youth Administration and WPA projects in both the school and community. WPA funds provided local labor for constructing the new Nambé school, and for a recreation director, a hot lunch program, and a nursery school. Lastly, the school became the community center for recreation and entertainment. The PTA sponsored dances, movies, speakers, and a library service; the school and the local fraternal organization, Sociedad Protectivo Mutual de Trabajadores Unidos, jointly sponsored fiestas, an annual Christmas program, theatrical productions, and music performances.[75]

These curricular and community outreach efforts, however, could not be sustained. One immediate problem was the high turnover rate of teachers. Of a total of twenty-one teachers on the Nambé faculty between 1937 and 1942, only two taught every year. Eight teachers did not last beyond one year and fifteen served two years or less. Most of the faculty was non–Spanish speaking. Nambé may have offered more rustication than many of the Anglo teachers were willing to tolerate. Frank Angel, for example, noted the difficulty he had finding a satisfactory residence in Nambé: "Looking for a place to move to, I found not a single house with a bath. The water in every house I've visited so far is all brought in from uncovered, unprotected outside wells."[76]

The teachers also had to contend with Tireman's combative personality. According to Tireman's biographer, David Bachelor, the hard-driving director was abrasive and heavy-handed with his subordinates, most of whom were women.[77] Historian Lynne Marie Getz observes a paternalistic-ethnocentric streak in Tireman's behavior at Nambé, which may have been a factor in ending the community school in 1942. Getz argues that Tireman imposed a romanticized version of Hispano culture on the school; like the Anglo literati in New Mexico generally, he chose to emphasize as valuable "the beauty-loving tendencies" (his phrase) of Spanish-speaking people, expressed in their folklore, music, and colonial arts. Tireman's approach was politically conservative and narrowly based on an Anglo standard of culture—any cultural attribute, real or imagined, that to his mind threatened the political status quo was anathema. While he sincerely wanted to improve the living conditions of Spanish-speaking subsistence farmers in the Southwest, he could not envision these people in the U.S. economic mainstream. His main interest in bilingualism was to promote the learning of English as a vehicle of assimilation for more effective and productive subsistence farming. Tireman failed to comprehend that many of the school's parents wanted their children to graduate high school and attend college. Regarding the low graduation rates of former Nambé students who attended the consolidated high school in nearby Pojoaque, he wrote tellingly: "Our job is not to prepare these children for college but to live happier and more efficiently in this community."[78]

After five years of operation, the Nambé Community School ended in the summer of 1942. Residents voted in a community meeting to return the school to the Santa Fe School District, in effect restoring its status as an ordinary rural school, even though Cyrus McCormick promised continued funding for the community school. The villagers had grown increasingly fearful that community-centered schooling was depriving their children of a demanding education. They were concerned about the lack of homework, and they had difficulty squaring their perception of "real school" with the Nambé School's activity curriculum. Here the villagers raised what has been a continuous issue with community schools—the danger that the school's emphasis on social issues will deprive young people of the knowledge and intellectual skills they need to become productive, socially mobile workers adaptable to a changing economy. Finally, a sense that the regional economy was on the upswing, especially after Pearl Harbor, made the community school's social service role more expendable for the villagers than it had been previously.[79] In the end Nambé was a client-centered project that offered its clients no means for political empowerment or democratic self-development, and it even worked to suppress their educational dreams. When the winds of fortune changed, there was little left to attract the villagers and much to repel them.

Arthurdale

The locale hardest hit by the Depression in the West Virginia coal fields was Scott's Run, named after a stream that carved out a narrow, five-mile-long coal hollow and joined the Monongahela River a few miles northwest of the state capital, Morgantown.[80] During the post–World War I boom in the bituminous coal industry, some thirty-six mines operated along the Run, and densely populated company towns sprouted on the hillsides up and down the hollow. By the mid-1920s, the coal boom had run its course; with production sharply curtailed, out-of-work miners began leaving the hollow. Those who remained in the crumbling company towns were consigned to lives of horrific poverty, filth, and disease.[81]

Appalled by the conditions she observed there in the summer of 1933, Eleanor Roosevelt used her formidable influence in Washington to have the first federal "subsistence homestead" built for the people of Scott's Run. (Section 208 of Title II of the National Industrial Recovery Act of 1933 set aside $25 million in a revolving fund for the subsistence homestead program, which was administered by the Department of the Interior; the Arthurdale homestead was created specifically to alleviate the social and economic plight of indigent coal miners and their families.)[82] The site chosen for the experiment was a tax-burdened farm consisting of 1,028 acres in Preston County seventeen miles southeast of Morgantown, an estate owned by Richard Arthur, a prosperous hotel proprietor in Pittsburgh and "gentleman farmer." Included with the sale of the property, purchased for $45,000, was a twenty-two-room Victorian mansion built in 1903.[83]

Considering Arthurdale's status as a "demonstration project" or "federal laboratory," the Arthurdale selection committee felt justified in exercising careful scrutiny to select 165 families for the new venture. Their careful scrutiny, however, was tainted by prejudice: Blacks and immigrant applicants were denied admission to Arthurdale; the project accepted native-born whites only. (According to the 1920 manuscript census, 60 percent of the Run's miners were immigrants, of whom 93 percent were southern or eastern European; nonforeign whites and blacks each made up 20 percent of the population.)[84] Disavowing any racial prejudice on their part, the first group of homesteaders themselves voted against including any blacks at Arthurdale, elliptically citing West Virginia's Jim Crow laws: "The admission of Negroes would necessitate the establishment of separate schools and churches, as our State laws forbid both races to attend the same schools."[85] "Surprised and dismayed," ER accepted the homesteaders' wishes—it was a price the pragmatic humanitarian would grudgingly pay to accomplish her other goals.[86]

Over a four-year period, 1933–37, a total of 165 houses were built in three groups of increasingly better design and construction. When it was finally completed in 1939, the town-center complex included an assembly hall, general store, barber shop, weaving room, post office, administration center, salesroom for the Mountaineer Craftsmen Cooperative Association, six school buildings, grist mill, health center, and three factory buildings.[87] The new community spread out about a half mile beyond the community center, the homesteads scattered among gently sloping meadows interspersed with small groves of trees. Subsistence family farming was expected to be the major activity. Yet as the federal planners knew only too well, the success of subsistence homesteading would be contingent on the availability of part-time industrial employment, which was expected to be the homesteaders' primary source of cash income.[88] (By World War II the failure to recruit a viable branch industry would be the homestead's undoing.)

From the outset, Arthurdale was beset with administrative and financial problems, not to mention an intensive and occasionally scurrilous media scrutiny because Arthurdale was regarded as Eleanor Roosevelt's pet project, hence grist for New Deal–hating conservatives.[89] Cost overruns propelled by major flaws in the first homestead houses inspired such embarrassing headlines as "Mud and Red Ink Flooding Utopia: Mrs. Roosevelt's

Subsistence Homestead Totters" and "Blunders and Waste Written Off as U.S. Expense."[90] New Deal administrative changes contributed to the project's instability—during the fourteen years of federal stewardship at Arthurdale, a total of four government agencies and five managers (four prior to 1941) administered the project.[91]

For all these problems, Arthurdale managed to create a viable communal life and spirit of cooperation. The major catalyst for community building was the Arthurdale School, which functioned as a community school from 1934 to 1936. On the strength of the First Lady's recommendation, Elsie Ripley Clapp was appointed by the ad hoc West Virginia School Advisory Committee in January of 1934 to organize and direct the new school. A graduate of Barnard College and Columbia University, as well as a former teaching assistant and lifelong devotee of John Dewey, Clapp was widely regarded as a leading expert on rural education.[92] She served as vice president of the Progressive Education Association and held several important committee positions in the PEA. Coming from a background of progressive teaching in elite East Coast private schools, from 1929 to 1934 she directed the Ballard School, a rural community school in Jefferson County, Kentucky, an experience she recounted in her 1939 book *Community Schools in Action.* Here Clapp's program included an agenda of health and social services for children and families, as well as a curriculum that was reminiscent of Dewey's Chicago Laboratory School in two key ways: an emphasis on active experiential learning ("learning by doing") and the spiraling of a general theme from lower to upper grades—in Dewey's case, U.S. economic history; in Clapp's case, Kentucky life and history. Clapp would recall that when she consulted Dewey about taking the position in Kentucky, he told her: "I cannot urge you to do it, because I think it would be difficult, but I have always hoped I would live to see such a dream come true. Before long we are going to need community schools in this country, and someone must learn by doing it just what a community school is and does."[93] In effect Clapp would act as Dewey's agent for ideas he had introduced in his 1902 essay "The School as Social Centre" and Laboratory School writings. More than Ballard, Arthurdale would involve an adventurous, logical extension of Dewey's Chicago theory.[94]

Preston County provided three local teachers, each handpicked by Clapp. Private donations arranged by ER paid for a group of supplementary teachers, six of whom accompanied Clapp from the Ballard School, "all steeped in progressive education."[95] As a "fund raiser, promoter, and guiding spirit," the First Lady not only organized a national advisory board, which included such luminaries as John Dewey and Lucy Sprague Mitchell, but also persuaded wealthy friends such as financier Bernard Baruch to make substantial donations to the school through the American Friends Service Committee.[96] Various buildings on the Arthur estate, including the Victorian mansion, were reconditioned for school use, and the jury-rigged facility opened in September 1934 with 167 pupils, reaching 246 by the end of the first year (the following year the number would total 317).[97]

The most pressing community need in Arthurdale was public health, as Preston County lacked any clinics, district nurses, and school dentists. To provide on-site health care, Clapp recruited a capable nurse who had worked at the Henry Street Settlement in New York City. In February 1935 a doctor joined the community-support staff, and a monthly dental service was also arranged. The main school building housed the community clinic, where public health services, including vaccinations, immunizations, and a well-baby clinic, were conducted.[98]

Building on and extending Dewey's educational theory, the curriculum at the Arthurdale School revolved around occupations and issues related to reconstructing the children's home community[99]—thus a fundamental distinction from Clapp's earlier initiative in Kentucky. Clapp's strategic conceptual (and instrumental) advance was both to construct her new school as a community problem–solving institution and, progressing beyond Dewey's Chicago theory, to illustrate concretely the principle of "community as text" as the basis of curriculum reconstruction.[100]

At Arthurdale ongoing community activities such as road building, house construction, barn raising, gardening, and well digging embedded the elementary school curriculum. Clapp introduced the phrase "socially functioning studies" to capture the interface of the curriculum and community development. For example, first and second graders "were in fact learning from the activities of their own fathers in farming, in trucking, in building construction. *What they studied everyone was learning and doing*" (original emphasis). In a study of traditional mountain culture and their own pioneer ancestry, fourth graders furnished an old log cabin on the Arthurdale property with furniture and utensils they made in the school shop; here they learned and practiced the Appalachian folk arts of weaving and cookery. Fifth graders' studies of West Virginia colonial life emphasized colonial handicrafts and food preparation, shop work, and the use of local materials and resources.[101] Ninth-grade science included the collection, mounting, and classification of local plants and the operation of a plant-and-shrub nursery—projects that contributed to Arthurdale's planned agricultural development. Eleventh- and twelfth-grade chemistry studies included glassmaking. After a trip to a local glass factory, the students designed and built an arc furnace, experimented with various fuels and chemical compounds, and spent "a great deal of time" on blowing glass.[102]

In the second year of the project, 1935–36, the Arthurdale community built a series of new buildings to permanently house the various components of the Arthurdale School, "a little village in itself," located in a "long sunny meadow under the lee of the Mansion hill and across the road from the Town Center." Clapp described the community uses of the new complex:

On the architect's plans the High School Building was labeled "Building for Older Students and Adults," which expressed the right idea, but
in truth every building was for their use and used by them: notably the
Nursery School, where the Well Baby Clinics were held, and where
the mothers—and fathers—came and went all day; the Recreation
Building, with its basketball floor—"the best in the State," the homesteaders declared—and its stage for plays and concerts used by adult
groups, and its orchestra practice room where the square-dance orchestra rehearsed; the School Center, in whose kitchen and lunchroom the
mothers prepared the School lunches, and which contained the doctor's offices, the savings "Bank" that carried community accounts, and
the Home Economics rooms—canning kitchen, sewing room, and food
demonstration room—used by the women in the afternoons and
evenings; as well as the High School Building itself, whose Science
room and greenhouse, and whose School and Community Library,
were frequented by the older men and women.[103]

While a genuine strength of the Arthurdale curriculum was its immediacy
in the life of the local community, Clapp's program was neither cosmopolitan
nor supportive of a broader democratic movement, unlike the Highlander Folk
School, which cast a wide net for social justice. Daniel Perlstein demonstrates
that the Arthurdale School muted class and race as issues for curriculum study.
Older students were not given the opportunity to examine how the corporate
coal interests wielded power to secure the miners' quiescence, or to study the
recent history of labor militancy in the central Appalachian coalfields. Children
who otherwise made explicit curricular connections with the old log cabin on
the Arthurdale estate, which was built as a slave quarters by the tract's original proprietor, learned nothing of slavery as an institution.[104]
    Samuel Everett, one of Clapp's reviewers, saw value in her book as a prac-
tical guide for rural community schools, yet he found the book lacking a "social
philosophy," a "weakness" (his term) that perhaps explains Clapp's absence in
Everett's book *The Community School.* Specifically Everett criticized Clapp's
programs for ignoring major societal issues, including, among others, race,
farm tenancy, and unionization.[105] Daniel Perlstein and Sam Stack argue that
Clapp failed to address how a "democratic community" might contribute to a
serious attack on societal problems when that community itself is enmeshed
in a "complex society marked by fundamental racial and class relations of dom-
ination and subordination."[106]
    After the 1935–36 school year, Clapp concluded the experimental phase
of her program and transferred administration of the Arthurdale School to
West Virginia state and county authorities. Barnard Baruch, the school's primary financial sponsor, had persuaded ER that continuing to support the community school with large private grants would create an island of dependency

in northern West Virginia—the time had come to make the school a locally funded operation.[107] Not surprisingly, in the absence of sustained institutional support and vigorous leadership, the school lost its community-centered focus. As the progressive educators left Arthurdale, traditional teachers replaced them. "As the school neared the war years," Stephen Haid observes, "it was increasingly the case that Arthurdale was just another rural school in Preston County."[108]

Undaunted by her setback at Arthurdale, Elsie Clapp turned to ER and Baruch for money to start yet another rural community school, this time at a more economically stable subsistence homestead, and to take Arthurdale's non–West Virginia teachers with her. Although Baruch had the highest praise for Clapp's work, he had lost faith in the homestead idea. ER demurred on the grounds that any money she might raise would be obligated to Arthurdale, even in its incarnation as regular state-run school.[109] Clapp's efforts to raise private foundation funds also failed, and she finally gave up on the idea.

Although lives were salvaged, the Arthurdale subsistence homestead was a failed national model. The project foundered on the shoals of the federal planners' misguided optimism that branch industry could be recruited and retained at Arthurdale, a hard and lonely place in the central Appalachian coalfields. Several industries, all of short duration, came and went at Arthurdale—an electric vacuum cleaner factory, a shirt factory, a farm-tractor manufacturing plant, and a radio and television company; federal work relief was the major and often only source of employment.[110] In 1942 the federal government began liquidating its interest and selling its entire inventory of properties to individual householders and outside investors—transactions that were finally completed in 1947.[111] The federal investment at Arthurdale far exceeded the return in homesteader earnings; the average selling price of the homestead houses was less than a third of the appraised value.[112]

The unfulfilled promise of democracy at the Arthurdale homestead and the pitfalls of the project's client-centered orientation, which may have encouraged dependency on federal largess, made it an inauspicious model for social reform. What about education reform? Briefly put, Clapp's approach to community school development had several idiosyncrasies that limited exportability of her ideas. In West Virginia she logically extended Dewey's educational theory in a real-world setting. Yet her work was not undertaken in an ordinary public school with ordinary teachers. Clapp had the luxury of selecting her own teachers, and she attracted extraordinarily capable women and men to Arthurdale who were experienced progressive educators. Moreover, she had a mandate to create a progressive school, and within her funding constraints she was free to create exactly the kind of school she wanted. While Clapp intended to demonstrate the feasibility of Deweyan principles in a public school, the relative artificiality of Arthurdale made it highly unlikely that less-talented educators in more traditional schools would attempt to replicate the project. Her work also had a utopian quality reminiscent of nineteenth-century communalist agricultural settlements such as Brook Farm and Oneida. With Eleanor Roosevelt, Clapp, like earlier utopians, envisaged Arthurdale as a beacon community that would light the way to the reconstruction of U.S. life and schooling in the twentieth century. It was beside the point to Clapp that Arthurdale was an isolated rural school.

As we describe in considerable detail in Part Two, Benjamin Franklin High School in East Harlem applied the community school idea in a "real" school—an ethnically diverse comprehensive high school that was subject to the bureaucratic constraints of the New York City school system. Unlike Clapp's, Covello's goal was not to create a lighthouse school or to demonstrate a particular set of educational principles, but rather to mobilize the revitalization of East Harlem under the aegis of a community school and to educate a leadership class to direct and sustain that effort. And unlike both Arthurdale and Nambé, Franklin was not the vision and product of an "expert" outsider—a southern Italian by birth, Covello came of age in East Harlem.

Our analysis thus far begs the question, Did in fact a community school "movement" actually occur in the 1930s? The answer obviously depends on how one defines the term. Historian Herbert Kliebard suggests that "the term movement may be applied to *a broad category of persons who share certain fundamental beliefs and who, over a sustained period of time, self-consciously act to gain public acceptance for those beliefs*" (original emphasis).[113] Certainly the community school organizers shared certain fundamental beliefs about the appropriate role, organization, and positioning of schooling in local communities. And they self-consciously acted to promote their ideas—through books, journal articles, and speeches—and in the case of Everett's book, to issue a manifesto. They did not persist, however, over a sustained period of time, at least not as a cohesive national group. Community schools were a trend, at best a nascent movement, which paradoxically declined just as it was gathering a head of steam, a casualty of wartime mobilization and better economic times, among other factors.

A Note on Community Coordinating Councils

Community schools coordinated community development in a small number of cities and towns of the Depression era. Another approach to community coordination, often involving local schools in a supportive role, was more widely adopted. In an effort to address problems like juvenile delinquency, which some observers saw as threatening to overwhelm individual agencies and schools, many communities formed "coordinating councils," efforts to coordinate all the youth-serving agencies in a community.[114] For some locales, a council's establishment reflected reactions to specific lurid events. For example, only after a twelve-year-old girl killed her playmate, fearful she would reveal the "sex play" into which they had been inducted by a local man, did the community of Hastings-on-Hudson decide to establish its coordinating council.[115] Most often focused on preventing juvenile delinquency, these councils generally conducted local social research, increased recreation programs, tried to control or remove destructive community influences, gave special attention to youth not in school or work, and sought to improve home environments through parental education.

While many communities had formed community councils as early as World War I, these tended to fall into disuse or to limit their attention to organizing athletic programs.[116] The Depression gave impetus to many more socially concerned coordinating councils under various names (on the East Coast, they were frequently councils of social agencies) designed to plan communitywide approaches to the crisis.[117] In 1929, the growth of Los Angeles Coordinating Councils for the Prevention of Delinquency, led by professional social workers, inspired imitations under lay leadership across the nation.[118] If schools were not often centers and catalysts of such coordinated community planning, they were frequently called upon to coordinate community efforts in particular areas such as guidance, juvenile delinquency prevention, adult education, or recreation.

Considerable disagreement about the school's role in community coordination, however, surfaced at the 1937 New York University Conference on Current Problems in Community Coordination. Some panelists argued that the schools were too often aloof and ill-disposed to allow the community use of school buildings and equipment. Others were skeptical that the schools could do a better job than could other organizations such as Community Chests, Councils of Social Agencies, Parents Associations, and settlement houses.[119]

Community coordinating councils relied on and often developed out of "fact-finding" surveys of local social conditions. The Yonkers Coordinating Council, in an industrialized town just north of New York City, developed out of two citizen groups, one of which, dominated by elementary school principals and directors, carried out a detailed sociological survey of the city that spurred wide community reaction. Initially led by principals from underprivileged areas, neighborhood councils formed even before the Yonkers council established itself. Bringing together some two hundred local organizations and representatives, the larger council included an "enthusiastic following from educational circles," leading the assistant superintendent to declare that "the traditional school isolation is permanently broken."[120] Down the Hudson River in Elizabeth, New Jersey, a council of social agencies began work in 1924, expanding until it required a full-time coordinator and National Youth Administration support by 1936. The council launched the "Elizabeth Plan for a Community-Wide Attack on Social Ills," supported by a central planning board and local neighborhood coordinating roundtables. The board of education assisted in educational programs and surveys, especially in areas of juvenile delinquency, and participated in the planning board's education section along with local churches, libraries, the PTA, the NAACP, the American Association of University Women, and others.[121]

Two other New Jersey districts developed coordinating councils out of surveys of local social conditions, a pattern similar to that which developed in East Harlem. In Madison, New Jersey, a youth survey by the local Rotary Club led to the formation of a social planning council. Under the leadership of the school superintendent, a broad group of community leaders met four times a year to discuss social concerns, carry out studies of local conditions, and coordinate solutions. A religious education committee sought to bridge the gap in character-building efforts of schools, churches, and agencies. A guidance committee, headed by the high school principal, developed lists of "citizen counselors," community adults willing to give advice to students about businesses and professions. Reflecting a growing trend in social work, the council formed a community case-study conference, bringing together a wide variety of local social agency representatives to assist specific "maladjusted" youth.[122] All the social planning council's efforts were enhanced by a detailed sociological base map of Madison, directed by the superintendent of schools with the assistance of New York University's Department of Educational Sociology. Nearby Summit, New Jersey, developed a coordinated community approach over an eight-year period, following a survey of local social conditions carried out by an external agency. The resulting council of social agencies, formally established in 1934, conducted studies and coordinated local agencies in addressing the problems uncovered. The school played a central role in the Mayor's Youth Welfare Council, formed two years after the council of social agencies. As in Madison, a case-conference committee was established to handle individual cases.[123]

And in East Harlem, Benjamin Franklin High School, a product of lobbying support by myriad local social agencies, at the outset joined the East Harlem Council of Social Agencies (EHCSA), a community coordinating council that had helped to organize and manage the high school campaign. Covello and his staff experimented with community coordination by organizing a community advisory council (CAC) at Benjamin Franklin, an entity that would include and complement the EHCSA. Implemented primarily through faculty outreach, the CAC provided a framework through which "every constructive agency in the community" could coordinate their efforts to address such local concerns as guidance, housing, health, race relations, citizenship, and adult education.[124] (See Chapter 4 for further details.)

Thus far our tracing of community school history has specified an important framework for our case study of Benjamin Franklin High School: a national context of ideas and concrete developments that culminated in a small set of community schools in the 1930s and the effort to build a national social movement. Various strands of the community school idea and related developments such as community coordinating councils would coalesce in the evolving conceptualization of community-centered schooling in East Harlem. Another critical framework for understanding Franklin High School is the history and demography of East Harlem in the 1930s. The next chapter looks at this particular context of local social forces and conditions to which Benjamin Franklin continuously struggled to adapt its programs and activities.

CHAPTER TWO

East Harlem in the 1930s:
Constraints and Opportunities

A LIFELONG OBSERVER OF EAST HARLEM affairs, a consummate cultural pluralist and an ardent democrat, Leonard Covello possessed a profound tacit understanding of the area and its complex social forces. He brilliantly crafted an institutional mechanism, community-centered schooling, expressly to respond to these factors. As two of its major evolving goals, Benjamin Franklin High School aimed to advance cultural pluralism and intergroup harmony, and to mobilize East Harlem's splintered ethnic groups in cooperative efforts that would solve pressing social problems and extract a measure of social justice from an insouciant city.

This chapter explores the forces and conditions that shaped East Harlem from the 1890s, when Pietro Coviello's family arrived in the district from southern Italy, to the 1930s, when Pietro's son Leonardo and his Italian American allies organized politically to create a boys high school for East Harlem. By the 1920s Italians, overwhelmingly from southern Italy, had become East Harlem's largest ethnic group;[1] by 1930, according to a count by Covello, Italians comprised about one-third of a total population of 233,400 in East Harlem.[2] In no small way Covello's plan for the new high school, both in its evolving conceptualization and in its operation in the years before World War II, grew out of the tensions that were inherent in the cultural experience of first- and second-generation Italian Americans.

Yet East Harlem was a culturally diverse terrain, and the experiences of other ethnic groups were also salient. Demographic change was an East Harlem constant in the first half of the twentieth century; ethnic groups were in motion and conflict, and the district was rife with intergroup hostilities that would emerge in and shape the community high school. Of these other ethnic groups, we give particular emphasis to the early growth of the Puerto Rican population because that group's ascendancy by the late 1940s would prompt a redirection of Benjamin Franklin's curricular and community programs.[3] We also consider institutions and agencies that were linked to particular ethnic groups, as well as ones that served a larger constituency, and we attend to other aspects of social life that would elicit an institutional response from the community high school. An overview of East Harlem's early development and immigrant history sets the stage for this discussion.

Early Growth and Development of an Immigrant Terminus

An area for farming and large estates well into the second half of the nineteenth century, East Harlem had become, as early as the 1830s, a "retreat for sportsmen and a haven of private estates and less a region given over to agriculture."[4] At midcentury East Harlem counted about 1,500 residents, with at least four hotels arrayed along the Park Avenue horse-car line, which extended north to the Harlem River. Brownstone houses, abodes of the wealthy, had begun to appear on Fifth Avenue, most prominently at 125th Street; concomitantly, Irish and German immigrants, refugees from the Lower East Side, were settling in crate-box shantytowns closer to the river.[5] By the 1860s, the area's remoteness had made it attractive first as a dumping site for city garbage, then as a slaughterhouse district. The worst section was the Harlem Flats, an East River marshland of tidal ponds and creeks east of Park Avenue between 98th and 113th streets, described by one observer as "a marsh in winter and an effluvia-emitting slough in summer," its stench detectable as far as Central Park.[6] This condition changed dramatically when extensions of the Second and Third Avenue railroads reached upper Manhattan in 1879 and 1880, respectively, connecting East Harlem by a forty-five-minute train ride to the business and industrial districts in lower Manhattan. Real estate developers reasoned that overcrowding in other areas of the city, particularly the Lower East Side, favored residential development in East Harlem. The availability of better housing and rapid transit meant that inner-city dwellers, even the working poor, could now reside in East Harlem and still work downtown. The realtors' calculated risk paid off handsomely even though the decision-making process leading to a move uptown was far more varied and complex than they had imagined.[7] In the early 1880s East Harlem experienced an unprecedented housing boom, especially in the Harlem Flats between Third Avenue and the East River above 100th Street, where low-cost four- and five-story tenements arose on landfill and the high ground of the flats. The stage was set for the arrival of thousands of southern Italian immigrants and the creation of an uptown Little Italy east of Park Avenue between 104th and 119th streets.

The building boom of the 1880s included West Harlem, an area that was bounded by 110th Street on the south, 159th Street on the north, and Fifth to Eighth Avenue on the east-west axis. Irish and Germans of means, including many German Jews, fled the downtown ghettos and relocated in Harlem. Between 1895 and 1910 the Jewish population of Harlem grew steadily, its numbers augmented and then dominated by an influx of eastern European Jews moving up from the Lower East Side. In 1923 approximately 176,000 Jews resided in Harlem; 75,500 lived in West Harlem, 101,000 in East Harlem (roughly 47 percent of the population). Harlem was predominately Jewish, and East Harlem was the largest Jewish section.[8]

Yet by this time an out-migration of Jews had already started in West Harlem, at first involving only a small number of families leaving for new residential sections in the Bronx. Later it sharply escalated as blacks began to enter the Jewish neighborhoods. Between 1910 and 1915, blacks moved into the neighborhood around 135th Street and Seventh Avenue; by 1920 they comprised 83.7 and 73.9 percent of the population in health areas 10 and 13, respectively—the area between Fifth and Eighth avenues from 126th to 142nd Street. And they had arrived as far south and east as 114th Street between Lenox and Fifth avenues. By 1930, blacks dominated West Harlem north of 118th Street, and they were a growing presence in the blocks around 110th Street.[9]

Recession of the Jewish population followed a similar pattern in East Harlem, where a small out-migration to the Bronx turned into a large-scale retreat in the face of the arrival of blacks and Puerto Ricans. In the 1920s Puerto Ricans and other Hispanic groups entered the area between Madison and Seventh avenues from 102nd to 119th Street. Blacks and Puerto Ricans filtered into neighborhoods east of Fifth Avenue, and Italians, who were prevalent in the blocks east of Third Avenue, pushed west of that boundary. The largest press by blacks was in health area 16, the area between Third and Fifth avenues from 119th Street to the Harlem River—where they constituted 31.9 percent of the population. By 1930, writes Ronald Bayor, East Harlem's Jewish population had dwindled to just 2,900, a 97.1 percent reduction since 1923.[10]

Italian Harlem: Rise and Domination

Italian immigrants were present in East Harlem as early as 1875, recruited as strikebreakers on the First Avenue horse-car line. Their employment engendered a longstanding conflict with the Irish working class, which was intent on establishing an ethnic niche in the New York City construction trades. The vilified strikebreakers were housed in single-story shanties built along the Harlem Creek in the vicinity of First Avenue and 106th Street. Their arrival in the Harlem

Flats set the stage for a much larger influx of Italians that would begin in the 1890s.[11]

By 1890, as a result of burgeoning immigration, New York's Italian population numbered 114,877 (foreign born and of foreign parentage), greater than a fivefold increase from 1880. In 1900 the Bureau of the Census counted 225,026 Italians in New York; less than four years later the total reached 382,775. The heaviest concentration of Italian settlement was the notorious Mulberry Bend area of lower Manhattan. "Mulberry Bend," George Pozzetta writes, "exhibited all of the worst characteristics of slum life. Cramped, overcrowded tenements, inadequate water and sanitation provisions, filth, squalor and crime were all in abundant example."[12] Bursting at the seams, Mulberry Bend began to disgorge its overflow population in the late 1880s. In the next decade many Italians left lower Manhattan for East Harlem. New arrivals, including Pietro Coviello, began to bypass Mulberry Bend altogether, heading directly to East Harlem from Ellis Island on the First Avenue horse-car line or the electric streetcar lines along Second, Third, and Lexington avenues.[13] By 1910 East Harlem's growing Italian population was concentrated along Second Avenue between 102nd and 116th streets, including the neighborhood around Thomas Jefferson Park at Pleasant Avenue. Increasingly thereafter, and most intensely after 1920, East Harlem's Italians were involved, directly and indirectly, in a pattern of neighborhood "invasion" and succession.[14]

Though the Italians were East Harlem's dominant ethnic group in the 1930s, their absolute numbers were declining. Two conditions explain the receding Italian presence. First, federal immigration laws after 1921, especially the Reed-Johnson Act in 1924, severely curtailed immigration. Second, scores of families, having accumulated sufficient savings, were leaving Italian Harlem's tenements in search of improved housing and social status in the Bronx and Queens. The Italians were not "ethnically displaced." Unlike the Jews, they were able to stave off the influx of other ethnic groups, in particular Puerto Ricans and African Americans, at least until after World War II. While Puerto Ricans were the dominant counterbalance to the Italian presence, they were unable to gain a foothold in the central zone of Italian settlement. A critical factor was the temporary halting of Puerto Rican migration in the 1930s and the return of many of the migrants to Puerto Rico. A large-scale recession of Italians was postponed until after the war, when Puerto Ricans arrived in East Harlem en masse and public housing projects, which proliferated in the district in the early 1950s, began to attract large numbers of poor blacks to the Italian section.[15]

By 1930 the Italians were heavily concentrated in health areas 21, 22, and 26 (roughly the blocks between 104th and 119th streets, from Third Avenue to the East River), where they comprised approximately 79.6, 78.6, and 84.3 percent of the population, respectively. (The main building and "street units" of the original Benjamin Franklin High School would be located in an Italian tenement neighborhood on 108th Street, between First and Second avenues.) Italians interfaced with Puerto Ricans west of Lexington Avenue, and with Puerto Ricans, blacks, and Irish between 104th and 100th streets. Beyond these interstitial blocks the Italian presence dissipated.[16]

The distinction made by historian Caroline Golab between "neighborhood" and "community" is useful to this analysis. As Golab's description of ethnic Philadelphia is apropos of intergroup relations in East Harlem, we quote her at length:

> The urban *neighborhood,* defined here as a physical or geographical entity with specific (subjective) boundaries, was always shared by two or more groups; or, to be more accurate, by three or four or more groups. Each group constituted its own *community* or network of social-emotional relationships. . . . *Neighborhood* and *community* were never synonymous. Diverse peoples shared the same city-space, but proximity did not lead them as a matter of course to interact with one another at the social or emotional level; rather, each group kept to its own network of affective structures. The distinction between neighborhood and community is critical, for it explains how neighborhoods could physically integrate diverse cultures and yet be "provincial" and "isolated" places. The provinciality and isolation of the immigrant resulted not from physical or spatial segregation but from the effectiveness of the many separate community networks, none of which needed or wanted to interact at the social or emotional level.[17]

Golab's categories are also descriptive of intragroup relations within East Harlem's zone of Italian settlement

Most East Harlem Italians traced their ancestry to southern Italy, where they or their parents had been rural peasants (*contadini*), or if they were extremely fortunate, artisans or small merchants; most Italian immigrants had experienced hardship in the old country—perhaps an exploitative landlord or the periodic droughts that made farming such a hazardous occupation in southern Italy. "The world the Italians entered in Harlem was recognizable to them," historian Robert Orsi has written. "It was a world of unemployment, overpopulation, disease, and exploitation."[18]

Southern Italian peasants were agrotown dwellers who toiled as day laborers, sharecroppers, or shepherds. Situated among agricultural lands, the *paese,* or agrotown, with as many as fifty thousand inhabitants, was typical of the Mediterranean region. Landless agricultural workers, the largest and lowliest element of the agrotown population, often had to labor on distant estates— and at irregular intervals depending on the season—returning to their families only on weekends. In 1901, according to Leonard Covello, fewer than 10 percent of contadini owned their land, and even then, in most cases, this was subsistence farming. "The main and often only source of income of southern Italian peasants," he writes, "was their employment by large estates or wealthier land cultivators. In other words, the majority of southern peasants were hired help."[19]

Above the peasantry, which had its own status hierarchy, stood the artisan class. The distinction between artisan and peasant was largely one of status and relative degree of freedom, not of material wealth—both were "terribly poor" by northern European and U.S. standards. Artisans and small merchants, unlike the peasants, controlled their own labor and typically worked in shops below their dwellings.[20] Literacy was another indicator of separation. Whatever books were to be found in the rural town belonged to the artisans, and most books had a religious content, primarily the lives of saints.[21] Covello's family belonged to Avigliano's artisan class. Pietro Coviello was originally a shoemaker by trade, as was his brother Domenico Canio, a master at his craft and the senior male of the family. The child Leonard attended a primary school in Avigliano, where he learned basic literacy skills—the mark of an artisan's son. Indeed a few books were to be found in the Coviello home, among them Giuseppe Mazzini's *Duties of Man*.[22]

Another factor distinguishing the two classes was the political activism of the artisans, who participated both in the Italian wars of liberation and the political unification of Italy after the Risorgimento. In the post-Risorgimento era, the artisans formed political clubs that challenged the power of the absentee estate holders, who composed the third, and dominant, social class in southern Italy. By contrast, the contadini had no political organizations. And when they voted, they sided with the landlords, upon whom they were economically dependent.[23] Covello's political activism was kindled by the rich traditions of his artisan family in Avigliano. "My uncles, cousins, and other relatives related stories about Mazzini and Garibaldi and particularly about the brigands who infested the region of Lucania, stories told around the fireplace with just the light from the burning logs," he recounted in his autobiography. "Children listened to their elders. We rarely ventured even a question and never offered a comment, for that was the way to absorb knowledge and wisdom."[24] In a sense Covello's struggles to galvanize a spirit of social activism in Italian Harlem involved a conflict of artisan and peasant values, the latter broadly entrenched. The problem, however, ran deeper than political apathy, for a deeply rooted devotion to the family group and the gemeinschaft network of *paesani* (townsmen) worked against larger communal values in East Harlem and an interest in societal affairs.

The southern Italian family (*la famiglia*) was an extended clan that embraced blood relatives and aunts, uncles, and cousins. Loyalty to the nuclear and extended family took precedence over social responsibility. Family honor, a source of kinship solidarity and clan feuds, had a prior claim over any claim the state or local community might presume to make.[25] Italian

Americans of the immigrant generation observed the "traditional patterns of respect [*rispetto*], familial obligations, and social behavior" of their native southern Italy—and they attempted to recreate that moral world and pass it to their children.[26]

As Miriam Cohen observes, southern Italy was a patriarchy whose private reality often belied its public rhetoric. Recent feminist scholarship such as Cohen's challenges the "conventional wisdom of patriarchal southern Italian culture," demonstrating that "married women played very active roles within the family and took part in important decisions about the behavior of its members." Cohen argues that while "southern Italian society was very much a patriarchy in the legal sense—males acted as official representatives of the family to the public world"—the private reality of family life presented a less hierarchical relationship of men and women than their public status and roles might suggest. The southern Italian wife and mother had not only a powerful domestic and moral influence, but also a decisive voice, at least equal to her husband's, in such important practical matters as the family budget, daily purchases, and dowry and inheritance planning. In many cases contadini women worked outside the home to support the family, either laboring in the fields at harvest time or selling produce and wares in the marketplace. When southern Italian men migrated—some on a seasonal basis and many others, like Pietro Coviello, remaining abroad for years—women assumed full responsibility for managing their households, combining economic projects with domestic tasks.[27]

Giving impetus to the migration of many thousands of contadini at the turn of the century was a congeries of push factors, among them the predictable chronic hardships of life in the Mezzogiorno; an unjust system of taxation imposed by agents of the national government who colluded with southern landlords; crises in the South's grain and wine markets; and a chain of natural disasters (for example, an earthquake and tidal wave in the Strait of Messina that killed as many as a hundred thousand people in the city of Messina).[28] There were strong pull factors as well, not the least of which was the prospect of economic opportunities in the United States.[29]

The first large wave of Italian immigration to the United States took place between 1890 and 1910; for most of these years, males accounted for about 80 percent of the total. As Thomas Kessner observes: "The Italian immigration was, by and large, a nonfamily movement of males in their productive years. These single men came to make some money and go home."[30] The small minority who decided to stay, however, formed "a critical mass upon which an increasing proportion of the later arrivals could rely to help find work and residence."[31] Pietro Coviello was part of this chain migration led by males, and his actions typified the dominant process involved in settling an Italian family permanently in the United States. After his arrival in East Harlem in 1890, Pietro took up residence as a boarder with the Accurso family. Vito Accurso, the head of the household, was a fellow townsman (paesano) from Avigliano, and he may have been a relative of Pietro's. Boarding of male paesani and relatives was a characteristic feature of the chain migration process. Once sufficient resources were accrued, the rest of the family could be brought over from Italy. Chain migration etched a pattern of residential clustering—Italian immigrants settled among their kin and paesani in New York and elsewhere.[32]

Notwithstanding the harsh conditions many of these immigrants were fleeing, they left their homelands with heavy hearts. The pain of separation was assuaged to some extent by the continuities the immigrants experienced "between the moral world of southern Italy and the emerging moral world of East Harlem."[33] Writing in 1935, Edward Corsi ruefully recalled the severe depression his mother experienced after the family's arrival in East Harlem in 1907: "She loved quiet, and hated noise and confusion. Here she never left the house unless she had to. She spent her days, and the waking hours of the nights, sitting at that one outside window staring up at the little patch of sky above the tenements. She was never happy here and, though she tried, could not adjust herself to the poverty and despair in which we had to live."[34]

Corsi's mother eventually returned to Italy, where she died of causes related to her depression. Her malady seems not to have been atypical. Covello's mother, like Corsi's, apparently wasted away in the throes of a long bout of severe depression. He recalled that "she had settled into a permanent kind of languor which slowly ate away the very life of her." As his wife lay dying, Covello's father lamented, "For what? Leave home. Come to a strange land. All the suffering. To what purpose? For an end like this?"[35]

Sociologist Robert Freeman's analysis of the 1900 federal manuscript census for four enumeration districts in East Harlem shows that Italians constituted 78 percent of the population in the blocks between 110th and 114th streets, roughly from Second Avenue to the East River. (Jews predominated in the area from 99th to 104th Street between First and Third avenues.) In 1910 the total Italian population of East Harlem was just over fifty-nine thousand, and the Second Avenue-East River corridor was 96 percent Italian. Between 1910 and 1920, the Italians consolidated their hold on the blocks east of Third Avenue. In the 1920s, concomitant with the departure of Jews and Irish, they were solidly entrenched from 104th to 119th Street east of Third Avenue. They were also moving west of Third Avenue along the same north-south corridor, and by the time Benjamin Franklin High School opened, they were the dominant national group in the area east of Park Avenue.[36]

Most Harlem Italians of the first three decades of the twentieth century fit the description of what demographers now call the "working poor." Freeman's analysis of the 1900 federal manuscript census for two enumeration districts in East Harlem shows that 54 percent of adult Italian males worked as day laborers, which for most reprised their occupational status in southern Italy. Approximately 70 percent of the Italian men were employed on the lower rungs of the construction trades, working as unskilled and semi-skilled laborers—many East Harlem Italians helped build New York City's elevated and subway lines. By 1910 their employment had become more diversified, with 28 percent involved in construction and most of the remainder working in factories (typically piano manufacturing), street trades, and small proprietorships (barbershops, shoe-repair shops, grocery stores, and the like). A not uncommon trajectory for Italian male self-employment led from pushcart peddler to garden produce concessionaire to grocery store owner.[37]

Similarly, Miriam Cohen's analysis of a 5 percent sample of the 1905 New York State manuscript census for three Italian neighborhoods in New York City, including a neighborhood in the heart of Italian Harlem, shows that approximately 44 percent of married Italian males in the three sampled neighborhoods were unskilled laborers (street cleaners, dockworkers, and construction laborers). About a quarter of the Italian husbands were skilled workers (barbers, tailors, and skilled construction workers); the remainder included semi-skilled laborers, shopkeepers and industrials, and white-collar workers. Cohen's sample analysis of the 1925 state census for these same neighborhoods shows that most Italian husbands had a low earning capacity, and their families were poor. Unskilled laborers represented 48 percent of the 1925 sample, and the percentages for the other occupational categories were about the same as 1905.[38]

The dire financial straits of most Italian families, whose fathers earned an average of $519 annually, necessitated the employment of women, who "flocked to work." Of Italian women sixteen years and older, 45.5 percent were gainfully employed, twice as many as the national average for all working women. The garment industry was the major source of employment for these women— in factories, shops, and home piecework arrangements, the latter involving about 25 percent of all Italian apartments. Italian women made up 36 percent of the entire workforce in this industry, and they dominated the occupational force in the artificial-flower and feather industries. Married women routinely cared for boarders, in addition to being occupied with domestic responsibilities and home piecework or other employment. As reported in a 1920 survey of Italian women in the Mulberry Street district's Little Italy, about 50 percent of fourteen- to twenty-year-olds, and 29 percent of twenty-one- to forty-four-year-olds, had jobs.[39]

Employment data collected from two large samples of Italian males are suggestive of the economic background of the Italian boys who entered Benjamin Franklin High School in the fall of 1934. In 1935 the Casa Italiana Educational Bureau enumerated the occupational trends of 31,556 and 16,945 New York City Italian males as recorded on marriage, birth, and death certificates in 1916 and 1931, respectively. According to John D'Alesandre, the author of the report, "the data concerning marriages in 1916 and births in 1916 may well be taken as typical of the parents of children now in our High Schools—ages 14 to 18." For each category of certificates Casa Italiana tabulated the thirty-six leading occupations of Italian males in 1916 and 1931. Significantly the occupation "laborer," the largest grouping for both years, showed a decrease from 50.4 percent in 1916 to 31.4 percent in 1931. Diversification of Italian male employment was shown to be a continuing trend. Of the top fifteen occupations listed in each of the three certificate categories in 1916 and 1931, tailors, barbers, shoemakers, carpenters, and painters appeared in the list; four new occupations—chauffeur, clerk, salesman, baker—appeared in the top fifteen in all three categories in 1931. Notwithstanding some employment gains for New York's Italian males by 1930, they remained preponderantly blue-collar workers, and their families always struggled to make ends meet.[40] To cite a rough index of family prosperity, Italian families paid a median rent of $32.59 in 1930, the second-lowest rent reported among twenty-eight ethnic groups in the city. As Cohen observes, even skilled workers, subject to the vagaries of seasonal employment, were prone to low incomes; "many jobs such as bricklaying, stonemasonry, and carpentry were particularly vulnerable to dips in the market and changes in the weather."[41] Sociologist Roger Waldinger describes the Italians as a "proletarian population" who "found themselves clustered in industries and occupations where they were bossed and directed by others"; often these "others" were Irish or Jewish.[42] Averting the hard living experienced by the overwhelming majority of their coethnics, a small coterie of Italian American professionals, including Covello and Marcantonio, resided in the so-called doctors and lawyers row, "a lovely stretch of limestone houses" on 116th Street between First and Pleasant avenues; given their immigrant backgrounds, however, none of them were strangers to poverty and hardship.[43]

The Great Depression took a heavy toll on Italian Americans. Ronald Bayor, who reviewed the Casa Italiana data, notes that "nearly half of the Italian-born fathers in 1931 were in occupations which were severely affected by the Depression," especially laborers in the construction industry.[44] According to a 1932 Mulberry Street survey, 48 percent of the Italian families lacked a full-time adult wage earner. As regular work was in increasingly short supply, married women turned to homework to keep their families afloat. "Indeed," according to Miriam Cohen, "during the height of the Depression, while the number of factory jobs shrank, the more poorly paid, irregular forms of employment—in particular, homework in the garment and artificial flower industries—rose dramatically."[45]

Economic hardship was associated with low levels of schooling among southern Italian immigrants. The contadino family regarded education as the prerogative of the home (*domus*), where training was informal and involved the transmission of family mores, traditional patterns, and work skills. In southern Italy formal education was restricted to elementary schooling and, in most cases, pursued only by the children of the artisan class.[46] While structural factors militated against formal education in the South—for example, lack of government support, nonenforcement of Italy's compulsory education law, lack of school facilities—entrenched cultural attitudes and practices also had harmful effects. The latter factors carried over to New York.[47]

Southern Italian children were expected to contribute to the family economy, a cultural expectation that collided with the American high school.[48] "While the *contadino* parents became, outwardly at least, adjusted to elementary education for their children, latent antagonism remained," Covello observed. "They delayed their plans for financial assistance from their children until their children might legally work. An antagonistic attitude toward high school education then developed with much the same intensity as the earlier antagonism toward the elementary school. The rejection of high school education is based upon old-world concepts of higher education, as well as upon economic factors. The Italian parent in America can see no moral or economic value in an expansion of the schooling period beyond the elementary school level. Contrarily, he considers the high school a place where time is spent in play or idleness."[49]

Cohen views school rejection in a somewhat different light, weighting her analysis toward the economic and social forces that impinged on New York's Italian American families. While Cohen acknowledges the "carryover of traditions," she suggests that familial attitudes toward schooling, in particular the high school, were also influenced by the conditions Italian immigrant families encountered in New York. For example, although the infant mortality rate was unacceptably high for Italians in East Harlem, that rate was not nearly as high as they had experienced in southern Italy. While health-service reformers in the 1920s succeeded in reducing infant mortality, their efforts were not matched by a reduction in the fertility rate. Accustomed to high mortality in their past experience, Italian immigrants continued to produce large families in New York, which stretched their resources and compelled them to put their children to work. "In short," Cohen writes, "the economic and demographic pressures encouraged parents to view their offspring as workers rather than school children."[50]

The educational levels of New York City's Italians lagged behind those of other groups, especially the Jewish population, whose traditional culture accorded learning "an honorable place" and a "special role."[51] In 1940, for example, 82 percent of adult second-generation New York Italians, as opposed to 33 percent of second-generation Jews in the city, had acquired only an eighth-grade education or below; whereas 20 percent of the Jews had some college or more, only 6 percent of the Italians had a comparable level of education.[52] In the 1930s second-generation Russian Jews in growing numbers achieved white-collar status through the apparel industry, public-sector employment, and the teaching profession. These jobs were staging grounds for the spectacular rise of Jews in the professions and higher education in the decades following World War II; anti-Semitism in the city's labor markets slowed but did not thwart this ascendancy. Higher education in municipal institutions became a Jewish trademark in the 1930s; all-male City College of New York, all-female Hunter College, and coeducational Brooklyn College were preponderantly Jewish institutions by 1940. By contrast, "schooling levels among native-born Italians were relatively slow to rise."[53]

From the southern Italian immigrant's point of view, the school, more than any other U.S. institution, jeopardized the integrity of the family and the core values of *via vecchia* (the old way). Robert Orsi's Italian American informants recalled the centrality of the domus in their lives and culture growing up in East Harlem. He writes: "A well-raised child, then, a young member of the community who was *ben educato,* was not one who had successfully completed the course of American schooling, for example, but one who had been successfully taught the values of the domus."[54] "A jarring note in the harmony of the family was struck when the child began to go to school," Covello declares. "It was at this moment that the parents felt the impact of an alien culture upon the child and very directly upon themselves. At this moment they clearly sensed the conflict between themselves and the American school. They became aware of the peril to their familial tradition and realized that the school implants into the child a different tradition; so different that there were only a few points of coincidence."[55]

Covello, who had a wealth of interview and life-history data at his disposal, found that the second generation's acculturation to U.S. mores was a topsy-turvy process that began with the child's temporary rejection of familial culture at the elementary age level.[56] One of Covello's informants recounted his experience of this process:

> Many of my Italian friends would say, "They have lived their own lives in their own way. We want to live our lives in our own way and not be tied down to fantastic customs that appear ridiculous not only to us but particularly to our 'American' friends." And I can assure you we were particularly keen about that ridicule. In fact so much so that we never invited our "American" friends to our home. And while "American" boys took their parents to some of the school functions, we not only did not take our parents but never even told them they were taking place. That was *our* life—exclusively ours and that of the other boys. The deadline [*sic*] was the threshold of the door of the house or the tenement in which we lived. Beyond that the older folks went their way and we went ours.[57]

The high school years, however, were marked by a "gravitation toward parental patterns" and the mores of *via vecchia*. "In high school there was a different atmosphere," the same informant recalled. "Somehow there was little that would make us ashamed of our origin. Probably the reason was that we began to distinguish between Jews, Irish, Germans, and so on. The Italian boys kept together in high school and felt at ease when in company with each other; we dared even to oppose an Irish clique that tried to make fun of us."[58] Covello noted "a high degree of retention by the [high school age] Italian children of the parental tradition."[59] One of these mores, which affected even third-generation Italian Americans, was the belief that education was primarily a family matter. It was, in Covello's judgment, the primary factor underlying the chronic truancy of many Italian American youths—a factor he believed was strongly correlated with the "comparatively high delinquency rates" of this group. "At least truancy, so far as seems to be evident in the high school, is not caused by a lack of parental control . . . . Truancy is the product of rather strict adherence of the Italian youth to the patterns of family life which *eo ipso* is detrimental to school attendance."[60]

Community norms in Italian Harlem tolerated teenagers "hanging around" at candy stores or other locales during school hours. Covello found that parent and child often colluded to violate the school law, especially when the family's interests were served by having the child at home.[61] This is not to suggest, however, that the domus was free of conflict between immigrant parents and their adolescent children. That was certainly not the case. As Orsi notes: "Often the two generations did not even speak the same language to each other: the immigrants might speak to their children in dialect and be answered in English, because their offspring could understand but not speak the tongue of the paese."[62] Intergenerational conflicts erupted over values and behaviors, no matter how trivial, that the parents believed threatened the primacy of the domus. Italian American young people, particularly the young men, sought a respite from domus pressures in what Orsi calls "a geography of rebellion"— parks, subways, elevated trains, buses, and social clubs—where young people held romantic assignations, young men joined gangs, and young women bobbed their hair. In most cases these "gestures of rebellion" were temporary, for "the most profound bond between the individual and the domus, . . . the link that frustrated all efforts to escape, was the fact that the men and women of Italian Harlem had deeply internalized the values and perceptions of the domus. They could not free themselves, however much they may have wanted to, because they bore the domus within."[63]

The Great Depression marked a turning point in the educational patterns of Italian American children. Structural changes in the economy prompted higher levels of high school attendance. In the mid-1930s New York State outlawed factory piecework in the home, established new restrictions on child labor, and passed a new compulsory-school law that required most children to remain in school, and out of the economy, until age sixteen. The disappearing youth labor market, indeed the paucity of regular employment for the ethnic working class, forced legions of older adolescents into the city high schools; they had nowhere else to go, as John Tildsley of the city's High School Division grudgingly acknowledged.

Following the Depression, Italian daughters, more than their brothers, had a strong economic incentive to continue their education. Reduced fertility rates, a by-product of hard times, freed them from many of their earlier domestic burdens. Increasingly a bustling market for female clerical and retail workers in New York attracted Italian women to enroll in commercial and business courses in the high schools. By 1950 these second-generation women, this time with the blessing of *la famiglia*, had outdistanced their male peers in high school attendance and were entering the white-collar ranks en masse. The majority of second-generation males continued to hold blue-collar jobs into the 1950s. In the second-generation fourteen- to twenty-four age cohort, 39 percent of females versus 34 percent of males had completed four years of high school or more.[64]

In the early years of Italian settlement in East Harlem, as we previously noted, immigrants from the same towns and provinces tended to cluster together. In the case of Covello's family and their paesani, "the idea of family and clan was carried from Avigliano in southern Italy to East Harlem. From the River to First Avenue, 112th Street was the Aviglianese Colony in New York City."[65] The spirit of regionalism, or *campanilismo*, made East Harlem a segmented community. Orsi has written that "extreme regional consciousness began to fade in the 1920s and 1930s, only to be replaced by an equally extreme neighborhood focus. Campanilismo was translated into a more American, urban, idiom as intense neighborhood loyalties developed. Little communities formed within Italian Harlem, each with its own traditions and sources of authority and maintenance. Strictly defined borders marked out the neighborhoods within Italian Harlem, and people tended to keep to their own blocks, choosing friends and spouses only from the immediate vicinity."[66]

As Orsi suggests, East Harlem's youth culture reflected these neighborhood divisions. Neighborhood-based gangs proliferated, and as sociologist Frederic M. Thrasher's East Harlem researchers discovered, juvenile delinquency was not stemmed by the Jefferson Park Boys' Club, which served six thousand youngsters. One of Orsi's informants told him: "You could do two things when we were kids—you either became a thief and eventually go to the rackets or you could go to school."[67] Covello believed that a community-centered high school in East Harlem would help ensure the latter option. In Italian Harlem this endeavor would confront a culturally defined skepticism of secondary schooling and, as historian Simone Cinotto argues, an Italian "family ideology" that was wary of involvement in public affairs.[68]

By 1930 a centralizing force and important source of Italian American identity was the popular devotion to Our Lady of Mt. Carmel (la Madonna del Carmine), an annual feast day (*festa*) that started July 16 and lasted as long as a week. The Church of Our Lady dominated the four hundred block of East 115th Street, less than a half block from the Pleasant Avenue site at which the new Benjamin Franklin High School would open in 1942. The festa reflected the prominent role of saint and Madonna worship in southern Italian and Italian American Catholicism. As Joseph Varacalli observes: "The worship and reliance on saints were part of a matrix of folk religiosity that fused with Catholic elements components of magic, superstitions, the occult, and paganism."[69] Saint worship provided a psychological buffer that helped assuage the vicissitudes and travails of peasant life in the Mezzogiorno. Southern Italians had a veritable directory of saints, each invested as a specialist in a particular category of miracles, each with his or her feast day on the calendar.[70] Closely related to and sharing many similarities with saint worship was the adoration of the Madonna, who assumed many manifestations and locally ascribed characteristics in southern Italy. More often than not the patron saint of a town or village was the Madonna. In 1882 a mutual aid society composed of immigrants from the town of Polla, in the province of Salerno, organized a feast day in East Harlem to honor Our Lady of Mount Carmel, the protectress of Polla. What started as a simple outdoor celebration in a tiny courtyard on 110th Street near the East River would, as more and more Italians arrived in East Harlem, grow into a great annual religious festival for all Italian Harlem.[71]

In 1884 the New York Archdiocese brought the fledgling lay celebration under ecclesiastical supervision, granting official sponsorship of the festa to the Pallotine order. That same year the church on 115th Street was completed, standing a few blocks north of the Italian neighborhood. From 1884 to 1919, Irish and Germans controlled the upper church; the Italians were treated as an "annex congregation," their worship restricted to a chapel in the church basement. From the outset the city's Irish-Catholic hierarchy was ambivalent toward southern Italian folk religion, which the church regarded as "the Italian problem," fearing that it would retard the assimilation of Italians, yet also recognizing that the Italians would abandon the church if it prohibited the festivals. Consequently, the prelates adopted a policy that treated the Madonna of 115th Street and similar popular devotionals elsewhere as a transitional stage toward full participation in American Catholicism. The separation of the devotion to la Madonna del Carmine from its original identification with a particular province of Italy had the long-term effect of contributing toward an Italian American identity. And it was a step toward overcoming East Harlem's fragmented community life.[72] Put another way, the devotion was an example of "cultural construction for purposes of ethnic community building."[73]

Before the turn of the century, the church acquired a luminous statue of la Madonna, which reposed in the basement chapel, the site of Italian worship. From 1920 to 1922, shortly after the Italians had moved their worship to the main sanctuary, the church interior was renovated through generous donations from the entire Italian Harlem community. In 1923, the statue of la Madonna was transferred upstairs and enthroned on the main altar. A bell tower was constructed in 1927, again through community donations, its chimes first tolling on Christmas Day. Like the festa, the campanile contributed to building an Italian American identity, as both a symbol of collective effort and a celebration of Italian heritage. "With the campanile, the church—and the neighborhood—looked more Italian," Orsi has written. "The street in front of the church now had the feel of an Italian village square."[74] (Fifteen years later the new Benjamin Franklin High School building would stand within a half block of the church, a secular beacon within the spiritual heart of Italian Harlem.)

East Harlem's festa had a "dense" street life, expressed on the occasion of an extravagant parade that was the highlight of the week. "The great Mount Carmel parade," Orsi remarks, "with thousands of marchers, trailing incense and the haunting sounds of southern Italian religious chanting, made its way up and down every block in the 'Italian quarter' of Harlem."[75] Regional social clubs were represented, as were Italian Harlem's youth gangs. Thousands of the devout watched the parade from crowded windows. Servicing the procession were myriad vendors, among them local merchants whose sidewalk booths "were filled with wax replicas of internal human organs and with models of human limbs and heads. Someone who had been healed—or hoped to be healed—by the Madonna of headaches or arthritis would carry wax models of the afflicted limbs or head, painted to make them look realistic, in the big procession. The devout could also buy little wax statues of infants. Charms to ward off the evil eye, such as little horns to wear around the neck and little red hunchbacks, were sold alongside the holy cards, statues of Jesus, Mary, and the saints, and the wax body parts."[76] While such practices mortified the Irish prelates, the festa, which Rudolph Vecoli calls "the most authentic expression of South Italian culture transplanted to the New World," evoked for its participants a warm memory of the old country.[77]

As we suggested, the devotional to the Madonna did not literally replicate an old-world folkway; it was a transmuted cultural practice, to which new elements were added in East Harlem. The festa was an amalgam that grew to represent the feast-day celebrations of all the particular villages of southern Italy. In effect, the Madonna of Polla became the matron saint of Italian Harlem. Other innovations crept into the festa to give it a peculiarly Italian American flavor; for example, the pinning of money, U.S. dollars, to the Madonna's effigy. Katherine Conzen and her colleagues write: "Inevitably, the campanilistic basis of the celebration became diluted, elements from the new-world setting were incorporated, and it became over time itself an expression of an emerging Italian American identity."[78] As Orsi puts it, the feast of Mount Carmel expressed "a nascent community consciousness. . . . It was a central communal event that mobilized the energies of all Italian Harlem and absorbed manifold conflicts and identities into a shared task."[79]

In the 1930s the East Harlem festa was still waxing strongly, although Italian membership in the Mount Carmel parish was waning—from about 6,800 in 1910 to between three and four thousand by the Great Depression. "The reason for this [decline]," a researcher for the Boys' Club Study observed, "is that as soon as the people have money enough they move to the Bronx, to Queens, to Long Island."[80] Yet the Italian American out-migrants and their children returned to the Madonna of 115th Street year after year, and the festa bands continued to play in East Harlem.[81]

The Catholic Church was not the only faith vying for Italian souls in East Harlem. In the 1890s the Protestant churches of New York began missionary efforts among the Italian immigrants and their children. These churches combined evangelism and philanthropy to win converts; the Protestant clergy used the social settlement as a proselytizing strategy, a tactic that incorporated both approaches.[82] The evangelical fervor of the Methodist missionary Anna Ruddy, director of the Home Garden settlement in Italian Harlem, will be described further in Chapter 3. Her proselytizing efforts converted Leonard Covello, whose family was nominally Catholic, to the Methodist faith. Beginning with Ruddy's tutelage, Methodism and the settlement house movement exercised a formative influence on young Covello, strengthening the service commitment imbued by the artisan traditions of his childhood in southern Italy. Deeply religious, Covello later (the precise year is not available; it was after the death of his first wife in 1914) joined the Jefferson Park Methodist Episcopal Church, founded in 1895. The church's cream-colored brick facade at 407 East 114th Street faced, and still faces, Jefferson Park, less than a block west of Pleasant Avenue and the site of the future high school. Covello and Vito Marcantonio assisted at Casa del Popolo, at 319 East 118th Street, which became the social service arm of the church in 1920.[83]

As we have seen, Italian Harlem in the 1930s was an established and evolving ethnic community. Italian American culture and identity were wellsprings on which Covello and his staff would draw in building their community high school. Embedded within this ethnic culture, however, were factors that would challenge this project, notably distrust of the U.S. school and a disinclination to participate in the public sphere. Italian American ethnicity also threatened to jeopardize areawide community building in East Harlem, where a growing Puerto Rican presence became a casus belli for a generation of Italian American youth.

Puerto Ricans in East Harlem:
The Early Settlement

In the early decades following the U.S. occupation of Puerto Rico in 1898, structural changes in the island's economy gave impetus to a migration of Puerto Rican workers to the mainland and New York City. Landholdings in the island's coffee sector, formerly the island's mainstay crop, were increasingly consolidated into "a mechanized, technologically advanced plantation system" that was dominated by four U.S. sugar corporations. Chronic unemployment, related primarily to the ascendancy of "mechanized capital intensive sugar production" that "displaced more workers than it incorporated into the system," and secondarily to changes in the tobacco industry, started gradually before World War I and accelerated throughout the 1920s.[84] When Bernardo Vega, a cigar maker (*tabacquero*) from the Puerto Rican highlands, arrived in New York in 1916, a small colony of about fifty Puerto Rican families lived alongside poor Jews in the vicinity of Park Avenue between 110th and 117th streets. At that time Jews and Puerto Ricans shared Park Avenue's open-air market (*marqueta*). Vega also observed that Puerto Ricans were interspersed in the blocks along Third Avenue between 64th and 106th streets; others resided downtown in Chelsea and a wealthy few had located on the Upper West Side.[85] According to Lawrence Chenault, the first large settlement of Puerto Ricans was in the vicinity of 101st and 102nd streets at Third Avenue, which was a poor tenement neighborhood.[86]

In 1926, an estimated 20,000 Puerto Ricans resided in the area bounded by 90th and 116th streets, First to Fifth Avenue; a total of some 40,000 had settled in upper Manhattan.[87] In 1930, according to Chenault, the line of Puerto Rican settlement extended "from about 97th Street up to and along 110th Street around the northern part of Central Park, northward to about 125th Street, and approximately from about Third Avenue on the east, to Eighth and Manhattan Avenues on the West."[88] The largest concentration appears to have been in health area 20, the neighborhoods around 115th and 116th streets west of Third Avenue.[89]

The Puerto Rican influx may have been the last straw for East Harlem's Jews, whose recession was completed by the end of the decade.[90] By the 1936s a new ethnic skirmish line had formed along the Park Avenue corridor, and the massive viaduct of the New Haven and New York Central Railroad, which ran between 96th and 111th streets (with openings at each crosstown street), became a contested boundary and visible symbol of this conflict; the occasional clashes that erupted along this border between Puerto Rican and Italian youth gangs would have harmful spillover effects on Benjamin Franklin High School.[91]

Most first-generation Puerto Ricans in New York had chosen to leave a badly deteriorating island economy for a mainland urban economy with relatively higher weekly wages. In the 1920s Puerto Rican migrants found jobs primarily in the garment trades and light industry, hotel and restaurant trades, cigar making, domestic service, and laundries. (According to one estimate, 60 percent of New York's working Puerto Ricans in the 1920s were employed in the tobacco industry.) Entry into these labor markets was eased by immigration restriction, which reduced competition for unskilled and semiskilled jobs that paid on average about twenty-one dollars per week.[92]

Employment of New York Puerto Ricans remained overwhelmingly blue collar throughout the 1930s. As reported for 1930–36, of 1,997 jobs obtained by Puerto Rican males under the auspices of the Puerto Rican Department of Labor's employment office in East Harlem, only about 8 percent were white collar; of 3,641 jobs reported for females, none of the positions were white collar.[93] The Depression forced about ten thousand Puerto Rican migrants to return to Puerto Rico. Virginia Sánchez Korrol writes: "Those Puerto Ricans who remained in New York, fortunate enough to be gainfully employed remained concentrated in the unskilled, semiskilled, blue-collar areas working at jobs basically similar to those held by immigrant groups during the past decade. But whereas during the twenties migrants were filling positions previously slated for newly arrived European immigrants, the decade of the Depression found Puerto Ricans competing with unemployed individuals for jobs as dishwashers, countermen, laundry workers, or in maintenance."[94]

Within their East Harlem zone of settlement, the Puerto Rican migrants established a cultural life of great vitality and sociality. In the 1920s and 1930s East Harlem's El Barrio (also *la colonia hispania*), the city's largest Puerto Rican colony, was New York's "mecca for Latin entertainment, shopping or professional services"—a status that greatly chagrined the Brooklyn colony's leaders, who suffered the indignity of watching boatloads of their compatriots dock in Brooklyn only to leave post haste for Manhattan. A small coterie of Puerto Rican professionals (physicians, dentists, lawyers), merchants, and restaurateurs stood at the apex of this vibrant scene.[95] Korrol argues that previous researchers, including Nathan Glazer and Daniel P. Moynihan, overlooked the rich associational life and communal organizational activity that flourished on the edges of El Barrio's bustling street life. For example, at least forty-three Hispanic organizations were active in New York by the mid-1920s, including "hometown or regional clubs; groups pledged to support island or continental political persuasions; Latin cultural societies or civically oriented associations."[96] Not surprisingly, these organizations provided leadership for the Spanish-speaking community. For example, the Porto Rican Brotherhood of America, founded in 1923, figured prominently in community affairs, striving "to be the type of group which could defend the Puerto Ricans within the political structure of New York City while maintaining links with Puerto Rico and acting as a watchdog in issues involving the United States and Spanish America." Indeed in the aftermath of what the *New York Times* called the "Harlem Riots" of July 1926, primarily a conflict between Jews and Puerto Ricans, the Porto Rican Brotherhood lobbied local police to increase their patrols in the affected neighborhoods; organized a media campaign with *La Prensa*, the city's major Spanish-speaking newspaper, to help ease tensions; and called on Mayor Jimmy Walker, Governor Al Smith, and federal officials to restore order and protection in the area.[97]

The Puerto Rican migrants brought with them a tradition of labor organizing and involvement in radical politics. Bernardo Vega and Jesús Colón, both socialist writers, described the *tabacquero* custom of *la lectura* as it was enacted in New York's Spanish-speaking cigar factories. A lector designated by the workers read aloud daily, one hour in the morning and one in the afternoon, to the cigar makers while they plied their craft; the morning session included news and current events, the afternoon session politics and literature. "And let me tell you," Vega proclaimed, "I never knew a single *tabaquero* who fell asleep."[98]

Notwithstanding a high level of cultural and communal identity, organizational activity, and social networking, daily life in El Barrio was "a struggle to survive on meager wages, inadequate health care, sub-standard housing, marginal educational and poor sanitation conditions" (conditions that afflicted all of East Harlem's groups, as we will see).[99] Nowhere was the plight of the migrants more poignantly evident than in the treatment Puerto Rican children received in the public schools of New York City. Not only were these youngsters routinely placed one or two years behind their mainland peers, but also they were labeled retarded or slow learners, both conditions reflecting the incapacity of the city schools to deal with "monolingual Spanish-speaking students." Consequently, many Puerto Rican youths failed to complete their secondary schooling.[100]

Italians, Puerto Ricans, and East Harlem's other ethnic groups, including "Negroes," Irish, Germans, British, Russian Jews, Finns, "Scandinavians," and "Slavs" (among the categories listed by the Casa Italiana Educational Bureau), were subject to similar deprivations in employment, housing, health and sanitation, schooling, public safety, and recreation. As a major immigrant terminus, East Harlem was a disempowered, highly stressed district where dire social conditions only worsened as the Depression deepened.

General Social Conditions: Hard Living and Malign Neglect

The Great Depression's effect on East Harlem may be likened to an earthquake sundering a rickety frame house. According to a report of the East Harlem Nursing and Health Service, by December 1931, 45 percent of East Harlem's male labor force was out of work, and 55 percent of heads of families were unemployed. Such were the hard times that men who worked as little as two to three days per week were listed as regularly employed.[101] East Harlem's poverty and tradition of hard living were longstanding and deeply entrenched; they could not be easily purged. The area remained a low-rent residential district for the working poor, with 229 of the district's 271 blocks devoted predominantly to housing. Of East Harlem's labor force of approximately seventy-five thousand, an estimated sixty-one thousand had to seek work outside the district; East Harlem produced only 14,700 jobs, according to the Mayor's Committee on City Planning. Business and industry serving the city as a whole largely bypassed the district; the seven north-south avenues mostly carried through-traffic, with only a small proportion of the vehicles arriving or embarking within the district. East Harlem was, the Mayor's Committee on Planning ruefully noted in 1937, "a local backwater with a dead-end psychology; a place from which to watch the swift stream of the city's life go rushing by." Most of the district's commercial activity—and the major source of local jobs—was quartered in storefronts on the ground floor of tenement buildings, typically small-scale businesses serving particular neighborhoods, or "ethnic villages," and contributing to the isolationist cast of the district.[102] By the midthirties, the district counted five hundred candy stores, 685 groceries, 378 restaurants, 156 bars, and 230 tailor shops, "a lot of small business in a good year."[103]

Notwithstanding East Harlem's multitudinous problems, city planners at the height of the Depression were optimistic that the district might, through a combination of progressive forces, break out of its historic isolation and ignominious status. They saw the looming presence of the Triborough Bridge, with a terminus in East Harlem at 125th Street and connections into Queens and the Bronx, as a propitious sign for future investment and commercial exchanges involving East Harlem across the metropolitan area; they saw New Deal housing legislation as a particularly ripe opportunity for a thoroughgoing refurbishing of the district's residential properties and "a new renaissance . . . of really good medium and low rent apartments."[104] By any measure, however, East Harlem was a far cry from realizing that felicitous vision when Benjamin Franklin High School opened in 1934.

Long before the Depression, acute poverty and hard times were endemic in East Harlem, perhaps an ineluctable consequence of the district's historic role as a conduit for the assimilation of low-status immigrant and migrant groups. In combination, overcrowding and a badly deteriorated housing stock were arguably the most deleterious manifestations of hard living in the district, given that they exacerbated other social conditions. Most East Harlem residents lived in "old law" tenement flats of two to five rooms, with no direct sunlight in at least two of those rooms; these flats were maintained in buildings that were long overdue for major reconstruction or replacement.[105] "A tenement built to accommodate sixteen families, houses over thirty," complained Angelo Patri, a contemporaneous observer. "The rooms are small, damp, dark, and sunless. The plumbing is bad, the ventilation abominable, the odors unbearable."[106]

The term "tenement," associated with housing for the urban poor, was in common usage in New York City by 1865. Since 1811 the city had subdivided its blocks into 25-by-100-foot lots; rising to five or six stories, the early tenements, called "railroad flats," often consumed about 90 percent of these lots, in the absence of any minimum standards for space, light, or ventilation. The Tenement House Law of 1867 provided a few minimal standards such as mandatory fire escapes and at least one water closet for every twenty tenants.

Yet, as housing reformers Lawrence Veiller and Hugh Bonner noted in their report to the New York State Tenement House Commission in 1900, architects frequently ignored the clause of the 1867 legislation that required fire escapes, perhaps because such appurtenances offended their artistic sensibilities. A revised act of 1879 restricted tenement house space to no more than 65 percent of the standard lot and added more toilets. Difficulties in enforcing the 1879 law eventually led to a compromise that was acceptable to realtors—the "dumbbell" or "old law" tenement, which covered 80 percent of the standard lot, with four dwellings per floor surrounding a common water closet and stairwell. By 1900, about 2.3 million people, two-thirds of the city's population, were housed in more than eighty thousand tenements, three-fourths of which were of old-law construction built after 1880. Old-law development was synonymous with overcrowding—one dumbbell-tenement block had a density of more than two thousand persons per acre. In 1900 pressure from the Charity Organization Society in New York City led to the appointment of a new tenement house commission headed by Robert DeForest and Lawrence Veiller. Their work resulted in the Tenement House Act of 1901, which legislated "new law" standards for tenements, restricting coverage to 70 percent, expanding the size of the dumbbell air shaft to courtyard proportions, and providing running water and a water closet for each dwelling and an exterior window for each room.[107]

In 1902 New York City established a tenement house department to ensure compliance with the new law. Good intentions, however, went awry from the start, as tenement housing reform failed to realize its promise of social amelioration. The "new law" apartments, some 117,000 in New York City by 1910, were priced beyond the means of the lowest-income families; the upshot was a high vacancy rate and doubling up of families in single apartments. Not that new-law housing marked any significant advance over its old-law predecessor, the dumbbell tenement—as historian Anthony Jackson puts it: "The improvements in lighting, ventilation, sanitary facilities, and fire prevention still left much to be desired." According to a tenement house department report of the 1930s, new-law buildings established in the trail of the 1901 reform act had "considerably deteriorated." Aggravating the problem was an unsavory combination of corrupt municipal officials, unscrupulous and incompetent builders, and negligent landlords.[108]

East Harlem residents of means took advantage of expanding subway lines and moved to the Bronx, Astoria, and other outlying areas. Yet the filtering process by which habitable old-law buildings would pass down to lower-income groups largely did not occur. Many sweatshops replaced the larger housing units, as few of the existing residents, particularly in the Depression period, could afford the rent of these larger units—by December 1931 the number of "totally unemployed men" represented 45 percent of the male labor force in East Harlem, an increase of 100 percent in one year.[109] Consequently as the

Depression deepened, more and more East Harlemites were pressed into overcrowded living arrangements. A researcher for the Boys' Club study in 1932 wrote: "On one 'social block,' two facing sides of one street, for the distance of one block, there are three thousand individuals, and no tenement in this block is over four stories high."[110]

In 1934 East Harlem had a population of about 201,000 people that was compressed into 947 acres, a density of 212 persons per acre. The continuing out-migration of families, including nine thousand Italians since 1930, coupled with immigration restriction, contributed to the declining population base and a 21.5 percent vacancy rate in East Harlem's tenements. Approximately 90 percent of the district's rental housing was priced in the "low or lower medium rent" group, that is, less than thirty dollars per month; by contrast, less than 4 percent was priced above sixty dollars per month. In its 1937 survey of East Harlem, the Mayor's Committee on City Planning commented tersely: "Most of the buildings have seen their day," and the committee recommended large-scale demolition between Third and First avenues.[111]

Housing conditions exacerbated problems of health and sanitation. A student researcher in 1936 gave the following report of "very lamentable and very unhealthy" conditions in the five and six "walk-up" tenement buildings: "Bath tubs are more of an exception than a rule; in many case toilets are located in the hall-way or on the corridor of each floor. The tenants on each floor keep a key to such places where sanitary measures are very much needed. Radiators are almost unknown as the houses are not supplied with steam heat equipment. The old system of the coal stove is still predominant."[112] Similarly, a student essayist wrote: "When Johnnie, 'a typical East Harlem boy,' wants to go to the toilet, he must use one that is in the middle of the whole floor. It is placed there for the use of the entire floor, which has seven families on it. He waits sometimes for one-half hour. Besides this it is filthy, unsanitary, and a place one doesn't like to use."[113]

A Union Settlement informant related a story of comparatively better living conditions in another tenement building:

My recollections of East Harlem date back to 1923. We lived at 451 East 115th Street, across from Holy Rosary Church. [I remember] the cold water flat in which we lived—four families on each floor and each two families shared a hallway closet. We had a bathtub for "Saturday Nite" baths that was located in our kitchen. The tub was covered by a tin enamel plate. We had gas but no electricity—the gas was not billed monthly—if you wanted gas, you fed the meter 25 cents for 20 minutes. For bright lights we depended on a very delicate gas mantel. If a fly hit the mantel, that was the end of the bright light. Our food was all purchased from pushcarts and stores on 1st Avenue from 100th to 116th Street. No Supermarkets! If you wanted milk and the store was closed, the storekeeper had a panel in the door that you could push in, and use his milk scoop to fill your pot and leave 6 cents for every quart you took.[114]

Sanitation, even in the district's best sections, was always problematic. A Boys' Club Study researcher, an East Harlem native, wrote that the district's streets, teeming with pushcarts, were "quite filthy with garbage and waste."[115] East Harlem's riverfront was dilapidated and noxious, a canker sore of urban blight.[116]

Infectious and communicable diseases were legion and deadly. From 1916 to 1925 East Harlem's general mortality rate stood at 15.3 per thousand, versus 14.7 for New York City; pneumonia was the leading cause of death in East Harlem, with heart disease, pulmonary tuberculosis, and diarrhea/enteritis ranked second, third, and fourth respectively.[117] In 1930 the East Harlem District had the city's highest rates for typhoid fever, measles, scarlet fever, diphtheria, whooping cough, influenza, and pneumonia—and it had the third-highest mortality rate for tuberculosis; the Mayor's Committee on City Planning reported in 1937 "above average death rates" for influenza, pneumonia, and tuberculosis in East Harlem.[118] From 1916 to 1920, the infant mortality rate stood at an appalling 100.6 per thousand live births, versus 94.3 for Manhattan and 88.2 for the city as a whole. On a positive note, following an intensive campaign by the East Harlem Health Center, the rate for 1920–25 was reduced by more than 23 percent to 76.7 per thousand live births; for 1925–30, infant mortality declined further to 71 per thousand.[119] This downward trend continued in the 1930s, especially after 1934, when La Guardia began to increase public funding for the city's health district programs. For example, Health Districts 21 and 22, in the heart of Italian Harlem, showed declines in infant mortality from 60 and 57 per thousand in 1931–35, respectively, to 55 and 42 per thousand in 1936–40, respectively.[120]

Growing up in East Harlem was risky business. For example, the high volume of vehicular traffic posed an enormous safety problem, given that East Harlem's children habitually used the streets as playgrounds. Mapped in 1811 for horse-drawn vehicles, the city's avenues were, by the mid-1920s, in the grip of "strangling traffic congestion," a half-million cars daily. In 1926 an estimated 859,600 daily commuters traveled the north-south arteries from the Bronx or Upper Manhattan to areas below Fifty-ninth Street.[121]

According to a New York University researcher, "hordes of [children] are seen after school hours and on holidays playing ball, craps, and cards. They become expert in dodging traffic and are oblivious to the casual passer-by for play engrosses their entire attention for the time being." In 1927 cars and trucks killed fifteen of these children, primarily on Second and Third avenues.[122] The abysmal lack of playground space on public school property was a key indicator of the recreation crisis; according to the Mayor's Committee on

City Planning, "the sixteen public schools of East Harlem, taken together have only sufficient play space [5 acres] for one modern school of normal size."[123] East Harlem had nineteen play streets, a makeshift solution that created a noisy and hazardous ambience for the residents whose flats fronted the designated blocks. Even more unsatisfactorily, along Park Avenue from 121st to 124th Street the city jury-rigged play spaces dangerously abutting these cross-streets as they passed under elevated the railroad.[124]

Public parks were also scarce. The only general-use park located completely within East Harlem was Thomas Jefferson Park, which stood near the East River and after 1942 adjoined the southern boundary of the new Benjamin Franklin High School building at 114th Street and Pleasant Avenue. The Department of Parks officially opened the park in October 1905 "with a chorus and mass flag and dumbbell drills by thousands of neighborhood children." In the 1930s, the WPA constructed an enormous swimming pool in Jefferson Park—a resource that would be hotly contested by East Harlem youth gangs in the 1940s, with serious ramifications for the community high school.[125] Writing in 1961, urban-planning critic Jane Jacobs decried the park's shortcomings: "Its location is at the far edge of its community, bounded on one side by the river. It is further isolated by a wide, heavy traffic street [First Avenue]. Its internal planning runs largely to long, isolated walks without effective centers. To an outsider it looks weirdly deserted; to insiders it is the focus of neighborhood conflict, violence and fear."[126]

Crime was another factor associated with hard living and the risks of making a safe passage through adolescence in East Harlem. Crime had long plagued the district, as had its reputation as a criminal hotbed; homicide rates were perennially high, gangs claimed turf block by block, and organized crime had flourished in various guises since the turn of the century. In the Prohibition era, East Harlem racketeers prospered from lucrative bootlegging and speakeasy operations, morphine and cocaine distribution, gambling, and prostitution.[127] New York University sociologist Paul Cressey noted that from East Harlem "had come many of New York's youthful gunmen and desperadoes of recent years." Having worked their way up through local street-corner gangs, some had ended up "in gang-land's one-way auto rides," while others "graduated" successfully to live "palatially on suburban estates far from the scene of their early activities."[128] While by modern standards of urban aberrancy the overall male juvenile delinquency rate for East Harlem in 1930 was comparably low, less than 3 percent, some streets, particularly in the Italian neighborhoods east of Third Avenue below 119th Street, were "very thickly populated with delinquents."[129] The New York State Crime Commission reported a "major arrest" rate of 4.78 percent for youths (male and female) aged sixteen to twenty in health area 21, the neighborhood bounded by First and Third Avenues between East 114th and 109th streets, the heart of Italian Harlem.[130]

Italian Harlem's approximately fifty storefront social and athletic clubs "linked the world of street gangs, racketeers, and politicians." The underworld contacts some youths made in these venues likely led them to illegal activities, although some also used the clubs as pathways to careers as upstanding citizens. "Social and athletic clubs, street gangs, and the rackets defined East Harlem's public space as a masculine, defended, segmented, and bounded domain," writes historian Eric Schneider. "Not every individual had to belong to such groups, but everyone owed them deference."[131]

These trenchant problems notwithstanding, East Harlem offered an array of organizational and political resources that would be available to Covello and his staff at Benjamin Franklin High School. These resources represented existing social networks in East Harlem, some of which served the needs of particular ethnic groups, others of which had a districtwide approach.

Organizing East Harlem: An Infrastructure

In its 1937 report, *The East Harlem Community Study,* the Mayor's Committee on City Planning focused primarily on the district's deficits, highlighting, for example, the egregious absence of a public hospital and the need for "at least one truly modern high school."[132] Leonard Covello, who served on the sponsoring committee for the study, had a heavy hand in determining the agenda for the final report. A consummate pragmatist, Covello recognized the manifest and latent strengths that were represented in the twenty-six pages of the report that adumbrated the myriad social services and resources available in East Harlem. No matter how sparse, these assets and the organizing infrastructure that supported them provided the community building blocks for Benjamin Franklin High School.

East Harlem enjoyed a rich and varied tradition of social welfare activity and community organizing. For example, no fewer than 110 mutual benefit societies provided recreational and religious activities, death benefits, and occasionally sickness and accident benefits to the Italian community.[133] At least forty-three political, cultural, and civic organizations served the Spanish-speaking populations of New York City, and of East Harlem in particular.[134] As many as fourteen social settlements and multiservice organizations were active in the district in 1930. Three of these organizations were closely linked to Covello and Benjamin Franklin: Union Settlement, Haarlem House, and the Heckscher Foundation.[135]

Founded in 1895 by graduates of Union Theological Seminary, Union Settlement at 237 East 104th Street provided, among other services, a playground and gymnasium, a health clinic, a music school, social clubs for children and adults, and a program for the aged.[136] Haarlem House developed out of the Home Garden, the Methodist mission founded by Anna Ruddy, who had inspired Covello's commitment to a life of dedicated Protestant stewardship. Incorporated in 1901, the Home Garden, after two moves, found a permanent home in 1917 at 311–313 East 116th Street, where in 1919 it was incorporated as Haarlem House. (In 1957 Haarlem House was rededicated at the same site as La Guardia Memorial House.) This settlement offered educational and recreational services and served as a valuable training ground for Italian American leaders, among them Vito Marcantonio, the future congressman from East Harlem, and Edward Corsi, who served in various government posts, including commissioner of immigration in the Hoover administration.[137] The Heckscher Foundation at 104th Street and Fifth Avenue, founded in 1921 by the German-born industrialist August Heckscher, served as a recreational center that boasted a marble pool on the sunlit top floor and one of the finest gymnasiums in the city. Located on the western edge of East Harlem and serving both boys and girls up to age sixteen, the foundation also provided free dental clinics, dance classes, music lessons, vocational guidance, an employment bureau, and emergency relief, as well as a camp program outside Peekskill, New York.[138]

The East Harlem Health Center at 160 East 115th Street, one of Covello's closest allies and an influential voice on the high school's community advisory committee, pioneered innovative community health programs, services, and materials that were adopted in other cities. The health center regularly sponsored public health campaigns, and its affiliated agency, the East Harlem Nursing and Health Service, at 454 East 122nd Street, provided districtwide prenatal and well-baby care.[139] Sophie Rabinoff, director of the health center and cochair of Benjamin Franklin's health committee, led the high school's East Harlem health and hospital campaigns (see Chapter 6).

Serving as an umbrella group for twenty-seven local agencies, the East Harlem Council of Social Agencies coordinated various neighborhood efforts in social work, health care, recreation, and education. Chaired by Grace Anderson of the East Harlem Nursing and Health Service, the council provided a loose network that proved critical in mobilizing support for the establishment of a high school in the area. Selina Weigel, for example, a representative of the East Harlem Health Center and a member of the council's executive committee, did recruitment work and served as secretary to two key committees on the high school campaign. The council sent a resolution to the board of education calling for the establishment of the high school.[140]

An infrastructure strength that worked to Covello's advantage was East Harlem's tradition of political associations, clubs, and parties, which provided a broad political education to their constituents.[141] At one time a center of Socialist Party strength, East Harlem, and especially the Italian section, lacked an entrenched Tammany machine and resisted loyalty to any single political party. Thus, while the Democratic and Republican parties figured prominently in local politics, third-party and fusion politics also played a role. Third parties rose and fell in the 1930s: American Labor Party, Progressive Party, Progressive Labor Party, Wet Party, Liberal Party, All People's Party, City Fusion, and Communist Party.[142] Of fourteen political clubs in East Harlem, the club of Fiorello La Guardia, which Vito Marcantonio, Covello's former student and La Guardia's protégé, inherited, dominated the district's political life. From the mid-1930s to the late 1940s, Marcantonio developed a political machine that paid meticulous attention to local residents' concerns; it was a fine-tuned, compassionate variation of a *padrone* system that appealed to Italian and Puerto Rican voters alike. While the "God of the Churches" might stay in "celestial splendor far above the earth," proclaimed a former minister of the East Harlem Protestant Parish, "the God of this life is Vito Marcantonio and his kingdom is the American Labor Party. Obviously, the God who can get the plumbing fixed becomes the center of faith for the great majority."[143]

This is not to suggest that East Harlem residents did not participate in church or synagogue life. In May 1932, May Case Marsh documented thirty-three religious institutions within a 180-block area of East Harlem, roughly one for every five-and-a-half blocks.[144] Largely divided along ethnic lines, the churches appeared to cooperate minimally with other community agencies and even less with each other, concerned primarily with an individualistic gospel and the internal conditions of their institutions. The Italian-dominated churches were particularly reluctant to embrace other national and racial groups.[145]

In its informal organization, East Harlem was also a place busy with the local markets, quotidian distractions, and petty amusements of a crowded urban neighborhood. With good reason youth workers and school officials cast a jaundiced eye at the allurements. Five hundred candy stores dotted the area, serving as hangouts for youth while selling sweets, the latest news, and school supplies—and housing the occasional bookie operation. Boys' Club Study researchers observed that "these stores are meeting places for suggestible children who are contaminated by the undesirable crowd which usually hangs out there." Shoe-repair shops and "shoe shine parlors" were also adolescent hangouts. A drink could be had on almost every corner, with at least 160 speakeasies flaunting the Eighteenth Amendment. There were also sixteen motion-picture theaters, five taxi-dance halls, and fifty public pool halls, not to mention numerous private billiard operations in the district's fifty social and athletic clubs. Junkyards, some two dozen of them, held an allure as venues for danger and adventure. Covello could not have been pleased with the ambience of vice and temptation that beckoned his students at the very doorstep of Benjamin Franklin's main building on East 108th Street. Within a four-block area that included the fledgling high school, from 107th to 109th Street between First and Third avenues, Frederic Thrasher's social-base maps for the Boys' Club Study show one movie theater (the Verona Theater, standing catty-corner to the main building), three pool halls, five speakeasies, three saloons, and nineteen candy stores.[146]

To summarize, East Harlem in its full panoply of social forces and contexts encompassed a vast array of educational influences. Some of these influences constituted or reflected major social problems; others carried a strong positive valence for educational purposes. After 1934 community-centered schooling would evolve as a formal educational strategy to help East Harlem's diverse citizenries surmount their cultural differences, mobilize collectively to overcome the negative social forces that impinged so forcefully on their lives, and achieve a more democratic, cosmopolitan community. Coeval with this evolving vision, Covello, his teachers, and community allies would harness East Harlem's social problems, as well as its trove of cultural and organizational resources, to the curricular and extracurricular programs of the new high school. Covello's background and preparation for this effort forms the core of the next chapter.

CHAPTER THREE

Leonard Covello:
The Heart of the Matter

T HE DEPRESSION ERA called forth powerful social forces that galvanized a small but hardy band of progressive educators to keep the reformist vision of community-centered schooling alive in the 1930s and early 1940s. Working in disparate locales and circumstances, their projects often unbeknownst to one another, these reformers built community schools and educational programs designed to improve the quality of local community life. The common ground of their diverse projects was the prevalent poverty and unemployment within their respective localities and their shared belief in the primacy of neighborly, face-to-face relationships, the efficacy of community problem-focused learning, and the potential of community-centered schools as integrative centers and catalysts for constructive social change.

The largest and most important community school experiment was Benjamin Franklin High School in East Harlem. More than any other community school, Franklin had an explicit agenda of democratic community development. It would strive to create a leadership class for East Harlem and to build and extend social networks and norms of trust and reciprocity among East Harlem's dozens of ethnic groups. The making of this high school was inextricably linked to the life and career of Leonard Covello, Franklin's founding principal, a native son of both Italy and East Harlem. In this chapter we examine particular elements of Covello's biography from his early life to midcareer that shaped his understanding and vision of community-centered schooling and led to the realization of the community school idea in East Harlem. Coming of age as a first-generation Italian American, Covello encountered, in highly formative ways, full-throttle assimilation for Anglo conformity in the youth-serving institutions he entered. Pulled, like many first- and second-generation immigrant youth, between the values taught in public schools and settlement houses and those learned from parents and community, he experienced cross-cultural conflict that permanently shaped his educational vision and professional life. In addition, exposure to the new field of educational sociology and the broader "progressive" emphasis in schooling, combined with his frustration with the bureaucratic impersonality of public high schools and the isolation of Columbia University's ivory tower, pushed Covello to sharpen his vision of the school as a community and civic center.

The Early and Formative Years: 1887–1913

Leonard Covello (formerly Coviello) was born on 26 November 1887 in the ancient walled town of Avigliano, located in the Apennine hills of Southern Italy's Basilicata region. Leonard's father, Pietro Coviello, had first tried his hand at shoemaking, a trade he learned from his older brother, then switched to upholstery for several years, though with little success. Evidently disgruntled with village life and his grim economic prospects, the adventurous Pietro set out for the United States in 1890, leaving his wife and three sons behind until he could raise the money to send for them. Leonard received some formal elementary schooling in Avigliano, imparted in a rigidly didactic, authoritarian fashion by a male schoolmaster who wielded a heavy ruler for the slightest infraction. His school experience, the benign influence of his extended family (his mother, two uncles and paternal grandmother), and the daily life of the town itself imbued the young Covello with a sense of duty and service and an appreciation for the virtues of struggle and sacrifice. Reflecting his artisan class provenance, he was also strongly influenced by Giuseppe Mazzini's *Duties of Man*. When he later embarked on his teaching career in New York City, he built his educational philosophy around these core values.[1]

By 1896, according to Covello's autobiography, his father had finally earned enough money as a common laborer in East Harlem to send for his wife and children, who arrived in New York City after a harrowing twenty-day trip from Naples aboard an old freighter. Following a nerve-wracking stay of two days and two nights on Ellis Island spent "sleeping on hard benches, while my mother hardly closed her eyes for fear of losing us in the confusion," the family was finally reunited in East Harlem. The Coviellos resided in a humble tenement flat on East 112th Street, part of "the endless monotonous rows of tenement buildings that shut out the sky," within range of the smell of the East River at ebb tide.[2] They lived in close quarters with the Accurso family, also from Avigliano, who had taken in Pietro during his six-year separation from his wife and the children; the crowded Coviello flat "had a water pump and a toilet in the hallway that served four families on the same floor."[3]

Leonard, now nine years old, first experienced U.S. schooling at the Soup School at 116th Street and Second Avenue. "The Soup School," he recalled, "got its name from the fact that at noontime a bowl of soup was served to us with some white, soft bread that made better spitballs than eating in comparison with the substantial and solid homemade bread to which I was accustomed. The school itself was organized and maintained by the Female Guardian Society of America. Later on I found out that this Society was sponsored by wealthy people concerned about the immigrants and their children. How much this organization accomplished among immigrants in New York City would be difficult to estimate. But this I do know, that among the immigrants of my generation and even later *La Soupa Scuola* is still vivid in our boyhood memories." In his autobiography Covello remarked that he had "not the faintest idea" why his father had picked the Soup School for his son instead of one of the area's regular elementary schools, "except that possibly the first Aviglianese to arrive in New York sent his child there and everyone else followed suit— and also possibly because in those days a bowl of soup was a bowl of soup."[4]

Covello spent two years at the Soup School, where the stocky and severe Mrs. Cutter, armed with a bamboo switch and "ever alert and ready to strike at any infringement," drilled the immigrant children unremittingly in the rudiments of English, geography, arithmetic, penmanship, and spelling. Whereas the brutalizing schoolmaster of Avigliano was simply mean, Mrs. Cutter was "meanly anti-immigrant" and pro Anglo conformity.[5] Yet Covello recalled that the Soup School "was not an unpleasant experience," and he praised its "forceful and vitalizing influence."[6]

Covello completed his elementary education at P.S. 83, a five-story building at 110th Street between Second and Third avenues, where teaching, as at the Soup School, remained largely a stiff affair of memorization and recitation. Covello reflected that the teaching "was thorough for those who could learn and who wanted to learn."[7] He would later acknowledge, however, that the elementary schools he had attended in New York were culturally depriving institutions. In 1964 he told Robert Peebles: "In all the four years I was in this school (P.S. 83), as well as the 'Soup School,' I do not recall one mention of Italy or of the Italian language, or what famous Italians had done in this world. Pretty soon we got the idea that Italian meant something inferior."[8] To Americanize his name, Leonard dropped the *i* from Coviello, driving a wedge between himself and his anguished parents.

The most important influence in Covello's formative years was Anna C. Ruddy, who directed the Home Garden Association, a Protestant settlement house located on two floors of a brownstone tenement on 115th Street at First Avenue, in the heart of Little Italy. The zealously religious daughter of a Canadian pioneer, Ruddy had arrived in East Harlem in 1890 intending to do missionary work among the Italians. "Apart from a rudimentary knowledge of the Italian language," Covello recounted, "she had absolutely no preparation for the tumultuous existence of crowded tenements, sidewalk pushcarts and the violence of life in the city's streets. But somehow she knew that she had to be there. Most missionaries were so concerned with carrying God's message to distant lands that they quite forgot the good they could do close to home. The Lord had directed her footsteps to East Harlem, she used to say." Established in 1898, the Home Garden took its name from "a garden in back where the children could read and play their games in the midst of flowers and green plants."[9] According to a contemporaneous source: "Here fifty or sixty children gathered daily to read, play games, or sew. . . . The house was filled with books, toys and games, while flowers of every description bloomed in the yard and were tended and watered by the children themselves."[10]

The Home Garden was dedicated to serving the physical and spiritual needs of the Italian community, saving souls, especially young souls, for Christ. Covello's circle of friends formed a cadre of exuberant Anna Ruddy recruits. In Ruddy's book *The Heart of the Stranger,* written in 1908, the reader hears an echo of Covello's circle in her tales of the juvenile "River Gang" members and in the conversion stories she relates in "How the Gang Came to Sunday-School."[11] (Not coincidentally, when one of those strangers, Covello, wrote of his life in teaching fifty years later, he entitled his book *The Heart is the Teacher.*) One of Covello's first Aviglianese friends in East Harlem, Vito Scallatore, introduced him to the remarkable Miss Ruddy. Covello recalled being fascinated upon first seeing this "tall, imposing looking woman, . . . her voice, low, strong and compelling," with "eyes which seemed to take in all of us."[12] Covello spent every Sunday afternoon and several nights a week at the Home Garden. Ruddy relentlessly proselytized Leonard and the other Italian children, her Sunday school, Bible lessons, and weekly prayer meetings leaving a profound impression. That Anna Ruddy was Protestant in Catholic East Harlem did not alarm the Coviello family at all. As Leonard's father declared: "A woman in a million. Protestant! Catholic! Egyptian! In the end, what difference does it make? Religion is a matter of the spirit and the heart. I take my hat off to Signorina Ruddy."[13]

Ruddy made a vigorous Protestant of Leonard, who remained deeply religious for the rest of his life. As an adult he taught Sunday school at the Jefferson Park Methodist Church and the Presbyterian church of Norman Thomas, presided over the former's missionary advisory board, and served on the interdenominational East Harlem Protestant Parish, which operated storefront churches in the district. Described as "a deeply religious man," Covello was known to many of his friends as "the Bishop of Harlem." The affectionate title referred both to his religious activities and to the service ethic he brought to Benjamin Franklin High School. Like his high school's famous namesake, Covello understood service to humankind to mean service to God.[14]

Undeniably, the Protestant values Ruddy so successfully inculcated distanced Covello from the Catholic Church; whether that experience was an internal source of tension for Covello or promoted conflict between him and practicing Italian Catholics, however, is an open question. A reasoned speculation suggests that his disquietude about, and perhaps disdain for, the boisterous street religion associated with the Madonna of 115th Street can be traced to, among other influences, the Protestant settlement house.

Ruddy's Christian witness also inspired Covello's decision to become a teacher. "It was Miss Ruddy who gave me an idea of how important the influence of a teacher can be in the life of a growing boy. Of all of us who went to the Home Garden, not one, to my knowledge, ever became a criminal or ended 'bad' in the usual sense of the word."[15] When Covello married the girl next door, Mary Accurso, the couple decided to take their honeymoon in Toronto to visit Miss Ruddy, who had returned to Canada in poor health after retiring from settlement work. Ruddy felt that with Leonard and Mary, "God had given me children of my own to remember and to perpetuate the life I passed here on this earth."[16]

In an interview in 1949, Covello declared of Anna Ruddy: "I can truthfully say that her influence has been the strongest and most important ever to enter my life."[17] As a tribute to Ruddy, Covello helped establish a memorial award in her name, a gift of the Home Garden Alumni Association, more than a half century after the Home Garden had ceased to exist. The Anna C. Ruddy Memorial Award was given annually to a graduate of Benjamin Franklin High School who had "served his school and community."[18]

By the time he entered Morris High School in the Bronx in 1902, Leonard was too busy to be distracted by East Harlem street life (twenty-six saloons operated within a square block of the Home Garden's corner of 115th Street). In his autobiography, Covello described his adolescence as his "work years." To help support his struggling family, which had now expanded to five children, Leonard, at age twelve, took a delivery job in a bakery at Fifth Avenue and 112th Street. The job required him to be on the street with a pushcart at 4:30 every morning, arduous labor for which he received $1.75 a week. "It was not very much but it helped a great deal in days when meat was twelve cents a pound and milk six cents a quart." Until he completed high school, he continued to take jobs after school and during summer vacations. For several summers he worked in a baking-powder factory in lower Manhattan, a job that netted $1.20 a week after carfare and lunch money were subtracted.[19]

The main building of the coeducational Morris High School (a former elementary school, P.S. 62) stood at 156th Street and Third Avenue, where it had opened in 1897. Two annexes were opened to remedy the severe overcrowding that was typical of the urban high schools of that era.[20] In 1902, Morris freshmen and sophomores shared a building with elementary school students on Mott Avenue (today's Grand Concourse) at 144th Street in the Bronx. Covello and four of his Italian American friends walked daily from East Harlem to the Bronx; one of the boys was Garibaldi Lapolla, with whom Covello would attend Columbia University and later teach at DeWitt Clinton High School. Covello wrote: "For two years our little group crossed the bridges of the Harlem River, 1st Avenue, 3rd Avenue, and occasionally Madison Avenue, usually walking for even the nickel carfare was an item in our budget and could be put to better use in getting a more substantial lunch at the school."[21] In 1904, when Morris opened its new building at 166th Street and Boston Road, the distance got even longer for the East Harlem boys.[22]

In 1902 Superintendent William Maxwell instituted a standardized course of studies, an uncompromising liberal arts curriculum, for the city's public high schools.[23] Covello recalled the rigorous standards:

> There was one course—one track for all students: the academic course—a first language (Latin or German) and French as a second language, mathematics, through intermediate algebra at least; biology and physics or chemistry and physiography (now Earth Science); ancient History [sic], British and American History and English, Elocution, Music, Drawing and Physical Training. It was a stiff course. The teachers expected much, home work was practically a daily assignment in all major subjects, and Morris students had to dig hard and deep in their books in order to survive. Our principal, Dr. Denbigh, formerly an enthusiastic teacher of mathematics at Morris, was a man of great integrity, who spoke to us directly and forcefully of our social and civic responsibilities.[24]

In 1902 Morris was dominated by students of northern European origin. Most of the teachers, none of whom were Italian, claimed English or German ancestry; only six of more than two thousand students were Italian. Reinforcing Covello's earlier experience of cultural hybridity in city schools, at times his high school experience pushed him to question the benefits of his Italian heritage. He recalled the stigma attached to Italian culture, and the effort he and other Italian youngsters made to distance themselves from their cultural origins: "For instance . . . when it came to taking lunch to school, we did not want to bring our Italian bread. . . . You see, we felt we had to use American bread, and all that went with it. We were ashamed to reveal where we lived, because it was a sign of our inferior status. We were always trying to play up to what we thought was the *American* way. We did not want to take our parents to school, feeling that they would probably be ridiculed. They dressed differently and couldn't speak English. It was very serious, this feeling of inferiority and the resulting concealment."[25]

Covello's Italian upbringing had not prepared him for the shock of attending school with girls at Morris High School; he also discovered that most of his classmates were "well dressed and had spending money" and "a social life" with "little gatherings to which we were not invited." Covello recalled that "in fact,

we did not want to be invited for fear that in some way we might have to recip-
rocate. We did not want them to see our homes and our parents and how we
lived."[26] He had acquiesced in the dropping of the *i* in Coviello as a necessary
adjustment to U.S. ways and fought with his parents when they did not understand. He knew the impossibility of explaining certain U.S. practices to his
mother and father and began to feel he was living "what seemed like fragmen-
tary existences in different worlds. There was my life with my family and
Aviglianese neighbors. My life on the streets of East Harlem. . . . Life at the
local public school. Life at what job I happened to have. Life in the wonder-
world of books. There seemed to be no connection, one with the other; it was
like turning different faucets on and off."[27]

Leonard carried a stressful load—at school and at home. His mother's
health was failing (she would die in 1907), a medical crisis that exacerbated
the family's perpetual struggle to make ends meet. "Whatever I could earn
after school was not enough, despite the fact that my father was working and
my two younger brothers were also contributing," Covello recalled. "I was old
enough now to work as a man. I had to work." Although the date is uncertain—it was probably 1905–6—we learn that Covello dropped out of high
school for a year to take a job loading crates at a downtown brassware factory.
Withdrawing from Morris he experienced the impersonal nature of large city
schools, which left him feeling isolated and unrecognized, little more than a
cipher in a ledger. The insouciance with which the high school staff treated
his leave-taking contributed to his later desire to create community schools
that were more than impersonal bureaucracies: "What stands foremost in my
mind concerning this decision was the indifference and the lack of guidance
at the high school itself. I simply turned in my books at the school office and
went away. That's all there was to it. No one spoke to me. No one asked me
why I was leaving or discussed my problems with me."[28] Academic high
schools, he learned painfully, had little sympathy for the plight of the city's
immigrant groups.

Nonetheless Covello's determination ensured that he used the public
school system to his advantage. The following year the reflective Covello
returned to Morris, in his words, "with a greater assurance and confidence."
He compiled an excellent academic record, good enough to win a Pulitzer
Scholarship of $250 annually and free tuition at Columbia College. Covello
also excelled in sports, playing halfback on Morris's city championship soccer
team in 1906, and serving as the captain of the senior basketball team. Later
he proudly noted: "Members of the team were awarded the much coveted
'M' which adorned the maroon jersey that we wore in school as well as the
'beanie' that was the style in my day."[29] Gifted in languages, he was able to
earn family money giving English lessons to Italian immigrants, "twenty-five
cents for the man of private business and fifteen cents for the pushcart peddler and wage earner."[30]

In September 1907 Covello entered Columbia College with great expectations: "I, and just a few other young men from East Harlem, went everyday from the East Harlem community below the heights to Columbia University. We walked across town; we climbed, every morning, 172 steps up to Morningside Heights; and we felt—all of us—that we were preparing ourselves for service and for the yet larger opportunities for which we were always hoping, and which we expected would some day surely come to us. We had faith in ourselves and faith in our determination to find ways of being of service to our community beneath the heights."[31]

Although Columbia University was largely a disappointment to Covello, his experience there may have added to his educational vision, pushing him to value links between schools and communities that he found absent in his university experience. He told Robert Peebles that his undergraduate years were a desultory intellectual experience even though he was quite successful academically. "There seemed to be little opportunity for the kind of intellectual exchange between professor and student he had anticipated," Peebles writes. "The courses were a matter of taking notes during lectures and regurgitating them on examinations, little more. What Covello missed was any sense behind the whole process."[32] Covello also complained that the university cloistered itself from the problems of contemporary society; little more than a hodgepodge of courses, the curriculum lacked an integrative social purpose. The stark contrast between Columbia's affluence and the pampered frivolity of its students and the poverty, filth, and violence of East Harlem began Covello's political radicalization: "His political orientation, although not identified through overt campaigning, was gradually but discernibly and sympathetically moving toward socialism."[33]

While at Columbia College, under the auspices of the Harlem YMCA, Covello taught English two nights a week to Italian immigrants at the Aguilar Library on 110th Street. In 1910 he and several friends from the Home Garden petitioned, lobbied, cajoled, and struggled to establish an East Harlem branch of the YMCA. The drive succeeded, and the group opened the new branch at 322 East 116th Street. In addition to drama, music, and athletic clubs, the East Harlem YMCA sponsored lectures, language courses, and "intellectual discussions." The New York Public Library's traveling branch provided book loans, particularly books on Italian history and culture. By now Covello realized the importance of learning about his Italian heritage and Italians' place in U.S. history: "We needed to know as much as possible about ourselves before we could feel that our people and their culture were not inferior—only different."[34]

Continually strapped for funds, the East Harlem YMCA operated for only three years, yet it was a formative intellectual experience for Covello. Two friendships he made there greatly stimulated his thinking on education and cultural difference in the United States. Covello first met Leon Piatelli, a young

Italian immigrant poet who worked as a bookkeeper, when Piatelli wandered into an English-language course Covello taught at the YMCA. Piatelli, "a turbulent soul . . . searching for the purpose of his existence," excited Covello with his enthusiasm for Italian culture and his vision of an historical parallel between the development of liberty in Italy and in America.[35] "In his *Divina Commedia*, Dante lit the torch of civil liberty and national consciousness in Italy," exclaimed Piatelli. "The universality of [Dante's] dream asserted itself in Italy through such men as Giuseppe Mazzini—and in America through Abraham Lincoln." Covello recalled leaving Piatelli, "my mind tingling" and "with the desire to know more about the world of poetry and art and literature and to bring it all into relation to my own life," to address *"il mistero della vita."* Piatelli's ability to blend Italian and U.S. cultural icons impressed Covello deeply. "Dante, Mazzini, Lincoln! I never thought about them together before," he confided to Mary Accurso. "And now a casual meeting with a man who is almost a perfect stranger has given me a new feeling of direction."[36]

Shortly after meeting Piatelli, Covello met the New Englander John Shedd, secretary to a U.S. millionaire, who had been teaching Sunday school at an Italian mission downtown. Shedd's interest in working among Italians drew him to the East Harlem YMCA, and he quickly involved himself in the branch, serving on the board of directors. Middle-aged, "heavily built, and in appearance much like G. K. Chesterton with a massive head, flowing gray hair, straggly mustache, and bushy eyebrows curling out over the edges of the thick lenses of his pince-nez," Shedd brought a well-cultivated enthusiasm for Lincoln, Jefferson, U.S. history, and pithy aphorisms to the evenings of discussion with Piatelli and Covello.[37] Emblematic of the cultural exchange of these three men would be Covello's direction of DeWitt Clinton High School students in a production of Shedd's play *Up at Abe Lincoln's* at the Harlem YMCA in 1921, and the eventual bequest of Shedd's considerable library to Benjamin Franklin High School.[38] Decades later, Covello, still in touch with the Shedd family, described his continuing distribution of John Shedd's book of aphorisms, *Salt from My Attic,* the work of a man "overflowing with life and an ungovernable will to live and help others."[39] Influenced by both Shedd and Piatelli, Covello began to think more broadly about the context in which his own teaching might fit, about the rich cultural heritage of both the United States and Italy, and about the struggle for democratic development.

Covello's involvement with the East Harlem YMCA did not distract from his education project. He spent the summer of 1910 studying French at the Alliance Française in Paris, under the stern and haughty tutelage of L'Abbé Rousselot. In February 1911, he graduated from Columbia with a B.S. degree in French, a concentration in Romance languages, and a Phi Beta Kappa key. Next Covello enrolled in Columbia's graduate program in Romance languages, having decided to become a college professor. He subsequently turned down offers to teach French at Wesleyan and Syracuse because his family desperately needed his financial support, which he was able to provide by teaching French in Columbia's extension program and taking such part-time jobs as florist shop attendant, poll watcher, and counter of whistles and tugboat tootings for a midtown riverside hospital. In 1913, he married his childhood friend and neighbor, Mary Accurso. According to his resume, Covello taught French at New Utrecht High School in Brooklyn in 1913–14.[40] His marriage was tragically short-lived; in August 1914, a week or so after the outbreak of World War I, Mary, who was a teacher at P.S. 191 in lower Manhattan, died of nephritis.[41] In part to assuage his grief, Covello threw himself headlong into a teaching position at DeWitt Clinton High School on Manhattan's West Side, where he would remain for seventeen of the next twenty years and profoundly influence the teaching of foreign languages in the New York City public schools.

The DeWitt Clinton High School Years, 1914–1917 and 1920–1934

DeWitt Clinton High School had opened in Manhattan in 1897. When Covello arrived as an "assistant teacher in French" in 1914, the ornately crafted high school occupied a five-story building on the west side of the block of 59th Street and 10th Avenue, three blocks west of Columbus Circle in Hell's Kitchen. DeWitt Clinton was designated an academic high school, "with practically all students taking the prescribed academic course" and the commercial course enrolling only a small minority.[42] The principal who hired Covello was John L. Tildsley, a proponent of rigorous academic standards. The philosopher George Abernethy, who attended Clinton in the mid-1920s, recounts the powerful intellectual ethos of this high school:

> What distinguished the Clinton faculty was that a high percentage of them had graduate degrees in the subject-matter fields rather than in education in a day when few high school teachers had graduate degrees. They lectured like college professors and required students to keep notes. Unannounced quizzes were common. The grading was severe. We had half-year graduations. In my June [1929] graduating class of 550 I ranked 50th with an average of 80.5. Only 12 boys out of 550 had a 4 year average of 90 or above. There was not social promotion. It was hard serious work. I was in a home room once where I was the only boy who had passed all his subjects. . . . The result of this was strenuous competition, a very serious attitude toward the mastery of subject-matter, and yet a lively sense of intellectual life and discussion. This was, of course, reinforced by the fact that many of the boys came from Jewish homes which placed a high value on intellectual matters and kept before them the goal of becoming a doctor or a lawyer

or a rabbi——or as a last resort a teacher. Catholic students did not have the same motivation, altho in fairness I should note that Dr. Leonard Covello, Chairman of the Italian Dept. and father-confessor to the Italian constituency kept somewhat similar ideals before the Italian boys.[43]

Clinton was a hothouse for cultural politics and socialist political activity, as one historian puts it, a "radicalized ambiance."[44] For example, Henry Linville, a socialist teacher at Clinton, founded New York's Local 5 of the American Federation of Teachers in 1916 and played a key leadership role in the first two decades of both the city and national unions. Abraham Lefkowitz, a longtime friend of Linville, himself a Clinton teacher and vigorous municipal socialist, also figured prominently in the New York Teachers Union and its leftist orientation.[45] A U.S. history teacher who ran for Congress on the Socialist ticket in 1922, Lefkowitz inspired the future East Harlem congressman Vito Marcantonio, who attended Clinton from 1917 to 1921, to become a socialist. One of only eleven Italian Americans who graduated from Clinton in 1921, the young Marcantonio walked four miles every day from his family's East Harlem tenement apartment on 112th Street between Second and Third avenues to Fifty-ninth Street and Tenth Avenue, pocketing the nickel carfare. As Marcantonio biographer Gerald Meyer notes: "Lefkowitz probably significantly influenced Marcantonio's view of American history as a succession of struggles of the haves against the have-nots to extend the boundaries of democracy."[46]

Yet it was a quiet socialist, Covello, who enlisted the impressionable Marcantonio, first as a high school student, later as a rising political star, to collaborate with him to help improve the quality of life and schooling in Italian Harlem. A series of progressive undertakings organized or inspired by Covello at Clinton "gave form and direction" to Marcantonio's life.[47] Grounded in Covello's background and firsthand experience of the hardships of immigrant life in New York City, and developed from his occupational base as an activist teacher of Romance languages at DeWitt Clinton High School, these efforts, integral components of his educational mission, included Covello's successful campaign to achieve parity for the Italian language in the New York City public schools, the organization of a thriving network of Italian clubs (Circoli Italiani), the founding of an Italian social settlement (Casa del Popolo), and the development of an extensive data base on first- and second-generation Italian Americans.

From 1914 until 1917, when he enlisted in the U.S. Army in World War I, Covello taught French and Spanish at Clinton; he also held evening-school licenses in the two languages.[48] Nowhere in the city was Italian being taught, notwithstanding the provision of an examination in that language by the state regents.[49] Encouraged by his students of Italian origin, Covello set in motion a strategy to elevate the status of Italian language and culture, first among its legatees, Italian American youth, then more broadly among other ethnic groups in the city schools. That strategy would come to fruition in the early 1920s.

In 1915, Covello sponsored the creation of an Italian club, Il Circolo Italiano, at Clinton. Open to all students, but primarily attracting the Italian boys, the Circolo's mission was twofold: to promote Italian language and culture, and to engage youth in social service activities. A bulletin from 1921 describes the Circolo's English-language performance of *Il Ventaglio* (The Fan), a three-act comedy by Carlo Goldoni, the centerpiece of a varied and spirited youth production. The bulletin's writer assures us that the Circolo's thespians acquitted themselves well in their roles, that the Clinton orchestra performed with "spirit and vigor," and that between the acts two Hunter College girls danced the old-country "Tarantella" "with all the abandon and vim that youth and enthusiasm and the 'tarant Tarantella' music could give it." The playing of Signor Guido Agosti of Bologna University in Italy, hailed by the writer as a "rare treat" (although he fails to mention which instrument the signor was playing), concluded the performance. "For this delightful evening too much praise cannot be given to Mr. Covello," the bulletin waxes in its peroration. "He is giving the most unselfish service and devotion to bringing the Italian immigrant into contact with what is best in American life, and at the same time making use of that wealth of culture which Italy offers the world."[50]

The Circolo's social service program included citizenship training and English-language instruction for Italian immigrants. By 1921 the club had established services at Casa del Popolo in East Harlem and Mulberry Community House on Mott Street. The editors of *Il Foro*, the club's new magazine, reported that "two of the boys are assisting in boys' club work in the afternoon, five are teaching English to groups of twelve to fifteen men, two are teaching American Civics to groups which are preparing to take out second papers and five are observing and are preparing to take up work along similar lines."[51] Covello always insisted that the club's service function never be subordinated to social, literary, or intellectual activities, adjuring Italian American students: "We need work, more work, and still more work—slow, self-forgetting, self-sacrificing work; we need action along constructive lines. Let us carry on in the spirit of Mazzini—the spirit of service wherever service is rooted."[52]

That Covello would even continue teaching in the 1920s had been in doubt. World War I and its immediate aftermath gave him a moratorium to test other career options. In the summer of 1917 Covello directed the Farm Cadet Camp at Milton, New York, an employment program for high school students conducted under the auspices of the board of education's Special Committee on War Service; this program augmented other seasonal labor in the state's fruit and berry industry, which experienced a labor shortage because of the war. That summer Covello also began his courtship of Mary Accurso's younger sister Rose, which would lead to their marriage following the war. In December

1917 he enlisted as a private in the Fifty-seventh Artillery, Battery D, posted at Fort Hancock, Sandy Hook, New Jersey. Letters of support from Associate Superintendent John L. Tildsley (Covello's first principal at DeWitt Clinton) and DeWitt Clinton's current principal, Francis H. J. Paul, called the army's attention to Covello's exceptional linguistic skills. The summer of 1918 found Covello in the south of France, where he was transferred to the Corps of Intelligence Police in Hendaye as a linguist and promoted to the rank of sergeant. On orders he crossed the Franco-Spanish border to gather intelligence on German activity in neutral Spain, becoming so fluent in Spanish that he passed for a native speaker. Covello spent ten months wandering all over Spain following leads and relaying information back to Paris. In June of 1919, following the Versailles Conference, Covello left the service to join a New York City–based international advertising firm he had learned about from an officer in Hendaye. After a year of desultory work lining up U.S. advertisers with South American markets, working out of a plush midtown Fifth Avenue office, Covello returned to DeWitt Clinton High School. Compared to teaching, advertising work seemed pallid.[53]

After his return to Clinton, Covello married Rose Accurso. The couple took up residence in a small apartment near New York University, and Rose quit her job as a secretary at an export firm to continue her college studies to become a teacher. To fulfill their obligations to their East Harlem families, Covello had to moonlight for a few years. "I had to go back to private lessons and teaching evening school five nights a week. I stopped teaching at ten and never reached home before eleven o'clock at night and was out of the house in the morning at 7:30." He augmented his income from "this deadening routine" with earnings from six-week summer teaching stints at the YMCA.[54]

Somehow Covello managed to stay focused on what was dearest to him professionally. He inaugurated the study of the Italian language at Clinton with thirteen students in September 1920.[55] "We struggled and, by means of petitions, meetings, and organized efforts, managed to get one class in Italian. But it was on what they call a minor language status. You had to take another language for at least one year before you could take Italian. Therefore, our next battle was to give Italian parity with the other languages"[56] If they succeeded, Italian would become a "first language," meaning it would meet the city's foreign-language requirement for the academic high school diploma.

Covello believed that an Italian-language program in the high school would help bridge the generation gap in the Italian American family and contribute significantly to the preservation of Italian culture in the United States. To be effective, however, it had to have coequal status with other foreign languages. Covello and the well-financed Italy America Society, founded in 1918, embarked on an intensive lobbying campaign to persuade the board of education to grant parity to Italian. Italy's participation as an ally in the war established a favorable citywide climate for this initiative.

Since a chief argument against recognizing Italian was the claim that it would not help students in their applications to colleges, the Italy America Society sponsored a survey of the teaching of Italian across the United States. The survey, headed by Mario Cosenza, then director of Townsend Harris High School and later dean of Brooklyn College, indicated that hundreds of colleges accepted credit in Italian toward admission, as well as taught Italian language and culture courses.[57] Cosenza also chaired the education committee of the Order Sons of Italy, the "largest and most influential" of the Italian benevolent and fraternal societies.[58] Working side by side with Covello, secretary of the education committee, Cosenza enlisted the support of New York state senator Salvatore A. Cotillo, a native son of East Harlem who was then grand master of the Order Sons of Italy. Organizing proceeded apace at the grassroots level. "We invited parents to entertainments at which our students put on plays in Italian, we publicized the campaign in the Italian newspapers, and we had conferences at the Board of Education," Covello recalled. "The most effective part of the campaign was the home visits that we made—speaking to the individual parents about signing petitions to introduce Italian in a particular school."[59] To present the case for Italian instruction before the board of education on 24 May 1922, Covello came armed with "the Cosenza survey" and the support of such groups as the Italian Education League and the Italian Teachers Association. After a short speech by Cotillo, the board unanimously passed a resolution designating Italian a "first language" in the high schools.[60] The following month, Covello was officially appointed chair of the Italian Department at DeWitt Clinton High School.[61] That new role was only part of his teaching responsibilities.

An increase in Clinton's Italian American enrollment in the 1920s prompted Francis Paul, the school's principal, to establish a special counseling program to deal exclusively with the discipline problems associated with these youngsters.[62] Special programs such as this were consistent with the "social efficiency" reform ideology that held sway in the New York City schools in the 1920s. The reformers feared that the loosened moral climate of the "Roaring Twenties" would lead to a breakdown in social order. As the major target for programmatic reform, the high schools were expected to provide "the systematic education of urban youth *away* from the dangers of the unfettered city streets and *toward* civic and social cohesion."[63]

Paul charged Covello with organizing the new program at Clinton. In his autobiography, Covello recounted: "In an out-of-the way corner . . . I found a small room that was being used as a stock room. Together with some of my students I spent several Saturdays cleaning and painting and putting it in shape for an office. The room had a very narrow window and just enough space for a desk, a few file cabinets, some chairs, and a mimeographing machine. It wasn't much of an office, but it was good enough for a beginning. It was good enough for the first office of the first Italian Department in the public schools of New York City."[64]

Covello informally integrated the work of his counseling office, the Circolo, and the Italian Department as a comprehensive education and service program for Italian American youths, their families, and local neighborhoods. He worked day and night on myriad activities related to his new position, imbuing them with his characteristic admixture of toughness and compassion. Often in the late afternoon or early evening when the corridors of DeWitt Clinton were deserted, Covello would hear a hesitant knock on his office door that signaled a boy in trouble. One late afternoon Joe D'Angelo knocked. Fumbling with his words, Joe confided to Covello: "It's the old man. He keeps hittin' me all the time. No matter what I say or do he's gotta start cloutin' me. He's a big guy and he works on the docks, and it hurts, and I can't stand it no more." To Covello's surprise, Joe was worried about his father's safety, not his own. Holding out a bony fist, Joe related that he was, unbeknownst to his father, a semi-professional boxer earning "a couple of bucks" in New Jersey fight clubs under the name Kid Angel. He had kept this secret from his family, who wanted him to become a lawyer—a goal Joe aspired to himself. Covello advised Joe to spend the night with an uncle in the Bronx—in the meantime he would speak with the father.

Later that evening Covello took the downtown subway to Little Italy in Greenwich Village, where Joe's family lived in a red-brick tenement on Mac-Dougal Street, an ambience redolent of garlic and tomato sauce. When Joe's startled father and mother learned that Covello could speak their Neapolitan dialect, they plied him with a dish of sausage and peppers and a glass of wine. Assured by Covello that Joe was not in any trouble, Pappa D'Angelo, a short, muscular, hirsute man, proudly showed his fist to Covello: "So he is a good student, Guiseppe? And good he should be. With this instrument I have taught him right from wrong. Respect for his elders. For those who instruct him in school. In the old tradition. In this way he will become educated and become a lawyer and not work on the docks like his father." Covello replied candidly that Pappa D'Angelo's didactic violence was about to backfire. The father listened dumbfounded as Covello explained that Joe's extra money was not being earned in a factory, as Joe had led his parents to believe, but rather in a boxing ring. "But Joe does not want to be a fighter," Covello cautioned. "He fights so that he can earn money to be a lawyer. But he is afraid that when you beat him that someday he is going to forget you are his father." Rocking his head, then scratching it, a sheepish smile broadening into a wide grin, Pappa D'Angelo replied, "That lilla sonamangonia!"[65]

Covello imparted his ethic of duty and service to his students. The Italian Department organized afternoon "help classes," with "older boys looking . . . after the younger ones," tutoring in any subject that the younger students were failing.[66] Circolo members operated this program as part of their club's service mission as late as 1934. Even "former Clintonites and one time members of the Circolo Italiano" were involved, working as volunteers in Italian districts, in Covello's words, "carrying on Citizenship Classes, teaching English to Italian parents thus bridging the language gap between the parents and their children, acting as leaders of boys clubs and cooperating with us on the outside."[67] Vito Marcantonio represented the quintessential case of what Covello hoped to accomplish. Marcantonio cultivated an intimate, almost filial, relationship with Covello, whom he affectionately nicknamed "Pop." Under Covello's tutelage, "Marc" achieved a high level of proficiency in Italian, "an inestimable political asset in a community whose population as late as 1940 was almost one-third first generation."[68]

Marcantonio was an ardent participant in the cultural activities of the Italian Department and the Circolo, for example, playing the role of Evaristo in the school's 1921 production of *Il Ventaglio*. During his first year of legal studies at New York University, Marcantonio helped found the Circolo Mazzini, whose activities included tutoring East Harlem high school students. In the early twenties, he also taught citizenship classes at Casa del Popolo, an Italian settlement house that Covello helped organize at 118th Street near First Avenue.[69]

Covello encouraged Marcantonio's early socialist leanings. On one occasion Covello arranged for Fiorello La Guardia, then president of the board of aldermen of New York, to speak at a Clinton assembly. Marcantonio preceded La Guardia on the podium, giving a passionate speech to his spellbound peers on old-age pensions and social security—oratory that greatly impressed La Guardia and marked the beginning of a longstanding collaboration. Later as an attorney, Marcantonio would work in La Guardia's law office, manage his congressional campaigns in East Harlem, and in 1934 win La Guardia's congressional seat after the "Little Flower" became mayor of New York.[70]

The decade of the twenties was extraordinarily productive for Covello and his Italian program. Enrollments in the Italian Department increased from 62 in 1921 to 475 in 1924 to more than 600 in 1930; in 1933 the department enrolled 900 students.[71] By 1930, Covello had a staff of five teachers who provided a four-year course of study. In conjunction with the Italian Teachers Association, Covello and the Italian Department, the city's largest, promoted Italian-language study in the metropolitan area through a series of Feste Italiane and Italian Nights (Serate), theatrical and musical entertainments presented in schools, settlement houses, and churches.[72] Covello organized the Italian Parents Association, which met monthly at Haarlem House "to discuss ways and means of helping the Italo-American family guide its children successfully and thus make its way more effectively in America."[73] From 1921 to 1926, he published *Il Foro*, a polished literary and cultural magazine that featured articles by leading Italian scholars, as well as student essays.

Here it is important to note that Covello promoted a standard Italian language, when in fact there were numerous dialects and vernaculars spoken in Italy. Jonathan Zimmerman's pathbreaking research on ethnics and ethnicity suggests that Italians resisted the imposition of "a single form of ethnic speech," even in the face of concerted campaigns like those of the Order Sons of Italy and *Il Progresso* to boost citywide Italian enrollments in Italian-language classes after 1922. Although Covello's program at DeWitt Clinton was highly popular, his success was not repeated elsewhere. Covello acknowledged the difficulty when he commented that "the pupil of Italian parentage who studies Italian finds the language of Dante and Petrarch, of Mazzini and Manzoni far removed from the dialect which his father has brought from Calabria or Sicily or Piedmont"; more pointedly the dialect was a "distinct impediment" to "that liquid and musical Italian of which we read." Zimmerman argues that Covello's remarks illustrate "the central contradiction that plagued foreign-language activists in the early twentieth century. On the one hand, they said, language study would heal painful rifts between generations in immigrant families; on the other, it would teach children a classical tongue that their parents did not comprehend."[74]

As we have seen, Covello was involved in the operation of an Italian settlement house, Casa del Popolo, whose founding he credited to Amadeo Riggio, his pastor at Jefferson Park Methodist Church. In addition to Marcantonio's adult citizenship classes, Casa del Popolo offered a preparatory school for young Italian men and an afternoon recreational program for children.[75] Although this jury-rigged effort was short-lived, it suggests the powerful attraction the settlement idea had for Covello. In its heyday in the late 1930s, Benjamin Franklin High School functioned, in many ways, as a publicly funded social settlement. The path that led to the East Harlem community school crossed the New York City settlements; indisputably, that experience significantly influenced the educational and social programs that Covello and his staff negotiated for the school.

The Teacher as Sociologist

Covello's approach to the broader social problems that impinged on his students became more sharply focused in the late 1920s, in large part because of his growing involvement with the Department of Educational Sociology at New York University's School of Education.[76] There he learned how to translate his rich experience with Italian students into a working model for a revitalized relationship between public schooling and community life. Covello's studies at New York University resonated deeply with his personal experiences and provided a practical and systematic approach for the community development work he viewed as so critical to educational success in poor urban neighborhoods. His doctoral studies would pull together both the lessons of his personal odyssey and the main currents of East Harlem's community organizational life. Particularly through the Boys' Club Study, under the tutelage of Professor Frederic M. Thrasher, Covello developed the methods by which he would extend his work with Italian students into the school-community programs he would pioneer for an ethnically diverse student population at Benjamin Franklin High School.

Covello's studies at New York University provided him with a theoretical basis and a multifaceted method for local community research, which guided Franklin's school-community programs. His vigorous application of local social research as the underpinning of community-centered education distinguished Franklin among the nation's community schools of the twentieth century. Specifically, Covello extended to public school practice the urban ecology approach adopted by sociologists at the University of Chicago in the 1920s.

"I CAN STATE HERE what I have stated publicly," wrote Covello to E. George Payne, dean of the School of Education, "that it was it was my contact with New York University that gave me the idea and impetus to establish our work in East Harlem on a community basis."[77] Covello, who had been teaching Italian in New York University's School of Commerce since 1922, began taking courses at the School of Education in the summer of 1925, starting with a class taught by Payne in educational sociology.[78] That fall he met and studied with Professor Paul Radosavijevich, a professor of experimental and developmental psychology, a "hulking, articulate" Serbian immigrant who spoke three languages beyond his native Serbian. Covello, an immigrant who spoke three languages beyond his native Italian, took three of the popular "Rado's" courses in "experimental education" among his earliest studies in education. Covello credited Radosavijevich with persuading him to pursue a doctorate at New York University. The two would frequently stop off at Italian restaurants in Greenwich Village after class and discuss issues of education and immigration. "Study for your doctorate, Leonard," Covello recalled Radosavijevich advising him. "Concentrate on the ethnic factor in education. That is your field—the cultural factor in education—a subject a great many educators talk about, but very few actually understand."[79] Covello later would advocate the value of experimental education programs in an unpublished manuscript on community-centered schooling. Such programs, Covello claimed, promoted "closer contacts with the community," an "intimate understanding of students," and "greater participation by students and community in social, civic, and educational planning."[80]

The individual who would most influence Covello's graduate studies—and teach him the value of applied research as a mechanism for social change—arrived in New York in 1927, the same year Covello took his last course with Radosavijevich. Frederic M. Thrasher joined the faculty of New York University's rapidly growing School of Education as an urban sociologist specializing in juvenile delinquency. As a doctoral student at the University of Chicago's Department of Sociology, Thrasher had completed a seven-year dissertation study of 1,313 gangs in Chicago. The University of Chicago published the study as part of its celebrated Sociological Series edited by Ellsworth Faris, Robert E. Park, and Ernest W. Burgess (Thrasher's dissertation advisor).[81]

Orchestrating "one of the most important pioneering sociological studies of gang life," Thrasher used a multimethod approach, deriving data from studies of boys' gangs and information provided by a diversity of youth organizations: YMCA, settlement houses, schools, playgrounds, the Juvenile Court, and boys' clubs.[82] Thrasher concluded that gangs were symptomatic of community disorganization, "the general disorganization incident to rapid economic development and the ingestion of vast numbers of alien workers." The instability in many urban areas contributed to the lack of effective social controls on youth, leading to a "blind groping for order, without much understanding of the nature of the problems involved or their difficulties." Foreshadowing a similar emphasis in Covello's work, Thrasher attributed much to the adjustment problems of immigrant families. The language difficulties, the inability to understand a new world, and the grinding poverty created a gap between children and parents, lessening parental control, and thus making more attractive "the free life of the gang." Citing the work of Sophonisba Breckenridge and Edith Abbott (former Hull House residents and founders of the University of Chicago's School of Social Service Administration), Thrasher found the instability of immigrant communities contributing to the lack of "any consistent tradition with reference to family control. In this sense, then the gang becomes a problem of community organization." As immigrant youths quickly learned not only English but also the sordid side of U.S. life, the problem was also seen as "one of too quick and too superficial Americanization of the children of the immigrant."[83] The variety of ethnic groups clustered together further contributed to a "cultural lag," as "there has not yet been time for adjustment among these diverse [cultural] elements and for the development of a consistent and self-controlled social order."[84]

It is important to note that while Thrasher believed that biological and environmental factors played a significant role, he found delinquents' "inner promptings, their aspirations, and the 'pictures in their heads'" to be "of far greater significance."[85] Inadequate family life, poor and deteriorating neighborhoods, ineffective religion, dull schooling, and the "lack of proper guidance for spare-time activities," however, did form the underlying "matrix of gang development."[86] Programs for addressing youth gangs, therefore, required local sociological analysis in order to be effective.[87]

At Chicago Thrasher participated in a pathbreaking collaborative research effort, an interdisciplinary project generously funded by the Laura Spelman Rockefeller Memorial that became a key training ground for a number of prominent sociologists. This loosely organized group research program, developed two years prior to Covello's first course in sociology, would significantly shape the design of community-centered schooling in East Harlem.[88] Beardsley Ruml, the twenty-six-year-old director of the $74 million Laura Spelman Rockefeller Memorial, had begun to persuade the Memorial to shift its emphasis from applied social welfare to social research in the service of social welfare— this new role Ruml described as "the development of the social sciences and the production of a body of fact and principle that will be utilized in the solution of social problems."[89] Tapping close relations with the Memorial, the University of Chicago received more than $600,000 from the Memorial between 1923 and 1932 for an interdisciplinary social research program, a systematic and scientific investigation of the Chicago community. An executive committee that became known as the Local Community Research Committee (LCRC) was formed, composed of representatives from the departments of philosophy, political economy, political science, history, and sociology. Completed at the premier seat of modern urban studies under the guidance of the two names most associated with the field, Park and Burgess, the LCRC studies constituted, according to Martin Bulmer, "the core contribution made by Chicago sociology between 1918 . . . and the early 1930s."[90]

Chicago sociologists during the 1920s developed a hallmark "mosaic" methodology in their efforts to place urban social research on a more scientific basis, a more comprehensive method for grappling with the "human ecology" of the urban community, especially within the "zones of transition."[91] The Memorial's grants supported a variety of urban research projects towards this end, including detailed maps of local communities, studies of family disorganization and divorce, research on juvenile delinquency, and investigations of homeless men and rooming-house keepers. The resulting studies made extensive use of social base maps, local surveys, case studies, life histories, ecological analyses, interviews, statistical profiles, and participant observation. Frederic Thrasher's study of Chicago's delinquent youth, *The Gang,* for example, tapped a wide range of documentary sources, public records, photographs, personal interviews, observations, and consultations with local agencies and various local studies.[92]

Park and Burgess encouraged their students to engage in a close, intimate relationship with the world they studied. The first monograph, Nels Anderson's *The Hobo,* relied heavily on informal interviews and "participant observation" with transients. Anderson, living near Chicago's "Hobohemia," confessed that he himself "was in the process of moving out of the hobo world" and that "preparing the book was a way of 'getting by.'"[93] Harvey Zorbaugh studied the sharp contrasts of two neighboring districts, the "Gold Coast" along Lake Shore Drive and the "Little Hell" along its borders.[94] In addition to extensive use of documents and records, Zorbaugh maintained informal contacts with local newspaper reporters, "free ward" nurses of the local hospital, and the night-court personnel. The intimate involvement of these young sociologists with

Chicago's flophouses, Gold Coast settees, and taxi-dance halls reflected Park's imperative to his students: "Gentlemen, go get the seat of your pants dirty in research."[95]

Within a few years several of the research assistants of the Local Community Research Committee had found their way to the Department of Educational Sociology at New York University's rapidly expanding School of Education. Harvey Zorbaugh arrived in 1926 after his three-year fellowship at Chicago and advanced to full professor in educational sociology. Nels Anderson also came to New York University in the late 1920s, as did Paul Cressey, and both scholars worked closely with Thrasher. Cressey helped direct the motion-picture study component of Thrasher's Boys' Club Study in East Harlem.[96]

While the Boys' Club Federation of America and its many supporters promoted the utility of the Boys' Clubs in the fight against juvenile delinquency, no definitive sociological research had ever been undertaken to test the claim of efficacy. In 1927 Thrasher arranged with the federation to direct such a study under the institutional auspices of New York University; his extensive work on juvenile delinquency had brought him into close contact with Boys' Clubs in Chicago. With a gift of $37,500 from the Bureau of Social Hygiene of New York City and substantial scholarship support from the university, Thrasher launched the Boys' Club Study in the spring of 1928. His proposed study sites included six Boys' Club units, three within New York City and three in outlying areas.[97] Only one of these sites, however, became the focus of an intensive local community study, and that was East Harlem. Propitiously, this study involved Leonard Covello as a practitioner-researcher, a role that "would eventually lead me to Benjamin Franklin [High School]."[98]

The immediate background of the three-year East Harlem study was as follows. In 1927, the board of directors of the Boys' Club of New York opened a second branch of their organization near Jefferson Park at 321 East 111th Street, between First and Second avenues (the original branch was located on the Lower East Side, at Tenth Street and First Avenue).[99] A six-story building expected to serve six thousand boys was erected on the site at a cost of $735,000.[100] The board specifically chose East Harlem because of its putatively high incidence of juvenile delinquency. It was, in Thrasher's words, "a crime breeding area of New York City"—hence grist for his sociological mill. In 1928, Thrasher set out "to determine the effects of the Jefferson Park Branch of the New York Boys' Club . . . upon the boys of the community who participate in the program which the Club serves, and incidentally upon the community itself."[101] The boundaries of the study were to be roughly coterminous with those of East Harlem: "Fifth Avenue on the West, 98th Street on the South, the East River on the East, and the Harlem River on the North."[102]

The parallels of Thrasher's project to the Local Community Research Committee in terms of funding, personnel, topics, and methods were striking.

Outside funding, sustained over a period of years, brought together a large number of sociologists and graduate students in an intensive collaborative investigation of a local community. The Boys' Club Study produced some twenty-six subsidiary studies, ranging from morbidity studies, to a study of "big muscle" activities, to a study of the problems of a girls' club in the area. Under Thrasher's direction Nels Anderson wrote his doctoral dissertation on the history of East Harlem from the colonial period to the 1880s. Salvatore Cimilluca, a former DeWitt Clinton student, began his Master of Arts thesis where Anderson had left off and traced East Harlem's history into the 1920s. Paul Cressey directed a study of motion pictures in the informal education of boys in the district. And in "a very important phase of the Boys' Club Study," graduate student Leonard Covello developed his interest in cultural influences through a subsidiary study, "Italian Heritage in a Boys' Club Area," which analyzed "the way in which cultural backgrounds condition the success of boys' club and other educational programs."[103]

Thrasher selected Covello as a lead researcher for the study because of the latter's deep roots in East Harlem and close relationships with many of the Clinton boys who frequented the Jefferson Park branch.[104] In his autobiography Covello recalled: "This project fascinated me. It fitted in very well with my idea for a doctoral thesis on the social background of the Southern Italian immigrant. We would be studying every aspect of the life of the community of East Harlem which at that time consisted of ninety thousand Italian Americans— the largest community of its kind in the United States."[105] Covello invited Annita Giacobbe of the DeWitt Clinton Italian Department and Salvatore Cimilluca, a former pupil of Covello's at Clinton, to join the study.

The Boys' Club Study employed a wide range of methods and drew frequently upon concepts derived from the work of Park and Burgess. One such method, "ecological" analysis, or "a study of society in its distributive aspects," involved the development of extensive "social base maps." Some 170 blocks of the East Harlem area were illustrated on large wall maps, locating graphically more than eighty different kinds of institutions, from candy stores to junkyards, as well as ethnic group concentrations, housing conditions, and population.[106] Once a social base map was developed, the researchers began an extended series of visits, observations, and interviews in order to "get behind the formal names and superficial functions attributed to social groups and institutions." Photographs were taken of each kind of institution studied. Case studies were developed for selected institutions, such as a local school, church, settlement house, and foreign-language newspaper. Covello, assisted by Giacobbe, Cimilluca, and members of the Boys' Club staff, prepared and administered confidential questionnaires and interview schedules to the East Harlem boys at DeWitt Clinton High School. The "Covello cases" were compiled in each of three years from 1928 to 1931.[107]

The Boys' Club Study, in addition to gathering a wealth of information about the area Benjamin Franklin High School would serve, also provided an intensive training ground for the local social research methods that Covello would later adapt to develop community-centered schooling in East Harlem. The influence on Covello's work of Thrasher and New York University's educational sociology program, and indirectly of the "Chicago school" of urban sociologists, would be visible in the importance assigned to continuous social research at Franklin. (We take up this point again in greater detail in Chapter 4.)

We now turn to how the Boys' Club Study moved Covello toward strategies for counteracting the social problems confronting Italian Americans in East Harlem. Thrasher completed the Boys' Club Study in 1932. He concluded that the East Harlem Boys' Club, 1927–1931, had *not* been a significant factor in preventing juvenile delinquency. Although his study refuted exaggerated claims of the salutary effects of Boys' Clubs, Thrasher also believed that the clubs had an important role to play in community revitalization. He put it this way: "The Boys' Club has an essential function to perform as a unit in a *concerted community program* designed to achieve crime prevention rather than as a single preventive agency" (emphasis added).[108] For Covello, the Boys' Club Study not only identified the need for concerted community action but also sharply focused his thinking on the relationship of school and community: "In our participation in this study, in the numerous discussions, conferences and seminars at New York University and in the East Harlem community, the question constantly arose as to what should be the role of the school in relation to the many serious problems facing the East Harlem community."[109] The study also stimulated Covello's realization of the need for a permanent base for applied sociological research in Italian American neighborhoods. As he put it: "My association with Dr. Thrasher and the other sociologists opened a completely new vista in the field of education for me. I was now convinced that to achieve educational objectives, it was necessary to have complete and detailed knowledge of every aspect of the lives of the people to be educated."[110]

To begin to obtain such complete and detailed knowledge on Italian Americans, Covello established an institutional base for his research at Casa Italiana of Columbia University. In 1932 he approached Casa Italiana with a proposal to create an Italian American research and publication center for graduate students and teachers. Though his proposal was approved, Covello's social welfare project proved in the end a poor match for Casa Italiana, an institution that had been created to meet the status needs of leading Italian American scholars and professionals and their wealthy benefactors. Indeed as early as 1924, Judge John J. Freschi of the Court of Special Sessions had complained to Covello: "It may be said that when a distinguished French scholar comes to New York, he has immediate access to the MAISON FRANCAISE which becomes his headquarters during his stay in the United States. The contrast between the advantages offered the reputations of the two leading Latin nations is so obvious to warrant no further emphasis."[111] Funded in large part by the Paterno and Campagna families, Casa Italiana, a seven-story edifice built in the Florentine Renaissance style, opened its doors on Amsterdam Avenue and 117th Street in 1927 "as a center of Italian culture in America under the auspices of Columbia University."[112] Elegantly appointed with Italian Renaissance furniture, the Casa projected an aura of elitism consistent with the social class assumptions and status needs of its first director, Giuseppe Prezzolini, an expatriate northern Italian, and the Casa's affluent supporters. Francesco Cordasco has written:

> At best, the Casa offered Leonard Covello modest facilities to house his proposed Bureau; Giuseppe Prezzolini consented to be named one of the Bureau's directors; but neither the Casa Italiana nor Prezzolini participated (or, for that matter, encouraged) the work of the Bureau. It could not have been otherwise. An Italian professoriat (largely engaged in language instruction) had appropriated Casa Italiana for their own interests; separated by social class and origins from the teeming Italian masses of the City, these erstwhile Italian expatriate academicians (and non-Italians associated with the Casa) would not have understood what Leonard Covello proposed for the work of his Bureau, and had they understood, their reaction would have been one of disinterest and disinclination, if not disapproval.[113]

While Covello applauded the Casa's interest in promoting Italian literature and art, he believed that it also had a social responsibility to produce knowledge that would help ameliorate the problems of "the teeming Italian masses of the City." In May 1932 he organized the Casa Italiana Educational Bureau (CIEB) in two small rooms of the building. Covello stated the purposes of the CIEB as follows:

1. The Bureau will be a *fact-finding* organization. Its purpose is to gather and present social and educational facts for all agencies and individuals to whom such information may be of interest and value.
2. The Bureau will serve as a medium for *centralization of efforts* directed toward social and cultural advancement of the Italian American.
3. The Bureau will formulate and initiate a *promotional* program of educational and social activities. To this end it will concern itself with the establishment and guidance of similar organizations throughout the United States [original emphases].[114]

Early financial support ($3,000) came from the Italian government and the pro-
ceeds of social affairs that Covello and his colleagues organized on Italian
transatlantic liners. Covello would later recall that "we used our modest budget
in getting some office equipment, supplies and a few scholarships for graduate students who were taking special courses at Columbia University." In the
mid-1930s the Works Progress Administration (WPA) and the Federal Writers' Project provided the mainstay financial support and personnel for the
CIEB, including "a goodly number of former newspapermen and writers."[115]
(Covello used his personal contacts with influential New York liberals to leverage support from the WPA bureaucracy.)

Casa Italiana provided an institutional base for aggregate studies of the
social problems of poor Italian immigrants in New York City. Covello recognized, however, that specific social data at the level of local neighborhoods
would be necessary to sustain effective schools in poor districts of the city. He
discerned that local variations and idiosyncrasies, while perhaps not significant
at aggregate levels of social research, could have tremendous impact on a
school's educational programs. University-based cultural institutions such as
Casa Italiana, however, were unlikely candidates to support localized studies.
The school, according to Covello, must therefore develop a means of carrying
out community research so that the knowledge gained would directly serve the
needs of specific educational programs. Not to do this would be to pay lip service to the public school's mission to develop the local citizenry, while leaving
the school no systematic means of accomplishing this role.

Within the first year of Benjamin Franklin High School's opening, a continuing collaborative group study of East Harlem was initiated, guided by a
"sponsoring committee" composed of representatives of such community agencies as Union Settlement and Haarlem House.[116] Reflecting the general
approach if not the rigor of the earlier Boys' Club Study, Covello and his staff
wished to determine basic population data for East Harlem, investigate special problems relating to education, relate home conditions to school work,
identify special needs of the foreign-born, describe the typical leisure time
activities of students and the community's elderly, and study the social backgrounds of the various ethnic minorities of the neighborhood.[117] School staff,
including WPA workers assigned to Benjamin Franklin High School, neighborhood volunteers, and students carried out surveys on local delinquency,
motion-picture viewing, graduates and dropouts, students' racial attitudes, and
students' economic backgrounds.

This approach was different from the kind of abstract, theory-driven social
science that by the 1930s had become the central tendency in U.S. research universities.[118] Keenly aware of the tension between the local and nonlocal uses of
research, Covello unabashedly took the side of the former while recognizing the
value of sociological methods responsibly applied. The measure of genuine

knowledge, he believed, was its capacity to solve concrete social problems and advance human welfare. He argued that the school, as a "diagnostician," must "penetrate . . . into the 'sphere of intimacy' of community life and to follow, as far as possible, changes in the emotional life, as well as changes of a more material nature."[119] For this reason, "success in gathering the kind of data that is valuable to the school," Covello contended, "depends upon sincere friendliness in the approach, rather than upon sheer technical skill in making a physical or sociological survey."[120] While his dissertation indicated his technical virtuosity in sociology, he sought primarily to advance East Harlem's development with sociological tools, and only secondarily to advance sociology's development through an East Harlem case study.

One technical approach that Covello did use, particularly in the initial years of Benjamin Franklin, was social mapping, the use of local area street maps for the display of social data.[121] Social mapping was developed to its fullest extent in the work of Park, Burgess, and their students at the University of Chicago during the 1920s. Covello and his staff produced large wall maps, for example, placing a dot where every Benjamin Franklin student lived in a color corresponding to race or ethnicity and generation. In combination these social maps enabled the high school staff to locate any student not only in terms of geography, but also in terms of the social ecology of the area in which he lived. Block-to-block distinctions could inform the school's approach to community problems that might affect students' schooling, whether the problem concerned youth gangs, ethnic group border disputes, or intergenerational tensions within immigrant families. Small local details could have large educational implications and could determine the success of school-community efforts. Covello insisted that "the school . . . assume the role demanded by its very nature," namely to serve as "the leader and the coordinating agency in all educational enterprises affecting the life of the community." This role demanded intimate familiarity with the community because the "surging life of the community as a whole, its motion-picture houses, its dance halls, its streets, its gangs, its churches, its community houses, its community codes of behavior and morals—these will either promote or destroy the work of the school."[122]

While the influence of the "Chicago school" of urban sociology on the practice of community-centered schooling in East Harlem is clear, it is important to note that Covello's approach also grew out of older practices, absorbed through both his formal sociological studies and his participation in less formal community reform efforts. Covello's local social research reflected an inheritance from a research tradition that predated Park and Burgess at Chicago: the use of social surveys as a vehicle for local social change. Often an avowed mixture of social research and social reform, the social survey dated back at least to Charles Booth's *Life and Labour of the People in London*, a panoramic, multivolume account of that city's social conditions in the late

Victorian period.[123] In the United States Booth's project inspired *Hull-House Maps and Papers*, a richly descriptive account of social conditions in Chicago's Nineteenth Ward, published in 1895 by the residents of Hull House. Jane Addams and the women of Hull House were first and foremost advocates for social justice, and they reported their findings on such conditions as child and sweatshop labor in unmistakable tones of outrage.[124] *Hull-House Maps and Papers* was the first in a series of studies associated with a turn-of-the-century social survey movement that also included, prominently, W.E.B. DuBois' classic community study *The Philadelphia Negro* (1899) and the Pittsburgh Survey (1907–9), a study of social conditions in a steel-industry city.[125]

While it is impossible to separate completely the influences of the overlapping social survey and sociological survey traditions, Covello's design of Benjamin Franklin High School clearly reflected a number of characteristics more typical of the former than of the latter. Covello intentionally sought to advance local reform in East Harlem, from housing to community consciousness, and not simply to pursue the more abstract investigation of social laws that were increasingly emphasized by often nonlocal "professional" sociologists.[126]

Other agencies with which Franklin worked closely, such as the East Harlem Health Center, the Heckscher Foundation, and the Union Settlement, had been involved with reform-minded local social research for more than a decade prior to the development of the school-community committee system that would be the hallmark of Benjamin Franklin High School. Kenneth Widdemer, director of the East Harlem Health Center, for example, had most likely used local social research in his earlier work as a neighborhood organizer in Bowling Green, and as a trainer of community organizers at the People's Institute, years before he pioneered community research and organizing around health issues in East Harlem.[127] Thrasher referred to the East Harlem Health Center as an exemplar of social service grounded in sound social research—one that "has based its program on facts established by research and it has tested its results by the same method—a truly scientific procedure and one too often absent from educational and recreational programs."[128] Consistent with the wider historical pattern, this local health agency apparently initiated the use of social surveys in East Harlem, a practice Benjamin Franklin High School employed regularly.

Covello's methods, particularly the use of social base maps, while developed further at the University of Chicago, had their origins in the social survey movement. Even the symbols used on the Boys' Club Study's social base maps of East Harlem, a key source of information for Covello, were derivative, adapted from the Russell Sage Foundation, whose Department of Surveys and Exhibits was a longstanding supporter of social surveys.[129] Ernest W. Burgess had been involved in a Kansas survey just before his arrival at Chicago; he and Robert Park taught about social surveys to their students, citing the works of Booth and the Hull House residents.[130] Though Park and Burgess later distanced themselves from what they perceived as a lack of scientific rigor in many surveys, Burgess found surveys a useful means of raising community consciousness. "Community self-study under expert direction is democracy being at school to the social scientist," he declaimed. "The social survey is to the community what the demonstration center is to the farmer. . . . To the advanced student the social survey affords severe and stimulating training in the technique of investigation and in the art of social action."[131]

The influential role of settlement house workers in Benjamin Franklin's community research also reflected a pattern more typical of the social survey movement than of the emerging sociology profession. Social research provided the means to advance East Harlem, not vice-versa. Many of the key figures in the East Harlem study, for example, Helen Harris of Union Settlement and Miriam Sanders of Haarlem House, were women long active in settlement-based neighborhood reform efforts. Miriam Sanders's long tenure at Haarlem House, in fact, came after her work and study at Hull House in Chicago.[132]

Covello drew upon salient elements of his background and experience to create and sustain a particular vision of schooling, one that was community-centered and targeted toward the social regeneration of East Harlem. An impoverished immigrant who lived the traumas of assimilation, Covello knew the challenges of living in several distinct and separate worlds. Straddling very different worlds led him to view cultural differences as "something normal and wholesome, something to be respected, cherished and worthy of dignity."[133] His acute experience of cultural conflict and the impersonal bureaucracy of large city schools made a deep and lasting impression, spurring his commitment to create a more personalized and empathic kind of schooling. An early and enduring relationship with an imposing Canadian missionary and various Protestant institutions provided support at critical junctures of his life and combined with his deep East Harlem roots to imbue in him a strong commitment to serving that community. Friendships with the likes of an immigrant poet named Piatelli and a New Englander named Shedd helped ensure that democratic development would remain a wellspring of his service. Long experience teaching and counseling Italian students at DeWitt Clinton High School forged a clear appreciation of how students' social backgrounds influenced the work of schools.

But it was the Chicago school of urban sociology, refracted through New York University's department of educational sociology, that provided Covello with the tools he would need to put his commitment to community-centered schooling into practice. The multimethod approach he learned through the Boys' Club Study and his association with Thrasher, Zorbaugh, and Payne yielded a systematic means of continually gathering and analyzing the very local social data upon which the school's educational success would depend. As a principal and highly skilled practitioner-researcher, Covello could implement programs for "*living* democracy as a way of teaching democracy."[134] Practically capable of coordinating efforts within its sphere of influence, public education might effectively marshal forces for the development of that basic unit of democracy, the local neighborly community. We turn now to Part II and our case study of Covello's effort to organize and operate a progressive high school that would provide that kind of broadly based civic education, an institution that would be both a center and a catalyst for democracy, citizenship, and civic empowerment, though one that would continuously confront formidable obstacles and tensions that are perhaps endemic to community schools, at least those that would aspire to what Covello strived to achieve at Benjamin Franklin High School.

PART TWO

The Making of
Benjamin Franklin High School

CHAPTER FOUR

The High School on
East 108th Street

F ROM 1931 TO 1934, Leonard Covello was deeply involved in the successful campaign to acquire a boys' high school for East Harlem. The
Boys' Club Study, which revealed the complexities of East Harlem's
social problems, suggested the need for a collaborative, multi-institutional
approach. Envisioning community-centered schooling as the catalyst for such
a strategy, Covello and his staff, between 1934 and 1942, organized the key
structures and programs that marked Benjamin Franklin High School as a
community school. These components provided frameworks and mechanisms
for coordinating the positive educational forces in East Harlem toward
Covello's goal of democratic community development. More precisely, Covello and his associates organized a community advisory council and its subcommittees, a set of street units (social clubs and research bureaus), and WPA-
sponsored recreational and adult programs to build and strengthen social
networks in East Harlem, supporting and complementing Franklin's school-
day academic programs and civic education activities.

The outreach components developed at Benjamin Franklin's main building on East 108th Street and on the surrounding block were not simply Covello's invention (see Figure 4.1). Such activities as recreational programs, social
clubs, and formal adult education were introduced in the city schools at the
turn of the century, often through the medium of social settlements.[1] And as
we saw in Chapter 1, by 1918 community programs operated at scores of
schools under a citywide director of community centers. These centers were
expanded in the 1920s and 1930s, reporting aggregated attendance rates as high
as eight million a year after 1935.

FIGURE 4.1:   Street Map of Benjamin Franklin High School
and 300 Block of East 108th Street

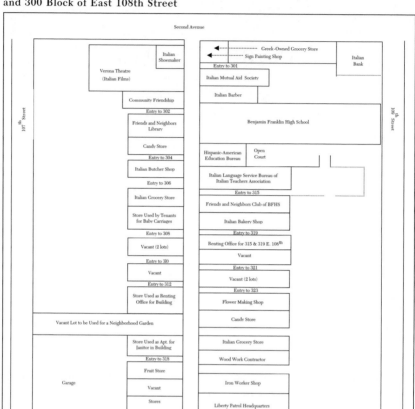

Source: Leonard Covello Papers, Balch Institute Collections, Historical Society of Pennsylvania, Philadelphia, box 18, folder 12.

   While Benjamin Franklin's community program was not distinguishable in *kind* from earlier "wider use" efforts; the program's comprehensiveness, theoretical sophistication, reliance on social research, and integration of underlying community issues with the school curriculum made it markedly different in *degree.*[2] Much more than recreating the school as a recreation or community-service center, Covello conceived of Benjamin Franklin as an agent of cultural democracy, situating the school centrally in the tradition of citizen-centered community schooling. The Benjamin Franklin example reveals the challenges of pursuing citizen-centered schooling within an academically rigorous, subject-centered education. And it discloses the tensions that arise from the extraordinary demands community-centered schooling puts on teachers, tensions that may be grounded in conflicting notions of teacher professionalism.

This chapter considers these and other issues in the context of a descriptive analysis of the various components of the community high school and its daily operations, with particular attention to the practical logic of Covello's strategy. Here we lay out the organization of the community program and its key subcomponents: community advisory council, "street units," and WPA adult education program. We also look at key aspects of the day high school: the curriculum, student outcomes (where available), and teachers. As Covello's philosophy of community-centered schooling was constantly evolving, interactively shaping and reflecting his practice, we include it in a section that follows our organizational analysis, acknowledging that some readers would prefer to have this material sooner.

This chapter sets the stage for a closer scrutiny in subsequent chapters of Covello's philosophy in action, the operation of particular curriculum programs, and the mobilization of school-based citizen action campaigns. We begin by tracing the origins of the East Harlem high school in a series of decisions and events that occurred during Covello's final years at DeWitt Clinton.

Creating Benjamin Franklin High School

By the early 1930s the threads of Covello's experience had begun to weave the complex tapestry that became Benjamin Franklin High School. "What was in the back of my mind," he remembered, "was a neighborhood school which would be the educational, civic and social center of the community. We wanted to go beyond the traditional subject-centered and the current child-centered school to the community-centered school."[3]

In the 1930s progressive intellectual ferment and social analysis fostered a climate of opinion that fortified activist educators like Covello who wanted to achieve social justice and a reasonable quality of life for all Americans, albeit without social upheaval. In New York City, where rampant unemployment propelled unprecedented numbers of youths into the high schools, Covello and his allies would receive a favorable hearing for a social innovation that had lost its constituency after World War I.

"THE WORLD IS ON FIRE, and the youth of the world must be equipped to combat the conflagration," Teachers College's Harold Rugg argued to the World Conference on the Educational Fellowship in 1932.[4] The same year his colleague George Counts stunned an annual Progressive Education Association convention with his clarion call for social reconstruction through the schools.[5] Historian Charles Beard, a frequent speaker to educational groups, warned school leaders of the "crisis in American thought" that lay behind the distress of the Depression.[6] Embedded within an increasingly strained, disturbed, and often displaced Depression-era populace, "the range of permissi-

ble socioeconomic dissent probably widened in the schools," cracking open the
door to what Herbert Kliebard has called the brief "heyday of social meliorism."[7] The "brute fact of the depression," claimed an Ohio superintendent, had
shocked Americans into reconsidering their "free-for-all race for special privilege" and "lip service to democracy." The economic crisis, this school official
insisted, forced Americans to rethink the foundations of their world, for "in
the matter of arousing the public mind, the end of our national joyride was the
beginning of our national schooling."[8]

In the thirties U.S. high schools experienced an unprecedented surge in
enrollments, from about 4.8 million in 1930 to more than 7.1 million in 1939.
As the youth labor market collapsed in the Depression, more and more youths
of working-class and poor backgrounds turned to the high school as an alternative to the breadline. They were hardly welcome. School leaders across the country recoiled at this onslaught of young people who were deemed unfit for the
high school. Yet leading educators and professional organizations were clamor-
ing for curriculum reforms to accommodate this army of presumed incapables.[9]

By the end of the 1930s, roughly 73 percent of fourteen- to seventeen-year-
olds were attending high school, up from just over half at the start of the
Depression.[10] Increasingly they came from Italian, Jewish, Slavic, and other
immigrant backgrounds. High school educators struggled to "Americanize"
these "new" students and address the challenges of what many referred to as
"the second-generation problem."[11] Confident in the science of education's
capacity to identify and address distinct mental abilities, educators also sought
to adjust the high school curriculum to the perceived talents and destinies of
children with different backgrounds.[12] In what Paula Fass refers to as "a new
common-school era," the arrival in high schools of so many immigrant children
changed the face of secondary education in the large cities and "replaced the
pious air of Protestant respectability with a complex cosmopolitanism."[13]

As more youth entered high school and stayed longer, the schools were
called upon to play a greater role in what Teachers College professor Paul
Hanna called "our youth problem."[14] With severe unemployment and more
employers demanding more years of schooling, high schools also took on a custodial function, keeping youth out of labor markets and off the streets.[15] The
concern grew that adults in already fragmenting urban communities, under the
extreme strain of the Depression, would be unable to nurture or even to control their youth properly. Many observers perceived a rising juvenile delinquency, especially among urban boys, and sought the high school's help in
combating this threat. The specter of troubled youth loomed large.[16] The
Depression seemed to target youth selectively, pushing their unemployment
to approximately 50 percent; some three million youth of high school age neither worked nor attended school.[17] Hanna, therefore, worried that "with no
sense of belonging to a great enterprise which demands their loyalties and
their labors, with no responsibility for making a contribution to the larger

group, the young develop few of those character traits which are so essential and basic in a highly interdependent modern society."[18]

Harvard criminologist Eleanor Glueck spoke more specifically of a disintegrating society's disastrous impact on the young, increasing "the restlessness of 'modern youth' in this age of 'jazz' and 'petting parties.'"[19] In a time of Fascist and Communist youth movements abroad, the possible radicalization of youth worried more than a few observers. As youth left schools only to find no jobs, lamented New York University sociologist Harvey Zorbaugh, more and more ended up in prisons or flophouses. Hundreds of thousands of others had decided to take to the road, "'thumbing' their way or 'riding the rods,' 'bumming' their living, sleeping in transient camps or in 'jungles,' keeping alive, but many of them trying to forget there was a tomorrow. Others sat at home, idle and brooding—insecurity and despair eating at their hearts like a rust."[20]

Nowhere were these issues more pressing than in New York City, which boasted the world's largest school system. To serve the enormous diversity of its school-age population—including, since the turn of the century, millions of newly arrived immigrants from southern and eastern Europe, a human tide that flowed unabated until the 1920s—the city built a variety of special schools alongside the regular elementary, junior, and senior high schools. The high schools were especially varied. By the 1930s, as Ruth Markowitz notes, "there were high schools for academically, musically, and artistically gifted students. There were numerous technical high schools, including one for the aviation trade, one for students pursing jobs in the textile industry, and even one for future homemakers."[21]

Between World War I and the mid-1920s, New York's high school enrollments more than doubled, from 61,000 to 125,000. What began as a surge in the twenties became a stampede in the thirties: by 1931, as the Depression deepened, citywide enrollments in the regular day high schools reached 178,000, an increase of 22 percent from 1925–26. By 1934, enrollments had increased another 54,000, or 30 percent. For the ten years before the 1934 opening of Benjamin Franklin, the largest proportionate increases occurred in the Bronx (280 percent), Queens (251 percent), and Richmond (221 percent); Brooklyn reported an increase of 110 percent; Manhattan, which had the largest average daily enrollments for the period, showed a 33 percent increase.[22] City enrollments steadily increased, albeit at a slower rate after 1934, until a pre–World War II high of 256,000 was reached in 1938–39 in the regular day high schools. Vocational high school enrollments, which had shown modest gains from approximately 4,000 students in 1925–26 to 8,000 in 1934–35, soared for the next six years, from 30,000 in 1935–36 to 56,000 in 1941–42.[23] Throughout the decade overcrowding in all these institutions was endemic—even the annexes were bulging.

The palpable symbol of the need for a high school for boys in East Harlem was overcrowding in DeWitt Clinton High School, which in 1929 moved from

59th Street and Tenth Avenue to Mosholu Parkway and Paul Avenue, in the North Bronx. In February 1931 Clinton recorded a total enrollment of 9,329 boys, with 6,164 located in the new main building and 3,165 in five annexes scattered across Manhattan. The largest annex, formerly P.S. 172, was located in East Harlem at 108th Street between First and Second avenues; it would be the first home of Benjamin Franklin High School. More than a thousand DeWitt Clinton students were listed at residences in the Yorkville–East Harlem area, east of Fifth Avenue from 59th to 110th streets; approximately 10 percent of the high school's total registration was Italian American.[24] The crisis at DeWitt Clinton sparked an organizing campaign to create a boys' high school in East Harlem—a campaign that Covello led and for which he helped effect a high level of grassroots organizing, building on his earlier successful campaign to establish parity for Italian-language studies in the city's high schools.

The nature of the East Harlem high school campaign, 1931–34, and its success reflected a community maturing in its organizational development and political clout. In particular the establishment of Benjamin Franklin reflected the growing political power of New York City's Italians, a change of leadership and direction within the board of education, and the growing ability of the school's advocates to take advantage of and to learn from changes in New York City politics. Covello would later recall that "a group of social-minded leaders in East Harlem" had been promoting an East Harlem high school for at least a decade prior to March 1931, when a committee of residents composed of educators and professionals met to draft a letter of appeal to public officials.[25] Thus began an intensive three-and-a-half-year organizing and lobbying campaign, the fate of which was in the end determined by the outcome of the 1933 mayoral election. Only after La Guardia became mayor, drawing his greatest percentage of support from East Harlem, did the long effort to create Benjamin Franklin finally come to fruition.

The leadership core of the East Harlem high school committee included Covello and three other noted Italian American educators: Angelo Patri, principal of P.S. 45; Anthony Pugliese, district superintendent; and Mario Cosenza, dean of Brooklyn College.[26] The group they led wrote letters, circulated petitions, called public meetings, held conferences with school officials, and passed resolutions from local organizations to the board of education. The new research from New York University's three-year Boys' Club Study provided ample data on local social conditions and needs. That study "was a potent factor in our argument," Covello noted, as it provided "data to prove that by working closely with students through the school, developing leadership, recreational programs, social awareness, we might be able to counteract disintegrating forces at work on the streets and even in the homes."[27]

The high school committee considered the rundown DeWitt Clinton annex in East Harlem an unsatisfactory long-term accommodation for the increasing number of Italian American youths who desired a high school credential. The committee advocated a "first class High School" for East Harlem—one that would diversify and make easily accessible curriculum programs tailored to the career interests of these students. Moreover, the committee wanted a "Community High School which the Community would feel was its own school—to which the parents could come easily and naturally."[28]

Citing the absence of a senior high school that was easily accessible to boys who lived on Manhattan's Upper East Side or in the lower Bronx, the committee noted that no high school for boys existed on the East Side north of Fifteenth Street or south of 166th Street in the Bronx.[29] "Many of the pupils in this Community," the East Harlem committee claimed, "because of lack of facilities, stop their education, or go to schools where they study the subjects that are taught but not necessarily the subjects they need or want." The upshot was increased juvenile delinquency: Unable to find work, these boys "turn to the street for recreation and activity which is often of an undesirable nature."[30] In a letter to Associate Superintendent Harold Campbell, Covello argued forcefully that "I can positively state that the beginnings of many a criminal could have been turned in the right direction if they had been kept in school doing work in which their interests were satisfied."[31] Covello and his allies envisaged "a high school that would take care of the boy that would want to go into the business life, the boy that had interests in the industrial field and the boy who would want to go into any of the professions:—in brief, a *General* or *Cosmopolitan High School*, that would give *industrial, commercial* and *cultural training*. Only by such an offering would it meet the needs of the Community and be a school *for all children of all the people*" (original emphasis).[32]

A long-term goal of the new high school, as viewed by the East Harlem activists, was to aid in the overall development of the district. The school would "coordinate and extend the limited facilities now available for the greater benefit of the children and the community." It would work with existing social agencies such as Haarlem House, the Heckscher Foundation, the Jefferson Park Boys' Club, and Union Settlement, which were already engaged in "extra curricular educational work with boys of high school age."[33] Beyond its benefits to local youth, the school would serve to bring all the members of a diverse community together. "The establishment of such a high school in this district," claimed the East Harlem Council of Social Agencies, "would aid in unifying and organizing a community social spirit and improving its civic life."[34]

The discussion given to the high school's expanded role in the community reflected the dramatic growth and heightened profile of that institution in New York City. Owing to the "greater holding power of the schools" and reinforced by a lack of options during the Depression, day high school enrollment jumped nearly eighteen thousand students in a single year, from March 1932 to March 1933.[35] Thus, the campaign for a boys' high school in East Harlem coincided with a general citywide need to address overcrowded high school facilities, if not also a need to reassess the role of secondary education. In many ways, it was a moment "propitious for radical innovations" in New York City school-ing.[36] The Depression compelled a reevaluation of old assumptions about the role of public institutions, including public schools. Many educators "specu-lated . . . about a boldly transformed social order . . . [and] were willing to lis-ten to different voices and entertain prospects of change that had been unthink-able in the profession only a few years before."[37] The need to build new high schools meant at least the chance that some new ideas for schooling might be realized. Recent New Deal funding had begun to provide resources outside the normal bureaucratic channels, allowing a new flexibility for experimenta-tion.[38] Finally, a state report published in 1933, while hailing many of the achievements of the city schools, recommended dramatic improvements, including a vastly increased guidance program and greater attention to "adapt-ing curriculum programs to the individual needs of the children."[39] In addi-tion, "teaching ability . . . should be evaluated not in academic terms but in [students'] growth in personality, character, social responsibility and those other characteristics which are essential to the desirable citizen."[40]

The East Harlem high school committee worked vigorously to enlist promi-nent Italian American political leaders in the campaign. Congressman Fiorello La Guardia, Vito Marcantonio, New York State Supreme Court Judge Salva-tore A. Cotillo, and Judge John Freschi of the General Sessions Court all lent their support to the effort.[41] Covello solicited Cotillo's support from the start, and La Guardia headed up a visit to Dr. Harold Campbell, then acting direc-tor of the High School Division, in the fall of 1931. Local agencies and foun-dations were soon brought into the campaign. A. Warren Smith, superintend-ent of the Jefferson Park Boys' Club in East Harlem, and his board of trustees had pledged support to the campaign as early as May of 1931. In the spring of 1932 Miriam Sanders of Haarlem House arranged to have Covello present the case for the high school to the influential East Harlem Council of Social Agen-cies, which endorsed and publicized the campaign.[42] Selina Weigel of the East Harlem Health Center served as secretary of the committee and played a critical liaison role in marshaling local agency support. Public meetings further galvanized local sentiment for the school.

The campaign revealed the committee's adaptability in the changing polit-ical climate of New York City. For example, Covello and his allies especially targeted Generoso Pope, an Italian with significant political and economic influence, to speak directly to the president of the board of education, Dr. George Ryan. Pope, publisher of the largest-circulation Italian daily, *Il Pro-gresso Italo-Americano,* was known as the "sand king"; he owned the largest construction-material company in the world, the Colonial Sand and Stone Company, and was a benefactor to various Italian American organizations.[43] Covello began cultivating Pope's support for the high school in October of 1931 and provided him letters and materials to facilitate his lobbying of board president Ryan and Dr. Howard Campbell, now associate superintendent in charge of high schools.[44] Pope's assistance apparently helped convince the board to appropriate funds in 1932 for the establishment of the high school, and to provide for an additional principal position in 1933 for the 1934 budget. Campbell indicated that a word from Pope to Ryan and Mayor O'Brien would cement the deal. Apparently Pope wrote Ryan but never spoke to him personally, and Ryan may have simply passed along Pope's letter. By July 1933 the campaign had stalled; a frustrated Covello wrote Cosenza that "it is a shame that we cannot put this thing over, especially as it is in our grasp. As a race, with exceptions, we do not seem to be able to strike opportunely."[45]

La Guardia's election as mayor in November of 1933 brought the school within closer grasp. "The possibility of establishing a cosmopolitan high school in East Harlem at this time is very good," declared Covello a month later.[46] Adjusting to the new political situation, the high school committee apparently eased their lobbying of Pope, whose pro-Tammany Democrat *Il Progresso* had not supported La Guardia in his earlier bid for mayor, and quickly sought out the mayor-elect's sponsorship. La Guardia had lobbied Campbell for the school two years earlier, and La Guardia's election meant that a number of the committee's allies would gain power. Marcantonio, who would win La Guardia's congressional seat in 1934, was a key supporter of the new high school.[47]

Key personnel changes at the board of education following La Guardia's election favored the success of the campaign. Harold G. Campbell, a favorite of the Progressive Education Association (PEA), was appointed superintendent of schools in January 1934, "a key landmark in the triumph of progressivism."[48] Characterized as a "conservative in education," Campbell nevertheless led the "labyrinthine city school system . . . hurtling along the road mapped out for it by the PEA."[49] Fortuitously, Covello's former principal at DeWitt Clinton, Dr. John Tildsley, was appointed acting head of the High School Division. Meeting with Tildsley to discuss the proposal, Covello and the representatives of East Harlem social agencies emphasized three points. First, the school would be "a community high school: a social center designed to serve the families living in its vicinity." Second, the school would open in an existing building, and the high school committee would "keep on from that beginning until a new building was procured." Third, the school's attendance zone would be drawn so as "to avoid a large influx of Negroes from the Central Harlem District."[50] This last, controversial point warrants an explanation.

The East Harlem delegation was afraid that the Italians would not tolerate a large African American presence at the new high school. It would be unfair and unconscionable to impute any ulterior motive to Covello or his East Harlem allies in this matter—as we show in subsequent chapters, they were deeply committed to social justice. On the other hand, their strategy may have played unwittingly into a larger pattern of restricted access for blacks to upper Manhattan high schools. By the early 1930s some Manhattan high schools, especially Julia Richmond, were overcrowded, and Harlem blacks applying there were funneled into "the unzoned, older buildings of Wadleigh and Haaren (as well as the various vocational annexes)." Wadleigh, located in Harlem, became a segregated high school. School Superintendent Harold Campbell "was sure that the zoning was not racial in origin, pointing to the permission given to some black students to cross zone lines as proof of a nondiscriminatory policy." Harlem parents, the NAACP, and the New York [State] Temporary Commission on the Condition of the Colored Population thought otherwise; to their minds the segregation was "obvious." Historian David Ment agrees: "The conclusion cannot be escaped that they [Campbell and the board of education] found acceptable or even desirable the segregation that they encouraged through official action."[51]

After a flurry of last-minute lobbying by Cosenza, the East Harlem Council of Social Agencies, Marcantonio, and numerous East Harlem organizations, the board of superintendents passed a resolution on 10 May 1934 for an Upper East Side high school, to be located in two annexes of DeWitt Clinton High School: P.S. 172 at 309 East 108th Street, and P.S. 53 at 211 East 79th Street.[52] The New York press reported that the new school would encompass the East Harlem and Yorkville districts. The superintendents were also reportedly looking for a site for the "eventual erection of a modern high school building."[53] On 23 May the board of education formally approved the establishment of the new high school.[54]

Tildsley authored the school district report that described the aim and purpose of the new East Harlem high school, as Tildsley put it, "a great social centre, open day and evening for boys and for adults to meet as many needs of this community as it can." The existing academic and specialized high schools had ill served Italian East Harlem, Tildsley stipulated. "Many of them [Italians] have been attending Clinton preparing for college and a professional career. Some of them have been enrolled in Commerce and quite a large number in the Aviation Annex of Haaren. But for very many of them no one of the existing high schools gives them just the training they need. These are not book minded nor definitely mechanically minded." The experimental comprehensive high school curriculum, giving students a choice among three courses of study—general (academic), commercial, and arts and crafts—would meet a broad range of needs and special interests.[55]

Tildsley and Covello had known each other for more than twenty years, dating back to Covello's early teaching days at DeWitt Clinton. A thirty-seven-year veteran of the New York City schools and a stalwart humanist, Tildsley believed that most of the new influx of high school students were "too inept or too indolent to master the time-honored subjects."[56]

Tildsley recognized that Covello would make the best of what Tildsley undoubtedly considered a Faustian bargain. For Covello a comprehensive high school was far preferable to a trade school, which some civic leaders in East Harlem had advocated. "An industrial high school," he had declared at public meetings, "presumes to make trade workers of our boys. It suggests that the boys of East Harlem are not capable of doing academic work. This is exactly the kind of school we do not want."[57]

Tildsley undoubtedly had Covello in mind when he wrote that "the man selected as principal should be a man with social vision, the attitude of the social worker, gifted with great sympathy and understanding of all kinds of boys. . . . He should understand the needs and possibilities of the various racial groups, especially of the Italian boys."[58]

Recommendations for Covello's appointment were received by the board of superintendents from the leaders of numerous organizations and constituencies in East Harlem and the city.[59] Although it is difficult to imagine any other serious candidate for this position, the board of superintendents interviewed five applicants in addition to Covello.[60] At the superintendents' meeting of 13 June 1934, Covello "received a majority of the votes cast for the principalship of the new high school and was therefore recommended to the Board of Examiners for examination for license as a high school principal."[61] Formally appointed by the board of education on 12 September 1934, Covello became New York City's first Italian American high school principal.[62]

The *New York Sun* described Covello's new position as "the most difficult ever assigned to a high school principal in this city. He will be required to organize a school that will be 'all things to all boys.' And he will long for the carefree days of 1917–18, when as a member of the Intelligence Service of the U.S.A., all he had to do was to keep track of thieves, deserters and spies."[63] Undaunted, Covello wrote La Guardia "to assure you that those of us who will have the privilege of working in this community which, for many years, has been your own home community, will do everything in our power to help the boys in this community to realize the best that is in them. We shall strive to instill in them a sense of civic responsibility and a desire for social usefulness."[64]

Covello had only the summer to organize Benjamin Franklin High School from scratch. Tildsley issued a call for volunteers to teach at the new school, which he advertised as "intended to meet the needs of the boys who have found it difficult to adjust themselves adequately to the general high school."[65] According to one newspaper account, twenty-six "inspiring" teachers were chosen from the volunteers list in Tildsley's office.[66] On that list were five outstanding teachers recruited by Covello from the DeWitt Clinton staff: Abraham Kroll, Annita Giacobbe, Michael Decessare, Morris Deschel, and Harry Levene. (By the end of 1934–35, Covello would have a staff of 102 teachers, many of whom were not at the school voluntarily.) Without compensation, Abraham Kroll, a general science teacher and Covello's new administrative assistant, worked throughout the summer helping the new principal get the high school ready for its September opening.[67]

Thus began one of the most adventurous experiments in the history of U.S. urban education. In addition to working with the large Italian community of East Harlem, Benjamin Franklin would have to work with the shifting variety

of ethnic and racial groups in the area, to "test in a living situation . . . the oft
discussed idea that it was possible for people of different origins, coming from
many countries with differences in language and customs, to work together
to improve community living." By "creating a united front," the school could
now apply what had been learned through research such as the Boys' Club
Study. But a matter of the heart also compelled Covello. After seventeen
years as a teacher, he would finally be coming home to the neighborhood in
which he had grown up, "for home is and always will be where you start."[68]
Reflecting later on his visit to what would be the main building of the first
Benjamin Franklin High School, Covello recalled: "I turned the corner of
108th Street and Second Avenue and walked east for a short distance. I knew
exactly where the Franklin main building was located. I had turned that corner many evenings as a boy to go to the evening recreation center. The main
door was open. I walked up a short flight of steps to the ground-floor—here
had been the recreation room—a piano, game tables; . . . over thirty years had
passed—nothing had changed—but nothing. . . . I had come back to the
schools of my earliest days in America—the America of East Harlem at the
turn of the 20th century."[69]

Organizing the New High School

Benjamin Franklin opened its main building and Seventy-ninth Street Annex in
September 1934 with an enrollment of some 2,000 boys. The new high school
was filled to capacity: By November 1935 the total registration had reached
nearly 2,600. In the fall of 1935, the main building at East 108th Street operated on a double session, and in 1936 the high school had to open a second, temporary annex on 117th Street.[70] Enrollments would peak between 1935 and
1937, with 2,482 students listed on the average daily register, a number that
dropped steadily from 2,079 registered daily in 1937–38 to 1,726 in 1940–41.[71]
      The tradeoff for the board of education's decision to locate Franklin in East
Harlem is evident in a report on the distribution of students by residence and
race as of March 1936. The high school was compelled to accept a sizeable proportion of its student body from outside East Harlem and Yorkville. In March
1936, approximately 44 percent of the students resided in East Harlem, 22 percent in Yorkville, 23 percent in the Bronx, 7 percent in downtown Manhattan,
3 percent in West Harlem, and about 1 percent in Queens and Brooklyn combined.[72] The school district's need for spaces for high school students clearly
took precedence over the concern that an imbalance of students from outside
East Harlem might jeopardize the project of community-centered schooling.
Covello and his allies may have won the political battle to site a new high
school in East Harlem, but henceforth they would have to do the bidding of

a massive school bureaucracy that was governed by an iron law of economy and efficiency.

Reports compiled in 1941 and 1942 suggest that East Harlem students became the majority at some point after 1936. There is no denying, however, the problem that faced Covello as he tried to create a community school that would be "all things to all boys," even boys from outside East Harlem. Unabashedly Covello's highest priority was "to develop some kind of East Harlem consciousness." Yet he was also painfully mindful that he would have to "correlate the communal backgrounds" of non–East Harlem students to that agenda.[73]

Every facet of the community high school's early operation was difficult, particularly the baleful condition of the buildings. Throughout its years as a scattered-site school, Franklin had continuous nagging problems with the out-moded physical plants at the East 108th Street and 79th Street locations. These problems were endemic citywide—the Depression forced severe cutbacks in the board of education's budget for school-building maintenance and renovation. With limited resources, Covello, his teachers, and workers provided by the WPA jury-rigged the former elementary school buildings as a high school. "Both buildings lacked, almost completely, adequate equipment for a modern high school," Covello wrote. "It was a makeshift arrangement, but the best that was possible under the circumstances."[74] (The main building was actually two buildings joined front to rear by a fourth-story bridge.)

Covello had to scrounge for furniture and equipment. The school library consisted of "three rooms thrown together."[75] An old toilet room in the open yard of the main building was pressed into duty as a sculpture and pottery class-room.[76] The Music Department had to use the facilities of the Neighborhood Music School at East 105th Street, where it "had the privilege of holding its concert in the auditorium satisfactory as to seating capacity and acoustics."[77] There were complaints of "drumming on the corrugated iron sheathing in stairways," "lassitude in keeping the building nominally clean," and "the lack of soap and towels in the school's toilet."[78] A teacher intern described the dismal annex: "The classrooms are so small that some of the boys must stand: a factor that leads to the distraction of the standing students. . . . The seats in many of the rooms are so small that the boys must keep their feet in the aisles."[79] A student complained: "We have been promised a basketball team. In this build-ing and at the seventy-ninth street annex there is not a proper court to prac-tice on. One cannot call a downstairs yard a proper gymnasium."[80] Lastly, there was the sheer ugliness of it all: "These buildings were not only unsuited to the requirements of our high school work from the standpoint of space and equip-ment but they were also unattractive. They needed thorough cleaning, remod-elling, and repainting. There was not a vestige of beauty about them. This very fact constituted a sort of damper on the enthusiasm of both students and teachers. One of the first jobs undertaken was the re-conditioning and beautifying of the buildings themselves."[81]

The unsuitability of the physical plant and the chronic paucity of resources notwithstanding, Benjamin Franklin, in its formative period, 1934–41, strived to create what Gerald Grant calls a "strong positive ethos"—an intellectual and moral climate that galvanized community participation and student loyalty and sentiment.[82] A graduating senior described his impression of the climate of the early high school: "The former annex on 79th Street was a hospital during the Civil War. Yet three years ago this same graduating class began its high school work in that antiquated structure. And the main building on 108th Street was not much better. Yet, it was there that we received the education of which we are now proud. No, it isn't the building, the furniture, the age and condition of the school that makes it live in the hearts of all its students. It is the spirit. And that spirit did exist in Benjamin Franklin regardless of the condition of the building. We felt that spirit—that spirit of friendliness, fraternity, tolerance, and community interest."[83]

Benjamin Franklin's organizational structure figured prominently in the development of this ethos. Covello and his staff divided the community high school into two intertwined spheres of activities: the community program and the day high school (the latter including the regular curriculum and conventional extracurricular activities).

Benjamin Franklin's Community Program

According to Covello's statement of aims, Benjamin Franklin would function as a citizen-centered community school. More precisely, it would provide "adequate service to the community along educational, civic, social, and welfare lines"; restore "communal living" to the extent possible in a beleaguered urban neighborhood; create "more harmonious" interethnic relationships; cultivate an East Harlem leadership core dedicated to "creating the finest possible background for the life of the community as a whole"; and extend the school's benefits to all members of the community.[84] Covello's rationale for the school as an enabling vehicle for these aims—and an integrative catalyst for constructive social change—is worth quoting at length:

> The Benjamin Franklin High School takes the position that the school
> is the logical agency through which these desirable ends may be
> achieved. Through it, all of the constructive forces in the community
> can be concentrated behind the movement for a better neighborhood
> life. The school touches practically every home in the community.
> It commands the respect of the community as a whole by reason of the
> fact that it is a school. It is non-sectarian and non-political. It represents an investment by the people. This investment should pay

dividends in service by which the whole school, adequately staffed, shall become available at all times for the use of the people of the community. The school has trained personnel at its command to guide the expressive activities of which the community has a great need. It has resources and technical equipment that permit intelligent planning and wise co-ordination of community resources and community activities.[85]

Covello and his associates created three community-centered structures for organizing citizen participation in the affairs of the high school and their project of local democratic development: the Community Advisory Council (CAC), the "street unit," and the WPA adult school. Each structure had an explicit educational role that supported and complemented the activities of the day-school curriculum. Although its influence would wane after 1942 , the CAC, the high school's entry portal to city and state politics, would indelibly stamp East Harlem's diverse social terrain.

Community Advisory Council

Within a year of Franklin's opening, East Harlem began an extensive neighborhood study, the first to receive the support of the Mayor's Committee on City Planning, in cooperation with the Works Progress Administration. This study was one of a dozen or more in the city intended to "lead to more active, intelligent and continuing efforts for the betterment of the community by the residents themselves."[86] Helen Harris, head worker at Union Settlement, served as chair until she was succeeded by Miriam Sanders of Haarlem House; Covello served on the sponsoring committee along with representatives from other local agencies.[87] East Harlem's community-coordinated approach, housed in the Union Settlement buildings, became a model for other New York City neighborhoods' social planning efforts. For Covello, "it established conclusively the idea that a continuing community survey is an essential part of the program of any community-centered school."[88] Covello quickly institutionalized a means for coordinating and acting upon such research, organizing Franklin's community advisory council (CAC) in the fall of 1935.

The stated purpose of the CAC was "to bring to the aid of the school all the constructive forces within the East Harlem district so as to combat the many disruptive forces of the community."[89] The council, which over the years comprised an array of school-community committees, each assigned to a specific problem area in East Harlem, coordinated the work of the various committees and mediated the ebb and flow of information and resources between the school and the community. The school-community committees were the task forces of the council, responsible for problem-solving initiatives and advocacy campaigns in their respective areas.

Covello's formulation of the CAC benefited from national and regional dialogues about coordinating councils.[90] For example, Covello tapped materials of the National Probation Association, a leading proponent of this approach, for a graduate course on community coordination that he taught at New York University in 1937–38.[91] When a key panel of a national conference addressed problems of community coordination, Covello joined nationally prominent figures in sharing their experiences.[92] At least some members of his staff were familiar with this trend as well.[93] In addition, Covello drew from the work of his dissertation advisor, New York University sociologist Frederic Thrasher, who advocated community approaches to preventing juvenile delinquency and played a prominent role in several initiatives in the New York/New Jersey area.[94] According to Thrasher: "Sociologically speaking . . . the individual delinquent is far less important than the community influences which create him."[95] Covello, in turn, urged schools to focus on the community's fundamental educational problems, broadly understood, in order to "correct the causes of maladjustment."[96] Thrasher cited Harvard criminologist Eleanor Glueck, who concurred with this view and argued that, in general, the public school was best poised to effect the "purposeful organization of social forces" and to "create an adjustment of relationships between the people."[97] Glueck further noted that the public school would prove "the most suitable center" because it was "non-sectarian, non-partisan, non-exclusive in character, and widespread in its influence upon the life of the people through their children."[98]

At its first meeting, 15 October 1935, the CAC reported a membership of 120 people and the participation of thirty-one organizations. The committees included representatives of social agencies, churches, and civic groups in East Harlem, as well as various community leaders. Covello even invited prominent officials from outside East Harlem to participate—Parks Commissioner Robert Moses politely declined the invitation to join the health committee.[99] Student leaders also joined the committees. Board of education president George Ryan and Congressman Vito Marcantonio led an impressive group of speakers in applauding the council's formation and in emphasizing the great need for "projecting the citizenship work of the school into activities of outside organizations," as well as "bringing welfare and civic groups into the curriculum of the school."[100] Five school-community committees were initially organized: Health, Citizenship, Parent Education, Correction and Guidance, and Racial.[101] Covello vested leadership of these and subsequently organized committees in his teachers, with the community's approval or at least its acquiescence. Harold Fields, one of Covello's stalwart teachers and chair of Franklin's Social Studies Department, served as the school's community coordinator and chaired the CAC executive committee.[102] By mid-October 1935, the CAC had gained the support of most East Harlem social and political leaders, and even the endorsement of Mayor La Guardia.[103]

By the spring of 1937, twenty-two committees were operating, "covering the full gamut of neighborhood needs,"[104] with considerable duplication of effort and attenuation of resources. Realizing that the school had too many committees, Covello and the council consolidated the work to some extent by reducing the number to eighteen in the fall of that year.[105] Several committees played key roles in major community-mobilization campaigns to improve the quality of life in East Harlem (for discussion see Chapter 6).

Street Units

One of the distinguishing features of Benjamin Franklin High School in the years 1934–41—and unique to that period—was the concept of the street unit; as Covello put it, "a unit that functions literally *in the street.*"[106] Directly challenging and bridging the spatial distinction between school and community, the Benjamin Franklin street units housed recreation, research, and educational activities that encouraged community members, business owners, parents, teachers, and students to work together to improve the quality of neighborhood life. The street-unit clubs and bureaus were located in reconstructed storefronts on the same block of East 108th Street as Franklin's main building. Some of the names—Friends and Neighbors Club, Old Friendship Club, and Association of Parents, Teachers, and Friends—unambiguously reflected the high school's stated goal of restoring "communal living" in East Harlem.

When the high school first opened, it operated, in addition to the day school, an afternoon community playground for neighborhood children and an evening community center for adults. Community-outreach activities were initially restricted to school property, as street units were not included in the original plan of the high school. Exigencies such as crowded space and inadequate equipment necessitated the development of exterior facilities. Organized in November 1934, with an early membership of 250 men and women, the Association of Parents, Teachers, and Friends (PTF) stimulated the development of street units and the expansion of the high school into the surrounding neighborhood.[107] Hearing of the PTF's plan for "a pleasant social center," interested neighbors in the surrounding blocks arranged for the communal use of one of the buildings adjacent to the high school. Nathan Jacobson, the owner of apartment buildings at 315–317 East 108th Street, donated two dilapidated storefronts rent free for one year for use as a social center. Neighborhood men and American Legion volunteers removed the partition between the two stores and performed cleaning and repair work; good-neighbor Jacobson provided wall paneling and painted the exterior of the stores. Annita Giacobbe, Covello, and Jacobson donated furniture for the clubrooms. The Friends and Neighbors Community Club opened on 25 September 1937, with Mary Carter Winter, a WPA employee assigned to Franklin's community-center program, serving as president (Winter was also president of the PTF).[108]

The Friends and Neighbors Club at 315 East 108th Street, just two doors removed from the high school, was the first of five "made-over" storefronts (formerly candy, cigar, and grocery stores) to be impressed for school use with the cooperation of neighborhood landlords who charged only five to ten dollars monthly rent. The club's calendar for the fall of 1938 indicates that the high school's Music Department used the clubrooms in the morning from 9:00 until 12:00; lunch was scheduled from noon to 2:30; an adult hand-sewing class met daily from 2:30 to 3:30 P.M. Tuesday through Friday the club remained opened the remainder of the afternoon for general community use. The storefront was reserved every Monday from 3:30 to 6:00 for school departmental meetings, and boys' and girls' social clubs used the facility on Tuesday and Thursday evenings.[109] The East Harlem Housing Committee and the PTF also scheduled meetings at the Friends and Neighbors Club, whose facilities were available free of charge to any club in the area. "Much thought goes into the fixing of the 'clubrooms,' reported the *New York Times* in 1939. "Soft plush chairs and sofas—gifts from the neighborhood—line the room. . . . A gas range and sink in the rear of the store provide an opportunity to make light lunches and serve refreshments. A few ferns, somewhat faded, in the windows give a quiet, homelike atmosphere. The neighbors got together and raised $34 for venetian blinds."[110]

Spearheading the high school's cleanup and beautification campaign in 1938–39, the Friends and Neighbors Club concentrated on building a neighborhood "friendship garden" on a vacant lot, the site of a demolished rookery, described as "an open space 60 by 125 feet, which had been filled in with debris and very poor dirt . . . [and was] a very unsightly blot upon the street."[111] Inaugurated in 1938, the garden project did not go smoothly, primarily because the project organizers could not locate sufficient topsoil, a problem that had not been resolved as late as December 1939, when Mary Carter Winter complained: "We have had great difficulty in securing dirt in New York City. I never realized how impossible it is to get just plain dirt in a city like this." Winter was more successful in locating plants for the new garden, requesting and obtaining free of charge three hundred hyacinth and three hundred tulip bulbs from the mayor of Haarlem, the Netherlands. She helped organize a Junior Garden Club of neighborhood children ages eight to sixteen, who potted the seedlings until topsoil for the garden could be located. When Winter requested cuttings from nearby Jefferson Park, however, she was stymied by a parsimonious bureaucrat in Robert Moses's office at the City Parks Commission: "You can readily understand that if this were started we would in the end be furnishing plants and other materials for many people in the city who might not have as good a reason for wanting them as you have."[112] In 1941, when Covello listed the projects that had been successfully completed with neighbors in the three-hundred block of East 108th Street, he did not list the "friendship garden."[113] The Friends and Neighbors Club was more successful in its "block beautiful" campaign, inspiring the school's neighbors to beautify their tenement apartments; as one report indicated: "Many of the families living on the block have already started window gardens and there are several roof gardens in the neighborhood."[114]

Four other street units followed the Friends and Neighbors Club— storefronts rejuvenated by students, teachers, and community members "with paint brushes swinging, plaster trowels wielded and hammers pounding."[115] One storefront was used as the Community Friendship Club, an association of Franklin graduates and dropouts. In the fall of 1936, Covello invited every Franklin dropout since 1934 to meet with teachers at the high school to explore ways to help dropouts with personal and employment problems. According to one participant at the November 5 meeting: "We feel that in the event . . . there should be an opening where we work or elsewhere, we should get in touch with other boys who have dropped out and thus help find work for them."[116] In 1937 the "Old Friendship Club" listed 150 active members, with Mary Giacobbe, a popular Franklin teacher, as its director.[117] This club was superseded by the Benjamin Franklin High School Alumni Association, which was established in October 1938. In March 1939 the Alumni Association reconstituted itself as the Community Friendship Club; the storefront it occupied at 302 East 108th Street was also the meeting place for community organizations that could not be accommodated by the overbooked Friends and Neighbors Club. Like the other storefront clubs, the Community Friendship Club was disbanded after the move to the new Benjamin Franklin High School in February 1942.[118]

A second storefront in the building at 302 East 108th Street housed the Friends and Neighbors Library, which operated five afternoons a week in 1940–41. Staffed by community volunteers, the library had no funds and only four hundred books, for which there was a surprisingly great neighborhood demand. "The interest created by this small library has been amazing," Covello remarked. "The children literally stormed the door to get in; and the problem has been to keep them out until we could count and list the books."[119] Covello and Mary Carter Winter headed a publicity campaign to obtain books and games for the library. Station WQXR told its listeners on 11 June 1940: "If you have old books to give away here is the place for you to send them. Children's books, stories, and books simply told but finely written in which American tradition, American history and American folk tales have been given meaning. Incidentally, jig-saw puzzles are welcome, too. You, who like books, will soon understand what a good deed you can do by giving away spare books—a good idea with many sides to it. It can help to fight the isms, too."[120]

The two other street units on the three-hundred block of East 108th Street, located in the same building as the Friends and Neighbors Club, were the Italo-American Educational Bureau and the Hispano-American Educational Bureau, which planned educational programs and provided employment and citizenship/naturalization services to Italian- and Spanish-speaking people, respectively.[121] Covello transferred the files of the by then defunct Casa Italiana Educational Bureau to the Italo-American Educational Bureau in the late 1930s. In December 1940 he incorporated the East Harlem Educational and Research Bureau as a nonprofit umbrella organization for the street units, the *East Harlem News*, and a new community research bureau, which he housed on the third floor of the National City Bank, at 357 East 116th Street. Coupled with individual contributions, the proceeds from the social activities of several Italian American groups, and from dances and *feste* at the high school, provided limited funding for these organizations, which, with the exception of the *East Harlem News*, were terminated after the move to the new Benjamin Franklin High School.[122]

The *East Harlem News* operated under the auspices of the East Harlem Educational and Research Bureau as a nonprofit, bipartisan publishing venture from March 1941 to January 1943. When he first broached the idea of a school-based community newspaper in 1939, Covello envisaged a medium that would foster a sense of community among the district's variegated and often contentious ethnic groups, particularly the Italians and Puerto Ricans. It would be "a home-town newspaper"—a vehicle "to promote community pride and cooperation, interracial good will, and good citizenship," supported by local advertising, subscriptions, and donations. The newspaper staff assembled by Covello included faculty and community members and students in the high school's journalism class. Fifteen thousand strategically distributed leaflets advertised the *East Harlem News* before the release of its first issue. "To finance our introductory issue," Covello recalled, "we held a folk festival in the grand ballroom of the Yorkville Casino. The Coro d'Italia I had organized at Columbia was there under the direction of Maestro Benelli. We had Negro dances and folk songs and spirituals, Irish jigs and ballads, Czechoslovak polkas, a German chorus, and the Pan-American singers of Benjamin Franklin. This festival netted us several hundred dollars and set the presses running for the *East Harlem News*." The first issue inaugurated a campaign for a hospital in East Harlem (see Chapter 6). Over a two-year period, the staff published twelve issues, with a respectable circulation ranging from five thousand to ten thousand copies per issue. Discontinued in 1943 "because of the financial bugaboo," publication of the *East Harlem News* was never resumed.[123]

The WPA And Adult Education At Benjamin Franklin

In April 1935 the U.S. Congress authorized $4.8 billion to create the Works Progress Administration. Fiorello La Guardia's close relationship with Franklin Roosevelt, coupled with his tireless lobbying of New Deal potentates in Washington, assured that New York City would garner a large share of the WPA relief monies. By October 1935 "the New Deal's favorite municipal officer" had leveraged more than two hundred thousand WPA job slots for New York City, far ahead of any other municipality; in 1936 one-seventh of all WPA relief monies went to New York City.[124] WPA largesse supported the labor force that made possible many of the community programs at Benjamin Franklin High School. As of 1938, sixty-nine WPA workers, thirty-eight of whom were listed as teachers, were assigned to the high school for sundry jobs.[125] Significant as the WPA was in providing assistance to the high school in the areas of research, recreation, counseling, remedial reading, and adult education, it proved, as we will soon see, to be a mixed blessing from Covello's perspective.

Of the twenty-five research projects undertaken at Benjamin Franklin High School by 1942, the WPA was involved in nine; two of these WPA-affiliated projects were sponsored by the Casa Italiana Educational Bureau. The WPA projects included a study of delinquency among Italians and non-Italians based on 1916 and 1931 records (showing a disproportionately high rate among Italian boys and the reverse for Italian girls); a block-by-block study of ethnic distribution in East Harlem; a study of motion pictures in the life of Benjamin Franklin High School students (highlighting attitudes and preferences); a study of leisure-time patterns of high school students; a sociological study of an Italian neighborhood in East Harlem; a study of patterns of delinquency in East Harlem; a study of dropouts and graduates of the high school (highlighting the role of parents in the decision to drop out); and a study of the home backgrounds of "problem" students at the high school. National Youth Administration workers participated in two studies; personnel from the Italo-American Educational Bureau, faculty of the school, and (in two cases) students provided the working staff for other studies. At the same time, Covello was disappointed because constant changes in WPA personnel and planning disrupted school activities and because many WPA research projects had to be abandoned before the research was completed.[126]

That Covello could keep the main building open continuously from 8:30 in the morning until 10:00 each evening was attributable to the WPA, which supplied the supervisors for the community recreation program. He described the afternoon and evening programs this way: "Practically every square inch of space in the school building is in use in the evening. The lower floor is given over to a recreational program for children and for grownups. Children under fourteen use the indoor playground in the afternoon from 3 to 6 P.M. From 7 to 10 the older boys and girls and the adults are admitted. A 'Kindergarten Group' of young children have been given a 'club room' in the evening also because they are always at the door of the school pleading for admittance."[127] In 1938, two youth clubs, the Silver Hordes and the Zeniths, held regular meetings at the recreation center; in the summer the center operated a vacation playground and "wholesome activity and hobbies" for the children of East Harlem and Yorkville, whom Covello wanted "off the streets and in the playgrounds." The recreation center operated "in the face of overwhelming obstacles—lack of space and equipment"—until about November 1939, when WPA cutbacks forced suspension of the program.[128]

WPA personnel also operated counseling and remedial reading programs in the day school and, under the aegis of the Federal Music Project, the high school's Vigo Drum and Bugle Corps and student music programs. In 1938 school counselor Elizabeth Roby summed up the WPA's contribution to the guidance office, where thirty-eight workers held jobs as typists, clerks, counselors, and messengers: "The chief benefit has been that the assignment of these workers has enabled us to keep complete records of work done for the student, regarding cutting, lateness, attendance, guidance, interviews, home visits, contact with Social Agencies, book records, etc."[129] In 1937 a remedial reading bureau staffed by nineteen WPA teachers reported an average reading increase of two-and-a-half years in the fall term alone for 160 boys enrolled in the special program; in 1938, the bureau reported 279 teaching periods weekly, serving between 177 and 208 pupils.[130] Needless to say, these day-school services were not extended beyond the period of WPA support. WPA personnel staffed the adult afternoon and evening school, as well as the adult summer school at Benjamin Franklin High School, offering courses ranging from English and citizenship aid to bookkeeping, stenography, and homemaking, to Italian, history, art, and music. When the adult education program opened in the summer of 1936, it registered only 63 students. Under Mary Carter Winter's leadership, the program increased from a registration of 260 in the summer of 1937 to 2,300, with an average daily attendance of 1,233 by January 1939.[131] One WPA senior official proclaimed Benjamin Franklin High School "one of the sensational successes in the present Adult Education Movement in the City."[132] Covello described the program as it stood early in 1938 as follows: "Today more than seventeen hundred adults have been registered. There are forty-six classes and twenty-six teachers in the school. It is of interest to note here that five teachers of English to the foreign-born have been assigned to the Adult School and that three naturalization aid experts, who speak several languages, are assigned to the school. So that we are prepared to give daily service along these lines to members of the community who do not speak English and who are having difficulties with their naturalization papers."[133]

Franklin's adult school was part of a larger citywide program of WPA education projects sponsored by the board of education, the adult education component of which employed 3,629 workers in 1937–38.[134] Concurrently with the WPA projects, the board maintained an evening elementary school division, which since the early 1900s had provided free schooling in English and citizenship training to the city's foreign-born adults.[135] In 1937, forty-four evening elementary schools were serving some twenty-three thousand adult learners in New York City; yet the board of education estimated that about 250,000 New

Yorkers were "just barely able to read and write English with a proficiency equal to that of the average nine or ten-year old child in our public schools."[136] By 1938, the board, perhaps anticipating the demise of the WPA adult school, had designated Benjamin Franklin High School as an evening elementary school.

The teacher allotment for the program included regular evening-school teachers assigned by the board of education and a supplemental allotment of WPA teachers. In 1939 Franklin's joint program offered thirteen classes in English and citizenship, seven in the evening elementary school, and six in the WPA adult school. It was not a peaceable arrangement. The licensed teachers who controlled the evening elementary school resented the WPA teachers and worked for their ouster. One evening elementary school administrator tactfully put the matter this way: "The WPA teachers were in the main inexperienced. They made up for that by their willingness to be guided and their devotion to the task. However, it is recommended that no WPA teachers be assigned to a regular class thereby displacing a licensed individual qualified to do the task. These WPA instructors should be assigned to help the regular staff by dealing with small groups of students who need special attention and individualized instruction."[137]

Covello's hope that the adult school would become "the center of many neighborhood activities"[138] was partially realized in the spring of 1938, when nine social clubs (choral, German, French, Hungarian, faculty players, American, Italian, journalism, and dance) were formed.[139] Yet Covello believed that WPA control of the adult school, separate from his management of the high school, thwarted the more effective integration of neighborhood activities, and he called for consolidating authority and supervision for the adult school in the office of the day-school principal. Moreover, community leaders, participating on advisory boards like Franklin's Community Advisory Council, should have "the power to plan specifically for neighborhood needs in each community on the basis of an actual survey of the neighborhood to be served by the adult center."[140]

The federal bureaucracy continually frustrated Covello. In 1939 he lost eight WPA teachers when Congress invoked the so-called eighteen-month rule, requiring the dismissal of all WPA employees who had worked for eighteen months or longer. The high school's WPA personnel manager complained to Covello: "By January we'll have no counselor, clerk, typist, assistant center head for the Adult Education unit—due to the 18 month rule and no replacements. This means I'll be tied hand and foot to the Adult Education classroom program, or will have to train volunteers, etc."[141]

Lamenting these vicissitudes, Covello argued that "the phase of the program undertaken by the WPA should be put on a stable basis and . . . it should not be subject to the disintegration that follows unexpected dismissals. Nor is it practical to project large and permanent plans of education when these programs are dependent upon personnel with no status in the regular school system."[142] (An adult high school sponsored by the board of education at the new Franklin building later in the 1940s would not be linked to the community program.)[143]

The Day High School

During Covello's tenure Benjamin Franklin High School was an all-male institution. A statement survives from 1938 suggesting that the grounds for this policy were pragmatic, not ideological. "The school is located in a foreign-born community," Covello noted. "The majority of parents of foreign origin are opposed to co-education. It is contrary to their established modes of thought. It violates codes that are still rigidly approved by the older generation."[144] By no means was a single-sex high school an anomaly in New York City, which had thirteen such institutions by the mid-1930s.[145]

Following the "cosmopolitan" model of the time, Benjamin Franklin High School sought to be "all things to all boys" by offering students a range of curricular options, including a traditional academic course of study, commercial subjects, industrial arts, and fine arts.[146] In practice, being all things to all boys did not diminish the difficulties that were endemic to efforts to provide a high school education for youth of the ethnic poor and working classes in Depression-afflicted East Harlem. While Benjamin Franklin pushed its students toward academic success through a variety of tailored programs and helping mechanisms, like many New York high schools of its day it had to fight continuously against low attendance rates, poor academic performance, and high incidences of dropping out. In the face of these challenges and the attitudes of "downtown" school officials who had written off many of his students as unfit for high school, Covello struggled to hold the high ground of academic standards in no small part to disprove the presumption of East Harlem youths' intellectual incapacity.

"We were determined to use all our resources to meet city and state requirements for graduation, including state Regents' Examinations for the academic diploma," Covello recalled in his autobiography. "In fact, a survey based on a questionnaire done by the mathematics department showed that many of our students wanted to feel they could continue on to college and would not have voluntarily accepted a modified course. The idea of a 'watered-down' curriculum, insisted upon for this type of community in so many quarters, was rejected by the pupils themselves."[147]

According to a scholarship report for the spring term 1936, foreign-language enrollments stood at 2,219, compared to an average daily register of 2,482 students for 1935–36. The 1936 report indicates that in addition to taking foreign languages (five were offered), more than 1,200 Franklin students took mathematics, with elementary algebra and plane geometry in the ninth and tenth grades respectively. Not surprisingly, the numbers dwindled in the higher-level math courses: trigonometry, advanced algebra, and solid geometry. Just over

1,100 students took science, with general science in ninth grade and biology in tenth. A smaller group of students took chemistry and physics in the final two years. By comparison, enrollments in "commercial" courses—business training, commercial arithmetic, and bookkeeping—and courses in stenography, crafts, and mechanical drawing were all significantly lower. Just under 200 students were enrolled in shop, woodwork, and printing combined.[148]

We speculate that Covello wanted to prove that "my boys," especially the Italians, could succeed on the same terms as New York's more advantaged high school students. Certainly many of the students graduated with high expectations. Of the school's 1,340 graduates between 1936 and 1939, 729, or 54 percent, applied to postsecondary institutions—612 to City College, 109 to Brooklyn College, 124 to NYU, 54 to Fordham, and 42 to Columbia.[149] According to a 1937 survey, 72 percent of Franklin graduates said they planned to continue their education; of this group slightly more than half planned to enter a profession, and about 6 percent were undecided.[150] Unfortunately, we do not know the actual rate of college attendance for these Franklin students; nor do we know the school's cohort graduation rates. Board of education reports for this period, problematically, did not include individual high school graduation data. Counts of senior photographs in Franklin's yearbooks provide a rough proxy, suggesting that 1936 through 1939 were the high school's watershed years for producing graduates.[151]

The available statistical reports suggest that the fledgling high school, for all Covello's prodigious efforts, fought a steep uphill battle to educate the youths, many of them overage for their grade, who thronged Franklin's main building and annexes. On the few performance rankings for which the board of education reported comparative data (arrayed in tables and graphs), the East Harlem high school held a number of lower-end citywide rankings. In 1937–38, for example, it ranked forty-fourth of forty-seven day high schools in average daily attendance. More pointedly, in the spring term it ranked forty-fifth of forty-seven day high schools in percentage of courses failed.[152] In the spring of 1941, Franklin had the highest percentage of courses failed among the day high schools.[153]

Dropouts appear to have been a serious problem, as suggested by the presence of the Old Friendship Club and dropout reports compiled in 1937–38. For the fall of 1937, 353 dropouts were reported versus 237 graduates for that term; 300 of the dropouts had four or more course failures on their record.[154] A WPA study of 322 dropouts and graduates released in the summer of 1937 showed "that almost half of the [125] drop-outs left school 'to go to work,' and less than a fifth because they 'disliked school.' . . . During an average time out of school of about one year, three-fourths of the drop-outs studied found jobs and held them for at least three months" (original emphasis).[155] A second report filed with the WPA study, however, identified school failure and aimlessness as prevalent factors in the decision to withdraw from school. In this case a guidance counselor interviewed 224 dropouts and found that 39 percent (87) were neither employed nor in a trade or night-school program. Of this group, the counselor wrote: "With the exception of a few I have to admit they are irresponsible and void of all ambition. . . . From this group I received the greatest number of reasons for leaving school and the reasons are all narrowed down to one. There is a strong dislike for school. . . . This group seems content to drift along with 'the crowd,' frequenting poolrooms, movies and street corners."[156] In his 1944 dissertation, Covello acknowledged that dropping out was "a conspicuous aspect of high school attendance in the East Harlem community"; here he made particular reference to Italian Harlem.[157]

Obviously, Franklin High School students' academic performance was not what it should have been. Yet for all these problems, Covello remained unflinching in his commitment to the community school idea. While his dissertation underscored the *domus* antipathy to secondary education, he optimistically pointed to a 1943 opinion poll at Franklin showing that "during the last ten years there has been an improvement in the school attitude and behavior of Italian students."[158] Covello apparently thought that his approach would eventually overcome the *domus* mindset, that given sufficient duration and sustained resources, community-centered schooling would turn the tide of educational failure in East Harlem.

That this ambitious endeavor did not achieve the academic outcomes Covello had hoped for (after all, these were extraordinarily parlous times) in no way diminishes the importance of his efforts. He astutely recognized that the school had an appropriate role to play in the reconstruction of urban communal life, in concert with other community organizations. Furthermore, he understood that the school's fulfillment of this role was a necessary condition for his students' academic achievement. With all its blemishes, Franklin High School illustrates concretely the range of complex issues that must be faced if we take seriously the advanced conception of democracy and citizenship Covello always held in view.

IN ITS QUOTIDIAN ROUTINES, which were spread across a seven-period day that began at 8:40 A.M. and ended at 3:00 P.M., Franklin's day school was not highly distinguishable from other New York City high schools. Although there were some powerful linkages to community issues and concerns, the curriculum was never reconstructed to be systematically progressive or community centered. As a general rule at Franklin, community studies were subordinated to subject-centered education. The community component functioned mainly on an ad hoc basis: As socially significant problems reached crisis proportions, they were integrated into the curriculum. Innovative curricular units on intercultural relations and housing (see Chapters 5 and 6, respectively), which were focal points of student interest and activism, were not expanded into sustained, problem-focused courses that integrated academic subject matter and higher-order intellectual skills. Teaching and learning at Franklin remained largely teacher and subject centered; "constructivist" or "authentic" teaching (to use the contemporary argot) and curricular integration were the exception rather than the rule.[159] Rather than experimenting with the difficult and perhaps risky multidisciplinary integration and pedagogical reorientation that would have been involved in building a curriculum that was more thoroughly community centered, Covello and his staff chose pragmatically to limit curricular experimentation to a single community studies course for a selective group of top students, as we will see.

By the mid-1930s, the climate of the New York City schools was such that Covello probably had a warrant to experiment more broadly. In rhetoric at least, the city schools were a hotbed of progressive activity, which originated with a large-scale program in the elementary schools and was targeted to percolate upward into the high schools.

In September 1935 Superintendent Harold Campbell, who was gravely concerned about rampant problems of "maladjustment" and "retardation" in the city schools, introduced an "activity program" in the city's elementary schools. Organized as a six-year experiment, the activity program involved sixty-nine schools (10 percent of all elementary schools), more than seventy-five thousand students, and 2,250 teachers; in these schools, 83 percent of the teachers and 83 percent of the pupils participated in the program. In theory at least, the activity program featured a greater emphasis on children's creative projects, for example, in art and poetry; more attention to class discussions and small group work; fewer restrictions on children's movement in the classroom; and a general shift from subject-centered to child-centered teaching.[160] To what extent did the so-called activity classrooms actually implement these progressive practices? The evidence is inconclusive and certainly did not warrant Campbell's claim in 1942 that significant change had occurred in the participating schools. Though a great deal of data was generated, little of it was based on direct observations of classrooms. It seems that most teachers in the activity classrooms incorporated some progressive activities but did not change their practice in fundamental ways. More germane here, to what extent did the philosophy of the activity program percolate into the city high schools? Based on an analysis of 152 descriptions and photographs of New York high school classrooms during the interwar years, historian Larry Cuban concludes that progressivism had little significant impact at this level—teacher-centered instruction was overwhelmingly the dominant instructional pattern.[161]

Whereas Campbell's version of pedagogical progressivism was child-centered, Covello's approach linked a particular curriculum unit or set of activities to a comprehensive social reform strategy. It seems reasonable to speculate that had World War II not intruded upon that strategy, Covello would have worked out a set of community problem-based courses to systematize what was to that point largely an ad hoc approach; in fact, he began that kind of systematic planning in the mid-1950s, albeit tentatively in a milieu that was no longer friendly to progressive education and lacking the federal support he had enjoyed in the late 1930s.

UNSURPRISINGLY, NEITHER BENJAMIN FRANKLIN'S community centeredness nor its "cosmopolitan" curriculum drew public attention to the high school beyond East Harlem and Yorkville. In the prewar years Benjamin Franklin achieved respectability in the pantheon of New York City's high schools largely on the strength of its day-school extracurricular program. In 1936 the school contributed seventeen singers and eight musicians to a student choir and symphony conducted by Walter Damrosch at the National Music Festival at Madison Square Garden—a distinction the student newspaper cited as "definite proof that our school has won a deserved recognition among the high schools of established standing."[162] Students further proclaimed that "Franklin has met the challenge of other high schools on the sport field and in the classroom, and has fought its way to the top. The 'critical period' is passed. We now emerge as a unified red-blooded member of New York's educational system."[163] In 1938, Franklin, "the smallest school of the school boy basketball circuit," won the city championship by defeating Newtown High School 29–27 in a game "played before a gallery of 3,700 excitement-mad fans." In the hyperbole characteristic of that era's student journalism, the Franklin *Almanac* proclaimed: "It was the result of hard work, against insurmountable odds, but our boys came through."[164]

In 1941 the high school listed forty-one extracurricular clubs and student groups. The General Organization (G.O.), a dues-paying student organization open to all students, coordinated extracurricular activities, club funds, and tickets to special events.[165] The Student Congress, with fifty-two elected representatives and an elected slate of four officers, was primarily an advisory body to Covello. Other prominent student groups included the Italian Club, orchestra and choral club, Arista (National Honor Society), and *Almanac* (student newspaper).[166]

Student participation in the deliberations of the Community Advisory Council committees was, as a rule, restricted to juniors and seniors in the Student Congress and seniors in the special leadership class at the high school. In other words, two paths led students to the CAC and a role in planning broadly based community initiatives, one extracurricular, the other curricular. Through the problem-based pedagogy of the leadership class, the curricular path to the CAC provided structured opportunities for learning participatory and problem-solving skills.

For the leadership class, teachers nominated boys "who seem to possess more than an ordinary amount of leadership ability. . . . The selection is made by our chairmen at a meeting at which the qualifications of proposed members of the group are freely discussed." In 1940 Covello described this class as follows: "Members of this class are given every opportunity to study the community, to make contacts with social situations conducive to leadership development, and to participate in radio broadcasts, neighborhood entertainments, community conferences, and all types of activity in the school and the community. In class, these boys are making a rather intensive study of contemporaneous American life. Members of this group are sent, as representatives of the school, to important meetings in New York City and elsewhere. Delegates have gone in this way to such meetings as the Constitutional Celebration for New York State at Poughkeepsie, to Albany for observance of Constitution Day, to Washington to various Youth congresses, to the World Youth Conference at Poughkeepsie, to local conferences in the metropolitan area, and to the recent conference on negro [sic] problems in Washington."[167]

A syllabus for the leadership class, "American History and Social Problems in Light of American Literature," describes what appears to have been the only course with a community problem-based approach that was integral to the course.

> Class Work—Each student will be asked to select a problem and follow it through in the field of American literature. Students will be grouped in accordance with the problem they have selected, and each group will report to the class at stated intervals on the results of and the inferences to be drawn from their reading.
>
> Field Work—Each group will be required to do actual field work in its own phase of the general subject. For example, the group studying problems of the slum will be expected to make personal investigation of actual slum conditions; the group studying the problem of the "melting pot" will be expected to ascertain through actual observation and personal investigation the difficulties presented in the adjustment of racial differences and animosities; and the group studying the problems of education under our American democracy will be asked to visit schools where noteworthy attempts are being made to achieve democracy in education—for instance, the Herman Ridder Junior High School. In other cases, as, for instance, in that of the problem of peace and war, students will be expected to get into personal touch with agencies working in the field, such as . . . World Peace Ways. The active assistance of the Department of Social Sciences will be enlisted in the attempt to make this field work fruitful of results.[168]

The leadership class was conceptualized as the kind of "project curriculum" William Heard Kilpatrick advocated in his "social frontier" essays at Teachers College, and Covello was undoubtedly influenced by Kilpatrick.[169] By the 1930s Kilpatrick, who inspired an "incredible spate of books" on the activity curriculum in the 1920s, had loosed his moorings in child-centered pedagogy and adopted a social-change approach to classroom project development. Aligning himself with Columbia University's social reconstructionists, the "Teachers College crowd," Kilpatrick emphasized the need for greater linkage between classroom work and the "purposeful activity" of the community. In his introduction to Paul Hanna's *Youth Serves Community,* Kilpatrick asserted that the truly educative situation brought youth and adults in a community together in a shared enterprise, one in which "each can have his own responsible part." Here was "the education in which democracy can most rejoice, particularly in these times when we must learn to put the public welfare first in point of time and importance. In solemn fact, *cooperative activities for community improvement* form the vision of the best education yet conceived" (original emphasis).[170] Beyond the leadership class, "cooperative activities for community improvement" infused other courses at Benjamin Franklin on an ad hoc basis in conjunction with the high school's intercultural program (Chapter 5) and the CAC's East Harlem campaigns (Chapter 6).

In December 1937, forty-one students were listed as participants and voting members of CAC committees; a revised list published around 1938 showed sixty-three students on fourteen committees.[171] The rest of the students participated in committee projects and activities. For the East Harlem housing campaign, "all students of the school filled out questionnaires on the housing conditions under which they live. Committee members helped to prepare a chart of living conditions in the community from these questionnaires. The chart gave helpful information in the fight for a low-cost housing project in East Harlem. Essays on housing as well as models and scenes of the community were prepared by the boys." With respect to health issues: "Two student members of the School-Community Health Committee are members of the East Harlem Health Center Committee. They attend meetings and report to the school committee the latest information of interest to the community on the vital question of health. Visits of the entire student body to the Health Center have been arranged. A faculty conference at the East Harlem Health Center at which the Health Commissioner of the City spoke was attended by student representatives. The boys of the committee were pioneers in the drive for the administration of the Tuberculin Tests and Chest X-Ray examinations."[172]

In his speeches and writings, Covello eschewed au courant psychoanalytic and deterministic interpretations that portrayed youth as inherently volatile, tumultuous, and untrustworthy. He believed that adolescence was a period of benign growth, when young people acquired large capacities for sociality and empathy. The high school's role was to develop these natural tendencies, to cultivate in young people a disposition joined with a capability for social service and civic action.[173] As suggested by the selective processes underlying student participation in the leadership class and on CAC committees, Covello's vision was also meritocratic: Participation at this level was an earned privilege. Covello wanted to train a leadership class for East Harlem, a service-minded elite that W.E.B. DuBois elsewhere designated "the talented tenth." A former student who remembered his own role as "a kind of liaison man between the student body and the community organization proper [CAC] and so served on almost all the committee panels—health, citizenship, racial relations, education"— explained to Covello: "I don't have to tell you about how the inspiration of us Franklin students were [sic] fired by the thought that we would be able to participate in something bigger than ourselves that would allow us to translate into action some of the things we had been hearing about and seeing in books."[174]

Covello and his teachers paid a great deal of attention to the rank-and-file students, particularly those with behavioral and attendance problems, to such an extent that several student leaders complained to Covello: "Attention has been given only to the delinquent students. The normal student and the student who is slightly above normal are almost completely neglected."[175] This criticism exaggerated the situation, but Covello and his staff did make a considerable effort to help troubled youngsters. For example, the teachers held meetings with the parents of students who failed two or more subjects in a marking term. Covello and two or three Spanish- and Italian-speaking teachers reserved every Wednesday evening, 8:00 to 10:00, to meet with parents who could not come in for interviews during the school day. An informant told Robert Peebles in 1965 that Covello "was always concerned when students dropped out. He would personally interview the student and then find the means for the boy to continue, whether this be social, economic, psychological, or otherwise. I was fascinated by the efforts of Dr. Covello with one boy in particular who was graduated at the age of 20 or thereabouts. I am sure that but for Dr. Covello, this boy would not have completed more than two years of high school."[176] As noted previously, the Old Friendship Club provided counseling and employment assistance to dropouts. The guidance and placement service was "an intensely crowded office," which in 1937–38 reported interviews with three hundred potential dropouts, job placement for seventy dropouts, and part-time placement for 402 currently registered pupils.[177]

Covello organized a Student Aid Fund, based on a program he had created at DeWitt Clinton High School in the 1920s, which provided eyeglasses, shoes, clothing, and medical assistance to needy Franklin students. "With the winter approaching the problem of student aid becomes a very pressing one," Covello told his faculty. "We know that you doubtlessly have other responsibilities but we feel that our boys need help so badly that we must appeal to you. We have very little on hand, yet the number of boys who need help is increasing daily. Money is spent only for the most needy and only after the cases have been thoroughly investigated. To cover the cost of such things as clothing, shoes, glasses, etc. we need about $35.00 a month."[178]

Funding sources for the Student Aid Fund included PTF card parties, Italian *feste,* and contributions from faculty and students. In the fall of 1939, the fund disbursed $387.35 for items ranging from shoes (sixty-four pairs) to eyeglasses (twenty-three pairs) to underwear (eleven suits). That term the high school's Social Welfare Office, which housed the Student Aid Fund, provided free lunches for 362 boys.[179] A neighborhood optometrist recalled Covello's work: "I was then, as now established as an optometrist on Lexington Avenue and East 106th Street, a stone's throw from the school. It was here that I first got to know what Dr. Covello was doing besides teaching. He would refer his students who were too poor to take care of their visual problems to me and made sure that they were not handicapped by poor vision. Their dental and medical needs were not overlooked. He knew that a physically neglected child could not profit from the best education."[180]

Covello also worked closely with the National Youth Administration, which provided jobs to some 3,500 students in uptown senior and junior high schools. In the fall of 1939 the NYA disbursed $3,655 to boys at Benjamin Franklin High School. In 1940–41 Franklin's total NYA appropriation was $13,950. A report from May 1941 shows that 257 boys held NYA jobs at the high school, serving as teachers' assistants, clerks, and printshop workers, and Covello created an NYA "service squad" to check for student passes to leave the building and to monitor the lunchroom line. He justified these jobs as necessary to advance the community school in the face of dwindling WPA support: "Lack of funds for activities outside the prescribed routine of a senior high school and lack of additional personnel to carry out the school-community program constitute a great handicap in trying to carry forward the program at Benjamin Franklin H.S."[181]

Covello's Evolving Philosophy of Community-Centered Schooling

Covello envisioned schools in polyglot immigrant communities as functioning as hubs for the delivery of education, health, social, and recreational services to all members of their constituent neighborhoods. They would be public spaces for organizing communitywide citizen action projects, such as campaigns to improve housing, educational services, health, and sanitation in the blocks and neighborhoods served by the school. Urban community schools would also be catalytic hubs for democratic participation and intergroup cooperation. "By a Community-Centered School," Covello stated, "I mean one in which there is a thorough inter-action between the school and its neighborhood in meeting needs of both the child and community. I take it for granted that all progressive minds are now committed to the idea that the school of today should be—and the school of tomorrow must be—the educational and social center of its community. We have been moving toward this newer concept ever since the subject-centered school yielded to the child-centered school in our advancing educational methods. The school, which occupies a unique and strategically important position because of its relationship to practically every home in the community, should be a guiding influence not only in the life of the child but of his family and community as well." In rhetoric that Jane Addams might have found appealing, Covello also envisioned the community-centered school as a moral force. "The responsibility of the school as an educational factor does not cease at the hour of dismissal in the afternoon; it extends far beyond the walls of the school," he declaimed. "The child does not appear from *nowhere* in the morning nor does he vanish into *nowhere* in the afternoon hours. He comes from, and goes back into the surging life of the community in which the streets, motion pictures, dances, gangs, social clubs, churches, settlement houses, communal codes of morals and behavior are making daily and hourly impacts upon his mind and consciousness. These impacts educate—either for *good* or for *bad.* It is one of the primary duties of the school to see that the constructive forces in the community are drawn solidly together in support of educational programs for the development of the child and in behalf of a more wholesome community life" (original emphasis).[182]

This analysis, of course, begs the question: How did Covello define and use the term "community"? Was it more than simply a rhetorical device? What, realistically, is the school's area of effective community service? Ever the reflective practitioner, Covello wrestled with the implications of the term, always eschewing casual usage, as evidenced by an intriguing passage from a remnant manuscript:

When we first began to project the school-community program, we found it necessary to formulate a definite opinion as to what really constituted "the community," as far as the school and our work was concerned. We leaned somewhat to the idea of the "broad community," with the East Harlem-Yorkville Community as a sort of island to be explored in a wide expanse of interests and problems. This meant that we were undertaking to reach an area 200 city blocks long and eight city blocks wide. Within this space, about 400,000 persons are living. Below 96th Street, the population is mostly German and Slavic. Above 96th street, more than thirty different racial strains are represented in the congested population. Scarcely realizing the magnitude of the task of education in relation to an area so large and diverse in its population and interests, a base sociological map was made of the entire East Harlem-Yorkville territory with an idea that this was our sphere of action.

At the end of the first six-months [*sic*], it was decided that we would do well to concentrate on East Harlem alone, with its 200,000 and more people. Later still, we were talking in terms of "the neighborhood" meaning by that term, the area immediately contiguous to the school. Later still we were thinking in terms of the "social block," and were convinced that we should have rendered a valuable service to the larger community if our school could work out a satisfactory, rounded program that would meet the needs of even the 2,000 and more people living in the "social block" of which the Benjamin Franklin High School is a part.

By degrees, as our program began actually to evolve, the wisdom of making the social block the basis of community-centered education became apparent. By a block to block progression, any community, of any size whatsoever, may eventually be reached. We projected, therefore, the "street unit" program of the Benjamin Franklin High School.[183]

Here Covello used the term "community" "in a descriptive sense," much as "sociologists engaged in community studies . . . use the term to mean something like 'small town' or neighborhood." As philosopher Iris Marion Young observes, the term can also be understood as "a normative model of ideal social organization." It is this idealized, normative sense of community that emerges in other writings and in the structures, roles, and programs that Covello built for the high school; community thus understood, to borrow Young's apt phrase, is "the concept of social relations that embody openness to unassimilated otherness with justice and appreciation."[184]

Consistent with this understanding of community, the "community-centered school" rested upon a view of education as inherently a civic function. Covello began with the premise that education signified "a *leading forth*, from within, of latent abilities, and of a process of *guiding* such abilities" (original emphasis). The kind and quality of this dual development, he implied, would have significant repercussions for both community and national life. Covello argued that education must "broaden the child's intellectual grasp and the horizon of his mind," while building disciplined study habits, as well as logical and coherent thinking. In addition, education should enable a student not simply to tap current knowledge, but also to begin "branching out along lines that are original and constructively valuable; [education] must encourage initiative in discerning and deciding problems of practical importance in relation to the life he is to live." Yet education does not stop there, as its twofold nature carries its influence into the wider community. The child's status as tomorrow's adult citizen implies education's socially constructive role, as schools should "sense in the growing child, the citizen of to-morrow." It is upon that future adult citizen, insisted Covello, that "both his small community and the nation must depend for intelligent contributions to civic progress, for the nation is but the sum total of its small communities, and the communities themselves are but the sum total of homes from which school children come."[185]

Covello saw no inherent conflict between these two aspects of education—on the contrary, they served to enhance each other. The community-centered school built on academic education and broadened it considerably on the basis of "knowledge of, and experience in, the community."[186] Centering the school on the local community, he argued, advanced traditional academic goals by investing academic work with an immediate relevance and "attaching a sense of importance to the individual himself as well as to his education for a larger responsibility. . . . [This] sense of reality and of unity with large aims, and important activities provides the best incentive for the student, particularly the high school student. Moreover, community centered education develops ability as well as interest and prepares for democratic participation in community life." The underlying cause of school failure, in Covello's judgment, was the lack of "programs through which interest can be developed."[187]

Not only did Benjamin Franklin staff members understand community-centered education as a leading forth of the individual into civic participation, but also they viewed the community as exercising a broad set of educational influences on the individual. Contrary to the assumptions of "the traditional type of academic isolation, . . . the school child does not live in a social vacuum; . . . his educational process involves not only the home and the school but the total community." This general condition required that the school establish "an 'education for social living' as a process in which the child in the school must be considered in relation to his entire background, i.e., his home, his groups, and his community."[188]

The community that Benjamin Franklin engaged suffered from an impoverishment of social capital (our term for Covello's meaning), a "general problem of maladjustment," a broadly felt resentment, and a creeping indifference—factors that imposed a "weight upon the progress of the community."[189] Covello assigned great importance to community-centered schooling as a catalyst for local democratic development, applying a "galvanizing stimulus" to counteract the negative social forces that produced such alienation and despair. In order for the local public school to perform that role, it "must find its way back to active and intimate identification with the daily life of its community."[190] Inspired by the examples of George Washington and Abraham Lincoln, Covello insisted that the way to educate young people for effective citizenship was to involve them in solving real problems in the local community. His yardstick was Lincoln's civic education.[191]

At a time when books were difficult to obtain, the adolescent Lincoln not only read and studied but also participated fully "in the life and tasks of the community." The wilderness did not allow a theoretical democracy; citizenship meant knowing what the community needed and shouldering one's fair share of the work. Young Lincoln, a sixteen-year-old boy, "was expected to measure up to the demands of the situation the same as the older members of the community. In other words, there was a complete integration of the educational process with the practical life of the community." This may explain, Covello noted, the quality of many leaders during that period, and why "men with aptitude for leadership were able to measure up to their times and to make great contributions to democracy and to the world, after having first made their contributions to the smaller communities to which each belonged."[192]

By cultivating such a problem-solving orientation and relationship, Covello wrote, the community-centered school could fulfill its central role as a local public institution dedicated to the democratic development of the community. Specifically, the school must operate as a "socializing agency in intercultural relationships and the expansion of the local social world; in the development of community-consciousness and communal cooperative effort"; and as "a testing ground for leadership ability within the school, and for training community leadership."[193]

Covello portrayed the community-centered school, in all its interactions, as a microcosm of U.S. democracy, contending that it transcended parochialism, its immediate focus on local issues and concerns notwithstanding. "If human relationships are to be developed on the basis of civic responsibility, they ought to embrace the entire community of East Harlem, then the city, then the state, then the nation, and should probably include the world," he wrote. "But a start has to be made somewhere. In East Harlem there is sufficient justification in emphasizing the need for the people to become aware of the common ties of the local community, the need, so to speak, for sensing the community of interests within the boundaries of East Harlem. The point of view is admittedly a narrow one, but it has the advantage of permitting concrete exemplification of a basic democratic principle, with the possibility of launching programs that, though limited in scope (in a geographical sense) carry the elements of enterprises that are valid for larger human aggregates. Simply stated, a developing social consciousness within the limits of East Harlem contains on a small scale all the aspects of democratic life in larger social groups, and is therefore conducive to becoming expanded."[194]

To achieve its goals, the school needed to recognize that it was part of the community being educated, a "part of the general educational process." Benjamin Franklin's staff would also have to show the East Harlem community concrete results, "not lip service but genuine help to the community."[195] That friendship would include helping to counter the low self-esteem that many East Harlem residents felt—a feeling reinforced by negative media stereotypes of the district. No one understood this more clearly than Benjamin Franklin students. In an article describing the community-centered approach at the high school, three students expressed youthful optimism that the school's community programs would revitalize East Harlem by addressing its "defeatism," by providing "a feeling of hope and pride." "Then they would no longer be obsessed with the idea that a community such as East Harlem offers absolutely no means for advancement in the world. For the old, worn-out philosophy of defeatism would give way to a new feeling of optimism and a will to take an active part in improving their conditions."[196]

Democratic development would mean the education and mobilization of diverse cultural groups around shared political goals, creating new networks of social capital. The cumulative successes of cooperative planning across ethnic, racial, and class boundaries would, in theory at least, contribute to greater tolerance and respect of cultural differences. In this way civic empowerment would be entwined with broadly based community building in East Harlem. In his salutatory address for the spring commencement of 1938, senior Salvatore Canino recounted: "Throughout our high school career we have been taught our science, our mathematics, history, French, economics and other truly useful subjects—but we are leaving Franklin with a far better education, a far better training than the knowledge of these subjects gives us as a result of our extra-curricular activities in the community. From these activities we have learned the importance of co-operation in the solution of such pressing problems in our community as housing, illiteracy, and racial prejudice."[197]

Covello cast the community-centered school in many roles: as social center, as stimulus for communal action, as research agency, as guardian of the prestige of the community, to name but a few. Covello underscored the centrality of the research role ("the school as explorer"), which he described as "the indispensable factor" in the success of its other functions. Knowledge of the community, "a comprehension by the faculty of the total community situation," was the driving engine.[198]

Benjamin Franklin's Teachers

Community-centered schooling in East Harlem required teachers who subscribed to Covello's philosophy and supported his community agenda. Covello was able to build an inner circle of committed activists of this ilk. Yet he regarded community as a professional obligation of all teachers.

The New York City schools of the 1930s were a megabureaucracy whose managers expected city teachers to be all things to all children. City teachers were socialized in both their teacher training and professional practice to be social workers, to attend scrupulously to the physical and mental health needs of their pupils, and to work extended hours without wage compensation. Their work conditions, however, undercut the board of education's goal to "supplement the home."[199] Most city teachers were already overburdened by overcrowded classrooms, unremunerated extracurricular assignments, and mountains of paperwork: "forms, reports, censuses, surveys, grading, tests, and scores to far greater degree than teachers elsewhere." To understate the point extravagantly, teachers had "a very long day."[200]

Viewed from this perspective, the internal contradictions of the board of education–sponsored Activity Program appear in full relief. The board wanted to fuse child-centered education onto social efficiency schooling, and to do that it imposed an additional burden at a point where teachers badly needed relief from the minutiae of their professional lives. Absent citywide systemic reform—realigned priorities and adequate support structures for progressive education—teachers inevitably downgraded or co-opted the reform. At the high school level this "grammar of schooling" was even more entrenched by virtue of departmentalization, Regents' examinations, and work-entry and college-entrance requirements.

Educational economies during the 1930s affected all New York City schools and teachers, Benjamin Franklin being no exception. On 1 January 1933, the state legislature authorized what amounted to an average reduction of 6.5 percent of all salaries in the city schools; the following year the total salary budget was cut by another 10 percent.[201] The sixteen salary scales on which these reductions were apparently based ranged from $2,148 (level 1) to $4,500 (level 16).[202] Teachers were doubly burdened—their class sizes increased as new teacher hires did not keep pace with burgeoning enrollments. In the high schools 1932–33 was a particularly stressful year, with an increase of some eighteen thousand students that was matched by a net gain of only 323 teachers.[203] Unfortunately, we do not know what, if any, effects beleaguered district finances had on hiring or retention of regular teachers at Benjamin Franklin from the fall of 1934, when the high school opened, to July of 1937, when the salary schedules were reinstated.

Educational historians have noted the high quality of New York City teachers in the 1930s, a few even hailing it as the city's "Golden Age" of education."[204] In the first in-depth treatment of the subject, Ruth Markowitz attributes this efflorescence in no small part to the entry of highly educated female Jewish teachers into the city schools—by 1930, 40 percent of entering teachers were Jewish women; by 1940, 56 percent. Graduates of the liberal hothouses Hunter and Brooklyn colleges, many of these teachers were dedicated activists, either by virtue of their immigrant family's participation in eastern European socialist or labor movements, or their exposure to the Depression era's "unemployment, marches, picketing, breadlines, evictions, and labor strife." Fearing for their jobs, however, in many cases these teachers were constrained from enacting their social critiques in city schools by bureaucrats who were punitively hostile to such agendas.[205]

In various ways Benjamin Franklin was a rare exception to the "real-school" script in the New York City Schools. Primarily through the agency of the Community Advisory Council, the community high school offered a select group of teachers a school-based venue and encouragement for their social activism. Throughout his twenty-two-year tenure as Franklin's principal, Covello was blessed with a core of exceptional teachers who shared his dedication to young people and his vision for community building and social justice in East Harlem. Five of these teachers—Abraham Kroll and Morris Deschel in science, Michael Decessare in economics, Annita Giacobbe in Italian, and Harry Levene in math—were among the seventeen transferees who joined Covello from DeWitt Clinton.[206] Kroll served as Covello's assistant principal, and Deschel was the "teacher in charge" of the high school's Yorkville annex; Giacobbe had helped Covello with the struggle to win parity for Italian in the 1920s and with the Boys' Club Study. The Clinton expatriates were the first of a line of distinguished teachers who would make distinctive contributions to community-centered schooling in East Harlem. These teachers, whose nonremunerative school-community work is documented in the next several chapters of this book, made extraordinary sacrifices on behalf of the community school, working late into the night at the high school side by side with Covello; chairing CAC school-community committees; leading community campaigns for better housing, health, schooling, and citizenship; supervising school clubs and special programs; and serving as foreign-language translators for the school and community and as public speakers to explain the school's program to community organizations.[207]

This is not to suggest that all Franklin teachers adhered to the high standard of public service set by Covello and his hardy band of committed activists. "Many of our teachers have entered generously into the work of the school and community," Covello noted in a five-year report on the progress of the high school to Benjamin Franklin faculty and staff, written in September 1939. This report suggests (elliptically, given its generally positive tone) that he was not yet satisfied with the level of teacher participation. After announcing that a Faculty School-Community Committee had been formed "for the purpose of working out plans for greater participation on the part of our teachers in the community program," he adjured all his teachers to "realize that there is a pressing need to make more and better contacts with the community in which we are working. . . . We cannot really do satisfactory professional work if we continue to ignore the community." Put differently, community work is integral to professional work.[208]

Though documentation is lacking, we surmise that some teachers resisted this calculus, regarding community work as just another "pressing need" to complicate their already intensified work lives. The problem of Franklin teachers' "greater participation" in the community program may also have been an issue of teacher professionalism. Many teachers would increasingly distance themselves from the social-worker role; they would define their professional role as classroom teaching and, in the second half of the twentieth century, specify their expectations for that role in the legal-bureaucratic language of union contracts. Given Covello's expectations for teachers' community involvement, it is not difficult to imagine a Franklin teacher saying, "I'm a mathematics teacher, not a social worker."

To summarize thus far, by the end of the 1930s, as Covello worked on
a plan to move Benjamin Franklin to a new building above East River Drive,
a thriving community school operation, coordinated by the CAC, guided by a
core of dedicated teachers, and bolstered by street units and WPA educational
resources, was in place—although the future was uncertain, given the instability of WPA programs and the gathering storm in Europe. During Franklin's
pre–World War II halcyon years, the committees of the CAC had begun to
coordinate educational resources within East Harlem's existing social networks,
the East Harlem Council of Social Agencies, for instance, and to fuse them
into a set of programs and citizen-action projects that would contribute to
bringing important new resources to the district and building and strengthening social capital in the wider community. As we learned, the making of Benjamin Franklin was always a hard-fought, terribly difficult struggle, especially
when it concerned wedding students and parents to the school's academic goals;
poor academic performance and a high dropout rate were continuing problems.

And yet for all the attendant problems, something bold, adventurous, and
visionary, without parallel in the history of American urban education, was
unfolding in this East Harlem high school in the late Depression era. We turn
now to consider a critical aspect of Covello's project, the high school's curricular strategy to educate East Harlemites for "cultural democracy," the most
prominent element of which was an intercultural education program that Covello organized with Rachel Davis DuBois of the Service Bureau for Education
in Human Relations.

CHAPTER FIVE

Community Schooling for Cultural Democracy: Premises and First Steps

RESPECTED PUBLIC SERVANT Edward Corsi, commissioner of immigration at Ellis Island under President Hoover, described the East Harlem he knew in the decade prior to the founding of Benjamin Franklin as a profoundly international corner of a great cosmopolitan metropolis: "Perhaps in few other spots throughout the world are so many races to be found in so small an area. The life in many parts of the Old World is re-enacted here. Were it not for the 'flappers' and the 'cake eaters' of the younger generation, 'Americans' to the core, the illusion would be complete."[1]

East Harlem's shifting mix of ethnic and racial groups provided a rich context and constant challenge for community-centered schooling. "At Benjamin Franklin High School," noted Covello, "we have known for some time that some of the major problems of the school are connected with the need for establishing tolerance and friendly relationships among the differing groups of students in our school."[2] Influenced by both local and nonlocal developments, including community coordinating councils, diverse traditions of social research, and national discussions of social reconstruction and intercultural relations, Covello and his staff attempted to deal institutionally with this challenge through an effort that revealed a complex interplay of goals and underlying tensions in the school's mission—the desire to respect pluralism versus the need for common values, the school's democratic aims versus the reality of ethnic divisions in East Harlem, and the school's curricular goals versus a community studies approach. Despite these tensions Benjamin Franklin's leaders developed an evolving vision of cultural democracy that addressed community problems as educational challenges broadly understood. To clarify and advance this evolving goal, they developed a local research agenda, mobilized and extended a social network of local service agencies and community activists to support the high school, introduced a community-planning mechanism (the CAC), and created programs and structures for formal and informal intercultural education.

Building on lessons derived from local experimentation, the community high school established a mix of intergenerational, cross-group, and cross-institutional approaches to educate East Harlem's diverse groups to accept and work past their cultural differences. In the mid-1930s Franklin students participated in a cocurricular program of intercultural education organized by Rachel Davis DuBois of the Service Bureau for Education in Human Relations, and in various classroom activities involving intercultural themes (though curricular efforts never sought to reformulate the prescribed subject-centered curriculum in a radical way). Activities of the CAC subcommittees, street-unit social clubs, and a web of service agencies provided informal intercultural education to the wider community. Educating parents was an ongoing project—not without accompanying tensions, however, as Covello's cultural pluralist approach to Americanization involved both affirming and challenging immigrant culture.

Unlike Tireman at Nambé and Clapp at Arthurdale, Covello was an indigenous leader. A southern Italian by dint of birth, childhood, and early education, he spent his formative years in Italian Harlem, where the influences of his native region were dominant, and in that profound sense he was "of the people." Yet he was also a member of southern Italy's artisan class, which distinguished him from the *contadino* majority in Italian Harlem, and as an adult he rose into an emergent Italian American professional class, a new American *prominente.* And as we have seen, his "high culture" version of Italian American ethnicity conflicted with the way most of his coethnics constructed their cultural identity.

Covello would later explain that he had no set plan, no clear formula for action, when he began his experiment at Benjamin Franklin.[3] Perhaps this was true, though as Chapter 3 illustrated, prior to his arrival he certainly had developed a number of supporting concepts and personal beliefs that he sought to implement at Benjamin Franklin. Benjamin Franklin offered the opportunity to "test in a living situation . . . the oft discussed idea that it was possible for people of different origins . . . to work together to improve community living."[4] The tensions and opportunities presented by the ethnic mosaic of East Harlem provided an anvil upon which Covello's notions of community schooling would be forged, strengthened at times and weakened at others. This chapter describes the community high school's struggles to develop effective school-community approaches to intercultural relations, and it illuminates the complex construct of community schooling that ultimately evolved.

Forging Cultural Democracy

We have less to fear from frontal attacks than from ambuscades. When we see our foes before us we can arm ourselves and fight back. It is the subtle and hidden thrusts which menace our liberties most, . . . the insidious sowers of anti-social seeds which are planted in the wind and in the air around us; whose stench pervades the atmosphere, stifling our social sensibilities; whose roots penetrate our homes and our schools.
Louis Relin, English teacher, Benjamin Franklin High School[5]

The first issue of the *Social Frontier* appeared one month after Benjamin Franklin High School opened in 1934. The founders of the journal at Teachers College, Columbia University, shared with the founders of the high school a belief "that education would inevitably play a vital role in the social and economic reconstruction that was needed" in the "age of transition" in which the nation found itself.[6] Many Franklin faculty were familiar with the social thought of Harold Rugg, John Dewey, George Counts, Goodwin Watson, and other writers in the social reconstructionist wing of the progressive education movement. A high school staff committee that included Harold Fields, Austin Works, and Walter Wolff invited Rugg to speak on the topic "The Making of a Good Teacher" at a faculty conference in 1936.[7] Covello made *Democracy and Education* required reading in his in-service course for teachers.[8]

George Counts, the chief architect of social-reconstructionist ideology, emphasized the leadership role of teachers in societal change. "To the extent that they are permitted to fashion the curriculum and procedures of the school [teachers] will definitely and positively influence the social attitudes, ideals, and behavior of the coming generation," he asserted.[9] Counts imagined that teachers, unleashed from their bureaucratic chains, would constitute the avant-garde of social democracy, and he charged them to inculcate their vision of a democratic way of life in their pupils. In this fashion, he envisaged, teachers would play a prophetic role, calling the nation to be faithful to its democratic creed.[10] Directly or indirectly, these ideas influenced Covello. "The larger task of the teacher," he wrote, "is the building of a better society . . . the importance of this should draw the teacher into more active service to the community."[11]

Accordingly, Covello and his staff sought to reconstruct East Harlem's civic life through the agency of a public high school, building the processes and even the public spaces where a broad civic spirit could support the finest qualities of a pluralistic democracy. In the 1930s, developing local democracy in East Harlem meant, among other things, negotiating the neighborhood's diverse and at times volatile ethnic and racial mix. Given the shifting ethnic and racial profile of East Harlem during a tense and troubled era, interethnic relations presented a pervasive and daunting challenge to Franklin's efforts at community-centered schooling.

Discussions and controversies concerning ethnicity and race flourished among educators in the 1930s.[12] A survey of educational magazines and journals turned up some 220 articles related to intercultural education published between 1934 and 1944, not including technical scientific works and more narrowly political or economic essays.[13] The survey, conducted under the auspices of the American Council on Education, revealed that many of the articles were published by professional sociologists and centered on "intergroup relations and characteristics and problems of special groups."[14] In general the number of articles increased until 1940, declined in the early war years, and then began to rise again in the last year of the survey. Most essays treated ethnicity and race in fairly general terms for educators; only 9 percent of the articles treated intergroup factors specifically within schools.[15]

Three competing ideologies or conceptual models were in play by the 1930s to explain how immigrants and their descendants came to be absorbed in the U.S. population: Anglo-conformity, the melting pot, and cultural pluralism. These ideologies, as sociologist Milton Gordon explained in his seminal 1961 essay "Assimilation in America," have been used "as explanations of what has happened—descriptive models—and of what should happen—goal models."[16]

Anglo-conformity, with roots in colonial times, has been the most prevalent ideology, reaching a high-water mark in the virulent Americanization campaigns of World War I, yet continuing to draw "numerous and powerful adherents" up to and beyond World War II.[17] Writing in 1915, Horace Kallen, a philosopher at Columbia University, was moved to declare that "the 'Anglo Saxon' . . . constitutes, in virtue of being heir of the oldest *rooted* economic settlement and spiritual tradition of the white man in America, the measure and the standard of Americanism that the newcomer is to attain."[18] As we have seen, Covello's own experience of schooling in turn-of-the-century New York illustrates how conformity to strictly Anglo American cultural values worked insidiously to rive the children of immigrants from the culture of their ancestral homelands.

A second ideology, the melting pot, can be traced to the eighteenth century and the writings of J. Hector St. John Crevecoeur, a French-born agriculturalist and close observer of American life, who declared in *Letters from an American Farmer* that "here individuals of all nations are melted into a new race of men, whose labours and posterity will one day cause great changes in the world." Wending its way into nineteenth-century literary and academic circles, the melting pot drew adherents as diverse as Ralph Waldo Emerson and Frederick Jackson Turner.[19] In 1908 the term achieved the status of a catchword following the appearance of Israel Zwangwill's eulogistic play about the immigrant experience, *The Melting Pot*, whose Russian-Jewish protagonist giddily proclaims:

America is God's crucible, the great Melting Pot where all the races of Europe are melting and re-forming! Here you stand, good folk, think I, when I see them at Ellis Island, here you stand in your fifty groups, with your fifty languages and histories, and your fifty blood hatreds and rivalries. But you won't be long like that, brother, for these are the fires of God you've come to—these are the fires of God. A fig for your feuds and vendettas! Germans and Frenchmen, Irishmen and Englishmen, Jews and Russians—into the Crucible with you all! God is making the American.[20]

The third ideology is cultural pluralism, a term Horace Kallen coined in "Democracy Versus the Melting-Pot," an essay published in the *Nation* in 1915. Kallen became the leading theorist and proponent of cultural pluralism, giving it an idiosyncratic interpretation. Rejecting the melting pot, which he feared was Anglo-conformity in another guise, Kallen asked pointedly: "What do Americans *will* to make of the United States—a unison, singing the old British theme 'America,' the America of the New England School? or a harmony, in which that theme shall be dominant, perhaps, among others, but one among many, not the only one?" He envisaged a democratic commonwealth, whose "form would be that of the federal republic; its substance a democracy of nationalities, cooperating voluntarily and autonomously through common institutions in the enterprise of self-realization through the perfection of men according to their kind." Kallen likened this federation to a symphony: "As in an orchestra every type of instrument has its specific timbre and tonality, founded in its substance and form; as every type has its appropriate theme and melody in the whole symphony, so in society, each ethnic group may be the natural instrument, its temper and culture may be its theme and melody and the harmony and dissonances and discords of them all may make the symphony of civilization."[21]

What Milton Gordon called "draconic Americanization" was softening in the Depression era. Cultural pluralism, although not necessarily Kallen's version, gained a tenuous foothold in both the media and the academy.[22] Louis Adamic, a Slovakian American journalist widely cited by advocates of intercultural education, extolled the achievements of recent immigrant groups through books, speeches, magazines, and pamphlets.[23] Unsurprisingly, social reconstructionists aligned themselves with this position. Responding to "the dangers of racial conflict and forced 'melting pot' assimilation processes," they endorsed cultural pluralism—and intercultural education—in the service of "a welfare state which practices social planning" to overcome "cultural lags."[24] Covello himself was committed to the ideal and strategy of "cultural democracy," a position that differs from Kallen's pluralism. Cultural democracy not only recognizes that ethnic attachments are important as sources of self-esteem, group identification, and social capital, but also subscribes to the principle of a unifying set of national goals and values.[25] Thus, while Covello shared Kallen's views on the importance of ethnic attachments, he was not a cultural pluralist in the separatist sense of Kallen's proposed federation of cultures.[26] Covello's democratic project was to foster tolerance, respect, and mutual adjustment across racial, ethnic, and social class lines; community-centered schooling was to contribute to a strong "civil society" (our term for what he intended) and a rejuvenated "American" nation.[27] When Covello spoke of assimilation, he meant inclusion; he shared Dewey's vision of "genuine assimilation *to one another*—not to Anglo Saxondom."[28]

Of immediate practical use for educators interested in these matters were the descriptions of actual school programs attempting to encourage greater tolerance of ethnic and racial diversity. Before World War II, communitywide educational approaches that promoted cultural democracy could be found on the New York side of the Hudson River in Hastings-on-Hudson, the Lower West Side, Queens, Hempstead, and Yonkers. In New Jersey, efforts were underway in Madison, Jersey City, and Bloomfield.[29] Interested educators were surfeited with information about the programs in Springfield, Massachusetts, for example, where a communitywide effort began in 1939. The Springfield Plan for "living, learning, working and thinking together" was featured in *Newsweek, March of Time, We the People, Woman's Home Companion,* and the *Harvard Educational Review;* presented on RCA television; described in at least two books; and even made into a Warner Brothers' film, *It Happened in Springfield.*[30] What happened, according to one of the plan's directors, was that "education for democratic citizenship" became "accepted as a first objective" and was "on its way to becoming the core of the curriculum."[31] Organized from the elementary grades upward to adult education and public forums, Springfield's "total war against prejudice" sought to counter intolerance by a thorough adoption of "the democratic process of group thinking about the needs of the community and the best ways to meet them."[32] A new wing for a local hospital became a special study of community cooperation for a neighboring grade school. The Labor Relations Forum brought nearly two hundred representatives of labor and management together in discussion once a week.[33] Pittsburgh, along with other school districts, sought to implement programs modeled on Springfield's.[34]

Local Research Guides Local Action

If Benjamin Franklin High School were to address intergroup relations in the complex ethnic mosaic that was East Harlem, it could not simply adopt another community's program. Instead, thorough and continuous research into local conditions would need to be developed.[35] Speaking to the National Education Association in 1938, Covello emphasized the need for schools to know their communities "intimately," especially in heavily immigrant neighborhoods.[36] East Harlem's foreign-born community, a community which understood internal boundaries, included many ethnic elements, many of them scarred from the immigrant experience, stymied by language barriers, and frustrated by past encounters with public schools that did not meet or even attempt to understand their needs. Many southern Italians, raised in a "domus-centered" culture fiercely loyal to kinship groups, profoundly distrusted the authority of public institutions and feared their corrupting influence on the young.[37] Adding to this complexity, the local population constantly shifted, its second generation presented increasingly new challenges, and its economic conditions changed month to month.[38]

Franklin's involvement in local social research and planning reflected the fluid state of social research at the time and the variety of organizing efforts through which activist educators were formally and informally trained. The "plural worlds" of social research and activism afforded a variety of research traditions and organizing efforts to assist community-centered approaches to schooling.[39] Teachers, community activists, and social agency directors often appear to have shared similar vocabulary and notions regarding the "organic" nature of community and the "ecology" of urban problems—reflecting a rich and dynamic milieu that drew from various emerging professions and established practitioners. The tradition of settlement house investigators and survey-wielding community activists, for example, informed early developments in the emerging subfields of educational sociology and rural sociology, areas that had a significant impact on community schooling.[40] Among Franklin staff, several key members were trained in educational sociology. Covello and Italian-language teacher Marie Concistre completed their dissertations in educational sociology at New York University in studies growing out of Thrasher's Boys' Club Study; and science teacher and community coordinator Salvatore Cimilluca wrote his M.A. thesis under that project's auspices. Activist Rita Morgan, speech teacher and community coordinator, completed her dissertation in the same field at Teachers College, where she analyzed the educational effects of industrial arbitration, and the ways schools might better prepare workers for the new industrial democracy.[41] Social studies teacher Layle Lane gained organizing experience from her extensive work with the American Federation of Teachers and her efforts to organize Southern rural schools for blacks. Rachel Davis DuBois, who helped organized Franklin's intercultural program, appears to have been influenced by the work of rural sociologists, especially Mabel Carney of Teachers College, with whom DuBois worked.[42] That Covello listed Elsie Clapp's book *Community Schools in Action* and Lloyd Cook's rural sociology text *Community Backgrounds in Education* as required reading in his in-service teacher-training courses suggests the serious attention he paid to "progressive" rural developments and rural sociology.[43]

As we noted previously, Franklin could not rely on general studies or surveys and expect to be effective in a neighborhood as complex as East Harlem. Most surveys, cautioned Covello, "deal with large areas of space or thought," which meant that "local differentiation peculiar to the small communities are overlooked. . . . Special community problems are omitted in the larger scope of the work. . . . The people of the community are disregarded, to a large extent, in their individual human relationships and in their civic and community importance as factors of progress or retardation and . . . no intimate, friendly, enduring contacts are established within the community by outside research workers whose interest is limited to the particular objectives of a current survey."[44]

In addition to standard census data and municipal reports on East Harlem, local research conducted under New York University's auspices for the Boys' Club Study provided a wealth of relevant information to the early staff of Benjamin Franklin. Some fifty-five researchers produced nearly fifty reports, articles, theses, and dissertations concerning the impact of the Boys' Club in East Harlem, as well as intensive research into the area's youth, families, history, and institutions. Nearly every report provided details useful to understanding the wider life of Franklin's boys. A dissertation study by Irving Sollins, for example, while analyzing the Boys' Club membership, detailed activities and status levels within the local and influential Federal Athletic Club, "no more than a highly organized criminal gang," according to the report. The study described the Athletic Club's efforts at "boring-from-within" to take over the Boys' Club facility.[45] Another investigator, May Case Marsh, explored thirty-three East Harlem churches and synagogues, describing their respective membership, activities, and rituals in more than six hundred pages of elaborate detail. Marsh's notes on religious services included dress, ethnicity, gender, and generational breakdown, complete with explanations of where second-generation youth of various ethnic groups preferred to marry and why.[46] The extensive social base maps completed for the Boys' Club study yielded a treasure trove of social geographic detail, ranging from which ethnic groups dominated what blocks to which areas contained what recreational facilities and dangerous lures for youth.[47]

The Educational Bureau of Casa Italiana, where Covello directed some fifty researchers in 1932, produced a number of studies of some general use to Franklin's community work.[48] One of the "pioneering" efforts in Italian American studies, the bureau produced reports on Italian contributions to the United States, health conditions of Italian New Yorkers, language usage in Italian families, and Italian occupational trends, along with pertinent demographic data. The research added specific details to the many general impressions of New York Italian life and thus aided Franklin staff in their work with a heavily Italian community. Unfortunately, this research assistance did not survive World War II. Money soon ran out for the bureau when the WPA ended, and though the bureau and its research briefly became the Italian-American Educational Bureau on East 108th Street, and then the East Harlem Educational and Research Bureau on East 116th Street, its fifty-four transfer files of work ultimately found their way into a Sanitation Department drive for old paper by 1945.[49]

While the data gathered through these investigations provided important information to Covello and his staff, they were not "sufficient to meet the actual needs of the school in its effort to create a school-community program."[50] Convinced that "the school is too vital a force to permit a lag in its knowledge of the neighborhood," Covello and others, with the support of the Mayor's Committee on City Planning, launched a community survey of East Harlem soon after Benjamin Franklin opened, seeking both "thoroughness" and "informality" in their effort at "getting acquainted" with the community they wished to serve.[51] At the top of the list of research concerns was the pattern of ethnic distribution throughout East Harlem.[52] With the critical support of volunteers, city planning staff, and WPA workers, detailed demographic data were gathered through block-to-block studies, house-to-house surveys, interviews with community elders and prominent residents, and reports by participant observers.[53]

Benjamin Franklin students contributed to these local research efforts. Students supplied and helped compile information on parents' citizenship status, health problems, and housing conditions and were consulted as essential sources for understanding youth perspectives in community affairs. For a study of student leisure-time activities in 1936, for example, 620 diaries chronicling a week of free time were analyzed to determine how Franklin might help meet the recreational needs of youth in East Harlem. The research found that students spent more time at the movies than at all the recreational centers combined, that local agencies could hardly compete with movies in influence, and that "systematic explorations of the submerged influences not definitely recognized as of educational importance" needed to be carried out and applied by the school.[54] In the special English class for boys who showed leadership potential, students performed fieldwork as a part of their analysis of local problems, especially those "difficulties presented in the adjustment of racial differences and animosities."[55] As another example, Franklin students assisted Covello in constructing a large wall map of the streets of East Harlem; they marked each East Harlem student on the map according to his place of residence. One dot represented each student, with different colors designating ethnicity and different dot designs indicating generation. At a glance Franklin staff could see the ethnic group variability and distribution of these students across East Harlem's blocks.[56]

Although student involvement in community research was subordinate to the role of adults, it represented, nevertheless, a valuable contribution and gave Franklin youths, at least on occasion, direct experience in cooperative social problem solving. Franklin star senior Albert Hemsing proclaimed in an NBC radio speech in 1937: "We are educated for a democracy only insofar as we have learned to work in cooperation with others," and on the school-community committees, "there is always student participation."[57] Student Donald Merit, president of the Club Crusaders, gathered some one thousand signatures for a petition urging racial equality in the armed forces. Student Frankie Tartaro, after surveying housing conditions firsthand, was "surprised there were not more delinquent young people." Robert Alleyne concluded from his housing survey research that "delinquency knows no race or color, it is present wherever conditions encourage it—poverty, bad housing, poor opportunities for work or play, broken or unhappy homes."[58]

The school's local research program allowed Franklin staff and students to begin to understand the richness and idiosyncrasies of the community they strived to serve, and it began to facilitate the school's efforts to improve intercultural relations among its students and within East Harlem.[59] With so much research activity taking place in the neighborhood, Covello felt it necessary to caution researchers against haughtiness or insensitivity. Distinguishing the school's work from other research approaches, Covello emphasized that the school "must attain a certain degree of sociological data with scientific accuracy without making the community feel that it is merely a 'social laboratory' for the school and its faculty. It must preserve the warmth and courtesy that mark all true social contacts between neighbors and friends."[60]

Local Networks

Benjamin Franklin's various research efforts were linked to the school's wider relationship with the community and to local social action in a number of formal and informal ways. Among those linkages were the longstanding ties among East Harlem community activists and progressive organizations. Covello, for example, had worked at the Jefferson Park Methodist Church, Haarlem House, Casa del Popolo, and the short-lived East Harlem YMCA long before the Benjamin Franklin era. The fledgling high school soon joined the East Harlem Council of Social Agencies, which held its annual meeting at Franklin in 1935 and enlisted Covello as its vice president for a time. Franklin faculty served on committees of the East Harlem Council, as well as the Yorkville Civic Council, broadening their knowledge of the local community and developing personal contacts valuable to the school's community functions. But Franklin staff, and particularly Covello, did not want to leave the school's relationship to the community solely to such informal, though often quite effective, ties. Thus, for the school visibly to assume leadership in developing the democratic community life of East Harlem, and to put together a coordinated approach to meeting local needs, Covello sought a more formal mechanism. The school could not hope to face the challenges posed by interethnic tensions, for example, if it did not have the organizational infrastructure through which to both gather research and coordinate action.[61]

During the summer of 1935, following Franklin's first year, Covello, assistant principal Abraham Kroll and social science chair Harold Fields sketched the outlines of such an infrastructure, the Community Advisory Council (CAC)—a central mediating body through which local needs could be presented, and where research and programs to meet those needs would be coordinated. The CAC was seen as central to carrying out the fundamental mission of the school, namely "to develop a sense of practical and personal citizenship among the boys . . . through the co-operation of civic and welfare organizations."[62] The council allowed the school "to touch and build up citizenship through precept and aid rather than through instruction."[63] Fields took the lead in gaining the support and participation of the East Harlem Council of Social Agencies.[64] Local agencies were to be represented on the Community Advisory Council's committees and would provide direct assistance to the school under CAC auspices. The school would open its facilities to the agencies and provide the framework for a communitywide coordination of educational efforts, not unlike community-coordinating council structures that were emerging across the country.[65]

Initially the CAC comprised five major committees, designated as the Health, Citizenship, Parent Education, Correction and Guidance, and Racial committees. The CAC grew to twenty-two faculty-chaired committees of teachers, students, and community members by 1937—an unwieldy, inefficient arrangement that necessitated a consolidation and reduction of committees in subsequent years.[66] The various CAC committees formed essential bridges between the high school and local service agencies, facilitating the coordination of in-school activities with communitywide efforts. The council's role as a mediating structure is illustrated by its coordination of activity around the problem of juvenile delinquency.

The sensitive area of juvenile delinquency, so often linked to interethnic tensions, posed a particular challenge to Franklin and tested the school's ability to work cooperatively with the service agencies. Since Franklin and the local Juvenile Aid Bureau shared a concern about juvenile delinquency in East Harlem, for example, they decided to cooperate under the CAC's auspices in investigating the problem, classifying offenses, and gathering third-party research.[67] A set of 748 cases reported to the bureau were plotted on an area wall map according to residence and nationality, allowing the school to trace the relationship between ethnicity and delinquency, as well as to anticipate and address likely trouble spots in East Harlem. The school's reclassification of delinquency found that only 2 percent of the cases qualified as "real delinquency" (one stage beyond "malicious mischief"), and that "delinquency" was a relative term. Covello noted what many already suspected, namely, an apparent link between ethnicity and chance of arrest: "An Irish boy in an Irish community has less chance of being dragged into court than an Italian boy in an Italian community."[68] The school then channeled its findings into the committee system headed by the CAC, through the Juvenile Aid and Big Brother Committee, Guidance Committee, and Social Welfare Committee. Concluding that "the street is the true generator of anti-social behavior," the CAC redirected the in-school guidance programs as well as their various community outreach efforts in light of the study's findings.[69]

The Challenge of Diversity

Benjamin Franklin had to face the challenge of cultural diversity from the out-set. Franklin's students reflected the diversity of the district. At least thirty-four ethnic groups were represented among the students who first entered the high school in 1934.[70] In 1930 the total area east of First Avenue between 99th and 104th streets and east of Third Avenue between 104th and 109th streets was 84 percent Italian; and the area within that boundary up to 119th street was 79 percent Italian. Across Third Avenue, the Italian numbers dropped to between 12 and 21 percent of the population. Puerto Ricans were prevalent in the blocks above 108th Street between Lexington and Fifth avenues, while the blocks along Fifth Avenue below 104th Street remained predominately Jewish.[71] The notorious "Chinese Wall" of the Park Avenue Viaduct was East Harlem's most conspicuous social border, the neighboring blocks on both sides delineating a zone of confrontation between Italian and Puerto Rican youth gangs. Just south of 103rd Street along Third Avenue, the summit of a steep hill marked a social border separating pockets of Irish and German settlement from the Italian neighborhoods. To the north, the elevation of Mount Morris Park served a similar purpose, dividing East and West Harlem.

As we noted in Chapter 2, within Italian Harlem itself regional differences often dictated immigrant settlement patterns—although extreme regional con-sciousness (*campanilissmo*) had diminished by the 1930s. For example, Italians from Bari settled on 112th Street, the Sarnesi on 107th Street, immigrants from Piscento, in northern Italy, on 106th Street, and the Calabrians on 109th and 111th streets.[72] Status distinctions were also prevalent; the professional class (mainly doctors, lawyers, and brokers) tended to reside in the brownstone blocks along 116th Street, "a sort of main street," while poorer Italians lived in tene-ments to the south, closer to the borders of other ethnic groups.[73]

The high school students reflected the diversity and divisions of East Harlem and the neighborhoods south of the district in Yorkville. As of the spring of 1936, 1,680 students, approximately two-thirds of Benjamin Franklin's total daily registration, resided east of Fifth Avenue between 59th and East 142nd streets. Table 5.1 specifies the ethnic and racial composition of the scat-tered-site high school for the East Harlem–Yorkville student census. Roughly half the students were of Italian working-class background, some 14 percent were Jewish, and the rest largely were Irish, German, and Slavic; only about 2 percent were "Negro" and 4 percent "Latin American & Spanish."[74]

TABLE 5.1   1936 EAST HARLEM–YORKVILLE STUDENT ETHNICITY BY
BRANCH OF BFHS

	ANNEX	MAIN BUILDING	ANNEX		
	117TH	108TH	79TH	TOTAL	% OF TOTAL
	%117TH	%108TH	%79TH		
Italian	335	365	155	855	**50.89**
	88.16	**53.91**	**24.88**		
Jewish	11	99	121	231	**13.75**
	2.89	**14.62**	**19.42**		
Irish	7	36	106	149	**8.87**
	1.84	**5.32**	**17.01**		
Slav/	5	52	67	124	**7.38**
Hungarian	**1.32**	**7.68**	**10.75**		
German	3	30	49	82	**4.88**
	0.79	**4.43**	**7.87**		
L. American/	7	26	26	59	**3.51**
Spanish	**1.84**	**3.84**	**4.17**		
Negro	5	15	17	37	**2.20**
	1.32	**2.22**	**2.73**		
Others	7	54	82	143	**8.51**
	1.84	**7.98**	**13.16**		
Total	380	677	623	1,680	**100.00**
	100.00	**100.00**	**100.00**		

Differences among the school's three sites—a main building at East 108th
Street and two annexes, one at 117th Street and one at 79th Street—illustrated
the ethnic settlement patterns of East Harlem and Yorkville (see Table 5.1).
While the 79th and 108th street sites were of similar size, the 79th Street
Annex, located thirty blocks south in Yorkville, enrolled three times the percentage of Irish students in the census, nearly twice the number of German
boys, and less than half the number of Italians. By contrast, nearly 90 percent
of the East Harlem–Yorkville census at the 117th Street Annex, less than ten
blocks north of the main building and in the heart of Italian Harlem, came from
Italian backgrounds; of all the Italians in the census, only 18 percent attended
at the 79th Street Annex. Of the Jewish students less than 5 percent attended
at the 117th Street Annex. The high school reported a total of 2,551 students
on the daily register for March 1936. Italian students comprised 42.5 percent
of the register, Jews 22.5 percent, and "Others" 35 percent.[75] In March 1936,
East Harlem claimed 44 percent of BFHS students; in September 1941, 61.6
percent; in May 1942, 60 percent.[76]
    In the 1930s East Harlem, the focal point of community-centered school-
ing, was changing in two fundamental ways—the total population was declining as the ethnic mix shifted, and in the process East Harlem's internal frontiers were changing. While New York City's total population had risen to nearly
seven million in 1930, Manhattan, including East Harlem, had dropped below

FIGURE 5.1

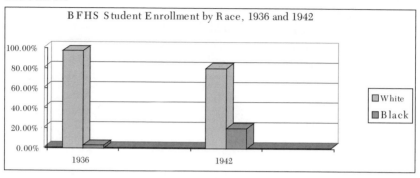

two million residents for the first time since 1900, largely owing to movement to the outer boroughs.[77] From 1930 to 1940 East Harlem's population shrank by 10.6 percent, continuing a decline from the 1920s. Seventy-five percent of the census tract areas lost population in the Depression era, with approximately 77 percent of the decline occurring east of Third Avenue in blocks that were overwhelmingly Italian—a net loss of more than 15,700 residents. The five census tracts that comprised Italian Harlem (170, 188, 180, 178, 162) lost, on average, 14.7 percent of their population. Census tract 170, which included Franklin's main building on East 108th Street, lost more than three thousand residents, nearly 19 percent of its population. By contrast, all census tract increases in population over this period occurred west of Third Avenue, though that half of the district experienced a net decline as well.[78]

One of the great difficulties confronting Covello and his staff as they targeted community needs was East Harlem's shifting racial and ethnic composition in the 1930s—the target was moving. The white population in the core health areas dropped by about 30,000 residents in ten years, a decline of 19 percent, whereas the black population rose by more than 7,700 residents, an increase of 30 percent.[79] In the northwestern corner of East Harlem, contiguous with West (by the 1930s called Central) Harlem, blacks increased from 31.9 percent of the population in 1930 to 47.5 percent by 1940. In Health Area 20, the East Harlem blocks between Fifth and Third avenues from 112th to 119th Street, the black enclave grew from 27.4 percent of the population in 1930 to 44.7 percent in 1940. Across Fifth Avenue, in Health Areas 24, 19, and 15 (Central Harlem between 110th and 126th streets), blacks constituted 84.8, 92.6, and 93.8 percent of the population, respectively—from 1930 to 1940 a leap from 41 to 90 percent of the total population in these blocks.[80] Over a six-year period, 1936–42, Franklin's racial mix began to reflect the size of the increasing black population in East Harlem (see Figure 5.1).

Racial and ethnic tensions in East Harlem worried Franklin's staff. Young males often came into conflict along contested borders. Italian and Puerto

Rican youth gangs in particular clashed along the border carved by the Park Avenue Viaduct. Covello put the matter this way:

> The "Chinese Wall" is a term applied to the solid wall of Masonry built around Park Avenue to support the railroad tracks over which all trains pass into Grand Central. Built of heavy blocks of gray granite with arched openings at street intersections, this wall is a community landmark that has had a recognizable influence as a dividing boundary line in the community. In the area between this wall and Central Park, particularly in the neighborhood of East 110th Street occur many of the tensions characteristic of the unadjusted community groups in their inter-actions with each other. It is one of the "Social frontiers" along which take place the clashes that are a part of the impenetration [sic] of an older established community by a newer and a different type of people.[81]

Robert Orsi suggests that this in-group/out-group hostility contributed to the "ethnic self-constitution" of Harlem Italians as Italian Americans. As we have seen, the annual festa of the Madonna of 115th Street provided a shared public space for worship and celebration and helped build that identity. Casting Puerto Ricans as "the other" also played a part in this process. According to Orsi, the route of the Madonna's procession symbolically delineated the boundaries of "Italian Harlem"; on the days of the festa, no Puerto Rican, even those living in the neighborhoods traversed by the celebrants, dared to cross the Madonna's path. "This sense of exclusion was so forceful that Puerto Ricans came to hate the celebration." Harlem Italians of the parental generation "scapegoated" the migrants in the sense that they blamed Puerto Ricans for their children's leaving East Harlem, thereby violating the sacred norms and values of la famiglia and the domus—when, in fact, the younger generation was following the path of upward mobility to the Bronx and other areas.[82]

Occasionally the tensions along borders erupted in open conflict, as in the fall of 1938, when a series of clashes occurred between Italian and Puerto Rican youths. In one of the "riots" more than a hundred Italians and Puerto Ricans skirmished on 107th Street between Park and Madison, tossing garbage and stones from windows, heaving chimney bricks from rooftops, and battling with fisticuffs in the streets until police squads arrived to break up the melee. The Bronx Home News reported: "Since the start of the fighting, Park Ave. has been the recognized boundary line." The city sent extra police to East Harlem, and seven days of street fighting ended with a total of thirty-five arrests. No Franklin students were arrested in these incidents.[83]

Covello and his associates in the Harlem Legislative Conference (HLC) took remedial action to head off further rioting and to blunt media criticisms of East Harlem.[84] On 26 October the HLC held a mass meeting at Odd

Fellows Hall at 106th Street and Park Avenue, attended by hundreds of East
Harlemites.

> Those in the assembly were of both Italian and Spanish origin. The
> Italian societies and the Spanish and Puerto Rican societies were
> represented by able men who spoke on the need for understanding and
> friendliness between the two groups. Even our High School students
> spoke at this meeting. At the end the assembly, as a whole, voted to
> request the mayor to withdraw extra policemen from the community
> and pledged themselves to handle the situation in a manner that would
> demonstrate the friendliness of the two groups to each other. Out of
> that meeting came a better understanding between the two groups. It
> was an excellent illustration of the democratic process functioning in
> the interest of unity through the will of the people at large.[85]

Ethnic tensions in East Harlem reflected broader trends in intergroup relations
in the United States and abroad. The foreign conflicts endemic in the 1930s rip-
pled into East Harlem. "The Ethiopian War had raised the question of tensions
between Negro and Italian," Covello recounted, "and the persecution of Jews
by Hitler raised questions of tensions between Germans and Jews, particularly
in Yorkville. The Christian Front [a virulently anti-Semitic group] was active in
the lower Bronx and in Yorkville. . . . Our boys lived in this atmosphere."[86] In
the fall of 1938, in the aftermath of Kristall Nacht and the nationwide burning
and looting of Jewish stores in Germany, the board of education mandated
assemblies in all city schools to stress "tolerance and freedom for all men."[87]

Even when not the proximate cause of violent outbursts, international events
were often conflated with domestic conflicts, adding a dangerous patina to
diverse neighborhoods like East Harlem. For example, on the afternoon of 19
March 1935, after rumors had circulated in Harlem that a young black man suspected of shoplifting had been beaten by white employees of the Kress Five-
and Ten-Cent Store on 125th Street, rioting broke out in Harlem and continued into the early morning hours. Nearly one thousand police patrolled the
streets; some one hundred blacks and whites were shot, beaten, or clubbed.
Pleading with Governor Herbert Lehman for military protection, panicked store-
owners whitewashed their store windows with hastily contrived signs, for example, "This shop is run by COLORED people" or "This store employs Negro workers." Adam Clayton Powell, Jr., assistant pastor at Abyssinian Church, attributed
the outbursts primarily to the dearth of employment opportunities for African
Americans in Harlem stores, but he also noted that the Scottsboro Boys case and
the Abyssinian trouble were contributing factors. As a result, claimed Powell,
blacks initially embroiled for other reasons in the riot recalled the "Italian affront
to Abyssinia" and then proceeded to wreck every Italian grog shop they could
find in Harlem.[88] Later that same year, on 3 October, some 1,200 police were

placed on special duty in Harlem and Brooklyn "following the outbreak of trouble between Italian-Americans and Negroes in Harlem and Brooklyn . . . as a result of the Italo-Ethiopian hostilities."[89] African Americans picketed the King Julius General Market occupied by Italian meat and vegetable shops at 118th Street and Lenox Avenue; scuffles outside the market brought in the police. Across the street from the local police station in Harlem, a man stayed after the crowds had dispersed and slowly waved the red, orange, and green flag of Ethiopia.[90] As a Franklin faculty committee reported some years later: "The Italo-Ethiopian conflict appeared to exercise an appreciable effect upon the attitudes of Negroes and Italians toward one another, and the racial theorists of fascist countries, abetted by their friends here, most probably have had some effect upon the attitudes toward the Jewish group."[91]

It is important to note that the Italian fascists' rise to power had a divisive effect on Italian Americans. During a particularly bitter battle within the Order Sons of Italy during the 1920s, Congressman La Guardia and state senator Salvatore Cotillo led the New York State branch to break with the national organization and to establish the anti-Fascist American Sons of Italy Grand Lodge. Luigi Antonini, president of Local 89, the Italian Press and Waist Makers Union of the ILGWU, spoke out strongly against fascism in weekly radio talks.[92] Fascism, however, had a strong following in Italian Harlem. *Il Progresso*, the city's major Italian-language newspaper, was pro-Fascist and supported Mussolini during the Italo-Ethiopian crisis—a position that was probably approved by most East Harlem Italians.[93] After Vito Marcantonio, Covello's close ally, denounced fascism at a Madison Square Garden rally in August 1935, fascist supporters burned Haile Selassie in effigy on Marcantonio's lawn in East Harlem.[94]

Marcantonio was publicly anti-Fascist until he lost the 1936 congressional election (*Il Progresso* supported his opponent) and took a pragmatic view of the matter. "After his defeat in 1936 until Italy's capitulation in 1943," Gerald Meyer writes, "he rarely publicly attacked Mussolini or Italian Fascism. Rather, he dissembled."[95] Similarly, Covello acted pragmatically in a potentially volatile situation by not taking a public stand against Mussolini or by directly challenging pro-Fascist sentiments in his own Italian department. He chose, rather, to work behind the scenes against Fascism.[96]

From 1937 to 1940, Girolamo Valenti, editor of *La Parola*, an anti-Fascist Italian-language newspaper in New York, led a three-year campaign to ban *Andiamo in Italia* (Let's go, Italy), a high school textbook "replete with Fascist propaganda."[97] At issue was chapter 7, "L'Avvento Dello Stato Corporativo," which proclaimed that "the results [of Fascism] obtained in every field of civil progress are absolutely impressive."[98] Covello became involved in the controversy when the assistant superintendent of the high school division asked him to review the contested material and to render a judgment on the textbook.[99] In addition to advising "a more faithful translation in several spots," Covello tersely responded that the "laudations" of Fascism should be removed.[100]

TABLE 5.2   PUPILS AT BENJAMIN FRANKLIN HIGH SCHOOL BY
NATIONALITY (1,846 STUDENTS), MAY 1940

COUNTRY	# OF STUDENTS	% OF TOTAL STUDENTS
Algiers	2	0.1
Austria	45	2.4
Canada	6	0.3
Central America	9	0.5
Canary Islands	2	0.1
China	4	0.2
Czechoslovakia	19	1.0
Denmark	2	0.1
England	19	1.0
Estonia	4	0.2
Finland	6	0.3
France	2	0.1
Germany	58	3.1
Greece	17	0.9
Hungary	41	2.2
India	2	0.1
Ireland	86	4.6
Irish Free State	15	0.8
Italy	750	41
Lithuania	4	0.2
Mexico	2	0.1
Netherlands	4	0.2
Panama	2	0.1
Poland	43	2.3
Portugal	2	0.1
Puerto Rico	9	0.4
Romania	4	0.2
Russia	73	3.9
Scotland	2	0.1
South America	15	0.8
Spain	24	1.3
Sweden	2	0.1
Turkey	4	0.2
U.S. (White)	333	18.0
U.S. ("Negro")	117	6.3
Virgin Islands	2	0.1
West Indies	115	6.2

Experimenting with Intercultural Education

Table 5.2, a snapshot of Benjamin Franklin in the spring of 1940, illustrates
the ethnic composition of the student body in the late Depression era.[101] Con-
stituting some 41 percent of the students, the Italians, virtually all from East

Harlem, were far and away the dominant group. Their proportion was growing in the latter part of the decade, a time of declining enrollments in the total school population. In 1936 the East Harlem Italian registration was 772, or 30 percent; six years later, with more than 500 fewer students at the high school, the Italian figure was 782 (45 percent). African American representation grew steadily from the mid-1930s, from 74 (2.9 percent) in 1936 to 117 (6.3 percent) in 1940, to 350 (20 percent) in 1942. Jewish representation declined from 574 (22.5 percent) in 1936 to "a few in 1942." In 1940, the first year a disaggregated figure appears for the high school, only nine Puerto Ricans (0.4 percent), a disproportionately low number, were enrolled.[102]

Ethnicity and race were powder-keg issues at the East Harlem high school. From the start, the Racial Committee (also called the Committee for Racial Cooperation) was one of the most active in the school-community committee system coordinated by Franklin's CAC. This committee investigated how the school might play a role in resolving ethnic and racial tensions in East Harlem, starting first with the students. Addressing interethnic and interracial relations required an investigation into both the attitudes of the students and the possible remedies these attitudes suggested. In particular, Franklin staff felt a need to determine:

1. The age at which intercultural reactions begin to occur and the causes by which unfavorable reactions are set up on a purely racial basis.
2. Particular attitudes by which the reactions of the high school student are conditioned, and suitable types of education programs whereby young people, on the eve of mature participation in community and national life, may be prepared to assume civic and social responsibilities in a manner that will contribute to intercultural harmony and civic and social development, among individuals and in the community.
3. The method by which the community can be drawn into full participation in the movement for intercultural harmony and cooperation, with the school itself as a center through which both school and community can function effectively.[103]

The challenge of improving intercultural relations, then, could provide "practical experience in working out the problems of democratic living in a democratic manner."[104]

In an initial effort to understand how intergroup relations at Franklin and in East Harlem might be improved through community schooling, Covello invited the Service Bureau for Education in Human Relations, whose executive secretary was Rachel Davis DuBois, to carry out an experimental program in intercultural education in the spring of 1935.[105] Covello had met DuBois at a conference sponsored by the YWCA's International Institute in Philadelphia, at which they shared the same platform and addressed the question "The Melting Pot—Yes or No?"[106] At the invitation of Mabel Carney of Teachers College, Columbia University, Covello joined the founding board of the Service Bureau, and thus began a lifelong friendship with DuBois.[107]

A Quaker of Welsh ancestry, a longstanding pacifist, and a "gadfly for interracial understanding," Rachel DuBois had worked out various methods for intercultural education over the course of a decade before the Service Bureau's efforts at Benjamin Franklin. As a social studies teacher at Woodbury High School in southern New Jersey, she had developed an assembly-program approach for improving intergroup relations—one that appealed to students' emotions by combining "song, dance, drama and oratory." She refined her methods as a doctoral student at Teachers College, Columbia University. For her dissertation, DuBois applied her program to four thousand students in nine suburban Philadelphia schools in 1931–32. She used an attitude test developed at Teachers College and an experimental research design to measure the effectiveness of her approach. Her findings demonstrated the superiority of the assembly program over a series of pamphlets conveying the same information, and the latter's superiority over doing nothing; she obtained the best results, however, from a combination of assembly programs and written materials. As the Great Depression deepened, DuBois, allied with Louis Adamac, turned to the problem of ethnic and racial alienation.[108]

With critical assistance from several Columbia University faculty and the financial support of the American Jewish Committee, the Service Bureau was founded in early 1934, its purpose to design curricular materials, operate an educational clearinghouse, and provide guidance to educators and community leaders. Housed in an apartment around the corner from Teachers College, the Service Bureau quickly began work in fifteen schools in the metropolitan New York area, aided by Civil Works Administration workers assigned to the bureau through Columbia University. The only New York City high school involved was Benjamin Franklin, which became one of the Service Bureau's seven "demonstration centers" during the 1934–35 school year.[109]

The Service Bureau's program at Benjamin Franklin allowed the school to begin to gather information on student attitudes about ethnicity, and to start experimenting with methods of addressing these attitudes. Covello knew that he needed to "grow into" any program that would confront such a difficult area as ethnic tensions, and the Service Bureau's track record provided credibility and a measured start.[110] After a preliminary meeting in February 1935, the bureau staff and select Franklin faculty decided to focus on four ethnic groups—Italian, Latin American (especially Mexican and Puerto Rican), Slavic (especially Polish and Czech), and Japanese, the last added because by choosing a group so far removed from East Harlem, "it would not seem as though any particular group was being singled out in the school."[111] Working with about five hundred of the older students, the Service Bureau pretested the students with an attitude and knowledge questionnaire designed by William Hinckley of Columbia University. A control group of about a hundred students was also tested.[112]

The Service Bureau then developed and implemented a program based on coordinating intellectual, emotional, and situational approaches to intercultural education.[113] The intellectual approach included meeting with teachers, advising them on discussion methods for homerooms, and providing special materials about each ethnic group that might be incidentally woven into class work. Assembly programs on each ethnicity included an emotional appeal and featured such activities as jujitsu exhibitions, Puerto Rican dances, and folk songs by Dvorák. Finally, the situational approach involved two students from each homeroom meeting with the invited guests in Covello's office after the assembly. After a series of miscellaneous follow-up programs, posttesting revealed significant increases in students' factual knowledge of the four ethnic groups and an improvement in the attitudes represented by their responses.[114] Pleased by the overall results for both students and faculty, Covello ecstatically wrote that the school "had broken out in a difficult and vital area—fears had been allayed and difficulties overcome." He had seen the data and was now convinced that "the job could be done—if we willed it strongly enough."[115]

Applying Lessons: Entering the "Sphere of Intimacy"

Franklin's brief experiment with intercultural education helped convince Covello and many of his staff to move forward in several new directions to improve intergroup relations in East Harlem. They came to believe that interethnic tolerance had to suffuse all the school's efforts and affect all sectors of the community. The value of indirect efforts to change attitudes was now clear to them. Efforts designed to combine the goals of intercultural education with the broader school-community aim of East Harlem's democratic development had the best chance of success. A report of the Committee for Racial Cooperation several years later explained this lesson: "The program must not be overstressed [a criticism which might, with some truth, have been leveled against the Franklin experiment]. A subtle approach is necessary. Ours is a fight more difficult than an open battle. We must not conquer and subdue those with undesirable intercultural attitudes; we must rather persuade and win them over as ardent converts to the idea of intercultural democracy."[116]

In terms of DuBois' framework, the experiment encouraged a combined emotional-situational approach using events and activities aimed at the community's democratic development. Neighborhood folk festivals sponsored by

the school provided social events while also promoting the celebration of ethnic heritages. Community bulletins in English, Italian, and Spanish discussed
local news while emphasizing every group's membership in the community. By
sponsoring naturalization drives through multilingual mailings and evening citizenship classes, Benjamin Franklin established closer relations with various
community ethnic organizations. Working to bring the first public housing to
East Harlem, the high school placed itself at the center of myriad community
groups, transcending ethnic boundaries in pursuit of a goal held in common
(for details see Chapter 6).

Emblematic of Franklin's approach to intercultural education, and indicative of the staff's commitment to intensive local research, was the series of
"street units" established after 1936. It was not enough for the staff to know
about the cultural or social backgrounds of students, Covello claimed. The
school must also understand "the individual child in his social relationships outside of school . . . and must play an active and aggressive part in the affairs of
the community."[117] The street units—clubs and bureaus housed in area storefronts and managed in part by community representatives—helped Franklin
comprehend those relationships, embed itself further within East Harlem life,
and enter in yet another way the community's "sphere of intimacy."[118]

Housed in converted storefronts, these novel off-site social and educational centers extended the school's presence closer to the corner hangout and
illustrated the linkage between local research and social action that the entire
school-committee system sought to facilitate. The Association of Parents,
Teachers, and Friends encouraged the opening of the first such unit, the
Friends and Neighbors Club, in 1937. Overcoming language obstacles and
cultural restraints against women participating in activities outside the home,
Franklin staff organized a relatively small but active association. The group soon
developed the club idea: "a little family club . . . where the older people, the
children, and the young people of the neighborhood can meet and plan various kinds of activities."[119] The high school and community residents renovated
an adjacent store in exchange for the first year's rent. Located at 315 East 108th
Street, next door to Franklin's main building, the club was generally open for
student and faculty use during the day. The club held an open house every Sunday evening. "Anyone passing by may enter, read a magazine, play the piano,
listen to the radio or even dance an old-fashioned jig. Tea and cake are served
by volunteer teachers or mothers of the neighborhood," reported the *New
York Times*. During the week, children attended daily story hours, and teenagers
learned classical music or played in a fife-and-drum corps.[120] Local boys' clubs,
as long as they maintained order and a democratic procedure, could use the
facilities. Every Monday, the Housing Committee met at the club to plan its
next move in securing the East River Drive Low Rent Housing Project (later
called East River Houses; see Chapter 7). All money for light, rent, and other
necessities came entirely from donations.[121]

In addition to serving as a local social and organizational center that would bring different neighborhood groups together and offer youth a recreational alternative to East Harlem street life, the street unit served the CAC's need for local research concerning intergroup relations. Once Benjamin Franklin became an active part of the community and entered its "sphere of intimacy," it had to constantly engage in social experimentation and consistently test the effects of different approaches. The street units allowed that experimentation to take place off school grounds. When the Friends and Neighbors Club experimented with community gardening, not only did the club seek to understand the finer agricultural points of collective urban gardening, but "the work was at the same time an exploration of specific attitudes and behaviour of the people." Although the garden failed, the project provided new knowledge to the school about its varied constituency, part of an intentional drive by the school to constantly push its understanding of this diverse community further. "Begun for the purpose to gather information, the work was in the nature of research; the garden project itself was an experimental program."[122]

The street units also allowed the school to play an active role in the community, coordinating on relatively neutral ground the educational forces affecting interethnic relations. While not physically a part of a public school building many residents might see as alien, the street units were also not private local facilities in which some faculty might feel uncomfortable and that might fail to convey the clubs' nonprivate status. In the storefront clubs, an undefined common "turf" was created, part of the school enterprise but not actually the school, a social club in a neighborhood fond of such institutions.[123]

In this spirit, on 17 February 1939, some seventy representatives from all of East Harlem's ethnic groups met at the Friends and Neighbors Club for a program sponsored by the school-community Committee for Racial Cooperation. Welcoming everyone to the club, Covello indicated that the club's very existence showed the promise of interethnic cooperation. Recalling the street conflict of the previous October, Covello urged local leaders that "our great task is to find some means of removing intolerance." He warned that the United States could not afford to fail as Europe had in maintaining "tolerance and comradeship in community and national life."[124] Lee Lombard of the Franklin faculty presented the program of the Committee for Racial Cooperation, followed by Austin Works's description of the work in intercultural education featured in the special Franklin course for leadership training. A general discussion ensued in an effort to develop a "practical program for interracial understanding and cooperation in East Harlem."[125]

At least five street units were organized in the early years of Benjamin Franklin High School—Friends and Neighbors Club, Italo-American Educational Bureau, Hispano-American Educational Bureau, Community Friendship Club (or Old Friendship Club), and Association of Parents, Teachers, and Friends. Each club provided a vehicle for the intellectual, emotional, and situational approaches of intercultural education. While the specific goals of the five clubs differed, as did their success in reaching these goals, each helped Franklin reach out into East Harlem, gather "intimate" data, experiment with novel approaches, offer a forum for local residents, and plan a coordinated program for improving East Harlem's intergroup relations.

Curriculum Provides a Tool

Another lesson learned from Franklin's 1935 experiment with the Service Bureau, and from the school's early years in East Harlem, was the need to revise systematically its formal curriculum in light of the aims of intercultural education.[126] Some progressive schools had transformed the organization of their studies in dramatic ways, following the Dalton (Massachusetts) Plan of Helen Parkhurst and E. D. Jackman, the Denver (Colorado) project of Jesse Newlon and A. L. Threlkeld, and the Winnetka (Illinois) Plan of Carleton Washburne, among other innovations. By the 1930s, notes educational historian Herbert Kliebard, "change had definitely permeated the curriculum atmosphere." Bellwether high schools, especially some of the "unshackled" high schools participating in the Progressive Education Association's Eight-Year Study, organized their curricula around core themes ("the problems and issues of modern life," the twelfth-grade program at one Denver high school) or correlated studies.[127] Following this trend, for example, teachers in California's Santa Barbara County developed a problem-solving curriculum around a set of common social activities and competencies; grade ten, for instance, revolved around the theme of "learning to live in a changing world through investigating problems arising from a shift from an agrarian way of life to a highly industrialized way of life."[128]

For Covello, furthering the aims of intercultural education did not imply any such radical reconstruction of the traditional curriculum, but rather its adaptation to the aims of community schooling. "There was no attempt to change completely the traditional curriculum," recalled Covello. "After all Franklin was an integral part of the New York City public school system as well as the N.Y. State Dept. of Education."[129] Franklin's formal curriculum framework was consistent with the standard for "cosmopolitan" (comprehensive) high schools in the city—and, in terms of school ethos and course enrollments, the day school was not highly distinguishable from an academic high school.

Nevertheless, Franklin staff showed considerable effort and innovation in suturing intercultural themes into the curriculum. Perhaps the most ambitious effort took place during the 1938–39 school year. This was later referred to as the Second Intercultural Experiment, modeled in part on the earlier effort led by the Service Bureau for Intercultural Education. The school-community Committee for Racial Cooperation led the schoolwide initiative.[130] The committee—composed of Franklin faculty, student representatives, and a variety of community representatives—decided first to carry out an experimental program at the 117th Street Annex, taking advantage of its smaller size, before considering whether or not to expand it to the main building on 108th Street as well as the other annex on 79th Street.[131] Faculty at the 117th Street location, with the assistance of a National Youth Administration researcher, carried out pre- and posttesting of freshman and sophomore student attitudes, using selected students from the main building as a control group.[132] Implementing the three-pronged factual-emotional-situational approach advocated by the Service Bureau, faculty modified their courses in English, civics, biology, art, Italian, and French and then coordinated these changes with several assembly programs, radio programs, and films.[133] During the fall of 1938, the racial committee decided to extend the intercultural curriculum revision work to all subjects and all grades. By June 1939 "almost every department was participating in the intercultural program according to planned teaching units."[134] The faculty report that chronicled and analyzed the 1938–39 curriculum work ran to several hundred pages and included intercultural syllabi from fine arts, Italian, French, mathematics, science, social studies, and English. While all the curricula noted the contributions of diverse peoples and sought to broaden student appreciation for different ethnic and racial groups, the social studies and English curricula embodied more than the others an activist approach to intercultural education, one oriented more explicitly toward social change.[135]

The outbreak of street clashes between Puerto Rican and Italian youth took place in the midst of this experiment, in October 1938. Although no students from Benjamin Franklin were among those arrested, Franklin students apparently took part—they bore the evidence of evenings in the streets the mornings following the clashes. English teacher Louis Relin, who recalled his own injuries from the Jewish-Irish battles during his youth in East Harlem, noted the daily "quota of lacerations and bruises," as well as his own hesitation as to how to deal with the interethnic violence in the midst of a curriculum experiment on racial tolerance. "In that hectic week," Relin noted, "a number of lads came to school with bandaged heads, black eyes and other battle scars which they displayed with the proper pride of valiant warriors." Nervous as to how the street battles might affect a curriculum through which he was "still feeling [his] way along in the dark," Relin cautiously proceeded: "At first, while feelings were at fever pitch, I sought to evade a head-on collision with the problem in the classroom, but the boys pressed for discussion. Hoping our classroom might serve as an outlet for some of their emotion, I did at length consent to this discussion, with the understanding that we try to meet the situation as mature, thinking people—not as 'bull-headed kids.' I must hand it to the boys. They displayed a remarkable restraint and self-control which, I wish, could have been present in the electric atmosphere of their streets."[136]

That Puerto Rican students stayed away from school that week may also have helped calm Relin's classroom. In any case, consistent with the goals of its curricular efforts, the Committee for Racial Cooperation worked with other community groups in organizing and cosponsoring the mass meeting at Odd Fellows Temple that helped calm neighborhood tensions that fall of 1938.

For the rest of Franklin's first decade, curricular reform efforts are less evident; the record is simply incomplete, if suggestive. Faculty coordinated a series of intercultural assemblies in 1939–40, though whether these were a part of board of education–mandated "tolerance" assemblies is unclear.[137] The English Department appears to have adopted a continual curriculum revision process. An English Revision Committee was organized in 1939, though a revised English syllabus did not appear until 1945 and was first used in the 1945–46 school year.[138] The outcome of a joint curriculum reconstruction effort between Teachers College and Franklin, discussed in 1942, remains unclear, though "enough freedom [very likely] existed at present for very considerable innovations to take place."[139] The strain of World War II, the turnover of some key Franklin faculty, and the challenge of continuing to refine a newly revised curriculum may have led to less dramatic curricular efforts during the early and mid-1940s.

To whatever degree their curriculum innovations succeeded, Franklin faculty viewed curriculum as a component of a broader community-schooling effort to promote intercultural harmony.[140] To that end, they felt that an intercultural curriculum had to respond to the demands of the era—at the time, the rise of antidemocratic forces, continuing widespread economic insecurity, and negative racial stereotyping in propaganda. The local context demanded close attention to the challenges of a heavily immigrant and migrant population. Given this large foreign element, the Franklin faculty sought to accomplish locally what the country needed to do nationally and in a more balanced manner, namely, "to interpret to newcomers the ideals upon which the country was founded, . . . to use most effectively the cultural contributions of the racial and national groups represented here, . . . and to develop harmonious and fruitful relations among all elements in the population."[141]

In terms of curriculum, these needs translated into a set of operating guidelines evident at least in the best of Franklin's efforts. A student-focused pedagogy should train young leaders through their participation in community problem solving. Across the curriculum and beyond it, the school must trumpet the community's development and impress the community that the school plays an integral role in that development. The "project method" should be used to stimulate community action; the school-community committee system provided the means for informing students and faculty of projects authentically needed by the community. To aid in studying the community's needs, students should be trained as "participant observers"; they could often reveal aspects of community life that no external or adult observer would likely capture. Following these guidelines, the curriculum could then begin to fulfill its role in helping to cultivate the dispositions of the students toward community service. In Covello's view it was the task of Franklin's curriculum "to find ways and means of educating our boys in understanding and in concerning themselves about improving community life—developing their responsibility to help in solving community problems. We realized that actual accomplishments would be slight—but I was interested in the process, in the changes that would take place in the students' thinking and attitudes."[142]

Franklin faculty devised various curricular strategies to engage their students' interest in intercultural affairs. Some, such as fine-arts teacher Bernard Saxon, preferred to maintain an indirect approach, incorporating art from diverse origins but never focusing on racial or ethnic tolerance as a topic. Others like English teachers Louis Relin and Austin Works developed special units and curricula on racial and ethnic tolerance. English teacher William Hayett, for example, held "town hall meetings" one period a week as an exercise in oral English; students came prepared with "elementary research" to debate such topics as "Should Negro ball-players be allowed in the Big Leagues?" or "Changes that Should be Made in the Curriculum."[143] As a part of his research class in social studies, Morris Cohen invited a school counselor from all–African American P.S. 184 in Harlem to discuss the effects of school and job discrimination on the education of young blacks.[144] Teacher Maurice Bleifeld, later to succeed Covello as principal, developed a biology unit treating intercultural and racial relations; the *American Biology Teacher* featured the curriculum unit, which included analysis of "current conceptions of race supremacy."[145] The English Department incorporated one immigrant student's autobiographical essay into the department's curriculum, a course of study that was noted in the *English Journal*.[146] Some English classes collected oral history and constructed scrapbooks of essays, photos, and memorabilia. One class of students read John Galsworthy's play *Justice,* and they studied delinquency and recreation problems in the neighborhood, reporting their findings on the city's public radio station, WNYC.[147] Other students presented their research on the need for social facilities at a local public housing complex to the New York City Housing Authority. During World War II, a student drama group took to the streets of East Harlem to raise local morale.[148]

Of course, outcomes among students could be expected to vary. For example, hoping to engage students in creative solutions to interracial tensions, one English teacher assigned essays on the question "How I think discrimination can be stopped." One student's response, a straightforward answer the teacher might welcome, also revealed an immediate and personal motive for eliminating discrimination, one the assignment itself created: "Discrimination can be stopped only if every race participates in helping. . . . I feel that there are too many race conscious things in the United States to stop and think that the fellow opposite him has flesh covering his bones too. If people were to stop and use common sense, there would be no need for me to be writing this composition."[149]

Though Franklin faculty and staff drew curriculum ideas from the varied and vibrant discussions concerning intercultural education in the 1930s,

the early role of the Service Bureau for Intercultural Education had an especially prominent influence on the school's approach. DuBois, who guided the
bureau's initial work at Franklin, also helped out in the Fall 1938 experiment
while she was working briefly with the Progressive Education Association.[150]
One of DuBois' strong allies, if an uneasy one at times, was the National Conference of Christians and Jews (NCCJ). Dr. Everett Ross Clinchy, chair of
NCCJ in the early 1930s, had long lent DuBois critical support in her work,
as he strongly believed that "cultural pluralism [was] an essential characteristic of genuine democracy."[151] Franklin faculty invited Clinchy to speak at a
school conference open to all Yorkville and Harlem teachers and to the special English class, "especially as a preparation and an inspiration for [the Fall
1938] program in interracial relations."[152] One of the school assemblies at the
117th Street Annex that fall embraced the "trialogue" approach to intergroup
harmony that Clinchy had helped pioneer at NCCJ; Rabbi Neuman, Reverend Del Campo, and Father Osterman discussed tolerance and pluralism,
as did so many "tolerance trios" sponsored by NCCJ in the mid-1930s. A letter that Covello wrote about interethnic relations to the Franklin faculty in
the fall of 1938 included a summary of Dr. Carlton Hayes's radio remarks
regarding the NCCJ; Hayes, a Columbia University historian, was the first
Catholic cochair of the NCCJ.[153] Covello's work with the bureau included collaboration with Bruno Lasker, who headed a committee that looked into producing manuals on intercultural education for teachers. Author of the influential *Race Attitudes in Children*, Lasker at the time had recently assumed
responsibility for the preparation and distribution of the Service Bureau's
publications.[154]

The 1940 Children's Crusade for Children recognized Benjamin Franklin
High School's "integrated program on intercultural education" in its list of
"what some schools are doing" to promote interethnic understanding.[155] Paul
Robeson described his participation in a Negro History Week assembly as "one
of the most inspiring afternoons of my career."[156] Franklin faculty were invited
to share their work with other teachers through conferences, in-service workshops, and publications. Yet Benjamin Franklin's curricular efforts in intercultural education never sought to reformulate the prescribed course of studies
in any radical way. Nor is it clear that many teachers at Franklin would have
welcomed a significant reorganization of the curriculum. When the board of
education suggested to Franklin teachers in 1942 that they could gain wide lat-
itude from official regulations, the kind of leeway the Lincoln School of Teachers College enjoyed, Franklin faculty representatives were lukewarm. Wild
enthusiasm was certainly lacking for the additional work that would be
required, as was confidence that many faculty would welcome the effort.[157]

On the other hand, a substantial core of faculty and students did not flinch
in the face of volatile and at times violent issues of intercultural relations in
East Harlem, not a small accomplishment. They faced seemingly intractable

local tensions, creatively carried out research into sensitive local issues, adapted the curriculum in imaginative and inspiring ways, and built the premises and structures for sustained community-centered schooling. Above all, they struggled to stay the course of a school-coordinated community-development effort, despite a community that was often profoundly uneasy with itself.

Educating the Other Teachers of
Benjamin Franklin Students

As Covello and his staff struggled to implement intercultural education via committees, street units, and curriculum, they recognized that they were not the only, or even perhaps the most significant, teachers of their charges; formal schooling was only one of many competing educational influences in East Harlem. Clearly many of their students' attitudes and behaviors toward members of different ethnic groups reflected the views of their parents and adult neighbors, for good and for ill. If the teachers hoped to foster tolerance among their students, here was an educational force that had to be marshaled toward the amelioration of intercultural conflict. "We feel that we can do something in the school situation," declared Covello. "We also feel that the home, too far removed, is often the point where prejudice starts. Therefore it seems what we must do is to see to it that the school is opened to the people in the community where they and the teachers can work together on common problems."[158] "This means," Covello told the *New York Times*, "that we as educators must extend our program in intercultural education beyond the walls of the classroom and the school."[159]

Extend they did. Information about school programs went out to parents in English, Italian, Spanish, and German. WPA workers of various ethnicities visited the homes of students from the same background.[160] Adult summer-school staff wrote articles about their program in English, Italian, Russian, Hungarian, Spanish, and German and sent them off to foreign-language newspapers. A movie trailer plugged Franklin's adult summer school in the local cinema.[161] Students and staff regularly placed posters around East Harlem, spoke to area groups and schools, sent mailings to local residents, and visited local establishments—all to promote awareness of adult program activities. S. Alexander Shear, a leader in adult education in New York City, established Benjamin Franklin's Institute for Adult Education, a program that offered area residents fifteen-week courses in subjects from art appreciation to typewriting.[162] WPA staff ran a series of adult education clubs as yet another extension program for adult residents; within a few years, adult community members sang, danced, wrote, acted, and celebrated in their native languages under the aegis of nearly a dozen active clubs.[163] Ranging in age from seventeen to eighty, neighbors met neighbors in a variety of courses, clubs, and social events, extending Franklin's message of intercultural cooperation to the broader East Harlem community.[164]

Though the classes and clubs brought many adults to Franklin and convinced many others that the school seriously wanted to serve the community, Covello, WPA adult-school director Mary Winter, social studies chair Harold Fields, and others felt it was not sufficient to help build bridges among adults of different backgrounds. Interethnic tensions and youth delinquency reflected the lack of control many adults, especially recent immigrants, exercised over their children. As described earlier, many observers saw the maladjustment of adult immigrants to be a major cause of juvenile delinquency and youth gangs, which only fanned interethnic tensions. If Franklin wanted to counter those tensions, it would have to help parents control their children, and that meant bridging the generational and cultural divide between adults and youth.

Parents and their children both needed first to appreciate the strengths of the two worlds they now inhabited: the old country of parental memory and the new country to which these families had somehow to adapt. Immigrant parents were often bewildered or alienated by the individualist-materialist culture they encountered in the United States; their children often felt caught between Scylla and Charybdis. The old-country culture, redolent with the smell of familiar foods and rekindled in tales told and retold, had the pull of parental affection. But the children did not look backward. Their American world was exciting, varied, and immediately known—the brash clamor of the Third Avenue El was a beckoning call. For them the old world was often a remote and backward place accessible only through the memories of their parents and perhaps a framed photograph on a small table in a tenement dwelling.[165]

As we have seen, Covello grew up with this turbulent tension. From his own life and from his experience with Italian youths at DeWitt Clinton, Covello had concluded that schools could play a critical role in bridging the cultural gap between adult immigrants and their children, even though they often contributed to the problem. "It is pathetic," Covello told the Progressive Education Association in 1934, "to see how sometimes the school itself creates in the child the disrespect which later breaks up the immigrant home."[166] He was convinced that the school's effectiveness depended upon both affirming the parental culture and easing the immigrant family's assimilation into the U.S. mainstream.

Benjamin Franklin affirmed immigrant culture by insisting on multilingual presentations and materials, by frequently enlisting the foreign-language press and associations, by offering adult courses on immigrant languages and cultures, and by treating parents as resources in their children's education. As an example of this last type of affirmation, social studies teacher Harold Fields counted some of his department's homework assignments as part of an effort to improve family relations. Students, for example, were asked to find out what their parents had known about Abraham Lincoln and George Washington before arriving in this country—more than 1,500 reports were submitted. Russian boys heard parents speak of references to Lincoln in letters to Russia from emigrants in the United States. Irish students heard praise for Washington as a freedom fighter against the British. A German grandmother recalled having read the special edition of a Berlin newspaper reporting Lincoln's assassination. A Hungarian mother's doctor had proudly hung portraits in his office of Washington, Lincoln, and Lajos Kossuth. Southern Italian parents recalled streets and squares named after Lincoln. Fields claimed that the students' discovery engendered a new respect for their parents; "an assignment in history became the common denominator for a reciprocal lesson for parent and child." The assignment also stimulated linkages with other community efforts at Franklin; one student asked: "Where can my parents learn English? They ought to be able to tell others what they told me in Italian."[167]

As they sought to bolster parental pride and authority, Franklin's staff also highlighted the second generation's mastery of the dominant U.S. culture and of English, tapping this strength to help assimilate and even to naturalize their parents through the school's citizenship program. Students helped translate for their parents, spoke to local elementary and junior high school assemblies, made class presentations on the positive and negative reasons for citizenship, and assisted parents with naturalization processes and papers.[168] The children of adult evening-class students were invited to attend the graduation exercises held for their parents.[169] In such nonthreatening ways Franklin staff tried to locate the school's programs within the context of family relations.

The high school's role as a coordinating institution for solving local problems created a critically important venue for informal adult education. The CAC was a cross-generational, cross-sector, collaborative leadership training ground; in this sense, adult education went far beyond the adult classes offered by the high school. The CAC provided a structure and process for East Harlem adults to "approach [real problems] from the point of view of the community as a whole," and "instead of confining themselves to discussion of these problems, . . . to reach decisions as to what is to be done and then carry out their decisions through cooperative action."[170] This mechanism enabled the conjoint activity of East Harlem residents of diverse backgrounds and reference-group identifications; it is beside the point whether, as one proponent claimed, the process created a "fellowship."[171]

ON THE EVE OF THE SECOND WORLD WAR, Covello and his staff had in place a set of school and community programs, activities, and structural supports that promoted tolerance, respect, and mutual adjustment among East Harlem's diverse social groups. Their incipient project of cultural democracy included school-based research activities to study East Harlem's social conditions and their effects on youth development, supportive networks of progressive organizations and social agencies in East Harlem whose work was integrated with the community school, a formal intercultural education program for students and related school assemblies that targeted problems of diversity at Benjamin Franklin, adult-education classes and related clubs, informal intercultural education conveyed through street-unit social clubs, and CAC committee work and sponsored activities. These programs and activities proceeded in the face of persistent challenges posed by a shifting demographic base in East Harlem, the district's history of volatile ethnic and race relations, and the intergenerational stresses of immigrant assimilation.

In the next chapter, we turn to Benjamin Franklin's East Harlem campaigns, community mobilization efforts that sought to unify the area's diverse groups to solve mutually shared problems. Directed toward East Harlem's democratic development and civic/political empowerment, these campaigns were organized to build participatory citizenship skills, to strengthen East Harlem's social and political capital, and to advance the pluralist vision of "assimilating *one to another.*"

CHAPTER SIX

The East Harlem Campaigns

B Y THE LATE 1930S, Covello had great hopes that the prospect of dramatic improvements in the quality of life in East Harlem would stimulate interethnic cooperation, at least to the extent that the various groups would rally to these goals, show respect and courtesy to each other, draw on each group's unique capacities, and work to solve problems of compelling interest to all the groups. Contemporary democratic theorists call such conjoint activity "public work," which is work that harnesses the cooperative efforts of diverse categories and groups of people, ones that are often in conflict, to accomplish shared civic and political goals.[1] In East Harlem public work was a strategy to coalesce the agendas of subordinate groups around shared goals, to build a unified base, and to create power vis-à-vis entrenched dominant interests. Covello and his allies recognized that for East Harlem to press effectively its claims for housing reform, health care, education, and economic development on the state and city, diverse ethnic and racial groups would have to speak as one voice on those issues.[2]

Four broadly based East Harlem campaigns, examples of public work, were organized, in whole or part, under Benjamin Franklin's auspices in the late 1930s. Activities related to these campaigns infused both the community program and the regular curriculum, providing a hopeful glimmer of cultural democracy in action on the eve of World War II. More than any other aspect of the community high school, public work made Benjamin Franklin more than just a slum high school that happened to offer a diversity of services to its clientele.

top, Another reason not to be in school.
(Leonard Covello Photographs (PG 107), Balch Institute Collections, Historical Society of Pennsylvania.)

middle, East Harlem tenement scene.
(Leonard Covello Photographs (PG 107), Balch Institute Collections, Historical Society of Pennsylvania.)

Covello, *left*, in an East Harlem store.
(Leonard Covello Photographs (PG 107), Balch Institute Collections, Historical Society of Pennsylvania.)

DeWitt Clinton High School, a "cathedral of culture," at Fifty-ninth Street and Tenth Avenue, 1920, where Covello created the Department of Italian. *(NYC Municipal Archives.)*

The "Chinese Wall," Park Avenue in East Harlem, May 1948, which Covello called a "dividing boundary line" in the community. *(Photo by Arnold Eagle; Museum of the City of New York.)*

P.S. 172 in 1933, a former elementary school, later an annex of De Witt Clinton High School, at 309 East 108th St., which served as the main building of Benjamin Franklin High School from Fall 1934 to Winter 1942; tenement storefronts were located on both sides of the five-story building. *(NYC Municipal Archives.)*

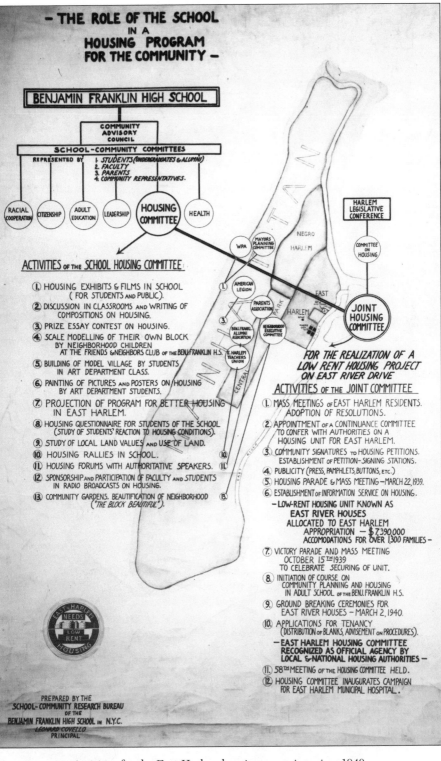

Activities for the East Harlem housing campaign, circa 1940.

(Leonard Covello Photographs (PG 107), Balch Institute Collections, Historical Society of Pennsylvania.)

Covello addresses a meeting of the Association of Parents,
Teachers, and Friends at the main building on East 108th Street.
(Leonard Covello Photographs (PG 107), Balch Institute Collections, Historical Society of Pennsylvania.)

Groundbreaking ceremony for the new BFHS, 17 April 1940; Covello, second from left;
Christina Claxton, a descendant of Benjamin Franklin, center;
Mayor La Guardia with shovel; Superintendent Harold Campbell, far right.
(Leonard Covello Photographs (PG 107), Balch Institute Collections, Historical Society of Pennsylvania.)

Cornerstone-laying ceremony for the new BFHS, 23 May 1941.
(Leonard Covello Photographs (PG 107), Balch Institute Collections, Historical Society of Pennsylvania.)

The boys of BFHS.
(Photo by Podell & Podell, New York City; Balch Institute Collections, Historical Society of Pennsylvania.)

Covello, left, and Mayor La Guardia, third from left, onstage at BFHS, 1942.
(Leonard Covello Photographs (PG 107), Balch Institute Collections, Historical Society of Pennsylvania.)

A "new school in a new community": The main entrance to
Benjamin Franklin High School at Pleasant Avenue and 115th Street.
(Leonard Covello Photographs (PG 107), Balch Institute Collections, Historical Society of Pennsylvania.)

Graduation Day at the new Benjamin Franklin High School.
(*Leonard Covello Photographs (PG 107), Balch Institute Collections, Historical Society of Pennsylvania.*)

The Carmine Luongo Playlot, circa 1950.
(*Leonard Covello Photographs (PG 107), Balch Institute Collections, Historical Society of Pennsylvania.*)

The Church of Our Lady of Mount Carmel, a centralizing force in Italian Harlem and the subject of Robert Orsi's luminous book *The Madonna of 115th Street.*
(Leonard Covello Photographs (PG 107), Balch Institute Collections, Historical Society of Pennsylvania.)

A street parade for the East Harlem sanitation campaign, 1948.
(Leonard Covello Photographs (PG 107), Balch Institute Collections, Historical Society of Pennsylvania.)

Frank Sinatra addresses Franklin students following the incident of racial violence in October 1945.
(*Photo by Edward Ozern; Balch Institute Collections, Historical Society of Pennsylvania.*)

Anna Ruddy, founder of the Home Garden and Covello's early mentor.
(*Leonard Covello Photographs (PG 107), Balch Institute Collections, Historical Society of Pennsylvania.*)

Covello and the students of Club Borinquen.
(*Leonard Covello Photographs (PG 107), Balch Institute Collections, Historical Society of Pennsylvania.*)

Covello and the plaque in his honor,
Covello Hall, BFHS.
(Leonard Covello Photographs (PG 107), Balch Institute Collections, Historical Society of Pennsylvania.)

Covello in military uniform, circa World War I.
(Leonard Covello Photographs (PG 107), Balch Institute Collections, Historical Society of Pennsylvania.)

Covello with students at the Friends and
Neighbors Club, circa 1939.
(Leonard Covello Photographs (PG 107), Balch Institute Collections, Historical Society of Pennsylvania.)

Congressman Vito Marcantonio speaks on 105th Street in East Harlem, 1943.
(Photo by John Albok; Museum of the City of New York.)

East River Houses, 1941, First Avenue, East River Drive, 102nd to 105th Street;
"1170 apartments, 2–to 6–rooms, renting from $3.85 to $7.30 per week."
(New York Housing Authority; Museum of the City of New York.)

East River Houses Campaign and
Vito Marcantonio

The most dramatic achievement of the Community Advisory Council (CAC), indeed perhaps of Benjamin Franklin High School as a community-centered school, was the East Harlem housing campaign, a collaborative effort with the Harlem Legislative Conference, which obtained the East River Houses, the district's first low-income housing project. The housing campaign richly exemplified the aims of the CAC, and Covello proudly showcased it as the quintessence of his community school program. More than any other community project, the housing campaign was linked to the high school curriculum, albeit not as an integrative strategy for curriculum reorganization, but rather as a set of curriculum activities appropriate to a number of discrete subject areas.

In 1934 adequate, decent, affordable housing was in sort supply in New York City. In January the Roosevelt administration announced that the city would be eligible for $25 million in Public Works Administration (PWA) funds, contingent on the creation of a municipal public housing authority. In February, following the passage of state enabling legislation, the New York City Housing Authority (NYCHA) was founded to build, own, and operate public housing.[3] Between 1934 and 1941, operating in an appallingly sluggish housing market, NYCHA built 23 percent of the total 55,465 new housing units constructed in New York City; that is to say, in relative if not absolute terms, public housing made a significant contribution. It is important to note, especially in light of trends in urban development after the Second World War, that at the outset "public housing was not . . . low-quality housing for lower-class people, but middle-class housing for working people."[4]

The Wagner-Steagall Bill (or U.S. Housing Act) of 1937 made support of public housing a permanent federal responsibility and created the U.S. Authority (USHA) to supervise federal programs administered by state and local authorities. In 1938 the congressional allocation for public housing expenditures was $800 million. USHA disbursements financed 545,594 low-rental apartments in the United States between 1937 and 1957; 33,355 units were built with federal dollars by NYCHA (in combination with state and city housing programs, a total of 87,743 units were administered by NYCHA in this twenty-year period).[5]

The first public housing in upper Manhattan was Harlem River Houses, a PWA-NYCHA project whose announcement was precipitated by the Harlem riot of 19–20 March 1935. Built on a vacant site at 151st Street between McCombs Place and Seventh Avenue (property formerly owned by the John D. Rockefeller family), Harlem River Houses was a successful venture from the standpoint of architecture and social planning. The buildings were attractive four- and five-story red-brick walk-ups whose grounds included recreational and community spaces—small playgrounds, a wading pool, a nursery school, a health clinic, social rooms, rooms for occupational use, and laundries; also, the city maintained a riverfront park and amphitheater adjacent to the project. Harlem River opened in September 1937. Applications, some fifteen thousand of them, for the 574 units were subjected to a careful scrutiny that excluded the unemployed and poorest workers, as well as unrelated occupants.[6] On the downside, consistent with Interior Department secretary Harold Ickes's commitment to maintain neighborhood racial preferences in the PWA housing program, Harlem River was racially segregated, for blacks only.[7]

At the inception of NYCHA it was unclear whether public housing projects would be built on vacant sites on the periphery of the city or on slum-clearance sites in the central city. The Regional Planning Association of America (RPAA), whose membership included, among other luminaries, Lewis Mumford, Catherine Bauer, and Clarence Stein, advocated the former strategy, arguing for low-rise, low-density development conducive to the building of "community." Powerful real estate interests championed the latter strategy, purporting that slum clearance would shore up real estate values (conversely the realtors feared a devaluing of slum property if the RPAA strategy were adopted). In the end slum clearance and a central city strategy claimed the higher priority at NYCHA, and the USHA acquiesced in that decision.[8]

Government loans and grants for public housing were a coveted resource, highly selective and subject to the whims of powerful political forces. Of the $800 million appropriated by Congress under the U.S. Housing Act of 1937, $80 million went to New York State, of which $53 million was allocated to New York City. That amount was exasperatingly small given the city's need for $2.9 billion for an adequate housing program. A proviso in the U.S. Housing Act that limited any state to a maximum of one-tenth of the total appropriation meant, in effect, that "the city's housing need was too great to be significantly remedied."[9] In the case of East Harlem, ensuring a piece of the federal housing pie would require an unprecedented level of community organizing and political mobilization. Covello and his staff recognized that community-centered schooling could be a powerful catalyst in this effort.

In the mid-1930s, old-law tenements continued to dominate East Harlem's housing market. According to a report of the New York Tenement House Department, between 1918 and 1929 developers constructed only 110 new-law buildings between 86th and 130th streets east of Lennox Avenue—an area that included, yet encompassed far more territory than, East Harlem.[10] In 1934, of a total of 4,044 old-law structures in East Harlem, more than half (2,043) were listed in poor condition; even more alarming, 35 percent of the 844 new-law tenements, structures no more than thirty years old, also had a poor rating. Apparently the most dilapidated housing was in the blocks east of Third Avenue: Italian Harlem.[11]

At this time East Harlem had a high vacancy rate (21.5 percent) tethered to high population density, a seeming paradox attributable to multiple factors, including families' doubling up to make ends meet or to avert unlivable tenement conditions. Comprising only 6.6 percent of Manhattan's total area, East Harlem contained over 10 percent of the island's total population and had a population density more than 50 percent higher than the borough average; in fact, over 90 percent of the district's population was squeezed into about 60 percent of its blocks, and almost one of every six blocks in East Harlem was devoid of any residential population.[12]

Covello observed these conditions firsthand, and he participated in the research that brought them to public light.[13] High-quality public housing was a deeply felt personal issue. As a youth Covello had watched his chronically depressed mother pine away amid the dark squalor of an Italian Harlem tenement. And he always sensed that the death of his first wife, Mary Accurso, was somehow related to tenement life. Though Mary died of a form of nephritis (as Covello learned long after the event), the prescribed treatment for her malady suggested a misdiagnosis of tuberculosis, "the scourge of the tenements at the time," for she was whisked off to the Catskills for fresh air, sunlight, and milk.[14]

The chance of obtaining federal money for an East Harlem public housing project sparked a vigorous awareness and advocacy campaign for low-income housing that radiated from the high school outward to the community. Covello, the lead agent in this campaign, believed that East Harlem residents, as part of their own civic empowerment, should share the responsibilities of securing high-quality housing, lest these projects become a form of government paternalism and contribute to the further debasement of poor immigrant groups; as he saw it, public housing rightly construed was a technical, civic, and, above all, educational enterprise—or tersely put, "an instrument of assimilation."[15] Covello also believed that the involvement of East Harlem residents in every phase of the campaign would instill a sense of ownership and acceptance of public housing.

The first step was to call the community's attention to the problem of squalid, congested, and dilapidated housing in East Harlem, a problem that the occupants of such housing were not fully aware of. For example, student responses on a 1937 Franklin housing survey showed that the students were far less concerned about the type or quality of their housing than about the low social prestige associated with an East Harlem address. Moreover, East Harlem tenement conditions, for all their misery, were a notch above what the parents of foreign-born students had experienced in the old country; hence parents were unlikely to complain and might even be expected to resist a radically "foreign" innovation. For example, Covello noted that "congestion—several families living in one apartment, or a family of eight members living in two and a half rooms—is to them not a housing evil, but a very prudent and thrifty arrangement. They are bewildered, for instance, by the regulations in low rent housing units, limiting the number of people who occupy the apartment."[16]

As early as 1935 Covello and his teachers targeted housing as a community issue worthy of their students' attention. In October 1935 the Lennox Hill Neighborhood Association helped the high school prepare a "metropolitan housing exhibit," an array of models, graphs, drawings, and photographs depicting good and bad housing conditions. In the fall of 1937 another housing exhibit, supplemented by motion pictures and community lectures, was displayed at the high school; concomitantly, as part of the mobilization campaign, Franklin teachers integrated housing concepts on an ad hoc basis into the curriculum, a process Covello described in his report on the housing campaign.[17]

> In our school departments, primarily those of social science, languages, English and art, the usual curricular contents were as far as possible oriented toward the housing problem. The English department, for example, sponsored the writing of essays on housing in the form of a prize contest under the title, "What East Harlem Needs." The department of social sciences devoted some lessons in the history, civics and economics classes to the problems of housing, such as property taxes and rentals, questions of sanitation, relationships between poor housing, illness, crime, etc. The art department invited the students to make models of their own showing what they would like to see in better housing and better use of space. This department also produced posters in large quantities to publicize the idea in the school and in the community. The language department did the translations in Italian and Spanish, in order to reach our non-English speaking people. The result of all this was to heighten the interest of our boys and to increase the consciousness of the situation in the community.[18]

As students carried the message for low-rent housing back to their homes and neighborhoods, Franklin's housing committee joined forces with the housing committee of the Harlem Legislative Conference (HLC) to form the East Harlem Housing Committee. This would be the agent to "stimulate, direct, inform" the people of East Harlem.[19] The history of the HLC, 1937–43, an organization that played a key role in the success of the housing campaign, warrants an explication here, as does the congressional career of Vito Marcantonio, with whom the HLC and housing campaign were inextricably linked.

Briefly viewed, between 1935 and 1951, Marcantonio served seven terms in the U.S. Congress, six of them consecutively. He was a politician who "knew East Harlem house by house and floor by floor. He knew New York politics in the whole and in particular, clique by clique and deal by deal."[20] A "people's politician," Marcantonio's signal approach was to meet individually with constituents on a first-come, first-served basis at one of his political clubhouses. One journalist likened the clubhouse scene on the occasion of a visit by Marcantonio to "a busy day in the clinic of a great city hospital. Marcantonio and three or four secretaries sit at desks on a platform in the front of the main hall. Before them on wooden camp chairs are about a hundred constituents, many of them cradling infants in their arms." Each of them received a personal hearing and action on his or her case.[21] Marcantonio's fluency in Italian, achieved under Covello's tutelage, proved to be an enormous political asset in East Harlem. As Marcantonio biographer Gerald Meyer observes: "The devotion of his Italo-American constituency could only have been strengthened by his ability to deliver speeches in Italian and, for example, to refer to his inept Democratic opponent in 1948, Jim Morrisey, as a *testa di cappuccio* ('cabbage head')."[22]

Marcantonio took full advantage of an anomaly in New York State's election laws that allowed a candidate to run on more than one party ticket simultaneously—in two elections he campaigned on three party tickets. Until 1944, he remained, nominally at least, a Republican although his allegiance was to the American Labor Party (ALP). In 1944, the year Marcantonio became undisputed leader of the state ALP, the Republican-controlled state legislature gerrymandered his East Harlem district, the Eighteenth Congressional District, into a new district, the Twentieth, which included both East Harlem and Yorkville, a neighborhood of German and Irish constituents. As Alan Schaffer notes, Marcantonio consistently took a "radical," that is an antiwar, prolabor, pro–civil rights, and after 1945, anti–Cold War, stand on national and international issues, occasionally voting as the lone dissenter in Congress. He was finally ousted from political office when he ran unsuccessfully for mayor of New York City in 1949 on the ALP ticket only. His untimely death from a heart attack in 1954, at the age of fifty-one, came just as he was about to campaign as an independent to recapture his old congressional seat.[23]

Founded in 1937, with Marcantonio as its first and only chair, the Harlem Legislative Conference was dedicated "to bettering the conditions of the community of Harlem through progressive legislation and better administration, both in the New York State Legislature and in the Congress of the United States." An avowedly "nonpartisan" umbrella organization (its affiliation with left-wing organizations notwithstanding), the HLC represented 165 organizations in Central and East Harlem, with 565 delegates.[24] As Meyer suggests, the HLC had close ties to New York City's Communist Party, primarily through the conference's executive secretary, Emmett M. May, a black Harlem Communist; Vito Marcantonio, while not a Communist Party member, was in political agreement with the Communists, who supported his congressional campaigns with labor and money, and had a foothold in the American Labor Party, which was a bastion of Marcantonio support in East Harlem.[25] Covello himself chaired the East Harlem Housing Committee in 1941 and worked for the conference in various other capacities; while he undoubtedly voted for Marcantonio and probably for the ALP ticket, he was not visibly involved in political campaigning.[26]

The East Harlem Housing Committee held more than seventy meetings between 1938 and 1941. The upshot of its planning was a vigorous campaign that included petitions, mass meetings, parades, and even housing buttons.[27] The committee advertised a Housing Parade as follows:

HORROR AND DEATH STRIKE TWICE IN A WEEK!

FOUR CHILDREN, FOUR VICTIMS, FOUR DEATHS

Yes—the people of East Harlem were again witness to a tragedy, a tragedy which this time took as its victims five innocent children peacefully at sleep, but suddenly awakened by the noise of roaring flames, which led to their destruction and death. This tragedy happened on East 112th Street—who knows when or where the next one will occur? The East Harlem Housing Committee of the Harlem Legislative Conference is fighting for a low-rent housing project. You can win this fight by—coming to the Monster Housing Parade. Mobilize at Benjamin Franklin High School.[28]

The *Building Trades Union Press* reported that two thousand East Harlemites, including five building trades locals, participated in the parade, which was held on 25 March 1939 and led by Leonard Covello along a two-mile route from Franklin to 110th Street and Fifth Avenue.[29] A year earlier, Covello had addressed "a Monster Mass Meeting to fight for a low-cost housing project for East Harlem," where two thousand signatures were collected for a petition addressed to Mayor La Guardia.[30] Marcantonio was also in contact with La Guardia; as he told Covello: "I had a long discussion with the Mayor about a week ago with regard to the housing problem in Harlem. Confidentially, he is with us. He asked me to submit to him right away land values along the East River. Will you please get these for me at once?"[31]

English teacher Louis Relin described the part his students played in the housing campaign:

My boys rolled up their sleeves and ploughed into this community work with enthusiasm. All took part in collecting signatures for the petitions which enjoined the proper authorities to provide East Harlem with a much-needed housing project such as had been built in Williamsburg. My boys canvassed their tenements and their blocks. Volunteers undertook to publicize the gala parade for housing which was to take place on Saturday of that week. One afternoon I found several of the least active boys distributing notices of the parade at the subway entrances of 116th Street and Lexington Avenue. Scores of boys, with the assistance of our art teachers, painted colorful posters for the demonstration. Negro, Jewish, Puerto Rican, Italian, Irish, Russian lads—all knew they had a common stake in this campaign. They worked together, united in a common cause; past grievances seemed to be forgotten.[32]

The slogan for the long campaign, which was linked to the effort to secure a new building for Benjamin Franklin High School, was "A New School in A New Community."[33] Throughout this period the East Harlem Housing Committee continued to hold regular meetings and work in is subcommittees. In addition to the parade of 25 March 1939 a "huge mass meeting" was held on 28 April in the Verona Theater on Second Avenue and 108th Street. The petition campaign produced twenty thousand signatures. On 1 May Emmett May addressed the New York State Legislature on the need for low-income housing in East Harlem. Finally, on 18 September 1939, a jubilant Vito Marcantonio, the Twentieth District's congressman, announced that the federal government had agreed to subsidize the building of low-income housing between 102nd and 105th streets near East River Drive.[34] Marcantonio wrote Covello ("my dear Pop") the following letter from Washington, DC, dated 2 October 1939:

> By this time you have already read in the press of the housing project which will be built in East Harlem. The application for this project was made February 25, 1939.
>
> The total cost of the project will be $7,368,000 of which the Federal Government has made a loan of $6,631,000. The site will be the north side of 102nd Street to the south side of 105th Street, from the east side of First Avenue to the East River Drive. It will house 1,326 families.
>
> It will consist of 14 six story buildings with apartments of 2 $\frac{1}{2}$ to 6 $\frac{1}{2}$ rooms. The rent will be no more than $5.00 per room. Each apartment will be supplied with a Frigidaire, gas range and all modern equipment. The basement of the buildings will be used for a gymnasium and other recreational purposes.
>
> At the southeast corner of the project there will be a park consisting of 42,000 square feet. There is also a possibility of a foot bridge from the project to Wards Island which will become a park.
>
> I take this occasion to thank you as a member of the Harlem Legislative Conference for your cooperation and effort in this achievement which will bring a measure of happiness to the people of my district.[35]

The HLC was effective only in the area of public housing; its efforts in other social sectors—education, health care, recreation, welfare, and WPA funding—failed to produce the intended results. For example, in 1941, it could not get a bill out of the Rules Committee of the New York assembly to provide a publicly supported hospital for East Harlem. That five hundred people showed up at a "memorable mass meeting" at Benjamin Franklin High School, chaired by Covello, in support of an East Harlem health care facility had scant bearing on the deliberations in Albany. In 1942 the HLC was subsumed by the Harlem Victory Council, and its work was redirected toward eliminating discrimination in national defense employment in Central Harlem. In 1943, the voluntary organizations that had previously cosponsored HLC meetings and parades in East Harlem withdrew their support. In the end, the HLC's real legacy was not the East Harlem housing campaign, but its role as an indispensable political base for Vito Marcantonio, the lone radical politician in the U.S. Congress. As Meyer has noted: "The HLC was of inestimable value to Marcantonio. Its countless meetings, at which he was invariably the main speaker, and endless mailings, all of which went out over his signature, projected Marcantonio as the preeminent and undisputed leader of the community. . . . Without an exceptional orator and charismatic leader, the HLC might never have taken root; but without the HLC Marcantonio might not have found the means of integrating himself quite so completely into East Harlem."[36]

The close relationship between Marcantonio and Benjamin Franklin High School did not escape the notice of New York's right-wing press. On 16 May 1941 the Hearst-owned *Journal American* falsely charged that the high school was a hotbed of Communist activity:

> Teachers praise Soviet Russia in the classrooms, while students sell the Communist paper, *The Daily Worker,* in the halls. Clippings from the *Daily Worker* are posted on the school's bulletin boards. Communist organizations receive publicity in the official school calendar. The school auditorium on at least two occasions served as a campaign hall for Representative Vito Marcantonio, named by the Dies Committee as a leader or member of more than 20 Communist "front organizations."

Several days later, the high school's department chairs resolved that "from their own observation and to their best knowledge and belief the allegations in the article in the *Journal American* were *untrue.*" In an open letter, Marcantonio called the *Journal American* a "scandal sheet" and its article "a typical Hearst piece of yellow journalism." "Hearst hates a school that believes in democracy, that has faith in the people," he assured his readers. "That is why he is trying to discredit the school and through the school our people who have the most progressive and most democratic civic life in the country."[37] The high school's patriotic stance during World War II (as the headquarters for the East Harlem Defense Council, it helped mobilize community resources for the war effort) and its reduced level of activism perhaps buffered Covello and his teachers from further attacks from the Right. Vito Marcantonio, however, remained in the eye of the storm.[38] In 1944, his veritable lock on a congressional seat began to break apart when the New York legislature, hostile to his politics, created a new congressional district, the Twentieth, to include East Harlem and Yorkville, the latter a more affluent, predominantly German-American district from 96th to 79th Street east of Lexington

Avenue to the East River, where many voters found Marcantonio's politics unpalatable. Unfavorable national publicity also sullied his reputation. For example, *Time* magazine castigated Marcantonio as "the little *padrone* . . . the 18th's new-style ward boss and idol," a pro-Communist "who ladles out jobs, pocket money, speeches—anything for votes."[39]

As the saga of East River Houses is inextricably linked to the history of Benjamin Franklin High School, a short digression is warranted here to consider the long-term ramifications of that project. Briefly put, as a harbinger of future public housing, East River Houses turned out to be a mixed blessing. The fifth of New York's USHA-financed developments, it was noteworthy as the city's first high-rise tower project, inspired by Le Corbusier's "city in a park" image. The East River architects quirkily positioned the project's twenty-eight buildings, six of which were ten- and eleven-story high-rises, at a forty-five-degree angle in relation to the city gridiron—ostensibly for aesthetic reasons. (A small triangular park built by parks commissioner Robert Moses fronted the project on East River Drive; later a footbridge was added above the East River to connect the park to Ward's Island.)[40] Completed in 1941, East River Houses was a larger project than the one Marcantonio had forecast in 1939.

In 1948 a second high-rise project, the James Weldon Johnson Houses, rose on a bulldozed landscape between Park and Third avenues from 112th to 115th Street. Thirteen more public housing sites were subsequently developed and East Harlem experienced in no small way the disruption of slum clearance. As one journalist noted in 1954: "In many blocks, houses have been torn down, leaving gaping apertures full of rubble and rubbish, so that the area resembles London after the blitz."[41] By the mid-1960s high-rise towers sprouted across East Harlem, in Robert Freeman's words, "a virtual avalanche of public housing projects," probably the largest single concentration of housing projects in the United States: Some sixteen thousand families were being housed on 164 acres of redeveloped slum land.[42] For better or worse, East River Houses had set this frenzied redevelopment in motion. And, as Richard Plunz notes: "The high-rise, government-subsidized precedent set by East River Houses remained the exclusive model for housing development in East Harlem."[43]

It is beyond the scope of this book to provide a detailed analysis of the myriad disasters that befell high-rise public housing in East Harlem.[44] A description of several central tendencies freely drawn from Robert Freeman's magisterial study of East Harlem must suffice. First, redevelopment and slum clearance in the postwar years displaced a disproportionate number of blacks and Puerto Ricans. Displaced families either moved into public housing, where they came to be represented in disproportionate numbers, or—in cases where they were ineligible for public housing (for any number of possible reasons)—often had no alternative but to move to private housing in areas targeted for future slum clearance and redevelopment. As East Harlem had multiple development sites, the movement of displaced residents from site to site, always a step ahead of the bulldozer, was especially prevalent. The presence of frequently relocated families, in many cases stigmatized by poverty and racial stereotypes, on particular housing sites in East Harlem may have been the final straw for the Italians, who were stampeding out of the district by the mid-1950s. Second, while East River and other early projects provided far more apartments than the number of families displaced on those sites, the trend was soon reversed: By the midfifties the number of families originally on site exceeded the number of new units in East Harlem. The district appears to have been a terminus in a citywide chain reaction of one slum replacing another. Third, the racially charged practice of redlining, banks' refusal to insure mortgages in areas designated as blighted or undergoing urban renewal, virtually guaranteed East Harlem's continuing deterioration.[45]

Hindsight, of course, is always 20/20. Certainly the East River Houses campaign and the subsequent history of New York City public housing illustrate the law of unintended consequences; In the long term things did go badly awry in East Harlem. It is important, however, to view the East Harlem housing campaign as Covello did: as a civic, technical, and educational catalyst for constructive social change. He makes this point in "A Community-Centered School and the Problem of Housing," written in 1943 for the *Educational Forum*. "The greatest achievement lies in the fact that no activity involved in the program occurred without the participation of the community in it," he declared. "Through mass meetings, rallies in the school, and participation in various subcommittees, impetus was given to greater communal consciousness." Moreover, "simultaneous participation of diverse racial and nationality groups blunted the prejudices and antagonisms common to their every-day [*sic*] patterns of life. There was wholesome interaction between these groups, and the nature of this interaction was to us a potent means for education in intercultural relations." It was, Covello claimed, "an educational process toward acquiring the rudiments of democratic procedure, of tolerance, and of other valuable prerequisites."[46]

Considered theoretically, Covello's project was to form a "larger public" from the "little publics" of East Harlem's competing ethnic and racial groups.[47] The housing campaign instantiated this goal and a model of public work citizenship as the practical means to achieve it. More pointedly, in the housing campaign BFHS institutionally modeled this kind of citizenship through school-based applied research, community organizing, and curricular and cocurricular activities. This approach to larger-public building and civic development was foundational for Franklin's other prewar community campaigns.

Community Health and Hospital Campaigns

The Community Advisory Council's Health Committee became a potent force for improved health and sanitation under the leadership of Sophie Rabinoff, director of the East Harlem Health Center, and her cochair on the CAC Health Committee, Dr. Herman Dlugatz, chair of the Benjamin Franklin High School

Science Department. (This was the only CAC committee with cochairs.) Health Committee members spearheaded campaigns to eradicate tuberculosis in East Harlem and to acquire adequate health care for the area's residents. Throughout these campaigns, the Health Committee had the cooperation and close-at-hand assistance of the East Harlem Health Center at 160th East 115th Street.[48]

By the late 1930s, East Harlem had the highest rate of tuberculosis in New York City. The problem was particularly acute for the area's young people. From 1933 to 1937, 41 percent of all deaths in the age group fifteen to twenty-four years were attributed to tuberculosis; in January 1941, East Harlem had nearly eight hundred *known* cases of the disease.[49] In the spring of 1937, the East Harlem Health Center and the CAC Health Committee launched a cooperative attack on the problem, working in and through the high school to educate the community about the problem and to identify cases for treatment. As part of the health center's Early Diagnosis Campaign, the Health Committee did "pioneer work" by arranging for free tuberculin tests and X rays for students and teachers at the high school. Over the next several years, in addition to the free testing program, the health center and Herman Dlugatz, the Science Department chair, conducted an annual weeklong health education program, featuring three day-school assemblies on various health subjects and an evening parents' meeting. Increasingly tuberculosis became the focus of the annual health program. By the fall of 1940 the health program was being integrated with the work of the high school departments, the goal being "the recognition of early symptoms of tuberculosis to combat the disease in its incipient stages as well as a recognition of preventive hygiene." The strategy was to educate the students in the main building and the 79th Street Annex to educate the community. As Sophie Rabinoff described it:

> The tangible objective of the project was to create posters in English, Spanish and Italian based upon the material submitted by the students in the form of slogans. Unification of this work demanded the fullest cooperation of the chairman of six departments—Physical Education, Science, English, Spanish, Italian and lastly, consummation in the Art Department. This was attained admirably through the good offices and encouragement of the principal of Benjamin Franklin High School, Dr. Leonard Covello. A conference was arranged early in the term [Fall 1940] by the principal, the various heads of the departments, the Health Officer [Rabinoff] and Mrs. K.Z.W. Whipple, in charge of Health Education at the New York Tuberculosis and Health Association. The latter was instrumental in supplying tuberculosis material in the form of posters and literature as well as teaching units, and information regarding experience elsewhere in the integration of teaching on tuberculosis into the curriculum.[50]

The CAC Health Committee also played an instrumental role in the 1941 campaign to acquire a hospital and related clinical services for East Harlem.

The campaign, which included a "monster mass meeting" held at Benjamin Franklin High School on 14 March, sought "the erection and construction in our community of a hospital fully equipped with 500 beds and with a general clinic and dispensary services."[51] Later in the spring, state senator Dr. Charles Muzzicato, a member of the CAC Health Committee and the Harlem Legislative Conference, introduced Senate Bill No. 282 for the construction of a five-hundred-bed hospital in East Harlem, at a cost of $7 million. Although the state senate passed the bill, the Rules Committee of the assembly buried it, citing "heavily military expenditures as the reason for its defeat."[52] East Harlem would not have its own public hospital until the mid-1950s.

Citizenship Campaign

As we previously noted, Leonard Covello believed that the cultural rift between first- and second-generation Italian Americans contributed to, if not caused, juvenile delinquency in the immigrant community. The primary source of that rift was the domus centrality of the first generation, which precluded, in Covello's view, even a rudimentary assimilation of U.S. norms and values. It followed that naturalization was a critical step toward a sympathetic understanding of U.S. culture: "Naturalization is necessary, because it not only places our people on a more equable plane politically but also because the family of foreign origin is apt to develop more of unity and stability when *all* members belong to America."[53] The high school's citizenship campaign in the 1930s and early 1940s was predicated on Covello's vision of the school as a cultural bridge between the generations; the school's relationship to the home was defined in terms of a set of educational activities that promoted intergenerational respect and mutuality.[54]

The high school provided two mechanisms for advancing U.S. citizenship within the immigrant community. First, the WPA adult school and, later, the board of education evening elementary school, offered English and citizenship classes for the foreign born.[55] Second, under the auspices of the high school, naturalization secretaries representing immigration agencies helped prospective citizens with paperwork and problems related to naturalization. As early as the fall of 1935, Covello and his staff were involved in citizenship recruitment in East Harlem. Between 1935 and 1937, more than 1,500 applicants for naturalization aid were processed at the high school.[56] The general strategy was a series of citizenship campaigns ("Citizenship Weeks") directed by the CAC Citizenship Committee. These campaigns involved Franklin faculty organizing a group of speakers from among the students to explain to peers the importance of obtaining citizenship, to build interest that would filter back to the immigrant families; then the teachers sending out letters in English and other languages to inform parents of the citizenship campaign, to urge them to register, and to apprise them of the school's schedule of free naturalization services.[57]

In 1938 the Citizenship Committee, which included, among others, Covello and Harold Fields, formed a New Citizens League of men and women who had received their first or second papers through the high school's free naturalization service. The league was a recruitment mechanism for the WPA adult-school citizenship classes. In 1940, the Citizenship Committee instituted the East Harlem Festival for New American Citizens, held on Flag Day, 14 June, to honor five hundred new citizens and young people voting for the first time. The 1942 Flag Day celebration included a parade led by Covello and the Mt. Carmel Cadets along ten blocks of Lexington Avenue and, at the high school, the awarding of certificates to newly naturalized citizens and first voters by Ed Sullivan, the Broadway columnist and producer.[58]

"A New School in a New Community"

No sooner had Benjamin Franklin High School opened its doors in 1934 than a hue and cry went up for a new high school. As one student sardonically put it: "The 79th Street Annex is absolutely unfit for even an elementary school. Our Main Building is unfit as an annex. If the Board of Education has started something, they should finish it properly."[59] An angry open letter to La Guardia published in the Franklin *Almanac* declared the current arrangement a "disgrace to a community's dignity."[60] Ironically, it would take nearly eight years for the board to "finish it properly," notwithstanding that it began casting about for a site as early as 1934.[61] Not until 1938 was an appropriation passed that would pay for the new building; even then, the location was undecided. The Community Advisory Committee, the Harlem Legislative Conference—indeed, almost everyone associated with Benjamin Franklin—wanted the new building placed on a two-block vacant site between Pleasant Avenue and East River Drive, adjacent to Jefferson Park. The CAC Housing Committee linked the campaign for low-rent housing to the new school campaign, using the slogan "A New School in a New Community." The term "East Riviera" was coined to describe the projected development along East River Drive.

The board of education considered three possible locations for the school. In his autobiography, Covello recalled that students persuaded La Guardia to sponsor the most attractive location, a lot bounding Pleasant Avenue and East River Drive at 114th–116th streets, comprising 164,000 square feet. At a radio panel discussion, the students had an opportunity to speak with the mayor about the site, calling La Guardia's attention to a study of East Harlem land values they had compiled in their social studies classes. According to Covello, La Guardia, who had previously demurred on the site because he thought it was too expensive, reconsidered his position when confronted with assessed valuations indicating that the Pleasant Avenue site, assessed at $562,000, indeed was the least expensive of the three locations.[62]

For Covello and his allies, the East River Drive location symbolized a new beginning. The high school was to be located on a campus landscaped with-tree-lined sidewalks at the northeast boundary of Jefferson Park. The entrance stairway, colonnaded portal, and cupola would face Pleasant Avenue at 115th Street, with a view to the campanile of the Church of Our Lady; the rear of the building, which included the library terrace and school parking lot, fronted East River Drive, with a view across the river to Randall's Island and the Triborough Bridge. By the time the building site was approved, the first section of East River Drive, the approach to the Triborough Bridge from 92nd to 125th Street, had been completed. With the exception of a one-mile stretch between 30th and 49th streets, by June 1940 East River Drive, a restricted access expressway, was open to traffic from Corlear's Hook on the Lower East Side to 125th Street.[63] The new high school would open to the muffled drone of fast-flowing traffic, barely notice-able within the classrooms and offices on the building's river side.

The groundbreaking ceremony for the new Benjamin Franklin High School took place with great fanfare on 17 April 1940. Father Duffy's Cadets, the Vigo Drum and Bugle Corps, St. Ann's Drum and Bugle Corps, and the Benjamin Franklin High School Band played and marched before 1,800 Franklin students and hundreds of spectators. Accompanied by Christina Clax-ton, aged fifteen, a descendant of Benjamin Franklin, Mayor La Guardia turned the first spade of earth, telling his audience: "I don't have to tell you what a dump this was down here before I took office. I still have twenty more months to go in office, and we're going to do a great many more things to make New York City more beautiful before I go." In his speech, Leonard Covello remarked: "Once . . . the Mayor . . . told the boys that we . . . wanted a fine new building . . . 'on the EAST Riviera.' It seemed a joke then, at which all of us laughed; but today, we have broken ground for our new school on the 'East Riviera.' . . . It is our hope that this new school of ours shall be to our commu-nity a symbol of all that is fine in life and achievement."[64]

The new building took two years to complete. Covello recalled complaining to Rose, his wife: "At the rate they're going I'll be ready to retire before they finish." His students importuned him: "What goes on, Mr. Covello? They build-ing Rome all over again?" Construction delays in the summer of 1940 especially annoyed Covello, who called upon Vito Marcantonio to intercede with La Guardia to keep the city from dragging its feet on the new high school; for exam-ple, on 5 June 1940: "The work on the new building has ceased as far as I can judge. They have dug out the foundation and then stopped and nothing has been done for two weeks. You can do a great deal by letting the mayor know what is going on. If we are going to get in by September 1941—and for many reasons we should—the work should not stop except for bad weather." Covello told Marcantonio that if the board of estimate delayed approving the general con-struction appropriation for the new building in the early summer, "the matter will not be taken up again until September or October, and that would indeed be very deplorable." In late July, Marcantonio sought to assuage Covello's anxiety: "I flew down with the Mayor this morning and had a very satisfactory talk with him in regard to the school. I will explain in detail to you when I see you. I am confident everything is going to be all right." However, a general construction contract was not issued by the board of estimate until 12 September 1940, and completion of the new building was delayed throughout 1941.[65]

The new high school building finally opened its doors in February 1942. It was a red-brick and limestone structure quite unlike any previous building in East Harlem, of British, not U.S. architectural lineage, of "late Georgian" inspiration. The entrance façade included a stairway that ascended to a portico framed by Corinthian columns, reminiscent of a Greek temple. A Greek Revival–style cupola, the building's signature detail, ascended high above the central roof. Deeply recessed wings, which included four floors of classrooms, fanned out on each side of the building, each ending in a tall pavilion that included a large rounded-headed window set in a shallow recess. Visually the building conveyed elegant simplicity and balance.[66]

Just before the move to the new Franklin, Richard Bauman, a senior and president of the Student Congress, reflected on the old building at East 108th Street:

> Isn't it strange but now that I have been assured that Benjamin Franklin will be housed in that new, magnificent schoolhouse on 116th Street and the East River Drive . . . I still can't help feeling sorry that I have to leave that old building on 108th Street. Maybe I haven't exactly liked the place while I have been here. Perhaps I even went so far as to wish the old place would burn down. But now that I am about to leave it, I begin to reminisce and become a little sorry. Many students, however, are probably glad that Franklin is moving from that prehistoric structure to the most modern school in the city. Many students, I bet, will purposely take walks past the new building with some of their friends so that they may proudly say, "This is my school!"
>
> But I don't think we all feel that way. Some of us remember this old dilapidated building with a feeling of . . . of nostalgia. True, it was old; it was dirty; why even the paint (where there was any) was peeling off the walls. I distinctly remember the broken windows; the broken desks; and the broken chairs. But it was my school. And I was proud of it. I know, you are going to tell me that I am foolish to think this way when we have that beautiful new building. I can't help it though; I had become so used to it. I became used to walking the five flights of stairs between periods. I enjoyed the mad rush through the only bridge, which was bottled up every once in a while as if by a stopper when somebody who was slightly overweight attempted to pass through. And

the occasional fracas in the halls, when some students collided as they raced from room to room, added zest to the trek from the fifth floor of the 108 Street building to the fourth floor of the 109 Street building. Why if the Science teacher didn't have a look of exasperation upon his face when he couldn't finish the experiment because of the lack of supplies, I felt that the day just wasn't right. And I remember the days during the months of April and May when the class had to compete with the noise (Music, if you will) of the "juke boxes" in the street. True, it made it difficult for the teacher to talk to the class. But what teacher can compete with Benny Goodman? The noise, the rush, the lack of supplies; that was unimportant as I really didn't mind. I was getting an education—as fine an education as any high school boy in the city.[67]

On 23 May 1941, New York City Council president Newbold Morris laid the cornerstone of the new Benjamin Franklin facility before a gathering of four thousand spectators.[68] Less than a year later, 16 April 1942, La Guardia and an assemblage of dignitaries that included Covello, Marcantonio, and Manhattan borough president Edgar J. Nathan dedicated the new Benjamin Franklin High School, completed at a cost of $3,250,000. Yet for all the anticipation and genuine cause for celebration, the happy occasion was tempered by the nation's involvement in World War II. The mayor spoke presciently of the difficulties about to confront the new high school and its students as the war effort increasingly demanded the lion's share of the nation's resources:

You boys are getting a tough break. You are at an age when, if the war continues, you will be called. You have to prepare so much more because of the great responsibility that is going to be yours. And when we come through it, you will have to face another war—a dislocated world.

I sympathize with you. You have it hard through the accident of age. Yet it is something that could not be avoided. You have to realize the enormity of your responsibility and prepare yourselves for it. If you are called, it will be for a great cause and one which is the hope of the entire world. I know the boys of Benjamin Franklin will be the first to respond when the call comes.[69]

Ironically this "new beginning" was in many respects an untimely ending: Franklin's heyday as a community high school was over. The Second World War would mark a turning point in the history of the school. The forces unleashed by that conflict would drain Franklin of critical resources and forge new social and political contexts that would make community-centered schooling in East Harlem a very difficult proposition.

CHAPTER SEVEN

The High School on
Pleasant Avenue

HE NEW BENJAMIN FRANKLIN High School opened on 2 February 1942. The country was at war when Franklin staff and students moved seven blocks northward into the stately Georgian building next to Jefferson Park and East River Drive. The fourteen and a half years that Covello spent at the Pleasant Avenue building, up to his retirement in 1956, were years of struggle and decline for the community high school, precipitated first by the war, then by seismic demographic shifts and mounting ethnic conflict, and finally by a conservative postwar zeitgeist that militated strongly against progressive education.

The war, of course, was the decisive event, influencing all that followed, calling to mind the corrosive effects World War I had in accelerating the movement away from democracy in the nation's community centers (see Chapter 1). War and its aftermath, the "dislocated world" La Guardia gloomily forecast on the new high school's inauguration day, would irreparably damage the community school and Covello's project of local democratic development—the social forces unleashed or given increased impetus by the war simply could not be restrained. This chapter traces these developments, underscoring the high school's vigorous efforts, despite a precipitous curtailment of resources, to adapt its programs to new constituencies and to reposition itself in a community that was increasingly Puerto Rican and African American, and more and more riven by cultural tensions.

The War Years

Designed by board of education architect Eric Kebben, the new Franklin building, which could accommodate 3,350 students, featured an auditorium with a seating capacity of 1,250; two gymnasiums; a student cafeteria seating 1,500; a library; a teachers' lunchroom; shops and laboratories for biology, chemistry, physics, electricity, mechanical drawing, pottery, photography, printing, wood and metal work, remedial reading, and social studies; a museum; a roof playground and greenhouse; a science weather station and observatory; and a community lecture/forum hall seating 125. On paper the new high school listed six courses of study: academic, general, commercial, major art, major music, and industrial arts. In practice, four programs were offered during the war years—academic, general, commercial, and industrial arts.[1] In the spring of 1942 the board of education authorized custodial service to keep the new building open twenty-four hours daily for community purposes.[2]

The war had an immediate effect on the community program, which geared its activities to civil defense, gasoline rationing, and bond and salvage drives. The high school housed the East Harlem Neighborhood Volunteer Defense Council, which coordinated rationing, war bond drives, and metal and paper salvage drives in East Harlem. The Community Advisory Council organized a defense program that contained thirteen committees, ranging from Defense Savings to Moral and Public Relations to Knitting.[3] As late as the spring of 1942, the reduced WPA continued to offer some evening courses at the high school, but only courses "which have a bearing to the national emergency and make for unity." A "typical [daily] program" in 1942 listed evening civilian defense activities in both the Defense Council office (Room #107) and the community room.[4]

A field study by Franklin teachers in 1943 concluded that war effects exacerbated truancy at the high school. Students under sixteen were leaving the school to take jobs (illegally) in manpower-depleted retail and wholesale businesses; other students were dropping out to enjoy themselves until they were eligible for the draft.[5] Truancy hearings in 1942–43 were up nearly 56 percent in the city schools, with court prosecutions more than doubling the prewar rate.[6] Regarding the "disturbing rise in juvenile delinquency," Covello was convinced "that the social and moral dislocations due to the war are producing the appalling behavior we are concerned about." "In war time," he continued," such factors as emotional excitation, dislocation of family life, increased freedom because of acquisition of youth of financial means, and others are evidently causing a greater inclination to misbehave."[7]

In May 1942 enrollment at Benjamin Franklin High School stood at 1,743, a loss of 808 students (32 percent) since March 1936.[8] By 1944, Franklin enrolled only about 1,112 students, a disturbingly low figure that Covello attributed to the draft (many of the students were overage for their grade level) and to the inflated wartime job market, which siphoned off many students.[9] The New York Times wrote of the new high school building: "Constructed at a cost of $3,429,000 and two-thirds empty, it is the most expensive white elephant in the history of the city school system."[10] Confronted with such disappointing enrollment figures, Superintendent of Schools John E. Wade took action in the spring of 1944 to consolidate Benjamin Franklin High School with Junior High School 172, a move that was expected to raise the total student population at the high school to approximately 1,900. (JHS 172 occupied the former Franklin building at 309 East 108th Street.) Given that Franklin's enrollment problems were reflective of a citywide loss of high school students in large part attributable to the war, Wade had no plans to remove Covello, arguably New York's most respected principal.[11] The merger of Franklin and JHS 172, now called James Otis Junior High School, was achieved in the fall of 1944. This arrangement established Franklin as "a six-year secondary school, accommodating pupils from the seventh through the twelfth year."[12] As having two principals in the same building was an expensive, inefficient arrangement, the board of education appointed Covello principal of both schools. In 1946, Covello reported a joint enrollment of 2,200 boys ("it is a man's world up there, I assure you").[13]

In the face of enormous difficulties, Covello managed to hold together Franklin's community program during the war years. There is no denying, however, that it was a truncated version of the original program at East 108th Street. No attempt was made to revive the Friends and Neighbors Club or the other street-unit activities that had contributed such great vitality to the original Franklin. The new location on East Harlem's periphery was one problem—the high school lost its neighborhood base of support; diminished resources was another problem—the WPA's withdrawal drained the high school of scores of support personnel.

In the spring of 1942 the board of education officially blessed Covello's program by declaring Benjamin Franklin High School "a twenty four hour school," an honorific that had little practical value other than eliminating custodial fees for community groups using the building.[14] Such groups that spring included Holy Rosary Cadets, City Patrol Corps, NYA Symphony Orchestra, East Harlem News, Red Cross, City History Club of New York, and Association of Italian Social Workers; activities ranged from drilling to first-aid classes, concerts, and exhibits; Franklin also served as a "general clearing house for information and service in the community."[15]

Instituted at the old Franklin building in the spring of 1941, Community Nights, "a series of monthly Community-Get-Togethers," continued throughout 1942. The primary aim of these meetings was to provide a regular time and place for CAC committee work.[16] The program for Community Night, 24 April 1941, listed a general meeting in the auditorium at which state senator Dr. Charles Muzzicato spoke on the topic "Health Needs in East Harlem," followed by meetings of eight CAC committees on the second and third floors, and then refreshments in the school lunchroom.[17] Community Night also became the occasion of such events as the annual "I am an American" ceremony for new citizens and twenty-one-year-old first voters, and the East

Harlem Festival. In November 1942 Covello divided responsibility for Franklin's community and adult programs between Spanish-language teacher Emilio L. Guerra and English teacher Rita Morgan. Guerra had general oversight of twelve specifically "school committees" (Alumni, Social Affairs, Social Welfare, Assembly, Scholarship and Arista, Building Decorations, Film-Radio, Student Congress, General Organization, Cafeteria, Publications, and Service Squad (NYA); seven "defense committees" (Salvage, Defense Savings, Air Raid Precautions, Publications and Posters, Publicity for Defense, and Block Captains and Messengers); student teachers; and building use up to 3 P.M. Morgan had responsibility for eight specifically "community committees" (Adult Education, Health, Housing, Recreation, Racial Cooperation, Consumer Education, Citizenship, and Juvenile Aid); the adult education program; community use of the building; public relations; and the Association of Parents, Teachers, and Friends.[18] For the war years, however, there would be no heated crusades like the housing, high school, and hospital campaigns of the late thirties; indeed, it would not be until the late forties that an issue of similar magnitude would capture the community's imagination.

The major school-community activity from 1942 to 1945 was the Benjamin Franklin High School Summer Session, initiated by Covello to promote civilian defense and to help stem the rising tide of juvenile delinquency in East Harlem. Over three summers, the high school provided classes, workshops, and supervised recreation programs that addressed felt community needs. In 1942, fifty-five summer staff members conducted activities in music, dramatics, art, tutoring, guidance, printing, speech correction, publications (*East Harlem News*), adult education, civilian defense, general recreation, community dances, and singing. Student teachers from Teachers College and New York University joined with the Italian Social Workers Association, Franklin faculty, and teachers from other high schools to staff the program, which served more than one thousand youngsters and adults. In his report on the summer of 1942, Covello wrote: "The building was in constant use from 8:30 A.M. to 5 P.M. and from 7:00 P.M. to 10:00 and later. Hundreds of children, young people and adults used the building freely. The behavior of all . . . was exemplary in every respect—not one untoward incident marred the program. The building was taken care of by all—nothing was touched or defaced."[19]

In the summer of 1943, the high school operated a day-care center for children ages six to twelve, staffed by student teachers from Teachers College, in the south wing of the basement. Dr. Rita Morgan directed an academic high school in the new Franklin building, which registered 302 students in fourteen academic courses (U.S. history, Italian, chemistry, trigonometry, etc.) and typing and stenography. Other activities included citizenship aid, civilian defense, farm garden, health education and supervised recreation, music, and arts and crafts. A total of thirty-five student teachers, twenty-three from Teachers College and twelve from NYU, participated in the 1943 summer program.[20]

In 1944 in addition to the children's center, the academic program, and adult activities, Franklin provided a summer "teen-age canteen." The canteen opened on 18 July at the close of the Feast of Our Lady of Mount Carmel with 250 teenagers "dancing under the stars" to jukebox music on the school terrace. The dances were held three times weekly that summer. The high-water mark was reached on 3 August, when 589 young people danced to the music of Sonny Donofrio's band; on other occasions attendance averaged about 400. While he was pleased with the large turnout, Covello expressed disappointment that black youth stayed away:

> The Canteen was to have been an inter-racial, intercultural venture. In this respect it failed. After two incidents involving both threat and attack—both occurring outside the Canteen area and away from the school—the small group of the Negro attendants remained away from the dancing and Negro members of the Youth Committee became absent. The Committee was reluctant to accept this turn of events but felt that the mores of the predominant group within the community [Italian Americans] would make any attempt at corrective measures during so brief a period very difficult.[21]

During the war race relations in East Harlem grew increasingly tense, although they would not flare in the high school until the fall of 1945. Blacks continued to settle in East Harlem during the 1940s, growing to 26 percent of the population by 1950.[22] Of Benjamin Franklin High School's 1,743 students in May 1942, 782 (45 percent) were Italian American. Blacks constituted the second-largest ethnic group with 350 (20 percent), compared with only 74 (less than 3 percent) of 2,551 total students in 1936.[23] By 1945 blacks made up 30 percent of the students.[24]

The growing tension between whites and blacks within his own institution may have spurred Covello in 1942 and 1943 to host two conferences at Franklin on race relations. Convened on 12 December 1942, the "Greater New York Conference on Racial and Cultural Relations in the United States," held under the aegis of the American Jewish Conference, NAACP, National Conference of Christians and Jews, National Urban League, and other progressive groups, assembled as panel leaders such national educational luminaries as William Heard Kilpatrick and Ruth Benedict of Columbia University, Eduard C. Lindeman of the New York School of Social Work, Harry Overstreet of City College, Constance Warren of Sarah Lawrence College, and Kimball Young of Queen's College. The keynote speakers were Algernon D. Black of the Ethnical Culture Society and Channing Tobias of the National Council of Young Men's Christian Association. Kilpatrick and Covello presided over panel sessions that addressed the following questions: "What are the prevalent American attitudes which threaten national unity and international understanding? What can be done about these attitudes? What are the techniques that may be used to build better inter-group attitudes?"[25] Representing the CAC Committee on Racial Cooperation, Franklin senior Daniel Patrick Moynihan, a future U.S. senator from New York, presented several resolutions that were formally adopted by the conference, notably integration of the armed forces and merger of black and white Red Cross blood banks.[26]

The "Conference on Racial Conflict" was held at Franklin on 21 July 1943 in response to race riots in such cities as Beaumont, Mobile, Los Angeles, and Detroit (which saw the worst violence, with thirty-four people killed, mostly blacks, on 21 June). The conference featured adult and student panels addressing two questions: "What immediate steps can teachers take in the present critical situation facing many communities? How can school and community, working together, meet this crucial test of democracy?" The adult panel included Covello, Stewart Cole of the Service Bureau for Intercultural Education, Alain Locke of Howard University, Dan Dodson of New York University, and Arthur Linden of Teachers College; Algernon Black of the Ethical Culture Society directed the student panel discussion. Ironically, within a few weeks of the conference, a race riot broke out in Central Harlem on 1 August 1943 in which 6 blacks were killed and 185 injured; property damage was estimated at $5 million.[27]

Perhaps ineluctably given the volatile demographics of East Harlem, racial violence disrupted Benjamin Franklin High School, where the racial mix by the fall of 1945 was 50 percent Italian, 30 percent Negro.[28] On Saturday, 29 September 1945, the New York Times reported "a flare-up of riot proportions" on the previous day at Benjamin Franklin High School. "Twice during the day," the Times article continued, "street fighting broke out in which knives flashed, stones and bottles were flung from roof-tops and 500 white and Negro students and their elders battled eighty uniformed and plainclothes policemen." The Daily News reported that "fully 2,000 surging students joined in the brawls—a morning affair and an afterpiece." Over the next few days, four hundred police officers and plainclothes detectives "blanketed the area extending from Lenox Avenue to the East River and north as far as 125th Street." (No deaths or serious injuries were reported.) The Times reported that more than a third of Franklin's 2,196 students stayed away from the building on the Monday following the riot. High-ranking police officials, school board representatives, and even Walter White, secretary of the NAACP, gathered at the high school to assess the violence of 28 September. White told a Times reporter: "Our association is seeking to learn the identity of the person or persons who last Friday went about the section in which the school is located spreading such wild rumors among mothers as that the principal had been stabbed and that three teachers had been slain. The campaign was fairly well organized and industrially pursued."[29] On the other hand, Covello averred that the incident was not "a planned racial disturbance" but rather the result of a scuffle between white and black students in the gymnasium on 27 September. On 2 October, Franklin faculty and student representatives reported their own investigation of the incident, supporting Covello's claim and playing down the magnitude of the riot—if indeed it were a riot—implying that the *Times* and *Daily News* accounts were greatly exaggerated. These investigators also proclaimed Franklin to be free of racial animosity "among colored and white students."[30]

On 7 October, Dorothy Dunbar Bromley, a reporter from the *Herald Tribune* who spent a full day at Benjamin Franklin High School, gave a persuasive account of the situation:

> My talks with teachers at Benjamin Franklin and observation of the students themselves convinced me that the intercultural program at the school has made somewhat more progress in the last eleven years than the first sensational news stories would have indicated. But it was also evident from the teachers' frank disclosures that under-surface tension does exist. It is largely ascribable, they believe to strong anti-Negro prejudice felt in this Italo-American community, a prejudice which the principal, Dr. Leonard Covello, has not been able to break down, for all this valiant struggle to build "a community school." . . .

> Last week the student body as a whole seemed quiet and ashamed. The seventy-some elected members of the student organization, white and Negro boys, who met on Wednesday, listened to speeches by their leaders that could not have been more liberal in character. But the purpose of the meeting was a bit blurred. . . .

> A Negro boy proposed a resolution that all the boys of the school, to demonstrate their unity to the entire city, march en masse in the city's Columbus Day parade. This project, the idea for which had emanated, I gather, from Dr. Covello was indorsed.

> The emphasis on getting good publicity for the school seemed to me understandable but of relatively little therapeutic value under the circumstances. A second proposal, for a school parade in the neighborhood, which the principal hopes to see carried out, seemed of more fundamental value.[31]

Covello unleashed a counterattack on the negative media publicity surrounding the incident. On the evening of 8 October 1945 he convened a mass meeting at the high school attended by as many as a thousand community members, mostly Italian Americans. Vito Marcantonio implored the audience: "We've got to fight the Bilbos and Rankins [an allusion to two Mississippi Democrats in the U.S. Congress] all over the world. We of Italian origin know the meaning of discrimination because we have been exploited, so we refuse to discriminate against others. We have no quarrel with Negro people." The meeting adopted a resolution denouncing sensationalized accounts of the racial incident by "certain newspapers of this City," which were "tendered to damage the fine reputation for interracial harmony and good will built up by the school over a period of years."[32]

As reported in the *Times,* a delegation of five hundred Franklin students marched in the 12 October Columbus Day parade up Fifth Avenue, "led by their principal, Dr. Leonard Covello, and flanked by parents. The students and parents, white and Negro, marched in a demonstration of unity, signalizing the restoration of interracial harmony and goodwill at the school where disorders occurred on Sept. 27 and 28."[33] The marchers carried placards "showing that they were of various races and nationalities," and they "stepped along behind a huge banner which proclaimed that they were 'Americans All.'"[34] On 23 October, Covello convened a special assembly at the high school, featuring pop singer Frank Sinatra as the keynote speaker on behalf of racial tolerance.[35] On 9 November, at an Armistice Day ceremony, Covello told 1,100 senior high school students that racial hatred was an "atomic bomb" in their midst and adjured them to help root it out in their own neighborhoods. A troupe of white and black actors performed *Skin Deep,* a one-act play on racial prejudice by Charles Polacheck. "The play caused particular interest at Benjamin Franklin since its action took place in a bus, and a bus had been the scene of one of the disturbances between Negro and white boys in which the school became involved on Sept. 28," the *Times* reported.[36]

The Mayor's Committee on Racial Unity and the recently formed East Harlem League for Unity issued separate reports of investigations of Benjamin Franklin High School. The Committee on Racial Unity stated: "Our hearings brought out the fact that there is an exceptionally high degree of cordial integration of the youths of all races into the total program of the school. In every phase of its activities, including class dances and parents association activities, the Negroes participate without any apparent difficulties except that it is reported that the Wednesday Evening Community Dances are not attended by Negro students for fear of their safety in the neighborhood after the dances are over. This leads us to the conclusion that the incident was *not a race controversy but a dispute growing out of a fight*" (emphasis added).[37] Similarly, the East Harlem League for Unity concluded that "the occurrences at the school were of comparatively minor importance, but that the conditions under which the school and other community agencies are working should be made known to the public. . . . There was nothing of any startling nature that happened Sept. 27 or 28, but the possibilities of serious happenings in the community are not only present but growing greater month by month. The incident may well be forgotten, but the need for city-wide attention to the problem cannot be ignored."[38]

In his own report, Covello remarked sadly that sensationalized newspaper accounts "gave the incident nation-wide publicity and gave the school an ill-deserved notoriety and brought out the statement that if a race riot could happen at Franklin where an intercultural program had been attempted for so many years and apparently so successfully, then what was the use of encouraging intercultural educational programs." He stipulated, however, that beyond the schoolyard, racial prejudice was rending East Harlem's social fabric: "The [weekly community] dances are publicized in our school's Weekly Bulletin and over the Public Address System, but Negro young people do not come because on going home after the dances, on several occasions when these dances were first started, Negro boys going home late at night, have been attacked by white hoodlums. As a result, the Negro young people do not attend this particular dance but they do attend all class dances and other school functions."[39]

The Postwar Puerto Rican Migration

In the postwar years, Covello and Benjamin Franklin High School confronted a major transition that would define the ethnic contours of East Harlem for the next forty years—the great Puerto Rican migration of the forties and early fifties. Between 1940 and 1950, New York's Puerto Rican population increased dramatically from seventy thousand to two hundred and fifty thousand. Most of the influx came after the war, on the wings (literally) of cheap air travel, usually fifty dollars for a one-way ticket from San Juan to New York and installment plans for those without cash. Of the postwar migration, Nicholas Lemann has written: "In general what brought people there were economic prospects vastly less dismal than those in Puerto Rico. Back home, at the outset of the migration, industrialization was still in its very early stages, sugar prices were depressed, and thousands of people who had moved from the hills to the lowlands a generation earlier now had to move again, to notorious slums on the outskirts of urban areas, such as La Perla ('the pearl') and El Ganguito ('the little mudhole')."[40] The first terminus of the great migration was 116th Street and Third Avenue in East Harlem (in the late 1940s, the center would shift two miles north to 149th Street and Third Avenue, in the South Bronx, where it is currently located). In 1950, 60,380 Puerto Ricans comprised 33.42 percent of East Harlem's total population—figures that would reach 63,375 and 42.6 percent in 1957.[41] Needless to say, the effects of the "internal migration" reverberated in the hallways of Benjamin Franklin High School.

In June 1947, the board of education reported an enrollment of 13,914 newly arrived Puerto Rican children in the city's public elementary and secondary schools. In a statement that might have described an earlier generation of Italian immigrants to East Harlem, the board stated: "There is no doubt but that many pupils coming from Puerto Rico suffer from the double handicap of unfamiliarity with the English language and lack of previous educational experience, sometimes approaching complete illiteracy. Malnutrition and other health deficiencies contribute to the educational problem of the schools. The overcrowding at home and the restlessness on the street carry over into the school in the form of nervousness, extreme shyness, near tantrums, and other behavior characteristics which are the more difficult for the teacher to understand because of the language barrier."[42]

Until his retirement in 1956, Covello devoted much of his time toward helping Puerto Rican youngsters and their families make the difficult adjustment to East Harlem.[43] In the summer of 1947, Covello accepted an invitation from the University of Puerto Rico to deliver a lecture series on such topics as community schools, intercultural education, and the problems of minorities in the United States. He extended his visit an extra two weeks to make a study of the island. The *Herald Tribune* reported: "Carrying forty-seven letters from his pupils to their relatives and friends, he saw Puerto Ricans at home—in impoverished parts of San Juan and also on the farms and in remote mountain hamlets."[44] Upon his return to New York, Covello visited other schools to share his newly acquired insights. He wrote a colleague at the University of Puerto Rico: "I know I can do a lot to help change people's opinion about the Puerto Rican people and make them more sympathetic with their problems."[45]

At Benjamin Franklin High School, Covello and Emilio L. Guerra instituted special orientation classes for newly arrived Puerto Rican students. As Guerra noted:

These classes are conducted entirely in Spanish because those boys who are placed in the classes cannot express themselves adequately in English, although they may understand a little English if it is spoken slowly. The orientation class attempts to make the pupil's adjustment to his new environment a pleasurable experience during which his customs, traditions and languages are treated with a sympathetic understanding that makes it unlikely that the pupil will experience those frustrations which are generally the cause of maladjustment. With his dignity and prestige assured, the new arrival is asked to fill in a questionnaire (in Spanish) through which the teacher attempts to determine what the pupil's previous educational experience has been and also to learn something about his home background. Then a non-verbal intelligence test (in Spanish) is administered. This is followed by an achievement test to determine literacy in Spanish.

In general the aim of the course is to orient the Puerto Rican pupil to the school community, to East Harlem, to his city, state, and nation; to explain the duties and responsibilities of the good citizen and to

acquaint him with the educational and vocational opportunities offered
by the school and the city. The major emphasis in the course is on attitudes and skills rather than on purely factual understanding.[46]

In 1947 and 1948 Guerra and Michael Decessare, another Franklin
teacher, helped organized the Club Borinquen at Benjamin Franklin High
School, the purpose of which was to study Puerto Rican culture, to identify
the problems and needs of East Harlem's Puerto Rican community, and to "outline ways and means in which the students and the school can be of help to
improve our community." The high school also formed an Association of Puerto
Rican Parents, which worked with the Club Borinquen to leverage financial
support from *El Crisol,* a Spanish-language newspaper in East Harlem.[47] From
1948 to 1953, Covello and Club Borinquen, in conjunction with *El Crisol* and
later *El Diario,* sponsored a Latin American Festival held annually in the high
school auditorium. These festivals, which supported a student-aid fund for
Puerto Rican youngsters, featured "the best known stars of stage, night club
and radio in the Hispano-American entertainment world."[48] In 1950 Covello
wrote Babby Quintero, who recruited talent for the festival and served as the
master of ceremonies: "Since you were there, it is unnecessary for me to
describe to you the tremendous crowd which filled our vast auditorium far
beyond its capacity; the deeply appreciative and joyous reception which was
given every artist and every group of artists who during a period of *five* hours,
performed generously and superbly; the expressions of appreciation which
were tendered through me for you and for our artist friends by so many in the
audience. This wonderful experience, I can say, we shared together."[49]

In 1948–49 Covello and Club Borinquen officers met bimonthly at the high
school with representatives of New York City's Spanish-language press. The
"Puerto Rican press conferences," as they were called, also included leading
members of the Puerto Rican community and featured guest speakers from
social welfare, police, education, health, child welfare, and labor agencies. The
purpose of the meetings was to develop an agenda of information and guidance about social services for dissemination by the Spanish-language press.
Dina Caputo, faculty advisor to Club Borinquen, described the meeting of 7
March 1949, at which Dr. Sophie Rabinoff, district health officer of the East
Harlem Heath Center, was the guest speaker:

> Dr. Rabinoff spoke of the different City clinics that have been estab-
> lished for both child and adult, of the special classes conducted on
> food and proper clothing (this is important for the Puerto Rican whose
> native climate is a tropical one and who is used to a somewhat differ-
> ent diet), of the T.B. X-Ray campaign that was to take place in P.S. #101
> on March 14 and 15th. The importance of this campaign was realized
> when Dr. Rabinoff stated that one-half of the T.B. cases in East Harlem

were Spanish ones and urged the Spanish press to exhort all people in the Community to be X-Rayed. Dr. Covello asked the members of the Club Borinquen to act as interpreters and clerks in this campaign.[50]

The territory from East 96th to East 112th Street, from Fifth to Third Avenue, was known as El Barrio, with a market district located under the Park Avenue "Chinese Wall" from East 111th to East 116th Street. As with previous immigrant groups (although Puerto Ricans, as U.S. citizens, were not technically immigrants) East Harlem proved to be a way station, as substantial numbers in the second generation found the means to move to the South Bronx, at that time the route of upward mobility.[51] Yet by any standard, relative or absolute, for those Puerto Rican migrants who arrived and left, as well as for those who stayed, living conditions in East Harlem were harsh. Contemporary accounts described Spanish Harlem in much the same terms as earlier writers had portrayed Italian Harlem: putatively vermin-infested, rotting brownstone tenements; "cramped, scabrous rooms"; garbage-strewn sidewalks and alleys; vacant lots cluttered with blackened cans and broken glass; idle groups of men gathered around storefronts; boys playing stickball in busy streets, et cetera.[52]

A mid-1940s report of the Urban League of Greater New York estimated that more than one hundred youth gangs operated in East and Central Harlem. "There seem to be more gangs among Puerto Ricans per square inch than in any other group . . . because they are probably worse off economically."[53] In the late 1940s, Italian youth gangs controlled the area around Benjamin Franklin High School, frequently attacking blacks and Puerto Ricans who wanted to use the nearby Jefferson Park pool. In the early 1950s Puerto Rican and other Hispanic students complained to *El Diario de Nueva York* that Italian gangs operated inside the high school and assaulted the Spanish-speaking students.[54]

Benjamin Franklin High School increasingly lost students in the 1950s, to the extent that by the spring of 1956, the year of Covello's retirement, the high school registered only 652 students (by contrast James Otis Junior High School, in the same building, registered 1,092 students).[55] The primary factor in Franklin's diminished enrollment seems to have been ethnocultural conflict— a factor suggested by the disproportionately low enrollment of Puerto Rican boys, who constituted just 17 percent of 730 total students in 1955.[56] Writing in 1959 Dan Wakefield, in *Island in the City*, observed that Italians maintained the high school as their "turf," even as the surrounding neighborhoods were becoming Puerto Rican. "Not only the high school but also the blocks around it were looked upon as Italian territory and Puerto Rican kids were anxious to avoid even going near the school, much less going into it. In 1957 the newspaper *El Diario* carried the story of a sixteen-year-old boy named Frank Martinez who was knifed while walking past the high school. When asked by the police if he knew who had knifed him, Martinez answered, '*Un Italiano.*' The answer was almost automatic and was no surprise to the neighborhood."[57]

Though Franklin's Puerto Rican population had grown over the years, their numbers were far below the proportion of Puerto Ricans entering the former stronghold of Italian Harlem. For even as the Italians flocked out of East Harlem, Franklin's reputation as an Italian school lingered and served as a bar to Puerto Rican enrollments. Unlike the high school, zoning laws were applied to Junior High 172, and Puerto Rican youngsters had no choice but to attend. Yet even with counseling support, many of them chose not to enroll in the high school.

The Postwar Curriculum

How did these changes impact Franklin's day-school curriculum? The Covello Papers provide only glimpses of how Covello and his staff adjusted the curriculum to the multiple crises of the 1940s and 1950s. The limited available evidence suggests that Franklin teachers, feeling a heavy strain, retreated from the academic standards of the prewar high school toward life adjustment education, an educational policy trend that emphasized adolescents' personal growth needs, as opposed to intellectual development.

During the war some teachers complained that "an academic curriculum" dominated the high school, suggesting at least a short-term carryover of the high school's nonvocational orientation from East 108th Street.[58] Desperate for students by 1944, Covello planned to introduce a "general vocational course" (recently authorized by the board of education) as a recruitment tool, although he lacked the shop teachers to run it. In addition to losing students to Manhattan's vocational high schools, Franklin fought a losing battle with academically elite Stuyvesant High School for the "mental cream" of East Harlem and Yorkville boys.[59]

Downgrading their expectations of students, Franklin teachers, often grudgingly, gravitated toward life adjustment education. It is difficult not to conclude that the East Harlem high school became a custodial institution in the postwar years, joining a national trend toward lowered expectations in the U.S. high school.[60] In 1947, noting the "high percentage of failure under the present curriculum," the school's scholarship committee called for revised courses of study "to make them more suitable to the needs, interests and capacities of the students" (a life adjustment mantra associated with a lack of academic substance).[61] A defeatist tone pervaded the annual departmental reports of the 1950s. In his 1953 report Mathematics Department chair Henry Levene, one of Covello's stalwarts, lamented that "the hundred percent promotions . . . have produced hidden deficiencies in many of our boys, which we find difficult to eliminate." Even in the upper-level math courses, remediation was needed for students "who declare they 'never learned' how to add $\frac{1}{2}$ and $\frac{1}{4}$, or how to divide a number by 12.5. . . . Such difficulties are not peculiar to Franklin boys, they are becoming general in our high schools." The Commercial Department, which Levene also chaired, had downgraded its formerly rigorous business arithmetic course. Once "geared to the state Regents examination," it "would have disappeared from our Department if we had not modified the subject along lines less rigid, more practical, more interesting for our students. It has become indeed, a course in 'Arithmetic for Daily Living.'" Comments from other departmental chairs are also telling, for example, Foreign Language, 1953: "One of the most serious problems facing our teachers has been that of retardation in reading ability among our students. Students who find it difficult to read English, find it even more difficult to read a foreign language"; Science, 1955: "The work we do must be based on the nature and capacities of the students"; English, 1956: "Our pupils, in the main, are not academic minded. Unfortunately so many come to us with such deep-seated reading difficulties that we are unable to provide more than slight amelioration and adjustment."[62]

Having noted this retreat from standards in Franklin's postwar curriculum, we are also mindful of a longstanding maxim that "if one wishes to create high standards of quality in public schools in a popular democracy, one has a hope of success only if the standards are broadly established and if the populace as a whole may therefore become committed to them."[63] In the New York City school district in the late 1940s and 1950s, as in other parts of the country, high standards were neither broadly established nor was the populace committed to them. In a climate where social promotion and life adjustment were the prevailing norms, Covello and his staff received neither resources nor encouragement for pressing a more rigorous agenda. And reflecting the shortcomings of the broader "system," the students who found their way into Franklin in the postwar era were increasingly appallingly ill-prepared for an academic program. Unsurprisingly, even the best of the high school's beleaguered teachers veered toward life adjustment education—by their lights it was the only game in town.

The Community Program: The Last Decade

After 1945 until Leonard Covello's retirement in 1956, Benjamin Franklin High School maintained a simulacrum of its former community program. The Community Advisory Council lapsed after the war, and its committee functions were incorporated by default into the East Harlem Council for Community Planning, a consortium of fifty-three agencies, including Benjamin Franklin and eleven elementary and secondary schools, chaired by the durable Rita Morgan.[64] The high school operated a truncated version of the old WPA recreation program with the support of community volunteers. One volunteer group, Veterans of Company K, New York City Patrol Corps, provided games, sports, and movies and sponsored the East Riviera Youth Council at the high school. In 1946 three community organizations used the building as their headquarters for periodic meetings and conferences: East Harlem Schools Committee, East Harlem Council for Community Planning, and Italian Social Workers, Inc.[65] Yet the daily program noticeably lacked the intensity of neighborly involvement characteristic of the old Franklin or the vibrancy and sheer quantity of people who crowded the storefronts along East 108th Street long into the evening or flooded into the school for a myriad of purposes. It is instructive to note that Covello himself recalled the prewar Franklin as the highwater mark of his efforts to create a community high school in East Harlem:

> The Wednesday night "open house" sessions in my office at the old building at Franklin came closest to fulfilling my dream of the school as an integral part of the community. Throughout the building, classes were in progress. I could sit in my office and listen happily to the hum of knowledge. Young men and adults who for one reason or another had been unable to graduate from day school were now completing their high-school education at night. In other rooms immigrants of varying ages and nationalities struggled with the complexities of the English language, sometimes taught by their own sons, while still others prepared for citizenship tests. In the gymnasium a basketball game was in progress, as often as not involving two Jews, two Italians, three Negroes, two Puerto Ricans, and a fellow named O'Reilly. In the library, the Parent-Teachers Association was holding a meeting, while from the auditorium might come the shrill sounds of an argument that meant that the Community Advisory Council was in session.[66]

Sanitation and playlot campaigns in the late 1940s, and a school-directed project to rescue small businesses in the path of East Harlem's housing projects in the early 1940s, recalled the spirit of the East Harlem campaigns of the 1930s. In a sense they were the last hurrah of Franklin's community program. They are explicated here both as part of the historical record and because they illustrate the variety of citizen-action projects that is possible in a community-centered approach.[67]

Sanitation Campaign and Carmine Luongo Playlot, 1948–1950

Simon Beagle, the school-community coordinator at James Otis Junior High School, 1947–53, directed the sanitation campaign and the Carmine Luongo Playlot projects, which were carried out by the Otis Youthbuilders, a school civic club organized in the fall of 1945 to help clean up East Harlem, alleviate racial tensions, and reduce juvenile delinquency.[68] The Youthbuilders extended their mission to counteracting negative press reports about East Harlem, revived by the polling-place murder of Joseph Scottoriggio, a Republican Party election-district captain, and sensationalized in press accounts (the *New York Times* published fifty-nine articles about the murder and subsequent grand jury investigation) that charged Vito Marcantonio with racketeering and linked him to the murder.[69] As the *Times* noted: "To them [Otis Youthbuilders] East Harlem means homes, school, churches, jobs and families—not racketeers, gangs and juvenile delinquency."[70] At the opening of the 1948–49 school year, the Youthbuilders walked the streets of East Harlem to determine if recent negative press reports about "dirty streets and lots" were true and what might be done about them. At the club's next meeting, "most members agreed with the newspapers. After each boy described what he had seen on his tour of conditions on his own block, one member said, 'The truth is the truth, and instead of complaining about the press, we should see if we can do something to clean up our neighborhood.'"[71]

The East Harlem sanitation campaign got under way in September 1948 and ran until February 1949. In conjunction with the city Sanitation Department and the East Harlem District Health Committee, the Youthbuilders helped organize the following activities: a parade, featuring a fifty-piece band donated by the Department of Sanitation, seventy placards provided by the high school Art and Shop departments, and five thousand leaflets printed by the city Sanitation Department and distributed along the line of march; a student and community leaders conference led by Vito Marcantonio; a cleanup contest in a six-block area sponsored by the *Daily News;* an educational campaign, including sound-truck broadcasts in the streets of East Harlem and a science and social studies lesson plan, "Sanitation in East Harlem"; and a (successful) campaign to change the City Sanitary Code to effect more frequent and efficient garbage collection.[72]

Pitting block against block, the five-day cleanup contest, the centerpiece of sanitation campaign, started on 6 December 1948 with Mayor William O'Dwyer, Commissioner of Sanitation William J. Powell, and the borough presidents of Manhattan and the Bronx presiding. The *Daily News* donated five thousand dollars in prizes (small appliances) to be awarded to each family living on the blue-ribbon block. Four judges—a representative of the Outdoor Cleanliness Association, a supervisor from the Newark Department of Sanitation, and two sanitary engineers from Columbia University and NYU, conducted the block inspections. At the outset, "the judges heartily agreed with Mayor O'Dwyer, who, after one look at 110th Street between Second and Third Ave., one of the six test blocks, littered with paper and cardboard and strewn with garbage and cans, declared: 'It's frightful.'" Most of the mess was attributed to what East Harlemites called "airmail delivery," garbage flying from windows into the streets, tenement courtyards, and alleyways. One woman at 210 East 113th Street told the *Daily News*: "Every time I see a bundle of garbage come splashing down in the street it makes me mad. It's dangerous to health, I have six children, and I tell my children never should they throw anything from the windows." Similarly, a woman at 215 East 112th Street remarked: "You should see this block in the Summer time. The flies are everywhere. They breed in the garbage in the gutters and backyards. Even at this time of year the neighborhood is so dirty I'm ashamed to invite my relatives to visit me. My son spends his time in Yorkville, where we lived before we came here. He says: 'Mother, I can't ask my friends to come into this neighborhood. Too dirty.'"[73] After several days, the judges noted great improvement in the blocks: "As we walked through the blocks from 110th to 115th St. between Second and Third Aves. on our tour today, the difference in the appearance of them all from last Monday was that of night and day."[74] According to one description of the contest: "East 111th Street was jubilant on the morning of the announcement that every family living on East 111th Street between 1–2 Avenue would receive a gift certificate, courtesy and compliments of the New York Daily News, for an electric percolator, table radio, lamp, waffle iron or toaster at Vim's."[75]

In the spring of 1949 and in 1950, the Otis Youthbuilders renewed their sanitation campaign in East Harlem. On 2 May 1949 students from James Otis Junior High School, Benjamin Franklin High School, and other East Harlem schools cleared two tons of garbage and rubbish from a vacant lot at 410 East 116th Street in just over a half hour, proclaimed by the *New York Times* as "the fastest clean-up job in recent sanitation history."[76] On 20–21 June, Franklin and Otis students inaugurated the summer sanitation drive in East Harlem with a sound truck and float loaned by the Department of Sanitation. The 1950 campaign targeted a "garbage ridden dump" at 115th Street between First and Pleasant avenues as the site for developing a "fully equipped recreation area." In the fall of 1949 Carmine Luongo, a florist and father of seventeen children, transferred the lot to the city for development as a vest-pocket playground for young children, with the simple justification: "I've been in the neighborhood twenty-seven years. My own kids are eight months to twenty-three years. I know it's no good for kids to play in the street, get run over, or play in the dirt."[77] A citywide collaboration of agencies built the Franklin Playlot. The Otis Youthbuilders cleared rubbish from the 50'x100' lot, where two buildings had formerly stood; the Sanitation Department collected the trash, the Manhattan Borough president's office paved the lot, the city Fire Department installed a circular shower and drains; and the Police Athletic League provided the playground supervisor. More than five hundred children marched into the playground on 16 July 1950 accompanied by the music of the Benjamin Franklin High School Band; after a round of obligatory speeches by government and civic leaders, the children "swarmed over the newly paved playlot to take up game equipment and start playing."[78]

Small-Business Survey, 1954–1955

In December 1954 Leonard Covello participated in the last community project of his remarkable tenure as principal. The small-business survey of 1954–55 also marked the end of the Benjamin Franklin community school. The survey was conducted to assist small-business owners who were being displaced by East Harlem's plethoric public housing developments—ten more projects since the East River Houses opened in 1941! (A student at Otis whose family fruit-and-vegetable business was displaced by a housing project after thirty-seven years at the same location on East 115th Street brought the problem to Leonard Covello's attention.) William Kirk, director of Union Settlement; Joseph Monserrat, director of the Puerto Rico Labor Department's Migration Division (a 1939 graduate of Benjamin Franklin High School); and Covello headed a planning committee that included East Harlem business leaders and representatives of social work and educational agencies. To gather information on the crisis in local small-business ownership, the planning committee assigned an extensive survey to the James Otis Social Studies Department, headed by Leon Bock, the current school-community coordinator.

The East Harlem Small-Business Survey had two phases. In the first phase, 150 pupils in Otis social studies classes surveyed seventy-seven blocks in the area between 106th and 125th streets, from Third Avenue to the East River, recording the names and addresses and type of business of 1,056 stores. Social studies pupils from JHS 83 conducted a similar survey of fifty-three square blocks, recording the location and type of business of another 762 stores. Union Settlement personnel surveyed 932 stores in the area below 106th Street. The final tally was 2,750 businesses. Data reported in 1956 revealed that at least 1,500 retail stores employing 4,500 people had been eliminated by the projects. The Franklin Houses, located from 109th and 106th streets between First and Third avenues, displaced 169 stores (2,873 years on the same spot) and 529 employees. Of the student role in the first part of the survey, Covello wrote: "The participating students received valuable citizenship training and experience in this survey activity. The students functioned in leadership positions managing the survey and in a creative capacity in map-making, illustrating and filing the survey results." In the second phase, Otis students "distributed and collected 1,200 questionnaires in English and Spanish" to identify consumer preferences about type and location of stores in relationship to the growing housing-project area. This survey revealed a "desire for an increased number of small neighborhood stores for *credit,* food, and *closeness to project*" [original emphasis].[79]

The Small-Business Survey and Planning Committee epitomized the catalytic role of the school as a "stimulus to community action, speeding and ener-
gizing the solutions of problems that might otherwise long handicap or retard
considerably the growth of an organization." The process of organization building would lead outward from the principal's office into the community, where
leadership of the project would eventually repose. First, Covello organized a
temporary Executive Committee, including social workers, teachers, and a student representative. The committee's role was "to bring business people into
the committee, to offer temporary leadership and guidance and then to transfer leadership completely to the people directly concerned—the East Harlem
businessman." The committee targeted a cross-section of East Harlem businesses. "Utilizing the material on locations and types of business catalogued
by the students, the Committee sent out invitations to 100 businessmen—50
chosen to cover a representative area on the principle of at least one businessman from each block and another 50 chosen to cover representative types of
business on the principle of at least one businessman from every important kind
of commercial venture."[80]

One meeting held in Covello's office on the evening of 25 May 1955 drew
forty participants. After Executive Committee members introduced the meeting and reviewed the committee's activity to date, including the survey work
of students, the participants discussed the question, "What can the committee
do to aid the city government in planning for the placement of the local storekeeper on the sites of the new housing projects?" Covello described that discussion in telling detail (punctuation emendations added):

> The living experiences behind the displacement statistics come to the
> fore here. . . . Mr. Frank Ascione, a druggist in the neighborhood for
> 33 years, tells his story: "For 29 years I had one place of business on
> the corner of East 115th Street and Second Avenue. I had a good drug
> store with friends and customers coming to me for years and years.
> Then the City gave me notice to get out to make room for the proj-
> ects. The projects are fine . . . they're good for the people to have a
> chance to live in new houses. But what about me? Where can I go to
> build up a new place? All the rents went way up wherever I tried to
> move in the neighborhood. Finally I was able to start a new place going
> on First Avenue near East 116th Street *only* because some good friends
> were able to loan me money. And now how do I know the City won't
> throw me out again—after all, look what happened to our good friend,
> Mr. Lopez. He had his Army and Navy store on East 112th Street near
> Lexington Avenue for years—then the James Weldon Johnson Houses
> pushed him out so he set up his business a few blocks further East on
> 113th Street and boom—another blockbuster came along and the Jef-
> ferson Houses evicted him. The man gave up—he gave up completely

and moved to Queens. We've lost a good man who served this community for many years. We have got to protect ourselves against this sort of thing."

"Absolutely right," said Mr. Rosenberg, proprietor of a clothing store on Third Avenue for over 50 years and head of a family active in East Harlem business affairs when the neighborhood still knew the one-story brownstone house and an Irish-German population. "How can we plan our business future when we don't know from month to month whether we will be allowed to remain where we are? Let's do something."

In answer to the business people's question, "What can be done?" the committee proposed the following strategy:

a. let us invite other local business people to join the Committee. Act energetically through personal contacts and visits to spread word of the next meeting.
b. let us draw in other community leaders to broaden our power: the minister of the Church on East 106th Street—a block marked for a future project; the lawyer for the Legal Aid Society, who has shown an interest in the human problem; the President of the Spanish Grocers Association on Madison Avenue; the Head of the Third Avenue Businessmen's Association. These names are noted; assignment for bringing these into the Committee is allotted.
c. let us plan to send a delegation to visit Mr. Warren Moscow, Executive Director of the New York Housing Authority, to present our views.
d. let us form a committee to seek favorable publicity for our viewpoint in the Press of the City of New York by presenting letters and news releases; with emphasis on the local neighborhood and foreign-language papers (Italian and Spanish).
e. let us plan for a large mass meeting of East Harlem Business people and consumers to dramatize our aims and show the united community feeling supporting our program.[81]

A total of fourteen meetings were held within a period of seven months, from December 1954 to June 1955, "to introduce the work of the committee to successive groups of business people in the natural community-areas of East Harlem." The latter's full participation, however, was problematic. Covello noted "fluctuations in attendance"—that "the people most concerned in the affairs of the committee, the *business-people,* found it difficult to maintain a regular attendance." Irregular attendance complicated the transfer of leadership responsibility to the small-business community. "The main sources of early leadership of the Committee could be traced to the School Principal, Dr. Leonard Covello, the Director of Union Settlement, Mr. William Kirk, and the Director of the Puerto Rican Migration and Labor Bureau, Mr. Joseph Monserrat. It was felt and expressed all along that leadership in this committee must come from the people most directly concerned: the business people. 'They cannot be dragged to salvation against their will' was the theme of the expectation that the merchants would accept and carry out the leadership roles." An effort to share these leadership positions with counterparts in the business community foundered when the businesspeople deferred to the presumed authority and expertise of the "nonbusiness" committee leaders. "They waited for signals from the co-leaders before proceeding with any action and allowed the items of letter-writing, money-raising and agenda-planning to be performed by the School or Settlement House personnel on the Committee." Now cognizant of these shortcomings, the school leadership on the committee resigned to force the merchants to take charge themselves—sink or swim. "An owner of a barber shop, Mr. Michael Di Silvestro, eloquent and energetic with the conviction that fair play be given to the small businessmen, joined Mr. Pedro Canino, business leader in the Spanish speaking section, as Co-Chairmen of the Committee. Other business people accepted Executive positions."[82]

Near the end of his tenure as principal Covello expressed optimism that the "East Harlem Small Businessmen Association," controlled exclusively by local merchants, with the school in an advisory role, would be a going concern. "Under the stimulus of their manifest self-interest and with the sense of the undivided responsibility for accomplishment on their shoulders," Covello wrote, "the business people moved ahead and are moving ahead today." The most propitious indication was the city Housing Authority's commitment to give displaced storekeepers priority consideration for commercial sites in the Taft and Franklin Housing Projects.[83]

A Note on McCarthyism and Benjamin Franklin

How did McCarthyism and Cold War tensions, evident in New York City's antisubversive campaign, which started in the 1940s, affect the community high school, which had a social-activist orientation and longstanding ties to Vito Marcantonio? While Benjamin Franklin was not unscathed by the witch-hunts, the damage was surprisingly minimal. In fact, the only incident we can document occurred in 1951, when the *Herald-Tribune* accused Speech Department chair Rita Morgan of being "red" for having spoken at a peace rally attended by Communists. Morgan successfully defended herself against the charge on First Amendment grounds, aided by the intercession of Covello and Superintendent of Schools William Jansen. In Morgan's case Superintendent Jansen played the role of a benevolent despot.[84]

In the summer of 1952 Jansen appointed city corporation counsel Saul Moskoff to investigate suspected Communist party activity among the city's teachers. According to labor historian Marjorie Murphy: "Moskoff collected all the lists he could find, from Communist party nominating petitions to license-plate numbers of cars observed at rallies for the Rosenbergs, and he looked for teachers' names."[85] Moskoff and the board of education's primary target was the heavily Jewish Teachers Union, which as Local 5 had been ousted from the American Federation of Teachers in 1941 because of members' ties to the Communist Party. Most of the teachers who were dismissed in the late forties and fifties were Jewish unionists; indeed, as one student of the purge argues, the inquisition had a strong anti-Semitic flavor.[86] While Superintendent Jansen would on occasion intercede on behalf of an accused teacher, as Rita Morgan's case illustrates, more often he endorsed the racking and head-chopping; in one notorious case, Jansen sent a teacher to the block for refusing to participate in a celebration the superintendent had ordered in honor of General Douglas MacArthur's homecoming.[87] Greasing the skids for the purge was a New York Supreme Court justice's ruling in 1950 that allowed the board of education to dismiss teachers under Section 903 of the City Charter of 1936 for refusing to answer questions.[88] By the end of the fifties Moskoff and his henchmen had extracted a pound or more of flesh from 447 teachers: Thirty-eight of these teachers were fired, 283 resigned or retired either before or after being interrogated, and 126 were reinstated only after completely and convincingly repudiating their former ties to the Communist Party.[89]

Other than the Morgan case, the antisubversive campaign appears to have bypassed Benjamin Franklin. In the absence of school-specific documentation, we can only speculate as to why that was the case. Apparently the critical factor weighing in the purges was membership in the Teachers Union, the board of education's bête noire in the McCarthy era. Given the union's past association with the Communist Party, it was a magnet for harassment and public humiliation, if not dismissal by the board. By contrast, membership in the Teachers Guild probably signified one's good standing with the board.[90] The union teachers who were fired worked in high schools and grade schools in Brooklyn and the Bronx, in particular Brooklyn Technical High School, Franklin Lane High School, Abraham Lincoln High School, and Jefferson High School.[91] In short, the topography of the witch-hunt suggests that Franklin teachers were not strongly associated with the Teachers Union.

Some Franklin teachers had impeccable anti-Communist credentials and the high school may have benefited from their reputations. Layle Lane, a socialist African American teacher at Franklin in the 1930s and 1940s, and Simon Beagle, the community coordinator in the 1950s, played leading roles in the AFT's ouster of the Local 5 Communists and the establishment of the Teachers Guild, the forerunner of the United Federation of Teachers. Covello, an old Teacher Unionist himself, broke with the union to join the fledgling guild, which was headed by his former DeWitt Clinton colleagues Abraham Lefkowitz and Henry Linville.[92] As for the Benjamin Franklin–Marcantonio connection, those ties were sharply attenuated following the high school's move to Pleasant Avenue. The time when a Hearst newspaper would describe Franklin as a bastion of the *Daily Worker* quickly passed.[93] This is not say that the Franklin teachers were unaffected by the hysteria, which had an incalculable ripple effect across the city schools. With a precarious toehold on the ladder of social mobility, teachers of immigrant origin felt particularly vulnerable. The 1940s generation of teachers interviewed by Ruth Markowitz claimed that "almost all Jewish teachers, Communist or not, believed themselves to be potential suspects."[94]

Sadly, Louis Relin, the former Benjamin Franklin English teacher who had played such a prominent role in the high school's intercultural programs and the East Harlem housing campaign, fell prey to the anti-Communist dragnet at Abraham Lincoln High School in Brooklyn. After nineteen years of teaching, Relin, a Teachers Union member, was fired by the board of education on 2 October 1952 for violating Section #203 of the New York City Charter: "Any city employee refusing to testify about his work before a legally constituted body . . . shall be dismissed." Standing on the principle of academic freedom, Relin had pleaded the Fifth Amendment before a subcommittee of the U.S. Senate Judiciary Committee, which was charged to investigate "subversive activities" in the New York City schools. Relin, who would later list his occupation as "salesman," bitterly recounted: "I am teacher. I was a darned good one as my supervisors would tell you. . . . The hundreds of us dismissed without justification, victims of McCarthyite lunacy, were the very ones most dedicated to the welfare of our young citizens of tomorrow."[95]

Valedictory

Leonard Covello retired as principal of Benjamin Franklin High School following the spring semester of 1956. There is evidence that he was moving toward a reconstruction of the curriculum—toward a three-tiered curriculum of core intellectual skills (reading, social studies, applied mathematics and science-consumer education, music and art appreciation, and health education), community problems (discussion groups, service at community centers, charitable work, nurses' aids, school community committees, community research, etc.), and elective specializations (college preparatory, vocational, commercial).[96] Yet a genuine integration of community issues and academic learning continued to elude him. Covello retired early, his hopes apparently frustrated by low enrollments and rife speculation that the high school would be turned over to the junior high division of the board of education. He wrote Leon Bock: "About my retirement from Franklin—I would have stayed on for the two extra years possible but I felt it was better for me to go since the plan I proposed for Franklin apparently is not forthcoming in the near future."[97]

At age sixty-nine, Covello retired from the public schools to an active part-time career as the educational consultant to the Commonwealth of Puerto Rico's Migration Division, headquartered in New York City and directed by Joseph Monserrat, a 1939 Benjamin Franklin High School graduate. The Puerto Rican government established the Migration Division, which employed 105 persons in eleven U.S. cities to provide employment assistance, educational services, community leadership development, and public relations work.[98] Covello's longstanding involvement with Puerto Rican youngsters and more recently his service on the Mayor's Committee on Puerto Rican Affairs (he authored the committee's 1951 report "Puerto Ricans Pupils in New York City" and coordinated the New York Puerto Rican Scholarship Fund established in 1952), not to mention more than twenty years of work as one of the leading proponents of intercultural education in New York City (he chaired the Board of Education Committee on Intercultural Relations in a Post-War World and the High School Principals' Committee on Intercultural Education), well qual-ified him for that position, which he held for more than a decade.[99] Covello's work included, among other activities, coordinating the Migration Division's in-service courses for New York City teachers (for example, "Practical Tech-niques for Working with Puerto Rican Families in New York City"), directing a teacher-exchange program, and speaking in communities in the New York City metropolitan area.[100] In 1960 he told friends:

> My work with the Puerto Rican government is becoming more and more involved. There is so much to be done. At present Rose and I are planning to chaperone a group of 12 high school students who are going to Puerto Rico as guests of the Puerto Rican government dur-ing Xmas week. These students were chosen from schools where there is a large percentage of Puerto Rican students. We want these 12 stu-dents to see Puerto Rico and get a different view of the people there so they can come back and be goodwill ambassadors to make for bet-ter relations between the Puerto Rican students and those of other eth-nic backgrounds. Last year 7 Italian boys went to Puerto Rico and came back with a completely different viewpoint and one that has been most beneficial in smoothing out tensions and difficulties. [101]

In 1961 Covello reported spending two to three days a week at the Migra-tion Division, located at 322 West 45th Street, and one day a week at the East Harlem Day Center for Older People, housed in the old Franklin High School building at 309 East 108th Street, where he served as chair of the center's board of directors.[102] He also chaired the East Harlem Good Neighbor Committee, which sponsored an annual open-air "Good Neighbor Week," and the education committee of the East Harlem Council for Community Planning. Although he had lived in Westwood, New Jersey, since 1950, his "first love *was, is* and always will be EAST HARLEM" (original emphasis).[103]

In 1966 Leonard and Rose left Bergen County and moved back across the Hudson to an apartment at 975 Walton Avenue in the Bronx, one block from the Grand Concourse. The pensioner Covello had too much work in the city to be bothered with a daily commute across the George Washington Bridge from Bergen County. For office space he rented the parlor of a brownstone at 319 East 116th Street, just fifteen minutes by cab from his apartment, where he moved his professional papers and books, including the files of the newly incorporated Italian-American Historical Association, which he helped organize, pending transfer of the archive to Casa Italiana, Columbia University.[104]

Covello quickly acquired legendary status at Benjamin Franklin High School, where the Leonard Covello Scholarship Fund was established in 1957; the high school auditorium dedicated as Covello Hall in 1961, replete with a bronze plaque of Covello's profile in bas relief; and the plaque replicated as the Covello Medal, to be awarded annually to "a Franklin student that had to overcome the greatest difficulties to achieve graduation."[105] Periodically, Covello returned to the high school for graduation days and informal visits. "I do miss my boys and my school very much," he confided to a friend in 1958. In 1960 he wrote Layle Lane, remarking wistfully: "I spent the morning at Franklin the other day, seeing old friends and wandering around the building to see what our boys are up to."[106]

In 1972, at the age of eighty-five, Covello left New York for the last time (Rose Covello had died), returning to Italy for the last decade of his vigorous life to work with the Sicilian reformer Danilo Dolci at Dolci's Center for Study and Action in western Sicily. He died in Messina on 19 August 1982.[107] The *New York Times* carried Covello's obituary, citing Nathan Glazer and Daniel P. Moynihan's salute to him as "one of the great educators of New York City."[108]

After Covello's retirement, Benjamin Franklin High School became an ordinary comprehensive high school. Given the low enrollments, its status as a high school remained uncertain until 1960, when the board of education "saved" Franklin by making it coeducational.[109] By then Covello's community school program had vanished. (In Chapter 8 we discuss national trends that explain why this idea failed to inspire a social movement.)

By 1966, reflecting East Harlem's postwar demographic profile, the student population at Benjamin Franklin was approximately 97 percent black and Puerto Rican. Over the years the post-Covello Franklin would be described as the "worst high school in the city"—by 1966 the average Franklin tenth grader read at a fifth-grade level—and labeled "the Drug Store."[110] Between 1976 and 1980 the high school lost more than a thousand students and in 1981 graduated only forty-six seniors. Its 1981 the attendance rate was 59 percent, 20 percent below the citywide average, and the school's 290 suspensions in 1980 were four times the citywide average. The *New York Times* attributed the school's demise to "a debilitating pathology of ethnic politics, shifting population and that intangible ingredient essential to the health of every New York City public school: 'reputation.'"[111]

The board of education decided to close the high school in June of 1982, ironically just a few months before Covello's death, because of "dwindling enrollment, declining achievement and poor attendance record."[112] The building would continue to serve as a city high school, although it was divested of any association with the former occupant. In September 1983, the city's chancellor of schools, Anthony J. Alvarado, reopened what was formerly Benjamin Franklin High School as the Manhattan Center for Science and Mathematics, a selective academic high school in District 4, which graduated its first class of 143 students in 1986 with only one dropout to report for the cohort. The class valedictorian was headed to Yale.[113]

The irony of Benjamin Franklin High School as a community school is not that it failed in the end, but that no one even bothered to ask why it failed or how it managed to accomplish as much as it did. This book seeks to redress this loss of historical perspective. We conclude this chapter with a brief assessment of factors that in combination worked to undermine the East Harlem community high school.

Even at its high-water mark in the late 1930s, Benjamin Franklin High School faced formidable, if not insuperable, obstacles as an institutional catalyst for social reconstruction in East Harlem. Visionary, charismatic, indefatigable, Leonard Covello became East Harlem's Lone Ranger. Covello envisaged concentric circles of reconstructed social blocks progressively radiating outward from the high school across the neighborhoods of East Harlem. The limitations of this vision were manifested in the enormous investment of time, energy, and resources needed to organize just one local neighborhood. Bluntly stated, Franklin's reach exceeded its grasp. Functioning as community schools, the area's elementary and junior high schools might have interacted with their own neighborhoods in a fashion similar to Franklin's community program, relieving the high school of a districtwide burden it was ill-equipped to assume and expanding the ambit of community-centered schooling. The fact remains, however, that Covello's was the *only* commitment by an East Harlem principal to the community school idea. Furthermore, there existed no school district infrastructure or even a core of support to encourage the development of a network of community schools in East Harlem or anywhere else in the city. The board of education lacked sustainable resources to support even Covello's community school, let alone an East Harlem network. The WPA case makes the point.

As indicated previously, the WPA provided numerous workers to the high school for a plethora of activities: teaching, research, counseling, record keeping, recreation, et cetera. The curtailment of the community program after 1940 reflects in large part the withdrawal of WPA workers from the high school.

The absence of sustained governmental funding was never counterbalanced by indigenous institutional support or an outpouring of community volunteers. Columbia University and New York University qua institutions viewed the high school as an exciting vehicle for training student teachers yet never acknowledged Franklin's program as somehow integral to their own mission and self-interest. Columbia's neglect was arguably egregious given its close proximity to the high school, its vital self-interest in a sane and healthy Harlem, and the presence of an influential cadre of "social reconstructionists" on the Teachers College faculty who heralded schoolteachers as the vanguard of radical social reform.[114]

We suspect that social class differences between the high school's founders and their Italian constituents worked to some degree against Covello's democratic project. His high-culture version of Italian ethnicity, if not his strategy of guided democracy, was likely off-putting to some Italian Americans. By the same token, the East Harlem housing campaign was undoubtedly resented in some quarters, especially by those who were to be displaced by the bulldozers of the East River Houses and already had, by their lights, satisfactory living or business arrangements.

Ethnic differences were more clearly a decisive factor in the community high school's decline. Covello's considerable efforts to build a sense of community in East Harlem were inadequate to stave off ethnocultural conflict, in either the local community or even his own building. The high school reflected the shifting frontiers of ethnic settlement in East Harlem and attendant ethnic clashes along those borders. Cultural conflict exacted a heavy toll on student enrollments, especially among the Puerto Ricans. Because of its location in the spiritual heart of Italian Harlem, standing cheek by jowl with the Madonna of 115th Street, Benjamin Franklin retained a residual Italian identity that in the 1950s discouraged many Puerto Rican youngsters from attending the high school even as the surrounding neighborhoods burgeoned with Puerto Rican tenants. By 1956, the year Covello retired, enrollments had plummeted to 652. By that time in a very real sense Benjamin Franklin was *in,* but no longer *of,* East Harlem.

PART THREE

The Community School Idea
since World War II

CHAPTER EIGHT

Drift and Renewal:
Community Education and
Community Schools

THE PARTICIPATORY DEMOCRATIC reform tradition of community-centered schooling promoted by Samuel Everett in his 1938 book, *The Community School,* and richly expressed in Covello's East Harlem project, faded after World War II. Nothing recognizable as a community school of this genre would appear for decades thereafter, not even in the community-control battles of the late 1960s. Starting in the late 1980s, however, a core of university faculty activists and community organizers, if not always consciously, embraced this tradition and linked it to a broader renewal of interest in community schools.

This chapter looks at the last sixty years of the community school idea, which we divide into two stages: the rise and persistence of the community education movement, a diffuse, ill-defined, often conservative trend, from 1942 to 1990; and the emerging movement toward community schools since 1990. In the early years of the twenty-first century, community education remains a strong continuing trend, paralleling and in many cases converging with the recent movement toward community schools. Proponents of the participatory democratic tradition of community-centered schooling have staked a vigorous claim within the new emergent community school movement. They advocate what we call *citizen-centered* community schools, a conception that differs markedly in kind from the *client-centered* (service-center model) community schools that in contemporary practice are the dominant version of the community school idea.

We precede our analysis of post–World War II developments with a discussion of John Dewey's problematic role in community school history. After his Chicago period and for the rest of his career, Dewey distanced himself from the idea of schools as social centers or community schools, having little to say on the subject and ultimately repudiating community schools as an appropriate strategy for cities. If community schools were such a good idea, why did Dewey downgrade them? What role did his "defection" play in the failure of community schools to enter the mainstream of U.S. education?

Dewey: Missing in Action

From 1902, when he delivered his paper "The School as Social Centre" to the National Council of Education in Minneapolis, until his death in 1952 Dewey had little more to say about school social centers, school community centers, or community schools. In fact, beyond the 1902 piece, Dewey published no more than three short essays related to any of these topics. The first essay appeared in *Schools of To-Morrow,* which Dewey wrote in collaboration with his daughter Evelyn in 1915 at the high tide of the school social center movement.[1] The second piece was his revealing introduction to Elsie Clapp's 1939 book *Community Schools in Action,* in which he applauded Clapp's rural community school experiments yet eschewed potential urban applications of community schooling.[2] The third essay, his very last publication on education, served as an unsatisfactory introduction to Clapp's second book on community schooling, a 1952 work entitled *The Use of Resources in Education,* in which Dewey hardly even mentioned community schools.[3]

That Dewey abandoned, in all but a token way, community-centered schooling is also evident in his absence in key archival records related to the community school idea and a deafening silence in his correspondence. The Speyer School of Teacher's College, hailed by Harold Rugg as the nation's first community school, is an exemplary case: Even at home Dewey was in absentia.[4] Dewey is missing in extant documents that likely would have recorded his activity at Speyer had there been any, including annual publications of the *Dean's Report* and articles in *Teachers College Record;* his letters mention no involvement and suggest only a passing interest in the school.[5]

Why then did Dewey, the nation's preeminent educational philosopher, pay such short shrift to an idea that once loomed so large in his theory? The answer is to be found in large part in Dewey's change of venue from Chicago to New York in 1905. Dewey resigned his chair at the University of Chicago in the spring of 1904 following an acrimonious dispute with Chicago's president, William Rainey Harper, over the administration of Dewey's Laboratory School. It also deprived Dewey of the powerful influence of Jane Addams, the founder of Hull House, an activist with brilliant educational insights who worked closely with Dewey, and Ella Flagg Young, an extraordinary teacher and practical thinker who studied with Dewey at the University of Chicago and helped him link the workings of the Laboratory School with his theoretical pursuits.[6]

Another factor intruded in the summer of 1904: Dewey's homelife began to deteriorate. During a family trip to the British Isles his eight-year-old son, Gordon, contracted typhoid fever and died, an event that devastated Dewey and even more his wife, Alice, who suffered a mental breakdown from which she apparently never recovered (another son, Morris, had died nine years earlier of diphtheria in Milan).[7] Max Eastman saw Alice, who was principal of the Dewey School and a major irritant to Harper, as the indispensable activist in Dewey's life, without whom the Dewey School would never have happened; Dewey's wife, he tersely notes, "kicked" him to become an activist. From his vantage point as a close friend of Dewey, Eastman wrote tellingly: "Nothing seems important to him but thinking. He is as complete an extrovert as ever lived, but the extroversion all takes place inside his head. Ideas are real objects to him, and they are the only objects that engage his passionate interest."[8] Of Alice Dewey's influence Eastman observed: "Mrs. Dewey would grab Dewey's ideas—and grab him—and insist that something be done. . . . She kept pulling him down into the real world."[9] But after they left Chicago, Alice became far more a burden than an inspiration to Dewey; she lost her zeal and grew increasingly resentful and caustic.

It might be said, of course, that Addams and Young had also pulled Dewey into the real world. As a result, without the benefit of their influence and insights and Alice's exhortations, and lacking a supportive institutional venue, Dewey turned, as if by default, to scholastic writing and publication.[10]

In 1905 Dewey joined the faculty of Columbia University, where until his retirement in 1927, he retained an endowed professorship in the Department of Philosophy and Psychology and a joint appointment at Teachers College. At Columbia he withdrew from practical activity to improve the U.S. schooling system.[11] While he continued to write from the treasure trove of experiences and ideas cultivated at the Chicago Laboratory School, he ventured no new school experiment or educational project to build, test, or refine his educational theories. *How We Think,* Dewey's brilliant disquisition on reflective thinking published in 1910, "is essentially a Chicago work."[12] To a certain extent, this is also true of perhaps his most famous work, *Democracy and Education,* published in 1916, which revisits and extends many of the ideas expounded in *The School and Society* (1899), *The Child and the Curriculum* (1902), a raft of other Chicago essays, and *How We Think* (1910). Though Dewey added some new writing on education in the 1920s and 1930s, these essays contributed little more than a clarification of ideas that Dewey's disciples had distorted into a romanticized view of children.[13] And in the main these ideas were essentially derived from Dewey's Chicago years.

That Dewey made no effort to develop the social center idea any further than the germ he planted in 1902 is suggested by his relationship with Elsie

Clapp. Clapp was Dewey's most astute disciple, the one who best understood his educational philosophy and its implications for practice. Clapp was Dewey's student at Columbia University as early as 1908 and a graduate assistant in his course on educational philosophy at Teachers College in the summer sessions of 1911 and 1912. This was the start of a longstanding professional relationship and friendship: Clapp would assist Dewey with his course in various sessions in the 1920s before undertaking her Ballard School experiment and the Arthurdale School.[14] From 1913 to 1924 she taught in public and private schools, the latter including the Milton Academy of Milton, Massachusetts, 1921–23; and the City and Country School of New York City, 1923–24. From 1924 to 1929 she served as head of the Rosemary Junior School of Greenwich, Connecticut, where she worked, at Dewey's suggestion, on "modern methods" of teaching and curriculum in a college-preparatory upper school.[15] In her private life Clapp participated in labor strikes and suffrage campaigns and cultivated "a growing sympathy with the plight of the working class."[16] Not until she moved to Kentucky and West Virginia, however, would these pedagogical and social-activist strands of her progressivism be united in a single approach.

Clapp's community school experiments were directly inspired by Dewey. In her acknowledgments to *Community Schools in Action,* she emphasized: "The work which is here described is itself a tribute to John Dewey, whose philosophy and whose vision of the school as a social institution prompted our efforts to create a community school and to participate in community education. Although he is no way responsible for what was done, everything that we have learned from our experiences in this attempt we learned in a special sense from him. The work and the book which records it are to be counted among the numberless expressions of appreciation in this country and abroad of one of the greatest thinkers of our time."[17]

Regarding the Ballard School in Jefferson County, Kentucky, we do not know whether Clapp actually communicated her plan to Dewey or his role in its development. But a note in her resume suggests that Dewey may have encouraged her to launch the Ballard project: "Work undertaken because John Dewey wished to have worked out for educational use [a] plan of community education, and the concept and operation of a community school."[18] Clapp's book and the archival record, however, are silent as to Dewey's further involvement at Ballard. We must surmise that he never visited the school.[19]

While Dewey was listed as a member of the Permanent Advisory Committee of the Arthurdale School in Arthurdale, West Virginia, his participation was, for all intents and purposes, nominal.[20] He did manage to visit the West Virginia project, and what he saw there made a strong impression. "Last week I visited for a few days a school in connection with the re-settlement project in Arthurdale, West Virginia," he wrote a colleague at Black Mountain College. "In many respects it is the best public school I have seen in this country."[21]

By the fall of 1939 Dewey was encouraging Clapp to write a second book. "You have the material for a noteworthy book on the subject of educational resources," he advised." It would use of course some of the same material you have in your report book—but in a different context—or rather a context that would seem to most readers to be different." Dewey exhorted Clapp that he felt "more and more strongly—and largely because of your own work—that the next educational step—or the completion of the one started—depends upon educators grasping the significance of the resources of their own communities for educational purposes."[22]

It would take Clapp thirteen years to complete the second book on Ballard and Arthurdale. This was undoubtedly a frustrating project for her, as it dragged on for years and in the end may have alienated her from the aging Dewey. Clapp always thought of Dewey as "my advisor," and this project was no exception.[23] Clapp was always the dutiful acolyte in this relationship; in this respect her query to Dewey upon completion of the third quarter of the manuscript is telling: "So this seems the time to ask you what you would like to have me stress—What points you would like to see brought out."[24] Although it apparently had been agreed, as late as October 1948, that Dewey would write the introduction to the book, a year later his endorsement was still in doubt. Clapp wrote several letters to Dewey, even offering to send Dewey a letter he had written in the early days of the manuscript to use as the main basis of his introduction.[25] In 1951 as Dewey, now in his nineties, entered a period of physical decline, he enlisted a colleague, Joseph Ratner, to assist him with the introduction and to deal with Clapp. For the first time in their long relationship, Clapp expressed dissatisfaction with Dewey and sent him a proposed revision of the introduction, which the combative Ratner asserted was "wholly unacceptable" to Dewey. Ratner enlisted William Heard Kilpatrick as his emissary to tell Clapp that Dewey "must decline to consider any further revisions"; Ratner added: "To put it more bluntly than Mr. Dewey would perhaps consider necessary . . . Miss Clapp is to feel free to accept or reject his Introduction but she is not to feel free to change it or to ask him to change it."[26] Kilpatrick ended the negotiations a week later in a letter to Ratner: "I cannot say that Miss Clapp is happy, but this seems the best solution to the problem."[27] Clapp must have been distraught over this slight.

Dewey's death from pneumonia in June 1952 concluded the more than forty-year relationship with her mentor. In a letter of sympathy to Dewey's second wife, Roberta, Clapp recounted Dewey's formidable influence on her life: "I would . . . just like to say what you already know—that no one outside my family has throughout my life been as close to my heart as Dr. Dewey. For over forty years, during the time I worked with him at the University and the active years which followed, he not only taught and counselled me, but shared with me currently some of his thinking and gave me the support of his belief in what I was doing. I have now an overwhelming sense of loss, but I know that he would expect me to go forward; it would be a poor return for his unfailing generous help and trust not to attempt to do so."[28]

It seems reasonable to conclude that "the school as social centre" would have disappeared from Dewey's radar screen altogether after 1915 had not Elsie Clapp been willing to invest her career in advancing the idea. Community-centered schooling was an evolving approach for Clapp; the distressed conditions that gave rise to Arthurdale required a more adventurous approach than she had taken in the Kentucky project. Clapp's conceptual advance and evolving strategy was a community problem–based curriculum.[29] Viewed in historical perspective, that strategy represented a "logical extension" and practical application of the body of theory that emerged from Dewey's Chicago years.[30]

By 1939 and Clapp's publication of *Community Schools in Action,* however, Dewey had so far distanced himself from his Chicago years and urban public schools in particular that he failed to see exactly where she was heading with his theory.[31] While Dewey recognized the distinct advantages of rural community schools organized à la Ballard and Arthurdale, he now rejected any suggestion that this approach might work in cities: "For I am convinced it is a mistake to believe that the most needed advances in school organization and activities are going to take place chiefly in cities—especially in large cities."[32] Yet had Dewey acted in ways consistent with his Chicago theory (thinking reflectively, integrating means and ends), he might have reached a far different conclusion about urban community schools—the very schools he recognized as having the "deepest need."[33] Leonard Covello might well have winced when he read Dewey's repudiation of urban community schools.

By 1952 and the publication of *The Use of Resources in Education,* Elsie Clapp had another good reason to be distraught with Dewey. His five-page "introduction" to her second book really had little to do with her text. In the opening paragraph he begged off from any discussion of community schools. "It would be to engage in a wholly superfluous performance," he wrote, "if I were to detain the reader with any restatement of the basic ideas Miss Clapp has so effectively stated in the context of describing the educational work actually done, where ideas take on life and their consequences become manifest."[34] Dewey then proceeded to defend "the ideas and principles I have had a hand in developing" and to criticize the tendency of teachers colleges to convert progressive education into "a fixed, self-sufficient subject matter."[35] We are reminded of the apocryphal theology student who turned the exam question on its ear: "Far be it for me to distinguish the major and minor prophets of Israel and Judah—but as for the kings."

It seems reasonable to speculate that had Dewey acted to realize his general ideas in concrete practice, the history of progressive education would have taken a radically different course than the one it followed in the 1920s and 1930s. Dewey would have recognized community schools as a primary means to his "Great Community" and "living democracy" (for further discussion, see

Chapter 9). As a proactive force he would have lent his enormous prestige and energy to the pre–World War I "school as social center" movement and made that social movement the main basis of progressive education in the Depression era and beyond. In that event the outrages committed in his name by disciples misled by his abstract prescriptions might not have taken place. In all likelihood, of course, for that development to have occurred, Dewey would have had to remain at the University of Chicago.[36]

The Community Education Movement

Rise of Community Education and the Mott Foundation, 1942–1960

In the 1940s the community school idea was conflated with the rhetoric of life adjustment education, a hybridized curriculum approach loosely based on social efficiency ideology and developmental psychology. Through catchphrases such as "life-centered education" and goal statements such as "genuine competence in successful living," community school proponents made this connection explicit.[37] "Community education" was coined as an omnibus term for community schools and community-based educational programs that operated outside schools. While "community ed" created a rhetoric and national discourse about community schools and related educational programs, it failed to inspire anything like Covello's citizen-centered community school. Indeed, the memory of that adventurous social experiment faded and then vanished in the community education literature of subsequent decades. A client-centered approach has dominated community education practice and rhetoric for the past fifty years.

In 1945 Edward Olsen joined the Washington State Department of Education as the nation's first state official "specifically assigned to promote development of community education in local school districts." For the next five years, Olsen and his staff "helped 21 local districts design systematic community surveys, compile directories of resource people and field trip opportunities, include lay people in school program planning, organize community-school councils, and establish routine procedures."[38] In 1953 Olsen edited *The Modern Community School,* a book that sharply distinguished the community-education movement from the 1930s community school movement. "Our earlier emphasis which seems to have gone," Olsen wrote, "is the matter of improving the social order. Apparently projects to make life better for members of the community in areas such as health, food, shelter, recreation, race relations, and international understanding are being accomplished without labeling them as attempts to bring about a new social order."[39] Olsen might have added, "and without an animating democratic vision."

The National Society for the Study of Education (NSSE) devoted part 2 of its 1953 yearbook to the topic of *The Community School*, a collection of twenty-seven essays. Maurice Seay, chair of the University of Chicago's Department of Education, who had authored the chapter "The Community-School Emphasis in Postwar Education" for part 1 of the 1944 NSSE yearbook, chaired the committee that organized the 1953 volume. Seay's earlier chapter provided the basis of the new book. He also contributed the introductory chapter to *The Community School*, in which he advocated a community problem–solving curriculum as a critical element of the community school. On his view, students' learning activity would be targeted directly toward "an improvement in the living conditions and standards of the community." Through the study of a local problem involving "different types of instructional materials," students would acquire "appropriate skills, values, and concepts" that would then be applied "to solve larger problems," adding in turn "more skills, enriched values and broadened concepts"[40]

The yearbook committee chose Paul Hanna and Robert Naslund to also define the community school. Beyond its community-service functions, Hanna and Naslund argued: "The [community] school is a center where children and youth become partners with adults in discovering community needs and problems, in analyzing them, in exploring and formulating possible solutions to them, and in applying the results of these co-operative efforts so that community living is improved. Thus, the community school is a unifying force *of the community* rather than merely *in the community*" (original emphasis).[41]

The contemporary programs described in the section on "educational and social experimentation reflecting community-school objectives," however, did not embrace this kind of school-based community organizing and activism. A case in point was the Michigan Community-School Service Program, which was sponsored by the Michigan Department of Public Instruction from 1945 to 1953 with support from the Kellogg Foundation. In eight northern Michigan towns and twenty-four local communities, program leaders organized study committees of local citizens to address problem areas in their communities. The committees functioned independently of the local schools and many of their activities did not even involve the schools. As the Michigan case suggests, community educators in their practice were beginning to attenuate the school's role in community-improvement efforts.[42]

Starting in the late 1940s and continuing in the 1950s, community education was swept up in an attack mounted by influential critics who charged that life adjustment education, by now the dominant version of progressive education, was diverting schools from teaching the liberal arts curriculum and depriving the nation of the scientists, mathematicians, engineers, and linguists it needed to win the Cold War. Life adjustment education, which, according to historian Herbert Kliebard, received "unprecedented support in professional educational journals and among highly placed school officials," often advocated frivolous, nonintellectual subjects as core curricular content, for example (notoriously), "Basic Urges, Wants and Needs, [and] Making Friends and Keeping Them," in Battle Creek, Michigan; and (vaguely) "problems 'meaningful to youth' and building the 'right attitudes'" in Minneapolis.[43] Though it is uncertain how extensive such programs were in actual practice, the ballyhoo behind them and the firestorm of criticism they unleashed set in motion a national rethinking of curriculum, which gained increased impetus from the Soviet launching of the Sputnik earth-orbiting satellite in 1957. Hundreds of millions of federal dollars supported a national "structure of the discipline" movement, which resulted in a spate of new voluntary national curricula in science, mathematics, foreign languages, and social studies. Associated with life adjustment education and lacking academic content, community education was out of step in this political climate.[44]

During the 1960s, community education retreated into an enclave, the state of Michigan, where the Charles Stewart Mott Foundation began building an infrastructure that would support a resurgent and reinvigorated community education movement after 1970, when a favorable political climate prevailed for the wider use of schools as community-service providers. (Community education is indicative of the influence of private foundations in shaping the development of schooling ideas.) Community education's client-centered version of the community school idea would gain widespread support from state education offices and a home base in state university systems.

The Mott Foundation's leadership of the community education movement after 1960 was historically rooted in the fissure of "community centers" and "community schools" in the 1930s. In the throes of the Depression, Flint, Michigan, a national center for automobile manufacturing, had ordered major cutbacks in the city's schools and social services. In 1934 Frank J. Manley, Flint's director of physical education and recreation, used New Deal funds to organize a citywide playground program. Impressed by this program, Charles Stewart Mott, a founder and senior vice president of the General Motors Corporation, met with Manley to discuss how best to invest the resources of the Mott Foundation, founded in 1926, to aid the revitalization of Flint.[45] Mott and Manley designed a plan to convert the city's forty public schools to community centers; they also arranged with the board of education to have the Mott Foundation provide trained recreation supervisors and materials for five demonstration centers, for which the board would pay custodial and building costs. On the heels of the 1935–36 demonstration centers, the Mott Foundation agreed to support fifteen community centers in 1936–37. The expanded program included activities for all age groups, ranging from recreation and athletics, to art and music, to English and citizenship classes for immigrants. In 1941 Flint's school community centers reported an aggregate attendance of more than 769,000 participants.[46]

In 1938 Manley and the Mott Foundation decided to hire and train a team of six visiting teachers who would report on the problems of families experiencing severe hardship and would work with Flint's social agencies and schools. Over a seven-year period these visiting teachers qua social workers assisted at least two thousand families; their reports spurred the creation of school-based adult-counseling and job-placement services and a raft of adult education classes.[47] In 1939 the foundation, in conjunction with the Genesee County Medical Society, established the Children's Health Center at Flint's Hurley Hospital, which provided medical, dental, and orthopedic care for the children of "border-line indigent families." The targeted children, whose families were not eligible for relief, were referred to the center by teachers, public health nurses, and school physicians; the center's coordinator was the director of health for the city schools. In 1947–48, the Children's Health Center reported 4,037 medical patient visits and 2,234 dental patient visits. The foundation also sponsored a "health-guarded child" program to treat each child's medical and dental problems, immunize her against diphtheria and smallpox, and provide a skin test for tuberculosis. When the program started in 1939, only 13.5 percent of Flint school children met every criterion for health-guarded children; by 1948, the total reached 7,438, or 45.6 percent.[48]

On 6 June 1950 Flint's citizens approved a $7 million program to construct new community schools, and the Mott Foundation provided a match of $1 million. The Flint community school building project lasted from 1951 to 1960, when nine new elementary schools were built with special facilities to accommodate community programs and older buildings were upgraded with the addition of "community wings." The board of education hired physical education teachers to plan and direct the new wider-use programs.[49] A 1961 report on the Flint community schools, authored by Manley and his associates, highlighted the city's myriad "wider use" programs for recreation, drama, music, arts and crafts, social clubs, and adult education (basic and vocational).[50]

Efflorescence, Consolidation, and Persistence of the Community Education Movement, 1960–1990

In the 1960s the Mott Foundation built an alliance with the schools of education at seven state-supported Michigan universities and orchestrated a network of community education projects and leaders.[51] The 1970s and 1980s would provide a congenial zeitgeist for the development, expansion, and persistence of that network. With Mott Foundation support, community education would become a minor social movement—an expression of what Harry Boyte has called the "new citizen movement."[52]

In 1964 the Mott Foundation established the National Center for Community Education (NCCE), a leadership training program, with Ernest Melby as its first director. Melby advocated an expansive notion of community education, centering education in institutions, organizations, and agencies beyond the school.[53] In 1966 the foundation created the Inter-Institutional Clinical Preparation Program for Educational Leadership, better known as the Mott Intern Program, as a major component of NCCE. Pat Edwards writes of the internship program: "The Flint Community Schools became an open laboratory. [The] universities collaborated in developing formal classes, colloquiums, and internships, and the granting of advanced degrees—master's, specialist's, and doctoral—in community education. During its ten-year existence, about 850 community education leaders emerged from this program to provide leadership to the community education movement."[54]

In 1966 the National Community School Education Association (NCSEA), a professional membership organization, was established in Flint under Mott Foundation auspices. In the 1970s the name was changed to the National Community Education Association (NCEA), with headquarters in Washington, D.C.[55] Another important component of the community education network was fifteen Mott-funded regional university centers, which became the major training and technical assistance centers for community education.[56] The foundation contributed approximately $125 million to community education programs in the 1960s and 1970s.[57]

In 1970 the first state-funded programs of community education were established in Michigan, Florida, Utah, and Maryland. In 1974 the Mott Foundation listed 2,771 local community education programs. Such was the lobbying effectiveness of this grass-roots movement that in 1974 Congress passed the Community Schools Act, which until 1983 provided an annual appropriation of $3 million to support community education offices in thirty state departments of education.[58] In 1985, the Council of Chief State School Officers reported that twenty-five of forty states surveyed indicated that they had allocated state education agency (SEA) funds for community education; twenty-one of those states had community education legislation.[59] In 1989 Minnesota was the national leader in state expenditures for community education with $18 million; of that state's 435 public school districts, 380 had community education departments.[60]

As described in issues of the *Community Education Journal* from 1971 to 1990, community education programs emphasized adult education, recreation, and youth-enrichment activities.[61] The absence of linkages to the K–12 program persisted throughout this period as a limitation of these programs. While community education advocates in universities and state departments of education frequently called for curriculum development, their efforts to influence curriculum and instruction were largely ineffectual.[62] A 1981 study of seventeen community education projects, one in each of seventeen states, documents that community education practitioners were not attentive to curriculum. In such places as Alamagordo, New Mexico; Newton, Massachusetts; and Upper Arlington, Ohio, community education was kept largely separate from the K–12 program; where there was curricular integration, it was restricted to ad hoc enrichment activities such as guest speakers and community field trips.[63] Entering the 1990s, community educators remained "primarily programmers,"[64] in the tradition of the recreation-oriented U.S. community centers of the 1920s and 1930s.

The durability of this movement can only be explained by the sustained participation of the Mott Foundation, which catalyzed community education, provided the major leadership and training, and supported countless local projects over a fifty-year period.[65] (State and federal support piggybacked on the shoulders of the Mott programs.) It is hardly extravagant to say that without the Mott Foundation, community education would have vanished from the scene long ago—and the revived movement toward community schools in the 1990s and early twenty-first century would have been, at a minimum, long delayed.[66]

Coalescing Movements toward Community Schools, 1990–2004

Full-Service Schools

In the 1990s a movement gathered significant momentum to create "full-service schools"—schools that provided integrated support services to help treat and counteract the "new morbidities" of substance abuse, unprotected sex, stress, school failure, "gangbanging," and increasing levels of violence. Proponents of full-service schools recognized that the new morbidities were rapidly undermining the social fabric of urban America. As of the mid-1990s, some five hundred school-based health and social service programs were in operation, funded largely through a creative packaging of state and federal categorical funds. (New York was the leading state, with 140 school-based clinics.) The range of these programs included school-based dental clinics, health centers, mental health services, family resource centers, and after-school centers; typically, the services were provided at a school center staffed by local health and social agencies. Philanthropic foundations such as Robert Wood Johnson, Pew, Stuart, and Casey helped stabilize these programs with essential funds and expertise; they also played a seminal role in the national diffusion of the concept of full-service schools. Joy Dryfoos, a researcher in the employ of the Carnegie Corporation, publicized these programs in a well-received book, *Full-Service Schools: A Revolution for Health and Social Services for Children, Youth, and Families,* published in 1994.[67] (Dryfoos reprised the role played by Clarence Perry, who rode circuit for the Russell Sage Foundation on behalf of school social centers in the 1910s and 1920s; see Chapter 1.)

Advanced full-service programs such as I.S. 218 in Washington Heights, New York City, offered "quality education" and "one-stop unfragmented health and social service systems that are consumer-oriented, developmentally appropriate, and culturally relevant."[68] Created through a partnership between the Children's Aid Society (CAS), a nonprofit charitable organization, and the New York City public schools, I.S. 218 (Salome Ureña de Henriquez Middle Academies) featured a school-based health and dental center, a multipurpose family resource center, and a surfeit of community educational and recreational programs—all funded by CAS at just below $1,000 above the city's $6,500 educational expenditure per child. A quality education program served 1,200 students who enrolled in one of four self-contained academies in the building and extended their studies through after-school educational programs.[69] Between 1992 and 2001 CAS opened a total of ten community schools in Washington Heights, East Harlem, and the South Bronx. Drawing from multiple public and private funding streams, the agency invested more than $125 million in two flagship schools, I.S. 218 and P.S. 5 (the Ellen Lurie School), both of which serve the largely immigrant Dominican population of Washington Heights. As of 2003, CAS reported more than 150 national and international adaptations of its full-service model.[70]

University-Assisted Community Schools

Of all the initiatives that carry the banner of community-centered schooling, the project of university-assisted community schools is the only one to ground its work in a historical analysis of community-centered schooling. This project originated in 1983 in the School of Arts and Sciences at the University of Pennsylvania. The project director was historian Ira Harkavy, who as a Penn undergraduate in the late 1960s had led a nationally publicized takeover of the main administration building—a protest that was directed against Penn's recent expansion into West Philadelphia, the university's immediate geographic community, a disadvantaged area of the city. Harkavy and two other Penn historians, Lee Benson and Sheldon Hackney (who from 1980 to 1992 was also president of the university), played instrumental roles in the creation of a coalition that included University of Pennsylvania faculty, staff, and students; West Philadelphia teachers and school administrators; and local governmental and community organizations. The West Philadelphia Improvement Corps (WEPIC) grew out of a jointly produced student paper in an undergraduate honors history seminar cotaught by Harkavy, Benson, and Hackney in the spring of 1985. The informal coalition launched by the seminar gained momentum in the aftermath of the notorious MOVE fire on Osage Avenue. The original project involved one West Philadelphia school (the Bryant Elementary School, located in the neighborhood of the fire) where WEPIC focused on organizing school and neighborhood beautification projects and developing youth employment opportunities for area high school students.

Although aware of community schools through the National Society for the Study of Education's 1953 yearbook, *The Community School*, WEPIC planners first began to explore the potential of the idea in a seminar of West Philadelphia school practitioners and academics, which met periodically in 1989. Informal discussions among university faculty colleagues in the seminar pointed to the need for research that would look backward to earlier comprehensive efforts to use schools as centers and catalysts for community revitalization efforts. Benson and Harkavy began to read the secondary literature on the history of schools as "social centers" and "community centers." At this time they also "discovered" Covello and Clapp, whose work convinced them that what they had been "groping toward" for the past five years was the community school idea.[71] Long persuaded that historical study should guide contemporary real-world problem solving, they called on one of us, John Puckett in the Graduate School of Education, to undertake a preliminary survey, which Puckett completed in 1992.

As faculty interest in developing undergraduate and graduate seminars related to WEPIC grew, the university created a campuswide Center for Community Partnerships, with a reporting line to the president and provost and the appointment of Harkavy as the founding director. Not surprisingly, the new center, which opened in 1992, adopted university-assisted community schools as its core strategy.[72]

At least four core assumptions have guided this effort. First, the neighborhood school can effectively serve as the core neighborhood institution and catalyst for social change—an institution that both provides services and galvanizes other community institutions and groups. Second, a community school is more than an accretion of interventions and support services; that is, it is more than the full-service (client-centered) model. A comprehensive community school approach makes the development of "cosmopolitan, neighborly, democratic communities" a primary focus of every component of a community school and designates space in the curriculum for community problem–based learning. Third, community schools require sustained institutional support and more resources than do traditionally organized schools—and far more resources than poorly funded urban school districts could realistically be expected to provide on their own. Universities, by virtue of their multifaceted disciplinary expertise and comprehensive approach, are uniquely qualified for this support role. Moreover, they have compelling institutional reasons to play this role, including public accountability, institutional self-interest (the safety, cleanliness, and attractiveness of the campus periphery, for instance), and a better integration of the university's research, teaching, and service missions. Fourth, reform of the university toward a greater social responsibility and integration with other levels of the pre-K–16 schooling system is a sine qua non for democratically transforming the schooling system, that is, achieving fully realized community schools.[73]

Penn's core strategy to support WEPIC community school development has been "academically based community service" (ABCS), a service-learning approach that involves the creation or redesign of university courses to incorporate a community problem–solving focus and, in a number of cases, the development of action research agendas and community school programs to help solve those problems. Since 1992, when only 4 ABCS courses were listed, approximately 150 have been developed—in education, social work, history, English, mathematics, engineering, fine arts (for example, landscape architecture, city and regional planning), communications, medicine, anthropology, sociology, linguistics, classics, environmental studies, and biology. Other strategies include direct traditional service (for example, mentoring and tutoring) and community development.[74]

After twenty years of energetic conceptual work, strategic organizing, and alliance building within the university and in its neighboring community, the Penn/WEPIC model is still in a developing phase. In the face of powerful entrenched obstacles, the Center for Community Partnerships and its WEPIC community allies have introduced elements of community-centered schooling in varying degrees at ten school sites. These elements include, among others, educational, recreational, cultural, health, and job-training programs that are available to all local community residents at the school site—programs that rely on volunteer resources from the university, as well as from the school and community. Every school is linked to InfoResources, a neighborhood-mapping, census-linked database for West Philadelphia, which is housed on the Penn campus. School and community projects supported by the WEPIC coalition include school and neighborhood beautification (cleanups, landscaping, gardening, and mural art); low-cost model-housing construction; computer repair and Web-page design; community arts performance; school-to-career internships (Penn's health-care system and university offices); and community publications (QWEST, a community newspaper at West Philadelphia High School, for example). Six schools have community advisory councils, although this component has been slow to develop. Also, while the overall WEPIC initiative is conceptualized as an "ongoing communal participatory action research project," the level of democratic participation, from planning to implementation, varies from site to site.

A key factor is an array of curricular and cocurricular programs that bring disciplinary perspectives to schoolchildren's studies in nutrition and disease detection/prevention, urban environmental issues (lead toxicity, brownfields, submerged urban floodplains, urban gardening, and landscaping, for example), social-base mapping, and African American culture and history in West Philadelphia. Research projects at the sites have programmatic components that contribute directly to teaching and learning. For example, a study of reading difficulties among West African American children at the Wilson Elementary School, directed by William Labov, a world-renowned professor of linguistics, led to the development of a reading improvement program that is being tested at this and other WEPIC sites—and in the Oakland, California, schools as well.[75] The Urban Nutrition Initiative at the Turner Middle School and other WEPIC sites, headed by Francis Johnston, one of the world's foremost physical anthropologists, translated research findings from nutrition studies of West Philadelphia schoolchildren into curricular materials that are used at several WEPIC sites.[76] And a study of the Mill Creek submerged floodplain in West Philadelphia, directed by Ann Spirn, a leading historian of urban landscape design, resulted in the development of imaginative curricular activities at the Sulzberger Middle School related to the beautification and potential uses of abandoned property in the floodplain.[77]

Exemplifying the concept of "One University," faculty and students from the schools of Medicine, Nursing, Dentistry, Law, Graduate Education, Social Work, and Arts and Sciences collaborate to provide health screenings and primary care referrals at the Sayre Middle/High School, as well as health education for students and their families, "with an overarching goal of reducing health disparities in West Philadelphia." On the curriculum side, the Health Promotion and Disease Prevention Program is designed to integrate community health themes with the core academic subjects (science, English, social studies, etc.) and to train Sayre students to be "active agents of change," "providers of information and deliverers and coordinators of service" in their home neighborhoods. The university's academically based community-service courses buttress this citizen-centered curricular approach, which is part of a broader strategy to facilitate what Harry Boyte aptly calls "community capacity for self-action." As of 2004–5 curricular units link undergraduate studies in urban nutrition, neuroscience, and lead toxins to the middle school curriculum. Current plans call for continued growth of the program both at Sayre and Penn, and extension to other West Philadelphia schools in the WEPIC orbit.[78]

Safe Passage Schools, Beacons, and Other
Variants of the Community School Idea

In *Safe Passage*, a 1998 book sponsored by the Carnegie Corporation, researcher Joy Dryfoos looked at a range of schools that provide programmatic safeguards for children in high-risk environments—so-called safe passage schools. One of these schools, El Puente in New York City, had an explicit social reconstructionist ideology similar to Covello's—it trained young people to be community activists. Founded in 1993 by Latino activists Luis Garden-Acosta and Frances Lucerna in Community School District 14, and located in a converted church building at the Brooklyn entrance to the Williamsburg Bridge, El Puente, or the Academy for Peace and Justice, was a tiny high school for 130 ninth through twelfth graders (the first class graduated in 1998).[79] The school served Williamsburg's predominately Latino South Side, about which the *New York Times* reported in the mid-1990s: "If geography were destiny, it would not be too difficult to imagine feeling isolated and powerless in a place like Williamsburg's South Side. Crowded apartment buildings stand in the shadows of a bridge and highway that cut the neighborhood off from the rest of the borough. The sun sets behind a western waterfront covered with factories, vacant lots and waste-collection businesses."[80] The academy, which was an extension of a community center and after-school youth-development program, had an explicit community development focus, and local social issues were topics of classroom activity; for example, an epidemiology class studied the environmental impacts of lead-paint removal from the Williamsburg Bridge; a humanities class produced a documentary video on the dangers of a proposed garbage incinerator in the nearby Navy Yard; and a biology class participated in immunization drives.[81]

At the time, El Puente was one of some forty designated "Beacons" in the New York City Schools—a strategy created in 1991 by Mayor David Dinkins, who allocated $10 million from his Safe Streets, Safe Cities budget to create ten "schools transformed into community centers, available to children and adults 365 days a year."[82] The Countee Cullen school community center in Harlem, one of the original Beacon sites, attracted national attention on the strength of two books, Geoffrey Canada's *fist stick knife gun*, published in 1995; and Lisabeth Schorr's *Common Purpose*, published in 1997. Canada, who was president of the Rheedlen Centers for Children and Families, a New York social service agency founded in 1970, saw the Beacon concept as a promising strategy for infusing comprehensive services for children and their families in city schools that served disadvantaged neighborhoods. He decided to commit staff and resources to a test of that strategy. In *fist stick knife gun*, Canada relates the conversation he had with his associates Shawn Dove and Joe Stewart, who persuaded him that the Countee Cullen school would be an appropriate choice for Rheedlen's Beacon project:

> Shawn began the conversation. "Geoff, I think we found our school. It's an elementary school on 144th Street and it looks perfect. It's an old building on a block that's struggling to make it. There are several abandoned buildings on the block and people selling drugs on both corners." Joe continued without missing a beat. "It's surrounded by a housing project and has the highest number of children living in temporary housing in Harlem. There are junkies sitting on an old couch right outside, nodding while children come and go. Geoff, I think this is it."[83]

Housed in P.S. 194, a five-floor elementary school at 144th Street between Adam Clayton Powell and Frederick Douglass boulevards, Countee Cullen was open twelve hours daily, seven days a week. The project provided homework support and after-school sports and recreation for children; school-to-career classes for youth; parent support groups and services for high-risk families; African dance for children and adults; the Countee Cullen Teen Council and service-learning projects (Harlem voter registration, play street development, neighborhood beautification, food and clothing drives); and programs for adults (for example, Alcoholics and Narcotics Anonymous, aerobics, education work-shops). In 1998, the Rheedlen Centers opened a second Beacon, the Booker T. Washington Center, at J.H.S. 54 on West 107th Street, with services targeted primarily toward Upper West Side Latino children and their families.[84]

Starting in 2001 Canada boldly transformed the Rheedlen Centers into the Harlem Children's Zone (HCZ). Working with sizable foundation and cor-porate sponsorship and a projected budget of $46 million over nine years, the project targeted a sixty-block swathe of central Harlem and about 6,500 chil-dren for twenty after-school and parental support programs at school sites and other neighborhood locations. When Canada opened the Rheedlen Centers in the mid-1990s, he assumed that an array of external supports such as computer literacy training, recreation, preventive services, and family outreach programs would raise area children's achievement scores. Nearly a decade later, however, he had come to believe that such programs could only have a "fringe" effect on achievement in light of the dismal condition of Harlem's public schools. As this book was being written, the flagship program of the Harlem Children's Zone was a K–12 charter school, the Promise Academy, scheduled to open in the fall of 2004 with a cohort of kindergartners and one of sixth graders; the new academy was to be the first in a network of HCZ charter schools.[85]

As of fall 1997 more than seventy-six thousand youth and thirty-three thou-sand adults participated in the citywide Beacon program. By 2001 eighty Bea-cons operated in New York City, with a total program budget of $35 million a year and $400,000 allocated for each site, all of which was administered and funded by the Department of Youth and Community Development; the Youth Development Institute of the Fund for the City of New York provided ongo-ing technical assistance to the Beacons. A 2002 report summarized Beacon activity as follows: "Individual Beacons offer children, youth, and adults a wide range of recreational programs, social services, educational enrichment, and vocational activities in four core areas: academic support and enhancement, parent involvement and family support, and neighborhood safety and commu-nity building. Many Beacons also take an active role in the community by sponsoring activities—voter registration drives, clean-ups, and cultural events and celebrations—to make the neighborhood a better place to live."[86]

From 1997 to 2000, the DeWitt Wallace–Reader's Digest Fund sponsored the National Beacons Adaptation Project, which extended the New York City

Beacon model to schools in Denver, Minneapolis, Oakland, and Savannah, providing $1 million to each city for the three-year period.[87] From 1997 to 2002 the Wallace Fund (the foundation's new name) "awarded $19.6 million to help transform 57 underused school facilities in twenty low-income communities," allowing the communities to adapt any one of four "extended school" models— Beacon Schools, Bridges to Success, CAS, and WEPIC.[88]

Since the mid-1990s the Charles Stewart Mott Foundation has been increasingly involved in similar developments, including the foundation's sponsorship of *Community Schools across America,* which features 135 "community/school partnerships that are making a difference."[89] Mott's funding priorities in this arena are weighted heavily toward extended-day programs. In January 1998 President Bill Clinton announced the creation of Twenty-first Century Learning Centers, a pathbreaking public-private partnership between the Mott Foundation and the U.S. Department of Education to support after-school academic enrichment and recreation programs for some 500,000 children.[90] The Twenty-first Century Learning Centers were targeted at low-income communities. In 1999 the Mott Foundation's seven-year commitment to the project stood at $95.2 million.[91] Receiving strong bipartisan support in Washington, the federal appropriation grew from $40 million in 1998 to $1 billion by 2002, with grants awarded to 7,500 rural and central-city public schools in more than 1,400 communities.[92] In FY 2003 this federal program served approximately 1,325,000 schoolchildren. Citing the first-year results of a national evaluation study that showed "limited academic impact" for the program, the George W. Bush administration moved to cut the federal appropriation by 40 percent in FY 2004. Opponents of the cutback, however, were able to secure continued funding at nearly $1 billion through FY 2005.[93]

As of 2004 Chicago, Indianapolis, and Portland/Multnomah County, Oregon, sponsored programs for client-centered community schools. In 2002–3 the Chicago Public Schools inaugurated twenty community schools, each formed through a partnership with a local community agency and targeted primarily toward improving students' academic achievement; academic and extracurricular offerings included, for instance, pupil tutoring, adult education/GED preparation, computer training, health services, homework support, and childcare.[94] In Indianapolis the United Way–sponsored Bridges to Success program served forty-four schools through an array of local partnerships providing health, family-support, and youth-development services.[95] Founded in 1999, the SUN (Schools Uniting Neighborhoods) Initiative of Portland/Multnomah County involved forty-six schools in six districts in 2004; as in Chicago, a nonprofit organization played a lead role at each community school. Extended-day activities and services included, among others, homework clubs and drama classes, health vans, and family literacy nights; a goal is increased parental involvement in the schools, with particular attention to the districts' Latino and Asian/Pacific Islander families.[96]

Lastly, it is important to note the effort of the Annenberg Rural Challenge, a five-year (1995–99), $50 million grant program that was targeted at small schools in diverse rural communities in thirty-three states. The goal was to create a critical mass of networked rural schools that would be catalysts for community renewal and citizenship development. "A site that proposed primarily to increase test scores of school children by 10 percent, or even 50 percent, did not get much attention from the Rural Challenge," according to the program's lead evaluator. "A site that outlined its work as building powerful community-school integration, using the local environment, its physical, economic, cultural, linguistic and historical resources as a base for curriculum in the schools, seeing community people as important educators and its many institutions as educating agencies, seeing students in the schools as genuine resources for sustaining and revitalizing the local community, encouraging local people to understand, in fact, that the schools belong to them, received, on the other hand, considerable attention from the Rural Challenge."[97] While the Rural Challenge succeeded in spurring many educationally rich, interdisciplinary elementary and secondary curriculum projects that focused on community environmental issues, historic and cultural preservation, and economic development, and while it built active regional networks to support this work, the program's "pedagogy of place" concept, for the most part, played a distant second fiddle to conventional teacher-centered, textbook-based instruction in the grant-supported schools. These individual projects, though, had salutary impacts beyond the classroom, for example, focusing local attention on critical issues, building constituencies for local problem solving, and bridging generation gaps (the latter by involving community elders and local "experts" in the projects). In 1999 the Rural School and Community Trust was established to continue this school reform effort, which involved more than seven hundred rural schools.

Building Social Capital for a Twenty-first Century Community Schools Movement

In 1998 Joy Dryfoos coined the term "full-service community schools" as an umbrella category for the hundreds of programs that provide out-of-classroom educational, health, and social services to children, families, and neighborhoods, especially in disadvantaged communities. In *Safe Passage* Dryfoos writes: "What these programs have in common is the provision of services by community agencies in school buildings with a view toward the creation of new institutional arrangements, of comprehensive 'one-stop' educational and service centers." Dryfoos highlights school-based health clinics, school-linked (referral) services, school-based youth centers, family resource centers, and an array of other approaches, including Beacons, the Children's Aid Society's "settlement house-in-the-school approach" and "university-assisted schools." "For purposes of improved communication I call these efforts *full-service community schools,* or just plain *community schools*" (original emphasis).[98] *Safe Passage* is a modern analog of Samuel Everett's 1938 book *The Community School,* in the sense of being a conscious effort to unify often unrelated projects into a cohesive movement toward community schools. Dryfoos, who has written three major books on the subject with support from the Carnegie Corporation, and who reprises Clarence A. Perry's advocacy role in the 1910s social center movement, is the prophet of a new community school movement. There is a tendency in Dryfoos's work, however, to blur somewhat the different conceptualizations and often profound ideological differences that separate the various projects and approaches she describes and hails as community schools— a point we return to later.

In 1998 the Mott Foundation sponsored a conceptually sophisticated report on these projects, entitled *Learning Together: The Developing Field of School-Community Initiatives,* prepared by the Institute for Educational Leadership (IEL) and NCCE, and published in partnership with the Center for Youth Development Policy and Chapin Hall Center for Children at the University of Chicago. The same organizational players in Dryfoos's books—Beacons, Children's Aid Society, West Philadelphia Improvement Corps, for example— appear here in a framework called "school-community mapping," which, among other things, maps each project in terms of four approaches: youth development, school reform, community development, and services reform. Drawing on extensive survey data from twenty projects, the researchers also looked for central tendencies within their sample. For example, they found that "state legislative allocations to single departments—primarily education agencies and not-for-profit organizations including foundations, local United Ways and universities—together fund about two-thirds of this sample. . . . Local school districts are not a typical source of primary cash funding although they are an important source of redirected and in-kind services."[99]

With respect to services provided, the researchers reported that "averaging each activity in terms of its frequency, importance and likelihood of expansion suggests that tutoring and literacy, parent education, school-age child care, leadership development, and employment and job training are the five most salient areas of activity across the field. This array reflects each of the four major approaches and purposes connected with school-community initiatives and confirms the extent to which the field is characterized by blended and complementary purposes, strategies and activities."[100]

Building a National Coalition

IEL, with support from the Wallace—Reader's Digest Fund, the Mott Foundation, the Ewing Marion Kaufmann Foundation, and the Carnegie Corporation, serves as administrative headquarters for the Coalition for Community Schools (CCS), which was founded in 1997. The coalition's steering committee includes, among others, representatives from IEL, Penn's Center for Community Partnerships (Ira Harkavy is the CCS chairperson), the Children's Aid Society, the Fund for the City of New York (Beacon Schools), and the National Community Education Association. Engaging some 170 education, youth-development, family-support, and community-development organizations, CCS promotes a "broad vision of a well-developed community school." According to the coalition's three-paragraph statement, the "well developed" community school is established through a partnership arrangement involving the school district and one or more community agencies. Community artists, businesspeople, professionals, and college faculty and students support curricular and cocurricular programs to strengthen students' academic learning and service learning. Among other community-support activities, the school provides or arranges health, dental, and mental health services, with oversight provided by a community school coordinator. Over time the community school integrates "quality education, positive youth development, family support, family and community engagement in decision-making, and community development."[101]

Most of the community schools that are represented in the coalition's big tent are full-service or partially full-service schools of the type Dryfoos describes in her 1994 book on the subject. In some cases they hearken back to the "school as community center" idea, for example, the Stanley Elementary School of Wichita, Kansas:

> Evenings and weekends, the school hosts college classes, community programs and recreation for adults. At weekly Family Learning nights, parents come to Stanley with their children. Adults take part in English as a second language and other literacy activities. Their school-age children study with reading tutors while preschoolers play together in child care provided with Title I funds. Participants from Volunteers in Service to America (VISTA, a branch of the Corporation for National Service Americorps program) work with the CIS [Communities in Schools] site coordinator to organize literacy activities, raise funds and promote community service.[102]

The George W. Bush administration's heavy emphasis on standardized test scores has given increased impetus to the Coalition for Community Schools to demonstrate that the service-center model strengthens academic achievement. Evidence collected by the coalition from an array of school-based community-service programs associates some programs with children's gains in reading and math. More broadly, gains are shown in increased levels of parental involvement in children's schooling, improved parental relations with teachers, higher levels of student attendance, more positive attitudes toward school, reduced risk behaviors, and improvements in school climate. In 2003 the coalition reviewed twenty programs that have had close evaluative scrutiny: four national models, seven state-funded/statewide approaches, and nine school district/local initiatives. Seventy-five percent of these initiatives reported early gains in individual academic achievement, in addition to positive developmental indicators such as improved school attitudes and motivation.[103] Yet these studies lack rigorous statistical controls to demonstrate causal links between "full-service" variables and rising student test scores, and CCS makes its present appeal to federal policy makers on the basis of highly tentative evidence.

Undaunted and fiercely optimistic, CCS held its second biennial national conference in the spring of 2005 in Chicago, which drew some 950 participants representing the coalition's member organizations: foundations, professional associations, universities, and federal, state, and local agencies. The conference celebrated the recent release of *Community Schools in Action,* a book on the Children's Aid Society's community schools in upper Manhattan, coedited by Joy Dryfoos and published by Oxford University Press—a volume that further signals an incipient national movement toward community schools.

It is important to note that the varied projects and approaches that are represented in the network we have described have different conceptualizations of a community school—ones that are deeply rooted in ideological or philosophical commitments. Perhaps for tactical reasons, Dryfoos and other coalition builders tend to downplay these distinctions. The point is that there are very real differences among these approaches—differences that could fragment the broad alliance if not openly acknowledged, debated, reconciled, or at least recognized and cheerfully accepted.

One reform group in the new community school movement, for example, advocates parallel spheres of "full service" and "quality education" (standards-based instruction aligned with standardized tests). On this view extended-day programs and health and social services help ensure the integrity and success of the school's academic program. Family and community involvement is sought as a means to improve the service rendered to individual students; collective (i.e., community) benefits are indirect and collateral.[104] Allowing for some variation across sites, this is the dominant version of community school practice in the new community school movement. It is essentially a client-centered approach. While supportive of a vigorous program of school-based student and family services, another reform group seeks to strengthen the wider community directly through a "community-as-text" or "problem-based learning" approach (both curricular and cocurricular) that prepares young people to be active learners, democratic citizens, and local change agents.[105] With Covello, these reformers view community schools as community problem–solving institutions. Their position is essentially citizen centered; the unifying vision is the creation of "neighborly, cosmopolitan, democratic communities." Highlighting the centrality of this goal, the University of Pennsylvania/WEPIC coalition and their allies in other higher education institutions and cities identify local democratic development and neighborhood revitalization as core public purposes of a community school. The service role supplements these public purposes by providing essential supports to students and strengthening the community's positive identification with the school.

In the next chapter we explore in greater specificity the meaning of Covello's project for public schooling in the twenty-first century, building on the frameworks of practical democratic theory and contemporary debates about the state of civic education. We turn to this history in search of ideas that may point the way toward a reinvigorated democratic citizenry. To borrow an apt phrase, we "look backwards critically to look forward constructively."[106]

CHAPTER NINE

Learning from the Past:
Covello and Democratic
Citizenship in Perspective

O N A CHILLY SPRING DAY, 17 April 1940, a date that marked the 150th anniversary of Benjamin Franklin's death, Mayor La Guardia turned the first spade of earth for the new high school building on Pleasant Avenue. The ebullient mayor was accompanied by Christina Claxton, a fifteen-year-old descendant of the nation's founder. Rear Admiral Woodward of the Brooklyn Navy Yard brought a color guard. Father Duffy's Cadets provided a bugle-and-drum corps, and the Reverend Benjamin Franklin Farber delivered the invocation as thousands paid tribute to Franklin, the "great patriot" and "Prophet of American Education."[1] The public purposes of schooling reverberated in the pomp and patriotism on full display.

A "community-centered school" for boys, Benjamin Franklin High School suggested what a multiethnic public school might look like if it were to model participatory and public work citizenship. That public schooling should educate young people to be capable and willing change agents for a just and humane society, that education should foster local democratic processes and cultivate a richer citizen participation in resolving intercultural conflict—these were animating goals of this extraordinary urban social experiment. Covello and his allies built a community school infrastructure to secure these goals, including community advisory committees; WPA-supported adult education and recreational services; street units for social clubs, community research bureaus, and a community library; and a school-based community newspaper. Large-scale community-organizing efforts such as housing, health and citizenship campaigns, and partnerships with umbrella activist groups, such as the East Harlem Council of Social Agencies and the Harlem Legislative Conference were undertaken to mobilize the community's educational resources in the service of the high school. These efforts provided training for deeply engaged citizenship (for youth and adults alike) and unified East Harlem's competing ethnic groups on the common ground of a shared democratic vision.

These community activities were linked to the high school curriculum through a multicultural education program, a community social research agenda, and various classroom projects. Every facet of Franklin's community program focused on the civic education of East Harlem and reinforced the high school's instructional program and work with youth. Community advisory committees, social clubs, and antidefamation activities, for instance, educated East Harlem parents about interethnic tolerance and cooperation at the same time their sons were learning these lessons in the high school's intercultural education program.

Working largely within the financial constraints of the New York City public schools, a megabureaucracy, Covello applied the community school idea in a congested neighborhood. His goal was not to create a lighthouse school or to demonstrate the feasibility of a particular set of educational principles—Dewey's, for instance—but rather to organize schooling as a primary agency for East Harlem's revitalization. This was social reconstruction writ small. To Covello East Harlem's renewal and civic empowerment meant nothing less than achieving the promise of American democracy in a poor and ethnically diverse community. An essential step toward realizing that goal, he recognized, would be the cultivation of strong civic and moral leadership that would emanate from the community school and the informal learning networks fostered by community-centered schooling.

Franklin, though, never perfected citizen-centered schooling; East Harlem never became a Camelot of public work citizenship. However, their inspiring but imperfect achievements elucidate key tensions, core tradeoffs we still make as we implement, consciously or not, our present era's response to schooling's duty to train citizens. The first tension schools face is between a citizen-centered conception of community schooling and a client-centered approach. Grounded in the competing ideologies of social progressives and reforming professionals in the early twentieth century, this tension was evident in the nation's social/community centers on the eve of World War I, when claims for scientific expertise and social efficiency began to override the democratic purposes of these institutions. To some extent it appeared again in the Depression era when Benjamin Franklin and other social justice–oriented projects such as the Highlander Folk School stood in contrast to Nambé, where local democratic development was never an agenda, and Arthurdale, where it was truncated by law, custom, and political exigencies. It was muted during the long ascendancy of community education, which emphasized client services, especially community recreation and adult education, without a political agenda. This tension has reemerged at the opening of the new century under the big tent of the Coalition for Community Schools, where client-centered programs such as "school-based health and social services" stand uneasily beside the comprehensive citizen-centered approach advocated for university-assisted community schools.

Franklin High School also embodied the perennial tension in community-centered schooling between community problem–solving efforts and the subject-centered curriculum. Himself a liberally educated scholar-practitioner, Covello always respected the liberal arts and held them in view whenever he talked about community-centered schooling. In his practice he struggled to reconcile their tension, not by reconstructing the high school curriculum to achieve a systematic integration of problem-based learning and academic studies, but rather by leaving traditional curricular structures largely intact and infusing traditional academic coursework with civic/political themes such as intercultural relations and quality of life issues, often at crisis points in the life of the community. Social research, participation on school-community committees, and citizen action were largely extracurricular or informal activities conducted under the high school's aegis. In 1953, acknowledging that effective participatory skills require political knowledge and systematic cultivation, Covello sketched out, but never implemented, a multiyear, core civic education course that would involve *all* students under the watchful eyes of trained supervisors in participatory and public work activities in such venues as local research bureaus, community social agencies, and school-community committees.[2]

Today this tension is apparent in efforts by the Coalition for Community Schools to align its school-community agendas with the federal government's No Child Left Behind (NCLB) legislation, which defines school achievement exclusively in terms of students' scores on standardized tests of academic knowledge. The challenge NCLB poses for these community school proponents also illustrates in bold relief the perennial tension that we noted between local and nonlocal influences in community schooling. Perhaps as a pragmatic response to the present political climate, the coalition strives to show empirically that its agendas, especially health and social services, support a rigorous subject-centered and intellectual skills approach. The coalition provides, however, no examples or suggestions as to how community studies and academic studies might be effectively reconciled to support a citizen-centered community school.

Another tension that challenged Covello's project was inherent in the demands required by his citizen-centered conception, which defined teaching as public work. There is no denying that a stalwart core of Franklin teachers, dedicated to civic activism for democratic ends, were devotees of this version of community-centered schooling. They were emblematic of what some scholars consider a golden age of teaching in the New York City schools. Yet we surmise that for some teachers Covello's project posed an unwelcome intensification of their already hectic work lives as city teachers, or it hearkened to a conception of teachers as social workers. In our present era of accountability, as external pressures mount for strengthening "teacher quality" (meaning a combination of subject-matter expertise and professional acumen), teacher work is more and more intensified and increasingly focused on raising student test scores. To understate the point extravagantly, these factors outweigh proposals to reinvigorate citizenship development as a public purpose of American schooling, and thus outweigh citizenship training's claims on precious professional time.

This observation returns us to the true starting point of our book, the deepening crisis of U.S. citizenship in our present situation. How does Covello's theory and practice of community schooling speak meaningfully to the problem of Americans' hastening retreat from the public sphere? What lessons from his project, if any, might help us set this course aright and achieve a fuller realization of this nation's democratic promise?

Constructing a Usable Past

While it is no mine of panaceas to be unearthed, the past can expand our present imagination by engaging us with visions of the world significantly different from what our current practice allows. Community-centered schooling provokes our imagination at both theoretical and practical levels, responding to a longstanding challenge posed by Dewey and to the demands of the present policy environment.

At the level of theory, Covello seems to have solved a vexatious dilemma in Dewey's theory of democracy. In his years as Franklin's founding principal, Covello was groping pragmatically toward participatory democracy, an idea toward which Dewey himself groped theoretically.

Identifying democracy as "a mode of associated living, of conjoint communicated experience," Dewey argued in *Democracy and Education* (1916) that "the extension in space of the number of individuals who participate in an interest so that each has to refer his own action to that of others, and to consider the action of others to give point and direction to his own, is equivalent to the breaking down of those barriers of class, race, and national territory which kept men from perceiving the full import of their activity." According to Dewey, finding a common ground for conjoint participation in achieving goals shared by diverse groups, by implication groups in conflict, is a prior condition of a truly democratic society, the "more numerous and varied points of contact" the better as they "secure a liberation of [individual] powers."[3]

A decade later in *The Pubic and Its Problems*, Dewey identified the causes and harmful effects of the fragmentation of communal life in urban industrial (and postindustrial) society. Only by restoring local neighborly communities, he reasoned, might the public find itself and work as an integrated whole to achieve the full benefits of modern science and technology. "Democracy," declared Dewey, "must begin at home, and its home is the neighborly community."[4] Designating three preconditions for a democratic communal life—interaction, shared activity, and shared values—he wrote eloquently that conjoint activity in the service of a shared goal molds an aggregation of people into a community and leverages shared values.[5] Only in the neighborly community, he averred, could "effective regard for whatever is distinctive and unique in each [person], irrespective of physical and psychological inequalities," be achieved.[6]

Avoiding the question of how and by what agencies or institutions local community life might be restored in an advanced industrial (or postindustrial) society, Dewey nevertheless believed that the required conditions for reconstructing local communities as seedbeds of democratic participation and opportunity would somehow be realized. In his memorable peroration to *The Public and Its Problems,* he held out the utopian vision of somehow achieving a synthesis that would maximize the benefits of both past and present, a democracy of convergent pluralistic interests, which he associated with the Great Community. "Whatever the future may have in store, one thing is certain. Unless local communal life can be restored, the public cannot adequately resolve its most urgent problem: to find and identify itself. But if it be reestablished, it will manifest a fullness, variety and freedom of possession and enjoyment of meanings and goods unknown in the contiguous associations of the past. For it will be alive and flexible as well as stable, responsive to the complex and world-wide scene in which it is enmeshed. While local, it will not be isolated."[7]

Characteristically of Dewey, he sketched his vision of pluralistic democratic participation, or cultural democracy, in highly abstract terms, leaving it to others to work out the "practical means to realize his utopian end."[8] Serving a polyglot community, Benjamin Franklin High School suggested a practical strategy for educating young people to progress toward Dewey's democracy of convergent pluralistic interests. Covello's approach centrally located the public school as an agent of cultural democracy and as a catalyst for training the public work citizen Dewey's vision of the Great Community so strongly implied.

The distinction between bridging (inclusive) and bonding (exclusive) social capital provides insight into Covello's motivation and his evolving understanding of the purpose of a community school, including its role as public work. Franklin was an example of bridging social capital; it was, to use Robert Putnam's words, "outward looking and encompassing people across diverse social cleavages."[9] In this sense the community high school embraced the full range of East Harlem's ethnic and generational diversity. By comparison, the Church of Our Lady, literally a stone's throw from the "new" Benjamin Franklin, epitomized bonding social capital, which in this case contributed to the development of Italian American ethnicity and exclusive social networks (the bludgeoning of Puerto Rican onlookers at the church's annual festival revealed the dark side of this exclusivity).

Bonding social capital was critical to Covello's purposes—the social networking of Italian American business, professional, and educational leaders led to the first high school in East Harlem. As soon as the high school was established, Covello began to fashion it as an instrument of bridging social capital, extending its reach throughout multiethnic East Harlem. The school-community advisory committees, street units, intercultural education program, East Harlem campaigns, *East Harlem News*, and other activities conducted in alliance with umbrella organizations such as the East Harlem Council of Social Agencies and the Harlem Legislative Conference expressed this concept. Borrowing Putnam's language, norms of trust and reciprocity were created and strengthened. In turn social capital leveraged political capital to bring the East River Houses and the new Pleasant Avenue high school building to East Harlem.[10]

To our knowledge Covello never referred to community-centered schooling as "public work," a term that had currency among "ordinary people" in the 1930s and 1940s, albeit not among political theorists.[11] And though the construct "social capital" appeared as early as 1916 in the context of the social center movement, Covello apparently never used that term either. Irrespective of Covello's civic lexicon, Benjamin Franklin High School mirrored and embodied social capital and public work in much the way practical democratic theorists delineate these concepts. Covello's essay on the East Harlem housing campaign, among other documents, illustrates that his thinking about community-centered schooling fits logically in the bailiwick of these contemporary theorists, although it lacks systematic empirical verification: "Simultaneous participation of diverse racial and nationality groups blunted the prejudices and antagonisms common to their every-day patterns of life. There was wholesome interaction between these groups, and the nature of this interaction was to us a potent means for education in intercultural relationships."[12] Covello's project was to form a "larger public" from the "little publics" of East Harlem's competing ethnic and racial groups. In combination with the larger public–building activities of the East Harlem campaigns, CAC subcommittees, and street units, the treatment of race and intercultural issues across the curriculum differentiated BFHS as an institution from other progressive education programs of the 1930s, which tended to avoid underlying social issues.

In East Harlem in the 1930s and 1940s, Benjamin Franklin High School suggested what a public school might look like if it were to institutionally model public work citizenship, if it were seriously to hold itself accountable for training active citizens. To do so, Franklin acted as an institutional citizen, modeling the interconnectivity of the three domains of civic preparation and performance: knowledge, behaviors, and dispositions. Through its social research program, the high school was constantly improving its *knowledge,* which led it to adjust its *behaviors* to address its evolving role in engaging and reconciling civic and political issues. And through its behaviors—notably, the East Harlem housing campaign—it modeled the *dispositions* of engaged public work citizenship. Franklin, especially in its prewar heyday, conveyed "civic ideas" and "civic-mindedness" across classrooms.[13] The thought that "we would be able to participate in something bigger than ourselves" was a galvanizing sentiment for many Franklin students. Citing Hanna and Naslund, we have argued that a citizen-centered community school is "*consciously used* by the people of the community," meaning that "youth and adults together work to analyze the problems of the community, research and formulate solutions to those problems and mobilize resources and support for putting solutions into operation." Locating curricular space for active citizenship education and creating programmatic links with community agencies and venues of civic activism is a necessary start toward public schools that institutionally model the civic knowledge, behaviors, and dispositions we want our young, "strong" democratic citizens to hold.

But even if Covello's work provides a practical response to Dewey's challenge, how usable is this past today? How does it fit within the current policy environment? Some responsible school critics contend that schools already try to "do too much" and that only a heightened focus on the academic mission of the school will provide society with the skills and knowledge it needs in a brutally competitive global economy. As journalist Thomas Friedman stresses, the "young Chinese, Indians, and Poles are . . . racing us to the top," and it will take considerable effort and will for the United States to compete effectively.[14] Is citizenship preparation desirable but secondary to this challenge? Does it distract from a more fundamental need, as an ideal to indulge only after we bring academic achievement up to par? We now turn to a closer examination of this critical tension.

Reconciling Goals: Academic Achievement and Citizenship Preparation

Covello's intent in developing community-centered schooling was primarily to strengthen the school's ability to carry out its academic mission. (A linguist and teacher-scholar at DeWitt Clinton High School and Ph.D. student in educational sociology at New York University, Covello cultivated an abiding regard for liberal learning.) The campaign to establish a high school for boys in East Harlem insisted that the school have an academic curriculum, as distinct from a solely vocational focus. The community program, most notably the CAC subcommittees and street units, was organized to reinforce the high school's instructional program.

Today, U.S. schools face a bracing set of challenges in terms of their core mission in academic preparation. The current policy environment underscores significant inequities, and the rising international challenge highlights the scale of the issues. At present, "more than two-thirds of workers in growing, good-paying occupations have postsecondary education" compared to "only one-third of workers in declining, low-paying occupations."[15] Yet U.S. students rank sixteenth in high school graduation among Organisation for Economic Co-operation and Development (OECD) nations, down significantly since the early 1980s. Significant ethnoracial differences are evident in the percentage of students who graduate from high school with a regular diploma: for the class of 2002, 78 percent of white students versus 56 percent of African American students and 52 percent of Hispanic students. In terms of achievement, seventeen-year-old Hispanics and African Americans achieve at the level of thirteen-year-old whites and graduate "college-ready" at roughly half the rate of their white fellow students—and fewer than half of white high school graduates leave "college ready." The proportion of Hispanic kindergartners that will complete a B.A. is just one-third that of white kindergartners.[16] With so much to be done to improve academic achievement, would not attention to Franklin-style citizenship preparation only distract us from this pressing challenge?

One solution would be to find another institution or institutions able to take on the challenge of citizenship preparation. Schools can be asked to tackle the achievement gaps; another institution would tackle the citizenship gaps, such as those resulting in Hispanic voting rates half those of white citizens.[17] But which institution might pick up this massive task? To which public or even common institution are the vast majority of young citizens exposed today? As we stated at the onset, there is nothing in our historical or contemporary analysis that weds us to a particular configuration of educating institutions to accomplish citizenship training. Unfortunately for those who would excuse schools from the lead responsibility of citizenship training, there appears to us no plausible institutional option. Indeed, there appear to be fewer and fewer institutional experiences shared across a broad swath of our society. Our investment in the vitality of our citizenry suggests at least a leading role for schools.

Learning from the past, how then might schools balance citizenship preparation with academic achievement, clearly the present moment's policy priority? Might these two core goals actually reinforce each other rather than compete for the energy and focus of these strained institutions? Might a school that institutionally models public work citizenship actually improve its academic achievement by doing so?

Aware of the messiness of school change, we think so. Modeling public work citizenship could enhance the learning environment directly and indirectly, as well as improve the political and financial support schools enjoy.

One way community-centered schools advance their academic mission is by countering the negative impact of neighborhood effects on academic achievement. Covello recognized that he could not effectively teach neighborhood boys if he did not first understand and then address neighborhood and home factors that either supported or countered the educational impact of the school. He knew, for example, that intercultural education programs in the school were insufficient; he had to reach parents, and local informal leadership, in order to affect the educational impact he sought. The same applied to academic goals and thus necessitated an extensive adult education program. Neighborhood contexts currently figure prominently in the study of adolescent development, and researchers highlight two dimensions of neighborhoods as formative for young people. The first is neighborhood structure, broadly defined as demographic factors and socioeconomic composition; the second is "neighborhood processes," a term that includes social organization (for example, physical conditions and social interactions) and the quantity and quality of institutional resources. Unsurprisingly, studies associate low neighborhood SES with low school achievement and associate poverty with other factors that may jeopardize school achievement, such as delinquency, criminal behavior, and sexual activity, especially for older adolescents. Residential instability, a neighborhood structural variable, apparently has negative impacts that shape some of these behaviors and in some studies explains a major portion of variance in academic achievement.[18]

For just these reasons, Richard Rothstein has challenged educators and policy makers to broaden educational policy beyond the school to bring the relative influence of schools into greater balance. Rothstein characterizes as "out of balance" the widely held conviction of educational scholars and policy makers "that if only schools held all students to a single academic standard, students' subsequent success in higher education and in the labor market and, in consequence, their lifetime income and social standing, would be independent of racial status or of parental social class." This "myopia" will lead only to failure and thus will undermine public support. Indeed, "our national determination to reform only education and then expect all other forms of inequality and oppression to . . . take care of themselves will doom us to another half century of lack of progress."[19]

However, some educators resist mightily the Rothstein argument, fearing that this will distract attention from viable school improvement investments and mire educational policy in intractable broad social problems. Community-centered schooling, however, suggests a middle road for educators, integrating efforts to address those local community factors affecting achievement with schooling's core imperative of citizenship preparation. Students reinforce academic skills while they work to ameliorate factors diminishing academic achievement; both academic and citizenship aims are advanced in parallel, reinforcing rather than distracting.

Another way community-centered schooling reinforces academic achievement is via student motivation. Local public work citizenship requires authentic academic work, real audiences, and lived social problems. Since long before

Rousseau's *Emile,* student disengagement has presented a major obstacle to student achievement. Recent studies only reinforce the impact of low student motivation on lackluster achievement patterns, all the more acute for students buffeted by all-too-authentic socioeconomic challenges. This research highlights the centrality of "psychological mediators of engagement," namely "adolescents' needs for competence, control, and a sense of belonging." Here researchers underscore the primacy of well-constructed "authentic tasks" in activating high-school student engagement. This is product-oriented or "hands-on" intellectual work that speaks to an audience beyond the classroom and involves new conceptual challenges (higher-order thinking), collaboration, "meaningful connections to students' culture," and "autonomy in selecting tasks and methods." These learning-motivational factors assume heightened saliency with respect to the resilience and educational performance of African American and Latino youths in poor urban neighborhoods.[20] History suggests that citizen-centered community schooling can provide such intellectual work.

In addition to improving motivation and addressing local social conditions, both of which impinge on academic achievement, citizen-centered community schooling promises a way to balance local control with nonlocal educational forces. At present, the local versus nonlocal tension often arises in curricular terms, witnessed in recent debates regarding evolution. Local-control activists, for example, ally with those who inveigh against the dominant discourse of biology, a discourse that is international in scope. Protests to the contrary, the direction or discourse of academic communities will not be contained by local town imperatives. The tradition and impulse of local control, however, will not abate, nor will it be satisfied on curricular battlegrounds.

The resolution may be to move the debate off curricular grounds, and instead, to grounds of citizenship preparation. Indeed, local control speaks to the need for the autonomy of local citizens, and what better vehicle than the recognized public mission of schools to prepare solid citizens? Might not the strong impulse to local control be more productively directed toward enhancing citizenship training via community-centered schooling models, and away from whether or not topic X belongs in a course area that must, by its nature, ultimately derive direction from an international disciplinary community? Would not differences in local citizenship preparation, within the legitimate if contested bounds of democratic traditions, more productively engage the local/nonlocal tensions with which a republic must always grapple? While legitimate local curricular issues certainly arise, a local version of calculus makes little sense to debate; on the other hand, the issue of what democratic citizenship means in a local context could stimulate a fruitful proliferation of a variety of engaging models of public work preparation, accompanied by legitimate debate and diversity of view.

Finally, in a political economy with the potential to become increasingly unfavorable to financial support for compulsory schooling, community-centered schooling offers a common ground shared across generational cohorts competing for scarce public funds. The degree to which public schooling promotes individual economic advancement at the expense of citizenship is the degree to which it pits a public service aimed at youth against public services supporting an increasingly elderly, and politically powerful, population. The degree to which public schooling advances citizenship, with shared benefits across generations, including tangible improvements in local community life, is the degree to which cross-generational competition for scarce public funds can be diminished. The cross-generational tensions will never disappear, but reinforcing public schooling's contribution to a shared common good can only advance its interests in fiscally competitive times.

WEAK CITIZENSHIP PREPARATION endangers the vitality of this republic, threatening its ability to sustain its democratic traditions and to lead as a democratic society in the world community. The schools remain the only viable public institution to lead a revitalization of public work citizenship, the only way the United States could pretend to lead internationally in democratic reform. Our history does not lack exemplars or clear lessons for the present. Our history is without panaceas, though, and can only clarify our now largely muted and implicit responses to the inevitable civic challenge. That community-centered schooling can address this fundamental societal need while advancing the core academic mission of schools argues powerfully for our close consideration today.

We are optimistic that the national attention being paid civic education— a critical public purpose of public schooling—will grow in the coming years. Our book, we hope, will compel further attention to the crisis of diminishing citizenship and to a way out of this crisis through public schools that institutionally model an advanced form of democratic citizenship. We are also hopeful that this book will draw attention to the power and promise of the community school idea in the debates about public schooling's role in citizenship preparation. In *A Place for Us* (1998) Benjamin Barber writes that achieving strong democracy requires a reconceptualization and repositioning of existing institutions, not the creation of a novel civic architecture.[21] We agree. Citizen-centered community schools that model public work—embodying as institutions a civic ethos that includes focused, systematic development of strong democratic citizenship—should be central to that reconstruction. Only then will our civic performance meet the standards of our democratic dreams.

> They watch us all the time. The students, that is. . . . We are fallible, and should not pretend that we are anything else. But we ought to be aware of what we are doing. We have a profound moral contract with our students. We insist, under the law, that they become thoughtful, informed citizens. We must—for their benefit and ours—model such citizenship.[22]
>
> Theodore R. Sizer and Nancy Faust Sizer

NOTES

In citing works in the notes, the following abbreviations appear:

Almanac	Benjamin Franklin High School *Almanac* (Newspaper)
BOE	New York City Board of Education
CCS	Leonard Covello, *The Community-Centered School*, CP
CIEB	Casa Italiana Educational Bureau
CJD	John Dewey, *The Correspondence of John Dewey, 1871–1952,* electronic ed. Larry A. Hickman (Charlottesville, Va.: InteLex Corporation, 1999) (CD-Rom)
CP	Leonard Covello Papers (MSS 40), Balch Institute Collections, Historical Society of Pennsylvania, Philadelphia
JBOE	*Journal of the Board of Education of the City of New York*
JDP	John Dewey Papers, Special Collections Research Center, Morris Library, Southern Illinois University
MCCP	Mayor's Committee on City Planning
PER	*The Papers of Eleanor Roosevelt*, gen. eds. Anne Firor Scott and William H. Chaffee (Frederick, Md.: University Publications of America, 1986) (microfilm)

NOTES TO INTRODUCTION

1. "Program of the Ceremonies Incident to the Dedication of Benjamin Franklin High School," 16 April 1942, Leonard Covello Papers (MSS 40) [hereafter CP], Balch Institute Collections, Historical Society of Pennsylvania, Philadelphia, box 32, folder 6. See also See Robert Putnam, "Community-Based Social Capital and Educational Performance," in *Making Good*

Citizens: Education and Civil Society, ed. Diane Ravitch and Joseph Viteritti (New Haven, Conn.: Yale University Press, 2001), 58–95.

2. "Program of Ceremonies"; also in CP box 32, folder 6: [Leonard Covello], "Introductory statement—Presentation of presiding officer"; "Speech Delivered by Congressman Vito Marcantonio at the Benjamin Franklin High School Dedication Exercises on Thursday, April 16, 1942." Two versions of Covello's dedication speech appear in this folder; we have trusted the more eloquent statement.

3. John Dewey, *Democracy and Education* (1916; reprint, New York: Free Press, 1944), 214.

4. John Dewey, *The School and Society*, in *John Dewey: The Middle Works, 1899–1924*, vol. 1 (1899–1901), ed. Jo Ann Boydston (Carbondale: Southern Illinois Press, 1976), 8, 20.

5. David Labaree, *How to Succeed in School without Really Learning: The Credentials Race in American Education* (New Haven, Conn.: Yale University Press, 1997), chap. 1.

6. For democracy as a political versus an economic concept, see Michael W. Apple, *Educating the "Right" Way: Markets, Standards, God, and Inequality* (New York: RoutledgeFalmer, 2001), 18, 39.

7. See David Tyack, "Preserving the Republic by Educating Republicans," in *Diversity and Its Discontents: Cultural Conflict and Common Ground in Contemporary American Society*, ed. Neil J. Smelser and Jeffrey C. Alexander (Princeton, N.J.: Princeton University Press, 1999), 63–83.

8. Michael Walzer, "Citizenship," in *Political Innovation and Conceptual Change*, ed. Terence Ball, James Farr, and Russell L. Hanson (Cambridge: Cambridge University Press, 1989), 211–19. See also Will Kymlicka and Wayne Norman, "Return of the Citizen: A Survey of Recent Work on Citizenship Theory," *Ethics* 104 (1994): 352–81.

9. Michael J. Sandel, *Democracy's Discontent: American in Search of a Public Philosophy* (Cambridge, Mass.: Harvard University Press, 1996), chap. 1.

10. Benjamin Barber, *Strong Democracy: Participatory Politics for a New Age* (Berkeley: University of California Press, 1984), 4.

11. Ibid., 133.

12. Joel Westheimer and Joseph Kahne, "What Kind of Citizen? The Politics of Educating for Democracy," *American Educational Research Journal* 41, no. 2 (2004): 237–69.

13. Harry C. Boyte and Nancy N. Kari, *Building America: The Democratic Promise of Public Work* (Philadelphia: Temple University Press, 1996); Harry C. Boyte, *Everyday Politics: Reconnecting Citizens and Public Life* (Philadelphia: University of Pennsylvania Press, 2004), with a chapter on "citizenship as public work."

14. For further illustrations of community organizing for public work, see Roger Sanjek, *The Future of Us All: Race and Neighborhood Politics in New York City* (Ithaca, N.Y.: Cornell University Press, 1998), a multiyear ethnographic study of Elmhurst Corona, a neighborhood in Queens, New York City, described as "perhaps the most ethnically mixed community in the world" (1); Mark R. Warren, *Dry Bones Rattling: Community Building to Revitalize American Democracy* (Princeton, N.J.: Princeton University Press, 2001), an ethnographic study of Industrial Areas Foundation (IAF) organizations in Texas.

15. Westheimer and Kahne, "What Kind of Citizen?" table 1, p. 240—their typology is not a continuum. The critical factor that distinguishes education for participatory citizenship from a more politicized, social change conception is the latter's depth of attention to the structural causes of social problems. Westheimer and Kahne call it the "justice-oriented citizen," the third and most advanced category of their schematic. We believe, however, that public work citizenship is a more powerful conception, as it embraces the goal of "larger public" building and suggests a set of operational criteria for the justice-oriented conception. For the "larger public" and the problem of "little publics," see Walter C. Parker, "'Advanced Ideas about Democracy: Toward a Pluralist Conception of Citizenship,"

Teachers College Record 98, no. 1 (1996): 104–25. Parker updates the central argument of John Dewey's 1927 book *The Public and Its Problems* as the theoretical basis of a pluralist conception of citizenship.

16. For reference citations see Michael C. Johanek and John Puckett, "The State of Civic Education: Preparing Citizens in an Era of Accountability," in Susan Fuhrman and Marvin Lazerson, *Institutions of American Democracy: The Public Schools* (New York: Oxford University Press, 2005), 130–59.

17. Since its inception in 1987, the We the People program of the Center for Civic Education (Calabasas, California) has involved some twenty-six million students through its supplemental texts for elementary and secondary classrooms. *We the People: The Citizen and the Constitution,* the program's widely used high school text, provides conceptual scaffolding for students regarding the Constitution and the political process. Although it offers students some good opportunities to take a critical perspective on U.S. society through the lens of constitutional history, the text nudges them to take an optimistic view, conveying the positive message that the U.S. political system is fundamentally sound and just, that it is self-correcting by dint of a strong judiciary, and that violations of civil liberties are always, however gradually, weeded out.

18. Public Achievement, a youth initiative for ages eight through eighteen, is based on Boyte's theory of public work. Examples of children's public work include third and fourth graders organizing parents and neighborhood residents to march against violence, and fifth and sixth graders successfully campaigning to build a neighborhood park, raising $60,000 from public officials and businesses. Robert Hildreth, *Building Worlds, Transforming Lives, Making History: A Guide to Public Achievement,* 2nd ed. (Minneapolis: Center for Democracy and Citizenship, 1998); see also Boyte, *Everyday Politics,* chap. 5.

19. Paul R. Hanna and Robert A. Naslund, "The Community School Defined," in *The Community School, Fifty-Second Yearbook of the National Society for the Study of Education,* ed. Nelson B. Henry (Chicago: University of Chicago Press, 1953), 52–55. We are indebted to historian Lee Benson for introducing us to this important source. The citation in the form we present it here appears in several of Benson's publications, most recently in Lee Benson and Ira Harkavy, "Truly Engaged and Truly Democratic Cosmopolitan Civic Universities, Community Schools, and Development of the Democratic Good Society in the 21st Century," paper presented at the seminar "Research University as Local Citizen," University of California, San Diego, 6–7 October 2002. This definition has guided the university-school-community projects Benson, Harkavy, and John Puckett have worked on for more than fifteen years in West Philadelphia.

20. For discussion of ideal-types, see Edward Bryan Portis, *Max Weber and Political Commitment* (Philadelphia: Temple University Press, 1986), 63–65; cited in Benson and Harkavy, "Truly Engaged and Truly Democratic."

21. See and cf. Labaree, *How to Succeed in School,* chap. 1.

22. Albert H. Smyth, *The Writings of Benjamin Franklin,* vol. 2: *1722–1750* (New York: Macmillan, 1907), 396; James Campbell, *Recovering Benjamin Franklin: An Exploration of a Life of Science and Service* (Chicago: Open Court, 1999), chaps. 2.4, 5.3; John C. Van Horne, "Collective Benevolence and the Common Good in Franklin's Philanthropy," in *Reappraising Benjamin Franklin: A Bicentennial Perspective,* ed. J. A. Leo Lemay (Newark: University of Delaware Press, 1993), 425–40.

23. Arthur S. Link and Richard L. McCormick, *Progressivism* (Arlington Heights, Ill.: Harlan Davidson, 1983), 72–96.

24. Eric Schneider, personal communication, 24 February 2003. Dr. Schneider's thoughtful reading of the first draft of our book led us to highlight this tension.

25. The quote belongs to Frederic Ernst, Associate Superintendent of High Schools, from stenographer's notes, CP box 32, folder 6.

26. Citations of Leonard Covello's *Social Background of the Italo-American School Child: A Study of the Southern Italian Family Mores and Their Effect on the School Situation in Italy and America* (Leiden, Netherlands: E. J. Brill, 1967) are legion; see esp. Francesco Cordasco, ed., *Studies in Italian American Social History: Essays in Honor of Leonard Covello* (Totowa, N.J.: Rowman and Littlefield, 1975). Covello was an inveterate compiler and sorter of personal and public papers related to East Harlem and the history of BFHS—a treasure trove of documents and photographs that were housed at the Balch Institute until 2002 and are now located at the Historical Society of Pennsylvania. This collection has provided major source materials for such works as Robert Orsi's brilliant treatise on street religion in Italian East Harlem, *The Madonna of 115th Street: Faith and Community in Italian Harlem, 1880–1950*, 2nd ed. (New Haven, Conn.: Yale University Press, 2002); and Eric Schneider's illuminating history of New York City youth gangs, *Vampires, Dragons, and Egyptian Kings: Youth Gangs in Postwar New York* (Princeton, N.J.: Princeton University Press, 1999). For critical commentary on the Covello Papers, especially several hundred interviews he conducted for his dissertation, 1927–44, see Simone Cinotto, "Leonard Covello, the Covello Papers, and the History of Eating Habits among Italian Immigrants in New York," *Journal of American History* 91, no. 2 (2004): 497–521.

27. Nathan Glazer and Daniel P. Moynihan, *Beyond the Melting Pot: The Negroes, Puerto Ricans, Jews, Italians, and Irish of New York City*, 2d. ed. (Cambridge, Mass.: MIT Press, 1970), 184, 200.

28. David Tyack and Elisabeth Hansot, *Managers of Virtue: Public School Leadership in America, 1820–1980* (New York: Basic, 1983), 208.

29. Paula S. Fass, *Outside In: Minorities and the Transformation of American Education* (New York: Oxford University Press, 1989), 57.

30. Vito Perrone, *Teacher with a Heart: Reflections on Leonard Covello and Community* (New York: Teachers College Press, 1998), 74.

31. Robert W. Peebles, Leonard Covello, A Study of an Immigrant's Contribution to New York City (New York: Arno Press, 1978).

CHAPTER 1: THE COMMUNITY SCHOOL IDEA

1. Lee Benson, *Toward the Scientific Study of History: Selected Essays of Lee Benson* (Philadelphia: J. B. Lippincott, 1972), 334–40.

2. Ibid., 336.

3. Gertrude Himmelfarb, *Poverty and Compassion: The Moral Imagination of the Late Victorians* (New York: Knopf, 1991), 235–43.

4. Figures reported in Allen F. Davis, *Spearheads for Reform: The Social Settlements and the Progressive Movement,* rev. ed. (New Brunswick, N.J.: Rutgers University Press, 1984), 12–13; Judith Ann Trolander, *Professionalism and Social Change: From the Settlement House Movement to Neighborhood Centers, 1886 to the Present* (New York: Columbia University Press, 1987), 3.

5. See Marvin Lazerson, *Origins of the Urban School: Public Education in Massachusetts, 1870–1915* (Cambridge, Mass.: Harvard University Press, 1971), 191–97; Murray Levine and Adeline Levine, *A Social History of Helping Services* (New York: Appleton-Century-Crofts, 1970), 128–29; Morris I. Berger, *The Settlement Movement, the Immigrant, and the Public School* (1956; reprint, New York: Arno Press, 1980); Davis, *Spearheads for Reform,* esp. 40–59; Amalie Hofer, "The Social Settlement and the Kindergarten," NEA, *Journal of Proceedings and Addresses* (1895): 514–25; Isabel M. Stewart, "The Educational Value of the Nurse in the Public School," in *Health and Education,* pt. 1 of *Ninth Yearbook of the National Society for the Study of Education,* ed. Thomas Wood (Chicago: University of Chicago Press, 1910), 19–26.

6. Jane Addams, "The Objective Value of a Social Settlement" (1897), in *The Social Thought of Jane Addams*, ed. Christopher Lasch (Indianapolis: Bobbs-Merrill, 1965), 44–61.

7. Davis, *Spearheads for Reform*, 103–47; see also Kathryn Kish Sklar, "Hull House in the 1890s: A Community of Women Reformers," *Signs: Journal of Women in Culture and Society* 10, no. 4 (1985): 675–77; Mary Jo Deegan, *Jane Addams and the Men of the Chicago School, 1892–1918* (New Brunswick, N.J.: Transaction Press, 1988); Ellen Fitzpatrick, *Endless Crusade: Women Social Scientists and Progressive Reform* (New York: Oxford University Press, 1990).

8. Stanley Wenocur and Michael Reisch, *From Charity to Enterprise: The Development of American Social Work in a Market Economy* (Urbana: University of Illinois Press, 1989), 138–46; Louis Menand, *The Metaphysical Club* (New York: Farrar, Straus and Giroux, 2001), 306–16.

9. Ira Harkavy and John Puckett, "Lessons of Hull House for the Contemporary University," *Social Service Review* 67, no. 3 (1994): 299–321; see also John Puckett and Ira Harkavy, "The Action Research Tradition in the United States: Toward a Strategy for Revitalizing the Social Sciences, the University, and the American City," in *Action Research: From Practice to Writing in an International Action Research Development Program*, ed. Davydd J. Greenwood (Amsterdam: John Benjamins, 1999), 147–67; Ellen Condliffe Lagemann, *The Politics of Knowledge: The Carnegie Corporation, Philanthropy, and Public Policy* (Middletown, Conn.: Wesleyan University Press, 1989), 67. For "research done with a reformist and ameliorative purpose," see Martin Bulmer, "The Decline of the Social Survey Movement and the Rise of American Empirical Sociology," in *The Social Survey in Historical Perspective, 1880–1940*, ed. Martin Bulmer, Kevin Bales, and Kathryn Kish Sklar (New York: Cambridge University Press, 1991), 305.

10. Menand, *Metaphysical Club*, 308; the quote describes Hull House, not Dewey's opinion.

11. John Dewey, *John Dewey: The Middle Works, 1899–1924*, vol. 2 (1902–3), ed. Jo Ann Boydston (Carbondale: Southern Illinois Press, 1976), 80–93, quote from 80, 82. During his tenure at the University of Chicago, 1894–1904, Dewey was a frequent guest, observer, and lecturer at Hull House; Addams profoundly influenced his views on democracy and education. Lawrence Cremin, *American Education: The Metropolitan Experience, 1876–1980* (New York: Macmillan, 1988), 175–79.

12. Dewey, *Middle Works*, 2:91. In 1915, Dewey and his daughter Evelyn revisited these themes, declaring that "closer contact with immediate neighborhood conditions not only enriches school work and strengthens motive force in the pupils, but it increases the service rendered to the community." Maintaining that "the schoolhouse is the natural and logical social center in a neighborhood," the Deweys argued for the merger of schools and social settlements in "districts where the social and economic standards of living are so low that the people are not especially successful citizens, . . . using the activities of the community as a means of enriching the curriculum, and using the school plant for a neighborhood center." John Dewey and Evelyn Dewey, *Schools of To-morrow* (New York: E. P. Dutton, 1915), 205–28, quotes from 206, 224.

13. Lee Benson and Ira Harkavy, "School and Community in the Global Society: A Neo-Deweyan Theory of Community Problem-Solving Schools, Cosmopolitan Neighborly Communities, and a Neo-Deweyan 'Manifesto' to Dynamically Connect School and Community," *Universities and Community Schools* 5, no. 1–2 (1997): 32.

14. Alan Ryan, *John Dewey and the High Tide of American Liberalism* (New York: Norton, 1995), 133–42.

15. Dewey, *Middle Works*, 1:21–38.

16. We borrow liberally here from Benson and Harkavy, "School and Community in the Global Society"; the quote, which succinctly paraphrases Dewey's argument, is theirs,

32. See also Philip Jackson's introduction to the centennial edition of Dewey's *The School and Society* and *The Child and the Curriculum* (Chicago: University of Chicago Press, 1990), ix–xli; Robert B. Westbrook, *John Dewey and American Democracy* (Ithaca, N.Y.: Cornell University Press, 1991, 109–11; Aaron Schutz, "John Dewey's Conundrum: Can Democratic Schools Empower?" *Teachers College Record* 103, no. 2 (April 2001): 267–302. Our own close reading of Dewey's texts supports the critical observations of these authors.

17. In 1897 Aaron Gove, superintendent of schools in Denver, Colorado, in "The Proper Use of Schoolhouses," in NEA, *Journal of Addresses and Proceedings* (1898): 255, broached the idea of communitywide use of the school to the NEA, remarking: "Is it not reasonable and proper so to construct a schoolhouse, and with very little increased cost, as to afford to the people who pay for it, a literary home, an educational center for adults, including library where possible?"

18. Clarence A. Perry, *Wider Use of the School Plant* (New York: Russell Sage Foundation, 1913), chaps. 5–8, quote from 204.

19. William J. Reese, *Power and the Promise of School Reform: Grass-roots Movements during the Progressive Era* (Boston: Routledge and Kegan Paul, 1986), 187–96, quote from 190; Kevin Mattson, *Creating a Democratic Public: The Struggle for Urban Participatory Democracy during the Progressive Era* (University Park: Pennsylvania State University Press, 1998), 51–65, quote from 60. See also and cf. John S. Rogers, *Community Schools: Lessons from the Past and Present* (Flint, Mich.: C. S. Mott Foundation [1998]), sect. 2.1.

20. Edward J. Ward, ed., *The Social Center* (New York: D. Appleton, 1913), 179–99, quote from 187; and Ward, "The Rochester Civic and Social Centers," in *The City School as a Community Center*, pt. 1 of *Tenth Yearbook of the National Society for the Study of Education*, ed. Chester W. Parker (Chicago: University of Chicago Press, 1911), 51–57.

21. Ward, *Social Center*, 190–94, quote from 190.

22. Ibid., 198.

23. Reese, *Power and Promise of School Reform*, 196.

24. Ibid., 188, 194; Mattson, *Democratic Public*, 52, 59.

25. Ward, *Social Center*, 203–4; Reese, *Power and Promise of School Reform*, 201–2.

26. Reese, *Power and Promise of School Reform*, 197–98.

27. Ward, *Social Center*, 204–6, quote from 206. The conference papers are individually catalogued in the New York City Public Library. According to Ward, the "first large conference on social center development," the All Southwestern Conference for Social Centers, was held in Dallas, Texas, in the spring of 1911. The promoter was Colonel Frank P. Holland, owner and publisher of *Farm and Ranch* and *Holland's Magazine*. "The meeting brought hundreds of men and women from all parts of the southwest and served to give great impetus to the movement. To-day [Sic] schoolhouses are beginning to be used as centers of democracy, recreation, neighborhood through all that region" (204). Prior to World War I school social centers and community-centered schools associated with the country life movement appeared in rural districts of the Midwest and South. Examples include the Porter School, at Kirksville, Missouri, in Evelyn Dewey, *New Schools for Old* (New York: Dutton, 1919); the Penn School, at St. Helena Island, South Carolina, in Elizabeth Jacoway, *Yankee Missionaries in the South: The Penn School Experiment* (Baton Rouge: Louisiana State University Press, 1980); the James H. Stout School in Dunn County, Wisconsin, in Ann M. Keppel and James I. Clark, "James H. Stout and Menomonie Schools," *Wisconsin Magazine of History* 42, no. 3 (1959): 200–210. For the country life movement, see Paul Theobald, *Call School: Rural Education in the Midwest* (Carbondale: Southern Illinois University Press, 1995), chap. 5.

28. Mattson, *Democratic Public*, chap. 5; Follett quoted at 90.

29. L. J. Hanifan, "The Rural School Community Center," *Annals of the American Academy of Political and Social Science* 67 (1916): 130–38; also incorporated in Hanifan,

The Community Center (Boston: Silver, Burdett, 1920), 78–88. We are indebted to Robert D. Putnam's essay "Community-Based Social Capital and Educational Performance," in *Making Good Citizens: Education and Civil Society,* ed. Diane Ravitch and Joseph P. Viteritti (New Haven, Conn.: Yale University Press, 2001): 59, 87–88n3, for pointing out Hanifan's article and early use of "social capital" in the context of school community centers.

30. Edward W. Stevens, Jr., "Social Centers, Politics, and Social Efficiency in the Progressive Era," *History of Education Quarterly* (Spring 1972): 16. The social center movement gave impetus to such standard features of elementary schools as auditoriums, gymnasiums, shower baths, school libraries, restrooms and school health rooms. See Clarence A. Perry, *Social Center Features in New Elementary School Architecture and the Plans of Sixteen Socialized Schools* (New York: Russell Sage Foundation, 1912).

31. Quoted in Jesse F. Steiner, *Community Organization: A Study of Its Theory and Current Practice,* rev. ed. (New York: Century, 1930), 185.

32. Howard Gillette, Jr., "The Evolution of Neighborhood Planning: From the Progressive Era to the 1949 Housing Act," *Journal of Urban History* 9, no. 4 (1983): 421–44.

33. For a concise assessment of Perry's contribution, see Patricia M. Melvin, ed., *American Community Organizations: A Historical Dictionary* (New York: Greenwood Press, 1986), 146–48; see also John M. Glenn, Lillian Brandt, and F. Emerson Andrews, *Russell Sage Foundation, 1907–1946,* vols. 1–2 (New York: Russell Sage Foundation, 1947).

34. Clarence A. Perry, "The Community-Used School," in Parker, *City School as Community Center,* 66. Reese, in *Power and Promise of School Reform,* 203, 208, notes the "genuine ideological conflict" that existed in many of the nation's social centers between school board members who saw wider use as a way to maximize the productivity and efficiency of the "school plant" and communitarians who shared Edward Ward's philosophy and "the spirit of the little red schoolhouse."

35. Robert Fisher, "Grass Roots Organizing in the Community Center Movement, 1907–30," in *The Roots of Community Organizing, 1917–1939,* ed. Neil Betten and Michael J. Austin (Philadelphia: Temple University Press, 1990), 78–79.

36. Ibid., 80.

37. Fisher, "Community Center Movement," quote from 82. In 1916, 463 cities reported school-extension programs. Eleanor T. Glueck, *The Community Use of Schools* (Baltimore: Williams and Wilkens, 1927), 28. Clarence Perry noted the trend toward the professional organization of community centers in Cleveland. The board of education appointed a "supervisor of community centers" and assigned Division of School Extension staff to the city's sixteen designated community centers. Clarence A. Perry, *Educational Extension* (Cleveland: Survey Committee of the Cleveland Foundation, 1916), 94–96, 108–13.

38. Robert Fisher, "The People's Institute of New York City, 1897–1934: Culture, Progressive Democracy, and the People" (Ph.D. diss., New York University, 1974), 107–59, quote from 95.

39. Clarence A. Perry and Marguerita P. Williams, *New York School Centers and Their Community Policy* (New York: Russell Sage Foundation, 1931), 22.

40. Fisher, "People's Institute," 278–90, quote from 277–78; Clarence A. Perry, *Contributions to Community Center Progress* (New York: Russell Sage Foundation, 1920), 7.

41. Fisher, "People's Institute," 310–18, John Collier quoted at 313; Fisher, "Community Center Movement," 82–83.

42. The Speyer School of Teachers College, Columbia University, a combined elementary school, social settlement, and teacher-training facility from 1899 to 1915, was no exception. Incorporating settlement-style activities as early as 1902, several years ahead of the Rochester schools, the Speyer School was directed by a group of university professors and social workers whose goal was social meliorism, though lacking the grassroots political

orientation of the Rochester social centers and the early People's Institute. Housed in an elegant five-story German Renaissance–style building in Manhattanville, a working-class district north of the campus, the Speyer School was splendidly equipped to provide an array of community services, including, among other appurtenances, a gymnasium, recreation area, garden, and greenhouse pavilion. As Dean James Earl Russell noted in his annual report of 1904: "Besides the regular day classes of a kindergarten and elementary school, provision has been made for public lectures and entertainments, afternoon and evening classes in manual training for boys, sewing and cooking for the older girls and women, gymnastics and dancing, a savings bank for children, library and reading room for both adults and children, public baths for men and women, and numerous clubs and social organizations for both sexes of all ages." *Dean's Report, 1904,* Milbank Special Collections, Teachers College, Columbia University. The K–8 day school offered a program of "correlated" studies in language arts, mathematics, history, and geography, with an emphasis on liberal child development. Sometime in 1914 or 1915, Teachers College terminated its support of the school social center. *Dean's Report, 1914;* David Snedden, "Alumni Trustee's Report: Preliminary Report on the Speyer School and Industrial Arts Courses in Teacher's College," *Teachers College Record* 16, no. 1 (1915): 17–23. Representing a sizeable and putatively inefficient investment of academic resources, the school had become an ugly duckling in the research culture forged by Nicholas Murray Butler. In September 1915 the Speyer School reopened as an experimental junior high school under the direct control of the New York City Board of Education. All that remained of the Manhattanville social center was a cooking laboratory "reserved for classes of girls from the public schools who will be taught the household arts by students of Teachers College." *Dean's Report, 1915.* For a brief history of the Speyer School, see Lawrence A. Cremin, David A. Shannon, and Mary Evelyn Townsend, *A History of Teachers College, Columbia University* (New York: Columbia University Press, 1954), 104–6.

43. J. P. Lichtenberger, "The War Relief Work of the Council of National Defense," *Annals of the American Academy of Political and Social Science* 39 (1918): 229–32; quotes from 229. See also Hanifan, *Community Center,* chap. 1.

44. Glueck, *Community Use of Schools,* 32–36; Fisher, "People's Institute," 333–52; Fisher, "Community Center Movement," esp. 85–88; Robert Fisher, "Community Organizing and Citizen Participation: The Efforts of the People's Institute in New York City, 1910–1920," *Social Service Review* 51, no. 3 (1977): 474–90. For the "waning of the democratic republic," with particular attention to the fate of social centers, see Mattson, *Democratic Public,* chap. 6; for war nationalism and citizen mobilization, see Alan Dawley, *Struggles for Justice* (Cambridge, Mass.: Harvard University Press, 1992), 172–217; for the role of "experts," see John F. McClymer, *War and Welfare: Social Engineering in America, 1890–1925* (Westport, Conn.: Greenwood Press, 1980), chaps. 5–6.

45. Clarence A. Perry, *School Center Gazette, 1919–1920* (New York: Russell Sage Foundation, n.d.), 3–5; Glueck, *Community Use of Schools,* 31–36. In 1919–20, New York City listed ninety-six school community centers that were collectively open an average of 3.6 evenings per week; forty-four additional centers were "reported but not listed."

46. Glueck, *Community Use of Schools,* 36, 38, 40.

47. Progressives were heartened by Bernard Baruch's War Industries Board, which curtailed corporate privileges to an unprecedented extent. The *New Republic* viewed the war "as a pretext to foist innovations upon the country." Walter Lippman stated: "We shall stand committed as never before to the realization of democracy in America. . . . We shall turn with fresh interest to our own tyrannies—to our Colorado mines, our autocratic steel industries, our sweatshops and our slums." Quoted in Dawley, *Struggles for Justice,* 195–96. Social center activists were similarly optimistic. Mattson, in *Democratic Public,* notes that Ward and Follett endorsed the federal government's use of social centers during the war,

believing that "community councils could actually build a long-lasting democratic nation—not just a vehicle for propaganda during the war" (110). The outcome, however, was conformist, not participatory, citizenship. Frustrated that the public could be manipulated so easily and thoroughly by the federal government, Lippman and other intellectuals turned sour on public opinion and democracy in the 1920s (115–20).

48. Glueck, *Community Use of Schools*, 146; for a similar vision and disappointment, see Steiner, *Community Organization*, 199. In 1929–30, the community centers in 469 New York City schools had an aggregate attendance of about 5.5 million. The board of education distinguished between "official centers," which were operated by professional staff from the Bureau of Extension Activities; and "permit centers," which were recurrent meeting sites for outside organizations holding continuous permits issued by the bureau. Attendance at the former was roughly four times greater than at the latter. The official school centers were organized for citywide athletic competitions in the League of Neighborhood School Centers; 135 basketball teams from seventy-eight centers competed in the 1930–31 basketball tournament. Perry and Williams, *New York School Centers*, 1–30.

49. The fate of the Cincinnati Social Unit Plan, 1917–20, which was organized around community health needs, richly illustrates the repressive postwar political climate. See Patricia M. Melvin, *The Organic City* (Lexington: University Press of Kentucky, 1988).

50. Fisher, "People's Institute," 352. For more detail on New York, see Kevin Mattson, "Creating a Democratic Public: The Struggle for Urban Participatory Democracy during the Progressive Era, 1890–1920" (Ph.D. diss., University of Rochester, 1994), 249–86.

51. Gillette, "Evolution of Neighborhood Planning," 425–27.

52. Glenn, Brandt, and Andrews, *Russell Sage Foundation*, 2:449.

53. Quoted in ibid., 426.

54. Clarence A. Perry, *Housing for the Machine Age* (New York: Russell Sage Foundation, 1939), esp. 108–36, 209–14; quotes from 209. Eugenie Birch directed us to this volume. See also Birch's essay, "Five Generations of the Garden City: Tracing Howard's Legacy in Twentieth Century Residential Planning," in *From Garden City to Green City: The Legacy of Ebenezer Howard*, ed. Kermit C. Parsons and David Schuyler (Baltimore: Johns Hopkins University Press, 2002), 171–98.

55. Clarence A. Perry, "The Neighborhood Unit: A Scheme of Arrangement for the Family-Life Community," in *Neighborhood and Community Planning*, vol. 7 of *Regional Survey of New York and Its Environs* (New York: Committee on Regional Plan of New York and Its Environs, 1929), 20–140, quote from 51. See also Clarence A. Perry, "The Relation of School-Site Planning to Neighborhood Planning," *The American School and University*, 2d. ed. (New York: American School Publishing, 1929), 13–17; James Dahir, *The Neighborhood Unit Plan, Its Spread and Acceptance* (New York: Russell Sage Foundation, 1947), 2.

56. Perry, "Neighborhood Unit," 72–73. See also Glenn, Brandt, and Andrews, *Russell Sage Foundation*, 2:438–51.

57. Stanley Buder, *Visionaries and Planners: The Garden City Movement and the Modern Community* (New York: Oxford University Press, 1990), 165–75; Roy LuBove, *Community Planning in the 1920s: The Contribution of the Regional Planning Association of America* (Pittsburgh: University of Pittsburgh Press, 1963), chap. 7. In *The Culture of Cities* (New York: Harcourt, Brace, 1938), Lewis Mumford called the school "the essential civic nucleus of the neighborhood" (478). When Mumford wrote in 1968 that "the minimum requirements for a community center have now become a standard basis for school design in almost every part of the United States," he gave much of the credit for that salutary result to Perry, and by implication, the Russell Sage Foundation. Lewis Mumford, *The Urban Prospect* (New York: Harcourt, Brace and World, 1968), 56–77, quote from 64.

58. Gillette, "Evolution of Neighborhood Planning," quote from 438. See also Joel Schwartz, *The New York Approach: Robert Moses, Urban Liberals, and Redevelopment of*

the Inner City (Columbus: Ohio State University Press, 1993), chap. 4. Schwartz notes that "Metropolitan Life's decision to build Stuyvesant Town for whites only scandalized liberals and helped touch off the post-World War II fair-housing movement" (95). For a useful history, see Arthur Simon, *Stuyvesant Town, U.S.A.* (New York: New York University Press, 1970). For illustrations of alternative urban apartment housing designs that would have centered on elementary schools, see Perry, *Housing for the Machine Age,* 122–28.

59. Schwartz, *New York Approach,* 95.

60. See George Butler, *Introduction to Community Recreation* (New York: McGraw-Hill, 1949).

61. In 1925, there were 77 official centers, with an aggregate attendance of 3,327,258, versus 242 nonofficial (permit) centers, with an aggregate attendance of 1,270,083. In 1930, 112 official centers served 3,664,004 (47,035 nightly), and 312 nonofficial centers served 697,130 (20,577 nightly). In 1935, the combined aggregate attendance for official and nonofficial centers totaled 5,442,664; by 1939, the total had reached 8,019,868. Attendance remained strong during the war years, for example, 126 official centers drew an aggregate attendance of 3,385,459 in 1943–44. In 1949–50, an aggregate of nearly 8 million people (some 84,000 nightly) attended 240 official centers. In 1956 the board reported an aggregate attendance of over 7 million: "While some of these community centers offer a program of informal adult education . . . , *the major activities are recreational*" (emphasis added). *Annual Report of the Superintendent of Schools,* 1924–25, 1929–30, 1934–35, 1938–39, 1943–44, 1949–50, 1955–56; quote from *Fifty-Eighth Annual Report,* 1955–56, Stat. Sect., 251.

62. Paul Hanna and Research Staff of the Works Progress Administration, *Youth Serves the Community* (New York: D. Appleton-Century, 1936), 3–20.

63. Ibid., 259.

64. Ibid., 269–70.

65. In Samuel Everett, ed., *The Community School* (New York: D. Appleton-Century, 1938), 125–63.

66. Frank E. Midkiff, "Community Schools in Waialua, Hawaii," in Everett, *Community School,* 298–339.

67. For histories of Highlander, see Myles Horton, with Herbert Kohl and Judith Kohl, *The Long Haul: An Autobiography* (New York: Doubleday, 1990); John Glen, *Highlander: No Ordinary School* (Lexington: University Press of Kentucky, 1988); Frank Addams, *Unearthing Seeds of Fire: The Idea of Highlander* (Winston-Salem, N.C.: John F. Blair, 1975).

68. Myles Horton, "The Community Folk School," in Everett, *Community School,* 265–97. Over the years, militantly conservative Southerners, including the Ku Klux Klan, resorted to arson and other violent acts in unsuccessful attempts to drive out Highlander.

69. Descriptions of other rural community schools of the 1930s–early 1940s may be found in the following sources: for Holtville Consolidated School, in Deatsville, Alabama, see Leila V. Scott, "Holtville Youth Leads the Way," *The Rotarian* 67 (1946), reprint in Edward G. Olsen, ed., *School and Community Programs: A Casebook of Successful Practice from Kindergarten through College and Adult Education* (New York: Prentice-Hall, 1949), 12–17; for Pine Mountain Settlement School, near Harlan, Kentucky, and Norris School, near Knoxville, Tennessee, see Harold Spears, *The Emerging High-School Curriculum and Its Direction* (New York: American Book Company, 1948), 73–93, 163–78; for the Sloan Foundation experiment in Kentucky, which tested the effects of specially designed, community-based curricular materials on children and their families' dietary and sanitation practices, see Maurice F. Seay and Leonard E. Meece, *The Sloan Experiment in Kentucky,* Bulletin of the Bureau of School Service, University of Kentucky, vol. 16, no. 4 (June 1944). Recent studies of segregated African American schools in the Jim Crow South highlight the

community-building role of these institutions; see Vanessa Siddle Walker, *Their Highest Potential: An African American School Community in the Segregated South* (Chapel Hill: University of North Carolina Press, 1996).

70. L. S. Tireman and Mary Watson, *A Community School in a Spanish-Speaking Village* (Albuquerque: University of New Mexico Press, 1948), 1–9; originally published in 1943 under the title *La Communidad.*

71. Rita Carabajal Apodaca, "The Nambé Community School (1937–1942)" (Ph.D. diss., University of New Mexico, 1986), 54–59; Martin L. Berman, "Arthurdale, Nambé, and the Developing Community School Model: A Comparative Study" (Ph.D. diss., University of Mexico, 1979), 163–64.

72. Tireman and Watson, *Community School in a Spanish-Speaking Village,* 11, 22–24.

73. Ibid., 39–58, 74–89; Berman, "Arthurdale, Nambé," 152.

74. Apodaca, "Nambé Community School," 126–32, 153–56; Mary Watson Diaries, 25 September and 11 November 1937, 2 February 1938, Center for Southwest Research, University of New Mexico, University of New Mexico Department of Special Education Records, 1935–1942, box 4. Watson's diaries reveal frustration with the villagers, for example: "I have decided that all the adults must be handled as though they were children and be contented with simple thinking. They are all living in such a *personal world*" (original emphasis; 10 December 1940); "This is a group of simple, primitive people; . . . things of immediate time interest them. There is little or no planning for the future" (2 January 1941).

75. Tireman and Watson, *Community School in a Spanish-Speaking Village,* 90–131; Berman, "Arthurdale, Nambé," 148–58, 160–61, 164–66, 173–82.

76. Apodaca, "Nambé Community School," 66–69, 187–90; Angel is quoted on 84.

77. David L. Bachelor, *Educational Reform in New Mexico: Tireman, San José, and Nambé* (Albuquerque: University of New Mexico Press, 1991), 132, 142.

78. Lynne Marie Getz, in *Schools of Their Own: The Education of Hispanos in New Mexico, 1850–1940* (Albuquerque: University of New Mexico Press, 1997), 87–102; Tireman quoted at 89, 97. The perennial tension between disciplinary and community studies is suggested more recently in the controversy that swirled in the early 1990s around "community-based learning," among other contested factors in a set of sweeping innovations unsuccessfully proposed for a suburban Chicago community by a funded project of the North American School Development Corporation in the 1990s. See Jeffrey Mirel, "School Reform Unplugged: The Bensenville New American School Project, 1991–93, *American Educational Research Journal* 31, no. 3 (1994): 481–518.

79. Bachelor, *Educational Reform in New Mexico,* 97–101; Apodaca, "Nambé Community School," 134; Getz, *Schools of Their Own,* 101. A similar misalignment between the expectations of progressive reformers and the cultural norms and values of a marginalized group occurred in a New Deal–sponsored community school experiment on the Navajo reservation in Arizona and New Mexico. See Thomas James, "Rhetoric and Resistance: Social Science and Community Schools for Navajos in the 1930s," *History of Education Quarterly* 28, no. 4 (1988): 599–626.

80. Stephen E. Haid, "Arthurdale: An Experiment in Community Planning, 1933–1947" (Ph.D. diss., University of West Virginia, 1975), 1.

81. Ronald Lewis, "Scotts Run: America's Symbol of the Great Depression in the Coalfields," in *A New Deal for America,* ed. Bryan Ward (Arthurdale, West Virginia: Arthurdale Heritage, 1995), 1–23.

82. Haid, "Arthurdale," 1.

83. Blanche Wiesen Cook, *Eleanor Roosevelt,* vol. 2, *1933–1938* (New York: Viking, 1999), 134.

84. Lewis, "Scotts Run." Glenna Williams, who spent nine years of her childhood in a two-room hovel at Scott's Run, recalled: "On every little hill, there was a mine . . . and

people from all different nationalities, lots of people from Europe, from eastern Europe. . . . The only way I can describe it, I've never been to a third-world country, but I think it would have been something like going into something like that. And then, oh yes, there was the other race, there were the blacks." Glenna Williams, interview by Bryan Ward, 14 May 1999, Arthurdale Heritage, Inc., Oral History Collection, Arthurdale, W. Va.

85. Quoted in Cook, *Eleanor Roosevelt*, 2:139–40.

86. Ibid., 152. "Arthurdale," Blanche Wiesen Cook writes, "propelled the issue of race to the top of ER's agenda." Thereafter, a chastened ER worked vigorously publicly and behind the scenes for racial justice; for example, crusading for federal legislation to end racial violence and lynching (see chaps. 8–9).

87. Haid, "Arthurdale," 88–117.

88. Millard Milburn Rice, "Footnote on Arthurdale," *Harper's*, March 1940, 415; Clarence E. Pickett, "The Social Significance of the Subsistence Homestead Movement," *Journal of Home Economics* 26, no. 8 (October 1934): 479.

89. Daniel Perlstein, "Community and Democracy in American Schools: Arthurdale and the Fate of Progressive Education," *Teachers College Record* 97, no 4 (1996): 625–50. This incisive yet balanced reappraisal of the Arthurdale School directed us to the archives and collected papers cited in this section.

90. Scrapbook, Elsie Ripley Clapp Papers, Special Collections Research Center, Morris Library, Southern Illinois University Carbondale, collection 21, box 4, folder 2.

91. Stephen Haid, "Arthurdale's Greatest Failure and Arthurdale's Greatest Success," in Ward, *New Deal for America*, 65–97.

92. See Sam F. Stack, Jr., *Elsie Ripley Clapp (1879–1965): Her Life and the Community School* (New York: Peter Lang, 2004), chaps. 4–9.

93. Quoted in Elsie Ripley Clapp, *The Use of Resources in Education* (New York: Harper and Brothers, 1952), 8.

94. Clapp's development of ideas "logically entailed" in Dewey's theory appears in Benson and Harkavy, "School and Community in Global Society," esp. 32–36. We flesh out and amplify their point in our analysis of Clapp's relationship with Dewey in Chapter 8.

95. Elsie Ripley Clapp, *Community Schools in Action* (New York: Viking, 1939), 80–81.

96. Haid, "Arthurdale," 278–80, 292–95, quote from 278; Cook, *Eleanor Roosevelt*, 2:140–42; Bernard Baruch to ER, 18 December 1934, *The Papers of Eleanor Roosevelt, 1933–1945* [hereafter *PER*], gen. eds. Anne Firor Scott and William H. Chaffee (Frederick, Md.: University Publications of America, 1986), reel 1, 00220–21.

97. Clapp, *Community Schools in Action*, 83–86; enrollment figures reported in Berman, "Arthurdale, Nambé," 97.

98. ER to Bernard Baruch, 26 September 1935, *PER*, reel 1, 00236–37; see also ER's letter of 18 May 1935, reel 1, 0028–29. For Clapp's account of the health program, see *Community Schools in Action*, 89–99, 368–76. One of Clapp's letters suggests the deep gratitude that the homesteaders felt for the positive changes in their lives: "Mrs. Sissler (who sent you up earlier a jar of pickles) the mother of Elsie Eleanor, born December 25, has made for you a Christmas gift which I am mailing to you. The nurse has just been called off to welcome a baby in the Corley family, whose twins, Franklin and Eleanor, you may perhaps remember." Clapp to ER, [January 1935?], *PER*, reel 4, 00183. .

99. See Daniel Perlstein and Sam Stack, "Building a New Deal Community: Progressive Education at Arthurdale," in *"Schools of Tomorrow," Schools of Today: What Happened to Progressive Education*, ed. Susan F. Semel and Alan R. Sadnovik (New York: Peter Lang, 1999), 213–36.

100. These points are elaborated by Lee Benson, Ira Harkavy, and John Puckett in *Progressing beyond John Dewey: Practical Means to Realize Dewey's Utopian Ends* (Working title Philadelphia: Temple University Press, forthcoming).

101. Clapp, *Community Schools in Action,* chap. 3, quote from 131. For more on the curriculum, see Perlstein and Stack, "Building a New Deal Community."

102. Clapp, *Community Schools in Action,* chap. 9.

103. Ibid., 301, 303–4.

104. Perlstein, "Community and Democracy in American Schools." By contrast, residential workshops at Highlander were racially integrated, in open defiance of Tennessee's Jim Crow laws. Moreover, Highlander workshops and community performances celebrated labor militancy and featured protest music.

105. Samuel Everett, review of Clapp, *Community Schools in Action, Curriculum Journal* 2, no. 3 (1940), typescript in Elsie Ripley Clapp Papers, collection 21, box 2, folder 28.

106. Quoted in Perlstein and Stack, "Building a New Deal Community." 235. In a seminal essay, "The Progressive Educator, Race, and Ethnicity in the Depression Years: An Overview" (*History of Education Quarterly* 15, no. 4 [1975]: 365–94), historian Robert Goodenow criticizes Dewey, who consistently spoke out against racial intolerance and discrimination, for downplaying "the extent to which racism and ethnic conflict were outgrowths of the social-structural and institutional nature of American life" (366). By the late 1930s Dewey tended to view racism as "a problem of attitudes," one that "does not necessarily grow out of caste and class relationships" (370). Significantly, Roy Williams, acting secretary of the NAACP, described Dewey as "universally respected for [his] concern for civil liberties and the rights of man"; quoted in Jay Martin, *The Education of John Dewey: A Biography* (New York: Columbia University Press, 2002), 248. For a sympathetic appraisal, see also Steven C. Rockefeller, *John Dewey: Religious Faith and Democratic Humanism* (New York: Columbia University Press, 1991), 288–89.

107. Joseph P. Lash, *Eleanor and Franklin: The Story of Their Relationship, Based on Eleanor Roosevelt's Private Papers* (New York: Norton, 1971), 412. The Resettlement Administration agreed with Baruch: The homesteaders got their public buildings and a sizeable part of their mortgages gratis from the federal government. See J. O. Walker (Resettlement Administration) to ER, 13 April 1936, *PER,* reel 1, two letters: 0278–82.

108. Haid, "Arthurdale," 297; see also Perlstein, "Community and Democracy in American Schools." Observers from West Virginia University reported in 1940 that of seventeen teachers at Arthurdale, "practically half of the staff are new to the school, have come from traditionally organized schools, and have little or no sympathy with so-called progressive education. Of the 9 teachers who are in the high school, six . . . are there for their first year. It is not matter for wonder that the program of the high school is beginning to show a decided difference from that of the early days, nor is it surprising that the principal finds it an uphill task to maintain the ideas and ideals he first set out to maintain." Staff of the College of Education of the West Virginia University, "Report of the Survey of Arthurdale School," 31, West Virginia and Regional History Association, West Virginia University Libraries, Morgantown. ER would continue to support the school, making regular visits and giving the high school commencement address each June until 1945 (the exception was 1938, when FDR delivered the speech). Lois Scharf, "First Lady/First Homestead," in Ward, *New Deal for America,* 99–114.

109. ER to Bernard Baruch, 12 July 1936, *PER,* reel 1, 00292–96. Baruch would continue to donate to the Arthurdale School at least until the end of the decade, apparently seeking to ensure that the school had adequate resources. Local school authorities apparently resented Arthurdale—a not uncommon reaction to New Deal intrusions in public education. Clarence Pickett to Bernard Baruch, 12 July 1939, *PER,* reel 1, 00412; ER to Baruch, 2 December 1939, *PER,* reel 1, 00436–37.

110. Haid, "Arthurdale's Greatest Failure and Success."

111. Haid, "Arthurdale," 311–14.

112. Table found in John O. Walker to James T. Gobbel (Resettlement Administration), [1942?], *PER,* reel 1, 00533–36; see also Lash, *Eleanor and Franklin,* 416. Writing long after

Arthurdale's demise, ER continued to take a sanguine view of the matter: "Nevertheless, I have always felt that many human beings who might have cost us thousands of dollars in tuberculosis sanitariums, insane asylums, and jails were restored to usefulness and given confidence in themselves. . . . Ah yes, the human values were most rewarding, even if the financial returns to the government were not satisfactory." Eleanor Roosevelt, *This I Remember* (New York: Harper and Row, 1949), 131, 133.

113. Herbert Kliebard, *The Struggle for the American Curriculum, 1893–1958,* 2d ed. (New York: Routledge, 1995), 244.

114. Kenneth S. Beam, "Coordinating Councils," *Journal of Educational Sociology* 11, no. 2 (1937): 67–72.

115. Leonard Mayo, "Town and Village Councils," in *Yearbook of the National Probation Association,* ed. Marjorie Bell (New York: National Probation Association, 1936), 78–81.

116. Fisher, "Community Center Movement," 76–93; Glueck, *Community Use of Schools,* 33–36.

117. Beam, "Coordinating Councils"; the West Coast tended to use juvenile courts and probation departments, and other states varied; e.g., in Illinois the Department of Public Welfare authorized its state sociologists to organize groups of citizens and social workers into Big Brother and Big Sister Associations; in Pennsylvania, California, and Utah, the Department of Public Instruction encouraged the formation of these councils, especially for recreation; in Washington, the Department of Social Security established a Division on Community Organization to encourage such councils. Beam reported that a survey by the National Probation Association had found some three hundred councils in more than twenty states. Beam, "Community Coordination: Report of a National Survey of Coordinating and Neighborhood Councils," in *Coping with Crime: Yearbook of the National Probation Association, 1937,* ed. Marjorie Bell (New York: National Probation Association, 1937), 47–76.

118. Mayo, "Town and Village Councils," 82–83.

119. See the October 1937 issue of *Journal of Educational Sociology* 11, no. 2, dedicated to the results and issues of the conference, which was held 3 April 1937 at New York University's School of Education.

120. Bertha Smith, "The Yonkers Coordinating Council in the Yonkers Plan," *Journal of Educational Sociology* 11, no. 5 (1938): 296, 302; the council membership included the four superintendents, the twenty-six elementary principals, the vice principals, the nine directors, five high school principals, the principal of the continuation school, one teacher representative from each school and many special teachers, two board of education members, and representatives from the Yonkers Teachers' Association, the Yonkers Principals' Association, the Primary Teachers' Council, the special Class Teachers Council, and the PTAs. See also Smith, "The Yonkers Plan of Community Organization," *Journal of Educational Sociology* 11, no. 5 (1938): 257–64; Julius Yourman, "The Coordination of Education and the Community," *Journal of Educational Sociology* 11, no. 5 (1938): 304–20. This issue includes participant accounts of various neighborhood councils, as well as junior (youth) councils.

121. Ernest L. Chase, "The Elizabeth Plan for a Community-Wide Attack on Social Ills," *Journal of Educational Sociology* 11, no. 2 (1937): 77–96. The Elizabeth Plan later included five contiguous cities and became the Six Town Plan. Prior to the employment of a full-time coordinator, a Social Service Exchange was established in 1928 and the Community Chest was incorporated in 1932.

122. S. E. Witchell, "Community Organization in Madison, New Jersey," *Journal of Educational Sociology* 11, no. 2 (October 1937): 97–105; Harry Arthur Wann, "Social Planning in a Community," *Journal of Educational Sociology* 9, no. 8 (1936): 494–508.

123. John B. Dougall and Nora Alice Way, "How the Social Forces of a Community Are Coordinated to Serve Children," *Journal of Educational Sociology* 11, no. 8 (1938): 483–96.

124. Leonard Covello, "Neighborhood Growth through the School," *Progressive Education* 15, no. 2 (1938): 131; Leonard Covello, "The School as a Factor in Community Life," *School Executive* 59, no. 9 (1940): 20–21.

CHAPTER 2: EAST HARLEM IN THE 1930S

1. From 1900 to World War I, the major sources of Italian emigration were the southern provinces of Campania, Basilicata, and Calabria, and Sicily. A number of northern Italians settled in New York City in the latter half of the nineteenth century, on the periphery of West Greenwich Village. Many northerners had urban experience prior to emigrating, and they were generally more affluent than the southerners. Miriam Cohen, *Workshop to Office: Two Generations of Italian Women in New York City, 1900–1950* (Ithaca, N.Y.: Cornell University Press, 1992), 15.

2. Leonard Covello, "A High School and Its Immigrant Community—a Challenge and an Opportunity," *Journal of Educational Sociology* 9, no. 5 (1936): 331–46; see also and cf. Casa Italiana Educational Bureau (CIEB), "East Harlem Population by Nationality, Nativity and Color—1930," Leonard Covello Papers (MSS 40) [hereafter CP], Balch Institute Collections, Historical Society of Pennsylvania, box 6, folder 8, and box 77, folder 5. CIEB profiled ten health areas, including health areas 28 and 29, which encompassed blocks below 105th Street between Third and Fifth avenues. An authoritative source, Ronald H. Bayor, "The Neighborhood Invasion Pattern," in *Neighborhoods in Urban America*, ed. Bayor (Port Washington, N.Y.: Kennikat Press, 1982), 86–102, designates East Harlem as the area "from East 99th Street and 3rd Avenue on the south, traveling west to 5th Avenue at 105th Street and running north to the Harlem River" (88). In 1930 the total population in this area was 186,343; in the CIEB area, 233,400. Florence DuBois, supervisor, *Population in Health Areas, New York City, 1930* (New York: Welfare Council of New York City, 1931), table for Manhattan, pt. 1, pp. 3–4.

3. With Robert Charles Freeman, "Exploring the Path of Community Change in East Harlem, 1870–1970" (Ph.D. diss., Fordham University, 1994), we highlight, as descriptive categories, the centrality of Italian Harlem and, secondarily, the Puerto Rican settlement in the decades before World War II. Freeman's study is the most extensive analysis of East Harlem history and social topography to date.

4. Nels Anderson, "The Social Antecedents of a Slum: A Developmental Study of the East Harlem Area of Manhattan Island, New York City" (Ph.D. diss., New York University, 1930), iv. See also Jeffrey S. Gurock, *When Harlem Was Jewish, 1870–1930* (New York: Columbia University Press, 1979), 6–7. A wood-frame house at 17 East 128th Street survives from this era. A photograph at La Guardia Memorial House suggests that a farm stood at 116th Street and Lexington Avenue as late as 1889.

5. Donald Stewart, *A Short History of East Harlem* (New York: Museum of the City of New York, 1972), 33–35.

6. "A City Plague Spot," *New York Times*, 8 June 1875; quoted in Freeman, "Exploring Path of Community Change," 16.

7. Gurock, *When Harlem Was Jewish*, 14–15, 27–57.

8. Bayor, "Neighborhood Invasion Pattern," 86–102. Gurock, in *When Harlem Was Jewish*, 40, notes that poor East European Jews resided east of Third Avenue below Little Italy; the most affluent element settled into middle-class housing between Fifth Avenue and Morningside Avenue above 110th Street.

9. Bayor, "Neighborhood Invasion Pattern"; Walter Laidlaw, ed., *Statistical Sources for Demographic Studies of Greater New York, 1920* (New York: New York City 1920 Census Committee, 1922); DuBois, *Population in Health Areas*, table for Manhattan, pt. 1, p. 3; Frederic Thrasher, *The Final Report on the Jefferson Park Branch of the Boys' Club*

of New York, submitted to the Bureau of Social Hygiene, 21 October 1935, map 12A, p. 79-A, map 12B, p. 79B, Bureau of Social Hygiene Collection, Rockefeller Archive Center, Sleepy Hollow, New York, series 3, box 12, vol. 1; Ira Rosenwaike, *Population History of New York City* (Syracuse, N.Y.: Syracuse University Press, 1972), 132–33. In the lower blocks of West Harlem the transition was Jewish to Puerto Rican/Spanish American to black. Harry M. Shulman, *Slums of New York* (New York: Albert and Charles Boni, 1938), 55–70.

10. Bayor, "Neighborhood Invasion Pattern"; CIEB, "East Harlem Population by Nationality, Nativity & Color—1930," gives Jews a more salient presence.

11. Freeman, "Exploring Path of Community Change," 17–18. See also Suzanne Model, "The Ethnic Niche and the Structure of Opportunity: Immigrants and Minorities in New York," in *The "Underclass" Debate: Views from History,* ed. Michael B. Katz (Princeton, N.J.: Princeton University Press, 1993), 161–93.

12. George E. Pozzetta, "The Italians of New York City, 1890–1914" (Ph.D. diss., University of North Carolina at Chapel Hill, 1971), 76–77, 98–99.

13. Freeman, "Exploring Path of Community Change," 40.

14. Bayor, "Neighborhood Invasion Pattern."

15. Ibid.; Freeman, "Exploring Path of Community Change," 73–74. Boys' Club Study researchers noted that the Italians, even though they remained "the dominant and central group," were beginning to leave East Harlem by 1930 (Thrasher, *Final Report on Jefferson Park Branch,* 82).

16. Robert Orsi, *The Madonna of 115th Street: Faith and Community in Italian Harlem, 1880–1950,* 2nd ed. (New Haven, Conn.: Yale University Press, 2002), 17; Frederic Thrasher, *Final Report on Jefferson Park Branch,* serial map (no. 11), Local Neighborhoods, New York City, 1931, map 13, p. 84. As these percentages show, Italians never fully controlled any East Harlem neighborhood; for example, in health area 21, 151 blacks were counted.

17. Caroline Golab, "The Geography of Neighborhood," in *Neighborhoods in Urban America,* ed. Bayor, 72. For a similar definition of neighborhood, see R. Robert Huckfeldt, "Social Contexts, Social Networks, and Urban Neighborhoods: Environmental Constraints on Friendship Choice," *American Journal of Sociology* 89, no. 3 (1983): 651–69.

18. Orsi, *Madonna of 115th Street,* 28.

19. Leonard Covello, *Social Background of the Italo-American School Child: A Study of the Southern Italian Family Mores and Their Effect on the School Situation in Italy and America* (Leiden, Netherlands: E. J. Brill, 1967), chap. 3; quote from 57. Recent scholarship has challenged Covello's portrait of "stereotypical timeless peasants of a traditional and static society, untouched by social change." Kathie Friedman-Kasaba, in *Memories of Migration: Gender, Ethnicity, and Work in the Lives of Jewish and Italian Women in New York, 1870–1924* (Albany: State University of New York Press, 1996), 69–73, argues that four Italian provinces, including Cosenza in the south and Palermo in Sicily, "experienced long histories of seasonal migrations within Europe" long before the 1880–1920 period of mass migration; in the main these migrants were small landholders.

20. Donna Gabaccia, *From Sicily to Elizabeth Street: Housing and Social Change among Italian Immigrants, 1880–1930* (Albany: State University of New York Press, 1984), 40–45.

21. Richard Gambino, *Blood of My Blood: The Dilemma of the Italian Americans* (Garden City, N.Y.: Doubleday, 1974), 93–94.

22. Robert W. Peebles, *Leonard Covello: A Study of an Immigrant's Contribution to New York City* (New York: Arno Press, 1978), 40–50. In his autobiography, Covello describes the division of Avigliano into an upper town (*Il Castello*), the domain of the artisan class, and a lower town (*Bassa Terra*), where the contadini lived. The artisani lived in "substantial, several-storied houses" above and around the piazza; the contadini inhabited single-story hovels, often a single room, shared with their animals. Notwithstanding their relative affluence,

the Coviello family was poor; to make ends meet Covello's mother sold olive oil and bread from a booth in the piazza. Leonard Covello with Guido D'Agostino, *The Heart Is the Teacher* (New York: McGraw-Hill, 1958), 7–11.

23. Covello, *Italo-American School Child*, 95–96

24. Covello, *Heart Is Teacher*, 6.

25. Virginia Yans-McLaughlin, *Family and Community: Italian Immigrants in Buffalo, 1880–1930* (Ithaca, N.Y.: Cornell University Press, 1977), 61.

26. Orsi, *Madonna of 115th Street*, 20–21. East Harlem's most important street was 116th Street, home to doctors, lawyers, and brokers, which "signified to the Italian population a sort of main street, equivalent to the *il corso* of their native towns and villages." Francesco Cordasco and Rocco G. Galatioto, "Ethnic Displacement in the Interstitial Community: The East Harlem Experience," *Phylon* 31, no. 3 (1970): 303.

27. Cohen, *Workshop to Office*, 27–33.

28. Gambino, *Blood of My Blood*, 49–68. See also Pozzetta, "Italians of New York City," 10–20; Friedman-Kasaba. *Memories of Migration*, 77; Yans-McLaughlin, *Family and Community*, 32–33, adds declining child mortality rates and increased competition for land and work to the list of push factors.

29. See Yans-McLaughlin, *Family and Community*, 34–35.

30. Thomas Kessner, *The Golden Door: Italian and Jewish Immigrant Mobility in New York City, 1880–1915* (New York: Oxford University Press, 1977), 30–31. See also Nathan Glazer and Daniel Patrick Moynihan, *Beyond the Melting Pot: The Negroes, Puerto Ricans, Jews, Italians, and Irish of New York City*, 2nd ed. (Cambridge, Mass.: MIT Press, 1970), 184, 339fn7; Pozzetta, "Italians of New York City," 131, 172–75. Between 1906 and 1911, an average of 149,979 Italian immigrants returned to Italy. The trend toward family migration appears to have begun around 1915. Pozzetta, "Italians of New York City," table 3, p. 174. For the role of the labor boss (*padrone*) in recruiting Italian male labor in the United States, a system that had its most powerful influence in the 1890s but had virtually disappeared in New York by 1914, see Luciano J. Iorizzo, "The Padrone and Immigrant Distribution," in *The Italian Experience in the United States*, ed. Silvano M. Tomasi and Madeline H. Engel (New York: Center for Migration Studies, 1977), 43–75; Pozzetta, "Italians of New York City," 320–29; Freeman, "Exploring Path of Community Change," 22–25. The Italian government encouraged temporary migration, as emigrant remittances benefited both households and Italian banks. Friedman-Kasaba, *Memories of Migration*, 78.

31. Freeman, "Exploring Path of Community Change," 30.

32. Ibid.; Kessner, *Golden Door*, table 9, p. 101. Sociologist Douglas S. Massey writes: "Once someone in a personal network has migrated, . . . the ties are transformed into a resource that can be used to gain access to foreign employment and all that it brings. Each act of migration creates social capital among people to whom the new migrant is related, thereby raising the odds of their migration. Massey, "Why Does Immigration Occur? A Theoretical Synthesis," in *The Handbook of International Migration: The American Experience*, ed. Charles Hirschman, Philip Kasinitz, and Josh DeWind (New York: Russell Sage Foundation, 1999), 34–52, quote from 44. In the same volume, see also Alejandro Portes, "Immigration Theory for a New Century," 21–33, esp. 26. The percentage of females among Italian emigrants to the United States increased from 22.8 percent in 1900, to 22.9 percent in 1910, to 30.6 percent in 1920. Southern Italian women undertook a "delayed migration," following the men by an average of one year and two months. Many were joining their husbands and brought children with them; single women traveled in the path of parents, siblings, uncles, aunts, and fiancés. Friedman-Kasaba, *Memories of Migration*, 74; Cohen, *Workshop to Office*, 39–41, cited in Friedman-Kasaba; Yans-McLaughlin, *Family and Community*, 57–60, 99–100.

33. Orsi, *Madonna of 115th Street*, 23.

34. Edward Corsi, *In the Shadow of Liberty: The Chronicle of Ellis Island* (New York: Macmillan, 1935), 23; cited in Orsi, *Madonna of 115th Street*, 20; also in Freeman, "Exploring Path of Community Change," 27.

35. Covello, *Heart Is Teacher*, 58, 64.

36. Freeman, "Exploring Path of Community Change," 40–41; Kessner, *Golden Door*, 50.

37. Freeman, "Exploring Path of Community Change," 43–51. Italian families routinely sent all family members to work, and they exercised extreme frugality, saving from twenty-five to thirty dollars per month. Pozzetta, "Italians of New York City," 319.

38. Cohen, *Workshop to Office*, 41–45, appendixes A, B.

39. Miriam Cohen, "Italian American Women in New York City, 1900–1950: Work and School," in *Class, Sex, and the Woman Worker*, ed. Milton Candor and Bruce Laurie (Westport, Conn.: Greenwood Press, 1977), 120–43; see also, Friedman-Kasaba, *Memories of Migration*, 167–70. For a contemporaneous account, see Louise C. Oldencrantz, *Italian Women in Industry: A Study of Conditions in New York City* (New York: Russell Sage Foundation, 1919), 54–81; excerpted in Francesco Cordasco and Eugene Bucchioni, *The Italians: Social Backgrounds of an American Group* (Clifton, N.J.: A. M. Kelly, 1974), 397–412. Oldencrantz surveyed 1,095 Italian working women, of whom 1,027 were employed in diverse manufacturing jobs, primarily in the garment industry.

40. John J. D'Alesandre, *Occupational Trends of Italians in New York City*, CIEB Bulletin no. 8 (New York: Columbia University, 1935); reprinted in Cordasco and Bucchioni, *The Italians*, 417–31; Cohen, *Workshop to Office*, 44.

41. Cohen, *Workshop to Office*, 44–45; see also Roger Waldinger, *Still the Promised City? African-Americans and New Immigrants in Postindustrial New York* (Cambridge, Mass.: Harvard University Press, 1996), 102.

42. Waldinger, *Still Promised City*, 102–3.

43. East Harlem Historical Organization, "Rediscovering East Harlem," Union Settlement Association, New York City, 1997. During most of his mayoralty (1933–45), Fiorello La Guardia resided in East Harlem, at an address on Fifth Avenue between 108th and 109th streets. In 1943 he became the first mayor to live in Gracie Mansion.

44. Ronald H. Bayor, *Neighbors in Conflict: The Irish, Germans, Jews, and Italians of New York City, 1929–1941*, 2nd ed. (Urbana: University of Illinois Press, 1988), 18–19.

45. Cohen, *Workshop to Office*, 97–98.

46. Covello, in *Italo-American School Child*, 264, remarks that it was widely feared that literacy among women would foster a breach of the contadino code, which "forbade any kind of communication, whether by writing, speaking, or even glancing at each other, between girls and boys and particularly young men and young women of marriageable age." In 1907–8, according to the Italian government, only 20 percent of *all* Italian children, ages six to nine, was enrolled in elementary schools. These institutions were "underfinanced and badly organized." Cohen, *Workshop to Office*, 21–22. Daughters of the artisan class had access to some elementary schooling; for example, see Friedman-Kasaba, *Memories of Migration*, 82 (a gardener's daughter); Gabaccia, *Sicily to Elizabeth Street*, 39 (a shoemaker's daughter).

47. Joel Perlmann's thick statistical analysis of Italians' schooling in Providence, Rhode Island, presented in *Ethnic Differences: Schooling and Social Structure among the Irish, Italians, Jews, and Blacks in an American City, 1880–1935* (Cambridge: Cambridge University Press, 1988), chap. 3, lends support to Covello's "cultural heritage" interpretation of southern Italian immigrants and the American school. Using regression analysis Perlmann weighs such structural factors as family background (for example, father's occupation, length of residence in the United States), poverty, remigration and citizenship status, and contextual effects (for example, social class milieu) and finds "a considerable unexplained ethnic difference [for Italians] in patterns of schooling" (111). He then argues thoroughly and persuasively that one-half to three-quarters of this difference is likely

accounted for by "pre-migration cultural attributes" (112–13). Perlmann modifies Covello's interpretation to the extent that structural factors such as social class position, the economic order, and political arrangements "may have come together in a unique way in southern Italian culture" (118).

48. In the 1930s, when Covello collected most of the data for his dissertation, the junior high school was not yet a prevalent institution. See David Tyack and Larry Cuban, *Tinkering toward Utopia: A Century of Public School Reform* (Cambridge, Mass.: Harvard University Press, 1995), 69–76.

49. Covello, *Italo-American School Child*, 328–29. For a supportive argument see Selma Berrol, "Public Schools and Immigrants: The New York City Experience," in *American Education and the European Immigrant, 1840–1940*, ed. Bernard J. Weiss (Urbana: University of Illinois Press, 1982), 31–43. John Bodnar, in *The Transplanted: A History of Immigrants in Urban America* (Bloomington: Indiana University Press, 1985), 71–83, posits that an organizing principle of most immigrant groups was the family economy, an ethic of cooperative coping, similar to that described by Covello in his study of southern Italians, that pervaded the broader immigrant community between 1890 and 1940. Robert A. Orsi, in "The Fault of Memory: 'Southern Italy' in the Imagination of Immigrants and the Lives of Their Children in Italian Harlem, 1920–1945," *Journal of Family History* 15, no. 2 (1990): 133–47, argues that "perhaps coercive cooperation would be the best formulation," given the high level of generational conflict he found in his study of Italian family life in East Harlem in the 1920s and 1930s (143.)

50. Cohen, *Workshop to Office*, 121, citing East Harlem Health Center, *A Decade of District Health Center Pioneering* (New York: East Harlem Health Center, 1932). Stephen Steinberg, in *The Ethnic Myth: Race, Ethnicity, and Class in America*, updated and expanded ed. (Boston: Beacon Press, 1989), argues a strict social class interpretation: "To whatever extent Southern Italians exhibited negative attitudes toward education, in the final analysis these attitudes only reflected economic and social realities [in southern Italy], including a dearth of educational opportunities" (142); this argument, however, is speculative and based on existing literature. For further commentary, see Hans Vermeulen and Tijno Venema, "Peasantry and Trading Diaspora: Differential Social Mobility of Italians and Greeks in the United States," in *Immigrants, Schooling, and Social Mobility: Does Culture Make a Difference?* ed. Hans Vermeulen and Joel Perlmann (New York: St. Martin's Press, 2000), 124–49.

51. Perlmann, *Ethnic Differences*, 161. Cohen, in *Workshop to Office*, 139, notes that, in contrast to the Italians, Jewish immigrants "by and large . . . came from the ranks of artisans or small shopkeepers, literate segments of their community."

52. Waldinger, *Still the Promised City*, 345n14. Ruth Jacknow Markowitz, in *My Daughter, the Teacher: Jewish Teachers in the New York City Schools* (New Brunswick, N.J.: Rutgers University Press, 1993), 21, notes that the college attendance rate of Jewish women in the 1930s more than doubled the rate of the city's non-Jewish female population.

53. Waldinger, *Still the Promised City*, 97–101, quote from 102; Markowitz, *My Daughter, the Teacher*, chap. 2, esp. 21. See also Michael R. Olneck and Marvin Lazerson, "The School Achievement of Immigrant Children: 1900–1930," *History of Education Quarterly* 14 (1974): 453–82; Berrol, "Public Schools and Immigrants."

54. Orsi, *Madonna of 115th Street*, 79.

55. Covello, *Italo-American School Child*, 312. Simone Cinotto argues that Covello failed to recognize the consistency of Italian American family values with "Anglo-Protestant, middle-class values," for example, that "the gathering of all family members around the table every evening and every Sunday" was a practice the immigrant families shared with the white Protestant middle class. Cinotto, "Leonard Covello, the Covello Papers, and the History of Eating Habits among Italian Immigrants in New York," *Journal of American History* 91, no. 2 (2004): 512.

56. Life histories, for example, were drawn from three sources: Paul Cressy's Motion Picture Study at New York University; biographical and autobiographical writings submitted by Covello's students in the classes he taught at NYU from 1935 to 1941; and life histories written by various Italian Americans at Covello's request; Covello, *Italo-American School Child*, 8.

57. Statement authored by "L.C—E.H," in Covello, *Italo-American School Child*, 340.

58. Ibid., 349.

59. Ibid., 355. Covello also collected family survey data from Italian students at BFHS. To provide a comparative perspective, he surveyed students of other ethnic groups and did a cross-school comparison with a high school in Queens (360–61). Simone Cinotto, in "The Social Significance of Food in Italian Harlem, 1920–1940" (paper presented at the Balch Institute for Ethnic Studies, Philadelphia, 23 August 2000), cites the high frequency of second-generation Italian Americans marrying within their own cultural group as evidence of the internalization of "the ideology of the Italian family."

60. Covello, *Italo-American School Child*, 382.

61. Ibid., 383–89.

62. Orsi, *Madonna of 115th Street*, 111–12.

63. Ibid., 122–25.

64. Cohen, "Italian American Women," esp. 137; Cohen, *Workshop to Office*, 147–77.

65. Covello, *Heart Is Teacher*, 22; see also Pozzetta, "Italians of New York City," 95–96.

66. Orsi, *Madonna of 115th Street*, 34. Yans-McLaughlin, in *Family and Community*, notes that, in the Mezzogiorno, terms such as *paese* or *villaggio* "had spatial rather than social connotations. But in the anonymous American city, far from the homeland, the word *paesano* came to connote much more than someone born in the same geographic location; an emotional bond was implied" (64).

67. Orsi, *Madonna of 115th Street*, 32–33.

68. In "Eating Habits among Italian Immigrants," Cinotto challenges Covello's assumption that "immigrant family values . . . survived migration intact." He argues that, "more than defending a traditional family structure and ideology from the onslaught of traditional modernity, immigrants in East Harlem were constructing new ones to new needs" (511–12). In Italian Harlem the Old World family ideology was reconstituted around food practices and food-sharing rituals associated with "Italian" (ethnic) food. Activities around food helped to reconcile family tensions that were rooted in the second-generation's embracing of U.S. cultural practices; "food turned out to be a powerful means of negotiation in a widespread generational controversy" (515). This reconciliation, Cinotto explains, was not achieved through the public means Covello envisioned, i.e., collective political involvement, but rather through a private means that reinforced the centrality of the family at the expense of the public sphere.

69. Joseph A. Varacalli, "As the Saints (Apparently) Go Marching Out: Why Study Them?" in *The Saints in the Lives of Italian Americans: An Interdisiplinary Investigation*, ed. Joseph A. Varacalli, Salvatore Primeggia, Salvatore J. LaGumina, and Donald J. D'Elia (Stony Brook, N.Y.: Forum Italicum, 1999), 6.

70. Salvatore Primeggia, "The Social Contexts of Religious Devotion: How Saint Worship Expresses Popular Religiosity," in Varacalli et al., *Saints in the Lives of Italian Americans*, 68–92. For a detailed firsthand account of the East Harlem festa in 1930, see May Case Marsh, "The Life and Work of the Churches in an Interstitial Area" (Ph.D. diss., New York University, 1932), 439–45.

71. Mary Elizabeth Brown, "Italian Americans and Their Saints: Historical Considerations," in Varacalli et al., *Saints in the Lives of Italian Americans*, 35–67; Primeggia, "Social Contexts of Religious Devotion"; Orsi, *Madonna of 115th Street*, 51–52. Gerald D. Suttles reported a similar manifestation of "territorial unity" in Chicago, one that had emerged from separate paesani feasts around a single festival by the 1960s: "In this sense, their sole carnival

is only a final recognition that they form one *paesani* in Chicago rather than several in Italy." Suttles, *The Social Order of the Slum: Ethnicity and Territory in the Inner City* (Chicago: University of Chicago Press, 1968), 106n14.

72. Orsi, *Madonna of 115th Street*, 53–67; Silvano M. Tomasi, "The Ethnic Church and the Integration of Italian Immigrants in the United States," in Tomasi and Engel, *Italian Experience in the United States*, 163–93; Mary Elizabeth Brown, "Italian Immigrants and the Catholic Church in the Archdiocese of New York, 1880–1950" (Ph.D. diss., Columbia University, 1987), 166–67. Brown writes that Italians and Irish sometimes came to blows over church matters (199).

73. Joanne Nagel, "Constructing Ethnicity: Creating and Recreating Ethnic Identity and Culture," *Social Problems* 41, no. 1 (1994): 164.

74. Orsi, *Madonna of 115th Street*, 65–66.

75. Ibid., 2, 6. The main altar statue appeared in the parade only "on special occasions"; a second statue mounted on a flower-garlanded, beribboned float was used most years.

76. Ibid., 3.

77. Rudolph J. Vecoli, "Prelates and Peasants: Italian Immigrants and the Catholic Church," *Journal of Social History* 2, no. 3 (1969): 232. The prelates were undoubtedly not pleased to know that "penitents crawled up the steps [of the church] on their hands and knees, some of them dragging their tongues along the stone." Orsi, *Madonna of 115th Street*, 4.

78. Kathleen Neils Conzen, David A. Gerber, Ewa Morawska, George E. Pozzetta, and Rudolph J. Vecoli, "The Invention of Ethnicity: A Perspective from the U.S.A.," *Journal of American Ethnic History* 12, no. 1 (1992): 27. The "invention of ethnicity" helps us to understand the underlying social dynamics of "becoming Italian American" in East Harlem. Ethnicity is "a process of construction or invention which incorporates, adapts, and amplifies preexisting solidarities, cultural attributes, and historical memories. That is, it is grounded in real life contexts and social experience" (4–5). That is to say, ethnic content is not a whole-cloth replication of old-country folkways, but rather an adaptive response to conditions in the receiving country; as an evolving process, it continuously recreates itself as conditions change. William L. Yancey, Eugene P. Ericksen, and Richard N. Juliani, in "Emergent Ethnicity: A Review and Reformulation," *American Sociological Review* 41, no. 3 (1976), provided an early statement: "Thus, mounting evidence suggests that the examination of ethnic experience should use the urban American ethnic community, rather than the place of origin as the principal criterion of ethnic group membership. Integration into the mainstream of American life should refer to the American ghetto rather than the European rural village as the point of departure" (397). For the historiography of this construct, see Gary Gerstle, "Liberty, Coercion, and the Making of Americans," in Hirschman, Kasinitz, and DeWind, *Handbook of International Migration*, 275–93, esp. 282–85; in the same volume, Richard Alba and Victor Nee, "Rethinking Assimilation Theory for a New Era of Immigration," 137–60, esp. 140–41.

79. Orsi, *Madonna of 115th Street*, 180. Ethnic identity, of course, did not necessarily translate into community organizing. In 1960s Chicago, Gerald Suttles identified what he called "the spirit of *omerta*," a deeply rooted belief in the Italian American community that problems are best resolved through private settlements rather than public appeals. Suttles, *Social Order of the Slum*, 102.

80. Marsh, 'Life and Work of the Churches," 423.

81. Orsi, *Madonna of 115th Street*, 165, 171.

82. Brown, "Italian Immigrants and Catholic Church."

83. Marsh, "Life and Work of the Churches," 183–88; Betty Burleigh, "The 'Bishop' of Harlem," *World Outlook*, August 1949, 11–15. For all their missionary and outreach efforts, the Methodists, and the Protestants in general, lost the battle for Italian American souls to both the Catholics and mammon. Writing for the Boys Club Study, May Marsh surveyed

East Harlem churches that served Italian Americans. She reported an adult membership of 375 for Jefferson Park Methodist Episcopal in 1930, 400 for Ascension Presbyterian, 150 for Grace-Emanuel Episcopal, and 196 for St. John's Lutheran—a total of some 1,121 Protestants; Case reported 4,000 for Our Lady of Mt. Carmel (surely an estimate) and 800 for Our Lady of Angels—a total of 4,800 Catholics. In sum, fewer than six thousand East Harlem Italian Americans belonged to an organized church. Marsh, "Life and Work of the Churches," table 1, p. 489. Data reported for 1935 show that 98 percent of New York's Italian Americans, at least nominally, were Roman Catholic; only 1 percent were Protestant. As recorded by New York cemeteries in 1940, nearly 90 percent of Italian burials in each of four age categories, from one to sixty-five and over, were Catholic. Rosenwaike, *Population History of New York City*, table 59, p. 125; table 60, p. 126.

84. Virginia E. Sánchez Korrol, *From Colonia to Community: The History of Puerto Ricans in New York City, 1917–1948* (Westport, Conn.: Greenwood Press, 1983), 20–26, quotes from 22; Joseph P. Fitzpatrick, *Puerto Rican Americans: The Meaning of Migration to the Mainland* (Englewood Cliffs, N.J.: Prentice-Hall, 1971), 13–15.

85. Bernardo Vega, *Memoirs of Bernardo Vega: A Contribution to the History of the Puerto Rican Community in New York*, ed. Cesar Andreu Iglesias, trans. Juan Flores (New York: Monthly Review Press, 1985), 9–10.

86. Lawrence R. Chenault, *The Puerto Rican Migrant in New York City* (New York: Columbia University Press, 1938), 58.

87. Korrol, *Colonia to Community*, table 5, p. 59.

88. Chenault, *Puerto Rican Migrant*, 63.

89. CIEB, "East Harlem Population"; Korrol, *Colonia to Community*, 62.

90. See and cf. Bayor, "Neighborhood Invasion Pattern"; see also Korrol, *Colonia to Community*, 150–52, for an informed speculation about colonias as economic competitors with other ethnic groups.

91. Puerto Ricans, about one-fifth of whom were listed as "Negro" in the 1930 census, were far more likely to be accepted by non–Puerto Rican blacks than by Italians, notwithstanding labor competition between the two groups. Glazer and Moynihan, *Beyond the Melting Pot*, 92–93.

92. Korrol, *From Colonia to Community*, 29; Virginia Sánchez Korrol, "Puerto Ricans," in *The Encyclopedia of New York City*, ed. Kenneth T. Jackson (New Haven, Conn.: Yale University Press, 1995), 962–63. The 1917 Jones Act gave Puerto Ricans U.S. citizenship; accordingly they were recognized as legal migrants in the United States, subject to neither immigration laws nor immigration counts.

93. Chenault, *Puerto Rican Migrant*, table 18, p. 174. The percentage for male white-collar workers is drawn from a reconfiguration of this tabulation in Korrol, *Colonia to Community*, table 3, p. 33.

94. Korrol, *Colonia to Community*, 32.

95. Ibid., 57–66, quote from 57.

96. Ibid., 132–42, quote from 142.

97. Ibid., 142–52, quote from 148.

98. Jesús Colón, *The Way It Was and Other Writings*, introductory essay by Edna Acosta-Belén and Virginia Sánchez Korrol (Houston: Arté Publico Press, 1993), 15; Vega, *Bernardo Vega*, 21–22. "In 1918," according to the East Harlem Historical Organization, "there were more than 30 workers cooperatives, socialist organizations, political clubs, and labor protest and strike centers between 100th and 110th streets. These were dominated by Jewish radicals, although many of the early Puerto Ricans were cigar-maker artisans with leftist political affiliations." Before her deportation in 1919 the German-Jewish anarchist Emma Goldman published the radical journal *Mother Earth* from her residence at East 125th Street; Morris Hillquit, also Jewish, ran for Congress from East Harlem in 1918 and 1920,

losing by a narrow margin in both elections. Vito Marcantonio, elected for seven terms on the American Labor Party ticket, would boldly represent these earlier radical platforms in Congress from 1935 to 1950 (East Harlem Historical Organization, "Rediscovering East Harlem").

99. Colón, *Way It Was*, introductory essay, 17.

100. Korrol, *Colonia to Community*, 75–76.

101. "Status of Employment in East Harlem Families," data collected by field staff of the East Harlem Nursing and Health Service, 1 January 1932, cited in Irving Sollins, "A Socio-Statistical Analysis of Boys' Club Membership" (Ph.D. diss., New York University, 1936), 53–54.

102. Mayor's Committee on City Planning [MCCP], in cooperation with the Works Progress Administration, *East Harlem Community Study* (New York City, 1937), chaps. 2, 5; quote from 31. The first of a series of local surveys commissioned during the Depression by the Mayor's Committee on City Planning, the East Harlem study reported on many aspects of the district's infrastructure, from housing and property use, to transportation, to parks and recreation, to social services and resources. The subcommittee that actually conducted the survey was chaired successively by Helen Harris and Miriam Sanders (Vito Marcantonio's wife) of Union Settlement and included Leonard Covello.

103. Stewart, *East Harlem*, 47.

104. Ibid., 22.

105. Marsh, "Life and Work of the Churches," 46; MCCP, *East Harlem Community Study*, 36. Boys' Club Study researchers classified East Harlem as "a poverty stricken area." Thrasher, *Final Report on Jefferson Park Branch*, 130.

106. Angelo Patri, "Educational Forces outside of the Public School, Considered from the Standpoint of School Administration" (M.A. thesis, Teachers College, Columbia University, 1904), 11–12.

107. Richard Plunz, *A History of Housing in New York City: Dwelling Type and Social Change in the American Metropolis* (New York: Columbia University Press, 1990), 11–12, 22–30, 39–49.

108. Anthony Jackson, *A Place Called Home: A History of Low-Cost Housing in America* (Cambridge, Mass.: MIT Press, 1976), chap. 11, quote from 141.

109. "Status of Employment in East Harlem Families," in Sollins, "Boys' Club Membership," 53; the report further stated that "in December, 1931, our standards regarding *regular work* had decreased to the point where any man who had two to three days work a week was considered as *regularly employed*" (original emphasis, 2).

110. Ibid., 29. By the end of the decade the population density of East Harlem was 1,400 people per block; 50 percent of the blocks housed 90 percent of the people (forty-three blocks had no residential population). See Citizens Housing Council of New York, *Harlem Housing*, August 1939, CP box 43, folder 12.

111. MCCP, *East Harlem Community Study*, chap. 3, quote from 38. As of 1937, six hundred tenement buildings were "boarded up, ordered vacated, or abandoned by their owners." Citizens Housing Council of New York, *Harlem Housing*, 2–3.

112. Orsi, *Madonna of 115th Street*, 29.

113. BFHS, Community Advisory Council Report, June 1937, CP box 37, folder 14.

114. Interview with Frank Decorato, excerpted in La Guardia Memorial House, *100 Years of Service* (New York: La Guardia Memorial House/SCAN, 1999), 3.

115. Salvatore Cimilluca, "The Natural History of East Harlem from 1880 to the Present Day" (M.A. thesis, New York University, 1931), 4.

116. Robert A. Caro, *The Power Broker: Robert Moses and the Fall of New York* (New York: Knopf, 1974), 393. As reported by the Mayor's Committee on Property Improvement, 1938, the total assessed valuation of the area bounded by 96th Street and Park Avenue, 125th

Street and the Harlem River was $147,994,935. See Citizens Housing Council of New York, *Harlem Housing*.

117. East Harlem Health Center, *Casting the Life Lines for East Harlem: A Study of the Vital Statistics of the East Harlem District, New York City, 1916–1925* (New York: East Harlem Health Center, 1927), table 2a, p. 6; table 4, p. 11.

118. Health Center Districts, New York City, *Statistical Reference Data*, from the Committee on Neighborhood Health Development, a section of the Department of Health, New York City, 1931; cited in Sollins, "Boys' Club Membership," 55; MCCP, *East Harlem Community Study*, 20.

119. East Harlem Health Center, *Casting Life Lines*, table 3, p. 7; "Vital Statistics," 1931, CP box 77, folder 5.

120. Cohen, *Workshop to Office*, 149–54; table 11, p. 150.

121. Owen D. Gutfreund, "The Path of Prosperity: New York's East River Drive, 1922–1990," *Journal of Urban History* 21, no. 2 (1995): 147–83; quote from 148.

122. Cimilluca, "Natural History of East Harlem," 6.

123. MCCP, *East Harlem Community Study*, 46.

124. Ibid., 47.

125. East Harlem Historical Organization, "Discovering East Harlem." East Harlem residents also had access to the northeastern corner of Central Park, at Fifth Avenue and 109th Street, and to Mount Morris Park, east of Fifth Avenue above 120th Street. Mt. Morris Park (now Marcus Garvey Memorial Park) had two popular attractions: the Mount Morris Turkish baths, replete with sauna, steam, and therapeutic pool, which appealed especially to the residents of East Harlem's cold-water flats; and the Mount Morris watchtower, which was built on the district's highest point and displayed a large iron fire bell.

126. Jane Jacobs, *The Death and Life of Great American Cities* (New York: Vintage, 1989), 108.

127. Among a number of sources, Freeman, "Exploring Path of Community Change," 115–20. Gerald Meyer refers to Italian Harlem, especially East 116th Street, as "a major Mafia center" and cites David Durk's claim that the area was headquarters for those who processed and distributed more than half the heroin in the United States from the late 1940s until 1973; see David Durk, *The Pleasant Avenue Connection* (New York: Harper and Row, 1977), 26, 174; cited in Gerald Meyer, *Vito Marcantonio: Radical Politician, 1902–1954* (New York: State University of New York Press, 1989),127; see also the reference to the gang-controlled "Murder Stable" on East 125th Street and an East Harlem "overrun by gangs" in Luc Sante, *Low Life: Lures and Snares of Old New York* (New York: Farrar, Straus and Giroux, 1991), 232–33. For an excellent historical overview and counterstereotypic interpretation—Italian American organized crime as an adaptation of southern Italian culture to social and economic conditions in the United States—see Francis A. J. Ianni, "The Mafia and the Web of Kinship," *Public Interest* 22 (1971): 78–100.

128. Paul Cressey, unpublished ms, 1–2; cited in Sollins, "Boys' Club Membership," 46; see also references to youth gangs in Anna C. Ruddy (Christian McLeod, pseud.), *The Heart of the Stranger: A Story of Little Italy* (New York: Fleming H. Revell, 1908; reprint, Arno Press, 1975).

129. John E. Jacobi, "Statistical-Ecological Study of Juvenile Delinquency in Manhattan" (Ph.D. diss., New York University, 1933), 171–72. Juvenile delinquency was underreported, according to Schulman, *Slums of New York*, 172, reporting on a Rotary Club study of Manhattan slum areas in 1926 and 1931–32.

130. Data for 1931, cited in Citizens Housing Council of New York, *Harlem Housing*, 28. Of a total of 8,024 children arraigned by the Children's Court in 1929, nearly a third, 2,597, were children of Italian-born immigrants; arraignments for children of Russian-born immigrants were less than half the Italian number. Disorderly conduct and stealing were

the leading categories of crimes and misdemeanors for the Italian children. These patterns continued unabated into the 1930s. See *Annual Report of the Children's Court of the City of New York,* 1929, table 17, p. 25; 1930, table 16, p. 20; 1931, table 16, p. 32; 1932, table 17, p. 23. For East Harlem at 126th Street and the area from the East River east to Fifth Avenue between 119th and 108th streets, the Children's Court reported a 1930 delinquency rate of 11.5 per 1000 males aged seven to fifteen; the most delinquent was the thirteen–fifteen age group, with disorderly conduct, stealing, and burglary as the major crimes, respectively. See Irving W. Halpern, John Norman Stanislaus, Bernard Botein, and New York City Housing Authority, *A Statistical Study of the Distribution of Adult and Juvenile Delinquents in the Boroughs of Manhattan and Brooklyn, New York City* (New York: New York City Housing Authority, 1934), table 4, p. 86. According to the Boys' Club Study, the major crimes ascribed to East Harlem delinquent males were auto theft, burglary, and rape. See Thrasher, *Final Report on Jefferson Park Branch,* table 9, p. 184. For several interesting case studies that illustrate various factors contributing to the delinquent behavior of East Harlem Italian males aged ten to seventeen, on the eve of the Depression, see Crime Commission of the State of New York, *A Study of Problem Boys and Their Brothers by the Sub-Commission on Causes and Effects of Crime* (Albany, N.Y.: J. B. Lyon, 1929), section 3.

131. Eric C. Schneider, *Vampires, Dragons, and Egyptian Kings: Youth Gangs in Postwar New York* (Princeton, N.J.: Princeton University Press, 1999), 96–99. Gerald Suttles observed fourteen such male clubs in his report on Chicago Italians in the 1960s: "To my knowledge, not one of these older groups ever had a social or athletic event during the three years I was in the area. Mostly they gamble, drink and talk." Suttles, *Social Order of the Slum,* 89.

132. MCCP, *East Harlem Community Study,* 52.

133. Meyer, *Vito Marcantonio,* 114. See also Covello, *Heart Is Teacher,* 205–6. John W. Briggs, in *An Italian Passage: Immigrants to Three American Cities, 1890–1930* (New Haven, Conn.: Yale University Press, 1978), documents general-purpose, territorially based mutual benefit societies in southern Italy and Sicily in the late nineteenth century; as he puts it: "Southern Italians, by the time heavy emigration was taking place, possessed skills necessary to maintain voluntary associations and recognized the possibilities for promoting individual goals through associative endeavors" (17). Though these societies had few resources and "limited potency," their prevalence challenges Covello's claim, in *Italo-American School Child,* that "solidarity was comprehensible only within limits of [pre-emigration] familial existence; it did not apply to other aggregates" (152).

134. Korrol, *Colonia to Community,* 42.

135. Marsh, "Life and Work of the Churches," 65, lists nine settlement houses (65); Margaret Campbell Tilley, "The Boy Scout Movement in East Harlem" (Ph.D. diss., New York University, 1935), 38, lists fourteen. Tilley's list includes Jefferson Park M. E. Church and Casa del Popolo.

136. Catherine Quiggle, draft of preliminary inventory for Union Settlement records, 1947–1971, Social Welfare History Archives, University of Minnesota, 1; J. A. Lobbia, "100 Years of Settlement," *Village Voice,* 16 May 1995, 18; MCCP, *East Harlem Community Study,* 93.

137. See Harlem House Articles of Incorporation, 1901–1935, CP box 72, folder 6; "In Memory of Anna C. Ruddy," East Harlem Civic Association, Sixth Annual Dinner Dance, 25 February 1967; La Guardia Memorial House, *100 Years of Service.*

138. Tilley, "Boy Scout Movement in East Harlem," 36–38; MCCP, *East Harlem Community Study,* 94.

139. Interview with Selina A. Weigel, R.N., Director of the Health Shop, 4 September 1931, by May Case Marsh; cited in Marsh, "Life and Work of the Churches," 59–60; Kenneth D. Widdemer, *A Decade of District Health Center Pioneering: Ten-Year Report of the East Harlem Health Center* (New York: East Harlem Health Center and New York Chapter of the American Red Cross, 1932).

140. "History and Organization of the East Harlem Council of Social Agencies, 1931–35," CP box 70, folder 29.

141. Though public demonstrations were not common in socially conservative Italian Harlem, local political tradition managed to establish its own rich folklore, including such landmarks as the "Lucky Corner" at 116th Street and Lexington Avenue. Purported to bring good luck to candidates, the corner became a public gathering space and evoked shared political symbolism and memories among East Harlemites. See Meyer, *Vito Marcantonio*, 15, 101; also consulted were Salvatore John LaGumina, *Vito Marcantonio: The People's Politician* (Dubuque, Iowa: Kendall/Hunt, 1969), and Alan Schaffer, *Vito Marcantonio: Radical in Congress* (Syracuse, N.Y.: Syracuse University Press, 1966).

142. Local worker groups such as the powerful Italian Dressmakers Local 89 of the International Ladies Garment Workers Union often contributed to local political life. No fewer than eight labor organizations had offices in East Harlem. The International Workers Order's Italian-speaking lodge published *L'Unita del Popolo* for local consumption; its Spanish-speaking lodges organized in the sections west of Third Avenue. El Centro Obrero Espa?ol spread its message in East Harlem via its publication *La Vida Obrera,* later renamed *La Voz.*

143. Patricia Cayo Sexton, *Spanish Harlem* (New York: Harper and Row, 1965), 85; cited in LaGumina, *Vito Marcantonio,* 86

144. Marsh, "Life and Work of the Churches." The institutions were Eastern Orthodox (2), Jewish (3), Baptist (3), German Evangelical Synod of North America (1), Lutheran (5), Methodist Episcopal (4), nondenominational (1), Presbyterian (1), Protestant Episcopal (3), Reformed Church in America (1), Seventh Day Adventist (1), and Roman Catholic (8).

145. Freeman, "Exploring Path of Community Change," 359–61; Marsh, "Life and Work of the Churches," 608.

146. Thrasher, *Final Report on Jefferson Park Branch,* chaps. 8–10; quotes from 217, 218; for BFHS area, maps 27, p. 219; 30, p. 259. In the 1940s a BFHS student wrote ingenuously that in some candy stores "you may get marijuana, bad literature, meet fellows, and even girls who have had jail sentences, and get into the habit of excitement and disregard of law and decency which could start you on the road to crime." "General Leadership-Youth & Recreation in EH, from Rpt done by BFHS Students 1943–44 re NYHA proposal for James Weldon Houses, requesting space in project for youth center," CP box 36, folder 14.

CHAPTER 3: LEONARD COVELLO

1. Robert W. Peebles, *Leonard Covello: A Study of an Immigrant's Contribution to New York City* (New York: Arno Press, 1978), 40–50.

2. Leonard Covello with Guido D'Agostino, *The Heart Is the Teacher* (New York: McGraw-Hill, 1958), 20–21.

3. Peebles, *Leonard Covello,* 82. The Coviellos apparently formed a "partner household" with the Accursos, where the Accursos, while living separately, sublet rooms to the Coviellos and shared a kitchen with them. Donna Gabaccia, in *From Sicily to Elizabeth Street: Housing and Social Change among Italian Immigrants, 1880–1930* (Albany: State University of New York Press, 1984), 74–77, suggests that this was a common arrangement among Italian immigrant families.

4. Covello, *Heart Is Teacher,* 24.

5. Jeffrey Mirel called our attention to this distinction; personal communication, 14 February 2003.

6. Covello, *Heart Is Teacher,* 25–27.

7. Ibid., 41.

8. Peebles, *Leonard Covello,* 84. For details of the general pattern of cultural discrimination against Italians in the New York elementary schools, see Archie Bromsen, "The

Public School's Contribution to the Maladaption of the Italian Boy," in Caroline F. Ware, *Greenwich Village, 1920–1930: A Comment on American Civilization in the Post-War Years* (New York: Houghton Mifflin, 1937; reprint, New York: Octagon Books, 1977), appendix E, 455–61.

9. Leonard Covello to Lurton Blassingame, 23 March 1959, Leonard Covello Paper (MSS 40) [hereafter CP], Balch Institute Collections, Historical Society of Pennsylvania, Philadelphia, box 17, folder 34.

10. *The Home Garden* [1902?], CP box 72, folder 10.

11. Anna C. Ruddy (Christian McLeod, pseud.), *The Heart of the Stranger: A Story of Little Italy* (New York: Fleming H. Revell, 1908; reprint, Arno Press, 1975).

12. Covello, "Home Garden," Reminiscences and Autobiographical Notes, 3, CP box 20, folder 13; Covello, *Heart Is Teacher*, 32–35.

13. Covello, *Heart Is Teacher*, 32; Peebles, *Leonard Covello*, 85–88.

14. Covello to Marie Concistre, 24 July 1963, CP box 3, folder 28; Betty Burleigh, "The Bishop of Harlem," *World Outlook*, August 1949, 375–79.

15. Covello, *Heart Is Teacher*, 34.

16. Ibid., 102–3.

17. Burleigh, "Bishop of Harlem," 379.

18. Flyer announcing award, CP box 1, folder 15.

19. Covello, *Heart Is Teacher*, 36–39; quotes from 38.

20. Morris opened as the coeducational Peter Cooper High School in September 1897. (The name was changed four years later to honor Gouverneur Morris, signer of the Declaration of Independence and U.S. Constitution, who had lived in the area that became the Bronx in 1895.) By 1900 the three buildings of Morris High School housed a total of 2,136 pupils. In the summer of 1901 the cornerstone for a new high school building that would accommodate 2,500 students was laid in the Morrisana area at Boston Road and 166th Street. The splendidly appointed five-story building, replete with a 179-foot tower and 1,300-seat (1,700-person capacity) auditorium, opened in January 1904. Morris was the first high school designed by the renowned school architect C.B.J. Snyder, whose signature style was English Gothic Collegiate using an *H* shape. Gary Hermalyn, *Morris High School and the Creation of the New York City Public High School System* (New York: Bronx County Historical Society, 1995), 47–48, 73–107.

21. Leonard Covello, "Statement to Mr. Kern," 1, n.d., CP box 2, folder 20. See also Department of Education, *Directory of the Board of Education of the City of New York*, 1902, New York City Municipal Archives, 98.

22. The new Morris housed 2,101 students in 1904, with no annexes. Department of Education, *Directory*, 1904, 77.

23. Hermalyn, *Morris High School*, 133–34, 147.

24. Covello, "Statement to Mr. Kern," 2.

25. Robert W. Peebles, "Interview with Leonard Covello," *Urban Review* 3, no. 3 (1969): 14–15.

26. Covello, *Heart Is Teacher*, 48–49.

27. Ibid., 45.

28. Ibid., 50–52.

29. Covello, "Statement to Mr. Kern," 2.

30. Covello, *Heart Is Teacher*, 58.

31. Leonard Covello, "Memories from the Past and a Challenge for the Future," *L'Unita del Popolo*, 25 November 1939, newsletter, CP box 122, folder 12.

32. Peebles, *Leonard Covello*, 93–94.

33. Ibid., 96. In his autobiography, Covello stated that his work as a tutor in the home of a wealthy Long Island family in the summer of 1911 catalyzed his interest in the Socialist Party: "I read their literature. I kept seeing before my eyes the Johnsons, with their home

in the country and their mansion in town, and the people of East Harlem who worked all day long and were barely able to fill their stomachs and clothe their children." *Heart Is Teacher*, 87–89.

34. Peebles, *Leonard Covello*, 97–103; quotes from Covello, *Heart Is Teacher*, 81. In 1909 Pietro Coviello married a woman of contadino origins. The marriage was arranged by Leonard's uncles in Avigliano. Leonard's new stepmother, Carmella, won at first grudging and later full acceptance from Leonard, his five brothers, and his sister. Pietro retired from his café job in 1921, then tried unsuccessfully, at the age of sixty, to operate a corner candy store in East Harlem; shortly thereafter Pietro and "Momma-Nonna" moved to a small frame house on ten acres of land outside Bear Mountain. Covello, *Heart Is Teacher*, 77–78, 167–69.

35. Covello, *Heart Is Teacher*, 84.

36. Ibid., 81–82. See also Peebles, *Leonard Covello*, 97–103; Leonard Covello, "Background for tackling job of Princ[ipal] and intercultural Program he wanted to do," (handwritten), Reminiscences and Autobiographical Notes, 13–14, CP box 20, folder 16.

37. Covello, *Heart Is Teacher*, 82.

38. From materials in CP box 7, folder 1: correspondence with John Shedd (several letters, 1914–18), will, and legal documents following death of Annie K. Shedd, mother of John A. Shedd.

39. Covello to William Shedd, 12 March 1951, CP box 7, folder 1.

40. Covello, *Heart Is Teacher*, 85–101. Mary Accurso is listed as a 1900 graduate of Peter Cooper (later Morris) High School, a member of that high school's first graduating class. High Schools, Boroughs of Manhattan and the Bronx, "First Annual Graduating Exercises," 29 June 1900, reprinted in Hermalyn, *Morris High School*, 189–92.

The New Utrecht position is listed in "Record: Training and Experience: Leonard Covello," 5 January 1926, CP box 24, folder 2. There is some confusion in CP, however. Folder 2 includes a notification dated 10 July 1913, issued by the board of education, that appoints Covello to teach at Bay Ridge High School in Brooklyn; the notification for his transfer to DeWitt Clinton High School, dated 21 July 1914, shows Bay Ridge, not New Utrecht, as the sending school. In his 1926 resume Covello appears as a substitute French teacher at DeWitt Clinton High School, 1912–13; Peebles, in *Leonard Covello*, 105, suggests that Covello later parlayed that role into a full-time appointment.

41. Covello, *Heart Is Teacher*, 105.

42. Peebles, *Leonard Covello*, 106. The DeWitt Clinton High School building at 59th Street and Tenth Avenue, which today houses the John Jay College of Criminal Justice, opened in 1906. A "cathedral of culture," the Clinton building was created in the Snyder motif, a Collegiate Gothic edifice of red brick with limestone trimmings, six stories at the center, entered through a portal of rounded archways on Tenth Avenue. For school architecture, see William W. Cutler III, "Cathedral of Culture: The Schoolhouse in American Educational Thought and Practice since 1820," *History of Education Quarterly* 29, no. 1 (1989): 1–40, quote from 8; also Hermalyn, *Morris High School*, 44, 104fn40, 211.

43. George Abernethy, "Some Reflections on the Educational Process—Partly Autobiographical, Partly Sociological, Partly Philosophical," address to Faculty Research Club, Davidson College, 7 May 1984, 4, used by permission of the author. See also Peebles, *Leonard Covello*, 106–7. In 1934, Covello's final spring at the high school, the yearbook editors reported that only "twenty-four prodigies" had averages of ninety or higher, that "the average of Clinton's graduating classes in the past has invariably been between 73 and 74. This term, however, the average is the highest it has ever been—75.8%." *Clintonian*, June 1934, CP box 31, folder 13.

44. Gerald Meyer, *Vito Marcantonio: Radical Politician, 1902–1954* (Albany: State University of New York Press, 1989), 9.

45. See Marjorie Murphy, *Blackboard Unions: The AFT and the NEA, 1900–1980* (Ithaca, N.Y. Cornell University Press), 97, 101, 104–10, 151–61. In 1969 Covello told Robert Peebles that he had been involved in the union activity at DeWitt Clinton: "I've been a member of the teachers union since 1916, when about a dozen of us at Clinton formed one of its first chapters. I remember in those early days three of our members were thrown out of the school system for joining the union. I've been a member ever since." Peebles, "Interview with Leonard Covello," 17. Political activism was apparently muted at Clinton during World War I. As reported in Howard K. Beale, *Are American Teachers Free: An Analysis of Restraints upon the Freedom of Teaching in American Schools* (New York: Scribner's, 1936), 30–35, three Clinton teachers, all Teachers Union members, were fired for failing to support U.S. involvement in the war; six were transferred; and another six were investigated, including Lefkowitz, Covello's old friend Garibaldi Lapolla, and Austin M. Works, a future BFHS English Department chair.

46. Meyer, *Vito Marcantonio,* 9–10. Noted Trotskyist Max Schachtman, who gravitated to socialism as a Clinton student, recalled the high school's radical milieu, in particular the influence of a U.S. history teacher, probably referring to Lefkowitz (196n19).

47. Ibid., 11.

48. Licenses issued to Covello by the New York City Board of Education, CP box 24, folder 1.

49. Peebles, *Leonard Covello,* 113–14.

50. "The Italian Club of DeWitt Clinton Presents 'Il Ventaglio,'" *High Points,* February 1921, 24, CP box 6, folder 8.

51. *Il Foro* 1, no. 1 (1921), 1, CP box 26, folder 17.

52. Leonard Covello, "The Function of an Italian Circolo," Casa Italiana Educational Bureau (CIEB), Columbia University, n.d., CP box 92, folder 21. A transcript copy of this ms, dated 1921, may be found in CP box 20, folder 22.

53. For Covello's war record, CP box 8, folder 3; see also Covello, *Heart Is Teacher,* 113–28.

54. Covello, *Heart Is Teacher,* 163.

55. Covello to Dr. Pisani, 23 September 1925, CP box 24, folder 2. David Tyack and Elisabeth Hansot, in *Managers of Virtue: Public School Leadership in America, 1820–1980* (New York: Basic, 1982), credit Covello as "the first person, probably, to teach Italian in an American high school" (209).

56. Peebles, "Interview with Leonard Covello," 14–15.

57. John H. Finley, foreword to Mario E. Cosenza, ed., *The Study of Italian in the United States* (New York: Italy America Society of New York, 1924).

58. Federal Writers Project, *The Italians of New York* (New York: Arno Press, 1969), 106. In 1921 the Order Sons of Italy created the Dante Medals and $400 scholarships for young men and women excelling in the study of Italian. *Il Foro* 3, no. 3 (1925): 6, CP box 26, folder 6; Peebles, *Leonard Covello,* 161–63.

59. Covello, *Heart Is Teacher,* 136.

60. Minutes of 24 May 1922 meeting of the board of education, *Journal of the Board of Education of the City of New York* [hereafter *JBOE*], vol. 1 (1922), 1010–11, City Hall Library, New York City; as noted in the testimony, Washington Irving High School and DeWitt Clinton High School already offered Italian as a first-year elective to some 399 students.

61. Covello to Dr. Pisani. Covello's principal, Francis H. J. Paul, declared (unilaterally, it seems) Italian as a "first language" study in January 1921. In a letter to Paul dated June 1922, Covello wrote: "Although up to this time we have not had officially a Department of Italian, yet the function has been that of a Department." He concluded: "Since the Board of Education, on May 24th [1922], has placed Italian on an equal footing with all other foreign languages in the City High Schools, it would seem both proper and timely to have DeWitt Clinton, the High School in the City which has the largest number of students of

Italian [origin] (220), likewise establish this parity within its walls, by creating an independent Department of Italian." CP box 24, folder 2.

62. In 1920 Clinton's enrollment was 4,957, with two annexes. See Department of Education, *Directory*, 1920, 62.

63. Kate Rousmaniere, *City Teachers: Teaching and School Reform in Historical Perspective* (New York: Teachers College Press, 1997), 56.

64. Covello, *Heart Is Teacher*, 130.

65. Ibid., 131–34.

66. Yearly report of Department of Italian, 1 May 1922, 1, CP box 27, folder 20. See also *Clinton Alumni Journal* 2, no. 1 (December 1924), CP box 26, folder 15.

67. "Il Circolo Italiano," 1933–34, 1, CP box 26, folder 14. Covello stayed in touch with "my Clinton boys" for years after they graduated, observing "what an important influence in their lives and in their life work have been those experiences that we shared together. As a result of this personal experience, I am completely convinced that education—which is not the accumulation of knowledge and sharpening people's wits to prey upon their fellow man— can be a potent force in directing young people's lives to serve and not exploit a fellow human being." Covello, "Boys Club Study at New York University," n.d., CP box 78, folder 1.

68. Meyer, *Vito Marcantonio*, 11–13, quote from 11. The *Clinton News*, 16 October 1931, CP box 122, folder 10, reported: "'Pop' Covello, as he is known, is not far from being an idol of the Italian Students at Clinton."

69. Meyer, *Vito Marcantonio*, 11–12; Circolo program, 8 January 1921, CP box 26, folder 14; untitled ms fragment, probably authored by Covello, December 1940, CP box 36, folder 10; Covello, *Heart Is Teacher*, 152–54. .

70. Covello, *Heart Is Teacher*, 152–54.

71. Annual Report of the Italian Department, CP box 27, folder 20; Leonard Covello, "The Italian Immigrant and the Schools," address delivered at Twenty-fifth Annual Meeting of the American Sociological Society, Cleveland, 31 December 1930, CP box 8, folder 16; Covello to Mario Gulizia, 22 February 1933, CP box 41, folder 8. From 1923 to 1934, Covello served as a member of the College Entrance Examination Board for the Italian examination. See Thomas S. Fisk to Covello, 13 April 1934, CP box 26, folder 10. Covello and Annita Giacobbe published an Italian-language textbook, *First Reader in Italian* (New York: Macmillan, 1933), of which one reviewer remarked: "Certainly no text in Italian, to our knowledge, was ever so well adapted, organized and presented for classroom use." Peter M. Riccio, *Casa Italiana Bulletin* 3, no. 7 (1933): 9–10, CP box 17, folder 24. During his Clinton tenure, Covello made three summer trips to Italy—1921, 1923, 1926. In 1926 he directed the New York University Residential Tour to Rome. See "Record of Leonard Covello," [1956?], CP box 1, folder 20.

72. The Italian Teachers Association's Italian-language campaign, in which Covello played a leading role as vice president, succeeded to the extent that registration in New York City increased from 900 in February 1922 to 6,153 in October 1932—an increase, however, that paled in comparison to enrollments in French (107,000), Spanish (40,000), and German (23,500). Reported in Leonard Covello, "An Open Letter to Italian Societies and Clubs in Greater New York for the Study of the Italian Language in the Schools of the City," [1932?], CP box 98, folder 3.

73. Untitled publicity statement, DeWitt Clinton High School, [1930?], CP box 27, folder 13.

74. Jonathan Zimmerman, "Ethnics against Ethnicity: European Immigrants and Foreign-Language Instruction, 1890–1940," *Journal of American History* 88, no. 4 (2002). Zimmerman quotes from Covello, "Report on Italian Classes and Italian Club," CP box 27, folder 20. See also Simone Cinotto, "Leonard Covello, the Covello Papers, and the History

of Eating Habits among Italian Immigrants in New York," *Journal of American History* 91, no. 2 (2004): 506–7.

75. Covello, *Heart Is Teacher,* 154–56; *Casa del Popolo* 1, 23 (12 November 1920), newsletter, CP box 69, folder 8; in same folder, "A Good Education Pays."

76. Covello's academic transcripts indicate that he abandoned his graduate studies at Columbia University in 1913, the year he started teaching. From 1920 to 1928, he taught in various semesters as an evening instructor in French, Spanish, and Italian, holding positions at Columbia University, New York University, and Hunter College. After 1929, he largely restricted his university teaching to the School of Education at New York University. Transcripts, CP box 7, folder 16; "Record of Leonard Covello." As a lecturer in education, Covello taught the following courses at NYU, 1929–42, 1947: "Social Background of the Italo-American School Child," "Community-Centered School," "Administrative Techniques in the Community High School," "Culture and Civilization of Italy," "Methods of Teaching Italian." In 1946–47, he taught a sociology course, "Community Backgrounds of Education," at the Manhattan School of Music; in the summer of 1947, he served as a lecturer in education at the University of Puerto Rico; from 1953 to 1955 he taught "Community-Centered School" at Montclair State Teachers College, New Jersey.

77. Leonard Covello to E. George Payne, 27 October 1944, CP box 7, folder 16.

78. References to Covello's coursework are based on the authors' analysis of Covello's NYU transcript, CP box 7, folder 16; see also Irene Joseph Lawrence, "A History of Educational Sociology in the United States" (Ph.D. diss., Stanford University, 1951), 37; New York University School of Education Announcements, 1930–35, New York University Archives, Elmer Holmes Bobst Library, New York University, New York, School of Education Files. E. George Payne founded the Department of Educational Sociology in 1923, organized the first education section of the American Sociological Association, and established the *Journal of Educational Sociology* in 1927. Dan Dodson, John C. Payne, and Joseph B. Giacquinta, "A Brief History of the Department of Educational Sociology and Anthropology from 1923 to 1969," New York University Archives, School of Education Files, Departmental Histories, folder 8. An issue of the *Journal of Educational Sociology* (13, no. 1 [1939]) was devoted entirely to Payne's contributions to that field.

79. Covello, *Heart Is Teacher,* 165–67. See also Paul Radosavijevich, Biographical Files, New York University Archives.

80. "The Community-Centered School—Leonard Covello—Foreword" (outline notes), 1, CP box 18, folder 2.

81. Frederic M. Thrasher, *The Gang: A Study of 1,313 Gangs in Chicago,* 2d rev. ed. (Chicago: University of Chicago Press, 1936), originally published in 1927.

82. Martin Bulmer, *The Chicago School of Sociology: Institutionalization, Diversity, and the Rise of Sociological Research* (Chicago: University of Chicago Press, 1984), 100–101.

83. Thrasher, *Gang,* 487–90.

84. Frederic M. Thrasher, "The Gang as a Symptom of Community Disorganization," *Journal of Applied Sociology* 11, no. 1 (1926): 4.

85. Ibid., 6; citing Clifford R. Shaw, *A Problem Boy.*

86. Thrasher, *Gang,* 491–93.

87. Frederic M. Thrasher, "Social Background and Informal Education," *Journal of Educational Sociology* 7, no. 8 (April 1934): 470–84.

88. This account relies on Martin Bulmer, "The Early Institutional Establishment of Social Science Research: The Local Community Research Committee at the University of Chicago, 1923–30," *Minerva* 18, no. 1 (Spring 1980): 55–110; and Martin Bulmer and Joan Bulmer, "Philanthropy and Social Science in the 1920s: Beardsley Ruml and the Laura Spelman Rockefeller Memorial, 1922–29," *Minerva* 19, no. 3 (1981): 347–407.

89. Quoted in Bulmer, "Early Institutional Establishment of Social Science Research," 71.

90. Bulmer, *Chicago School*, 89.

91. See Robert E. Park, "The City: Suggestions for the Investigation of Human Behavior in the Urban Environment," in *The City*, ed. Park and Ernest W. Burgess (Chicago: University of Chicago Press, 1925), 1–46, first published in *American Journal of Sociology* 20 (1915): 577–612; Ernest W. Burgess, "The Growth of the City: An Introduction to a Research Project," in Park and Burgess, *The City*, 47–62. See also Bulmer, *Chicago School*, 108.

92. See sources, mostly in footnote references and bibliography, in Thrasher, *Gang*; see also Bulmer, *Chicago School*, 100–101.

93. Introduction to Nels Anderson, *The Hobo* (1923; Chicago: University of Chicago Press, 1961), xiii, quoted in Bulmer, *Chicago School*, 98.

94. Harvey W. Zorbaugh, *The Gold Coast and the Slum: A Sociological Study of Chicago's Near North Side* (Chicago: University of Chicago Press, 1929).

95. Bulmer, *Chicago School*, 100; Park recalled by Howard Becker, quoted in John C. McKinney, *Constructive Typology and Social Theory* (New York: Appleton-Century-Crofts, 1966), 71, cited in Bulmer, *Chicago School*, 97.

96. Paul Cressey authored *The Taxi-Dance Halls* (Chicago: University of Chicago Press, 1932); for the link to Thrasher's work, see Cressey, "The Motion Picture as Informal Education," *Journal of Educational Sociology* 7, no. 8 (1934): 504–15.

97. Frederic M. Thrasher, "The Boys' Club Study," *Journal of Educational Sociology* 6, no. 1 (September 1932): 4–16.

98. Covello, "Boys Club Study," 13.

99. Frederic M. Thrasher, "Preliminary Report on the Boys' Club Study of N.Y.U.," 15 March 1929, CP box 78, folder 3.

100. Frederic M. Thrasher, "The Boys' Club and Juvenile Delinquency," *American Journal of Sociology* 42, no. 1 (1936): 66–80.

101. Thrasher, "Preliminary Report on Boys' Club Study." See also Covello, *Heart Is Teacher*, 170. For methods used in the study, see Thrasher, "Boys' Club Study," and related articles in *Journal of Educational Sociology* 6, no. 1 (1932).

102. Irving V. Sollins, "A Socio-Statistical Analysis of Boys' Club Membership" (Ph.D. diss., New York University, 1936), 37.

103. Frederic M. Thrasher, "Related and Subsidiary Studies of the Boys' Club Study of New York University," *Journal of Educational Sociology* 6, no. 3 (1932): 184.

104. Three-fourths of the branch's membership was Italian American; see "Nationality Distribution of Parents of Boys' Club Members," in Sollins, "Boys' Club Membership," table 13, p. 79.

105. Covello, *Heart Is Teacher*, 171.

106. Frederic M. Thrasher, "Ecological Aspects of the Boys' Club Study," *Journal of Educational Sociology* 6, no. 1 (1932): 52–57. In 1930, DeWitt Clinton High School had a total enrollment of 8,500 boys; 5,400 of them attended the main building at Mosholu Parkway in the Bronx, with the remainder divided among five Manhattan annexes, the largest of which was the P.S. 172 building on East 108th Street between First and Second avenues. About 900 students, or 11 percent of Clinton's total population, were of Italian origin; of these about 200, or 22 percent, lived in the Boys' Club area, concentrated between 100th and 122nd streets. Seventy of the total were Boys' Club members. Covello and his colleagues collected survey data on all the Italian boys at Clinton. Leonard Covello, "Italian Boys at DeWitt Clinton High School," n.d., Bureau of Social Hygiene Collection, Rockefeller Archive Center, Sleepy Hollow, New York, series 3, box 11, folder 229.

107. Thrasher, "Related and Subsidiary Studies," quote from 176; Sollins, "Boys' Club Membership," 24.

108. Thrasher, "Boys' Club and Juvenile Delinquency," 66.

109. Remarks of Dr. Leonard Covello upon Acceptance of the Meritorious Service Medal of the Department of State of the State of New York, Benjamin Franklin High School, 15 December 1966, entered in *Congressional Record,* Proceedings and Debates of the 90th Congress, 8 March 1967.

110. Covello, *Heart Is Teacher,* 172. Thrasher and Covello agreed on this point. See Frederic M. Thrasher, editorial, *Journal of Educational Sociology* 7, no. 8 (1934): 1. For a restatement, see Leonard Covello, "A High School and Its Immigrant Community: A Challenge and an Opportunity," *Journal of Educational Sociology* 9 (1936): 336.

111. Freschi to Covello, 23 September 1924, CP box 82, folder 9.

112. Francesco Cordasco, "Leonard Covello and the Casa Italiana Educational Bureau," in Cordasco, ed., *Studies in Italian American Social History: Essays in Honor of Leonard Covello* (Totowa, N.J.: Rowman and Littlefield, 1975), 1–2.

113. Cordasco, "Leonard Covello and Casa Italiana," 2.

114. Leonard Covello, *The Casa Italiana Education Bureau: Its Purpose and Program,* bulletin no. 4, Casa Italiana Educational Bureau, CP box 5, folder 15.

115. Covello, "Boys Club Study," 20, 22.

116. "Sponsoring Committee for the East Harlem Community Study," backside of sheet, n.d., CP box 18, folder 3. Miriam Sanders of Haarlem House and Helen Harris of Union Settlement were the settlement-house representatives on the ten-member committee, which also included Covello. These women were friends and long-standing supporters of Covello. This committee apparently became formalized as the Mayor's Committee on City Planning.

117. Leonard Covello, "Research as the Foundation for Community-Centered Education," *The Community-Centered School* [hereafter *CCS*], remnant manuscript, chap. 2, corrected typescript, CP box 18, folder 9.

118. For example, in his 1929 presidential address to the American Sociological Society, William F. Ogburn declared: "Sociology as a science is not interested in making the world a better place in which to live, in encouraging beliefs, in spreading information, in dispensing news, in setting forth impressions of life, in leading the multitudes or in guiding the ship of state. Science is interested directly in one thing only, to wit, discovering new knowledge." Quoted in Bulmer, *Chicago School,* 182. For discussion of the shift from reform-minded social science in the Progressive Era to theory-driven social science after World War I, see Dorothy Ross, *The Origins of American Social Science* (New York: Cambridge University Press, 1991), 321–29; Dorothy Ross, "American Social Science and the Idea of Progress," in *The Authority of Experts,* ed. Thomas L. Haskell (Bloomington: Indiana University Press, 1984), 157–71; Bulmer and Bulmer, "Philanthropy and Social Science."

119. "Research and Its Aims" (outline notes, part 4), *CCS,* chap. 2, CP box 18, folder 9. Covello's conviction that such research was needed was strengthened as he attempted to implement BFHS's programs.

120. Covello, "Research as Foundation," 15.

121. Covello claimed that this research produced a collection of more than 120 "maps, charts, and graphs" regarding East Harlem. Ibid., 12.

122. Covello, "High School and Immigrant Community," 336–37.

123. Charles Booth, *Life and Labour of the People in London* (London: Macmillan, 1902). The first volume was published in 1889.

124. Residents of Hull House, *Hull-House Maps and Papers* (1895; New York: Arno Press, 1980), vii–viii, 5, 41. For an excellent history and exegesis of *Hull-House Maps and Papers,* see Kathryn K. Sklar, "*Hull-House Maps and Papers:* Social Science as Women's Work in the 1890s," in *The Social Survey in Historical Perspective, 1880–1940,* ed. Martin Bulmer, Kevin Bales, and Sklar (New York: Cambridge University Press, 1991), 111–47.

125. W.E.B. DuBois, *The Philadelphia Negro: A Social Study* (1899; reprint, with a new introduction by Elijah Anderson, Philadelphia: University of Pennsylvania Press, 1999). Sociologists Elijah Anderson and Douglas S. Massey, in "The Sociology of Race in the United States," in *Problem of the Century: Racial Stratification in the United States*, ed. Anderson and Massey (New York: Russell Sage Foundation, 2001), contend that DuBois "anticipated in every way the program of theory and research that later became known as the "Chicago school." Although not generally recognized as such, it represented the first true example of American social science research, preceding the work of Park and Burgess by at least two decades" (3–4). For a similar conclusion, see Martin Bulmer, "W.E.B. DuBois as a Social Investigator: *The Philadelphia Negro*, 1899," in Bulmer, Bales, and Sklar, *Social Survey in Historical Perspective*, 170–87. For the Pittsburgh Survey, see Steven Cohen, "The Pittsburgh Survey and the Social Survey Movement: A Sociological Road Not Taken," in Bulmer, Bales, and Sklar, *Social Survey in Historical Perspective*, 245–68.

126. For an excellent discussion of these distinctions, see Martin Bulmer, "The Decline of the Social Survey Movement and the Rise of American Empirical Sociology," in Bulmer, Bales, and Sklar, *Social Survey in Historical Perspective*, 291–315.

127. "The Training School for Community Workers of the People's Institute of New York. Announcement, 1917/18," 22, Milbank Special Collections (MSC), Teachers College, Columbia University. Widdemer instructed in a course entitled "Modern Forerunners of the Complete Community Center." Selected annual reports and other documents are available in MSC.

128. Thrasher, "Social Backgrounds and Informal Education," 481n7.

129. Thrasher, "Ecological Aspects of the Boys' Club Study," 54.

130. Bulmer, *Chicago School*, 68–74.

131. Ernest W. Burgess quoted in Bulmer, "Decline of Social Survey Movement," 303.

132. Meyer, *Vito Marcantonio*, 15, 131.

133. Covello, "Background for tackling job," 13.

134. "Community-Centered School—Foreword."

CHAPTER 4: THE HIGH SCHOOL ON EAST 108TH STREET

1. The Educational Alliance, a "somewhat special case" of the settlement movement, was particularly influential. Formerly the Hebrew Institute, from its five-story home at 197 East Broadway the Alliance sponsored myriad educational programs, kindergartens, vocational training, recreation centers, and adult-immigrant education. In 1902 Superintendent William Maxwell applauded the Alliance's role in the public adoption of its programs. Adam Bellow, *The Educational Alliance: A Centennial Celebration* (New York: Educational Alliance, 1990); see also Selma C. Berrol, "Julia Richmond: A Notable Woman" (Philadelphia: Balch Institute Press, 1993), chap. 4. In "Public Schools as Social Centres," *Annals of the American Academy of Political and Social Science* 23 (1904): 457–63, J. G. Phelps Stokes reported that "twenty-one of the public school buildings [of New York] are open after school hours, under suitable restrictions and supervisions, for the use of boys' and girls' clubs and other forms of youthful social life or recreation" (460). In 1908–9, 119 of the city's 610 school buildings were designated as school lecture centers, where experts of every conceivable sort, including professors, city planners, jurists, scientists, physicians, and "educators loaded with fresh spoils from the British museum," presented, often with stereopticon slides, lectures on more than 1,500 topics, drawing an aggregate attendance of more than 1.2 million, a "cosmopolitan multitude" of the city's immigrant working class." And in 1909–10, the board of education sponsored thirty-one evening recreation centers in the boroughs of Manhattan, the Bronx, and Brooklyn, with an aggregate attendance of 2.2 million and a nightly average of nearly 13,000 for all centers. The board also sponsored evening elementary schools, which

provided English-language and citizenship training for immigrants, with thirty-nine such schools in operation in 1895 and ninety in service by 1915. Clarence A. Perry, *Wider Use of the School Plant* (New York: Russell Sage Foundation, 1913), 201–39.

2. Jeffrey Mirel contributed this useful insight; personal communication, 14 February 2003.

3. Leonard Covello with Guido D'Agostino, *The Heart Is the Teacher* (New York: McGraw-Hill, 1958),, 182.

4. Harold Rugg, "Social Reconstruction through Education," *Progressive Education* 9/10, no. 8/1 (1932–33): 11.

5. See George Counts, "Dare Progressive Education Be Progressive?" *Progressive Education* 9, no. 4 (1932): 257–69; for a broader context for these remarks, see Ellen Condliffe Lagemann, "Prophecy or Profession? George S. Counts and the Social Study of Education," *American Journal of Education* 100, no. 2 (February 1992): 137–65.

6. Beard quoted in David Tyack, Robert Lowe, and Elisabeth Hansot, *Public Schools in Hard Times: The Great Depression and Recent Years* (Cambridge, Mass.: Harvard University Press, 1984), 57–58.

7. Ibid., 56; quotes from Herbert Kliebard, *The Struggle for the American Curriculum, 1893–1958*, 2d ed. (New York: Routledge, 1995), 155.

8. F. H. Bair, "The Beginnings of a School-Centered Community," *Clearing House* 9, no. 7 (March 1935): 421–22.

9. David L. Angus and Jeffrey E. Mirel, *The Failed Promise of the American High School, 1890–1995* (New York: Teachers College Press, 1999), 70–76.

10. Ibid., appendix A, 203.

11. Nicholas V. Montalto, *A History of the Intercultural Educational Movement, 1924–1941* (New York: Garland, 1982), 22–75, 102–23; Leonard Covello, "A High School and Its Immigrant Community: A Challenge and an Opportunity," *Journal of Educational Sociology* 9 (1936): 331–46; Leonard Covello, "Neighborhood Growth through the School," *Progressive Education* 15, no. 2 (1938); George E. Pozzetta, *Education and the Immigrant* (New York: Garland, 1991).

12. Paula S. Fass, *Outside In: Minorities and the Transformation of American Education* (New York: Oxford University Press, 1989), chap. 2; David B. Tyack, *The One Best System: A History of American Urban Education* (Cambridge, Mass.: Harvard University Press, 1974), 198–216.

13. Fass, *Outside In*, 74–75.

14. Paul Hanna and Research Staff of the Works Progress Administration, *Youth Serves the Community* (New York: D. Appleton-Century, 1936), 31.

15. Edward A. Krug, *The Shaping of the American High School*, vol. 2: *1920–1941* (Madison: University of Wisconsin Press, 1972), 307–36; Angus and Mirel, *Failed Promise*, 67–83.

16. See, for example, James Alfred Dickinson, "The Community-School Concept in Education" (Ph.D. diss., Ohio State University, 1942), 60–66.

17. Harvey W. Zorbaugh, "Which Way America's Youth?" *Journal of Educational Sociology* 2, no. 6 (1938): 322–34; in the same issue, Francis J. Brown, "How Fare American Youth?" 335–41; Edwin S. Fulcomer, *Secondary Schools as Community Centers* (New York: American Association for Adult Education, 1940), 15.

18. Hanna et al., *Youth Serves Community*, 33.

19. Eleanor T. Glueck, *The Community Use of Schools* (Baltimore: Williams and Wilkens, 1927), 1–2.

20. Zorbaugh, "Which Way America's Youth?" 325–26.

21. Ruth Markowitz, *My Daughter, the Teacher: Jewish Teachers in the New York City Schools* (New Brunswick, N.J.: Rutgers University Press, 1993), 93–94. For further discussion

see Josephine Chase, *New York at School: A Description of the Activities and Administration of the Public Schools of the City of New York* (New York: Public Education Association, 1927), chaps. 4–5.

22. New York City Superintendent of Schools [hereafter SOS], 36th *Annual Report* [hereafter *AR*], 1933–34, Stat. Sect., table 123, p. 189; table 124, p. 190, New York City Municipal Archives.

23. Ibid., 51st *AR*, 1948–49, Stat. Sect., table 2, p. 19.

24. "Distribution of Pupils of DeWitt Clinton High School by Residence," 20 February 1931, Leonard Covello Papers (MSS 40) [hereafter CP], Balch Institute Collections, Historical Society of Pennsylvania, Philadelphia, box 27, folder 13. See also untitled statement of DWCHS Italian Department, probably authored by Covello, [1930?], CP box 27, folder 10. DeWitt Clinton's enrollment would reach 10,368 by 1933, with four annexes. Department of Education, *Directory of the Board of Education of the City of New York*, 1933, 77, New York City Municipal Archives.

25. Leonard Covello, "The Benjamin Franklin High School: History and Inception of Program" (first draft), 3, *The Community-Centered School* [hereafter *CCS*], remnant manuscript, chap. 4, corrected transcript, CP box 18, folder 13.

26. See correspondence regarding the establishment of Benjamin Franklin, especially in CP box 32, folder 1; for example, Mario E. Cosenza, Leonard Covello, Angelo Patri, and Anthony Pugliese, "High School for Boys in East Harlem," petition on letterhead of Casa Italiana Educational Bureau (CIEB), 24 February 1934.

27. Covello, *Heart Is Teacher*, 182.

28. [Leonard Covello?], "A Boys High School for Harlem," n.d., 2, CP box 18, folder 13. In another document, Covello noted that the East Harlem Council of Social Agencies (EHCSA), a consortium of twenty-seven agencies that included such organizations as Haarlem House, the Heckscher Foundation for Children, the East Harlem Boys' Club, and Union Settlement, was moving in that direction in the early 1930s. "I attended one of the conferences," he wrote, "and before I knew it I [was] deep in the planning for the creation of a senior high school in East Harlem." "Casa Italian Educational Bureau and Italian Choral Society," CP box 5, folder 15. EHCSA records indicate that the conference to which Covello referred took place in the spring of 1932, where a "proposal for a Boys' High School in East Harlem was discussed and approved." "History and Organization of the East Harlem Council of Social Agencies, 1931–35," CP box 70, folder 29. The available evidence indicates that the idea of the community-centered school was largely, if not totally, Covello's brainchild.

29. The board of aldermen referred to the fact that "there is no high school within a three-mile radius of 125th Street and Madison avenue, Borough of Manhattan." Preamble and resolution adopted by the Board of Aldermen, 17 April 1934, *Journal of the Board of Education of the City of New York* [hereafter *JBOE*], vol. 1 (1934), 670, City Hall Library, New York City.

30. [Covello?], "Boys High School for Harlem," 2. See also "Dear Sir" letter, apparently from Covello to Dr. John Ryan or Dr. Harold Campbell, NYC BOE, dated 27 April 1931, CP box 32, folder 1; Covello to Dr. Harold Campbell, 17 June 1933, CP box 32, folder 1; Covello to Judge Salvatore A. Cotillo, 19 June 1933, CP box 32, folder 1; Cosenza et al., "High School for Boys in East Harlem"; "A Boy's High School for Harlem," report on the school campaign committee's progress, CP box 32, folder 1.

31. Leonard Covello to Dr. Harold A. Campbell, 17 June 1933, CP box 32, folder 1.

32. [Covello?], "Boys High School for Harlem," 2. The East Harlem committee complained: "There are much better High School facilities for girls for the Harlem Community"—i.e., Wadleigh High School at 114th Street and Seventh Avenue; Julia Richman High School at 67th Street and Second Avenue, with an annex at 86th Street and First Avenue. In New York's constellation of thirty-eight high schools and forty-five annexes, the descriptor

"general" referred to the academic high schools, which prepared students for college or normal school training; "cosmopolitan" referred to high schools that had academic, commercial, and industrial tracks. See Chase, *New York at School,* 52.

33. "Dear Sir" letter.

34. Quoted in Covello, "The Benjamin Franklin High School: History and Inception of Program" (second draft), 2, *CCS,* chap. 4, CP box 18, folder 13.

35. Frank Pierrepont Graves, *Report of a Study of New York City Schools, Part I: The Administrative-Supervisory Organization* (Albany: University of the State of New York Press, 1933), 36.

36. Sol Cohen, *Progressives and Urban School Reform* (New York: Teachers College, Columbia University, 1964), 160. Cohen cites as factors the "distractions of the Depression, the excitement generated by the mayoralty election, and the inauguration of a new city administration" (ibid.).

37. Tyack, Lowe, and Hansot, *Public Schools in Hard Times,* 57.

38. Ibid., chap. 3; John D. Millett, *The Works Progress Administration in New York City* (Chicago: Public Administration Service, 1938).

39. Frank Pierrpont Graves, *Report of a Study of New York City Schools: Part II: Evaluation of Achievement* (Albany: University of the State of New York Press, 1933), 6.

40. Ibid., 42–45.

41. Italian Americans, one in every seven New Yorkers by 1930, began to achieve commensurate political clout. Leonard Covello, "The Italians in America: A Brief Survey of a Sociological Research Program of Italo-American Communities," CIEB Bulletin Number 6, Columbia University, July 1934; data drawn from appended table. "Italian Stock of 1st and 2nd Generations over 5000 in Principal Cities of the United States," from *Italy American Monthly,* July 1934.

42. Sanders to Covello, 5 April 1932, CP box 32, folder 1; agency list on high school resolution, "A High School for Boys in East Harlem," CP box 32, folder 1. EHCSA records state that a "proposal for a Boys' High School in East Harlem was discussed and approved." "History and Organization of the East Harlem Council of Social Agencies, 1931–35," CP box 70, folder 29. In 1933–34 Covello was listed as council co–vice chair. East Harlem Council of Social Agencies Annual Report, 1933–34, CP box 70, folder 26.

43. For example, Pope was honorary president of the Italian Festa sponsored by Covello's Department of Italian at DeWitt Clinton High School in 1933. Copy of program flyer, Robert W. Peebles, *Leonard Covello: A Study of an Immigrant's Contribution to New York City* (New York: Arno Press, 1978), appendix O.

44. Covello to Generoso Pope, 9 October 1931, 10 June 1932, and 26 June 1933, CP box 32, folder 1.

45. Covello to Mario Cosenza, 1 July 1933, CP box 32, folder 1.

46. Covello to Anthony Pugliese, Mario Cosenza, Angelo Patri, 7 December 1933, CP box 32, folder 1.

47. Gerald Meyer, "Leonard Covello and Vito Marcantonio: A Lifelong Collaboration for Progress," *Italica* 62, no. 1 (1985): 56. According to Miriam Sanders, Marcantonio's wife: "He [Marc] was singularly fortunate in becoming associated with Covello. This friendship is continuing today. They live in adjacent houses on 116th Street and still see life as one. In the words of Tennyson they are 'twinned as horse's ear and eye.' . . . Marc was the chief instrument in establishing this school, vigorously promoting it after La Guardia, then mayor, had given it up." Personal Papers—Biographical Notes (apparently interview notes with Miriam Sanders), Vito Marcantonio Papers, New York Public Library, box 74, p. 2.

48. Cohen, *Progressives and Urban School Reform,* 159.

49. *School and Society* 39 (30 January 1934): 80–81; Cohen, *Progressives and Urban School Reform,* 160.

50. "Meeting of Special Committee in the Office of Dr. John L. Tildsley, Acting Head of the High School Division," 16 April 1934, CP box 32, folder 1.

51. David Ment, "Racial Segregation in the Public Schools of New England and New York, 1840–1940" (Ph.D. diss., Columbia University, 1975), 255–59. This zoning was apparently an exception to the practice of open admission that otherwise prevailed in the city schools in the 1930s; see and cf. Fass, *Outside In,* 272n23. By 1936 Benjamin Franklin would enroll a total of thirty-seven African American students, 2.2 percent of the school population.

52. Resolution of the Board of Superintendents, 10 May 1934, *JBOE.* 1 (1934): 796–97. The high school committee's first choice had been P.S. 99 at 100th Street and First Avenue; P.S. 172 was listed as the fourth choice in one of the planning documents. It should be noted that the board of superintendents, chaired by the superintendent of schools, had enormous power in the city schools; among other functions, it made recommendations to the BOE on changes in the boundaries of local school-board districts, courses of study, textbooks and supplies, licensing, and appointments to "the teaching and supervising staff"; it also determined the content of BOE-approved courses of study and was responsible to recommend transfer of teachers, principals, and other staff to the superintendent of schools. See Graves, *Report, Part I,* 31 (chart 2), 44–46.

53. "Cosmopolitan High School Planned for East Harlem," "High School Hunted by Board," *World-Telegram,* 10, 11 May 1934.

54. BOE, minutes, 23 May 1934, *JBOE,* vol. 1 (1934), 796–97. The school was formally named Benjamin Franklin High School the following month. Minutes of 27 June meeting, *JBOE* vol. 1 (1934), 1065–66. Whether or not the decision to name the high school after Benjamin Franklin was based on a consideration of Franklin's meaning of citizenship, it was certainly appropriate. (There is no discussion of this matter in either the Covello Papers or *JBOE.*)

55. John Tildsley to Board of Superintendents, 2 June 1934, quoted in full in "The Benjamin Franklin High School: History and Inception of Program" (second draft), 3–6.

56. John L. Tildsley, *The Inglis Lecture, 1936: The Mounting Waste of the American Secondary School* (Cambridge, Mass.: Harvard University Press, 1936), 63. As associate superintendent during World War I, Tildsley had orchestrated the dismissal of three DeWitt Clinton teachers and the transfer of six others who were accused of encouraging "unpatriotic sentiments" among their students. John F. McClymer, in *War and Welfare: Social Engineering in America, 1890–1925* (Westport, Conn.: Greenwood Press, 1980), 123–124, notes that "all of the dismissed teachers, and four of the six transferred were Jews" and all were members of the Teachers Union, putatively a hotbed of socialism; this tendency to use patriotism for other purposes would be repeated in the city schools of the McCarthy era (for more details see Chapter 7 in this volume). In most respects Tildsley and Covello were strange bedfellows, although they appear to have had a cordial working relationship and Tildsley obviously respected Covello.

57. Covello, *Heart Is Teacher,* 181.

58. Tildsley to Board of Superintendents; Peebles, *Leonard Covello,* 194–95.

59. Peebles, *Leonard Covello,* 194–95; letters in CP box 32, folder 1.

60. New York City Board of Education, *Minutes of the Board of Superintendents* (1934), 431–32, 451–52, City Hall Library, New York City.

61. Ibid., 451–52.

62. BOE, minutes, 12 September 1934 meeting of the Board of Education, *JBOE,* vol. 2 (1934), 1419.

63. Untitled clipping, *New York Sun,* 20 June 1934, CP box 122, folder 11.

64. Letter dated 20 June 1934, CP box 4, folder 24.

65. Tildsley to All High School Principals, June 1934, CP box 38, folder 24.

66. "200 More Teachers Shifted," *New York Sun*, 28 June 1934.

67. Covello to Harold J. Campbell, 22 October 1934, CP box 38, folder 10; "Teacher Transfers to Harlem HS," *JBOE* vol. 1 (1934), 1048–50, listed seventeen teacher transfers from DeWitt Clinton to Benjamin Franklin. Leah Kahnheimer, a teacher of Spanish who made her mark at Franklin, came from the High School of Commerce.

68. Leonard Covello, "Benjamin Franklin High School," typescript, 2–3, Reminiscences and Autobiographical Notes, CP box 20, folder 16.

69. Leonard Covello, "LC appraisal of his own background for tackling job of Princ[ipal] and intercultural Program he wanted to do," handwritten, 1–2, Reminiscences and Autobiographical Notes, CP folder 20, box 16.

70. "The Harlem Community Advisory Council," *Atlantica*, November 1935, 379, clipping, CP box 122, folder 11; "Meeting of Afternoon Session Teachers," 3 October 1935, CP box 34, folder 26; Benjamin Franklin High School *Almanac* [hereafter *Almanac*], 30 September 1936, CP box 131, oversize. In March 1936, the main building enrolled 1,576 boys; the Seventy-ninth Street Annex, 975; and the 117th Street Annex, 454. "Benjamin Franklin High School by Race or Nationality, Schools and Area of Residence, Spring Term 1936," CP oversize, folder 1.

71. Calculated from SOS, 37th *AR*, 1934–35, Stat. Sect., 199; 38th *AR*, 1935–36, Stat. Sect., 212; 39th *AR*, 1936–37, Stat. Sect., 236; 40th *AR*, 1937–38, Stat. Sect., 223; 41st *AR*, 1938–39, Stat. Sect., 211; 42nd *AR*, 1939–40, Stat. Sect., 216; 43rd *AR*, 1940–41, Stat. Sect., 226.

72. Calculated from data reported for March 1936 in "Analysis of Distribution of B.F.H.S. Students by Residence and Race," 1942, CP box 49, folder 14.

73. "Residences of B.F.H.S. Students (as of September 1941)," CP box 49, folder 13; "Analysis of Distribution of B.F.H.S. Students by Residence and Race." By 1943 Covello was concerned that the East Harlem proportion was declining ("Distribution of BFHS Students by Residence, February 1943," CP box 49, folder 13).

74. Untitled transcript, n.d., CP box 33, folder 7. See also Nina Cavaquaro and Virginia Bono, "Report on East Harlem," May 1939, CP box 78, folder 6.

75. Covello to Mrs. G. Robertson, 9 March 1936, CP box 44, folder 2.

76. Covello to John L. Tildsley, 11 May 1936, CP box 38, folder 24.

77. *Almanac*, 17 June 1938, CP box 131, oversize. Covello spent $430 of his own money for the purchase and repair of musical instruments. Irving Berman, Treasurer, BFHS, to Henry Smithline, 15 May 1938, CP box 31, folder 6.

78. Walter H. Wolff and Austin M. Works to All Section Officers, 18 February 1935, CP box 41, folder 2; Julius Cohen to Morris Deshel, 6 March 1936, CP box 44, folder 2; Joint Meeting of Health Education and Science Departments on Community Health Program, minutes, 3 April 1939, CP box 41, folder 9.

79. Michael Fabrizio, "Student Teaching," January 1941, CP box 36, folder 24.

80. *Almanac*, 23 November 1934, CP box 131, oversize.

81. Covello, "Neighborhood Growth through the School," 130. Students in the Art Department painted nine murals in the school auditorium, each depicting a great event in U.S. history, together forming a "continuous illustration to show the growth of American Democracy" (untitled, n.d., CP box 35, folder 15; *Almanac*, 16 June 1939, CP box 122, folder 13).

82. Gerald Grant, *The World We Created at Hamilton High* (Cambridge, Mass.: Harvard University Press, 1988), chap. 7.

83. Richard Bauman, BFHS, valedictory address, 2 February 1942, CP box 36, folder 18. Franklin graduated its first senior class in May 1936.

84. Covello, "Neighborhood Growth through the School," 128

85. Ibid.

86. New York City Mayor's Committee on City Planning, partial report on Project No. 165–97–6037, conducted under the auspices of the Works Progress Administration.

87. Materials in CP box 18, folder 3.

88. Covello, "Neighborhood Growth through the School," 133.

89. Covello, "High School and Immigrant Community," 337.

90. Several projects kindred in spirit to Franklin's community advisory council (CAC) appeared in and around the New York area. Harry Wann, principal of the high school in Madison, New Jersey, sought to move beyond narrow "institutional-mindedness" toward a communitywide coordination of educative factors. Based upon the belief that "every waking hour is part of education," the local social planning council conducted surveys of local educational influences and developed programs in order to "so integrate the various educative factors in the environment that the community will become an educative unity." Harry A. Wann, "Educational Leadership as Social Engineering" (Ed.D. diss., Teachers College, Columbia University, 1935), 97, iii–iv. The Community Service Council of Hastings-on-Hudson, New York, teamed up with the public schools to integrate efforts for community growth and organization. Starting with a social survey of the community, the council addressed local concerns from "worth-while forms of leisure-time activities" to housing and public relief, all in an effort to promote "a greater community consciousness and an effective program of community planning and improvement." Herman R. Otness, "The School and the Hastings Community Service Council," *Journal of Educational Sociology* 9, no. 6 (1936): 347–53. Across town from Benjamin Franklin, in the blocks just north of Teachers College, Columbia University, the Community Association for Cooperative Education (CACE), with the assistance of students and faculty of Teachers College's New College, sought to "promote such group activities as will teach its members how to work and live effectively together and to provide educational, recreational and material services on a non-profit basis." Though CACE did not operate through a regular public school, it did seek to construct a "community curriculum" that was rooted in the lives of community members and their environment; CACE carried out extensive studies of the educational, housing, and social needs of the Manhattanville neighborhood, provided a weekly "Open Night" forum for discussing residents' concerns, and operated both a local nursery school and a community farm in upstate New York. Wanda Sweida, "Cooperative Education through a Community Association: How It Functioned in a Metropolitan Area," *Progressive Education* 16, no. 7 (1939): 488–95. The principal of P.S. 81 in Brooklyn, Nathan Peyser, doubled as the executive director of the Flatbush Community League, a community supervisory and coordinating body composed of the Teachers' League, Mother's League, Men's League, and Junior Service League. With a membership of some 1,200 adults, the Flatbush Community League supported twenty-three adult classes, a local symphony orchestra, the Community Little Theater, the Civic Forum, and innovations within the day-school program. Concerned fundamentally with the prevention of juvenile delinquency since his school-community efforts twenty years earlier in East Harlem, Peyser viewed the school as the most appropriate "integrating agency" of the community, "whereby the family and community can be led to assume their responsibilities cooperatively." Nathan Peyser, "The School as the Center of the Community," *Journal of Educational Sociology* 9, no. 6 (1936): 354–58. Covello included Peyser's plan in the manuscript he was preparing on community schooling; see "Peyser Plan of Character Building and Delinquency Prevention," *CCS*, chap. 18, "Delinquency," CP box 20, folder 1. Similar efforts were under way in neighboring South Jamaica, New York City, through J.H.S. 40's principal Samuel Levenson and the South Jamaica Community League. Samuel M. Levenson, "The South Jamaica Community League," *Journal of Educational Sociology* 9, no. 6 (1936): 359–63.

91. The CP folder containing material for the course included, for example, a National Probation Association flyer entitled "Selected Reading: From Probation Officers and Others

Interested in Delinquency, 1937," and a copy of the April 1936 issue of *Coordinating Council Bulletin,* CP box 25, folder 1.

92. "Social Problems of Community Will Be Conference Theme," *Education Sun,* School of Education, New York University, New York, 31 March 1937, 1, CP box 122, folder 12.

93. Memo from Emilio L. Guerra to Leonard Covello, 13 February 1940, re: "Books Dealing with Community Coordination," including two by the National Probation Association, CP box 25, folder 10.

94. Frederic M. Thrasher and Julius Yourman, *Recent Experiments in Community Coordination* (New York: Prentice-Hall, 1937).

95. Frederic M. Thrasher, "Crime Prevention through Community Organization," *University of Chicago Magazine,* March 1935, 176.

96. Covello, "High School and Immigrant Community," 340. It should be noted that Covello, while concurring in the need to address maladjustments, warned against too great an emphasis on a community's pathological aspects. Leonard Covello, "The School as the Center of Community Life in an Immigrant Area," in *The Community School,* ed. Samuel Everett (New York: D. Appleton-Century, 1938), 137–42.

97. Glueck, *Community Use of Schools,* xi. Like Thrasher, Glueck studied with Chicago sociologists Park and Burgess.

98. Ibid. Covello expressed the same argument in "Neighborhood Growth through the School," 128.

99. Moses to Covello, 22 November 1935, CP box 41, folder 5.

100. Harold Fields to Covello, 31 October 1935, CP box 39, folder 1.

101. 102. Ibid.; Covello, "High School and Immigrant Community." For the early membership role, see "List of Acceptances to Membership of the Community Advisory Council of the Benjamin Franklin High School," 22 October 1935, CP box 39, folder 1.

102. The Covello Papers give no indication that a democratic process evolved in determining committee leadership roles; teachers chaired the committees in the 1930s and 1940s, and the issue of community control of the CAC was not raised. For the faculty's role, see "Committee Reorganization," 28 October 1937, CP box 40, folder 10.

103. "Mayor Endorses Advisory Body," *World-Telegram,* 15 October 1935.

104. "School Plan Helps Entire Community," *New York Times,* 6 June 1937. The twenty-two committees were: Parents Association, Adult Education, Juvenile Aid, Guidance, Good Form, Assembly, Decoration, Old Friendship, Teaching Rating, Senior Class, Scholarship, Faculty Conference, Big Brother, Racial, Housing, Community Health, Citizenship, Speakers, Peace, Service League, Student Aid, Film-Radio. Racial, Housing, Health, Citizenship, and Speakers were designated "community committees"; the others were called "school committees."

105. For reorganization of the committees in the fall of 1937, see documents in CP box 19, folder 1; box 40, folder 10; box 58, folder 1. The Juvenile Aid Committee provided special attention to "cutters, truants, habitual latecomers, boys who are beaten by parents and who leave home, and others with whom we may come in contact, and who often ask for help and advice." Juvenile Aid Committee, minutes, 26 January 1940, CP box 41, folder 11.

106. Leonard Covello, "Leadership among Minority Groups Developed through the Secondary School Program," address to annual meeting of the National Conference on Social Work, Grand Rapids, Michigan, 27 May 1940, 36, CP box 13, folder 32.

107. The Association of Parents, Teachers, and Friends (PTF) operated in many ways as a conventional PTA, e.g., fund-raising activities for the high school's Student Aid Fund. Attendance figures from a few meetings in 1936–37 suggest a modest average turnout of between eighty and ninety people. In 1943 Covello wrote: "Our Association has not been numerically strong; but it has made up what it lacked in numbers by the fine spirit which has prevailed and the many services which it has rendered the school and the community."

Covello to PTF, 9 December 1943, CP box 44, folder 8. The "Friends" in PTF denoted representatives of the nonimmigrant community, "older American" groups, invited to the meetings because "they represent a world of social ideas that is quite remote from the people of East Harlem." Covello, Report to Committee on Practical Democracy in Education, 13 January 1942, CP box 34, folder 11.

108. *Almanac,* 1 October 1937, CP box 32, folder 5.

109. Friends and Neighbors Club calendar, CP box 45, folder 13.

110. "Use Empty Stores for School Clubs."

111. Mary Carter Winter, "The 'Friendship Garden' Idea Finds Expression in a Different Type of Gardening in New York City," n.d., CP box 45, folder 17. In 1935 Covello had used his influence with local police to have 108th and 109th streets in the high school's block designated play streets—a designation that allowed only residents or persons having business on the block to drive there. Notes dated 3 January 1935, CP box 77, folder 12.

112. Mary Carter Winter to L. E. Van Etten, 14 December 1939, CP box 45, folder 17; C. G. Van Tubergen Ltd to Mary Carter Winter, 4 October 1938, CP box 45, folder 17; George Sprague to Mary Carter Winter, 16 August 1938, CP box 45, folder 17.

113. Covello, open letter, 1 April 1941, CP box 45, folder 21.

114. "Among the Italians in East Harlem," [1939?], CP box 44, folder 18. The "block beautiful" campaign had little impact beyond the immediate neighborhood around the high school. The "mothers of East 114th Street" wrote Covello complaining of street and sidewalk conditions on East 114th Street between First and Second avenues: "It seems that lately, there is a child run down by a motor vehicle on our street nearly every day. We find that it is due to the fact that the sidewalks are cluttered up with peddlars [*sic*] pushcarts, and the children have no place to play but in the streets. In most cases the drivers could avoid hitting anyone by swerving to the other side of the street, but this is impossible because they are blocked by the pushcarts. Not only are these pushcarts causing accidents but they are also very unsanitary. The streets are full of flies and insects, and at night when they leave, there are about 30 ashcans on the sidewalks full of garbage. Now that school is over, we really dread having the children around in such a filthy street and most of us cannot afford sending them away" (Mothers of East 114th Street to Covello, 30 June 1941, CP box 44, folder 13).

115. "Use Empty Stores for School Clubs." The main school building, as well as agency buildings in East Harlem, was also being used for various functions. For example, EHCSA held its annual meeting at BFHS in 1937 (Covello and Harold Fields served on the executive board). That year faculty conferences were held at Union Settlement and the East Harlem Health Center. "Community Advisory Council Report," June 1937, CP box 39, folder 2.

116. Letter dated 17 November 1936, in "An Experiment at the BFHS: The Old Friendship Club," 34, CP box 45, folder 20.

117. "Old Friendship Club Committee," [1937], CP box 45, folder 20.

118. Alumni Association file, CP box 44, folder 17; Covello, "Leadership among Minority Groups." The Alumni Association re-formed on 23 November 1945, at a meeting cochaired by Covello and Michael Decessare.

119. Leonard Covello, "The School as the Good Neighbor" (speech delivered to American Booksellers Convention, New York City, 12 May 1940), CP box 13, folder 20; "Friends and Neighbors Library," 30 April 1940; "Benjamin Franklin High School," 1939, CP box 38, folder 19.

120. Quoted in Peebles, *Leonard Covello,* 240.

121. For example, the Hispano-American Educational Bureau offered a course, "English for Hispanics," every Thursday evening in Room 224 at the main building, 309 East 108th Street, beginning 6 February 1941, open only to native Spanish speakers (press release, CP box 45, folder 18).

122. Certificate of Incorporation of East Harlem Educational and Research Bureau, 17 December 1940, CP box 45, folder 3; "East Harlem Educational and Research Bureau," 5 February 1941, CP box 45, folder 5. Francesco Cordasco, in "Leonard Covello and the Casa Italiana Educational Bureau," in Cordasco, ed., *Studies in Italian American Social History: Essays in Honor of Leonard Covello* (Totowa, N.J.: Rowman and Littlefield, 1975), relates that Covello continued the financially strapped EHERB from 1942 to 1944, at which time he finally disbanded the bureau. A letter from National City Realty to Covello, dated 16 March 1942, however, indicates that Covello terminated his lease with the bank effective 31 March 1942 (CP box 45, folder 17). The funding problems that had plagued Covello at Casa Italiana followed him into East Harlem. He sadly noted the failure of his fellow Italians to provide material support for his programs: "The Italian communities, I regret to say, never understood educational programs of this character. Their allegiance and their interest and involvement were with the political leaders and such things as educational research and educational programs even for the propaganda for the Italian language never had any financial support" (Cordasco, "Leonard Covello and Casa Italiana," 7).

123. Covello, *Heart Is Teacher*, 232–34; in CP box 43, folder 1: Covello, memorandum, 28 November 1939; Covello, open letter, [1939?]; "Announcing East Harlem News," [1939?]; Covello to *Bronx Home News*, 6 March 1942.

124. In New York City work relief and not public works received the primary emphasis. Originally headed by General Hugh S. Johnson, the NYC WPA started on a shaky footing on 1 August 1935. Hours of labor were fixed at 120 per month. The city's WPA employment reached a high on 19 February 1936 at 248,474. John D. Millett, *The Works Progress Administration in New York City* (Chicago: Public Administration Service, 1938); see also Thomas Kessner, *Fiorello H. La Guardia and the Making of Modern New York* (New York: McGraw-Hill, 1989), 336–42.

125. "Complete List of Names of All Workers Assigned by Works Progress Administration to the Benjamin Franklin High School and Annexes," 1938, CP box 47, folder 4. Board of education projects that drew on WPA funds included, among other categories, adult education and school community centers (a total of 114 citywide). By June 1938, 14,500 workers were employed on WPA education projects sponsored by the board; approximately 70 percent of them held jobs "of a professional or technical character, performing in the main direct teaching service." SOS, *All the Children*, 40th AR, 1937–38, 58ff.

126. Untitled report of research enterprises of Benjamin Franklin High School, [1942?], CP box 45, folder 13. Frederic M. Thrasher of New York University directed the motion-picture and leisure-time studies. The former entailed a questionnaire submitted to some eight hundred students; the latter included data from 620 student diaries covering a full week in February 1936 (untitled, n.d., CP box 117, folder 16). From the perspective of the adult researchers, the motion-picture survey yielded a disquieting result: Students ranked James Cagney as their favorite movie star; George Raft and Mae West ranked high as well. "We had our work cut out for us," Thrasher confided to a colleague. "Course in Motion Picture Appreciation," August 1936, CP box 49, folder 4; "Motion Picture Study," 1936, CP box 48, folder 37. The survey of dropouts and graduates is illustrative: "This survey has employed the services of about 16 [WPA] counselors in the field and 4 at the school. It has been carried forward by the use of a questionnaire in interviews at the school and in calls at the home of both parents and boys. From July 1st through August 13, 2,748 calls were made and 852 contacts. The low percentage of contacts is due to the fact that the nature of the study demanded separate calls on boys and parents, and so several recalls were frequently made in order to complete one questionnaire." The purpose of the study was "to discover, through a study of drop-outs and recent graduates, if the school is failing and if so, in what specific ways it is failing to meeting the needs of the people in this community." "Project 6155: Objectives of the Summer Program," 13 August 1937, 2–3, CP box 42, folder 1.

127. Covello, "Neighborhood Growth through the School," 136.

128. Covello, CAC reports, March–June 1938: "The Recreation Center," CP box 39, folder 15; Covello, open letter, 21 June 1938, CP box 39, folder 3; "Leadership among Minority Groups," 6; Arthur Schroeder to Covello, 3 November 1939, CP box 47, folder 1. Youth clubs made occasional use of Franklin's facilities. "Cellar social clubs" were a Depression-era phenomenon in New York City, distrusted by the police as alleged breeding grounds for vice and targeted by WPA youth workers for educational programs. See "Adult Education Finds New Outlet," *New York Times,* 21 February 1937; "300 Cellar Clubs Face Extinction," *New York American,* 8 March 1937.

129. Elizabeth Roby, memorandum, "Report on Circular 50, High School Division," 8 December 1938, CP box 47, folder 14.

130. "New Technics in Reading," *New York Sun,* 23 February 1937; Roby, "Report on Circular 50"; "Report of Remedial Instruction Unit in Reading for Term Ending January 31, 1938," CP box 35, folder 23. Covello cited "a remarkable improvement in the reading age levels of pupils assigned to remedial reading teachers. I am sure that without the opportunity for individual attention furnished to poor readers by this project many students who have acquired a reasonable degree of reading skill and improved reading would still be badly retarded in this important phase of school work." Covello to Brehm Somervell, WPA, 14 April 1939, CP box 47, folder 11.

131. Covello to Morris E. Siegal, WPA, 11 August 1937, box 42, folder 4. Mary Carter Winter, "Report of Summer Session, Adult School," 9 August 1937, CP box 42, folder 1; "Adult Education Program: Comparative Statistics on Adult Classes," [1940?], CP box 47, folder 11. Mary Carter Winter, "Final Report for Fall Term, Ending January 1939," CP box 45, folder 11. Winter had previously served as the WPA borough coordinator for Brooklyn's WPA adult education program. Before she took the reins (her title was assistant project supervisor), Franklin's WPA adult school, in Covello's words, "was practically non-existent because of ineffective management." Covello, open letter, August 1940, CP box 7, folder 10.

132. Abraham Cohen to Covello, 14 October 1937, CP box 42, folder 1. A less sanguine report appeared in 1939. The Franklin summer-school principal, Daniel F. Fitzpatrick, reported an enrollment of 1,121 (nine courses, thirty-one classes), but an average daily attendance of only 341. Fitzpatrick complained that the WPA adult school was not adequately serving the East Harlem community. He also indicated that the community did not have a say in what was being offered. "Report on the Summer Session of the Adult School at Benjamin Franklin High School," 5 July–18 August 1939, CP box 46, folder 3.

133. Covello, "Neighborhood Growth through the School,"136.

134. SOS, *All the Children,* 40th AR, 1937–38, excerpts in CP box 47, folder 4.

135. See Selma C. Berrol, "From Compensatory Education to Adult Education: The New York City Evening Schools, 1825–1935," *Adult Education* 26, no. 4 (1976): 108–225.

136. Abraham Cohen (WPA Adult Education Program), "Helping the Unlearned Men and Women of New York City: A Civics Project in Community Service Prepared for the Teachers and Pupils of the Benjamin Franklin High School," 15 February 1937, CP box 42, folder 1.

137. 137. Number of classes reported in Arthur Schroeder to Covello, 20 October 1939, CP box 47, folder 2. (Schroeder was "managing project supervisor" of WPA personnel at Franklin.) Mary Carter explained the WPA's side of the evening elementary school controversy in a lengthy memorandum, 31 October 1938, deposited in CP box 42, folder 6. Winter was frequently at loggerheads with BOE personnel. Faculty antipathies extended to the day-school WPA employees as well. For example, Abraham Kroll, Covello's administrative assistant, denigrated some of the WPA remedial teachers as "lazy workers." Kroll to Covello, 3 April 1939, CP box 47, folder 15. Covello clearly sympathized with the underpaid WPA teachers; as he told the Russell Sage Foundation: "It is to be regretted that these men and

women have been deprived of both the prestige and the fair remuneration to which they are entitled. Drawing a salary far below the salaries earned by others engaged in similar activities, they have not measured either the quality or extent of their services by the meagreness of their compensation. They deserve—and should receive—equal status with other teachers in the city system and fair compensation for professional work in the school and elsewhere. In emphasizing these points, I am quite mindful of the fact that not every person holding a WPA job has merited the full esteem that goes to those who have won the unqualified respect of their associates by the manner in which they have discharged their responsibilities under unusually difficult conditions. . . . The point of importance is that a noticeably large percentage of the men and women on the W.P.A. have made a real contribution to the educational activities of the city of New York." "How the WPA Education Project Helps the Community," WPA Conference, Russell Sage Foundation, 4 June 1938, 3, CP box 11, folder 10.

138. Covello to Gustav A. Stumpff, 28 September 1938, CP box 42, folder 1.

139. "Groups Formed at High School," *New York American*, 26 May 1938.

140. Covello to Stumpff.

141. Arthur Schroeder to Covello, 30 November 1939, CP box 47, folder 3.

142. Leonard Covello, "The Community-Centered School," CP box 18, folder 15.

143. According to a report from 1946, the evening high school, which catered largely to returning GIs, taught all high school subjects. Covello to Boris Tamler, Guldman Community Center, 18 November 1946, CP box 35, folder 10.

144. "New School: Co-Education," 25 March 1938, 1, CP box 10, folder 38.

145. In 1936–37, the superintendent of schools listed seven all-male high schools, among them BFHS and DeWitt Clinton, and six all-female high schools. SOS, 39th *AR*, 1936–37, Stat. Sect., 236, table 140.

146. A satisfactory description of the organization and specific content of Franklin's pre–World War II curriculum is not available in CP. "Benjamin Franklin High School Scholarship Report, Term Ending—June 30, 1936," CP box 18, folder 14, provides some illumination. Other statements are cursory, such as Leonard Covello, "The Benjamin Franklin High School—A Community High School," 2 February 1935, 4, CP box 9, folder 16; Leonard Covello, "The School as the Good Neighbor," presentation at American Booksellers Convention, New York City, 12 May 1940, 3, CP box 13, folder 20. The clearest statement of what Covello envisioned as a community school curriculum at Franklin is "Special Features of the New Building," [1941?], CP box 38, folder 2.

147. Covello, *Heart Is Teacher*, 203. As reported in 1940, for a diploma certified by the New York State Board of Regents, all students had to pass statewide tests in English and in U.S. history. SOS, *All the Children*, 42nd *AR*, 1939–40, 36.

148. "Scholarship Report." We cannot explain a discrepancy in the total registration count in this scholarship report (16,863) and the total count reported by the superintendent of schools (20,536), in SOS, 38th *AR*, Stat. Sect., 229, table 153. SOS, *All the Children*, 42nd *AR*, 1939–40, provides further insight into the academic content of the BFHS curriculum: "All candidates for a high school diploma in New York City must have four years of English, a year of American History, one-half year of Community Civics and Economics, a year of General Science, and Health Education throughout their four years" (36). The superintendent of schools recommended ability grouping in these nine "basic constants." Nine electives were taken according to "differences in interests and needs," for example, in foreign languages, science, commercial subjects, industrial arts, music, and fine arts. Franklin's course of study was 8 terms.

149. "Analysis of Graduates from June 1936 to June 1939," CP box 48, folder 18.

150. "Report of Leonard Covello, Principal of Benjamin Franklin High School, for 'All Our Children,'" 1937, CP box 47, folder 17.

151. Benjamin Franklin High School Yearbook Collection, Manhattan Center for Science and Mathematics (formerly BFHS). For most of the Covello era two yearbooks were

produced each year, one for January and one for June graduates. Our count includes only those years (a total of thirteen) for which both yearbooks are available or for which a full-year composite volume is available.

152. Franklin's attendance rate was 85.57, compared to the city mean of 88.94, SD=2.40 (SOS, 40th *AR*, 1937-38, Stat. Sect., 223, table 147), calculated from "percent of attendance" total per high school. Franklin's percentage of courses failed was 17.4, compared to the citywide rate of 10.7. (ibid., 229, table 152, "summary of passing ratings received by pupils in all subjects"); see also and cf. 230, fig. 30 ("percent of failures in all subjects").

153. SOS, 43rd *AR*, 1940–41, Stat. Sect., 233, table 150 ("summary of passing ratings received by pupils in all subjects"); 234, fig. 20 ("percent of failures in all school subjects"). Franklin's percentage of course failures for the spring term was 24.9, compared to the citywide rate of 10.4; its percentage of course failures for the school year was 22.3, compared to the citywide rate of 10.5. The superintendent of schools reported: "That as many as 20% to 25% of pupil subject ratings in some schools are failure ratings is cause for much concern" (232).

154. "Sectional Report on Analysis of Replies, Survey of Graduates and Drop-outs, Summer of 1937," attached summary, fall 1937, CP box 19, folder 8. Science chair Walter H. Wolff estimated that that "fifty percent [of the whole school] at most are not interested in the subjects or our course of study or not competent to master them." Letter to Covello, 10 May 1935, CP box 35, folder 27.

155. "Sectional Report."

156. Ibid., attached summary.

157. Leonard Covello, *Social Background of the Italo-American School Child: A Study of the Southern Italian Family Mores and Their Effect on the School Situation in Italy and America* (Leiden, Netherlands: E. J. Brill, 1967), 285.

158. Ibid., 286.

159. A curriculum report from the mid-1940s supports this conclusion, noting that over the previous decade "the fundamental task of curriculum reconstruction, involving not merely department revision but a cooperative job on the part of every department, cutting across department lines—that is an integrated plan and program in terms of the desires and needs, capacities and level of achievement of our students and our community—had not been undertaken." "Tentative Plan for Curriculum Reconstruction in Terms of School and Community," ms fragment, 19, [1947?], CP box 49, folder 5. A case in point was the Social Studies Department, which, as Covello told an audience at the University of Pennsylvania, followed the "usual Senior High School" curriculum. "How Social Studies Are Made to Function in the Benjamin Franklin High School at Its Community, East Harlem, New York City," 23 March 1939, CP box 12, folder 9. A student teacher's diary from the late 1940s provides shards of information about didactic classroom practice—for example, a social studies class on the Monroe Doctrine, in which "the teacher wandered from one topic to the other"; an English class on the poem "The Highwayman," in which the teacher had the students copy stanzas from the board into their notebooks ("Why the poem wasn't mimeographed for them is something of a mystery"). Robert C. Ten Eyck, "Daily Diary," 1948, CP box 36, folder 24.

160. Cohen, *Progressives and Urban School Reform*, 161–64; John Loftus, "New York City's Large-Scale Experimentation with an Activity Program: A Metropolitan School System Takes Stock," *Progressive Education* 17, no. 2 (1940): 116–24; Larry Cuban, *How Teachers Taught: Constancy and Change in American Classrooms, 1880–1990*, 2d. ed. (New York: Teachers College Press, 1993), 64–71

161. Cuban, *How Teachers Taught*, 71–75; for details of Cuban's methods, see his appendix, 291–93.

162. *Almanac*, 26 March 1936, CP box 131, oversize.

163. *Almanac,* 30 September 1936, CP box 131, oversize.

164. *Almanac,* 31 March 1938, CP box 131, oversize. In 1936 Franklin fielded a baseball team, which was disbanded when students refused to contribute $100 to suit up the team and pay the umpires. *Almanac,* 30 April 1936, CP box 131, oversize.

165. For discussion of General Organizations and citizenship training in New York City high schools, see Chase, *New York at School,* 65–69; for Arista, see Fass, *Outside In,* chap. 3.

166. "Around the Clock at Benjamin Franklin High School, [1938?], CP box 32, folder 1; "Club Directory," February 1941, CP box 35, folder 32; "Report of Leonard Covello."

167. "Leadership among Minority Groups, " 29–30.

168. "English 8B: American History and Social Problems in the Light of American Literature," [1938?]., 1, CP box 52, folder 2.

169. Covello played a leading role in two projects that included Kilpatrick as a major actor. Samuel Everett and his community school advisory board, which included Covello, enlisted Kilpatrick to write the introduction to the 1938 manifesto *The Community School,* which showcased one of Covello's best essays. And Kilpatrick served as a panelist and session leader at the 1942 Greater New York Conference on Racial and Cultural Relations, hosted by BFHS.

170. Kliebard, *Struggle for American Curriculum,"* 148, 169; Kilpatrick, introduction to Hanna et al., *Youth Serves the Community,* 20; see also William Heard Kilpatrick, ed., *The Educational Frontier* (New York: Appleton-Century, 1933).

171. Lists in CP box 58, folder 1. A number of the committees had exclusively school functions and probably did not involve community members, e.g., Lunchroom, Scholarship, and Assembly. Covello wrote of student participation in CAC committee work: "Responsibility for specific phases of the work is as a rule placed on individual student-committeemen or groups under their leadership." Report to Committee on Practical Democracy in Education, 13 January 1942, 17, CP box 34, folder 11.

172. "Student Participation in Community Activities," [1937?], 2, CP box 58, folder 1.

173. For example, "Democracy and Tolerance Program at Benjamin Franklin High School," spring 1939, CP box 34, folder 10.

174. Elmer Glaser to Covello, 30 January 1943, CP box 4, folder 17.

175. Albert Brewer, Elmer Glaser, and Paul Bilka to Covello, [1936?], CP box 4, folder 17.

176. Domenick A. Colangelo to Robert Peebles, 31 March 1965, CP box 6, folder 7.

177. "Report of Placement Counseling Activities in Benjamin Franklin High School," September 1937–June 1938, CP box 39, folder 15.

178. Covello, open letter to faculty, Benjamin Franklin High School, 21 October 1935, CP box 34, folder 26.

179. Student Aid Committee, CAC Report, June 1937, CP box 39, folder 4; Report of Social Welfare Office, 31 January 1939, CP box 47, folder 6.

180. I. I. Gredin to Robert Peebles, 19 September 1966, CP box 6, folder 7.

181. Report of Social Welfare Office; Mr. Heller to Covello, 9 May 1941, CP box 49, folder 1; quote from "Statement of Reasons Why the National Youth Administration Should Cooperate in Working Out the Experimental Program in School-Community Education at the Benjamin Franklin High School," 31 October 1939, 3, CP box 57, folder 16. Wadleigh High School had the city's largest program, with 593 students and a budget of $23,400. Superintendent Harold G. Campbell, who considered the NYA programs a boondoggle for students (in his words, "financial manna from heaven") appointed Covello to chair a special committee of secondary principals to "assure attention to details, habits of work, and the observance of all the requirements that would confront these young people in actual jobs." "Three Uptown Educators Named to Help Coordinate Work of City Students and NYA,"

Bronx Home News, 30 September 1940. National NYA director Aubrey Williams appointed Covello to the New York City and Long Island State Advisory Committee of NYA, 1941–42. Williams to Covello, 19 September 1941, CP box 57, folder 18.

182. WNYC broadcast, 29 January 1938, 3, CP box 10, folder 33; perhaps the most succinct statement of Covello's educational philosophy.

183. Leonard Covello, "The Community and Educational Needs," *CCS,* chap. 1 (corrected typescript), 19–20, CP box 18, folder 8.

184. Iris Marion Young, "The Ideal of Community and the Politics of Difference," *Social Theory and Practice* 12, no. 1 (Spring 1986): 1–26. Carol Merz and Gail C. Fuhrman, *Community and Schools: Promise and Paradox* (New York: Teachers College Press, 1997), 27, called our attention to this article.

185. Covello, "School as Center of Community Life," 126–27.

186. Covello, "The Community and Educational Needs," 2.

187. Ibid., 24–25.

188. Covello, *Italo-American School Child,* 413.

189. Leonard Covello, "The Development of the Community-Centered School Idea," *Understanding the Child* 11, no. 3 (1942): 5.

190. Covello, "The Community and Educational Needs," 3–8, 12.

191. Covello recalled that his interest in Lincoln began early, when he read a life of Lincoln given to him by Miss Quigley, a teacher at P.S. 83, as an award for getting the highest grade average. Leonard Covello, "LC appraisal of his own background for tackling job of Prin[cipal] and intercultural Program he wanted to do," 16, CP box 20, folder 16.

192. Covello, The Community and Educational Needs, 12.

193. Covello, *Italo-American School Child,* 414. The key principles of community-centered schooling are derived from statements of the founding principal of BFHS, as well as from the writings of others involved in the school during this period. See especially Covello, ibid., chap. 12.

194. Covello, report to Committee on Practical Democracy in Education, 13 January 1942, 10, CP box 34, folder 11.

195. Covello, "Neighborhood Growth through the School," 128.

196. Michael Lombardo, Joseph Bayza, and Leonard Kramm, "Franklin High Is Community Centered," *Junior Red Cross Journal,* October 1939, 54.

197. June 1938, CP box 36, folder 18. Covello articulated the pedagogical principle as follows: "The best method of encouraging initiative and of developing a proper sense of responsibility is to require decisions and actions based on definite problems and conditions. The power for critical judgment, self-discipline and intelligent action develops only through practice." Quoted in "School Restores Neighborliness to Congested Harlem District," *Herald Tribune,* 9 March 1941. Elsewhere he wrote: "Training for citizenship, achieving social competence must come—can only come—through actual service. . . . Knowledge must be used to create a fuller and better life for all people. The community—where men live and work and struggle—is basically the great teacher and the school must realize its educational aims and civic programs through active participation in the life of the community." "Leonard Covello Testimonial," *The Renewal [Il Rinnovamento]: A Magazine of Christian Thought and Ethics,* September–October 1960, 1–2.

198. Syllabus for "Course No. 425: In-Service Teacher Training Program of the Board of Superintendents: The Principal and His Community," 14 December 1943, quotes from 1, CP box 59, folder 14; quote from Covello, report to Committee on Practical Democracy, 18.

199. Kate Rousmaniere, *City Teachers: Teaching and School Reform in Historical Perspective* (New York: Teachers College Press, 1997), chaps. 2–3; see also Gerald Grant and Christine E. Murray, *Teaching in America: The Slow Revolution* (Cambridge, Mass.: Harvard University Press, 1999), 91–92.

200. Markowitz, *My Daughter, the Teacher,* chaps. 6–7, quotes from 106 and chap. 7, title.

201. SOS, *First Fifty Years,* 115.

202. Reported in SOS, *AR,* Stat. Sect., volumes for 1930s; see, for example, 37th *AR,* 1934–35, Stat. Sect., table 213, p. 306.

203. Graves, *Report,* 36; SOS, 35th *AR,* 1932–33, Stat. Sect., 709; see also Markowitz, *My Daughter, the Teacher,* 106–8.

204. Authors such as Selma Berrol, Sol Cohen, and Diane Ravitch cited in Markowitz, *My Daughter, the Teacher,* 114.

205. Markowitz, *My Daughter, the Teacher,* 2; chap. 3, with quote from pp. 51–52; chap. 6.

206. Teacher transfers to "Harlem HS," *JBOE,* vol. 1 (1934), 1048–50.

207. In the spring semester of 1937, Covello and nine Franklin teachers gave speeches to nineteen organizations and 1,644 people ("Community Advisory Council Report," June 1937, CP box 39, folder 14).

208. Covello, "A Glance Backward and a Look Ahead," 6, 12, September 1939, CP box 12, folder 35. In a speech to the Kindergarten–6B Teacher Association, Roundtable Conferences, New York City, 19 February 1938, Covello remarked: "The teacher has a definite obligation to the community. Despite [the] recognized fact that the teacher carries a heavy burden of school work, this obligation must be met," 1, CP box 10, folder 35.

CHAPTER 5: COMMUNITY SCHOOLING FOR CULTURAL DEMOCRACY

1. Edward Corsi, "My Neighborhood," *The Outlook,* 16 September 1925, 90–92, quoted in Margaret Campbell Tilley, "The Boy Scout Movement in East Harlem" (Ph.D. diss, New York University, 1935), 32.

2. Leonard Covello, "Inter-Racial Harmony through Co-Operative Leadership," special meeting, Intercultural Education Committee, Friends and Neighbors Club, 17 February, 1939, Leonard Covello Papers (MSS 40) [hereafter CP], Balch Institute Collections, Historical Society of Pennsylvania, Philadelphia, box 51, folder 19.

3. Leonard Covello, "LC appraisal of his own background for Tackling Job of Princ[ipal] and intercultural Program he wanted to Do," typescript, Reminiscences and Autobiographical Notes, 12, CP box 20, folder 16.

4. Leonard Covello, "Benjamin Franklin High School," typescript, 2, CP box 20, folder 16.

5. Louis Relin, "We Hold These Truths," n.d., report on intercultural education experience in English course, fall 1938, 1, CP box 51, folder 13.

6. Lawrence A. Cremin, *American Education: The Metropolitan Experience, 1876–1980* (New York: Harper and Row, 1988), 190.

7. Leonard Covello, "Making Education Real," guest editorial, *Yorkville Advance,* 4 December 1936; "Franklin's Faculty to Meet Welfare Worker," *New York Sun,* 23 October 1936. Other speakers invited for faculty conferences that year included Helen Harris, head worker of Union Settlement, "The Settlement's Approach to Education"; Fannie Hurst, author, "Literature in the American Scene"; and Stuart Chase, economist, "Economics in the Present Era."

8. Leonard Covello, "In-service Course—East Harlem; The Teacher in Relation to His Community," CP box 25, folder 10.

9. George Counts, *Dare the School Build a New Social Order?* (New York: John Day, 1932), from excerpt in *American Education in the Twentieth Century: A Documentary History,* ed. Marvin Lazerson (New York: Teachers College Press, 1987), 51. Years later, Covello recalled this work of Counts in describing the era in which Benjamin Franklin was organized. See "Remarks of Dr. Leonard Covello upon Acceptance of the Meritorious

Service Medal of the Department of the State of New York," 14 December 1966, CP box 6, folder 8.

10. Ellen Condliffe Lagemann, "Prophecy or Profession? George S. Counts and the Social Study of Education," *American Journal of Education* 100, no. 2 (1992): 137–65; Daniel Perlstein, "'There is no Escape . . . from the Ogre of Indoctrination': George Counts and the Civic Dilemmas of Democratic Educators," in *Reconstructing the Common Good in Education: Coping with Intractable American Dilemmas,* ed. Larry Cuban and Dorothy Shipps (Stanford, Calif.: Stanford University Press, 2000), 51–67.

11. Leonard Covello, "Teacher Responsibility to the Community," notes for roundtable discussion, kindergarten 6-B, Teachers Association, New York City, 19 February 1938, 3, CP box 10, folder 35.

12. See Robert Shaffer, "Multicultural Education during World War II: A Look at the New York City Public Schools," paper presented at the History of Education Society, Chicago, 23 October 1993.

13. Abraham F. Citron, Collins J. Reynolds, and Sarah W. Taylor, "Ten Years of Intercultural Education in Educational Magazines," *Harvard Educational Review* 15, no. 2 (1945): 129–33.

14. Ibid., 130. Sociology and social research were the largest single contributors. Background articles occurred frequently between 1934 and 1936, with a sharp decline in 1941; exhortatory articles began to appear in the late thirties, increased rapidly until 1941 and then dropped off until 1944. The lowest year overall, 1935, was the highest in terms of articles on methods and materials. The highest year overall was 1940.

15. Citron, Reynolds, and Taylor, "Ten Years of Intercultural Education," 130.

16. Milton M. Gordon, "Assimilation in America: Theory and Reality," *Daedalus* 90, no. 2 (1961): 263–85. It is worth noting how Gordon's typology and other conceptual models of immigrant encounters with American culture in the first half of the twentieth century compare with the work of contemporary anthropologists who are interested in processes of cultural formation among immigrant ethnic minorities of the post–Cold War era and "the types of cultural complexity generated by processes of globalization and local responses to such forces." Kathleen Hall, "Understanding Educational Processes in an Era of Globalization: The View from Anthropology and Cultural Studies," in *Issues in Education Research: Problems and Possibilities,* ed. Ellen Condliffe Lagemann and Lee S. Shulman (San Francisco: Jossey-Bass, 1999), 123. Hall's work is illustrative. In her ongoing study of British Sikhs since the mid-1980s, Hall finds that "young British-Sikhs encounter . . . two contrasting ideologies, two dominant ideas or conceptions of the social world; the first I will refer to as the ideology of family honor, and the second, the ideology of British nationalism or British cultural purity." Kathleen Hall, "'There's a Time to Act English and a Time to Act Indian': The Politics of Identity among British-Sikh Teenagers," in *Children and the Politics of Culture,* ed. Sharon Stephens (Princeton, N.J.: Princeton University Press, 1995), 248. These ideologies that British Sikh youth experience in their daily interactions, among other factors, position them "between two cultures" or, in Hall's phrase, "a cultural 'third space.'" Kathleen Hall, "British Sikh Lives, Lived in Translation," in *Everyday Life in South Asia,* ed. Diane P. Mines and Sarah Lamb (Bloomington: University of Indiana Press, 2002). Older conceptual models such as Gordon's, "the product of another historical moment," are no longer adequate to explain the cultural complexity of the era of globalization. Scholars of the "new immigration" are rethinking such processes as "assimilation" and "acculturation" through the use of new analytical tools ("hybridity," "migratory formations," "multiple cultural codes," for example). Marcelo M. Suárez-Orozco, "Globalization, Immigration, and Education: The Research Agenda," *Harvard Educational Review* 71, no. 3 (2001): 345–65; Suárez-Orozco, "Everything You Ever Wanted to Know about Assimilation but Were Afraid to Ask," *Daedalus* 129, no. 4 (2000): 1–30. For an excellent sociological survey, see Alejandro Portes and Rubén

G. Rumbaut, *Immigrant America: A Portrait,* 2d. ed. (Berkeley: University of California Press, 1996), esp. chap. 7 and the authors' discussion of "segmented assimilation"; and similarly, Rumbaut and Portes, eds., *Ethnicities: Children of Immigrants in America* (Berkeley: University of California Press, 2001).

17. Gordon, "Assimilation in America." John Bodnar, in *The Transplanted: A History of Immigrants in Urban America* (Bloomington: Indiana University Press, 1985), 189–97, notes that "Americanization . . . never elicited the constant attention of educational reformers as did the concern for vocationalism," and that immigrants often effectively resisted the Americanization/secularization efforts of the public schools, in part through the Catholic school system. John Higham, in *Send These to Me* (Baltimore: Johns Hopkins University Press, 1984), 181, finds a contradictory tendency in the schools: In the Midwest and "in other parts of the country assimilation through education was vigorously supported as a national goal but severely qualified in local practice."

18. Horace M. Kallen, "Democracy versus the Melting-Pot: A Study of American Nationality," *The Nation,* 18 February 1915, 192.

19. Gordon, "Assimilation in America."

20. Quoted in ibid.

21. Horace M. Kallen, *Culture and Democracy in the United States: Studies in the Group Psychology of the American Peoples* (New York: Boni and Liveright, 1924), 118, 124.

22. Louis Menand suggests "pluralisms" as a more accurate term. Menand, *The Metaphysical Club* (New York: Farrar, Straus and Giroux, 2001), chap. 14.

23. Louis Adamic, "Thirty Million Americans," *Harper's Magazine,* 169 (November 1934): 684–94; also, Adamic, *My America, 1928–1938* (New York: n.p., 1938); *America and the Refugees,* Public Affairs Pamphlet #29 (New York: Public Affairs Committee, 1940); *From Many Lands* (New York: Harper and Brothers, 1940); *Two Way Passage,* 3rd ed. (New York: Harper and Brothers, 1941); *Plymouth Rock and Ellis Island* (New York: Common Council for American Unity, 1940).

24. Ronald K. Goodenow, "The Progressive Educator, Race, and Ethnicity in the Depression Years: An Overview," *History of Education Quarterly* 15, no. 4 (1975): 366. Alexander Urbiel, in "High School Educators and the Changing Concept of Americanism: World War I to the Great Depression" (paper presented at annual meeting of the History of Education Society, Kansas City, Mo., 24–27 October 1991), identifies a similar consensus of the late twenties and early thirties as "scientific Americanization."

25. For discussion of cultural democracy, see James A. Banks, *Educating Citizens in a Multicultural Society* (New York: Teachers College Press, 1997), 47–49.

26. Werner Stollers, in "A Critique of Pure Pluralism," in *Reconstructing American Literary History,* ed. Sacvan Bercovitch (Cambridge, Mass.: Harvard University Press, 1986), presents evidence that "Kallen's pluralist orchestra did not have any room for Afro-Americans, among others" (262). As evidence, Stollers cites Kallen's 1907 correspondence with Harvard Brahmin philosopher Barrett Wendell, in which Kallen makes explicit statements about his dislike for African Americans. Racial exclusivity was also a hallmark of the melting pot, which "historically and institutionally had no place for African Americans." Desmond King, *Making Americans: Immigration, Race, and the Origins of the Diverse Democracy* (Cambridge, Mass.: Harvard University Press, 2000), 16.

27. Covello's approach bears strong similarity to what sociologists Portes and Rumbaut, in *Immigrant America,* call "selective acculturation." Referring to immigrant groups of the late twentieth century, they write: "Selective acculturation where learning American ways combines with continuing strong bonds with the ethnic community can also be expected to lead to a positive outcome," i.e., educational achievement (250–51).

28. John Dewey to Horace Kallen, 31 March 1915, quoted in Menand, *Metaphysical Club,* 400; see also Simone Cinotto, "Leonard Covello, the Covello Papers, and the History

of Eating Habits among Italian Immigrants in New York," *Journal of American History* 91, no. 2 (2004): 506–7.

29. E. George Payne, "Education and Minority Peoples," in *One America: The History, Contributions, and Present Problems of Our Racial and National Minorities,* ed. Francis J. Brown and Joseph Slabey Roucek (New York: Prentice-Hall, 1946), 496–506.

30. See League for Fair Play, "The Springfield Plan," n.d., CP box 56, folder 17; Clarence I. Chatto, "Springfield's Experience with Intergroup Education," *Harvard Educational Review* 15, no. 2 (1945); 99–103; Benjamin Fine, "The Springfield Plan," *Menorah Journal* 32, no. 2 (1944): 161–80; promotional brochure for *The Story of the Springfield Plan* (New York: Barnes and Noble, n.d.), CP box 56, folder 17; James W. Wise, with Alexander Alland, *The Springfield Plan* (New York: Viking, 1945); Clyde R. Miller, "Springfield, Massachusetts: A Whole Community Plans," in Annette Smith Lawrence, "American Schools Face the Minority Problem," *New Era in Home and School* 25, no. 6 (1944): 117.

31. Chatto, "Springfield's Experience with Intergroup Education," 99. The National Conference of Christians and Jews suggested initiating the Springfield experiment, with Clyde Miller to test the thesis that children could learn to accept ethnic and racial differences.

32. First quote: League for Fair Play, "The Springfield Plan," n.d., CP box 56, folder 17; second quote: Chatto, "Springfield's Experience with Intergroup Education," 99.

33. Chatto, "Springfield's Experience with Intergroup Education," 100, 102.

34. Fine, "Springfield Plan," 177–79.

35. It should be noted that a fair amount of research on the school's internal aspects (grading, student progress, intelligence scores, student evaluations of the school, etc.) also took place.

36. Leonard Covello, "Research and Development of the Community School," notes for speech presented to the "Parker Program," Atlantic City, NEA conference, February 1938, CP box 10, folder 36.

37. Covello, *Italo-American School Child;* Robert Orsi, *The Madonna of 115th Street: Faith and Community in Italian Harlem, 1880–1950,* 2nd ed. (New Haven, Conn.: Yale University Press, 2002); Joel Perlmann, *Ethnic Differences: Schooling and Social Structure among the Irish, Italians, Jews, and Blacks in an American City, 1880–1935* (Cambridge: Cambridge University Press, 1988).

38. Covello, "Research and Development of the Community School."

39. Ellen Condliffe Lagemann, "The Plural Worlds of Educational Research," *History of Education Quarterly* 29, no. 2 (Summer 1989): 185–214.

40. In addition to his work through the Home Garden, Covello worked at Casa del Popolo and served on the board of Hamilton House.

41. Covello, *Italo-American School Child;* Marie Concistre, "Adult Education in a Local Area: A Study of a Decade in the Life and Education of the Adult Italian Immigrant in East Harlem" (Ph.D. diss., New York University, 1943); Salvatore Cimilluca, "The Natural History of East Harlem from 1880 to the Present Day" (M.A. thesis, New York University, 1931); Rita Morgan, "Arbitration in the Men's Clothing Industry in New York City: A Case Study of Industrial Arbitration and Conference Method with Particular Reference to Its Educational Implications" (Ph.D. diss., Teachers College, Columbia University, 1940). Morgan also served as director of the James Weldon Johnson Community Center and was president of the East Harlem Council for Community Planning.

42. Rachel Davis Dubois, with Corann Okorodudu, *All This and Something More: Pioneering in Intercultural Education: An Autobiography* (Bryn Mawr, Pa.: Dorrance, 1984), 67, 72–73, 89, 239.

43. Elsie Ripley Clapp, *Community Schools in Action* (New York: Viking, 1939); Lloyd Allen Cook, *Community Backgrounds of Education: A Textbook in Educational Sociology* (New York: McGraw-Hill, 1938). Some early community school notions in the United States

may have been inspired by Danish folk schools through the work of rural sociologists such as Joseph Hart; see James Alfred Dickinson, "The Community-School Concept in Education" (Ph.D. diss., Ohio State University, 1942); Robert A. Naslund, "The Origin and Development of the Community School Concept" (Ed.D. diss., Stanford University, 1951); Neil Betten and Michael J. Austin, eds., *The Roots of Community Organizing, 1917–1939* (Philadelphia: Temple University Press, 1990), chaps. 5, 7.

44. Covello, "Research and Development of the Community School."

45. Irving V. Sollins, "A Socio-Statistical Analysis of Boys' Club Membership" (Ph.D. diss., New York University, 1936), 48–49.

46. May Case Marsh, "The Life and Work of the Churches of an Interstitial Area" (Ph.D. diss., New York University, 1932).

47. CP oversize, folder 1.

48. Covello is given credit for contributing to what was probably the first step in the founding of Casa Italiana, the organization of the Italian Club at Columbia University, in 1914. See Roger Howson, "Historical Survey of the Casa Italiana," n.d., folder "Casa Italiana," William F. Russell Papers, RG6, box 10, Milbank Special Collections, Teachers College, Columbia University.

49. The story of the bureau is most concisely available in Francesco Cordasco, "Leonard Covello and the Casa Italiana Educational Bureau: A Note on the Beginnings of Systematic Italian-American Studies," in *Studies in Italian American Social History: Essays in Honor of Leonard Covello,* ed. Cordasco (Totowa, N.J.: Rowman and Littlefield, 1975), 1–9.

50. Leonard Covello, "Research as the Foundation for Community-Centered Education," *The Community-Centered School* [hereafter *CCS*], remnant manuscript, chap. 2, corrected typescript, 14, CP box 18, folder 9.

51. "Sponsoring Committee for the East Harlem Community Study," CP box 18, folder 3, work undertaken in cooperation with the Mayor's Committee on City Planning, with Anthony Lombardi in charge of the local office; Covello, "Research as the Foundation." 14-15; See also Norman Studer, "The Community School," *New York Teacher* 4, no. 3 (1938): 25. (Inspired by Covello's ideas, Studer later modeled the Downtown Community School after Benjamin Franklin's design and became the school's director. A Covello lecture series was founded at the Downtown Community School; see "Lectures Given in Honor of Retired Principal," *4 for Better Education,* School District 4 newsletter, New York City, April 1970, 3.)

52. Mayor's Committee on City Planning, *East Harlem Community Study,* 1937, published as a partial report on Project No. 165-97-6037, conducted under the auspices of the WPA.

53. Covello, "Research as the Foundation," 16–19. Other initial surveys included a follow-up study of graduates and dropouts through interviews with the student and later his parents, a survey of the economic backgrounds of students, an analysis of the influence of motion pictures, a delinquency report, and a study of student leisure-time activities.

54. Ibid.; quote from Covello, "Research and Development of the Community School"; see also outline notes for Covello's NYU community coordination course, lecture of 25 April 1938, CP box 25, folder 10.

55. Edna G. Anderson, "Benjamin Franklin High School," apparently a paper submitted for a course at Teachers College, Education 233V and 183V, n.d., CP box 38, folder 13.

56. CP oversize, folder 1.

57. Albert Hemsing, "Does the School Provide Adequate Contact with Community Organizations?" CP box 36, folder 17.

58. Donald Merit, Frankie Tartaro, and Robert Alleyne were featured in *PM,* 14 June 1944 (title of article is unclear from available document in CP); Michael Lombardo, Joseph Bayza, Leonard Kramm, "Franklin High Is Community Centered," *Junior Red Cross Journal,* October 1939, 54–56.

59. Rita Morgan commented regarding student participation: "Only as these and similar plans are developed through the pupils themselves and in relation to their own lives and background, will citizenship be raised to the level of an integral part of students' lives, as real as their interest in a job, as personal as economic conditions at home, and as vital as the social and political forces that affect the life about them." Rita Morgan Papers, folder 5, Milbank Special Collections, Teachers College, Columbia University. Concerning a 1943 summer session Morgan added a further purpose: "To continue the constant study of the school in the interests of racial unity," Rita Morgan Papers, folder 1.

60. Covello, "Research and the Development of the Community School," 14.

61. Leonard Covello, "Neighborhood Growth through the School," *Progressive Education* 15, no. 2 (1938): 126–39; Leonard Covello, "A High School and Its Immigrant Community: A Challenge and an Opportunity," *Journal of Educational Sociology* 9 (1936): 331–46; T. J. Frontera, "Leonard Covello's Community Centered School: Italian-American Students at the Benjamin Franklin High School in East Harlem, New York, 1934–44" (Ed.D. diss., Harvard University, 1993).

62. Harold Fields to Leonard Covello, 31 October 1935, CP box 39, folder 1.

63. Ibid., 15 November 1935, CP box 39, folder 1.

64. See, for example, "Minutes of the Meeting of Mr. Covello and Mr. Fields with Members of the East Side Council of Social Agencies," 15 September 1935, CP box 39, folder 1.

65. Though the East Harlem Council of Social Agencies served as the larger umbrella council of the district, the CAC's growth and activity during its first few years put Benjamin Franklin at the center of many community reform efforts. Such a profile appears higher than most community coordinating councils of the decade maintained.

66. Memo to Chairmen of School Committees, April 1937, CP box 52, folder 30; BFHS organizational chart, n.d., CP box 8, folder 16; Covello, "Neighborhood Growth through the School" and "High School and Immigrant Community"; "Expanded Program at Franklin Is First Step of New Civic Council," untitled newspaper clipping, third week of October 1935, CP box 122, folder 4; "New Educational Plan Outlined by Covello," *Italian Review,* 29 October 1935, CP box 122, folder 11; "Communities Are Improved," *Christian Science Monitor,* 8 June 1937; flyers advertising CAC Community Nights, for example, 22 May 1941 (CP box 48, folder 1), 27 November 1941 (CP box 6, folder 8).

67. The Juvenile Aid Bureau was formerly called the Crime Prevention Bureau.

68. Covello, "Research and Development of the Community School," 9–10 (for quotes), 12.

69. Ibid., 13. This included the establishment of the street units discussed in Chapter 3.

70. "Distribution of Benj. Franklin High School Students by Race or Nationality, Schools and Area of Residence, Spring Term 1936," CP oversize, folder 1; Leonard Covello, "An Experiment in a NY City HS," address presented at the annual meeting of the Progressive Education Association, 1934, CP box 9, folder 9; Covello, "High School and Immigrant Community"; Leonard Covello, with Guido D'Agostino, *The Heart Is the Teacher* (New York: McGraw-Hill, 1958), 185.

71. "East Harlem Population by Nationality, Nativity and Color—1930," CP box 6, folder 8; Frederic Thrasher, *The Final Report on the Jefferson Park Branch of the Boys' Club of New York,* serial map (no. 11), Local Neighborhoods, New York City, 1931, map 13, p. 84, Rockefeller Center Archive, Bureau of Social Hygiene Collection, series 3, box 12.

72. Cimilluca, "Natural History of East Harlem," 3–6, cited in Sollins, "Boys' Club Membership," 43.

73. Orsi, *Madonna of 115th Street,* 34; quote from Francesco Cordasco and Rocco G. Galatioto, "Ethnic Displacement in the Interstitial Community: The East Harlem Experience," *Phylon* 31, no. 3 (1970): 303.

74. Numbers in table 5.1 are calculated from "Distribution of Benj. Franklin High School Students Residing in Yorkville and East Harlem by Race, Nationality and Schools, Spring Term 1936," CP oversize, folder 1.

75. "Chart I: Comparative Tables Showing Geographical and Racial or National Distribution of Students in Yorkville, East Harlem, The Bronx and Other Parts of New York," [1936?], CP box 19, folder 8.

76. Ibid.; "Residences of B.F.H.S. Students (as of September 1941)," n.d., CP box 49, folder 13; "Analysis of Distribution of B.F.H.S. Students by Residence or Race," 1942 [?], corrected typescript, CP box 49, folder 14. Writing after the U.S. entry into World War II, Covello worried that a "preponderant majority of students residing in outside areas" would impair the high school's capacity "to correlate the communal backgrounds of its students to the vital problems of East Harlem. . . . It would also be difficult indeed to continue any comprehensive community program, by offering students from other parts of the city social experiences in East Harlem" (2). This issue was muted by the community school's other problems during the war and its aftermath.

77. *Population in Health Areas: New York City, 1930,* prepared under the supervision of Florence DuBois (New York: Welfare Council of New York City, 1931), "Population: Color, Nativity, Parentage, Sex and Age, By Health Areas, New York City, 1930," Manhattan, pt. 1, in *Census Data with Maps for Small Areas of New York City: 1910–1960* (Woodbridge, Conn.: Research Publishing, 1929), microfilm, reel 8.5; Robert Charles Freeman, "Exploring the Path of Community Change in East Harlem, 1870–1970" (Ph.D. diss., Fordham University, 1994), table 4.1, p. 73; table 4.4, p. 82.

78. Freeman, "Exploring Path of Community Change," table 4.4, p. 82, including 16 census tracts east of Fifth Avenue from 98th to 126th street.

79. *Population in Health Areas, 1930*; Manhattan, pt. 1; Manhattan Borough Health Areas, 1940, table C.1, p. 108, in *Census Data*, reel 8.3. These calculations are for health areas 16, 17, 20, 21, 22, 25, 26, and 30.

80. *Population in Health Areas*; Manhattan Borough Health Areas, 1940, table C.1, p. 108.

81. Leonard Covello, "East Harlem," *CCS*, chap. 3, pp. 18, 20, CP box 18, folder 11.

82. Robert A. Orsi, "The Religious Boundaries of an In-between People: Street *Feste* and the Problem of the Dark-Skinned Other in Italian Harlem, 1920–1990," in *Gods of the City: Religion and the Urban Landscape,* ed Orsi (Bloomington: Indiana University Press, 1999), 257–88. Simone Cinotto, in "The Social Significance of Food in Italian Harlem, 1920–1940" (paper presented at the Balch Institute for Ethnic Studies, Philadelphia, 23 August 2000), notes that Puerto Rican food habits were a target of Italian American disdain, even as the diet of Italian Americans had been degraded by Irish and Germans earlier in the century.

83. See Dina DiPinto to Leonard Covello, 20 October 1938, CP box 53, folder 14, information collected from the local precinct station; "Italian Gang Battles Puerto Ricans; Nine Held after Skirmish in Harlem," *Bronx Home News,* 17 October 1938; "Youth Lies Near Death after Knifing by Gang at Harlem Racial 'Deadline,'" *Bronx Home News,* 18 October 1938.

84. An editorial in the 18 October 1938 *Herald Tribune* scathingly declared that "racial antagonism, which apparently was at the bottom of Sunday night's pitched brawl, exists there to a degree that is downright terrifying. . . . The section for the most part is sunk deep in squalor. It is not safe for a well dressed man to walk there at night. . . . Thousands of persons, most of them merely unfortunate but many of them vicious, live in the rows of dilapidated old houses which are unfit for human habitation." On 30 October, Covello broadcast a speech in English and Italian, "Racial Tolerance," over WOV, the city's Italian American station. His reply to the *Herald Tribune* editorial of 18 October appeared in that paper on 3 November. In his letter Covello charged that the editorialist had shown a tendency "to

exaggerate and dramatize pathological and criminal aspects of community life in a way that is positively injurious to the morale of the community as a whole."

85. Leonard Covello, "The Need for Racial Understanding and Appreciation," *Il Popolo,* clipping [1938], CP box 53, folder 13; see also BFHS press release, [October 1938?], CP box 53, folder 15.

86. Leonard Covello, "Intercultural Education," 3, CP box 51, folder 21. See also "Tentative Plans for Work in New York City High Schools," 1, Rachel Davis DuBois Papers, Immigration History Research Center, Elmer L. Andersen Library, University of Minnesota. "Very lately," Covello warned in early 1939, "I and others in the community have received information that leads us to believe there is a definitely organized movement to create differences among our people. This must not be allowed to happen." Covello, outline notes for an intercultural education committee meeting, 1, Friends and Neighbors Club, 17 February 1939, CP box 51, folder 19. The rise of virulent anti-Semitism helped spur the tolerance assemblies program mandated by Superintendent Campbell. Nicholas V. Montalto, *Intercultural Educational Movement, 1924–1941* (New York: Garland, 1982), 172–79, 218–20.

87. Montalto, *Intercultural Educational Movement,* 219. The use of community-centered schooling models in totalitarian regimes and their apparent effectiveness was not lost on advocates of community-centered schooling in the United States. See J. Morris Jones, *Americans All, Immigrants All: A Handbook for Listeners and Americans All, Immigrants All: Manual* (Washington, D.C.: Federal Radio Education Committee, 1939), a project in which Rachel DuBois played a central role. Montalto, *Intercultural Educational Movement,* chap. 6. See also Rachel DuBois, *National Unity through Intercultural Understanding* (Washington, D.C.: U.S. Government Printing Office, 1942).

88. "Police End Harlem Riot; Mayor Starts Inquiry; Dodge Sees a Red Plot," *New York Times,* 21 March 1935.

89. "1,200 Extra Police on 'War Duty' Here—Disorder Quelled in Harlem as Negroes Picket Italian Market—Two Hurt," *New York Times,* 4 October 1935.

90. Ibid. See also Arnold Shankman, "The Image of the Italian in the Afro-American Press, 1886–1936," *Italian Americana* 4, no. 1 (1978): 30–49.

91. BFHS Committee for Racial Cooperation, "Building Concepts of Racial Democracy," in *Americans All—Studies in Intercultural Education* (Washington, D.C.: Department of Supervisors and Directors of Instruction of the National Education Association, 1942), 52. The committee included Covello and Franklin teachers Lee Lombard (English), chair; Louis Relin (English); Daisy Katz (French); Nancy Zito (Italian); Bernard Saxon (art); and Maurice Bleifeld (biology).

92. Ronald H. Bayor, *Neighbors in Conflict: The Irish, Germans, Jews, and Italians of New York City, 1929–1941,* 2nd ed. (Urbana: University of Illinois Press, 1988), 79.

93. Guilds Committee for Federal Writers' Publications, *The Italians of New York* (New York: Random House, 1939), 124; Bayor, *Neighbors in Conflict,* 76–84, esp. 79; Nadia Venturini, "'Over the Years People Don't Know': Italian Americans and African Americans in Harlem in the 1930s," in *Italian Workers of the World: Labor Migration and the Formation of Multiethnic Studies,* ed. Donna R. Gabaccia and Fraser M. Ottanelli (Urbana: University of Illinois Press, 2001), 196–213; Herta Herzog, *Feeling among Four Minority Groups in New York City: Mayoralty Election as a Test Situation* (New York: Bureau of Applied Social Research, 1941). *Il Progresso* spoke against Fascism in September 1941 (Bayor, *Neighbors in Conflict,* 120).

94. Personal Papers—Biographical Notes (apparently interview notes with Miriam Sanders, Marcantonio's spouse), Vito Marcantonio Papers, New York Public Library, box 74; also mentioned in Gerald Meyer, *Vito Marcantonio: Radical Politician, 1902–1954* (Albany: State University of New York Press, 1989), 119.

95. Meyer, *Vito Marcantonio,* 119.

96. Deep political rifts over Mussolini may have trapped Covello between Scylla and Charybdis. Generoso Pope, publisher of *Il Progresso,* whose support Covello had enlisted to lobby board of education support for the East Harlem high school, was exuberantly pro-Fascist, to the extent that he sent $100,000 to Rome for the Ethiopian war. John P. Diggins, *Mussolini and Fascism: The View from America* (Princeton, N.J.: Princeton University Press, 1972), 303. *Il Progresso* journalist Armando Romano grandiloquently described Benjamin Franklin's Italian program, hailed Covello as "among the most tenacious defenders and promulgators of our language," and suggested that programs such as Franklin's reconnected Italian American youth to their "spiritual patrimony," whose legatee the writer obviously believed was the Fascist regime. Excerpts from an Italian Department syllabus that appear in Romano's piece contain language that suggests pro-Fascist sentiments in the department, for example, an admonition "to emphasize the great changes for the better which are evident in Italy since the advent of Fascism." Armando Romano, "A Spiritual Italian Conquest in the Greatest Metropolis in America," n.d., Rachel Davis DuBois Papers, box 17, folder 11. Calling Annita Giacobbe, the department's chairperson and Covello's close associate, "an avowed Fascist," the American League against War and Fascism complained to the board of education that her syllabus had been distributed to every New York high school. American League against War and Fascism, "Statement to the Board of Education of the City of New York," encl. accompanying open letter dated 7 June 1935, Swarthmore College Peace Collection, McCabe Library, Swarthmore College, Committee on Militarism in Education, reel 70.47. As we saw in Chapter 3, Covello was also affiliated with Casa Italiana, which "functioned as something of an overseas branch of Italy's Ministry of Culture and Propaganda," where "Fascism found a veritable home in America." Diggins, *Mussolini and Fascism,* 255. Although Covello intensely disliked Giuseppe Prezzolini, "a rabid nationalist," he appointed the Casa director to the executive board of the high school's CAC. Augustus Loschi, "Giuseppe Prezzolini," *Sons of Italy Magazine* 12, no. 2 (1939): 1–2; Prezzolini to LC, 11 November 1958, CP box 99, folder 19.

97. "City Schools Ban Italian Textbooks as Propaganda," *World-Telegram,* 10 October 1940. Jonathan Zimmerman called our attention to the *Andiamo* controversy and several archival resources.

98. Translation in CP box 97, folder 9.

99. Herman H. Wright to Covello, 14 December 1937, CP box 97, folder 9.

100. Covello to Wright, 3 January 1938, CP box 97, folder 9. In the late winter–early spring of 1938, Covello exchanged letters with the textbook's publisher, Henry Holt, endorsing the editorial position of the *Lincoln Guild News,* a bulletin published by Teachers Guild Group of Abraham Lincoln High School in Brooklyn: "We submit that this is sheer Fascist propaganda and does not belong in any text-book in a democratic school, least of all in a grammar text." Ralph B. Bristol to LC, 1 February 1938; Covello to Bristol, 26 March 1938; *Lincoln Guild News* 3, no. 4 (1938). Holt tried to get Covello to write a revision of chapter 7, which he declined to do. He did agree, however, to appraise the revised version that Holt arranged with the *Andiamo* authors. Covello to Bristol, 4 April 1938; Wright to LC, 2 November 1938, both in CP box 97, folder 9. He notified the assistant superintendent that the new version was not acceptable. "If the subject is to be treated at all, it should contain a statement pointing out that in the Corporative State there is a complete absence of all those things for which the American Bill of Rights has provided expression: freedom of speech, freedom of press, freedom of assembly, freedom from unwarranted search and seizure, and other guarantees of individual rights and liberties." Covello to Wright, 20 November 1938, CP box 97, folder 9. Subsequently, as the *La Parola* campaign escalated, the board of education withdrew *Andiamo* from city classrooms. Board president James Marshall stated: "This book is being stricken from the textbook list because it was found to contain matter which was not merely in praise of Fascism, but was derogatory to the parliamentary form of government."

"Italian Textbook Banned by Board," *New York Sun*, 10 October 1940; typescript copy in CP box 97, folder 9.

101. "Nationality of Pupils" according to country of birth of father, BFHS, May 1940, CP 49, folder 2.

102. "Analysis of Distribution of B.F.H.S. Students by Residence and Race"; "Distribution of Benj. Franklin High School Students by Race or Nationality, School and Area of Residence, Spring Term 1936," CP oversize, folder 1; "Nationality of Pupils."

103. Untitled, apparently a report to faculty and staff of BFHS, [1939–40?], CP box 56, folder 8,

104. Ibid.

105. Yoon Pak, in *Wherever I Go, I Will Always Be a Loyal American: Seattle's Japanese Americans during World War II* (New York: RoutledgeFalmer, 2002), documents the national appeal of intercultural education. For example, ideas of "tolerance," "intercultural education," and "character education" appeared in Seattle's curriculum guides as early as 1935. Two locally produced guides, *Successful Living* (1935) and *Living Today—Learning for Tomorrow* (1938) focused on these themes, with particular attention to democratic living; see 78–85.

106. DuBois, *All This and Something More*, 54. Their meeting apparently took place sometime between 1925 and 1928.

107. Mabel Carney to Covello, Casa Italiana, 18 October 1933; Covello to Mabel Carney, 22 October 1933, both in CP box 50, folder 9. After DuBois left the Service Bureau and set up the Workshop for Cultural Democracy, Covello joined the board of the latter.

108. Montalto, *Intercultural Education Movement*, 78–108; quotes from 83, 86.

109. *Montalto, Intercultural Educational Movement;* DuBois, *All This and Something More*; "History of the Service Bureau for Education in Human Relations," CP box 50, folder 9; biographical sketch in the guide to Rachel Davis DuBois Papers; Service Bureau pamphlet, CP box 50, folder 9; "The Need for Intercultural Education: A Petition for Support," General Education Board box 566, folder 6050, attached to correspondence from Rachel Davis DuBois to John Marshall, 27 March 1939, 3–5, folder 6048; General Education Board Records, Rockefeller Center Archive. The other six demonstration centers were in New Jersey.

110. Covello, "Intercultural Education," 3.

111. Rachel Davis DuBois, "Intercultural Education at Benjamin Franklin High School," *High Points in the Work of the High Schools of New York City* 19, no. 10 (1937): 25.

112. Service Bureau for Education in Human Relations, "Human Relations Project in Benjamin Franklin High School," 1935, 2–7, CP box 52, folder 10.

113. DuBois describes this approach in Rachel Davis DuBois, "Practical Problems of Intercultural and Interracial Education," *Clearing House* 10 (1936): 484–90.

114. DuBois, "Intercultural Education." Some staff involved noted that they could never be sure if the students' attitudes had really changed or if they simply understood what the "right" answers were supposed to be. In either case, the same staff reasoned, at least the students now realized more clearly the desired attitudes, and many might actually adopt them. Rita Morgan, "Benjamin Franklin High School Intercultural Program," 5, CP box 5, folder 19; later published as "A City High School's Contribution," *New Era in Home and School* 125, no. 6 (1944): 115–17 (featured within "American Schools Face the Minority Problem," a series of essays arranged by Annette Smith Lawrence, 115–21).

115. Covello, "Intercultural Education," 5. While reconstituting itself as the Bureau for Intercultural Education, the Service Bureau broke with DuBois in 1941 on the grounds that her "immigrant gifts" approach promoted ethnic distinctiveness and was out of step with the nation's wartime goal of social cohesion. In the late 1940s and 1950s social scientists, building

on a social-psychological model of prejudice, advocated more sophisticated approaches that would confront the underlying pathologies of prejudice. Social psychologist Gordon Allport, for example, developed an experimental workshop that brought participants from different racial, ethnic, religious, and occupational groups into extended contact through work on collaborative tasks and informal social activities. Proponents of this approach argued that the combination of cooperative work and interpersonal exchanges contributed to team building and overcoming prejudicial attitudes. Stuart Svonkin, *Jews against Prejudice: American Jews and the Fight for Civil Liberties* (New York: Columbia University Press, 1997), 1, 25–27, 66–67, 74–75. Researchers remain skeptical of "a direct path between knowledge of outgroup culture and attitudes towards the outgroup." Social psychologists Miles Hewstone and Rupert Brown note that "there is now ample evidence to show that intergroup discrimination and hostility are often caused by factors other than mere lack of knowledge or inaccurate perceptions"; also, "objective conflicts of interest are a potent source of mutual degradation." Hewstone and Brown, "Contact Is not Enough: An Intergroup Perspective on the 'Contact Hypothesis,'" in *Contact and Conflict in Intergroup Encounters*, ed. Hewstone and Brown (London: Basil Blackwell, 1986), 111.

116. BFHS Committee for Racial Cooperation, "Building Concepts of Racial Democracy," 69.

117. Covello, "High School and Immigrant Community," 336.

118. [Leonard Covello], "Research and Its Aims," outline notes, CP box 18, folder 9.

119. Covello, "Neighborhood Growth through the School," 135.

120. "Use Empty Stores for School Clubs: Teachers and Students of Benjamin Franklin High Renovate Eyesores," *New York Times*, 26 March 1939.

121. Lombardo, Bayza, and Kramm, "Franklin High Is Community Centered," 54.

122. [Covello], "Research and Its Aims," pt. 6.2. Covello considered the street units outposts of experimentation for the school-community program.

123. In 1930 some twenty-two private social clubs, secret societies, lodges, and social facilities were located within one block of where the Friends and Neighbors Club would be located seven years later. See Frederic Thrasher, *The Final Report on the Jefferson Park Branch of the Boys' Club of New York,* submitted to the Bureau of Social Hygiene, 21 October 1935, map 27, p. 219; map 29, p. 259.

124. Leonard Covello, outline notes for Intercultural Education Committee meeting, Friends and Neighbors Club, 17 February 1939, CP box 51, folder 19; see also letter from Covello to community leaders, 10 February 1939, CP box 52, folder 20.

125. Covello, quote from agenda for Intercultural Education Committee meeting, CP box 52, folder 20; see also in same folder, Committee for Racial Cooperation, minutes, 17 February 1939.

126. Recognizing the nearly impossible task of reconstructing "the curriculum" in the many senses in which it is used today—what teachers intend, what different students experience, what administrators perceive, what is stated on paper, etc.—we have chosen to concentrate on the formal curriculum, for which there is fairly clear written evidence. Other extant evidence does suggest, though, what classroom experiences might have been like—for example, informal memos from faculty explaining their activities, recorded remarks of students, reflections of graduates in letters, and so on. On varieties of curriculum, see Larry Cuban, "The Lure of Curricular Reform and Its Pitiful History," *Phi Delta Kappan* 75, no. 2 (1993): 181–85.

127. Herbert Kliebard, *The Struggle for the American Curriculum, 1893–1958*, 2d ed. (New York: Routledge, 1995), chap. 8, quotes from 178, 187; see also essays in *"Schools of Tomorrow," Schools of Today*, ed. Susan F. Semel and Alan R. Sadovnik (New York: Peter Lang, 1999).

128. Lelia Ann Taggart, "Curriculum Development in Santa Barbara County," *New Era in Home and School* 25, no. 6 (1944): 118–21.

129. Covello, untitled, handwritten, 1 (of 3 pp.), Reminiscences and Autobiographical Notes, CP box 20, folder 16.

130. Report of the faculty concerning intercultural education at Benjamin Franklin H.S. during 1938–39, box 52, folder 12. Headed by English Department chair Lee Lombard, this committee was first known as the Racial Committee.

131. Representatives were included from the board of education, Columbia University, Brooklyn College, Jewish Education Association, Salvation Army Welfare Department, P.S. 101, *Jewish Day* newspaper, *Il Progresso* newspaper, New York Public Library, Federation Settlement, physicians of East Harlem, real estate group of East Harlem, Italian Welfare League, City Department of Public Welfare, and Puerto Rican Service Center of New York. Ibid., 7.

132. The results of the pre-/posttesting had limited interpretive value. The meager sampling number, some poorly worded questions, second-language difficulties, and some evident "hesitation" and "instantaneous rectification" with responses led those coordinating the survey to claim "no authoritative pronouncements . . . about the 117th Street Annex. We can claim only that something 'appears to be' or 'is likely to exist' there." Faculty report of 1938–39, 28–29, CP box 52, folder 12.

133. Minutes of the 17 January 1939 meeting of the Committee for Racial Cooperation, 1, CP box 52, box 10. The Christmas assemblies that year featured "The Spirit of Good-Will in Many Lands" and included an introduction by student Joseph Monserrat, later a member of the BOE. The radio programs included the award-winning and highly acclaimed "Americans All" CBS radio series, to which Rachel DuBois served as special consultant; a series of pamphlets based on the series was also produced. See the debates involved in this production in Montalto, *Intercultural Educational Movement,* chap. 6.

134. Faculty report on curriculum work, 1938–39, 83, CP box 52, folder 12.

135. To invoke a useful typology, most of the formal curriculum material illustrated the "contributions" or "additive" approaches to "multicultural" curriculum development, whereas elements of the English and social studies curricula clearly were "transformation" and "social action" approaches. See James Banks, *An Introduction to Multicultural Education* (Boston: Allyn and Bacon, 1994), 24–27.

136. Relin, "We Hold These Truths," 13–15.

137. Teacher Layle Lane, an African American teacher union activist, sponsored an assembly entitled "Let Freedom Ring"; teachers Relin and Morgan sponsored an adaptation of *The Grapes of Wrath;* teachers Burnbinder, Guzy, and Lombard had their Special English Group present an assembly entitled "Bury the Dead." Spurred by such events as Kristall Nacht in Germany, the BOE mandated in 1938 that schools hold at least two "tolerance assemblies" every month, beginning in January 1939. General Circular No. 19, 1938–39, Office of the Superintendent of Schools, CP box 51, folder 18.

138. "Benjamin Franklin High School: English Syllabus," [1948?], 1, CP box 34, folder 15.

139. Rita Morgan, "Second Meeting: Group to Plan Cooperation T.C. and B.F. in an Educational Project," 1942, 2, CP box 36, folder 26.

140. The degree to which Franklin's black students were involved in particular extracurricular activities suggests the relative success of these efforts vis-à-vis other high schools. Paula Fass's analysis of extracurricular activities in seven New York City high schools of the 1930s and 1940s reveals an "exclusionary bias" against blacks: "No other group was absent in so many categories across schools." Fass finds their absence particularly conspicuous in student leadership roles and in Arista, the citywide honor society. Across the seven high schools, 1931–47, no black, male or female, was elected student or senior-class president; black males constituted only 0.6 percent of Arista membership. Paula S. Fass, *Outside In: Minorities and the Transformation of American Education* (New York: Oxford University Press, 1989), 81,

88 (table 4), appendix 1. These findings beg the question for the present study: Was the experience of blacks at Franklin any different from that at the other New York City high schools? Analysis of nine Franklin yearbooks (variously called the Franklin *Gazette* or *Yearbook*) for the years 1937–42, including January and June graduations, suggests a more facilitative climate for black male participation at the community high school than was available at the high schools in Fass's analysis. For example, in June 1937, 19 percent of the Arista society membership was black, compared to blacks' approximately 3 percent representation in the senior class. For January and June 1940, Arista counts of black membership were 11 percent and 10 percent, respectively, versus an approximate 7 percent representation for blacks in the senior class for the fall and spring semesters. For the five other yearbooks, black representation in Arista ranged between 3 and 9 percent. (A camera-shy category of missing senior photographs may signify a slight undercount of the black proportion in the senior class for any given semester.) On the other measure of interest, student government, there is no denying that blacks were less frequently—and in at least one semester, not—represented, although in a few cases their presence was conspicuous. In January 1937, for example, 33 percent of Franklin's General Organization representatives and 10 percent of the Student Congress delegates were black. In June 1939, the secretary of the senior class was black, as was the vice president of the G.O. in June 1940.

141. Report of the faculty concerning intercultural education at BFHS during 1938–39, CP box 52, folder 12. According to the report: "Only in so far as these purposes are realized, can there continue to emerge a nation *united* in the deepest sense. Throughout our history stress has been now upon one, now upon another of these objectives" (1).

142. These guidelines are drawn principally from curriculum descriptions throughout this time period, as well as the following: Committee for Racial Cooperation, minutes, 17 February 1939, CP box 52, folder 20; Leonard Covello, "The Community-Centered School," corrected typescript, sections noted 11, 12, 15, CP box 18, folder 15; agenda for the General Faculty Conference, 27 March 1939, CP box 51, folder 19; Covello, "Experiment." The quote is found in Covello, untitled, handwritten, 1 (of 3 pp.), Reminiscences and Autobiographical Notes, 1, CP box 20, folder 16.

143. Memo from W. Hayett to Covello and Joseph Gallant, 7 July 1941, CP box 51, folder 14.

144. Cohen apparently submitted an article to the NEA in the spring of 1941 describing the school's intercultural experiment in social studies; memo from Morris Cohen to Leonard Covello, 4 June 1941, CP box 51, folder 6. P.S. 184, J. Fenimore Cooper JHS, was located at 31 West 116th Street, east of Lenox Avenue; Abraham Cohen was the principal.

145. Maurice Bleifeld, "A Biology Unit Dealing with Racial Attitudes," *American Biology Teacher* 2, no. 1 (1939): 7. Bleifeld also worked on a unit for the New York Association of Biology Teachers; see Anthropology Study Group, "Outline of a Teaching Unit on Mankind," *Teaching Biologist* 9, no. 2 (1939): 27–45. Bleifeld was active in biology associations and published considerably; see Bleifeld, "Plant Hormones," *Teaching Biologist* 6, no. 1 (1936); "Plant Tissues Cultures," *Teaching Biologist* 8, no. 1 (1938); "Biological Effects of Flight." *Teaching Biologist* 12, no. 3 (1942); "Food Dehydration Joins the Colors," *Teaching Biologist* 13, no. 3 (1943).

146. The autobiography was written by Irving Danowitz; see memo from Lee Lombard to Leonard Covello, 7 March, 1950, CP box 51, folder 10. The four-year intercultural English curriculum elements are outlined in Joseph Gallant, "An Intercultural Curriculum," *English Journal* 33 (1944): 382. Gallant chaired the English Department, as well as the school-community Committee for Racial Cooperation. A Polish immigrant, Gallant later became English Department chair at Theodore Roosevelt High School in the Bronx, edited two student anthologies (*Essays in Today's Science* and *Stories of Scientific Imagination*, both

in Oxford Book Company's Student Pocket Library series), prepared two school editions of novels (*The Cruel Sea,* by Nicholas Monsarrat, and *The Light in the Forest,* by Conrad Richter), and served as a consultant on high school literature for Prentice-Hall.

147. Ethnic diversity among authors was emphasized in the English curriculum. Fifth-term English students, for example, were also assigned *International Short Stories,* a collection of stories from ethnic groups found in East Harlem, as well as *Story,* a "monthly magazine which publishes English translations of the best short stories in foreign languages," and *Magazine Digest,* which also published stories translated from foreign publications. See Covello, "Experiment," and various English Department syllabi and reports in CP.

148. "Benjamin Franklin High School: English Syllabus," [1948?], CP box 34, folder 15; further class activities may be found in Rita Morgan Papers, esp. the 1943–44 Curriculum Committee report in folder 1 and the English Department annual report of 1948 and *My Community Work Book* in folder 2.

149. Composition of Joseph Stule, English 402, 1 November 1944, CP box 53, folder 16.

150. Racial Committee, minutes, 30 March 1938, CP box 52, folder 20.

151. Clinchy quoted in Montalto, *Intercultural Educational Movement,* 206.

152. "Clinchy to Speak," press release for 21, 22, or 23 May 1938, CP box 52, folder 20.

153. Report of Racial Committee, September 1938–February 1939, 2–3, CP box 52, folder 20; Montalto, *Intercultural Educational Movement,* 188–205.

154. Bruno Lasker, *Race Attitudes in Children* (New York: Henry Holt, 1929); Leonard Covello, diary for 26 December 1940, CP box 1, folder 12; Montalto, *Intercultural Educational Movement,* 250–59.

155. Children's Crusade for Children, *Teacher's Handbook for Children's Crusade for Children, April 22–30, 1940* (New York: The Crusade, 1940).

156. Signed on program flyer for Negro History Week Assembly, 17 February 1948, CP box 42, folder 19. Franklin had very good fortune with celebrity singers; Frank Sinatra sang at a 1945 assembly meant to promote interethnic harmony. CP box 51, folder 18.

157. It is also unclear, though, whether the reaction was to curricular innovation or to undertaking the collaborative project with Teachers College and the board of education that was being proposed. Morgan, "Second Meeting." It should be noted that Franklin did obtain board permission for curriculum "reconstruction" in the following year and did pursue revisions in English.

158. "Report of a Discussion Which Took Place at Benjamin Franklin High School, Wednesday, June 3, under the Auspices of the Council Against Intolerance in America and Mr. Leonard Covello, Principal of the School," 3 June 1943, 2, CP box 50, folder 1.

159. "Prejudice Scored as Bar to Culture," *New York Times,* 14 May 1939.

160. Harold Fields, "Co-operating in Citizenship," *Social Education,* January 1937, 13.

161. Daniel F. Fitzpatrick, "Report on Summer Session of the Adult School at the Benjamin Franklin High School, Summer 1940, July 1–August 6. W.P.A.—Adult Education Program," 9 August 1940, CP box 47, folder 11.

162. Flyers describing the institute may be found in CP box 42, folder 4.

163. "Groups Formed at High School," *New York Advance,* 27 May 1938.

164. Mary Carter Winter, "Guest Editorial: Democracy and Education," *New York Advance,* 26 May 1938.

165. Covello, *Italo-American School Child;* Oscar Handlin, *The Uprooted,* 2nd ed. enlarged (Boston: Little, Brown, 1973); Bodnar, *Transplanted,* chap. 7.

166. Covello, "Experiment," 9.

167. Fields, "Co-operating in Citizenship," 13.

168. See Chapter 6 in this volume; see also Fields, "Co-operating in Citizenship," 11–15.

169. "Report of Discussion at Benjamin Franklin High School."

170. H. C. Hunsaker, "Community Councils," *Journal of American Education* 12, no. 4 (1940): 490.

171. H. Y. McClusky, "Community Councils," *Journal of American Education* 12, no 4 (1940): 491.

CHAPTER 6: THE EAST HARLEM CAMPAIGNS

1. Harry C. Boyte and Nancy N. Kari, *Building America: The Democratic Promise of Public Work* (Philadelphia: Temple University Press, 1996); Harry C. Boyte, *Everyday Politics: Reconnecting Citizens and Public Life* (Philadelphia: University of Pennsylvania Press, 2004); see also Benjamin R. Barber, *A Place for Us: How to Make Civil Society and Democracy Strong* (New York: Hill and Wang, 1998). Public work has theoretical and empirical warrants in social psychologists' research on superordinate goals and interracial conflict, spanning a fifty-year period. See Muzafer Sherif, "Superordinate Goals in the Reduction of Intergroup Conflict," *American Journal of Sociology* 63: 349–56; reprinted in Sherif, *Social Interaction: Process and Products: Selected Essays* (Chicago: Aldine, 1961), quoted at 445; Muzafer Sherif, O. J. Harvey, B. Jack White, William R. Hood, and Carolyn W. Sherif, *Intergroup Cooperation and Conflict: The Robbers Cave Experiment* (Norman, Ok.: University Book Exchange, 1961); Miles Hewstone and Rupert Brown, "Contact Is Not Enough: An Intergroup Perspective on the 'Contact Hypothesis,'" in *Contact and Conflict in Intergroup Encounters*, ed. Hewstone and Brown (London: Basil Blackwell, 1986), 1–44; Thomas F. Pettigrew, "The Importance of Cumulative Effects: A Neglected Emphasis of Sherif's Work," in *Social Judgment and Intergroup Relations: Essays in Honor of Muzafer Sherif,*" ed. Donald Granberg and Gian Sarup (New York: Springer-Verlag, 1992), chap. 4; Rupert Brown, *Prejudice: Its Social Psychology* (Oxford, U.K.: Blackwell, 1996), chap. 8; Miles Hewstone, "Contact and Categorization: Social Psychological Interventions to Change Intergroup Relations," in *Stereotypes and Stereotyping*, ed. C. Neil MacRae, Charles Stangor, and Miles Hewstone (New York: Guilford Press, 1996), chap. 10.

2. Our argument is richly informed by Nancy Fraser, in "Rethinking the Public Sphere: A Contribution to the Critique of Actually Existing Democracy," in *Habermas and the Public Sphere,*" ed. Craig Calhoun (Cambridge, Mass.: MIT Press, 1992), 109–42.

3. Rosalie Genevro, "Site Selection and the New York City Housing Authority, 1934–1939," *Journal of Urban History* 12, no. 4 (1986): 334–52. Peter Marcuse, in "The Beginnings of Public Housing in New York," *Journal of Urban History* 12, no. 4 (1986): 353–90, notes that 186,000 families received dispossess notices during an eight-month period between 1931 and 1932, and that 70 percent of the city's construction workers were on the welfare rolls by 1933.

4. Marcuse, "Beginnings of Public Housing in New York." The citywide vacancy rate for low-cost rentals dropped from a high of 20 percent in 1933 to 3.1 percent in 1939; an estimated half-million of these dwellings were substandard. Anthony Jackson, *A Place Called Home: A History of Low-Cost Housing in Manhattan* (Cambridge, Mass.: MIT Press, 1976), 221–22.

5. Richard Plunz, *A History of Housing in New York City: Dwelling Type and Social Change in the American Metropolis* (New York: Columbia University Press, 1990), 233–34.

6. Marcuse, "Beginnings of Public Housing in New York"; Genevro, "Site Selection."

7. Marcuse, "Beginnings of Public Housing in New York." Race, as Marcuse notes, figured prominently in the early New York City Housing Association projects; the principle of "separate but equal" applied to Williamsburg Houses in Brooklyn (white project) and Harlem River Houses (black project).

8. Genevro, "Site Selection."

9. Jackson, *Place Called Home*, 222.

10. Robert Charles Freeman, "Exploring the Path of Community Change in East Harlem, 1870–1970" (Ph.D. diss., Fordham University, 1994), 83.

11. Ibid., 84–88.

12. Ibid., 88–89. See also Citizens Housing Council of New York, *Harlem Housing*, 3–4, Leonard Covello Papers (MSS 40) [hereafter CP], Balch Institute Collections, Historical Society of Pennsylvania, Philadelphia, box 43, folder 12.

13. See Mayor's Committee on City Planning, *East Harlem Community Study*, 1937, published as a partial report on Project No. 165-97-6037, conducted under the auspices of the WPA.

14. Freeman, "Exploring Path of Community Change," 165.

15. Leonard Covello, "A Community-Centered School and the Problem of Housing," *Educational Forum* 7, no. 2 (1943): 136.

16. Ibid. See also and cf. Freeman, "Exploring Path of Community Change," 184–87.

17. The signal for the first housing exhibit may have been an article by Frederic M. Thrasher, "City Slums Are Shown as Breeders of Crime," *New York Times*, 5 August 1934. For the 1935 exhibit, see Walter Sanek, "The Metropolitan Housing Exhibit," 29 October 1935, student essay, CP box 43, folder 9; "Housing Exhibit Shown in School," press release, October 1935, CP box 43, folder 5. For the 1937 exhibit, see in folder 5: Harold Fields, "Benjamin Franklin Housing Exhibit of Vital Interest to Students," [1938?]; R. K. Schwartz, "Coordinated Plan for Housing Project for Entire School during Week of November 29 [1937]," 9 November 1937; Harold Fields to Adeline Hicks, New York City Housing Authority, 23 January 1936.

18. Covello, "Community-Centered School and Problem of Housing," 140. The American Legion's Thomas Jefferson Post 541 sponsored the widely publicized essay contest "What East Harlem Needs," awarding medals for the best essays at a public ceremony at P.S. 101, 111th Street and Lexington Avenue, 26 May 1937. "What East Harlem Needs," CP Box 75, Folder 16.

19. Covello, "Community-Centered School and Problem of Housing," 140–41.

20. Richard Sasuly, "Vito Marcantonio: The People's Politician," in *American Radicals: Some Problems and Personalities*, ed. Harvey Goldberg (New York: Monthly Review Press, 1957), 147.

21. Gerald Meyer, *Vito Marcantonio: Radical Politician, 1902–1954* (Albany: State University of New York Press, 1989), 94.

22. Gerald Meyer, "Leonard Covello and Vito Marcantonio: A Lifelong Collaboration for Progress," *Italica* 62, no. 1 (1985): 54–66.

23. Alan Schaffer, *Vito Marcantonio, Radical in Congress* (Syracuse, N.Y.: Syracuse University Press, 1966), chaps. 8–10.

24. Harlem Legislative Conference, open letter, 8 June 1938, CP box 72, folder 5. Of its first meeting, held 18 December 1937 at the Park Palace Casino on 110th Street near Fifth Avenue, the Conference reported: "Never before had the people of this community sat together with their legislative representatives, for the sole purpose of devising remedial legislation for the unbearable conditions in this community." Harlem Legislative Committee, 27 December 1937, CP box 72, folder 5. Conference subcommittees prepared resolutions for legislation that were taken to the plenary session for adoption. In addition to Marcantonio and Covello, other notable delegates included city councilman-elect and future congressman Adam Clayton Powell, Jr., and Manhattan borough president Stanley Isaacs.

25. Meyer, *Vito Marcantonio*, 53–54, 65–66, 70–71; Mark Naison, *Communists in Harlem during the Depression* (New York: Grove Press, 1984), chap. 9. Naison calls Marcantonio "the [Communist] Party's most reliable ally in Congress" (231). For useful general discussion, see Frank Warren's review of Meyer's book in *Socialism and Democracy* (Spring/Summer 1990): 189–99.

26. Covello's election as committee chair was unanimous (Sadie Jacobi to Covello, 11 January 1941, CP box 72, folder 6). Covello served as a member of the Harlem Legislative Conference's standing committee (Covello to Marcantonio, 4 January 1938, CP box 72, folder 5); three Franklin faculty and staff members served on the Conference's original housing committee. The Conference held one of its sessions in the Franklin auditorium at 309 East 108th Street, 17 December 1938. Covello backed numerous human rights organizations—from the American Committee for the Protection of the Foreign Born, which he served as a member of the board of directors, to the ad hoc Yorkville Joint Committee for Human and Religious Rights, which he publicly endorsed. He served as a pallbearer at Vito Marcantonio's funeral in 1954 and helped organize Marcantonio's memorial book, *I Vote My Conscience*. Covello's name generally does not appear on available documents that would suggest a public endorsement of Marcantonio. An exception is the letterhead stationery for the Non-Partisan Committee for the Re-Election of Congressman Vito Marcantonio, 1936, Vito Marcantonio Papers, box 45, Miscellaneous Campaigns file, New York City Public Library.

Like many of Marcantonio's constituents, Covello and his wife leaned on Marcantonio for personal political favors. For example, Rose Covello requested that Marcantonio write a letter of introduction to New York City congressman Martin J. Kennedy on behalf of her unemployed brother-in-law "with the possibility of his getting some of the Census work in that district." Letter dated 30 January 1940, Vito Marcantonio Papers, box 2, Covello file.

27. "East Harlem Housing Committee of the Harlem Legislative Conference," [1941?], CP box 43, folder 11. The merger that created the East Harlem Housing Committee took place at a meeting on 15 January 1938.

28. Meyer, *Vito Marcantonio*, 71–72. Meyer dates this leaflet approximately from March 1938. Other documents in the Covello Papers indicate that the housing parade referred to in the leaflet was actually held 25 March 1939.

29. "2000 in East Harlem Area Parade for Housing Project," *Building Trades Union Press*, 1 April 1939.

30. From Community Advisory Council documents, CP box 39, box 15. See also "Resolutions Passed by East Harlem Housing Committee at a Mass Meeting on March 22 [1938] at 8:30 P.M. in New York City," CP box 43, folder 5.

31. Marcantonio to Covello, 13 February 1939, Vito Marcantonio Papers, box 2, Covello file. For more on the Housing Committee, see Freeman, "Exploring Path of Community Change," 192–94.

32. Louis Relin, "We Hold These Truths," n.d., report on intercultural education experience in English course, fall 1938, 20, CP box 51, folder 13.

33. Covello, speech at Housing Celebration, 15 October 1939, CP box 43, folder 6.

34. "Housing," Community Advisory Council Report, June 1940, CP box 43, folder 5.

35. Marcantonio to Covello, 2 October 1939, CP box 5, folder 8. In 1937 Marcantonio and Covello were concerned that middle-class gentrifiers might use their wealth and political advantage to build segregated housing on the banks of the East River. Feeding that concern, a report of the Mayor's Committee on City Planning predicted "the erection of relatively high-cost apartments along the East and Harlem Rivers, where existing or projected waterfront improvements will make the site attractive." "East Harlem Close-Up," *New York Times*, 30 June 1937. In a speech Marcantonio decried "the [proposed] exploitation of this site by realty interests. We are opposed to the erection of another Tudor City along the East River. We do not want in our community penthouses and silk hats alongside tenements and people on relief budgets. We do not want Dead Ends. The East River is our river," Quoted in Meyer, *Vito Marcantonio*, 225n124. Covello wrote in 1939 that the East River Houses "will make it impossible for expensive apartment buildings to be erected on the desirable water-front, thereby crowding the people of East Harlem 'into back-yard tenement

areas' in which our old-law tenements will become more and more unfit to live in." Covello, "Our Friends and Neighbors in East Harlem," [May 1939?], CP box 43, folder 6. As the East River Houses went up, Marcantonio and Covello expressed a new concern: East Harlemites, especially Puerto Ricans, might not sign up or be assigned to the new units. With pressure from the Harlem Legislative Conference, and Marcantonio as the legislative watchdog, "it was possible to have a large percentage of the residents of the housing unit from East Harlem." Meyer, *Vito Marcantonio*, 72–73; quote from Covello, "Community-Centered School and Problem of Housing," 141. For a report on the completed East River Houses, see "East River Houses: Public Housing in East Harlem," New York City Housing Authority, June 1941, CP box 43, folder 11. By 1941 the Federal Housing Authority had erected thirteen separate public housing projects in New York City, totaling more than seventeen thousand apartments. See Robert A. Caro, *The Power Broker: Robert Moses and the Fall of New York* [New York: Knopf, 1974], 613.

36. Meyer, *Vito Marcantonio*, 78–79; see also *East Harlem News*, April 1941, CP box 6, folder 8.

37. "Statement by Chairmen of All Departments," 19 May 1941, CP box 51, folder 14; Marcantonio letter also in folder 14. This incident may have fueled a misunderstanding with the American Legion's Thomas Jefferson Post 541: "We had created the 'East Harlem News,' a school-community newspaper. The staff was composed of students, teachers and community representatives, with the students gathering the news and advertisements, and helping with the distribution. We received word that the American Legion had decided to boycott our paper because we had 'left wingers' on the staff. A teacher in the school arranged for us to meet with the Legion to discuss the matter with them. In the course of my remarks, I declared that I was principal of an American public high school and that neither the faculty nor I questioned the religious and political affiliations or the racial origins of my students, including the members of the newspaper staff. I told them: 'I don't know who these "left wingers" are, but if you are so concerned, by all means join with us and find out for yourselves the quality of the people who are helping us create a school-community newspaper, which you must concede is very much needed in our community.' I extended an invitation for anyone to join with us who was willing to make a contribution. We convinced the American Legion to support us. But we ran up against this misunderstanding and prejudice constantly." Robert W. Peebles, "Interview with Leonard Covello," *Urban Review* 3, no. 3 (1969): 16.

38. From the mid-1930s until the U.S. entry into the war, Covello encouraged and supported peace activities in BFHS. Although anti-Fascist, he publicly denounced war and advocated U.S. neutrality as late as 1940. For example, at a peace rally at the Little Red School House on Bleecker Street, described as a "non-political, non-partisan meeting," Covello told the audience: "Let us not endanger the strongholds of our national life by unwise entanglements with the wars of Europe." "Strength from Within," 12 April 1940, CP box 13, folder 23. Covello's views on the war paralleled Vito Marcantonio's; indeed, Covello wrote Marcantonio: "I would appreciate it very much if you would send me any material you have on peace and the reasons why American [*sic*] should keep out of the war, as I am going to speak on Friday and shall need this material in order to prepare my speech." Covello to Marcantonio, 1 April 1940, Vito Marcantonio Papers, box 2, Covello file. The high school organized a peace committee and conducted peace assemblies at which student leaders advocated international peace initiatives, sometimes in terms that were unabashedly Marxist. The student newspaper reported: "Following each speech, uncensored by the faculty, there was a question and open-forum discussion period. All points of view relating to the peace problem were addressed." *Almanac*, 22 April 1936, box 32, oversize. When the United States finally entered the war, Covello became a vigorous supporter of the war effort.

39. November 1946, quoted in Robert Orsi, *The Madonna of 115th Street: Faith and Community in Italian Harlem, 1880–1950,* 2nd ed. (New Haven, Conn.: Yale University Press, 2002, 44.

40. Plunz, *History of Housing in New York City,* 240–45.

41. Freeman, "Exploring Path of Community Change," 271–73.

42. Ibid., 273, quote from p. 296.

43. Plunz, *History of Housing in New York City,* 245.

44. See Jane Jacobs, *The Death and Life of Great American Cities* (New York: Vintage Books, 1961); Woody Klein, *Let in the Sun* (New York: Macmillan, 1964).

45. Freeman, "Exploring Path of Community Change," chap. 14. The ubiquitous Robert Moses played an important, if indirect, role in East Harlem in the 1950s and 1960s. As chair of the Mayor's Slum Clearance Committee, he administered Title I of the 1949 U.S. Housing Act, which provided for federally funded urban renewal by private developers under the auspices of a local redevelopment authority. As Freeman notes, notwithstanding the absence of any Title I project in the district: "Title I *did* have a lasting impact on East Harlem, for scores of families that had been uprooted from *other* neighborhoods by Title I redevelopment schemes were moved to the myriad East Harlem sites already earmarked for future bulldozing, while many other families from around the city who were ineligible for public housing and who chose to relocate themselves after their homes had been demolished were constrained by finances to re-settle in low-income neighborhoods like East Harlem." Ibid., original emphasis, 274.

46. Covello, "Community-Centered School and Problem of Housing," 141–42. See also Covello, report to Committee on Practical Democracy in Education, 13 January 1942, 11, CP box 34, folder 11.

47. For the "little public"–"larger public" problematic in John Dewey's *The Public and Its Problems* (1927), see Walter C. Parker, "'Advanced Ideas about Democracy: Toward a Pluralist Conception of Citizenship," *Teachers College Record* 98, no. 1 (1996): 104–25.

48. A smaller yet significant project was the Health Committee's lobby to demolish a vacant building at 2104–6 Second Avenue, a structure that, in the words of the Health Committee, "is definitely undermining the health and morals of the neighborhood. Not only is the appalling appearance of the structure an eyesore, but it has proved a hazard and a temptation to our high school boys, and has resulted in endless trouble to the school at large. This social menace necessitates the vigilance of the police at night." Covello, Sophie Rabinoff, and Herbert Lemuth to David A. Ostreicher, New York Housing Authority, 8 April 1938, CP box 43, folder 5. The city complied with the Health Committee's request to demolish the building.

49. Sophie Rabinoff, "A Cooperative Health Education Project on Tuberculosis by the East Harlem Health Center and Benjamin Franklin High School," 9 September 1941, CP box 80, folder 5.

50. Ibid. In 1937 the Health Center administered the test to all students. In the spring term of 1938, however, only graduating seniors took the test, with the Health Center providing the necessary follow-up. This policy continued until 1941, when the Health Center, acting on the high school's recommendation, began testing entering students as well, providing the follow-up under the school's jurisdiction. Boys at the 79th Street Annex received free testing by Kipps Bay–Yorkville health authorities. See "Report of the Work of the Health Committee during the Period from September 1940 thru January 1941," CP box 41, folder 10. A related activity on tuberculosis was the Health Center's program "Fighting Tuberculosis in East Harlem," featuring physicians speaking in English, Spanish, and Italian; and a performance of a one-act play, "Dress Rehearsal," by Franklin students, 21 April 1939 (CP box 77, folder 5). Concurrently with the tuberculosis campaign, the Health Center sponsored special health assemblies at the high school on such topics as cancer, industrial safety,

and accident prevention; e.g., see Sophie Rabinoff, "Health Program for September Term, 1940," CP box 41, folder 10.

51. *East Harlem News,* March 1941, CP box 6, folder 4.

52. Ibid., May 1941, CP box 131, oversize.

53. Leonard Covello, "Leadership among Minority Groups Developed through the Secondary School Program," address to annual meeting of the National Conference on Social Work, Grand Rapids, Michigan, 27 May 1940, 32, CP box 13, folder 32.

54. As Robert Orsi indicates, Covello assumed that intergenerational conflict was caused by the second generation's rejection of parental values and contemptuous treatment of the old country. Orsi challenges this interpretation—and most of the current immigrant historiography as well—by arguing that the parents *excluded* their children from "Southern Italy," an idealized construction used to discipline their Americanized children: "The immigrants were telling their children that 'never in a million years' could they live life as it was lived in that other place, because this place is not that place. The immigrants met every sign of change, every hint of autonomy, and each new idea or interest of their children's with the image of 'Southern Italy,' making it clear the whole time that they identified their children as 'Americans.' Covello and most subsequent historians of Italian-America have it wrong: the immigrants did not imagine 'Southern Italy' for their children, but *against* them." Orsi, "The Fault of Memory: 'Southern Italy' in the Imagination of Immigrants and the Lives of Their Children in Italian Harlem, 1920–1945," *Journal of Family History* 15, no. 2 (1990): 139–40.

55. Covello enlisted students to recruit friends and relatives for these classes. Across the five boroughs of New York City, some five hundred teachers taught English to foreigners in 335 centers. Covello, letter to students, CP box 42, folder 1.

56. Fiorello H. La Guardia to Harold Fields, 14 October 1935, CP box 42, folder 8; "Nationalities Represented among Applicants for Naturalization Aid at the Benjamin Franklin High School," 1935–37, CP box 42, folder 8.

57. Leonard Covello, "A High School and Its Immigrant Community: A Challenge and an Opportunity," *Journal of Educational Sociology* 9 (1936): 343–44. Franklin boys also promoted the high school's naturalization program as guest speakers at other East Harlem schools. In the spring semester of 1937, they made presentations at fourteen public schools. "Community Advisory Council Report," June 1937, CP box 39, folder 14.

58. East Harlem Festival for New American Citizens," June 1940, CP box 42, folder 9; "Flag Day Celebration," brochure, 14 June 1942, CP box 42, folder 9; Ed Sullivan, "Little Old New York," *New York Daily News,* 17 June 1942.

59. *Almanac,* 23 November 1934, CP box 131, oversize.

60. Quoted in Leonard Covello with Guido D'Agostino, *The Heart Is the Teacher* (New York: McGraw-Hill, 1958), 227.

61. "High School Site Hunted by Board," *World-Telegram,* 11 May 1934.

62. Covello, *Heart Is Teacher,* 228. Covello wrote erroneously that the board of education considered five sites. The board's records show discussion of only three sites: the strongly preferred Pleasant Avenue site and two sites on First Avenue assessed at $782,000 and $723,000, respectively. See *Journal of the Board of Education of the City of New York,* (1937), vol. 1, 1413–14, vol. 2, 3044–46, City Hall Library, New York City; also untitled city document, CP box 32, folder 3. In the early 1930s the Standard Gaslight Company occupied the land between 114th and 116th streets at Pleasant Avenue, which included coal yards and an ice plant. The Wards' Island Ferry stood at the terminus of 116th Street; Jefferson Park bordered 114th Street at Pleasant Avenue. Frederic M. Thrasher, "Social-Base Map of Local Neighborhoods, New York City, 1931," CP box 48, folder 1. In the mid-1930s, Triborough Bridge Authority president Robert Moses beautified the area as part of a deal he made with the city to build the East Harlem section of East River Drive See Owen D. Gutfreund, "The

Path of Prosperity: New York's East River Drive, 1922–1990," *Journal of Urban History* 21, no. 2 (1995): 147–83; Caro, *Power Broker*, 392–95).

63. Gutfreund, "Path of Prosperity."

64. "Mayor Defends School Budget at Ceremony," *Herald Tribune*, 18 April 1940; draft of Covello speech, CP box 13, folder 26, edited at later date by Covello, original text quoted here.

65. Letters in Vito Marcantonio Papers, box 2, Covello file.

66. We are indebted to architectural historian David Brownlee for his comments on Franklin's architecture; personal communication, 13 June 2002.

67. Richard Bauman, "On Leaving the Old Building," *Benjamin Franklin High School Yearbook*, January 1942, 5, Yearbook Collection, Manhattan Center for Science and Mathematics (formerly BFHS), New York City.

68. *East Harlem News*, June 1941, CP box 40, folder 6.

69. "Mayor Tells Boys of Facing 2 Wars," *New York Times*, 17 April 1942.

CHAPTER 7: THE HIGH SCHOOL ON PLEASANT AVENUE

1. "Special Features of the New Building," n.d., Leonard Covello Papers (MSS 40) [hereafter CP], Balch Institute Collections, Historical Society of Pennsylvania, Philadelphia, box 38, folder 2; in same folder, brochure advertising BFHS courses of study, dated 1942; John E. Wade, superintendent of schools, to Board of Education, 18 May 1944; "A Six-Year Unified Educational Organization at Benjamin Franklin High School," 30 October 1947, CP box 49, folder 16.

2. *Journal of the Board of Education of the City of New York* [hereafter *JBOE*] (1942), vol. 1, 656–57, City Hall Library, NYC.

3. Leonard Covello, "Report of the Activities of the Community Advisory Council," Fall 1941–Spring 1942, CP box 40, folder 8.

4. Mary R. Monforte, "Report on Field Work at Benjamin Franklin High School," [May 1942?], CP box 89, folder 2. According to Covello, a factor in the severe curtailment of the community school was "the loss of so many of our young teachers." Covello to D. Morrow, 21 February 1946, CP box 3, folder 13.

5. Marion Wolf, Harriet Beskey, and Pearly Harelick to Harvey Zorbaugh, 17 June 1943, CP box 117, folder 1. Nationwide the wartime economy had the greatest effect on declining high school enrollments; see David L. Angus and Jeffrey E. Mirel, *The Failed Promise of the American High School, 1890–1995* (New York: Teachers College Press, 1999), 79–80; William L. Tuttle, Jr., *"Daddy's Gone to War": The Second World War in the Lives of American Children* (New York: Oxford University Press, 1993), 24.

6. New York City Superintendent of Schools [hereafter SOS], *The First Fifty Years, 1898–1948: A Brief Review of Progress*, Fiftieth Annual Report (1947–48), 186–87.

7. Leonard Covello, "Adolescents in War," paper delivered to 11th Regional Conference on Social Hygiene, New York City, 3 February 1943, 3, 17, CP box 15, folder 2.

8. "Analysis of Distribution of B.F.H.S. Students by Residence and Race," 1942, CP box 49, folder 14. Sixty percent of the students came from East Harlem, 18 percent from West Harlem, 14 percent from Yorkville, 2 percent from downtown Manhattan, and the remainder from other areas of the city. In 1944 Covello's faculty cabinet reported that the high school's club program had suffered, citing "the difficulty of getting boys to stay after school." Cabinet Circular #6, minutes for meetings 6 and 9 March 1944, CP box 33, folder 29.

9. Leonard Covello, "Memorandum on a Six Year High School (Junior-Senior High School) at Benjamin Franklin High School," April 1944, CP box 49, folder 16. It is worth noting that Franklin had a disproportionately high failure rate, with 210 three-subject failures reported in 1943–44. "Report of the Curriculum Committee," CP box 41, folder 4.

10. "High Schools Face Shake-Up," *New York Times*, 16 May 1944.

11. Wade to Board of Education, 18 May 1944, CP box 49, folder 16; "Revamping Approved for 3 High Schools," *New York Times,* 25 May 1944; "Benjamin Franklin Institution to Become 6-Year Combined Junior-Senior High School," *New York Times,* 15 June 1944; "Schools Keep Supervisors," *New York Sun,* 14 July 1944.

12. *JBOE* (1944), vol. 1, 984.

13. "A Six-Year Unified Educational Organization at Benjamin Franklin High School," 30 October 1947, CP box 49, folder 16; Leonard Covello, "Building Concepts of Cultural Democracy through a School Community Program in a Large Urban Area Inhabited by National and Cultural Minorities," address delivered to Downtown Community School, New York City, 29 April 1946,3, CP box 15, folder 44.

14. *East Harlem News,* May 1942, CP box 43, oversize.

15. "The All-Year-Round Program at the Benjamin Franklin High School," CP box 38, folder 2.

16. *East Harlem News,* March 1941, CP box 6, folder 8. The community newspaper reported an estimated turnout of four hundred people at the first meeting. In May 1941 Emilio L. Guerra, then the school-community coordinator, concocted a scheme to "assure adequate attendance at committee meetings." Each committee chairperson would receive fifty tickets to be handed out to committee members present at the monthly meeting. They were good for refreshments in the lunchroom: No ticket, no refreshments. Guerra to BFHS faculty, 20 May 1941, CP box 39, folder 6..

17. Program for Community Night, 24 April 1941, CP box 39, folder 8.

18. "Benjamin Franklin High School Community and Adult Program," November 1942, CP box 5, folder 19. Teachers selected students as block captains, whose responsibilities included gathering the names and mailing addresses of soldiers from the block, collecting the latest news on the block, and mailing the *East Harlem News* to each soldier (presumably with the block news report). Documents from Block Organization file, 1942, CP box 57, folder 6.

19. Covello to Frederic Ernst, Associate Superintendent of Schools, 27 August 1942, CP box 46, folder 16. During the wartime emergency, the BOE required New York City teachers to spend two weeks of their summer vacation, 9 A.M. to 1 P.M., doing community service; one of the options at Franklin was to work in Dr. Herman Dlugatz's rooftop greenhouse and farm-garden project.

20. "Report of Summer Session Activities at Benjamin Franklin High School, Summer of 1943," CP box 46, folder 10. In 1943, Dlugatz's farm-garden project on the roof yielded approximately ten dollars' worth of weekly produce and provided vegetables and seeds for local residents' victory gardens. "Report of First Week of Victory Garden Projects," 8 July 1943, CP box 46, folder 10. Collins reported a total of forty-six student teachers and counselors from the two universities, as well as fourteen case workers from the East Harlem Youth Service; see Dwayne Rolland Collins, "A Plan for a Summer Community Guidance Program for the Benjamin Franklin High School in East Harlem, New York City for 1943" (Ed.D. diss., Teachers College, Columbia University, 1943), appendix 1.

21. "Benjamin Franklin High School, Summer Session, 1944," 6, CP box 46, folder 11. The Twenty-third Precinct Coordinating Council sponsored the 1944 youth canteen. Formed in December 1943 at BFHS in response to "the rising tide of juvenile delinquency," the council's purpose was to provide youth recreation and parent education programs. Its membership included clergy, educators, leaders of social organizations, police, and community members. "The 23rd Precinct Coordinating Council," [1945], 1, CP box 80, folder 26. The council was a cosponsor of the summer youth canteen in 1945, which drew three hundred teenagers to weekly Wednesday-evening dances and Friday movies. "Report of the Recreational Projects Jointly Sponsored by the Lion's Club, the Uptown Chamber of Commerce,

and the 23rd Precinct Coordinating Council, Summer 1945," 15–16 October 1945, CP box 80, folder 32.

22. "Characteristics of the Population by Health Areas, New York City, 1950, Manhattan Borough, Part I," table C-2, in *Census Data with Maps for Small Areas of New York City: 1910–1960* (Woodbridge, Conn.: Research Publications, 1979), microfilm, reel 7.3.

23. "Distribution of BFHS Students by Race and Nationality," 1942, CP box 49, folder 14; "Analysis of Distribution of BFHS Students by Residence and Race"; Benjamin Franklin High School Circular #97, 11 June 1943, CP box 49, folder 2.

24. Leonard Covello, "The Community School and Race Relations," 19 November 1945, CP box 22, folder 18.

25. *East Harlem News*, December 1942, CP box 131, oversize; *L'Unita del Popolo*, 19 December 1942, CP box 6, folder 8; "To Establish a More Perfect Union," conference program deposited in CP box 51, folder 19.

26. Robert W. Peebles, *Leonard Covello: A Study of an Immigrant's Contribution to New York City* (New York: Arno Press, 1978), 273.

27. Conference program, CP box 51, folder 19. For the Harlem riot of 1943, see Thomas Kessner, *Fiorello H. La Guardia and the Making of Modern New York* (New York: McGraw-Hill, 1989), 530–33; Cheryl L. Greenberg, *"Or Does It Explode?": Black Harlem in the Great Depression* (New York: Oxford University Press, 1991), 211–14; Nat Brandt, *Harlem at War: The Black Experience in WWII* (Syracuse, N.Y.: Syracuse University Press, 1996), 183–206.

28. Percentages reported in Covello, "Community School and Race Relations." Writing in 1944, Rita Morgan, by now director of community activities at Benjamin Franklin High School, described the propensity of community boys and girls to organize gangs along national and racial lines "for offensive and defensive purposes." Morgan observed that "certain streets are forbidden members of another racial or national group and members of that group who venture on them are attacked by organized gangs on the other side. In the Italian area there is resentment at the use of the school or other community resources by Negroes; in the Negro neighborhood, Italians are made to feel unwelcome, to put it mildly. . . . Italians and Puerto Ricans maintain a sharp dividing line which either group crosses at its peril. This strong feeling of animosity appears to exist in all age groups but overt expression in the way of physical attack appears to be most frequent in the 10 to 12 year group and in the older adolescent group." Morgan also described the high school's intercultural program, which in addition to intercultural course units and racially/ethnically integrated clubs included an annual "Brotherhood Week," celebrated with "appropriate ceremonies, displays, lessons in certain classes, discussions, etc." Covello, she noted, even larded the school building with visual appeals for racial tolerance: "The school is equipped with excellent display cases and bulletin boards in all the halls and with a museum. These are filled with books, posters, pictures, newspaper and magazine clippings etc. with suitable titles and slogans all emphasizing the contributions to American and world civilization of all racial groups. The Art department sponsors a contest for young artists for the best poster for use in this activity, and outside of the school in the community." "Benjamin Franklin High School Intercultural Program," [1944], quotes from 1–2, CP box 52, folder 16.

29. "2,000 High School Students Battle in Race Riot," *Daily News*, 29 September 1945; "Student Strikes Flare into Riots in Harlem Schools," *New York Times*, 29 September 1945; "400 Police Watch Harlem Students," *New York Times*, 2 October 1945; "Faculty, Kids Act to Thwart Racial Battles," *Daily News*, 2 October 1945.

30. "Statement of Facts Re Racial Incident at Benjamin Franklin High School," adopted 2 October 1945, CP box 54, folder 4.

31. Dorothy Dunbar Bromley, "Schools' Intercultural Program Seen in Need of Stronger Support," *Herald Tribune,* 7 October 1945. Bromley reconstructed the events of 28 and 29 September as follows:

The incident which set off the disturbance of Thursday, Sept. 27, was in itself not unusual. . . . A few white boys who were practicing with a basketball threw it off the court and one of a small group of Negro boys on the other side of the gym picked it up and instead of returning it to the players threw it in another direction. The coach explained that boys often act this way out of deviltry, but this particular incident started a fight, which he promptly stopped. Still riled, the white boys and a small group of their friends quietly laid plans to 'get' the Negro boys outside the building after school was dismissed. Hangers on in the neighborhood joined the fray, but it was broken up by the principal.

By this time the alarm had spread among the Negro high school students. The next morning, Friday, some seventy Negro boys, instead of coming by bus from Harlem, marched to the school in formation, some bearing arms of one kind or another. The police were notified and appeared just as the Negro boys broke ranks to chase a white boy. Five of the Negro boys were arrested and two who were over sixteen were held for a court hearing.

Covello's own account is similar: "I heard about this [the Negro youths' marching toward the high school] in time to go to meet the group within a block of the school, while they were pursuing a white boy. They stopped when they saw me, began to disperse and then two police cars came along and some the boys in the group were arrested. And *that* was the extent of the racial clashes." "Community School and Race Relations," 2.

32. "1000 Parents Again Uphold Racial Accord," *PM,* 9 October 1945; "Resolution at the Community Mass Meeting at the Benjamin Franklin High School," 8 October 1945.

33. "Unity and Plans for Aid to Italy Mark Columbus Day Fetes Here," *New York Times,* 13 October 1945.

34. "53,000 March in 2 Columbus Day Parades," *Herald Tribune,* 13 October 1945. That the sentiment was genuine is indicated in a letter submitted to the Columbus Day Parade Committee by Michael Falciano, an Italian American student, who averred that "there is really unity and brotherly love in Franklin and not race hatred." Quoted in Covello, "Community School and Race Relations," 9.

35. Special assembly leaflet, CP box 54, folder 6; *Band Leaders,* June 1946, photographic essay on Sinatra.

36. "Race Hatred Cited as Principal Peril," *New York Times,* 10 November 1945.

37. "Report of the Mayor's Committee on Unity on the Benjamin Franklin High School Incident," submitted to Mayor La Guardia, 1 November 1945, 5, CP box 54, folder 12.

38. "Unity League Sees Increased Tension," *New York Times,* 11 December 1945. Covello never denied that racial tensions existed in the high school, although he occasionally tended to mask their gravity. Faced with a cutback in his teacher allotment for 1946–47, Covello reminded Associate Superintendent Frederic Ernst that "we are dealing with difficult problems in this school, more difficult than is indicated by city averages. The nature of our student population in what is known and conceded to be a tension area, primarily Italian, Colored and Puerto Rican, presents problems of social adjustment, augmented by a lack of many of the essential elements of reasonable living conditions. These latter often include inadequate finances, and slum housing, and often offer conditions of congestion and squalor that few people can understand who are not intimately identified with the situation." Dated 29 May 1946, CP box 38, folder 5.

39. Covello, "Community School and Race Relations," 4. In part because he feared racial clashes with whites, in part because he disliked "colored people," Parks Commissioner Robert Moses discouraged blacks and Puerto Ricans from using the Thomas Jefferson Pool, located in the park next to Benjamin Franklin High School. Not only did Moses hire only

white lifeguards and attendants, but also, as one story has it, he did not heat the pool, convinced that blacks and Puerto Ricans would not bathe in unheated water. The point is that non-Caucasians did not use the pool, even on the hottest summer days; Puerto Ricans who lived only three blocks from the pool walked to Colonial Park at 146th Street in Harlem, three miles away, to swim. Robert A. Caro, *The Power Broker: Robert Moses and the Fall of New York* (New York: Knopf, 1974), 513–14.

40. Nicholas Lemann, "The Other Underclass," *Atlantic Monthly,* December 1991, 96–110.

41. Francesco Cordasco and Rocco G. Galatioto, "Ethnic Displacement in the Interstitial Community: The East Harlem Experience," *Phylon* 31, no. 3 (1970): 310.

42. BOE, *A Program of Education for Puerto Ricans in New York City,* 1947, 32, cited in Emilio L. Guerra, "The Orientation of Puerto Rican Students in New York City," *Modern Language Journal* 32, no 6 (1948): 416–17.

43. Covello wrote Ruperto Ruez, president of the Spanish-American Youth Bureau: "As a teacher for thirty-five years and principal of a high school in this community for eleven years, acquainted with the Spanish language and with some understanding of the Spanish-speaking peoples, I resent most strenuously the many injustices and adverse conditions which the Puerto Rican people in our community have to contend with, practically unaided except for a very limited number of institutions and even a more limited number of people who understand them, who appreciate their foreign qualities and potentialities and who are also willing to do something to help them take their place on the basis of complete equality in the New York community." Letter dated 5 January 1945, CP box 102, folder 13. Near the end of his career at Franklin, Covello made a telling statement to his friend Mario Cosenza: "In the Puerto Rican children, I see myself, my brothers, relatives and friends with whom we grew up in East Harlem trying to cope with many difficult situations with no one to turn to for guidance or help. I have occasion to interview many Puerto Rican parents who come to us for help, and in these patient, courteous and worried people, I can see our parents." Letter dated 5 December 1956, CP box 3, folder 13.

44. "Schools in City," *Herald Tribune,* 16 November 1947.

45. Covello to James Watson, 18 October 1947, CP box 106, folder 1. See also Covello to Juan Rivera, Department of Education, San Juan, Puerto Rico, 20 November 1947, CP box 106, folder 1. Covello and Robert Speer, professor of education at NYU, arranged for thirty to fifty New York teachers to study in the 1948 summer session of the University of Puerto Rico. See "Puerto Rican Study Set," *New York Times,* 5 August 1947. On 2 January 1949, Covello and his wife, Rose, attended the inauguration of Puerto Rico's first president, Luis Munoz Marin, as "official guests." Covello to Luisa Quintero, 4 June 1960, CP box 2, folder 14.

46. Guerra, "Orientation of Puerto Rican Students," 418–19. Entering Puerto Rican students were typically enrolled in the orientation class, a class in English for foreigners, a class in regular English, a class in Spanish, and classes in art, music, and health education. See Emilio L. Guerra, "The Role of the Teacher of Spanish in the Orientation of Non-English Speaking Pupils," *Hispania* 32, no. 1 (1949): 59–63. For more on Franklin's program, see Mary Finocchiaro, "A Suggested Procedure in the Teaching of English to Puerto Ricans," *High Points,* May 1949, 61–66, CP box 102, folder 18.

47. Quote from flyer in Club Borinquen file, 1947, CP box 104, folder 1. On those occasions when BFHS's Club Borinquen marched, e.g., the 1949 Pan-American Day Parade in honor of Simon Bolivar, club members carried a colorful banner, 21' by 4', on which, in orange letters, the terms *Club Borinquen* and *Benjamin Franklin High School* were sewn on a maroon background. A description of the club may also be found in "El Club Borinquen de la Escuela Benjamin Franklin," *La Voz de Puerto Rico,* December 1949, 14–15, 29.

48. Covello to Jose Quintero, *El Crisol,* 5 May 1949, CP box 106, folder 11.

49. Covello to Babby Quintero, letter dated 7 April 1950, CP box 106, folder 11.

50. "Report on the Puerto Rican Press and Leaders Conferences Held at the Benjamin Franklin High School during the Winter–Spring Sessions of 1948–49,"corrected typescript, 6, CP box 105, folder 17.

51. Lemann, "Other Underclass"; see also "Gains Made by Puerto Ricans Here," *New York Times*, 31 May 1957 .

52. "New York: World They Never Made," *Time*, 12 June 1950, 24–26. Cf. Winifred Rauschenbush, "New York and the Puerto Ricans," *Harper's*, May 1953, 78–83; "Flow of Puerto Ricans Here Fills Jobs, Poses Problems," *New York Times*, 23 February 1953.

53. Urban League of Greater New York, *Community Center for 31 West 110th Street*, May 1946, 7–8, CP box 73, folder 13. For discussion of East Harlem gangs and armed violence ("Luger pistols"), see "Boys Seen Growing More Anti-Social," *New York Times*, 29 April 1947.

54. Clyde Murray, East Harlem Council for Community Planning, and Simon Beagle, BFHS, open letter, 3 June 1948, CP box 58, folder 10; in same folder, "Minutes of James Otis Youthbuilder Conference on: 'How to Make Jefferson Park Pool Safe and Available to All Groups'" [June 1948]. In 1947, "working committees" at P.S. 171 and P.S. 172 prepared the following statement to city park officials: "May we earnestly suggest that, if it is at all possible, you assign more of your personnel to guard the pool and have among your personnel representatives of the three major groups using the pool, namely the Italians, the Spanish, and the Negroes. Such action on your part will do much to give each group a measure of security and thus help improve group relations in the East Harlem community." Simon Beagle to Leonard Covello, 3 June 1947, CP box 53, folder 16. For the students' complaint to *El Diario*, see "Pandillas italianas atropellan y roban estudinantes hispanos," *El Diario de Nueva York*, 2 November 1951.

55. [BOE], High School Division enrollment figures, February 1956, CP box 80, folder 10

56. "Number of Puerto Rican Pupils in the High Schools in New York City as of October 31, 1955," CP box 104, folder 10. The following ethnoracial percentages were reported for BFHS: Italian, 36.9; Puerto Rican, 17.3; Negro, 26.3. "Survey—National and Racial Origins," November 1954, CP box 49, folder 2. In contrast to BFHS, the percentage of Puerto Rican enrollment at James Otis JHS was 39—442 of 1,134 students (see folder 10, table for junior high schools). As of 1960 BFHS enrollments stood at a lowly 858, with Puerto Ricans representing 55 percent of the total register; see "Board of Education of the City of New York," February 1960, 4, CP box 104, folder 10.

57. Dan Wakefield, *Island in the City: The World of Spanish Harlem* (New York: Houghton Mifflin, 1959), 179–83, quotes from 181–82. In the 1950s East Harlem below 112th Street became Spanish Harlem. By 1960 the total population for East Harlem, not including the blocks below 99th Street west of Third Avenue or the blocks below 98th Street between Fifth and Third avenues (located in health areas 33 and 28.20, respectively), was 104,673 white and 64,300 black. The census counted 68,728 Puerto Ricans and 15,680 Italians. Puerto Ricans dominated East Harlem below 112th Street; in health areas 25, 26, and 28.10, they constituted 70, 48, and 51.9 percent of the population, respectively. Blacks were dominant in the neighborhoods north of 112th Street west of Third Avenue, accounting for 60 and 77 percent of the population in health areas 20 and 16, respectively. East of Third Avenue between 109th and 119th streets (health area 21), the heart of what was once Italian Harlem, the percentages for Puerto Ricans, Italians, and blacks were 38.1, 28.7, and 12.2, respectively. *Characteristics of the Population by Health Area, New York City, All Boroughs, 1960*, table P-1; in *Census Data*, reel 7.1.

58. Marion Wolf, Harriet Boskey, and Pearl Harelick to Harvey Zorbaugh, 17 June 1943, report of a field study on truancy, CP box 117, folder 1.

59. John E. Wade, superintendent of schools, to BOE, 18 May 1944; "A Six-Year Unified Educational Organization at Benjamin Franklin High School," 30 October 1947, CP box 49, folder 16

60. For excellent commentaries, see Arthur G. Powell, Eleanor Farrar, and David K. Cohen, *The Shopping Mall High School: Winners and Losers in the Educational Marketplace* (Boston: Houghton Mifflin, 1985), chap. 5; Angus and Mirel, *Failed Promise*, chap. 3.

61. "Report of Scholarship Committee," 9 June 1947, CP box 35, folder 26.

62. Annual departmental reports, 1953–56, CP box 32.

63. Powell, Farrar, and Cohen, *Shopping Mall High School*, 300.

64. Organizational chart for East Harlem Council for Community Planning, n.d., CP box 70, folder 25. Covello and his staff proposed "that our school organize 'local action sub-committees' composed of community people, teachers, and students. These sub-committees would meet with and be part of the full committees of the Council, but would deliberate and act further on specific local phases of general community problems. The rationale for such action is twofold: the Council hasn't the means, time or personnel for local action, and it is basically important to develop local, lay, leadership." Meeting of Covello, Simon Beagle, and Samuel Polatnick, 30 June 1949, CP box 70, folder 25. The East Harlem Citizens' Committee, which Covello chaired, lent its weight to council projects. For example, the Council and Citizens' Committee cosponsored the "House We Live in Rally" staged at BFHS, 24 April 1947. The council's housing committee prepared a fifty-three-item student-parent questionnaire for assessing housing conditions in the area. The high school published a mimeographed newsletter, *Housing News*.

65. Company K brochure, 1946, CP box 34, folder 7; Covello to Boris Tamler, 18 November 1946, CP box 35, folder 10.

66. Leonard Covello with Guido D'Agostino, *The Heart Is the Teacher* (New York: McGraw-Hill, 1958), 197–98.

67. There were other service projects of lesser magnitude. For example, in 1947 Franklin and Otis students compiled 1,300 pounds of food for shipment by American Relief for Italy, Inc., to the Enzo Drago Elementary School in Messina, Italy; in 1948 the students shipped $150 worth of school supplies (documents in CP box 35, folder 33). In 1950 the social welfare committee of the two schools collected discarded linen from Manhattan hotels and made one thousand pads for the Cancerous Poor Hospital, St. Rose's, on Jackson Street. Costadasi and Sabato, "The Community-Centered School," 7 May 1952, CP box 47, folder 20.

68. Early projects included a "town meeting" assembly at Benjamin Franklin High School, "How Can We Eliminate Racial Conflicts," moderated by Simon Beagle, with a panel of seven students and guest speakers Rep. Vito Marcantonio and Rep. Adam Clayton Powell; an assembly titled "A Clean City—Whose Responsibility?" (29 May 1946); an assembly titled "Why Do Some Children Become Truants?" (13 January 1947). In October 1947, the Youthbuilders helped raise $1,000 for a youth lounge for the Aguilar Branch of the New York City Public Library on East 110th Street near Third Avenue. Open for sixty evenings in 1947–48, the lounge served 2,884 young people, averaging 49 per evening, approximately half of whom were Spanish speaking. In January 1948, the Youthbuilders helped raise $150 to equip a "teen-age" lounge that opened in P.S. 80, 415 East 120th Street. In June 1948, they campaigned with the East Harlem Council for Community Planning for the safe, cooperative use of the Jefferson Park pool. See documents in Youthbuilders file, CP box 58, folders 10, 11.

69. Gerald Meyer, *Vito Marcantonio: Radical Politician, 1902–1954* (Albany: State University of New York Press, 1989), 34–35.

70. "Otis Jr HS Club Plans Program to Redeem Good Name of East Harlem," *New York Times*, 29 March 1947.

71. Leonard Covello, Simon Beagle, and Leon Bock, "The Community School in a Great Metropolis," in *Education for Better Living* (Washington, D.C.: Department of Health, Education, and Welfare, 1957) 193–212, reproduced by Migration Division, Department of Labor, Commonwealth of Puerto Rico, 1966, quote from 16, CP box 23, folder 4.

72. Ibid. Effective 14 February 1949, the city amended its Buildings Housing Law to require that landlords "provide one receptacle for every five living rooms in a building." See "New Clean-Up Set for Harlem Area," *New York Times*, 24 February 1949; see also Hariette Cohen, "A Report on a School-Community Sanitation Campaign; September, 1948 to February, 1949; Benjamin Franklin High School," 18 December 1952, 8, CP box 44, folder 14.

73. "E. Harlem Opens 5-Day Cleanup Test," *Daily News*, 7 December 1948.

74. "Cleanup Prize Winners to Be Picked Today," *Daily News*, 10 December 1948.

75. [Covello?], "School and Community," 11.

76. "Summonses Start 'Clean-up Weeks,'" *New York Times*, 3 May 1949. On 4 May city council president (and future mayor) Vincent B. Impelliteri installed Otis Youthbuilders officers at a special assembly in the Benjamin Franklin High School. The Youthbuilders designated themselves the school's Clean City League. The East Harlem Protestant Parish, established by an interdenominational team of black and white ministers in storefront churches in 1948, supported this work with its own cleanup project, a vest-pocket playground for baseball and other games, as well as summer evening movies for adults. Covello, himself a Sunday-school teacher at Jefferson Park Methodist Church, served as a member of the East Harlem Protestant Parish. "Their Brothers' Keepers," *Newsweek*, 31 October 1949; Betty Burleigh, "The 'Bishop' of Harlem," *World Outlook*, August 1949, 11–15.

77. "Father of 16 Gives City Use of $9,000 Lot as Playground," 28 October 1949, unidentified newspaper, clipping in CP box 44, folder 13.

78. "Playground Replaces Garbage on East Harlem Lot Lent to City," *Herald Tribune*, 17 June 1950.

79. Quotes from Leonard Covello, "East Harlem Small-Business Survey and Planning Committee: A Progress Report," October 1955, CP box 80, folder 2; displacement figures from "Fact Sheet," 16 January 1956, CP box 80, folder 2.

80. Leonard Covello, "Project No. 3: A School-Sponsored Plan to Aid the Neighborhood Merchant and Consumer," 6–7, CP box 23, folder 4.

81. Ibid., 8–10.

82. Ibid., 10–13.

83. Ibid., 13.

84. "High School Department Head Admits Talk at Red 'Peace Rally,'" *Herald Tribune*, 10 July 1951; "Jansen Upholds Right to Talk on Peace," *Herald Tribune*, 11 July 1951; Covello to Rita Morgan, 18 July 1951, CP box 5, folder 19.

85. Marjorie Murphy, *Blackboard Unions: The AFT & the NEA, 1900–1980* (Ithaca, N.Y.: Cornell University Press, 1990), 189.

86. David Caute, *The Great Fear: The Anti-Communist Purge under Truman and Eisenhower* (New York: Simon and Schuster, 1978), 437–38; Leon Bock, "The Control of Alleged Subversive Activities in the Public School System of New York City, 1949–1956" (Ed.D. diss., Teachers College, Columbia University, 1971), 154. Moskoff's actions were sanctioned by the state's Feinberg Law, enacted in 1949.

87. Caute, *Great Fear*, 435–36, 439.

88. Ibid., 434.

89. Ibid., 441.

90. Murphy, *Blackboard Unions*, chap. 8. The staunchly anti-Communist Teachers Guild implicitly accepted the board's right "to try teachers who refused to respond to questions on political grounds" but defended the union teachers' right to democratic process. Bock, "Control of Alleged Subversive Activities," 169.

91. Caute, *Great Fear,* 609n13.

92. The only extant record of Teachers Guild membership, a compilation from 1939, lists Covello and seven other Franklin teachers. "Guild Membership List," January 1939, provided by Kheel Center Archives, School of Industrial Relations, Cornell University. Layle Lane served on the Teachers Guild's executive board and as vice president of the American Federation of Teachers and chair of the Committee on Racial and Cultural Minorities; in 1943 she ran for New York City Council. See *Bulletin of the New York Teachers Guild* 3, no. 1 (1943): 1; United Federation of Teachers Collection, Robert F. Wagner Labor Archives, Tamiment Library, New York University. For more on Lane's political activism, especially her role as a strategist for A. Philip Randolph's March on Washington Movement, see Lauri Johnston, "A Generation of Women Activists: African American Female Educators in Harlem, 1930–1950," *Journal of African American History* 89, no. 3 (2004): 223–40.

93. One of the questions Moskoff posed to teachers in his "interrogation room" was whether they had voted for the American Labor Party. Caute, *Great Fear,* 438.

94. Ruth Jacknow Markowitz, *My Daughter, the Teacher: Jewish Teachers in the New York City Schools* (New Brunswick, N.J.: Rutgers University Press, 1993), 169.

95. Louis Relin, response to questionnaire from Paul Tillett, Paul Tillett Papers, Seeley G. Mudd Manuscript Library, Princeton University; also *JBOE* (1952), vol. 2, 2987–88.

96. For example, Leonard Covello and Samuel Polataick, "Metropolis USA: An Account of Community Living in the Twentieth Century," 1953, manuscript, CP box 22, folder 26.

97. Covello to Leon Bock, 8 August 1956, CP box 34, folder 26.

98. Migration Division brochure, 1957, CP box 111, folder 2. Monserrat recalled: "My deep interest in education started many years ago when I was a student at Benjamin Franklin High School and was lucky enough to have 'Pop' Covello as the Principal." Monserrat to Covello, 1 July 1969, CP box 5, folder 15. For Covello's comments on his appointment to the Migration Division, see "Immigrant Past Suits Educator," *New York Times,* 11 November 1956.

99. Leonard Covello, "Recommendations Concerning Puerto Rican Children in Our Public Schools," 1953, CP box 114, folder 10. Press release, Migration Division, Commonwealth of Puerto Rico, CP box 111, folder 19.

100. Covello to Layle Lane, 13 December 1957, CP box 4, folder 25.

101. Covello to Adeline and Frank Luini, 26 November 1960, box 4, folder 28.

102. *Covello Newsletter,* 1961, CP box 3, folder 12.

103. Ibid., 1962, CP box 3, folder 12.

104. Ibid., 1966, CP box 3, folder 12; Covello to David Impasto, 24 November 1967, CP box 4, folder 20; Covello, "Report of the American Italian Historical Association," delivered at Fourth Symposium on the Teaching of the Italian Language, Fairleigh Dickinson University, Teaneck, N.J., 21 October 1967, CP Box 17, Folder 19.

105. Announcement of reception honoring Leonard Covello, St. Moritz Hotel, 31 January 1957, CP box 2, folder 10; *Covello Newsletter,* 1961.

106. Covello to Mario Gulizia, 16 September 1958, CP box 4, folder 18; Covello to Layle Lane, 18 March 1960, CP box 4, folder 25.

107. Shawn Weldon, "Biographical Note," Register of the Papers of Leonard Covello, 1907–1974, Balch Institute Collections, Historical Society of Pennsylvania, Philadelphia; Leonard Covello to Verdi Long, 3 May 1970, CP box 3, folder 13.

108. "Leonard Covello, 94, Ex-Head of East Harlem High School," *New York Times,* 20 August 1982.

109. *Franklin Voice,* 2 June 1960, CP box 131, oversize. Franklin opened that fall with 1,400 students, 300 of whom were female, as a compared to a total of 800 students the previous spring. *Franklin Voice,* 22 December 1960.

110. Robert Charles Freeman, "Exploring the Path of Community Change in East Harlem, 1870–1970" (Ph.D. diss., Fordham University, 1994), 358 (citing Sandra Adikes,

"Academe's Groves in East Harlem," *Village Voice,* 20 January 1966); "A Failed High School Preparing for Renewal," *New York Times,* 11 July 1982.

111. "A Failed High School."

112. "Death of a High School," *New York Times,* 15 June 1982.

113. "East Harlem School, in First Graduation, Sees Dreams Thrive," *New York Times,* 30 June 1986.

114. According to Thomas Bender, in *New York Intellect: A History of Intellectual Life in New York City, from 1750 to the Beginnings of Our Own Time* (Baltimore: Johns Hopkins University Press, 1987), the university that Nicholas Murray Butler (1901–45) transformed and stamped with his own persona as a captain of erudition was "less and less a New York institution" (279) and increasingly a corporate, consolidated, cosmopolitan research institution with national power. In but not *of* the city, Columbia was "substantially built upon a denial of the city immigrants that surrounded it" (293). For the Teachers College social reconstructionists, see C. A. Bowers, *The Progressive Educator and the Depression: The Radical Years* (New York: Random House, 1969).

CHAPTER 8: DRIFT AND RENEWAL

1. John Dewey and Evelyn Dewey, *Schools of To-Morrow,* in *John Dewey: The Middle Works, 1899–1924,* vol. 1 (1899–1901), ed. Jo Ann Boydston (Carbondale: Southern Illinois Press, 1976), vol. 15, chap. 8. In this chapter, "The School as a Social Settlement," the authors highlight a school social center, P.S. 126, in a segregated black neighborhood in Indianapolis. In chapter 7 they write glowingly of the "platoon" schools of Gary, Indiana, under Superintendent William Wirt, which provided wider-use services to community residents; the authors stop short, however, of designating the Gary schools social centers.

2. John Dewey, foreword to Elsie Ripley Clapp, *Community Schools in Action* (New York: Viking, 1939), vii–x.

3. John Dewey, introduction to Elsie Ripley Clapp, *The Use of Resources in Education* (New York: Harper and Brothers, 1952), vii–xi.

4. For the Speyer School, an early school social center, see Chapter 1, this volume.

5. Dewey made an inquiry at Teachers College as to the possibility of his wife's appointment as principal of the Speyer School. He acknowledged that he had not conferred with Alice about this and that she might not be interested in any work of this sort. John Dewey to James McKeen Cattell, 21 April 1904, in *The Correspondence of John Dewey, 1871–1952* [hereafter *CJD*], gen. ed. Larry A. Hickman, vol. 1, *1871–1918* (Charlottesville, Va.: InteLex Corporation, 1999), CD-ROM, no. 0091.

6. For Addams and Dewey see Lawrence A. Cremin, *American Education: The Metropolitan Experience, 1876–1980* (New York: Harper and Row, 1988), 174–80. See also Ellen Condliffe Lagemann, ed., *Jane Addams on Education* (New York: Teachers College Press, 1985). For Young and Dewey see Ellen Condliffe Lagemann, "Experimenting with Education: John Dewey and Ella Flagg Young at the University of Chicago," *Journal of Adult Education* 104 (1996): 171–85; Joan K. Smith, *Ella Flagg Young, Portrait of a Leader* (Ames: Educational Studies Press and Iowa State University Research Foundation, 1979), chap. 6.

7. Robert B. Westbrook, *John Dewey and American Democracy* (Ithaca, N.Y.: Cornell University Press, 1991), 150–51.

8. Max Eastman, *Heroes I Have Known: Twelve Who Lived Great Lives* (New York: Simon and Schuster, 1942), 299.

9. Ibid., 299–300.

10. Robert L. McCaul, in "Dewey and the University of Chicago: Part III: September, 1903–June, 1904," *School and Society* 89, no. 2191 (1961): 202–6, notes by that by the time

Dewey broke with Harper and left Chicago in 1904, he was uniquely positioned as director of the School of Education, in charge of both an elementary school and a high school, to have a major impact on American education.

11. Dewey remained active in a quixotic pursuit of international democracy, peace, and the outlawry of war in the 1920s and early 1930s. Following the war and the Treaty of Versailles, Dewey and Alice spent more than two years in the Far East; most of this time was spent in China, where liberals gave a warm reception to his lectures on moral democracy. Dewey wrote extensively for the outlawry movement between 1923 and 1927 and after 1931 and the Japanese invasion of Manchuria. In the 1930s he was also involved in a project to create a third political party in the United States, serving as president of the League for Independent Political Action and the People's Lobby. Westbrook, *John Dewey and American Democracy*, chaps. 8, 12; see also Jay Martin, *The Education of John Dewey: A Biography* (New York: Columbia University Press, 2002), book 3.

12. Alan Ryan, *John Dewey and the High Tide of American Liberalism* (New York: Norton, 1995), 142.

13. See Lawrence A. Cremin on one of Dewey's most errant disciples, William Heard Kilpatrick, in *The Transformation of the School: Progressivism in American Education, 1876–1957* (New York: Vintage, 1961), 219–20.

14. Elsie Ripley Clapp, "Academic Records and Academic Correspondence," Elsie Ripley Clapp Papers, collection 21, box 1, folder 1, Special Collections Research Center, Morris Library, Southern Illinois University; see also ERC to Joseph Ratner, 22 October 1946. The preface to John Dewey, *Democracy and Education* (1916; reprint, New York: Free Press, 1944), iv, acknowledges Clapp's "many criticisms and suggestions."

15. Elsie Ripley Clapp, "Employment and Biographical Data," Elsie Ripley Clapp Papers, collection 21, box 1, folder 2.

16. Sam Stack, "Elsie Ripley Clapp and the Arthurdale Schools," in *Founding Mothers and Others: Women Educational Leaders during the Progressive Era,* ed. Alan R. Sadvonik and Susan F. Semel (New York: Palgrave, 2002), 96.

17. Clapp, *Community Schools in Action*, v.

18. Clapp, "Employment and Biographical Data."

19. In Clapp's "Notebook" on the Ballard School, 1929–30, she does not mention any contact with Dewey. She did meet with the faculty at Teachers College, including William Heard Kilpatrick, and the faculty of the Lincoln School (see 61–62). Elsie Ripley Clapp Papers, collection 21, box 4, folder 1.

20. Citing a previous speaking engagement in Cleveland, Ohio, Dewey sent his regrets to Eleanor Roosevelt in response to her invitation to a White House meeting of the Arthurdale advisory committee in October 1935. This is the only record we have found of a meeting of the board. The letter is John Dewey to Eleanor Roosevelt, 24 October 1935, *CJD*, vol. 2: 1919–1939, no. 07755.

21. Dewey to John A. Rice, 16 April 1936, *CJD*, vol. 2, doc. no. 08643 (custodian, Division of Archives and History, North Carolina Department of Cultural Resources). For similar praise, see letters to Albert C. Barnes, 12 April 1936, and Sabino Dewey, 8 May 1936, vol. 2, doc. nos. 04377, 06809. ER came the first day of the visitation. That evening Dewey attended a dinner party given by Clapp and a square dance at the homestead community center. Clipping, unidentified newspaper, 7 April 1936, Scrapbook, Elsie Ripley Clapp Papers, collection 21, box 4, folder 2.

22. Dewey to Clapp, 21 October 1939, *CJD*, vol. 2, doc. no. 07944 (custodian, John Dewey Papers, Special Collections Research Center, Morris Library, Southern Illinois University [hereafter custodian, JDP].

23. Clapp to Joseph Ratner, 22 October 1946, *CJD*, vol. 3, *1940–1952*, doc. no. 14831 (custodian, JDP).

24. Clapp to Dewey, 14 October 1948, *CJD*, vol. 3, doc. no. 14833 (custodian, JDP).

25. Clapp to Dewey, 27 October 1949, 8 October 1950, *CJD*, vol. 3, doc. nos. 14835, 14836 (custodian, JDP).

26. Joseph Ratner to William H. Kilpatrick, 29 October 1951, *CJD*, vol. 3, doc. no. 14884 (custodian, JDP).

27. William H. Kilpatrick to Joseph Ratner, 4 November 1951, *CJD*, vol. 3, doc. no. 14886 (custodian, JDP).

28. Clapp to Roberta Lowitz Grant Dewey, 10 June 1952, *CJD*, vol. 3, doc. no. 16113 (custodian, JDP).

29. Lee Benson, Ira Harkavy, and John Puckett, *Progressing beyond John Dewey: Practical Means to Realize Dewey's Utopian Ends* (Working title Philadelphia: Temple University Press, forthcoming).

30. Lee Benson and Ira Harkavy, "School and Community in the Global Society: A Neo-Deweyan Theory of Community Problem-Solving Schools, Cosmopolitan Neighborly Communities, and a Neo-Deweyan 'Manifesto' to Dynamically Connect School and Community," *Universities and Community Schools* 5, no. 1–2 (1997): 16–71.

31. Westbrook, in *John Dewey and American Democracy*, 508, notes "a substantial displacement of the classroom from the center of [Dewey's] reform vision" after World War I.

32. Dewey, foreword to Clapp, *Community Schools in Action*, ix.

33. Ibid.

34. Dewey, introduction to Clapp, *Use of Resources in Education*, vii.

35. Ibid.

36. This "reasonable speculation" draws on Puckett's frequent conversations with Lee Benson. See also Benson, Harkavy, and Puckett, *Progressing beyond John Dewey*. Perhaps the most important consideration, however, is not how we interpret the "Chicago Dewey" versus the "Columbia Dewey," but rather how we assess the validity of the claims Dewey made at these different points in his career. Were Dewey's claims about the relationship of school and society more theoretically and empirically valid in 1902 than in 1916? We are persuaded that the validity argument favors the Chicago Dewey.

37. Edward G. Olsen, *School and Community* (New York: Prentice-Hall, 1946), 17, 70. See also Olsen, ed., *The Modern Community School* (New York: Appleton-Century-Crofts), esp. 200–201.

38. Edward G. Olsen, "The Idea of Community Education," *Community Education Journal* 15, no. 3 (1988): 13.

39. Olsen, *Modern Community School*, 200–201. B. Othaniel Smith, William O. Stanley, and J. Harlan Shores, in *Fundamentals of Curriculum Development* (New York: Harcourt Brace Jovanovich, 1950), 532–52, noted that community school programs rarely achieved a synthesis of school and community; more often than not, community schools used community issues and concerns for school purposes—"the school-in-community-for-school purposes approach." These authors advocated organizing the school curriculum around large-scale community problems—deeply embedded structural problems that necessitated comprehensive approaches to problem solving and the cooperation of multiple interest groups, including local schools.

40. Maurice F. Seay, "The Community School: New Meaning for an Old Term," in *Fifty-Second Yearbook of the National Society for the Study of Education, Part II: The Community School*, ed. Nelson B. Henry (Chicago: University of Chicago Press, 1953), 11, 9.

41. Paul R. Hanna and Robert A. Naslund, "The Community School Defined," in Henry, *Fifty-Second Yearbook*, 55. Hanna, a professor at Stanford University from 1935 to 1967, is an enigmatic, contradictory figure in this history. He was a staunch social reconstructionist in the 1930s—he took his doctorate with William Heard Kilpatrick at Teachers College and as an assistant professor there was associated with the Social Frontier group. In

Chapter 1 we noted Hanna's contribution to the fledging community school movement, *Youth Serves the Community* (1936). In the 1940s, as social reconstructionism waned, Hanna turned to outside business ventures, including a series of lucrative contracts with the Scott, Foresman publishing company for no fewer than forty-nine widely used elementary social studies titles, which made Hanna wealthy and allowed him to maintain and renovate the famous honeycombed house that Frank Lloyd Wright had built for him and his wife, Jean, on the edge of the Stanford campus. Hanna unapologetically parlayed his frenetic entrepreneurship and string of textbook publications into an international reputation—he operated a powerful placement barony in the School of Education and for decades consulted on international development education in numerous countries, absenting himself from academic life for long stretches of time. Hanna and Naslund's 1953 statement on community schools is quintessentially social reconstructionist, yet it was published as Hanna himself was becoming increasingly conservative in his politics. In the fifties and sixties he was a consummate Cold Warrior, advancing American ideas and democratic values in developing nations from Southeast Asia to Africa, often with little regard to cultural contexts, always in conjunction with U.S. national security interests. In the 1950s Hanna promoted community schools as an instrument of American democratic values in the Philippines, albeit unsuccessfully. Critics viewed Hanna as a cultural imperialist, with some validity, as Jared R. Stallones acknowledges in his sympathetic portrait, "The Life and Work of Paul Hanna" (Ph.D. dissertation, University of Texas, 1999), our source for the information in this paragraph. Late in his life Hanna, a staunch supporter of Republican politics, was affiliated with the highly conservative Hoover Institution.

42. Edgar L. Grim and Eugene Richardson, "The Michigan Community-School Service Program," in Henry, *Fifty-Second Yearbook*, 195–211.

43. Herbert Kliebard, *The Struggle for the American Curriculum, 1893–1958*, 2d ed. (New York: Routledge, 1995), 217–18; Diane Ravitch, *Left Back: A Century of Failed School Reforms* (New York: Simon and Schuster, 2000), 341.

44. For an excellent description, see Daniel Tanner and Laurel N. Tanner, *Curriculum Development: Theory in Practice*, 2d ed. (New York: Macmillan, 1980), chap. 12.

45. See Peter L. Clancy, "The Contribution of the Charles Stewart Mott Foundation in the Development of the Community School Program in Flint, Michigan" (Ph.D. diss., Michigan State University, 1963), 40–50; Clarence H. Young and William A. Quinn, *Foundation for Living: The Story of Charles Stewart Mott and Flint* (New York: McGraw-Hill, 1963); Frank J. Manley, Bernard W. Reed, and Robert K. Burns, *The Community School in Action: The Flint Program* (Chicago: Education-Industry Service, 1961), 20–22.

46. Clancy, "Charles Stewart Mott Foundation," 52–61.

47. Ibid., 63–70; Manley, Reed, and Burns, *Community School in Action*, 33–42.

48. Clancy, "Charles Stewart Mott Foundation," 65–69. In 1945, the Mott Foundation instituted a fellowship program for University of Michigan resident physicians and dentists to ensure "a continuously flowing supply of pediatricians and pedadontic dentists" at the Children's Health Center (quoted at 70).

49. Manley, Reed, and Burns, *Community School in Action*, 59–60, 69–70, 74–80, 104.

50. See and cf. ibid., esp. chap. 8.

51. The seven universities in the Mott consortium were Michigan State, the University of Michigan, Wayne State, Western Michigan, Central Michigan, Eastern Michigan, and Northern Michigan—all of which provided graduate and in-service training programs in community education.

52. See Harry C. Boyte, *The Backyard Revolution* (Philadelphia: Temple University Press, 1980), esp. 187–208.

53. For example, see Ernest Melby, *Administering Community Education* (Englewood Cliffs, N.J.: Prentice-Hall, 1955).

54. Pat Edwards, "The Mott Network: In Transition," *Community Education Journal* 16, no. 1 (1989): 19. See also "National Center for Community Education," *Community Education Journal* 1, no. 4 (1971): 28–31.

55. For a twelve-year history of the National Community School Education Association, see Jack Minzey, "NCSEA: The Organization for Community School Educators," *Community Education Journal* 6, no. 2 (1978): 5–7.

56. Edwards, "Mott Network," 17–19. See also LeRoy Watt and Priscilla A. Lischich, "Community Education Training Programs in Colleges and Universities," *Community Education Journal* 5, no. 3 (1975): 12–15.

57. David S. Storey and K. Hugh Rohrer, *The Historical Development of Community Education and the Mott Foundation,* printed and distributed by Central Michigan University Center for Community Education, Mt. Pleasant, Michigan, 1979.

58. Edwards, "Mott Network," 19. The Community Development Act of 1974, through its program of community-development block grants, provided additional federal funds for school-community centers.

59. Jane Westbrook, "State Funding for Community Education," *Community Education Journal* 14, no. 1 (1986): 10–15. In 1988, the Mott Foundation awarded state planning assistance awards to forty-seven states "to develop or update a five-year plan for community education (1988–1993)." Larry E. Decker and Kim Biocchi, "The National Project for State Community Education," *Community Education Journal* 17, no. 1 [1989]: 8–11.

60. Donna Shoeny, "Community Education in the SEAs: Report on a Survey," *Community Education Journal* 17, no. 1 (1989): 28–29; Ruth Randall, "Education in the Community," *Community Education Journal* 17, no. 1 (1989): 26.

61. For example, see Robert L. Berridge, "Community Education is Enhancing Adult Education in Texas," *Community Education Journal* 14, no. 2 (1986): 22–23; Martin Brennan, "Community Education and Adult Education—Is the Distinction Getting Blurred in Michigan?" *Community Education Journal* 11 (1984): 25–27; Gary Welton, "Why People Participate in Community Education Activities," *Community Education Journal* 12, no. 4 (1985): 20–22. In the 1970s the term "community school" was applied to any school site where interagency services were provided. See several examples in Joseph Ringers, Jr., and Larry E. Decker, *School Community Centers* (Charlottesville, Va.: Mid-Atlantic Center for Community Education, 1995), 4–6. The most extensive of these projects was Boston's program of twenty "community schools" located in neighborhood elementary schools, inaugurated in 1971. Operated under the auspices of the Department of Public Facilities, the school centers provided such services as GED and ESL programs for adults, preschool and after-school child care, after-school reading programs, and summer camps and other youth programs. Neighborhood councils hired the community school coordinators and prepared center budgets. Solomon Fuller, "The Community School Movement in Metropolitan Boston: A Consolidation of Social Services," *Community Education Journal* 2, no. 2 [1972]: 20–21; William F. O'Neil, "Boston Community Roots from the Grass Roots," *Community Education Journal* 4, no. 5 [1974]: 29–30; Lee Warren, "To Make A Difference," *Community Education Journal* 12, no. 3 [1985]: 24–29. See also Atlanta's John F. Kennedy School and Community Center: R. C. Pendell, "Atlanta Pioneers a Community School-Center Complex," *Community Education Journal* 1, no. 2 (May 1971): 29–36. Undermined by the city's economic collapse in the 1970s, the community schools of Flint, Michigan, ceased to be a bellwether of community education. For a recent report on Flint, see Hugh Rohrer and Dan Cady, "Community Education—Restructured to Meet the Needs of an Urban Community in the 1990s and Beyond," *Community Education Journal* 19, no. 2 (1992): 40–41. Also see and cf. *Joining Forces: Communities and Schools Working Together for a Change,* special section reprint from 1993 Mott Foundation annual report, esp. 2–4.

62. Arguments for an integration of community education and the K–12 program were abundant. For example, see Phillip Clark and Kathryn Watson, "A Visit to a Community-Centered Classroom," *Community Education Journal* 6, no. 2 (1978): 4–8; Clifford L. Whetten, "Getting Involved with K-12," *Community Education Journal* 10, no. 1 (1982); Lawrence Senesch, "Redefining the Educational Environment," *Community Education Journal* 12, no. 3 (1985): 16–17; Kathryn Kulage, "Community Education and K-12," *Community Education Journal* 10, no. 2 (1983): 30–31.

63. George S. Wood, Jr., and Larry D. Carmichael, *Its Name Is Community Education* (Muncie, Ind.: Ball State University, 1981). There were no systematic evaluations of community education, and the few studies undertaken did not measure program outcomes. For example, an evaluation conducted by Development Associates measured compliance with federal guidelines for projects funded by the Community Education Program. U.S. Department of Health, Education, and Welfare, *An Evaluation of the Community Education Program* (Washington, D.C.: U.S. Government Printing Office, n.d.).

64. Quote from William M. Hetrick, "Community Education in Education Reform: How Have We Contributed?" *Community Education Journal* 19, no. 2 (1992): 9–10. For instance, see Larry E. Decker and Valerie A. Romney, *Community Education across America* (Charlottesville: University of Virginia, 1990), a survey of 132 local projects in forty-six states and the District of Columbia conducted by the University of Virginia's Mid-Atlantic Center for Community Education; and Linda Moore's critical review of *Community Education across America,* esp. Moore's caveat about "cookie-cutter programming," *Community Education Journal* 18, no. 1 (1990): 27–28. See also Lou J. Piotrowski, "Community Education and the Status Quo," *Community Education Journal* 9, no. 1 (1983): 4–8. Entering the 1990s theorists of community education deemphasized the role of the school, and such terms as "educative community" and "ecological education" were prominent in the literature. William H. Denton, "Restructuring through Community Education," *Community Education Journal* 18, no. 3 (1991): 17–20; Stephen Preskill, "Ecology of Education: A New Foundation for Community Education," *Community Education Journal* 18, no. 3 (1991): 13–14. Reviewing the performance of his field in the 1990s, William H. Denton, a thoughtful insider-critic of community education, renders the following verdict: "Community education as a comprehensive philosophy and practice for maximizing school-community connections seems to have little credibility"; Denton, "Community Education: On the Forefront of Educational Reform(?), Part II: Institutionalization of the Movement," *Community Education Journal* 26, no. 1–2 (1999): 28.

65. Our analysis of the community education movement has been influenced by research studies on voting behavior and the party process that call attention to "trends that persist over decades." Viewed thusly, community education is a "secular trend" that for more than a half century has moved beneath the cyclical variations of U.S. politics. See V. O. Key, Jr., "Secular Realignment and the Party System," *Journal of Politics* 21 (1959): 198–210, quote from 198; and Raymond E. Wolfinger, "The Development and Persistence of Ethnic Voting," *American Political Science Review* 59 (1965): 896–908.

66. Working outside the community education movement was the highly experimental, militant-led movement to establish community control of schools in the Ocean Hill–Brownsville District of Brooklyn in 1968–69. While Ocean Hill–Brownsville shares in the four tensions highlighted in this book, we have not developed it in our historical narrative. It is a complex and bitterly contested topic that is treated extensively in other books. Community-control activists, for the most part separatist proponents of Black Power, demanded locally elected, that is, African American, school boards that would control education policy, hiring and firing, curriculum, and the operation of schools in this disenfranchised, racially isolated district. The short-lived community-control struggle pitted in the main, though by no means monolithically, the predominately Jewish United Federation of Teachers against

African American community activists. This conflict and its unhappy outcomes have rami-
fied for decades in New York education politics, generated numerous analyses, and remain
a focus of heated debate. Daniel Perlstein, in *Justice, Justice: School Politics and the Eclipse
of Liberalism* (New York: Peter Lang, 2004), notes that militant activists, as an integral part
of their strategies for black self-determination and racial empowerment, envisioned community-centered curricula and an action-oriented pedagogy that would prepare young people to be effective social change agents; for example a science class to study "how to scien-
tifically eliminate rats from the community" (quoting activist Sonny Carson, 119; see also
127–50). Of broader significance, writes Perlstein, the conflict in Ocean Hill–Brownsville
"marked the eclipse of liberalism in American political life," more precisely, the rupture of
the social democratic political accord for racial justice in force since the New Deal, and the
abandonment of the "assimilationist liberal creed" that Gunnar Myrdal powerfully articulated in his 1944 book *An American Dilemma* (ibid., 2, 8, 24–25). See also Jerald E. Podair,
*The Strike That Changed New York: Blacks, Whites, and the Ocean Hill–Brownsville Cri-
sis* (New Haven, Conn.: Yale University Press, 2002); Jane Anna Gordon, *Why They Could-
n't Wait: A Critique of the Black-Jewish Conflict over Community Control in Ocean
Hill–Brownsville (1967–1971)* (New York: RoutledgeFalmer, 2001).

    67. Joy G. Dryfoos, *Full-Service Schools: A Revolution in Health and Social Services
for Children, Youth, and Families* (New York: Oxford University Press, 1994). For an example of foundation diffusion, see Richard E. Behrman, ed., *The Future of Children*, vol. 2,
no.1: *School-Linked Services* (Los Altos, Calif.: Center for the Future of Children, David
and Lucille Packard Foundation, 1992).

    68. Dryfoos, *Full-Service Schools*, 11.

    69. Ibid., 100–108.

    70. Joy Dryfoos, Jane Quinn, and Carol Barkin, eds., *Community Schools in Action:
Lessons from a Decade of Practice* (New York: Oxford University Press, 2005). From the perspective of our study, Children's Aid Society (CAS) activity at the Manhattan Center for Science and Mathematics (MCSM) in East Harlem is also noteworthy. Founded in 1998, the
CAS program at MCSM, the former Benjamin Franklin High School, provides extensive
after-school activities, including clubs, internships, SAT preparation, and a "freshman seminar" for a student population that is drawn from the city's five boroughs. Given its magnet
status, the Manhattan Center is *not* a community school, although CAS staff members refer
to it as such. See Hayin Kim, "Managing the Growth of Community Schools," in Dryfoos,
Quinn, and Barkins, *Community Schools in Action*, 141–56; Children's Aid Society, *Building a Community School*, 3rd ed. (New York: CAS, 2001), 8–13.

    71. See Lee Benson and Ira Harkavy, "Progressing beyond the Welfare State," *Univer-
sities and Community Schools* 2 (1991): 2–28.

    72. Ira Harkavy, Francis E. Johnston, and John L. Puckett, "The University of Penn-
sylvania's Center for Community Partnerships as an Organizational Innovation for Advancing Action Research," *Concepts and Transformations: Journal of Action Research and Organizational Renewal* 1, no. 1 (1996): 15–29.

    73. Drawn from Ira Harkavy and John L. Puckett, "Toward Effective University-Pub-
lic School Partnerships: An Analysis of a Contemporary Model," *Teachers College Record*
92, no. 4 (1991): 552–81; Lee Benson and Ira Harkavy, "1994 as Turning Point: The University-Assisted Community School Idea Becomes a Movement," *Universities and Community Schools* 4 (1994): 5–8; Ira Harkavy and John L. Puckett, "Lessons from Hull House for
the Contemporary Urban University," *Social Service Review* 68, no. 3 (1994): 299–321; Ira
Harkavy, "School-Community-University Partnerships: Effectively Integrating Community
Building and Education Reform," *Universities and Community Schools* 6 (1999): 7–24; Lee
Benson and Ira Harkavy, "University-Assisted Community Schools as Democratic Public
Works," *Good Society* 9 (1999): 14–20; Lee Benson, Ira Harkavy, and John L. Puckett, "An

Implementation Revolution as a Strategy to Fulfill the Democratic Promise of University-Community Partnerships: Penn-West Philadelphia as an Experiment in Progress," *Nonprofit and Voluntary Sector Quarterly* 29, no. 1 (March 2000): 24–45; Lee Benson and Ira Harkavy, "Higher Education's Third Revolution: The Emergence of the Democratic Cosmopolitan Civic University," *Cityscape: A Journal of Policy Development and Research* 5 (2000): 47–57; Lee Benson and Ira Harkavy, "Integrating the American System of Higher, Secondary, and Primary Education to Develop Civic Responsibility," in *Civic Responsibility in Higher Education*, ed. Thomas Erlich (Phoenix, Ariz.: Oryx Press, 2000), 174–96.

74. For the theoretical foundations of Penn's approach, see Lee Benson and Ira Harkavy, "Saving the Soul of the University: What Is to Be Done?" in *The Virtual University? Knowledge, Markets, and Management*, ed. Kevin Robbins and Frank Webster (New York: Oxford University Press, 2002), 169–209; Benson and Harkavy, "School and Community in the Global Society; Ira Harkavy, "De-Platonizing and Democratizing Education as the Basis of Service Learning," in *Academic Service-Learning: A Pedagogy of Action and Reflection*, ed. Robert A. Rhoads and Jeffrey Howard (San Francisco: Jossey-Bass, 1998), 11–19.

75. Benson, Harkavy, and Puckett, "Implementation Revolution."

76. Francis E. Johnston and R. J. Hallock, "Physical Growth, Nutritional Status, and Dietary Intake of African-American Middle School Students from Philadelphia," *American Journal of Human Biology* 6 (1994): 741–47; Lee Benson and Ira Harkavy, "Leading the Way to Meaningful Partnerships," *Principal Leadership* 2, no. 1 (2001): 54–58.

77. Anne Whiston Spirn, *The West Philadelphia Landscape Plan: A Framework for Action*, Department of Landscape Architecture and Regional Planning, University of Pennsylvania, 1991–1996; Spirn, *The Language of Landscape* (New Haven, Conn.: Yale University Press, 1998), 10–11, 161–63, 183–88.

78. Gina Greenberg, "Penn-Sayre Partnership: Better Health for West Philadelphians," *PennPulse* (University of Pennsylvania Medical Center), issue 98 (2003): 2–5, 21; "Sayre Health Promotion Disease Prevention Program: Progress Report: January 2003–April 2004," Center for Community Partnerships, n.d.; "Progress Report: Fall 2004–Spring 2005," retrieved from *http://www.upenn.edu/ccp/Sayre/overview.htm*, 10 December 2004; Harry C. Boyte, *Everyday Politics: Reconnecting Citizens and Public Life* (Philadelphia: University of Pennsylvania Press, 2004), 75.

79. Dryfoos, *Safe Passage*, 54–60.

80. "A Bridge from Hope to Social Action," *New York Times*, 23 May 1995.

81. Dryfoos, *Safe Passage*, 54–60.

82. Quoted in Lisabeth B. Schorr, *Common Purpose: Strengthening Families and Neighborhoods to Rebuild America* (New York: Anchor Books/Doubleday, 1997), 48. Schorr notes that the city established a Youth Development Institute to provide technical assistance, consulting, and research for the Beacons, all of which were located in poor and disadvantaged neighborhoods. See also Geoffrey Canada, "The Beacons—Building Healthy Communities," *Community Education Journal* 23, no. 3 (1996): 16–18.

83. Geoffrey Canada, *fist stick knife gun: A Personal History of Violence in America* (Boston: Beacon Press, 1995), 134.

84. Ibid., 137–42; Schorr, *Common Purpose*, 47–56; Harlem Children's Zone, *Beacons and Preventive Services*, retrieved from *http://www.hcz.org/beaconand preventive.html* 1 June 2004.

85. Paul Tough, "The Harlem Project," *New York Times Magazine*, 20 June 2004, 44–49, 66, 72–73, 75.

86. Constancia Warren, with Michelle Feist and Nancy Nevarez, *A Place to Grow: Evaluation of the New York City Beacons: Final Report* (New York City: Academy for Educational Development, 2002), 1.

87. Laura Samberg and Melyssa Sheeran, *Community School Models*, working draft prepared for Coalition for Community Schools, October 2000. For other "community school models" such as the United Way–sponsored Bridges to Success in Indianapolis, the state-funded Caring Communities in Missouri, and Yale University's CoZi, a model combining programs developed by Yale University professors James Comer (School Development Program) and Edward Zigler (School of the 21st Century), see Joy Dryfoos and Sue Maguire, *Inside Full-Service Community Schools* (Thousand Oaks, Calif.: Corwin Press, 2002), 18–21. See also Laura Desimone, Matia Finn-Stevenson, and Christopher Henrich, "Whole School Reform in a Low-Income African American Community: The Effects of the CoZi model on Teachers, Parents, and Students," *Urban Education* 35, no. 3 (2000): 269–323.

88. Wallace Foundation Web site, *http://www.wallacefunds.org/programs/programDetail.cfm?id_init=1172045161,* retrieved 25 May 2004.

89. *Community Schools across America: 135 Community/School Partnerships That Are Making a Difference,* compiled by Pat Edwards and Kim Biocchi (Flint, Mich.: National Center for Community Education, [1996]).

90. John S. Rogers, *Community Schools: Lessons from the Past and Present* (Flint, Mich.: C. S. Mott Foundation, [1998]), 3–4; Joy Dryfoos, "The Role of School in Children's Out-of-School Time," *The Future of Children*, vol. 9, no. 2: *When School is Out: Analysis and Recommendations* (Los Altos, Calif.: David and Lucile Packard Foundation, 1999); 117–33, esp. 123, box 1.

91. Charles Stewart Mott Foundation, *1999 Annual Report, www.mott.org/publications/websites/Annual1999/p-improving.asp,* retrieved 8 October 2003; see also Dryfoos and Maguire, *Inside Full-Service Community Schools,* 71–72.

92. Mathematica Policy Research, Inc., *When Schools Stay Open Late: The National Evaluation of the 21st-Century Community Learning Centers Program: First Year Findings* (Washington, D.C.: U.S. Department of Education, 2003).

93. See Mathematica, *When Schools Stay Open Late.* For proposed federal cutbacks, see Linda Jacobson, "'Community Schools' Earn Plaudits, but Face Perils," *Education Week,* 14 May 2003. For a neoliberal critique of the program, see Darcy Olsen, "12-Hour School Days? Why Government Should Leave Afterschool Arrangements to Parents," *Early Childhood Research Quarterly* 15, no. 2 (2000): 185–214.

94. Chicago Public Schools (CPS), Campaign to Expand Community Schools in Chicago: Request for Proposals to Transform Chicago Public Schools into Community Schools, 4 October 2002; CPS Office of Communications, "CPS New Community Schools to Offer Education Programs; Activities to the Community," press release, 19 September 2002; *Chicago Educator,* January/February 2003, *http://www.cps.k2.il.us/communications/Chicago_Educator/Community_Centers/community_centers.html,* retrieved 21 May 2004; Linda Jacobson, "'Community Schools' Cooking Up Local Support in Chicago," *Education Week,* 3 December 2003.

95. Bridges to Success, *Doing What Matters: The Bridges to Success Strategy for Building Community Schools* (Indianapolis: Bridges for Success, United Way of Indiana, 2004.

96. SUN Initiative, *http://sunschools.org/mission.shtml,* retrieved 24 May 2004; SUN Initative, *Schools Uniting Neighborhoods: Successful Collaboration in an Environment of Constant Change* (Baltimore: Annie E. Casey Foundation, July 2003), quote from 22.

97. Vito Perrone, *Living and Learning in Rural Schools and Communities: A Report to the Annenberg Rural Challenge,* Rural Challenge Research and Evaluation Program, Harvard Graduate School of Education, February 1999, 5n1. Matthew Riggan informed us of the Rural Challenge in his unpublished paper "Review of Annenberg Rural Challenge and Evaluation" (University of Pennsylvania, May 2004).

98. Dryfoos, *Safe Passage,* 72–75. See also Joy Dryfoos, "The Role of School in Children's Out-of-School Time," *Future of Children* 9, no. 2 (1999): 117–34.

99. Atelia Melaville, *Learning Together: The Developing Field of School-Community Initiatives,* Mott Foundation, September 1998, 40.

100. Ibid., 49.

101. Coalition for Community Schools, *Community Schools: Partnerships for Excellence,* publication of the Coalition for Community Schools (Institute for Educational Leadership, Washington, D.C., n.d. [2000?], 2–3, *www.communityschools.org/partnershipsforexcellence.pdf,* retrieved 8 October 2003. For a narrative of the coalition's history to date, see Martin Blank, "Reaching Out to Create a Movement," in Dryfoos, Quinn, and Barkins, *Community Schools in Action.*

102. Coalition for Community Schools, *Community Schools,* 2–3, 7.

103. Coalition for Community Schools, *Making the Difference: Research and Practice in Community Schools* (Washington, D.C.: The Coalition, 2003), chap. 3. See also Robert Halpern, "The Promise of After-School Programs for Low-Income Children," *Early Childhood Research Quarterly* 15, no. 2 (2000): 185–214, esp. 197.

104. The Children's Aid Society claims direct collective benefits from the two Washington Heights community schools. As discerned from Yvonne Green's essay, "Promoting Community Economic Development," in Dryfoos, Quinn, and Barkin, *Community Schools in Action,* 114–24, community economic development is, for the most part, a function of CAS funding priorities and not a process that is controlled by the Heights community or one that invokes the community school's agency or builds its constituents' organizing capacity. For example, Green cites CAS's hiring of "hundreds of community residents over the years" and the organization's purchase of services and supplies from local businesses as strategies for community economic development. The claim, though still attenuated, gains more solid footing with respect to other aspects of community development: for example, the Washington Heights schools are sites for building strong relationships among parents, local organizations, and institutions.

105. See Milbrey McLaughlin and Martin Blank, "Creating a Culture of Attachment: A Community-As-Text Approach to Learning," *Education Week,* 10 November 2004, 34–35.

106. Benson and Harkavy, "Saving the Soul of the University." As this book was in press, the Coalition for Community Schools released a report by Atelia Melaville, Amy C. Berg, and Martin J. Blank, *Community-Based Learning: Engaging Students for Success and Citizenship* (Washington, D.C.: Coalition for Community Schools, 2006), which was supported by the Mott Foundation. Endorsed by the Coalition's leadership, the report argues cogently for an integration of community-based learning within the school's regular curriculum. Of particular significance, it embraces community-based problem solving and citizenship preparation as core functions of a community school. The term "problem" is broadly construed, ranging in meaning from action on a social problem to the study of "the unique history, environment, culture, and economy of a particular place" (8). The authors ground their advocacy in a theoretical framework that includes, among other components, motivation research, neuroscience research, situated-learning theory, and resiliency research.

CHAPTER 9: LEARNING FROM THE PAST

1. Press release, 15 April 1940, box 4, folder 2; "Mayor Defends Schools Budget," *New York Herald Tribune,* 18 April 1940.

2. Leonard Covello and Samuel Polatnik, "Community Education in Metropolita," in *The Modern Community School,* ed. Edward G. Olsen (New York: Appleton-Century-Crofts, 1953), 26–46.

3. John Dewey, *Democracy and Education*, (1916; reprint, New York: Free Press, 1944), 87.

4. John Dewey, *The Public and Its Problems* (1927; reprint, Denver: Swallow, 1954), 213. Our analysis of this work draws liberally from Lee Benson and Ira Harkavy's stimulating essay, "Progressing beyond the Welfare State," *Universities and Community Schools* 2, no. 1–2 (1991): 1–27, and also benefits from Puckett's frequent conversations with Benson on Dewey.

5. James Campbell, *Understanding John Dewey: Nature and Cooperative Intelligence* (Chicago: Open Court, 1995), 174–75.

6. Dewey, *Public and Its Problems,* 151.

7. Ibid., 216, cited in Benson and Harkavy, "Progressing beyond the Welfare State," 25. Benson and Harkavy use the term "cosmopolitan local community" to describe Dewey's synthesis.

8. Lee Benson, Ira Harkavy, and John Puckett, *Progressing beyond John Dewey: Practical Means to Realize Dewey's Utopian Ends* (Working title Philadelphia: Temple University Press, forthcoming). See also and cf. Aaron Schutz, "John Dewey and a 'Paradox of Size': Democratic Faith at the Limits of Experience," *American Journal of Education* 109, no. 3 (2001): 287–319.

9. Robert D. Putnam, *Bowling Alone: The Collapse and Revival of American Community* (New York: Simon and Schuster), 22.

10. For the social capital–political capital nexus, see Kavitha Mediratta and Norm Fruchter, *Mapping the Field of Organizing for School Improvement* (New York: Institute for Education and Social Policy, New York University, 2001).

11. Harry C. Boyte and Nancy N. Kari, *Building America: The Democratic Promise of Public Work* (Philadelphia: Temple University Press, 1996), 8, 216fn9.

12. Leonard Covello, "A Community-Centered School and the Problem of Housing," *Educational Forum* 7, no. 2 (1943): 142.

13. See David T. Hanson, "A Renewed Call for Civic Education," *Insights: A Publication of the John Dewey Society for the Study of Education and Culture* 36, no. 1 (2003): 6–7.

14. Thomas L. Friedman, *The World Is Flat—A Brief History of the Twenty-First Century* (New York: Farrar, Straus and Giroux, 2005), 265.

15. Anthony P. Carnevale and Donna M. Desrochers, *Standards for What? The Economic Roots of K–16 Reform* (Princeton, N.J.: Educational Testing Service, 2003), fig. 4, p. 17.

16. Organisation for Economic Co-operation and Development, *Education at a Glance—OECD Indicators 2005—Executive Summary*, fig. A2.1, p. 10, retrieved 1 December 2005 from http://www.oecd.org/dataoecd/20/25/35345692.pdf; Thomas G. Mortenson, "Chance for College by Age 19 by State in 2000," *Postsecondary Education Opportunity: The Environmental Scanning Research Letter of Opportunity for Postsecondary Education,* no. 123 (Oskaloosa, La.: Mortenson Research Center on Public Policy, September 2002), retrieved 1 December 2005, www.postsecondary.org/last12/123902/ChanceForCollege19.pdf; Leadership Fund on Civil Rights, *Realize the Dream: Quality Education Is a Civil Right,* section titled "National Report Card on Education and Equal Opportunity," retrieved 3 October 2005 from http://realizethedream.civilrights.org/scorecards/national.cfm; Jay R. Campbell, Catherine M. Hombo, and John Mazzeo, *NAEP 1999 Trends in Academic Progress: Three Decades of Student Performance* (Washington, D.C.: National Center for Education Statistics, 2000, NCES 2000–469), fig. 2.1, p. 33; fig. 2.2, p. 35; fig. 2.3, p. 37; Jay P. Greene and Marcus A. Winters, "Public High School Graduation and College-Readiness Rates: 1991–2002," *Education Working Paper,* no. 8 (New York: Manhattan Institute for Policy Research, February 2005, retrieved 29 November 2005 from http://www.manhattan-institute.org/html/ewp_08.htm; John Wirt et al., *The Condition of Education, 2002* (Washington, D.C.: National Center for Education Statistics, 2002, NCES 2002–025), fig. "Bachelor's Degree or Higher (1971–2001)," p. 81.

17. Amie Jamieson, Hyon B. Shin, and Jennifer Day, "Voting and Registration in the Election of November 2000—Population Characteristics," *Current Population Reports* (Washington, D.C: U.S. Department of Commerce, 2002, P20–542), fig. 2, p. 3.

18. Tama Leventhal and Jeanne Brooks-Gunn, "Diversity in Developmental Trajectories across Adolescence: Neighborhood Influences," in *Handbook of Adolescent Psychology*, ed. Richard M. Lerner and Laurence Steinberg (Hoboken, N.J.: John Wiley and Sons, 2004), 451–86.

19. Richard Rothstein, "Out of Balance: Our Understanding of How Schools Affect Society and How Society Affects Schools," paper presented at Spencer Foundation 30th Anniversary Conference, 24–25 January 2002, 1–2, 24–25.

20. National Research Council and Institute of Medicine, *Engaging Schools: Fostering High School Students' Motivation to Learn* (Washington, D.C.: National Academies Press, 2004), 33–34, 49–53, 66, 173. See also Geoffrey D. Borman, Sam Stringfield, and Laura Rachuba, *Advancing Minority High Achievement: National Trends and Promising Programs and Practices, report prepared for the National Task Force on Minority High Achievement* (New York: College Board, 2000); Jacquelynne S. Eccles, "Schools, Academic Motivation, and Stage-Environment Fit," in *Handbook of Adolescent Psychology*, ed. Richard M. Lerner and Laurence Steinberg, 2nd ed. (Hoboken, N.J.: John Wiley, 2004), 125–53.

21. Benjamin R. Barber, *A Place for Us: How to Make Civil Society and Democracy Strong* (New York: Hill and Wang, 1998), 67.

22. Theodore R. Sizer and Nancy Faust Sizer, *The Students Are Watching: Schools and the Moral Contract* (Boston: Beacon Press, 1999), xvii–xviii.

INDEX